Studying Politics
An Introduction to Political Science

EDITION

4

Edited by Rand Dyck
Carleton University

NELSON / EDUCATION

NELSON / EDUCATION

Studying Politics: An Introduction to Political Science, Fourth Edition
by Rand Dyck

Vice President, Editorial Higher Education:
Anne Williams

Acquisitions Editor:
Anne-Marie Taylor

Marketing Manager:
Ann Byford

Senior Developmental Editor:
Linda Sparks

Photo Researcher:
David Strand

Permissions Coordinator:
David Strand

Content Production Manager:
Christine Gilbert

Production Service:
MPS, a Macmillan Company

Copy Editor:
Jessie Coffey

Proofreader:
Maura Brown

Indexer:
Edwin Durbin

Production Coordinator:
Ferial Suleman

Design Director:
Ken Phipps

Managing Designer:
Franca Amore

Interior Design:
Sharon Lucas

Interior Images:
2 discpicture/Shutterstock;
3 Paperboat/Shutterstock;
28 Marje/iStockphoto; 29 P_Wei/
iStockphoto; 100 Nejron Photo/
Shutterstock; 101 Devonyu/
Dreamstime; 162 Vlad Ghiea/
Shutterstock; 163 photostudio
7/Shutterstock; 280 Fuse/Getty
Images; 281 Fuse/Getty Images;
356: Yuri Arcurs/Shutterstock;
357: Jeffrey Coolidge/Getty
Images; 414: sb-borg/iStockphoto

Cover Design:
Sharon Lucas

Cover Images:
Young girls holding Facebook
signs - © Ron Haviv/VII/Corbis;
G20 Toronto Canada - Jemal
Countess/Staff/Getty Images;
Rally in Fayoum - REUTERS/Asmaa
Waguih; Southern women at
northern Sudan polling station -
YASUYOSHI CHIBA/Stringer/AFP/
Getty Images; Teenage girl at
computer (background image)
- Loisjoy Thurstun/Getty Images;
Iraqi fully-veiled woman after
voting - MUJAHED MOHAMMED/
Stringer/AFP/Getty Images.

Compositor:
MPS, a Macmillan Company

Printer:
Edwards Brothers

**Library and Archives Canada
Cataloguing in Publication**

Studying politics: an introduction
to political science/edited by Rand
Dyck.—4th ed.

Includes bibliographical references
and index.
ISBN 978-0-17-650342-0

1. Political science—Textbooks.
I. Dyck, Rand, 1943–

JA66.S84 2011
320   C2011-903982-6

ISBN-13: 978-0-17-650342-0
ISBN-10: 0-17-650342-0

We dedicate this book to those who are about to experience the joys and rigours of studying politics, in the hope and expectation that they will emerge stimulated by and committed to the subject, and thus become citizens capable of dealing with the domestic and global challenges of the 21st century.

Brief Contents

Contents

PART 5
Political Participation 280

Preface

That this text is entering its fourth edition is a sign it is holding its own among many other good introductory texts available in the field of political science in Canada. It is obviously fulfilling the hopes of its creators—to produce a fresh, new text for the new century. In 2002, we saw the need for a text that incorporated the best of the traditional approaches and subject matter of the discipline, but that at the same time acknowledged how patterns of domestic and global politics and the ways they are studied were changing at a rapid pace. The market was asking for a text designed for Canadian students, one that opened their eyes to important developments around the globe. In retrospect, we were correct in thinking that the resulting work would have wide appeal among students and professors alike.

The Development of *Studying Politics*

We originally canvassed a large number of professors of first-year political science courses and asked them what they wanted included in such a text. We then assembled an impressive array of leading Canadian political scientists from across the country, most of whom also taught the introductory political science course at their respective institutions, and asked each to write a chapter in the area of his or her expertise. We also put them together in a room and asked them to come up with common themes, common approaches, and a common format, so that their chapters would speak to each other and there would be a seamless transition from one to the next. Numerous other political science professors were then asked to review the work and to suggest revisions. One of the exciting things about politics, however, is that it is never static, and so we are now presenting a fourth, updated edition. We have added a new chapter on Political Economy to this edition, and several other chapters have been extensively revised.

A Text Written for Students

We believe this to be the most student-friendly text on the market today. *Studying Politics* starts out with a gentle introduction to the subject of politics and political science, mindful of the fact that many students will not have formally encountered this discipline before. We have tried to write at an appropriate level and avoid confusing jargon, even when we get into more difficult subject matter. Basic concepts are defined throughout each chapter and again in a glossary at the end of the book. Moreover, we have integrated into the text a large number of tables, figures, photographs, cartoons, and discussion boxes to clarify, stimulate, amuse, and add to the visual appeal of the book. Each chapter also begins with a list of its learning objectives, and ends with discussion questions, and suggestions for further reading. In addition, at the opening of each of the seven parts into which this book is divided, we have offered profiles, with photographs, of several political science graduates, illustrating how their study of politics contributed to their exciting and varied careers.

A Text Written for Professors

As for professors, *Studying Politics* provides the content and approaches that teachers of introductory political science courses are looking for, combining traditional and newer concepts. The book has a comparative/conceptual approach, but remains Canadian.

Studying Politics is accompanied by a wide array of ancillary materials:

NELSON EDUCATION TEACHING ADVANTAGE

The **Nelson Education Teaching Advantage (NETA)** program is designed to deliver research-based resources that promote student engagement and higher-order thinking and enable the success of Canadian students and educators.

Testing Advantage Resources

Nelson Education Ltd. understands that the highest quality multiple-choice Test Bank provides the means to measure ***higher-level thinking*** skills as well as recall. In response to instructor concerns, and recognizing the importance of multiple-choice testing in today's classroom, we have created the assessment component of the Nelson Education Teaching Advantage (NETA) program to ensure the value of our Test Banks.

The assessment component of our NETA program was created in partnership with David DiBattista, a 3M National Teaching Fellow, professor of psychology at Brock University, and researcher in the area of multiple-choice testing. All Test Bank authors have received training by Professor DiBattista in constructing effective multiple-choice questions and creating questions that assess higher-level thinking.

All NETA Test Banks are accompanied by David DiBattista's guide for instructors, *Multiple Choice Tests: Getting Beyond Remembering*. This guide has been designed to assist you in using Nelson Test Banks to achieve the desired outcomes in your course. Select the "NETA Assessment" button on the Instructor's Resource CD (IRCD) for a digital copy of this valuable resource, as well as the *Studying Politics* Test Bank and computerized Test Bank (see "Instructor's Resource CD/DVDs" below for more information).

Instructor's Resource CD/DVDs

Key instructor ancillaries are provided on the *Instructor's Resource CD* (ISBN 0-17-662820-7), giving instructors the ultimate tool for customizing lectures and presentations. The IRCD includes:

NETA Test Bank and ExamView® Computerized Test Bank. Test Bank files are provided in rich text format for easy editing and printing with all common word-processing formats. All Test Bank questions are also provided in the ExamView® computerized version. This easy-to-use software is compatible with Microsoft Windows and Mac. Create tests by selecting questions from the question bank, modifying these questions as desired, and adding new questions you write yourself. You can administer quizzes online and export tests to WebCT, Blackboard, and other formats. A copy of *Multiple Choice Tests: Getting Beyond Remembering* accompanies the testing materials.

Create, administer, and manage assessments effortlessly with ExamView® Assessment Suite, a complete toolset in three seamless applications.

Build comprehensive tests with ExamView® Test Generator, administer tests with ExamView® Test Player, and analyze results with ExamView® Test Manager.

ExamView® Assessment Suite is a product of eInstruction® and is made to work best with eInstruction's® complete family of instructional and assessment products. In fact, only eInstruction® products work seamlessly with publishers' content and question banks in both the oldest and newest versions of ExamView® files, and provide full support for educators' most requested features like dynamic questions, tables and graphics to make questions more engaging, and ExamView®'s complete meta-tag search capability.

Microsoft® PowerPoint.® Key concepts from *Studying Politics* are presented in PowerPoint® format, with generous use of figures, photographs, and short tables from the text.

Image Library. Customize your own PowerPoint presentations using figures, tables, illustrations, and photographs from the book. These items are provided in jpeg format for your use.

Instructor's Manual. The Instructor's Manual to accompany *Studying Politics* contains learning objectives and suggested classroom activities to give you the support you need to engage your students within the classroom.

Acknowledgments

With such guidance from the political science community, with such expert and enthusiastic contributors involved, and with a top-notch publishing team at Nelson Education, it was not a difficult job for me to coordinate the project. By way of acknowledgment, I must first thank the contributors to this book. It was a joy to work with these impressive and accomplished people. Busy as they were with their teaching and administrative duties and other writing and research projects, they were most faithful and cooperative in making this work a reality. We welcome Rodney Haddow, David Stewart, and Claire Turenne Sjolander to the group with this edition.

Then I wish to acknowledge the contributions of the many other political science professors who were asked for advice in the planning of the book or in reviewing draft chapters. Their recommendations led to many valuable changes. Among these reviewers over the years were Christopher Dunn, Memorial

University; Syed S. Islam, Lakehead University; James Kelly, Brock University; Dan W. Middlemiss, Dalhousie University; Eric Mintz, Sir Wilfred Grenfell College; Ross Rudolph, York University; David Winchester, Capilano College; Ken Woodside, University of Guelph; James Ferguson, University of Manitoba; John Sutcliffe, University of Windsor; Josie Hernandez de Leon, Laurentian University; Chaldeans Mensah, Grant MacEwan University; Logan Masilamani, Kwantlen Polytechnic University; Brian Tanguay, Wilfrid Laurier University; Myron Galan, Dawson College. The reviewers for the fourth edition included Amanda Bittner, Memorial University; Paul Hamilton, Brock University; Nilgun Onder, University of Regina; Daniel Preece, Grant MacEwan University; and Russell Williams, Memorial University.

Next, we thank the organizations, publishers, newspapers, photographers, and cartoonists who gave us permission to reproduce their work, which has so complemented our written words. We are also very pleased at the calibre of the seven individuals who agreed to be profiled as political science graduates to demonstrate the range of careers to which this discipline is open.

Finally, as a veteran author attached to Nelson Education Ltd., I wish to thank the wonderful people at that organization, whose daily assistance, encouragement, support, and advice have brought the four editions of this book to fruition. In this edition, I worked most closely with Linda Sparks, Anne-Marie Taylor, and Christine Gilbert, but they were supported by many talented, artistic people in the production department and beyond.

Rand Dyck
Carleton University

About the Authors

Yasmeen Abu-Laban is Professor and Associate Chair (Research) in the Department of Political Science at the University of Alberta. She has published widely on the Canadian and comparative dimensions of gender and ethnic politics, nationalism and globalization, immigration policies and politics, and citizenship theory. She is the co-author of *Selling Diversity: Immigration, Multiculturalism, Employment Equity and Globalization* (2002); the co-editor of *Politics in North America: Redefining Continental Relations* (2008); the editor of *Gendering the Nation-State: Canadian and Comparative Perspectives* (2008); and the co-editor of *Surveillance and Control in Israel/Palestine: Population, Territory and Power* (2011).

Christopher G. Anderson is an Assistant Professor in the Department of Political Science at Wilfrid Laurier University and received his Ph.D. from McGill University. He researches and has published on Canadian immigration, refugee, and citizenship policies, especially in terms of situating contemporary debates within a more extensive historical context, and exploring how the liberalness of the Canadian political system shapes policies toward noncitizens.

James Busumtwi-Sam is an Associate Professor in the Department of Political Science at Simon Fraser University, where he was a recent recipient of the Excellence in Teaching Award. He specializes in international relations and comparative development. He has published work on the politics of development finance and the role of international financial institutions; international organizations and regional security; the political economy of conflict and peacebuilding in Africa; and the politics of macroeconomic policy reform and financial liberalization in developing countries.

William D. Coleman is CIGI Chair in Globalization and Public Policy at the Balsillie School of International Affairs and Professor of Political Science at the University of Waterloo. He has written five books and edited the Globalization and Autonomy series with UBC Press (http://www.ubcpress.ubc.ca/books/series_globalization.html). Among his awards are: Member of the Royal Society of Canada, Lauréat Trudeau Fellow, the Konrad Adenauer Research Award from the Alexander von Humboldt-Stiftung in Bonn, the 3M Teaching Fellowship, and the Ontario Confederation of University Faculty Associations (OCUFA) Teaching Award.

Rand Dyck retired as Professor Emeritus in the Department of Political Science at Laurentian University, where he won the Teaching Excellence Award along with the OCUFA Teaching Award in 2002, and served as Vice-Dean of Social Sciences and Humanities. He is the author of several widely used textbooks in Canadian political science: *Provincial Politics in Canada* (1996), *Canadian Politics: Critical Approaches,* 6th edition (2010), and *Canadian Politics,* Concise 5th edition. (2011). He has also taught at Memorial University of Newfoundland and the University of Victoria, and is currently an Adjunct Professor at Carleton University.

Peter A. Ferguson is an Assistant Professor at the University of Western Ontario, where he teaches international relations and American politics. His research is devoted to the study of democratization, specifically the breakdown of democratic regimes. He has published a number of chapters and articles addressing democratization, as well as public opinion polls and the media.

Rodney Haddow teaches Canadian and comparative politics in the Department of Political Science at the University of Toronto. Among other publications, he co-authored *Partisanship, Globalization, and Canadian Labour Market Policy: Four Provinces in Comparative Perspective* (2006). His research interests are in the fields of Canadian and comparative political economy; he is currently writing a book on economic and social policy-making in Ontario and Quebec since the 1980s.

Andrew Heard is an Associate Professor at Simon Fraser University and an Honorary Adjunct Professor at Dalhousie University. He is a former parliamentary intern in the House of Commons. His research interests and publications include topics in Canadian constitutional law, parliamentary government, judicial behaviour, and electoral systems. Most recently, he has published a series of chapters and articles on Senate reform and on the powers of the governor general.

Brenda O'Neill is an Associate Professor of Political Science at the University of Calgary. Her research is devoted to the study of Canadian political behaviour, specifically gender, political opinions, and youth engagement. Recent publications include *Gender and Social Capital* (with Elisabeth Gidengil, 2006), and articles in the *Journal of Women, Politics and Policy*, *Party Politics*, *International Journal of Canadian Studies*, the *Canadian Journal of Political Science*, and the *International Political Science Review*.

Stephen Phillips teaches Political Science at Langara College in Vancouver. Trained in law as well as political science, he teaches Canadian government and comparative politics. His research interests include comparative parliamentary systems, political parties, and the Crown in Canada. He recently spent a year's leave in Ottawa studying Parliament.

Richard Sigurdson is Dean of Arts at the University of Manitoba, where he is also Professor of Political Studies. His areas of academic interest include contemporary political theory, Canadian politics and government, and the history of political thought. He has published a book on Jacob Burckhardt's social and political thought and numerous articles and book chapters on topics including nationalism, immigration, the Canadian Charter of Rights, multiculturalism, and provincial party politics in Canada.

Miriam Smith is Professor in the Department of Social Science at York University. She specializes in Canadian and comparative politics, social movements, public law, and public policy. Among many other works, she is most recently the author of *Political Institutions and Lesbian and Gay Rights in the United States and Canada* (2008) and *A Civil Society?: Social Movements in Canadian Politics* (2005), editor of *Group Politics and Social Movements in Canada* (2008), and co-editor of *Critical Policy Studies* (2007). She also served as President of the Canadian Political Science Association.

David Stewart is Professor and Head of the Department of Political Science at the University of Calgary. His research interests focus on political parties, leadership selection processes and provincial party systems. He is the co-author of *Conventional Choices: Parties and Leadership Selection in the Maritimes* and *Quasi-Democracy?: Parties and Leadership Selection in Alberta*, and has published in journals such as the *Canadian Journal of Political Science*, *Party Politics*, *Canadian Political Science Review*, and *Publius: The Journal of Federalism*.

Claire Turenne Sjolander is Director of the Institute of Women's Studies, as well as Professor of Political Science, at the University of Ottawa. A student of International Relations Theory and Canadian Foreign Policy, she has many publications in the area of gender and foreign policy. Forthcoming publications include *Gender Out of Bounds: Media Constructions of the War in Iraq* (with Kathryn Trevenen) and *Canada In the World: Perspectives on Canadian Foreign Policy* (with Heather Smith). Her impressive teaching has gained her the University of Ottawa's Excellence in Education and Professor of the Year awards.

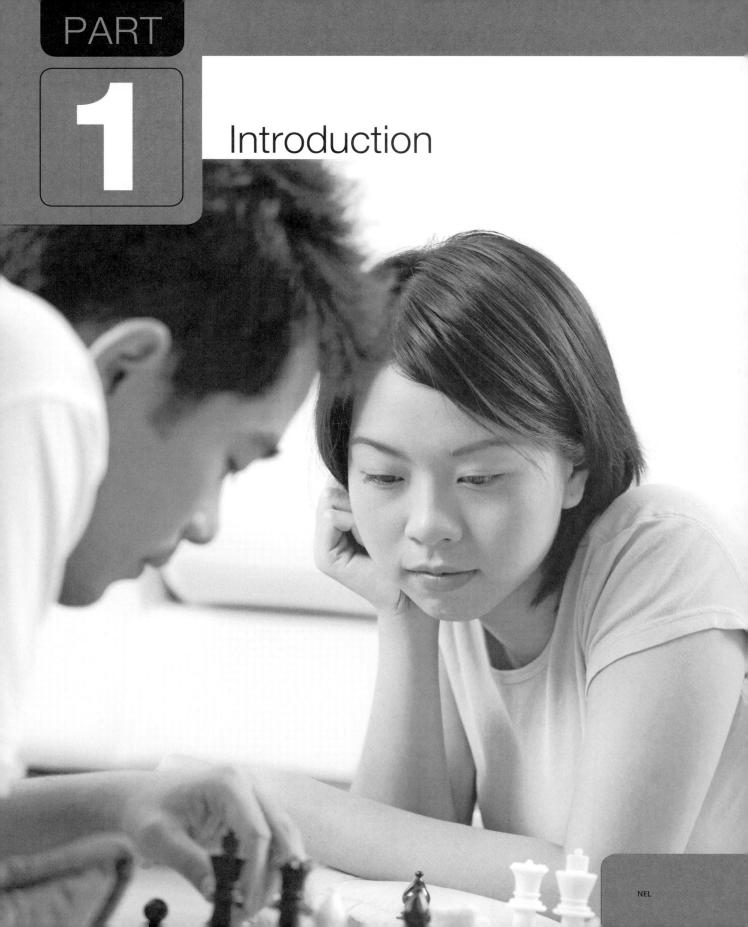

PART

1

Introduction

NEL

Alex Baumann adjusts his toque after carrying the Olympic Torch into Sudbury in January 2010.

The Canadian Press(Gino Donato)

ALEX BAUMANN

Alex Baumann is best known as one of Canada's most outstanding athletes but he is also one of our most distinguished Political Science graduates. While a degree in political science may not have had much to do with his athletic prowess, it is certainly relevant to his increasingly onerous administrative and leadership responsibilities in the athletic world, culminating in his successful current role as Chief Executive Officer of Canada's "Own the Podium" program.

Alex was born in what is now the Czech Republic but was raised in Sudbury, Ontario after his family moved in 1969. At the age of nine, he became involved in competitive swimming training at Laurentian University; by the time he was 17 he had set 38 Canadian swimming records and the world record in the 200-metre individual medley. Alex then enrolled in Laurentian in Sudbury and graduated with an honours degree in Political Science in 1990.

Alex's swimming career reached its pinnacle with two Gold Medals and two world records—in the 200 m and 400 m medley events—at the 1984 Los Angeles Olympics. He was the flag bearer for the opening ceremonies, was named Canada's male athlete of the year, and was awarded the Order of Canada. These medals and records were preceded and followed by countless others, until he retired from competitive swimming in 1987.

In 1988 Alex married Tracy Taggart, an Australian swimmer he had met at the Commonwealth Games in Brisbane. He moved to Australia, became a leading figure in the great success of that country's aquatics program, and eventually landed the position of executive director of the Queensland Academy of Sport.

After Canada's many mediocre Olympic results, Alex was recruited to return to this country and take over Canada's Road to Excellence program in 2007. He moved his family to Ottawa, and soon vaulted to the head of the Own the Podium program. Returning to the pool in 2009, Alex set a record for the 200 m individual medley in the 45–49 age-group and, not surprisingly, Alex and Tracy's two children are also competitive swimmers.

Alex says this about the role of his Political Science degree in this life so dominated by athletics: "My Political Science degree from Laurentian gave me the ability to critically analyze situations and make tough decisions based on the best information available at the time (not unlike politics itself). I also learned that in order to lead effectively, you have to follow your vision which may sometimes make you unpopular."

Studying Politics:
An Introduction to Political Science

Rand Dyck

CHAPTER OBJECTIVES

After you have completed this chapter, you should be able to:

- provide several good reasons to study politics
- describe the breadth of the discipline of political science
- discuss the changing nature of studying politics
- outline the principal fields of study within political science
- define such basic concepts as politics, government, power, influence, coercion, and authority

WHY STUDY POLITICS?

Before you commit yourself to studying politics, even in an introductory course in political science, you may well be asking the following three questions:

- Is it interesting?
- Is it important?
- If I decide to major in political science, is there a job at the end of the line?

This chapter and this book seek to assure you that the answer to all three questions is an unequivocal "YES!"

Politics Is Fascinating

That politics is important is the basic reason to study it, of course, but let us start with the fact that the subject is interesting—often fascinating and even entertaining.

This is partly because politics involves prominent individuals, with all their strengths, weaknesses, foibles, and idiosyncrasies, and we cannot help but be captivated by such colourful, intriguing people. For a time, for example, the charismatic Barack Obama lit up the political landscape of the whole world, although largely because of the Great Recession his record in office has been somewhat disappointing. Political leaders who have arguably left more meaningful legacies include Winston Churchill, in his determination to defeat the Nazi threat in World War II; Nelson Mandela, in his gracious stature as President of South Africa, devoid of bitterness even after having spent 27 years in prison for fighting against apartheid; Margaret Thatcher, with her "Iron Lady" determination to reduce the role of the state in the 1980s; Tommy Douglas, who as premier of Saskatchewan brought public health insurance to Canada; Pierre Elliott Trudeau, with his stylish, debonair, and often arrogant demeanour as Canadian prime minister; Martin Luther King, whose courageous leadership of the fight for racial integration in the United States had a tremendous impact; Mahatma Gandhi, in his effective pacifist resistance to British rule in India; and even Eva Peron, immortalized in the musical *Evita*, who fought for the rights of women and the poor in Argentina, however opportunistic her motives. One might also mention political leaders who had a devastating impact: Attila the Hun, Adolf Hitler, Joseph Stalin, Augusto Pinochet (in Chile), Ferdinand and Imelda Marcos (in the Philippines), and Saddam Hussein.

Part of the reason the subject is so interesting is that egos and ambition abound in political life, and the leading participants are usually involved in antagonistic relationships, either with colleagues or opponents. For example, the daily oral question period in the Canadian and British Houses of Commons and in provincial legislatures is often a great show. The personal characteristics of political leaders, their personality conflicts, and the peculiarity of many of their decisions provide daily fodder for cartoonists, comedians, and satirical radio and television shows. Every daily newspaper features a cartoon on its editorial page, and more often than not such cartoons reflect the humourous (or tragicomic) nature of politics. To brighten and lighten up the material in this text, we have included some of the best recent editorial cartoons. Canadians excel at political satire, exemplified by the popular CBC television program *This Hour Has 22 Minutes*.

Sue Dewar/Artizans

While political events and personalities are interesting and often entertaining to *observe*, many people prefer to take an active part rather than passively follow political developments. Politics offers many exciting opportunities for *participation*. Joining a political party or interest group, collecting names on a petition, going to a public meeting to discuss an issue of political importance, getting involved in an election campaign at any level, or taking part in a political demonstration—all of these can combine meaningful political participation with camaraderie, excitement, and fun.

Politics Is Important

More importantly, politics is important: it has significant implications for how we live our lives.[1] At its core, politics is about government actions and **public policies** that affect everyone in one way or another. When we consider environmental policy in the Alberta oil sands, social and health care programs for the poor, or foreign interventions in Afghanistan, for example, we can see that policies are often deadly serious. But there is even more to it than that. Because government actions and policies usually offer support for some people at the expense of others, they are normally accompanied by controversy and inevitably involve conflict. Such policy conflicts can be just as fascinating as the peculiarities of the individual policymakers involved.

Perhaps it is time to define the term *politics*. The word has its origins in Ancient Greece, which was characterized by such city states as Athens and Sparta. The Greek word for city state is *polis*, also meaning *community*. Thus, when Aristotle claimed that "man is a political animal," he meant that citizens were members of a community and had a responsibility for that community. Citing Aristotle in this way not only clarifies the meaning of politics, but also demonstrates its obvious importance.

In modern political science, one of the classic, catchy definitions of *politics* is Harold Lasswell's "who gets what, when, and how?"[2] Another widely used definition is that politics is "the struggle for power;" alternatively, we could call it the struggle for dominance or advantage. Lasswell adds that "the study of politics is the study of influence and the influential," the influential being those who get the most of what there is to get. Canadian-born political scientist David Easton defined politics as "the authoritative allocation of values for a society."[3] Although they use different terminology, there is a good deal of similarity among these varied definitions. For example, to talk about the allocation of values is basically to discuss the distribution of things that are valued in a society. Such desirable things include money, goods, services, jobs, favours, health, education, security, comfort, freedom, and so on. These are the "what" of who gets what, when, and how. They are also the things of which those who are influential want to get the most.

We should reemphasize that at its core politics involves a difference of opinion, a conflict, or interests that are opposed to each other. It does not arise where there is complete harmony between two or more individuals, two or more states, or two or more actors of any kind.

The other unstated premise here is that there is usually a desire to resolve such conflict, at least on the part of some of the actors involved. Politics is sometimes said to be "the art of the possible," or to be marked by compromise. Regardless of whether such a description is meant as praise or criticism, it is true that the public policies adopted are frequently designed to incorporate conflicting interests or to seek a middle ground. It is not always such a bad thing to develop a compromise policy that tries to bring together as many conflicting interests as possible, and it adds to the policy's legitimacy.

Politics thus seems to arise in a situation marked by conflict, in which attempts are made to resolve that conflict. Let us therefore define **politics** as "that activity in which conflicting interests struggle for advantage or dominance." In the context of government, we can add "in the making and execution of public policies." (The definitions used in this book are meant to help your understanding of the concepts involved, but you will likely encounter alternative definitions in other texts and from other authors.)

POLITICS: That activity in which conflicting interests struggle for advantage or dominance in the making and execution of public policies.

Governments could be said to exercise stewardship of a state; they provide the social, economic, and physical infrastructure that enables and protects country, citizens, and institutions, but every state decides how much government it needs. There is not much dispute about the idea that government should guarantee law and order in society by passing laws to make certain types of behaviour criminal and by hiring police officers and building jails. But beyond this basic consensus, political controversies immediately begin to arise. You may well have your own opinion on these matters. Does the Canadian government's antiterrorism legislation infringe upon civil liberties? Is it a crime to kill a severely disabled daughter, as in the case of Robert Latimer, or to demonstrate against the government or globalization, as in the case of the G20 in Toronto in the summer of 2010? You may be hoping for a career in policing, and whether the government should hire more women and visible-minority police officers may be of personal interest to you. Should the government be building more jails when the crime rate is declining? Should the penalty for murder be capital punishment?

It is usually assumed that national governments should establish armed forces to protect the country from external threats. But how large should such armed forces be? What kinds of armaments and equipment should be provided? Should a country require military training of all its citizens, especially those about the age of most readers of this book? Even in the case of internal and external security—a seemingly straightforward issue—politics becomes quite complicated because there are many conflicting ways of proceeding.

Beyond the commonly accepted notion of providing for law, order, and security, the question arises as to whether the government should intervene in society any further. Generally speaking, government action was limited until about 1900; the extent of government intervention then increased over the first eight decades of the 20th century, but after 1985 or so it began to recede. In the early part of the 21st century, most governments seemed to be less reluctant to spend or otherwise intervene, especially in the context of the Great Recession of 2008–2010. But if a government decides to get more involved, what form should such intervention take? We are all familiar with myriad government regulations that constrain individual, group, and corporate behaviour, for example, and with government programs that provide many kinds of services and money transfers to individuals, groups, communities, provinces, and corporations. In order to finance such regulation, services, and transfers the government normally has to engage in taxation. Occasionally, though less frequently than in the past, governments go beyond regulation, services, transfers, and taxation;

they actually buy or establish corporations and have them function as public- or state-owned enterprises. In Canada, these are called Crown corporations.

There is still virtual unanimity that government provision of a public education system is beneficial for society as a whole. But the consensus immediately breaks down around questions of what should be taught in such schools. For example, whether to teach evolution or creationism remains an issue for some people. This also leads to the question of whether there should be only one public education system or whether private institutions can be established. What about religious schools and home schooling? Should public funds be available for schools that are not part of the public system? As a recent secondary school graduate, you may well have opinions on these matters. Postsecondary education issues include the level of tuition fees, grants, and loans, and the recruitment of large numbers of students from overseas.

As costs escalate, the role of government in the provision of health services has also become particularly controversial. To what extent should there be a universal, public healthcare system? What health services should people have to pay for outside that system— chiropractic care, or circumcisions, or eyeglasses? Should people who can afford it be allowed faster or superior service, as the proponents of the so-called two-tier system believe? Should the universal system be extended to cover pharmaceuticals and dental care? What about deterrent fees?

Education and health are two of the most expensive public services provided by governments today, but the array of other social services is also extensive, although far from unanimously supported. Should the government ensure that no one goes hungry through initiatives such as public pensions for the elderly and disabled, child benefits, employment insurance, or social assistance? Should the government ensure that no one is homeless? Should single mothers who want to pursue postsecondary education be provided with child-care services? Should governments establish a reasonably priced universal childcare system, as exists in Quebec?

The preceding sketch of public programs leads to the question of how to finance the operations that government decides to undertake. Who should pay what kinds of taxes? Should there be a flat rate for everyone or should richer people pay at a higher rate? Should all forms of income be taxed equally or should capital gains, for example, be taxed at a lower rate? What about

lottery winnings? Should business people be allowed to deduct entertainment expenses from their income tax? What about individual charitable donations, political contributions, and interest paid on loans to buy stocks and shares?

The implications of the issues just raised are of considerable importance. Political decisions on these issues influence, if not determine, what kind of lifestyle a person or a family may possess; they can certainly make life easier or more difficult, as you as a student, can attest. While they are significant, such decisions, actions, and policies rarely constitute matters of life and death in the generally comfortable Canadian context. Canada ranked first for seven consecutive years in the United Nations **Human Development Index (HDI)** in terms of life expectancy, literacy, and income, as Prime Minister Chrétien never tired of pointing out. By 2010, however, Canada had fallen to eighth place on the general index, 16th on the gender equality index, and 12th in terms of reducing human poverty. Some of these statistics are revealed in Table 1.1.

When looking beyond Canada and the other industrialized democracies, the decisions made by governments often have much more serious implications. Huge portions of the global population suffer from the insecurities of poverty, malnutrition, illness, and homelessness sometimes, but not always, caused by natural disasters. In many cases, national governments might improve the situation with a fairer distribution of income; this is an internal political decision. Other cases require a helping hand from richer, industrialized countries. Many corners of the world are engaged in civil wars or military conflicts with external enemies in which government decisions or terrorist retaliations put lives in danger daily. These include Afghanistan, Iraq, the never-ending Israeli–Palestinian conflict, other parts of the Middle East, and many parts of Africa. In short, politics is a matter of life and death in a large part of the globe. The study of this important subject may serve as the first step in trying to solve such problems.

The Question of Citizenship Another aspect of the importance of politics revolves around the obligations of citizenship. Simply put, citizens of a democracy are expected to develop the best understanding they can of the political system in which they live, in return for the right of having a say in its governance. Studying politics is hard intellectual work that will make students better thinkers and better citizens.

Table 1.1 Top 16 Rankings in Various United Nations Human Development Indexes		
Human Development, 2010	**Gender Equality, 2008**	**Least Poverty, 2009**
1. Norway	1. Netherlands	1. Sweden
2. Australia	2. Denmark	2. Norway
3. New Zealand	3. Sweden	3. Netherlands
4. United States	4. Switzerland	4. Denmark
5. Iceland	5. Norway	5. Finland
6. Lichtenstein	6. Belgium	6. Germany
7. Netherlands	7. Germany	7. Switzerland
8. Canada	8. Finland	8. France
9. Sweden	9. Italy	9. Austria
10. Germany	10. Singapore	10. Luxembourg
11. Japan	11. France	11. Czech Republic
12. South Korea	12. Japan	12. Canada
13. Switzerland	13. Iceland	13. Japan
14. France	14. Spain	14. Australia
15. Israel	15. Cyprus	15. Belgium
16. Finland	16. Canada	16. Slovakia

Sources: United Nations Human Development Report (UNHDR), 2010, Tables 1 and 4, and UNHDR, 2009, Table I-2. Reproduced by permission of UNDP.

The concept of citizenship has changed considerably over time. In ancient Athens, for example, citizenship was severely restricted and excluded women, labourers, slaves, and foreigners. Propertied male citizens, on the other hand, were expected to play a direct, almost full-time part in the governing of their city-state.

Early in the 20th century, in most civilized countries, women and the working class forced their way into becoming part of the electorate, and other exclusions from the right to vote were gradually eliminated. **Citizenship** became virtually universal and it came to mean membership in a nation-state that entailed rights and responsibilities, including that of political participation. On the other hand, a very small proportion of citizens made political life a full-time preoccupation. The direct democracy of ancient Greece evolved into a representative democracy, in which periodic elections became the main focus of political activity for the general population. In an ideal case everyone would at least cast an informed vote in such elections.

In the period between 1945 and 1985, often called the period of the **welfare state**, the concept of citizenship in industrialized countries changed again. Citizens came to expect the state to provide universal programs of social security to overcome the negative effects of economic uncertainty associated with private-sector market forces. After 1985, however, an increasing consensus developed throughout the Western world that citizens should be more self-reliant. Led by Margaret Thatcher in Britain and Ronald Reagan in the United States, the balance between individual and collective responsibility underwent a major shift, as governments balanced their budgets by dismantling social programs while also lowering taxes. In almost every state, the government plays a smaller role today than it did in 1985 in terms of regulation, ownership, taxation, and provision of social services.

A rather dramatic development in such industrialized democracies as Canada, the United Kingdom, and the United States is the declining voter turnout rate in recent elections. Although this trend has many causes, it may be partially attributed to the fact that as the government becomes less involved in society citizens in turn decide that it is not as important to vote.

On the other hand, participation in what is sometimes called "small-p" politics, that is, being engaged in non-electoral activities such as working for local community betterment in charities, community groups, advocacy groups, and in political protests seems to be increasing.[4]

In this book, we take the position that governments continue to make a wide range of crucial decisions for society, even in the advanced, industrialized democracies such as Canada. Therefore, it is still an important obligation of citizens to cast an informed vote in elections, as well as to try to influence government decisions during the inter-election period. Indeed, a high level of civic participation is now considered to be a specific component of the Canadian Index of Wellbeing.[5] Studying politics is the most logical route to developing an understanding of our political system and of how to make an impact upon it.

Moreover, besides being a citizen of a specific state, we are all now citizens of the world, and we are all subject to unprecedented global forces. The question is often raised as to whether individual states are still as capable of providing for their own citizens as in the past. We are all affected by worldwide environmental developments, massive migrations of dispossessed people, and the concentration of capital in an ever-decreasing number of rapidly expanding **transnational corporations**. By studying politics, global citizens can help meet their obligation to understand as much as they can about the condition of the globe and to do their part to try to improve it.

In other words, studying politics can also lead to *solutions* to society's problems. Political science tries to make sense of and to solve the kinds of complicated ethical and organizational problems that must be overcome for large numbers of people to live and cooperate successfully with one another in a common state, as well as the problems associated with the complex interactions between states. In practice, politics is very much concerned with how best to achieve desirable values, such as political freedom or equality. Likewise, politics analyzes the relative merits of different forms of government and international organization. The aim of studying politics is to build up a more reliable systematic knowledge of the way political organizations emerge, develop, function, and co-exist, ultimately hoping that this knowledge will

assist in developing more attractive and more viable societies in the future.

Political Science Graduates Get Jobs

But does anybody hire students who decide to study and graduate with a degree in political science? The answer is yes, and the diversity of the jobs would probably astound you. This book will introduce you to several young people who have gone beyond the introductory course to specialize in political science in Canadian universities and show you the range of their career experiences, starting with those careers listed in Box 1.1.

When you tell someone that you are studying political science, chances are they will jump to the conclusion that you plan to become a politician. That may well be your intention, and a noble calling it is, however much abuse politicians take in the media and in public discussion. Many political science graduates *do* become politicians, and many politicians are political science graduates. Speaking only of Canada, many of those elected to the House of Commons, provincial legislatures, municipal councils, and other political posts have graduated in this field. We give you the examples of Keith Hutchings, a member of the Newfoundland and Labrador House of Assembly, in the introductory vignette to Part 5 of this text, as well as that of former member of Parliament, Wendy Lill, in the introduction to Part 3.

The number of politicians is fairly limited, however, and not all political science graduates can or want to choose this option. Many are employed as *assistants* to politicians, be they MPs, senators, members of provincial legislatures, or cabinet ministers. Very often, a period of employment in this capacity leads people to seek political office on their own, as in the case of Mr. Hutchings.

Another career avenue is to work for the government—federal, provincial, or municipal. These three levels of government employ over three million people in Canada, and a good proportion of these employees are political science graduates. Such graduates typically work in management positions or are involved in policy development. That is, they advise on which policies should be pursued and work

BOX 1.1

COMMON OPTIONS FOR POLITICAL SCIENCE GRADUATES

Campaign/Elections Officer	Public Relations
Market Researchers/Analyst	Human Rights Officer
Diplomat/Embassy Officer	Labour Relations Mediator
Legislative/Parliamentary Assistant	Lobbyist
Journalist/Reporter	Political Activist
Public Policy Analyst	Intelligence/Security Agent
Public Opinion Pollster/Analyst	Consumer Advocate
Professor/Teacher	Media Analyst/Researcher
Political Strategist	Labour Organizer/Negotiator
Public Administration (all levels of government)	Law Enforcement
Lawyer/Paralegal	Corrections Officer
Community Worker	Immigration Officer

to implement these policies once they are adopted. Kathryn Royal, profiled in the introductory vignette to Part 4, is an excellent example. With government downsizing and privatization characteristic of the post-1985 period, few such positions have been available but if you are graduating in the early years of the 21st century your prospects are much brighter. In the next five years or so, governments at all levels will be replacing thousands of employees who will have reached retirement age.

In addition to jobs at regular government departments, there are many employment opportunities in semi-independent government agencies, boards, commissions, and Crown corporations, such as Elections Canada, Statistics Canada, or indeed, the House of Commons or the Senate. A good example is Alex Baumann, who was introduced at the beginning of this chapter. Mr. Baumann heads the "Own the Podium" program, a complex organization involving Sport Canada, the Canadian Olympic and Paralympic Committees, and many other stakeholders, which aims to make Canada a world leader in high-performance sport.

One aspect of government employment that many political science graduates find attractive is the foreign service—the diplomatic corps. Some people are particularly excited about the prospect of serving at embassies, consulates, or high commissions around the world and of advising on Canada's foreign policy. Once again, a degree in political science is the most appropriate entry to such a career, although a postgraduate degree in international relations and the ability to speak at least two languages is an additional asset. We give the example of Katrina Burgess in the introductory vignette to Part 7. Related to this career is work for an international organization such as the United Nations, or for a **nongovernmental organization (NGO)** such as Greenpeace, the Red Cross, Amnesty International, Oxfam, or others involved in Third World development. Grant Budding, introduced in Part 6, has worked for the United Nations and plans to find employment there again or in some other international organization upon completing his graduate studies.

In addition to NGO employees, many political science graduates prefer to work *close* to the government rather than *for* the government. They are employed by political parties, for example, as researchers, recruiters, organizers, policy advisors, and campaign managers. Political science graduates also possess the skills to seek employment in the media as radio, television, and newspaper reporters and commentators, or with polling firms, as public opinion and voting analysts. Wendy Lill, mentioned earlier, combines a political career with that of a playwright, and her creative work often deals with political issues. Another related line of work is with interest groups, advocacy groups, and think tanks. In their attempt to analyze or influence government policy, these organizations also value the knowledge and skills acquired while obtaining a political science degree. Some graduates actually establish their own lobbying and consulting firms and provide policy advice for a fee.

Political science is also an appropriate background for a career in law. Although law schools welcome applicants from a wide range of disciplines, it is safe to say that they accept more applicants with political science degrees than from any other educational background. A large proportion of political science graduates from every university in Canada have gone on to law school.

Political science graduates can also become teachers. Some provinces hire political science graduates in their secondary schools and all provinces teach a certain amount of political science at the college level. Individuals intensely dedicated to the discipline can also become university professors. We provide 14 examples in the form of the contributing authors of this book!

So far we have mentioned careers that put a premium on a specific *political* component but political science is so broad in its scope and in the skills the graduates of this discipline develop that such a degree is valuable in a much wider range of occupations. Renny Khan, for example, whom we profile in the introductory vignette to Part 2, works in university administration as Director of International Programs for the Faculty of Medicine and Dentistry at the University of Alberta. Political science graduates also find a ready market in business—in corporations of all kinds at national and multinational levels, from banks and insurance companies to public relations firms.

The political science curriculum that you are about to embark upon, both in this book and possibly beyond, will help to open your eyes to what is happening at home and abroad. You will be required to analyze public issues from a variety of points of view, and in the process you will learn to think clearly and

BOX 1.2

SKILLS ACQUIRED IN STUDYING POLITICAL SCIENCE

Thinking Skills
- The ability to "think on your feet"
- Exposure to new, unfamiliar, and alternative perspectives on issues or problems
- The ability to develop logical arguments and assess or evaluate the arguments of others

Research Skills
- Identifying and locating sources of information
- Collecting, analyzing, and interpreting data to support or refute arguments
- Critical understanding of the uses (and potential abuse) of statistics
- Computing skills

Communication Skills
- Making oral presentations and engaging in debates
- Writing reports, summaries, and essays
- Communicating ideas clearly and concisely, whether orally or in writing
- The ability to listen

Source: Department of Political Science, Brock University website; cited on June 15, 2001; available at http://www.brocku.ca/politics/whypoli.htm. Reprinted by permission of the Department of Political Science, Brock University.

communicate effectively. Your studies will also make you a valuable commodity to an array of employers whose focus is not strictly political. The Brock University Department of Political Science website once identified the skills acquired in pursuing a degree in political science as those listed in Box 1.2.

You will often hear that in the modern world few people will retain a job with a single employer or even have the same kind of job with different employers until retirement and that you will have to be flexible in today's labour market. That is another way of saying that employers are not so much seeking job-specific abilities as transferable skills that allow an employee to adapt to the changing workplace and the changing world. Box 1.3 elaborates on the transferable skills that political science students will acquire over the course of their degree and that will prepare them for a variety of careers.

TRANSFERABLE SKILLS ACQUIRED IN THE STUDY OF POLITICAL SCIENCE

An Analytical Capacity
- An ability to draw relevant or significant distinctions between different classes of information
- An ability to arrive at decisions based on the analysis of information and data
- An ability to sort things, categorize them, or impose some scheme on what is otherwise an overwhelming set of materials
- An ability to compile and organize facts and information and to comprehend and apply new and/or unfamiliar information to different situations and settings

A Synthetic Capacity
- An ability to see connections; the skills required to identify and access a wide range of relevant information and resources
- An ability to make surprising or unexpected connections by grouping like with unlike according to conceptual or classificatory schemes you are able to construct

The Skill of Critical Perspective
- An ability to separate oneself and one's emotions from events, coupled with the need to escape the pressures of immediacy, to see the background to the events, and to see the broader chain of cause and effect
- An ability to engage with political events and gain a greater understanding of the processes involved in different political systems around the world

THE BREADTH OF THE STUDY OF POLITICS

If we have convinced you that you are on the right track in thinking about studying politics, let us spend the rest of this chapter introducing the subject of politics. Let us show you the breadth of the field and the central concerns of the discipline, and let us provide greater proof that the subject is both interesting and important. We will do so in terms of the organization of this book.

Governments, States, Nations, and Markets

Governments, states, and nations have always been core subjects of politics, and remain so today. Part 2 of this book—Chapters 2, 3, and 4—deals primarily with these concepts. We will leave it to those chapters to define *state* and *nation*, but here we will connect the concept of **government** to that of politics, cited above. Government can be defined as the set of institutions and practices that makes and enforces collective public decisions for a society. Government is the body that decides who will get what, when, and how; government reflects the interests of the influential; government represents those who have succeeded in the struggle for power; government makes the authoritative allocation of values for a society. Although the two terms—government and state—usually go together, some governments in the world are not closely identified with a state. Thus, Chapter 2 elaborates on all aspects of government, including those that do not take the form of the government of a state.

> **GOVERNMENT:** The set of institutions and practices that make and enforce collective public decisions for a society.

Chapter 3 concerns itself to a great extent in distinguishing between states and nations and clarifying the concepts of nationalism and cultural pluralism. We seem to have moved from a world made up of nation-states in which the population was quite homogeneous to a situation where most states are characterized by ethnic diversity. The world has seen huge waves of migration in the past 50 years, leaving few states without the problem of accommodating a variety of cultural groups within them. In many countries, Aboriginal populations have also become much more self-conscious and assertive. Such cultural groups that exist within a society often wish to practise as much self-government as possible. This is true even in a traditional multiethnic state, such as the United Kingdom, where Scotland and Wales are granted more autonomy. The place of Quebec in the Canadian federation also comes to mind.

Chapter 4 deals with the relationship between the state, or the public sector, and the private sector,

TYPICAL RESEARCH QUESTION

Will the various religious and ethnic groups within Iraq ever be able to work together in a common government, or should the country be divided into several small homogeneous states?

otherwise known as the "market." In modern western systems, at least, goods and services can be distributed in two basic ways: through the market forces of capitalism or through the government. The study of the relationship between state and market is usually termed "political economy," and is of much interest in contemporary political science.

Political Values, Ideas, and Ideologies

Studying politics also means studying political values, ideas, and ideologies, and these concepts are the subject of Part 3 of this book, which comprises Chapters 5 and 6. Values, ideas, and ideologies can be seen as the inspiration for much of what takes place in the realm of politics, even when it seems to centre on more trivial issues.

Political Socialization and Political Culture Most citizens have certain political values and ideas whether they realize it or not. Where do these values come from? Political science uses the term **political socialization**

to refer to the process of acquiring such values and ideas. Think about your own case: What are some of your own political values and ideas? Can you figure out where they came from? Common agents of political socialization are families, schools, peers, and the mass media, although there are many other sources.

Political science focuses primarily on those values and ideas that relate to the role of government in society. Figure 1.1 indicates an interesting difference of opinion on this role among Canadians of different party preferences. What this figure shows is that New Democrats are more committed to spending on social programs, while Liberals and supporters of the two parties that later combined to form the new Conservative Party of Canada emphasize reduction of the public debt. (The figure also indicates a subtle difference between those two partners.)

If we can find values and ideas that are widely held in any political system, we call such a collection the **political culture**. In other words, the political culture sets the context or the limits for what actions are considered appropriate for consideration in the political system. The politics of any society takes place within a

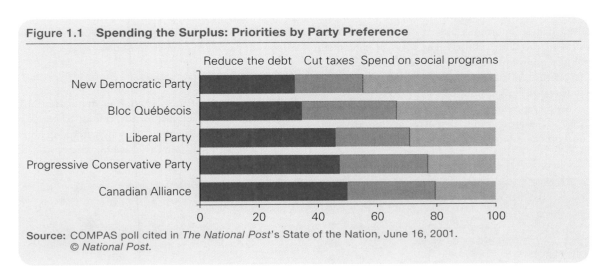

Figure 1.1   Spending the Surplus: Priorities by Party Preference

Source: COMPAS poll cited in *The National Post*'s State of the Nation, June 16, 2001.
© *National Post*.

distinctive context of values and attitudes; For example, Switzerland prefers to have citizens make decisions by way of regular referendums, whereas Canada has held only three national referendums in 145 years. Chapter 5 deals with both political socialization and political culture.

Political Ideas and Philosophy Just as we can ask where an individual's basic values and ideas came from, so we can inquire about the origins of the basic concepts in the study of politics. This inquiry usually takes us back to ancient Greece. There we find philosophers such as Socrates, Plato, and Aristotle asking questions such as "What is justice?"; "What is the best form of the state?"; "Who should govern?"; and "What are the obligations of citizenship?" When you start to think about them, none of these questions is easy to answer, but the ancient Greeks were among the first ones to try.

Other political philosophers later added their thoughts on these and other questions. Machiavelli told us how he thought a prince should govern, and Jean-Jacques Rousseau, Thomas Hobbes, John Locke, and John Stuart Mill all contributed profound ideas about the relationship between the individual and the state and about the concepts of citizenship, equality, and freedom. Even if these writers were not widely read by the general public, some of their ideas greatly influenced political developments such as the French and American Revolutions and the evolution of democracy. Similarly, Karl Marx's call for a working-class revolution to overthrow the alleged evils of capitalism had an enormous impact on the shape of the world in the 20th century. The ideas of subsequent political philosophers also influenced the way in which that century ended, and the new century will doubtless produce political philosophers of its own.

Studying politics, therefore, includes studying the ideas of the great minds that have addressed various concepts central to political thought over the centuries.

It cannot be complete without examining what these thinkers had to say, and hence some of their views are discussed in Chapter 6.

Political Ideologies When a person or group holds a consistent set of ideas about the objectives of political life, we often call it an **ideology**. An ideology usually includes a collection of related thoughts on the respective roles of the individual and the government in the state. In the daily battle among politicians and among political parties, we expect their respective words, promises, and decisions to reflect a basic ideological framework. The labels we apply to such sets of ideas include liberalism, conservatism, socialism, communism, fascism, nationalism, individualism, collectivism, feminism, environmentalism, populism, and radicalism, among others,[6] and political scientists are always on the lookout to classify politicians and parties in terms of such ideologies.

It is often expected, for example, that democratic political systems will be characterized by two or more political parties with at least slightly different ideological orientations. In a two-party system, one party might emphasize equality and collectivism while the other might favour individualism and privilege. In a three-party system, there might be a third party occupying a central ideological position between these two. In a multiparty system, there might be four or more parties, each claiming a narrow part of the ideological continuum: communists, socialists, social democrats, liberals, conservatives, neoconservatives, and so on. Even if such ideological clarity and consistency are often lacking in the real world, the subject remains an important part of the study of politics.

Political Institutions

Politics is also about the operation of the institutions of government. In fact, historically, this aspect was the very essence of the discipline. Although studying politics has a wider focus nowadays, we must never forget

TYPICAL RESEARCH QUESTION

Do social democratic Scandinavian countries have models of healthcare policy that are worthy of North American emulation?

that the ways in which government institutions function and the ways in which they might be reformed in order to operate more effectively are highly important topics. These subjects are contained in Part 4 of this book, which comprises Chapters 7, 8, 9, and 10.

Constitutions Government institutions are normally provided for in a state's **constitution**, which is the subject of much study in itself. In some countries, such as the United States of America, the constitution is a single comprehensive document. In contrast, as Chapter 7 of this book shows, the Canadian constitution is an unusual combination of written and unwritten parts.

Another interesting aspect of constitutions is the ease or difficulty with which they can be amended. The process of amending the Canadian constitution is rather complex, and after the experiences of the Meech Lake and Charlottetown Accords, we know that it is almost impossible to get agreement on comprehensive changes.

Most modern constitutions also contain some kind of bill or charter of rights that prohibits the government from interfering with the basic freedoms or liberties of its citizens. Canada added the Charter of Rights and Freedoms to its Constitution in 1982, but that did not mean that Canadians had no such rights beforehand. When there is a question about whether the government has overstepped its bounds, for example in curtailing freedom of expression in terms of terrorism or pornography, it is usually up to the courts or judiciary to decide the issue.

The Political Executive and the Bureaucracy The constitution normally establishes institutions that embody four branches of government: the executive, the bureaucracy, the legislature, and the judiciary. The **executive** branch of government usually consists of a head of state—a president or a monarch—who may be largely ceremonial, as in Britain and Canada, or imbued with great power, as in the United States or Mexico. In the case of a country with a ceremonial head of state, there is also an effective decision-making body, often called a prime minister and cabinet. As in the case of any organization, as you may know from your own experience, the executive provides leadership and makes many of the key decisions. Studying politics

includes examining how such executive bodies function, including the question as to who *really* makes the big decisions in running a government.

Nobody expects those politicians who make up the executive branch of government to be able to solve all of society's problems single-handedly. For the most part, they are fairly ordinary mortals without a profound knowledge of the issues they are called upon to address. But in modern political systems, these politicians are assisted and advised by permanent, professional employees of the state whose job is to answer whatever questions the politicians ask. The members of the public service or **bureaucracy** advise the politicians on which policies to pursue and how to pursue them, and then administer the policies adopted. The bureaucracy is the largest branch of a 21st-century government, and no successful politician would go very far without asking the bureaucrats for advice. Studying politics therefore means spending considerable time in assessing the role of the bureaucracy in the policy process. Chapter 8 of this book examines both the political executive and the bureaucracy.

The Legislature Almost every political system has a legislative chamber made up of the elected representatives of the people, variously called the House of Commons, House of Representatives, Chamber of Deputies, etc. If chosen in free and fair elections, this chamber is a defining sign of a democracy. In some countries, including Canada, the members of the executive branch also sit in the **legislature**, but in others, as in the United States, they are separately elected. In either case, it is essential that the legislative branch give approval to laws, whatever their origin. Many Canadian members of parliament, feeling that they have little influence in the making of government policies, look longingly south of the border at the real power of members of the House of Representatives and Senate in the United States. On the other hand, American observers often envy the efficiency with which the Canadian government can make decisions, at least in a majority government situation. Studying politics means examining legislative chambers and assessing the functions they perform, as well as understanding the logic of single-chamber and dual-chamber legislatures. These topics will be covered in Chapter 9 of this text.

The Parliament Buildings in Ottawa are the seat of the Government of Canada.

Maclean's/The Canadian Press(Peter Bregg)

The Judiciary Ideally, every state should have an independent **judiciary**, a system of courts that aim to make impartial decisions when it becomes necessary to interpret the law in cases of dispute. Studying politics has not always paid much attention to judicial interpretation, but this may have been a serious oversight, and the judiciary has now become intensely scrutinized as an integral part of the political process. The courts seem to be making more significant decisions than previously, partly because most states have some version of a bill of rights that has to be interpreted. Are judicial decisions impartial? How should judges be chosen? When should they be removed? Such questions are discussed in Chapter 10.

Studying politics thus includes examining how presidents, prime ministers, cabinets, councils of ministers, houses of commons or representatives, senates, bureaucracies, and courts function individually and how they interact with each other. It involves looking for the strengths and weaknesses in each national set of government institutions and tackling the question of whether what has proved to be successful in one country might be adopted or adapted elsewhere.

Political Behaviour and Participation

Many observers would regard political behaviour and participation as the most interesting part of the study of politics. Whether or not this includes you, these subjects are addressed in Part 5 of the book, which comprises Chapters 11, 12, and 13.

Voting and Elections In large part politics is about political behaviour and participation. One main aspect of this domain is voting and electing candidates to public office. Politics is also about deciding what kind of electoral system to use, and nearly every country has a distinctive process to choose its politicians. Especially in countries where **elections** are free and fair (a characteristic of democracy), they are usually exciting, entertaining experiences. If you have not been involved in an election campaign, you might wish to track down a candidate and volunteer for action! Of course, you might even become a candidate yourself.

But elections are also very serious events, since the leader or the political party that emerges victorious can have a profound effect on the public policies later adopted. The winning party normally proceeds to reward its supporters, whether in the appointments it makes or in the policies it adopts. When George W. Bush succeeded Bill Clinton as president of the United States, for example, his reversal of many of his predecessor's policies had implications far beyond American borders: he reneged on the Kyoto Protocol, denied federal aid to groups that promoted abortion overseas, went to war in Afghanistan and Iraq, and generally threw American weight around throughout the world. Barack Obama later reverted to many Clintonesque policies.

The role of the **mass media** in the election campaigns is also of interest to political science. Do the media give equitable coverage to all parties? Do they encourage an emphasis on image rather than substance? Does television advertising make elections too

TYPICAL RESEARCH QUESTION

In which states do the courts have the most power to overturn decisions of elected politicians?

Table 1.2 Voter Turnout Rates in 20 Selected Countries, 1945–2001			
Country	Percent	Country	Percent
Australia	94.5	Greece	79.9
Belgium	92.5	Finland	76.0
Austria	91.3	United Kingdom	75.2
New Zealand	90.8	Canada	73.9
Italy	89.8	France	73.8
Netherlands	87.5	Spain	73.6
Sweden	87.1	Ireland	73.3
Denmark	85.9	Japan	69.5
Germany	85.4	United States	66.5
Norway	80.4	Switzerland	56.5

Source: Reproduced by permission of International IDEA, from *Voter Turnout Since 1945: A Global Report*, Rafael López Pintor and Maria Gratschew, eds. © International Institute for Democracy and Electoral Assistance 2011, <www.idea.int>.

expensive and take away from their democratic character? Somewhat similarly, public opinion polls have come to figure prominently in election campaigns. Political science is interested in whether they are accurate, whether they favour one party over another, and whether they influence the results.

While being intensely interested in political participation, political science is also concerned with non-participation. As mentioned, the voter turnout rate in Canada, the United States, and the United Kingdom seems to be dwindling. Who is not voting, and why? Table 1.2 provides the voter turnout rates in selected countries in the post-World War II period, and in most cases the rate has decreased somewhat over this period, and since. On the other hand, as noted earlier, political participation in "small-p" activities is probably increasing.

Political Parties Politics is also about **political parties**, which seem to crop up in virtually every political system. In most cases, candidates run for office on a party banner and as a member of a party team. Studying politics involves investigating the number of parties (one, two, three, or more) present in what is usually referred to as the party system. Political science is also interested in why established parties sometimes founder and why new parties form. In Canada, for example, we are interested in whether the Liberal Party will regain its traditional dominant position or whether we have moved to a new era of party competition with a stronger presence of Conservatives and the NDP.

Studying politics involves examining how democratic political parties are organized, how they choose their candidates, how they select or remove their leaders, and how they develop their policies. Has increased public financial support affected their operations?

All of these aspects of political parties are discussed in Chapter 12 of this text. Again, most parties would welcome your own participation, and you might even want to become involved in the creation of a new one.

TYPICAL RESEARCH QUESTION

Do proportional electoral systems generally result in higher voter turnout rates and a larger representation of women and minorities?

Interest Groups and Social Movements Many people join together with others who share similar interests to establish organized groups. They may organize simply to promote their common interests without any thought of becoming political. But even if this is the case, such groups often find themselves drawn into the political process when they begin to see defects in government policies. Thus, countries that value freedom of association are characterized by hordes of **interest groups** that at least occasionally try to put pressure on the government to change public policies. Other groups may be formed with a more deliberate political purpose, and they may spend most of their time trying to influence such policies. Individual corporations regularly attempt to influence government policies and actions, and often band together in industry-wide interest groups to communicate their demands to government, frequently paying consultant lobbyists to get them in the door. For example, tobacco companies pressure government

to delay new warning labels on cigarette packages, coal and petroleum companies pressure government to dilute environmental standards, and manufacturers of military equipment pressure government for a piece of any new defence procurement contract. On another front, the Canadian Federation of Students (CFS) is primarily concerned with influencing the policies of federal and provincial governments that affect postsecondary students. More active participation in the CFS by a greater number of students would no doubt make it a stronger political force. On the local level, the student organization at your college or university may often function as a pressure group on your own campus.

The Summit of the Americas meeting in Quebec City in April 2001 and the G20 summit in Toronto in June 2010 both attracted thousands of protesters from both Canada and abroad—often young people who could be said to be part of the anti-globalization movement. Similar **social movements** include the

The Canadian Federation of Students demonstrates against rising tuition fees.

The Toronto Star/The Canadian Press (Steve Russell)

women's movement, the environmental movement, the gay and lesbian movement, and the animal rights movement, among many others. Studying politics also means studying such social movements, whether they operate in a single country or, as is increasingly the case, network with each other around the world. Possessing such resources as information and time, professors and students are often active in their communities in organizing demonstrations to articulate their opinion on contentious issues. Engaging in pressure group activity or protests can be a rather enjoyable social activity at the same time as it seriously tries to influence public policies that are felt to be detrimental. Interest groups and social movements are the subject of Chapter 13 in this book.

Political Development and Change

At one point in time, studying politics may have been largely confined to studying political ideas, institutions, and behaviour in the advanced, industrialized, often democratic states. But it cannot be so restricted any longer. Today, the study of politics must include what is often called the Third World or developing world, the concern of Chapter 14. Why are some countries rich and others poor? Why are some advanced and others underdeveloped? Is it a question of resources, distribution, or colonialism and exploitation? Should we expect every country to embrace the kind of democracy that we think is best? Perhaps the events of September 11, 2001 provided the most dramatic impetus for everyone to become more familiar with that part of the world.

As for political change, some observers note a general movement from nondemocratic to democratic regimes around the world. Is this really true, and if so, what are the factors behind this fundamental transformation? How are democratic regimes consolidated in such situations, and what are the consequences? On the other hand, is there any movement in the opposite direction? Another aspect of political change relates to questions of dissent, protest, rebellion, and violence, including terrorism and revolution. Why do some countries manage to change in a peaceful fashion, while others resort to radical, often violent change? These questions are addressed in Chapter 15.

International Politics and Globalization

So far we have concentrated primarily on domestic politics, that is, politics within any given country or state. But studying politics has always gone beyond the internal operation of individual states to include the international dimension. If we define politics as the activity in which conflicting interests struggle for advantage or dominance, then there is probably just as much politics involved between states as within them.

International politics has always been important, partly because conflict between states has often led to war, a dimension of violence usually much more serious than what is experienced within a single state. Studying politics involves examining the factors that lead to conflict between states and searching for mechanisms to moderate or prevent international violence, as shown in Chapter 16. The first half of the 20th century witnessed the two most horrible wars in human history, while the second half was dominated by the Cold War between the United States and the Soviet Union, in a kind of balance of terror. But if the Cold War is over, what are the new dimensions of international security in the 21st century? Was U.S. President Bush correct in proposing that the United States should try to extend its brand of democracy throughout the Arab/Muslim world? Or is the war against terrorism, especially after September 11, 2001, more a matter of improving intelligence capabilities?

Finally, as we have mentioned, individual states in the 21st century are increasingly subject to the forces of

TYPICAL RESEARCH QUESTION

Why are a number of Asian states undergoing massive economic development while, generally speaking, African states are not?

Table 1.3	The 10 Largest Transnational Corporations in the World, 2010
Corporation	**Sales (US$bil)**
1. Wal-Mart Stores	$408.2
2. Royal Dutch Shell	278.2
3. ExxonMobil	275.6
4. BP	239.3
5. Toyota Motor	210.8
6. Sinopec-China Petroleum	208.5
7. ING Group	167.5
8. Total	160.7
9. Chevron	159.3
10. PetroChina	157.2

Source: Reprinted by permission of Forbes Media LLC © 2011

globalization, the subject of Chapter 17. One aspect of globalization is that the global economy is increasingly dominated by huge multinational or transnational corporations. They operate around the world, have little or no allegiance to a specific state, and are often so mobile that they can move operations from one state to another. To minimize costs and maximize profits, such firms pressure the countries in which they operate to sign free trade deals with each other. Such agreements prevent the states involved from protecting their own interests and prohibit them from imposing barriers that would reduce the worldwide flow of the corporations' goods and services. Transnational companies also abhor taxation, ownership restrictions, and regulations such as environmental controls and labour standards. The 10 largest transnational corporations in the world in 2010 are ranked in Table 1.3 by total revenue. The annual revenues of some of these companies equal or exceed the total value of all goods and services produced (the gross domestic product) in many industrialized countries, such as Belgium ($394.9 billion), Sweden ($354.0 billion), Switzerland ($326.9 billion), Finland ($185.4 billion), and New Zealand ($119.2 billion), not to mention most underdeveloped countries.[7]

Thus, pressured by such transnational corporations, organizations such as the World Trade Organization (WTO) and treaties such as the North American Free Trade Agreement (NAFTA) can force states to repeal laws and policies that favour their own companies and residents or that otherwise infringe the principles of the trade agreement. It is these aspects of globalization that are so controversial and that have led to violent clashes between demonstrators and police officers at many recent international gatherings.

Studying politics includes assessing the benefits and drawbacks of such globalizing forces, as well as inquiring about how much discretion states continue to possess in designing their own policies. Since up to now politics has been studied primarily in terms of the internal or external functioning of sovereign states, globalization requires quite a shift in our orientation. It raises the basic question of whether electorates can still hold their governments democratically accountable.

The Changing Nature of the Study of Politics

The study of politics is now a much broader enterprise than it used to be. Today it embraces the whole world, paying attention to developing countries as well as advanced, industrialized democracies. It now must contend with multinational states, that is, states that are no longer embodiments of a single ethnic group, language, or culture, but instead are characterized by cultural pluralism. In many cases Aboriginal peoples are part of these pluralistic states and, in almost all

TYPICAL RESEARCH QUESTION

What would be the consequences of enlarging the Security Council of the United Nations to include India, Japan, Germany, and Brazil?

cases, the question of gender is of increasing significance. Studying politics must now address questions of political change, especially the general move toward democracy in the developing world. At the same time, it must examine the breakdown of former multinational states (often called "state failure") and the role of rebellion, terrorism, and civil war. Finally, studying politics means coping with all the forces of globalization that impinge upon states as they try to make collective decisions for their own citizens. Who could deny that this broad undertaking is both fascinating and important?

THE STUDY OF POLITICAL SCIENCE

Most university departments in this field call themselves **political science**, but some prefer the label *political studies*. This is a point that requires elaboration. Most teachers and researchers attached to the discipline believe that they should be as "scientific" as possible in the sense of searching for explanations, being as unbiased as they can, employing numerical measures wherever practicable, looking for causal relations between variables, and even enunciating theories. Few believe, however, that all aspects of the discipline can be subject to the same stringent "scientific method" standards as are practised in the natural sciences. You will regularly encounter the debate between political science and political studies if you proceed with further courses in the discipline.

In the process of discussing the breadth of the discipline, we have, to a large extent, already outlined the subfields within political science or political studies. Not every university department breaks the subject down in the same way. Until recently, however, there has been a general consensus about the chart below. Studying politics involves examining most or all of these aspects of the subject, usually in specialized upper-year courses.

For people who are studying politics in Canada, one of the subfields of the discipline is obviously *Canadian politics*. If you were studying politics in another country, such as the United States or Britain, that country's politics would substitute as this first field. We have already seen the breadth of the discipline as it relates to a single state, as well as what is involved in the study of international relations. *Comparative politics* compares a number of states instead of concentrating on only one. *Political development* is essentially the study of the Third World or developing countries.

Studies in the stream of *political theory* begin with an examination of the evolution of political philosophy or political thought, and then branch out into various aspects of modern political theory and analysis. *Public administration* is often separated out from a study of national politics and concentrates on the operation of the bureaucracy and the policymaking process.

Political science is, of course, one of the social sciences, and it can be easily combined with any of its cognate disciplines, especially political economy, political sociology, political psychology, or political geography (or geopolitics). Of these combinations, *political economy* is probably most common, as it studies the close connection between the political and economic realms of life. This connection can be seen at both the national and the global level, as revealed in Chapter 4.

BASIC CONCEPTS IN THE STUDY OF POLITICS

One of the charms (or curses!) of the discipline of political science is that almost every concept is open to debate. Not everyone agrees on what the basic concepts of the subject are, and not everyone agrees on how to define them. Nevertheless, we do need a common starting point.

We have already defined "politics" as the activity in which conflicting interests struggle for advantage or dominance in the making and execution of public policies,

Political Science					
Canadian Politics	Comparative Politics	Political Development	International Relations	Public Administration	Political Theory

and "government" as the set of institutions that makes and enforces collective public decisions for a society. The central concepts that emerge from these key definitions of politics and government are power, coercion, influence, and authority, so let us focus on these four terms.

Power is often defined as the ability of one actor to impose its will on another, to get its own way, to do or get what it wants. Such an imposition of will can be readily seen in the relations between states: for example, when Hitler's Nazi forces invaded Poland, or when Canada succumbed to American pressure to open up its magazine industry to foreign competition. Within a single state, we can witness a power relationship when a government extracts taxes from its citizens, imposes environmental controls on corporations, or rewards its friends with appointments or contracts. In all of these cases, those in a position of power impose their will, whether on another country, on society in general, or on individuals or other entities within that society. In Jean Chrétien's memoirs, he comments as follows on the question of power:

> To be frank, politics is about wanting power, getting it, exercising it, and keeping it. Helping people comes with it naturally, because you'll never be elected if you treat people badly. But no one will ever convince me, with all the experience I've had, that the motivations are strictly altruistic.[8]

POWER: The ability of one actor to impose its will on another, to get its own way, to do or get what it wants.

Most political scientists are inclined to subdivide the concept of power into three parts.[9] The first kind of power is **coercion**, which involves threats of harm, penalties, violence, or punishment. This is the kind of power that Russia uses to put down separatist sentiment in Chechnya or that George W. Bush employed in spearheading an armed invasion of Afghanistan and Iraq. When the United States pressures Canada to change its policies on any matter, what is left unsaid is that economic penalties might follow if Canada resists. Coercion is also what Canadian governments do when the police break up a demonstration or put people in jail, or what governments in the United States do when they carry out an execution. While democratic countries are entitled to use coercion when imposing their

will on dissident citizens, they are expected to do so only as a last resort.

COERCION: The imposition of one's will on another by the use of penalty, force, or the threat of force.

The second kind of power is **influence**, which is usually seen as involving persuasion and voluntary compliance. One actor imposes its will on another by making arguments that the latter finds convincing. Within a single state, a bureaucrat tries to influence a minister to adopt a certain policy, a party member tries to persuade a party leader to resign, or the government pays for television advertising to try to convince smokers that it is time to quit. On the international level, the Secretary General of the United Nations appeals to the United States to pay the arrears in its dues, for example, and states regularly try to persuade each other to change their policies. It is now common in international relations to distinguish between "hard power," such as military threats and invasions, and "soft power," in which one state tries to persuade another of the superiority of its approach. It is often said that Canada has primarily relied on soft power in its foreign policy, and that the United States should follow our example.

INFLUENCE: The imposition of one's will on another through persuasion and voluntary compliance.

The third aspect of power is **authority**. This is often called **legitimate** power; that is, one actor imposes its will on another because the latter regards the former as legitimate, as having a right to impose its will. It is a kind of power that we have agreed to be bound by because it comes from a respected source; it stems from the acceptance of an obligation to obey. It is not always easy to explain why we give certain political institutions or figures authority, or why we view them as having authority.[10] Such authority is particularly relevant to democratic governments because, having had a say (by way of elections) in who makes the decisions, citizens generally accept the decisions even when they do not entirely agree with them. When governments extract taxes most people pay them, however reluctantly, because elected politicians have a right to make such decisions. Another factor that may propel people to obey the government is the charisma of the leader. And, of course, it is also natural to obey if we agree with the decision or the action being taken.

AUTHORITY: The imposition of one's will on another by reason of legitimacy—because the subject regards the decision-maker as having a right to make such a binding decision.

We can witness power, coercion, influence, and authority in our daily lives in areas that do not necessarily involve government. The Mafia and other criminal elements, for example, are infamous for committing crimes and causing injury and death in order to impose their will. Parents sometimes resort to coercion by grounding their children in their room. Friends influence each other about what movie to see; transnational corporations try to influence what clothes we buy; and you yourself may have pleaded with someone to go out on a date. We obey our parents because we love them or feel that they have a right to make certain decisions; we do what our bosses or union leaders demand because they are legitimately in control; and we follow the dictates of respected religious authorities. The "politics of the family," the "politics of the workplace," "corporate politics," "union politics," the "politics of religion"—all such activity may involve power, coercion, influence, or authority. Politics surrounds us! Everywhere we turn we see relationships involving power, coercion, influence, and authority.

Generally speaking, however, if for no other reason than to keep the subject within manageable proportions, it is advantageous to develop a narrower concept of politics for the purposes of this book—what might be called "large-P politics." What political science is mostly interested in are the conflicts in society that need a society-wide, authoritative resolution and that result in the authoritative distribution of valued things. That is, in fact, what we mean by public policies: an authoritative distribution of things that are valued, such as wealth, freedom, and security.

In making and enforcing public policies, government draws on all three aspects of power: coercion, influence, and authority. Government has the ability to impose its will by means of sanctions or penalties, relying on the armed forces, the police, and punishments such as fines or jail. Indeed, as a general rule, *only* the government is allowed to use force or coercive power in society. But, especially in democratic societies, governments try to minimize their use of coercion in seeking compliance with their decisions. They would prefer to have citizens respond voluntarily, after they have been persuaded or influenced. Merely asking citizens, corporations, or other groups to refrain from smoking, from polluting, from discriminating, or from asking for too much money may sometimes have an effect, but such voluntary compliance is not usually effective.

That leaves authority as the leading ground on which democratic governments rely to impose their will. If the citizens have had a hand in choosing the government, if the government at least appears to listen to the electorate, if the government gives the impression that it is taking all interests into account in its public policies, then the people will probably feel that the government is legitimate and that they should abide by its authority. Canadians have been seen as particularly deferential to authority and are almost always ready to obey whatever policies the government adopts. Whether or not such deference is on the decline, as is now commonly claimed,[11] we are instinctively inclined to do what the government says because we have put it there and because we feel it has a right to make such decisions. Of course, we may also remind ourselves that if we disobey such policies, whether by speeding, stealing, or not paying taxes, the government can come down on us with coercive measures involving police, fines, and prison.

These definitions of politics, government, and power may betray a bias in favour of peaceful, domestic, democratic political systems. When political science turns its attention to such subjects as political change, political violence, state failure, and international politics, some of the wider definitions previously outlined may be more appropriate. There are many aspects of political activity, especially in relations between states, in which authority—agreement on who has a right to make collective decisions—is severely lacking. In such contexts, it may sometimes be more appropriate to revert to the idea of politics as a struggle for power or dominance, and the use of coercion in relations between states is often called "hard power." On the other hand, even at the international level states make treaties with each other and usually respect the authority of such agreements, such that "soft power," based on influence and authority, is also evident.[12]

THIS BOOK

This book seeks to meet the demand for an introductory political science textbook for the 21st century—fresh and yet classic in its approach. It aims to be a definitive introductory text, marrying traditional and contemporary approaches and appealing directly to the learning demands of modern students.

We have already outlined the basic contents of the book. Every effort has been made to provide a solid background in the traditional subjects, while at the same time offering material that covers emerging themes and issues in political science. Chapters that deal with these newer issues include Chapter 3 (States and Nations: Cultural Pluralism, Nationalism, and Identity), Chapter 4 (States and Markets: The Study of Political Economy), Chapter 14 (The Politics of Development and Underdevelopment), Chapter 15 (Regime Change in an Era of Globalization), and Chapter 17 (The Politics of Globalization). We wish to emphasize the cultural pluralism of most modern states; we try to promote a greater understanding of the Third World; we want to ensure that students are aware of the massive aspects of political change currently taking place around the world; we have included women's issues wherever relevant; and we insist that the entire study of politics be enveloped within the context of globalization. Yet, going farther in unorthodox directions would probably have disturbed those who value the important material contained in the other chapters. We have tried to make the material relevant to Canadian students' lives with stimulating examples, and we are conscious of the fact that many of the students using the book will be relatively recent immigrants to Canada. We also profile a number of recent graduates in political science to show what kinds of careers they are pursuing and how their degree in this discipline got them to where they are today.

The chapters are intended to be discrete units, allowing professors to cover the material in a different sequence or omit certain chapters entirely. Nevertheless, we hope that the chapters jibe with each other, having certain common themes and coverage but minimal overlap. The book might be said to have a conceptual/comparative approach, working outward from Canada to other industrialized, developed democracies, then to the developing world, and finally to the global scene.

We have put considerable effort into the visual attractiveness of this text. These visual features—photographs, cartoons, graphs, charts, and boxes of various kinds—animate the material and allow an examination of alternative viewpoints. We have also tried to include many pedagogical features that make the book more interesting: learning objectives for each chapter; discussion questions; and web links. At the end of the book is a full-fledged glossary of all the key terms used.

For the benefit of professors selecting this text, we have also prepared an Instructor's Manual and a Test Bank, PowerPoint slides, and an accompanying video. There is also a book-specific website—http://www.studyingpolitics4e.nelson.com, supplemented by Nelson's comprehensive, general political science website.

In other words, this is a cutting-edge textbook supplemented by helpful teaching materials and ready to meet the demands of 21st-century students and instructors.

CONCLUSION

This chapter has tried to show you that studying politics is both interesting and important, and that if you go beyond a single course, it also leads to jobs. The chapter has sketched the broad lines of the scope of the discipline of political science, outlined how the field is changing, and detailed its subfields. It concluded with definitions and explanations of some of the key concepts in political science, namely politics, government, power, coercion, influence, and authority.

DISCUSSION QUESTIONS

1. Think about your most recent personal experiences (unrelated to government) involving relationships of power. Did they involve coercion, influence, or authority?

2. Think about your most recent experiences involving government. Did any of them include aspects of coercion, influence, or authority?

3. Consider the question posed in Figure 1.1: How should government divide a budget surplus among cutting taxes, reducing the debt, or spending on social programs? Why?

4. In what kinds of political activity have you been engaged in the past, and in what kinds do you see yourself involved in the future? Why?

5. What do you think are the most pressing public issues facing Canada in the early 21st century?

6. What do you think are the most pressing issues facing the rest of the world?

FURTHER READING

Barber, Benjamin R. *Jihad vs. McWorld*. New York: Ballantine, 1996.

Bateman, Thomas, et al. *Braving the New World: Readings in Contemporary Politics,* 4th ed. Toronto: Nelson, 2008.

Charlton, Mark, and Paul Barker, eds. *Crosscurrents: Contemporary Political Issues,* 6th ed. Toronto: Nelson Education, 2009.

Chrétien, Jean. *My Years as Prime Minister*. Toronto: Knopf Canada, 2007.

Huntington, Samuel P. *The Third Wave: Democratization in the Late Twentieth Century*. Norman: University of Oklahoma Press, 1992.

Miliband, Ralph. *The State in Capitalist Society*. London: Weidenfeld and Nicolson, 1969.

Sens, Allen, and Peter J. Stoett. *Global Politics: Origins, Currents and Directions,* 3rd ed. Toronto: Thomson Nelson, 2005.

Simpson, Jeffrey. *The Friendly Dictatorship*. Toronto: McClelland and Stewart, 2001.

ENDNOTES

1. The great political philosopher Michel Foucault once wrote: "...why am I so interested in politics? If I were to answer you very simply I would say this: why shouldn't I be interested? That is to say, what blindness, what deafness, what density of ideology would have to weigh me down to prevent me from being interested in what is probably the most crucial subject to our existence, that is to say, the society in which we live, the economic relations in which it functions, and the system of power which defines the regular forms and regular permissions and prohibitions of our conduct? The essence of our life consists, after all, of the political functioning of the society in which we find ourselves." Michel Foucault, "Human Nature: Justice versus Power," in Fons Elders, ed., *Reflexive Water* (London: Souvenir Press, 1974). I would like to thank Jesse Schmidt for this quotation and other improvements to this chapter.

2. Harold Lasswell, *Politics: Who Gets What, When, How* (New York: Meridian Books, 1958).

3. David Easton, *The Political System: An Inquiry into the State of Political Science* (New York: Knopf, 1967).

4. See, for example, Jacquetta Newman, "Should Women Focus on Small-p Politics?," in Mark Charlton and Paul Barker, eds. *Crosscurrents: Contemporary Political Issues,* 6th ed. (Toronto: Nelson Education, 2009).

5. The Canadian Index of Wellbeing at http://www.ciw.ca/en/Home.aspx has adopted the following as its working definition of wellbeing: "The presence of the highest possible quality of life in its full breadth of expression, focused on but not necessarily exclusive to: good living standards, robust health, a sustainable environment, vital communities, an educated populace, balanced time use, *high levels of civic participation*, and access to and participation in dynamic arts, culture and recreation."

6. Roger Gibbins and Loleen Youngman, *Mindscapes: Political Ideologies Towards the 21st Century* (Toronto: McGraw-Hill Ryerson, 1996).

7. Although the comparison between corporations and countries can be problematic, recent GDP figures can be found at in the CIA *World Factbook*, available at http://www.cia.gov/library/publications/the-world-factbook/rankorder/2010rank.html; accessed January 10, 2011.

8. Jean Chrétien, *My Years as Prime Minister* (Toronto: Knopf Canada, 2007), p. 2.

9. Mark O. Dickerson and Thomas Flanagan, *An Introduction to Government and Politics: A Conceptual Approach*, 5th ed. (Toronto: Nelson Thomson Learning, 1998).

10. Discussions of authority almost always centre on Max Weber's distinction among rational-legal, charismatic, and traditional authority. The first is based on rules, the second on personal devotion and trust, and the third on unwritten custom.

11. Neil Nevitte, *The Decline of Deference* (Peterborough: Broadview Press, 1996).

12. Joseph S. Nye, Jr., *The Future of Power* (New York: Public Affairs, 2011).

WWW For various weblinks discussed in this chapter, please go to the book's website at **www.studyingpolitics4e.nelson.com**

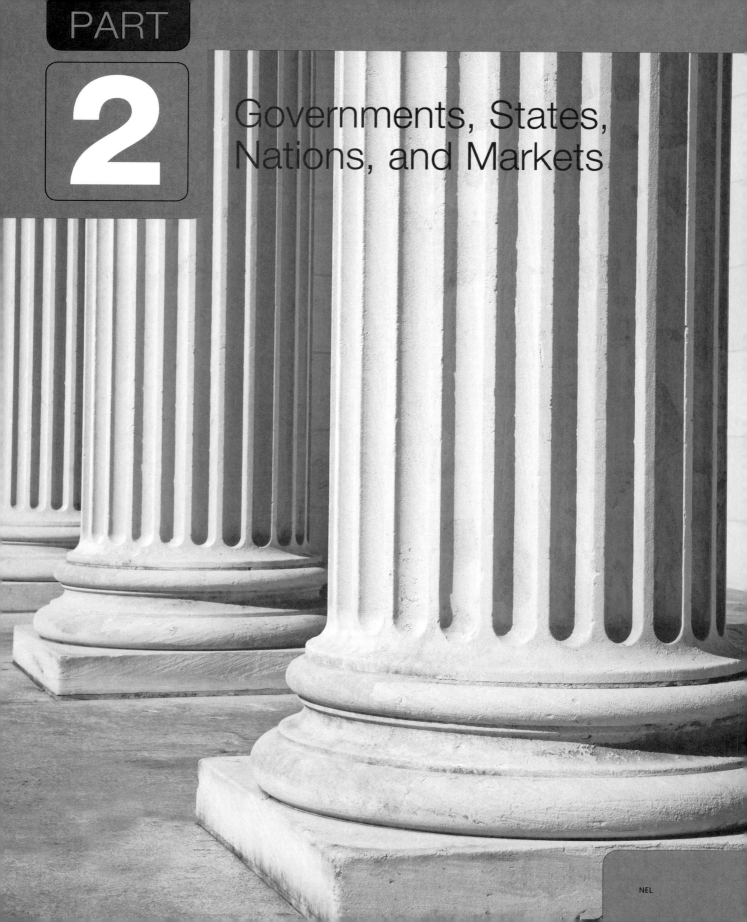

PART

2

Governments, States, Nations, and Markets

Courtesy of Renny Khan

RENNY KHAN

Renny Khan was born in Trinidad and Tobago, after which his family immigrated to Canada in the 1980s. He grew up in Montreal, completing his high school education in French. Renny holds a bachelor's degree in Political Science and History from McGill University, where he studied on an entrance scholarship, and a master's degree in International Relations from the University of Alberta.

Renny's degrees in Political Science have provided the foundation for an illustrious career in university administration. He joined the University of Alberta in 1999 after working for a few years in the Alberta Ministry of International and Intergovernmental Relations, and is currently the Director of International Programs for the Faculty of Medicine and Dentistry. Through collaborations, internally with senior administration, faculty, and staff, and externally with organizations, foundations, and governments, Renny works to facilitate the international strategies and initiatives of the institution.

Renny has played a key role in negotiating and implementing agreements between the University and several European and U.S. institutions and foundations, leading to the creation of successful research partnerships visiting professorships, student fellowships, and innovative international curriculum. Over the past three years he worked to develop a new model for strategic international support to Faculty units at the University, having previously served as the Director of International Programs for the Faculty of Agricultural, Life, and Environmental Sciences and the Associate Director for International Relations and Recruitment with a strong emphasis on European partnership.

Among other capacities, Renny served as project leader of a multisector provincial science and technology team to promote Alberta's national leadership in nanotechnology in Europe. In recognition of his work, he received a European Union Visitors Award (2005) co-sponsored by the European Union Commission and the European Parliament, and he also received an International Visitors Award from the U.S. State Department (2001).

Renny is married and has four beautiful children.

Governments and States: Perpetual Works in Progress

Christopher G. Anderson

CHAPTER OBJECTIVES

After you have completed this chapter, you should be able to:

- elaborate on the basic functions of government
- differentiate between government forms identified by classical scholars
- trace the evolution of the concept of democracy and the emergence of nation-states
- discuss principal features of the modern state, democratic government, and nondemocratic government
- exemplify and explain forms of non-state governments
- identify possible conditions and consequences of state failure
- consider the role of government and the state in a globalized world

INTRODUCTION

Imagine a political system in which there is no government and no state, a society where everyone has an equal say over decisions that affect individuals, groups, or the full community, in which people hammer out the details of these decisions in person and on a regular basis. Although there have been repeated attempts throughout history to create such political systems on the basis of the principles of **anarchy**, in which authority is not entrenched in established institutions and practices but rather is made to justify itself over and again, they have proved to be quite difficult to set up, much less maintain, and therefore have remained more of a philosophical ideal than a sustained reality.[1] Instead, governments and states—as structures of *governance*—have long been prevalent in the lives of human beings, locally, nationally, and even internationally.

It is difficult to contemplate modern life without taking into account the role of governments and states. Consider what you do on a daily basis. The hour at which you awake may be influenced by whether there is legislation concerning Daylight Saving Time. The ingredients in your breakfast are subject to bureaucratic regulation. The clothes you wear are taxed by the state. The frequency with which the bus arrives to take you to university or work is affected by the level of public funding that the transit system receives. The list seems endless. If you live in a less democratic political system, the nature of government and state intervention in your life is probably even more dramatic, censoring the news that you read, limiting the range of jobs that you can hold, curtailing your ability to travel freely inside or outside the country, and—in the extreme—determining whether you live or die because of who you are or what you believe. No matter where we live, then, governments and states figure extensively and intensively in our very existence.

For this reason, states and governments are an essential focal point when studying politics, as you will see not only in this chapter but throughout the remainder of this book. In part we study governments and states because we want to understand why some things happen and why others do not. In short, we hope to create and accumulate knowledge about the world around us. This might help us to become better informed as citizens, whether locally or globally, and gain the potential not only to interpret the world but to change it as well. Indeed, by studying governments and states, we soon learn that no political system is perfect, that each has strengths and weaknesses in varying proportions, but that all can be improved. Governments and states have the potential to be powerful vehicles for positive change, but this seems at least to require that we constantly ask what they do, why they do it, and how they might do it better.

While pondering these questions, we will repeatedly encounter the fact that governments and states are often—quite justifiably—subject to considerable criticism. For example, in many of the long-established democracies of the world, including Canada, there is evidence of a **democratic deficit**, in which citizens feel that the actions of government and state do not meet their expectations, either in terms of the accountability of the political system to "the people" or its responsiveness to their interests. In nondemocratic regimes, where there are far fewer mechanisms through which public preferences can be brought to bear on those who rule, serious concerns exist over the prevalence of human rights abuses. In some countries, there is talk of failing or failed states, where violent conflicts rage between state and non-state forces, and governments are unable to provide basic services in such areas as education and health. Sometimes such struggles are rooted

Democratic deficit: The perceived gap between the theoretical principles of democracy and the actual practice of ostensibly democratic institutions, including national governments and international organizations.

in the demands of people looking to create their own state in order to meet certain group-based needs as part of a process of liberating themselves from oppression. At the global level, in turn, there are increasing discussions about the necessity—or even inevitability—of a system of **global governance** to bind governments and states more closely to a commonly derived set of laws and norms of behaviour.

In this chapter, we will explore these and many other features of governments and states at the outset of the 21st century, and this will require that they be placed within both historical and comparative contexts. Governing institutions do not appear before us wholly formed, and neither do they remain the same for very long—rather, they evolve within a variety of economic, social, and political circumstances. A historical perspective reminds us that the institutions and practices through which we are governed are not—and have never been—set in stone. In a global age, when the barriers between states are thought to be ever more permeable, the task of tracing such patterns of continuity and change is both more difficult and more important. Moreover, in an increasingly interconnected world, we need to think about the foundations of governing institutions and practices that differ from our own, that originate in alternate political traditions, such as those in China or Iran, for example. As the Canadian political scientist Alan C. Cairns suggests, societies, governments, and states are embedded in one another, both nationally and internationally, and an important aspect of studying politics is determining the nature of this embeddedness and its effects on politics.[2] While we cannot fully cover the great variety and complexity of forms that this might take, we can establish some general terms and ideas to help us study governments and states in a more systematic manner.

STUDYING GOVERNMENTS

Using the definition of government from Chapter 1 as the set of institutions and practices that make and enforce collective public decisions for a society, we can attest that human beings and **government** have long been related in close, complicated, and enduring ways. Indeed, everyone in the world today falls under the purview of some governing authority. Even those who have been rendered stateless, or who live in one of the estimated 100 "uncontacted" tribes left in the world, fall within the ambit of one government or another, even if they are unaware of it! Because governments can affect most every aspect of our lives, the ways in which they are set up and in which we interact with them are multiple and complex. An important first step, therefore, is to make some sense of what governments do—their functions within a political system.

> **Government:** The set of institutions and practices that make and enforce collective public decisions for a society.

We can start by turning to the work of the political scientist Gabriel Almond, who proposed a checklist of functions performed by all governments: rule-making, rule-application, and rule-adjudication.[3] Although governments take on a great number of forms, they all share these three tasks. While citizens in democracies can readily connect these three functions with the main branches of government—the legislature, the executive, and the judiciary—in many political systems they may not be so clearly divided and allotted to separate institutions. For example, in the last remaining **absolute monarchy** in Africa—Swaziland—the king has extensive powers to make and interpret rules, and to see them implemented through a process of rule by decree. Even among democracies, significant differences exist in how these functions are institutionalized, as seen in the contrasting examples of parliamentary and presidential systems, details of which can be found in Part 4 of this book, "The Structure and Operations of Government."

> **Absolute monarchy:** A system of government ruled, at least in name, by one individual whose authority is unchecked, final, and permanent.

This diversity in the 21st century can be explained by the fact that each system of government has evolved within its own historical conditions and political traditions, some of which stretch far back in time. Indeed, in some parts of the world—such as China, India, and the Middle East—we can trace histories of government for several millennia. Thus, the forms that governments have taken, and the justifications advanced to support them, have varied greatly over time, and continue to do so.

Sue Dewar/Artizans

A BRIEF HISTORY OF GOVERNMENT

Our knowledge of how people have been governed only really stretches as far back as the written word. We can certainly speculate about what happened before that time—based, for example, on archaeological evidence or more contemporary forms of tribal societies—but this leaves us with enormous gaps in our understanding of the economic, social, and political lives of such communities, and of the institutions and practices through which they were governed. Even where written records and archaeological findings coexist—as they do for the first time with the Sumerian and Egyptian civilizations as early as c. 3500–3000 BCE (in what is now called the Middle East)—our knowledge remains quite impressionistic.[4] In both cases, we know that absolute monarchs with a mandate that was said to come from the gods ruled over large peasant populations and at times quite extensive territories with the support of a relatively small number of court officials and temple priests, alongside a select and well-trained staff of accountants and scribes. While certain features of these early governments may seem familiar to us today—there were, for example, repeated concerns over corruption and attempts at reform to improve the administration of government—there were also significant differences. Perhaps most importantly, these governments did not rule *for the people* but ruled *over the people* to ensure that they obeyed the gods. Thus, the people were subjects, not citizens, and they had little or no say over how they were governed. Although the precise configurations would change over time, and while new governments emerged, evolved, and disappeared in the Middle East (e.g., in Assyria, Babylonia, and Persia) and beyond (e.g., in present-day India and China), each presents us with a variation on this original form—absolute monarchy. It was not until the formation of the **republics** of ancient Greece that a radically different type of relationship between the rulers and the ruled takes root in the historical record.

> **Republic:** A system of government ruled by a head of state who is not a monarch (generally, in modern times, a president), in which citizens are entitled to participate in decision-making.

The Legacy of Government in Ancient Greece

Within the broad scope of the history of government, from the Sumerian city-states of 3500 BCE to the acceptance of South Sudan as the latest (and 193rd) member state of the United Nations in 2011, the rise and fall of democracy in the Greek republics from about 600 BCE to 300 BCE constitutes a relatively brief moment in time—but it has nonetheless had a profound influence on how we think about and practise government today.[5] Most of the 1,500 or so city-states that existed within ancient Greece were already notable for having instituted and developed republican governments, in which subjects (at least some of them) were transformed into citizens who participated in collective decision-making for society. Thus, government in the Greek city-states had generally shifted from the palace of the monarch to the *polis*, which consisted of both the city (along with the lands surrounding it) and its citizens. This was in and of itself a radical break with the past. The Greeks, however, also originated the word as well as the practice of democracy, both of which have come to permeate modern politics, albeit with important modifications. Although

earlier political systems (in Mesopotamia and India, for example) had certain democratic features,[6] it is with the ancient Greeks that we first see it named, described, analyzed, debated, and even celebrated (see Box 2.1).

BOX 2.1

PERICLES' FUNERAL ORATION

In *The History of the Peloponnesian War*, Thucydides (460–395 BCE) recounts a speech given by Pericles (495–429 BCE), who ruled in Athens for more than 30 years, in memory of those who had died during the first year of what would become a 27-year war between Sparta and Athens.

> Our constitution does not copy the laws of neighbouring states; we are rather a pattern to others than imitators ourselves. Its administration favours the many instead of the few; this is why it is called a democracy. If we look to the laws, they afford equal justice to all in their private differences; if to social standing, advancement in public life falls to reputation for capacity, class considerations not being allowed to interfere with merit; nor again does poverty bar the way, if a man is able to serve the state, he is not hindered by the obscurity of his condition. The freedom which we enjoy in our government extends also to our ordinary life. There, far from exercising a jealous surveillance over each other, we do not feel called upon to be angry with our neighbour for doing what he likes … But all this ease in our private relations does not make us lawless as citizens. Against this fear is our chief safeguard, teaching us to obey the magistrates and the laws … whether they are actually on the statue book, or belong to that code which, although unwritten, yet cannot be broken without acknowledged disgrace.

Source: Robert B. Stassler, *The Landmark Thucydides: A Comprehensive Guide to the Peloponnesian War* (New York: Free Press, 1996), 112.

In broad strokes, the institutional arrangement of the *polis* consisted of an executive, a select council, a general assembly, and, as democracy took hold, decision-making increasingly shifted toward the Assembly. For example, in Athens, which was considered to be the centre of democratic life in ancient Greece, all citizens could participate in the Assembly, where they could discuss and judge proposed legislation, decide questions of war and peace, and, indeed, debate any issue that a citizen deemed proper. Moreover, they might be chosen by lot to participate in the select Council of 500 or the Law Courts. Although similar to modern democracy in privileging the voice of "the people" in the political process, this was nonetheless a very different democracy than that which we find in the world today. First, it occurred on a much smaller scale: at the height of democratic Athens there were perhaps 30,000 citizens, and only a few thousand would take part in the meetings of the general assembly or would be selected by lot each year to serve as potential jury members, and just a few hundred would serve in various public posts. Second, citizen involvement was much more prominent—this was **direct democracy** in which citizens participated as rulers as well as the ruled. Third, citizenship was limited to adult males of Athenian parents, thereby excluding some 220,000 foreigners, women, slaves, and children. Furthermore, just because the *polis* was democratic did not mean that everyone agreed that it was the best system of government (indeed, it was overthrown for a period in Athens), and while the historian Thucydides provides us with a glimpse of the pride that democracy could engender in its advocates, it was not uncommon to hear it denounced as an unstable, and therefore dangerous, form of government.

Although numerous figures from ancient Greece discussed and wrote on the nature of government (along with Thucydides we could add the playwright Sophocles and the philosopher Plato, for example), Aristotle provided one of the more systematic analyses of the different forms of government known to the Greeks during this period. In *The Politics*, he famously states that "man is a political animal in a sense in which a bee is not, or any other gregarious animal," because men possess a "power of speech" that allows them "not only to feel pleasure and pain but to communicate these feelings to each other."[7] As a result, they have a unique ability to consider what is right and what is wrong, what is just and what is unjust, and do so to greatest effect in association with one another. While this leads Aristotle to claim that government is, therefore, a natural phenomenon—indeed, that it is the means by which men can not only live but also pursue the "good life"—there remains the vital question of which form of government is best.

To address this issue, Aristotle undertook a political analysis to determine which form was most likely to produce the stability required for the contemplation and achievement of the good life. He did so by collecting the political constitutions of 158 city-states and then organizing and comparing them across certain core characteristics. Specifically, he separated his cases according to whether they were defined by the rule of one, a few, or the many, and then he distinguished between systems in which those in power ruled in the common interest from those in which they ruled in their own particular interests. This produced a six-fold classification (see Table 2.1) from which—after having considered the nature of the cases in each—he drew a number of conclusions. While democracy was not

Table 2.1 **Aristotle's Typology of Government Forms**		
	RULE IN THE INTERESTS OF:	
Number of Rulers	**All Citizens (common interests)**	**The Rulers (particular interests)**
One	Monarchy	Tyranny
A few	Aristocracy	Oligarchy
The many	Polity	Democracy

Source: Adapted from Nicolas Baxter-Moore, Terrance Carroll, and Roderick Church, *Studying Politics: An Introduction to Argument and Analysis* (Toronto: Copp Clark Longman Ltd., 1994), 4.

considered by Aristotle to be the worst form of government (this was tyranny, which replicated a master–slave relationship between ruler and ruled), neither was it the best because it was prone to instability when demagogues courted popular support against the wealthy few, eventually leading to an **oligarchy** as the rich seized power and governed to protect their interests. Aristotle did, nonetheless, speak of the need to incorporate democratic elements into any stable system of government. As for monarchy and **aristocracy**, they were ideal forms only when controlled by people truly able to define and reflect the common interest. However, when this was not the case, they were likely to slide into tyranny and oligarchy. Instead, Aristotle pointed to the benefits of a **polity**, with the rule of the many (but not all), on the grounds that its deliberations were more likely to reflect the common interest consistently over time: "As a larger amount of water is less easily polluted, so the multitude is less easily corrupted than the few."[8] Thus, he saw in a polity the potential to balance the interests of the many who were poor with those of the few who were wealthy, integrating the best features of both oligarchy and democracy, and thereby increasing the likelihood of political stability.

Oligarchy: A system of government ruled by a few and, according to Aristotle, in their own interests.

Polity: A system of government ruled by the many but not—as in a democracy—by all; according to Aristotle, this was the most stable system of government when it was able to balance the interests of the wealthy with those of the poor.

Because he approached the study of government systematically—as a comparative examination of political institutions—Aristotle's work is often seen as an early example of political science in action. Moreover, as was the case with other Greek thinkers of the day such as Plato, the vocabulary he employed and the ideas he explored have influenced political thinkers through the ages to the present. As just one example, we can look at the term *oligarchy*. Robert Michels, a German sociologist, was confronted with an important puzzle when he noticed that all the political parties he studied—even those that were democratically structured—wound up being dominated by party leaders. In an effort to explain this, he proposed the existence of an "iron law of oligarchy," in which all organizational forms eventually become oligarchic, not simply because leaders seek to consolidate power but because those who are led permit them to become so. "Who says organization," he famously wrote, "says oligarchy." This idea, while seeking to explain a particular aspect of organizational behaviour, speaks directly to the study of governments and states, especially those that are democratic, because it challenges the idea that modern democracies are simply based in the will of the people and suggests instead that power may often reflect the narrower interests of leaders and political parties.

Other Ancient Government Traditions

What is most surprising about ancient Greek democracy is not that it ended, as the various city-states were eventually subsumed within the expanding power of Rome around 150 BCE, but that it so completely disappeared as a form of political organization for centuries before rising to such prominence in the recent past. While Rome itself emerged with a republican form of government, it never became a democracy but perhaps resembled more an oligarchy, with a relatively entrenched elite dominating public affairs, before it took on more tyrannical forms with the arrival of emperors claiming to descend from the gods. Nonetheless, Rome also left its mark on the subsequent development of government, initially at least in Europe. Aside from providing the staging ground for the eventual expansion of Christianity as a major religious and political force in the world, the Romans developed complex systems of both public and private law—the former giving definition to government, and the latter setting out rights and obligations between persons—that were both **secular** and rationally developed. As well as contributing to the expansion of the legal profession, this began the process of transforming government from something personal

Secular: Not connected to or founded on religious beliefs or institutions; in political terms, the separation of church and state is often thought to produce a secular state, which remains neutral on, and does not reflect, issues of religious belief.

(i.e., embodied in a monarch or particular individuals) to something more abstract. Thus, the essence of political authority was increasingly seen to exist more in the laws than those participating in decision-making. When European nation-states began to emerge in the 16th century, they drew considerably upon this tradition.

However, with the decline and eventual fall of the Roman Empire from about the 5th to 7th centuries, political life in Europe generally became quite fragmented and local. Alternative forms of political organization elsewhere in the world thrived, some of which continue to shape the nature of governments and states, and thus politics, at the outset of the 21st century. For example, the roots of Chinese political life can be traced back thousands of years to around 2000 BCE, after which time it became one of the most developed and durable forms of political organization until the late 18th century. By the time of the Han dynasty (206 BCE–220 CE), the basic contours of a form of government that combined an absolute monarchy with a Confucian system of belief were in place, from which have evolved a number of democratic and nondemocratic governments in East Asia today (see Box 2.2).

Confucianism is not a religion or a systematic code of law, but instead is rooted in a set of ethical assertions originating with the Chinese sage/philosopher Confucius (551–479 BCE) concerning the correct ordering of society, and thus politics as well. According to his teachings, the best way to achieve social harmony, and therefore the best form of government, is through rituals that reflect and reinforce ordered and hierarchical relationships— between government and the people, between parents and children, and between friends, for instance. Those in positions of authority are duty-bound to lead by example and to care for those under their charge, while those subject to such authority are obliged to revere and obey those in command. As opposed to the ancient Greeks, then, there is no sense of political power residing with a citizenry of equals; at the same time, the boundaries to the power of rulers is much more clearly defined than was the case in many other monarchical systems. In part, this stemmed from another distinctive feature of government in China: the elevation of scholars into the highest ranks of social and political life on the basis of merit. This left them in a relatively privileged position from which to influence decision-making. In comparison, the

---

BOX 2.2

CONFUCIAN IDEAS IN MODERN EAST ASIA

Although there is a tendency in the West to see liberal-democratic traditions as providing the key to successful economic and political organization, other traditions continue to prevail in much of the world, some of which—such as Confucianism— can also lay claim to having achieved considerable accomplishments in these areas.

The East Asian countries that have been strongly influenced by Confucianism … offer an interesting variation on the theme of halting development in the so-called Third World. Consider how they have fared as regards the three modern challenges of unity, prosperity, and democracy. First, all the Confucian countries of the region, including massive China as well as the smaller societies of Taiwan, the two Koreas, Vietnam, and Singapore, have succeeded in establishing powerful, centralized bureaucratic states undergirded by robust national sentiments. Second, many of them have

succeeded, often dramatically, at the task of generating economic growth: Taiwan, South Korea, and Singapore have become famous as "tigers" while more recently China has been astonishing the world in this field. Third, South Korea and Taiwan have not only maintained stable governance and economic development, but have made full-fledged transitions to democracy.... If one puts Japan back into the picture, it becomes apparent that, aside from Western Europe and the lands of its wider historic ambit, no region has been more successful than East Asia when it comes to achieving political and economic modernization.

Source: Chaibong, Hahm. "The Ironies of Confucianism." *Journal of Democracy* 15:3 (2004), pp. 93-94. © 2004 National Endowment for Democracy and the Johns Hopkins University Press (JHUP). Reprinted with permission of JHUP.

idea of a merit-based bureaucracy would not really take hold in the West until the 19th century—some 2,000 years later. Of course, the history of Chinese government reveals periods of both relative stability and instability (both through civil war and external conflicts), and many Confucian ideas were explicitly rejected with the rise to power of the Communist Party in 1949. Nonetheless, in recent years, they have experienced resurgence as an emphasis on harmony and order, as well as hierarchy and responsibility, have been seen to offer the possibility of a greater sense of certainty as China undergoes a massive social upheaval with its rise to prominence as one of the foremost economic and military powers in the world.

Elsewhere, with the emergence and consolidation of Muhammad as a prophet and political leader at the outset of the 7th century, the roots of a new religion and a new form of political organization took hold. From its origins in what is now Saudi Arabia, Islam rapidly spread within 100 years to encompass the Middle East, Northern Africa, and parts of South and Central Asia, Portugal, and Spain, and in doing so it provided the foundations to one of the most extensive empires in human history. Although the Empire of the Caliphate lasted for just about 250 years (c. 630–870 CE), it has had a profound influence on politics and government in these regions and beyond through to the present. Indeed, today there are nearly 50 countries in the world in which Muslims represent a majority of the population, mostly in the Middle East, Northern Africa, Central and South Asia, and Southeast Asia, constituting almost a third of the world's population, and a number of these countries—such as Indonesia and Mali—have become relatively stable democracies. Probably the most distinctive feature of Islam's influence on government has been the role of **sharia law**, which—as the command of God—regulates aspects of both public and private life, including features of worship and interpersonal relations. Since its inception, the existence of sharia law, and the role of religious scholars

Sharia law: The Muslim or Islamic system of law, both civil and criminal, based on a collection of ancient teachings, the Islamic holy scriptures, the Qur'an, and later scholarly writing, prescribing how people should behave and what punishments are appropriate for particular transgressions.

in interpreting its meaning, has raised a question of great political significance, namely, that of the appropriate balance between political and religious authorities in governing. In practice, from the Empire of the Caliphate to modern-day Islamic republics such as Iran and Pakistan, this has not been easy to settle: should a more secular political authority exist, and, if so, should its authority be higher than or merely different from that of religious authorities? As with political systems based on Confucianism, there have been periods of relative stability and instability in the Islamic world over time, but we can certainly contrast the often high degree of sophistication of its government forms up until the 17th century as opposed to those prevalent in Europe during much of this time.

EUROPEAN NATION-STATES

Indeed, the contrast with Europe (with the exception of the Byzantium Empire, which from its base in Constantinople would last almost 1,000 years as an absolute monarchy after the fall of the Roman Empire) was stark. It was not really until the late Middle Ages that government began to coalesce around a series of feudal kingdoms on the continent which, despite their diversity, shared several common characteristics. Although the pinnacle of political authority resided with kings, they often depended on the support of local landholders, powerful and armed, who could choose with whom they wished to be aligned. Within such a relatively decentralized system of power, towns came to take on a greater importance, often acting as essentially self-governing republics. In general, however, the population had reverted from being citizens to being subjects of their respective feudal lords. Alongside this more secular system of political organization, Christianity became an integral thread in the weave of political life in Europe during this period, as the Catholic Church worked hard to carve out and develop a political space for itself that was superior to that of kingly governments, representing—in the person of the Pope—a higher (indeed, heavenly) authority. Thus, the Middle Ages were defined by a complex, evolving patchwork of relations of authority, responsibility, and rights, and it was far from democratic. Indeed, it was only in a few small areas, such as a handful of Swiss cantons, that democracy could be found.

Nonetheless, within a few centuries, key features of modern democratic government emerged and challenged the political authority of established monarchies as well as the papacy, and a new form of political organization—the **nation-state**—appeared. This occurred at a time when European governments were beginning once again to become active on the world stage, and when European society was experiencing an incredibly dynamic period of economic, social, and political development. It is difficult to do justice to the breadth and speed of the changes that took place in Europe from the 14th to 18th centuries. With the rise of Protestantism, the religious and political authority of the Catholic Church came under attack. When combined with a new age of secular thought that blossomed throughout the Reformation and Renaissance, radical transformations took place in terms of how the authority of governments was conceptualized. This process was facilitated by the invention of the printing press, which resulted in widespread debate of competing economic, political, religious, and social ideas. The emergence of capitalism and industrialization, urbanization, and a period of rapid technological development in such areas as transportation and weaponry can be added to this mix, which facilitated both commerce and conquest. Indeed, during this period European governments began not only to centralize and institutionalize their authority as nation-states, but also to expand their economic and political ambitions vis-à-vis the rest of the world. By the 19th century much of Africa, the Americas, and South and Southeast Asia had been brought under their control under the aegis of **colonialism**. Altogether, this constituted perhaps the most rapid and extensive spread of political ideas and influence since the Empire of the Caliphate.

Nation-state: A term sometimes used synonymously with state, but implies that the citizens share a common ethnic or cultural background. In the modern world, few such homogeneous states remain, most either being multicultural, multiethnic, or multination states.

Nowhere were these rapid changes more apparent than in 17th-century England. A number of ingredients came together to challenge the domination of English politics by the monarchy. First, the enclosure movement produced profound changes in English society. Landlords were allowed to "enclose" or fence off lands that had been formerly available for public use, so that they could be turned towards increased agricultural production. As people were forcibly displaced from the country to the city centres, this provided a ready-made working class for the Industrial Revolution. Second, a new entrepreneurial or bourgeois class began to oppose the power of the monarchy to control lands and tax at will. As their demands for greater private property protection increased, so did tensions with the landed aristocracy, who had long benefited from close proximity to the crown. In their mobilization against one another, and vis-à-vis the crown, the origins of the party system that defines modern democratic government can be found. Third, religious toleration became socially and politically acceptable. The uncoupling of England and other emerging nation-states from the power of the Catholic Church in Rome led to an increasing awareness of the power of new ideas. Along with this spiritual liberation came a scientific freedom that assisted in shifting attention away from the divine right of kings and toward the terrestrial and rational interests (individual and collective) of the population.

These ingredients came together to produce a new political culture, one that the traditional political institutions associated with the monarchy could not represent. Although the power of the crown had been circumscribed—and many of the rights of the people asserted—through the *Magna Carta* as early as 1215, it would take centuries for the institutions and practices of government to reflect this shift in power more accurately. The calls and struggles for political reform that emerged from both workers and the bourgeoisie from the 17th century onwards, which were encouraged by the air of toleration and liberation of the times, put into motion a series of important institutional transformations. The concepts of representative democracy, free speech, the right to rebel against bad government, freedom for the accumulation of profit, human rights—all of which are now hallmarks of many modern systems of government—developed in a political renaissance that found inspiration in ancient thinkers and innovation in a new intellectual class that promoted the values that would underpin a new age of democracy. A prime example would be John Locke, a philosopher and activist whose ideas would be reflected in both the American Revolution and its *Declaration of Independence*. In his *Two Treatises on Government*, Locke contested the notion of the divine right of kings, arguing instead that against the uncertainty inherent in a "state of nature," a people will submit to government as long as it is directed toward "the mutual preservation of their lives, liberties and estates, which I call by the general name, property."[9] When such property rights were not respected, however, Locke argued that the people had the right to rebel against the government—that is, the right of **revolution**.

Two of the most significant political revolutions of the period took place during the late 18th century in the American colonies and France. In each, a fiery rhetoric arose in which the rights of citizens within and over the government were placed at the foundation of a new political system (see Box 2.3). Moreover, as can be seen in the American case in particular, this was to be a democratically elected government, a notion that resonated with the democracy of the ancient Greeks but also altered it in significant ways. On the one hand, the commitment to what Abraham Lincoln would one day call in his famous Gettysburg Address "government of the people, by the people, for the people" harked back to the ideas of the Greeks, as did the notion that only a select group of citizens (in this case, property and/or tax-paying white males) should participate. It was radically

different, however, in two related ways: first, it was to be a large-scale political system, and second, it would be based not on direct but indirect or **representative democracy**. Thus, the vast majority of citizens would be ruled, but not rulers as well. Although it would take some time, democratic forms of government would increasingly take hold in Europe after the American and French revolutions, and while the paths would vary considerably, they would all exist within a new form—the nation-state.

STUDYING STATES

Just as it is difficult to imagine modern life without governments, it is hard to overlook the presence of states in our world, especially when we discuss international politics. However, the historical survey presented above reveals that the world has not always been organized into a system of states. Indeed, for centuries—millennia, even—vast areas of the globe were left relatively unstructured in political terms, even during the rule of some of the most highly developed governments of the ancient world. This began to change with the emergence and expansion of European nation-states from the 17th century onwards, although, as will be seen below, degrees of uncertainty remain. What, then, are the basic features of a state?

BOX 2.3

RIGHTS, GOVERNMENT, AND REVOLUTION

The American *Declaration of Independence* of 1776 is quite a radical document, both for its time and in the present day. Building on the ideas of philosophers such as John Locke, its authors provided a justification for the removal of any government that did not adequately reflect the people's will:

> We hold these truths to be self-evident, that all men are created equal, that they are endowed by their Creator with certain unalienable Rights, that among these are Life, Liberty and the pursuit of Happiness. That to secure these rights, Governments are instituted among Men, deriving their just powers from

the consent of the governed. That whenever any Form of Government becomes destructive of these ends, it is the Right of the People to alter or to abolish it, and to institute new Government....

A similar commitment to the sanctity of political rights can be seen in the French *Declaration of the Rights of Man and of the Citizen* of 1789:

> Law is the expression of the general will. Every citizen has a right to participate personally, or through his representative, in its foundation. It must be the same for all, whether it protects or punishes.

First and foremost, a **state** needs a constitutive population; there must be a people over which rulers can rule. In the contemporary period, we can point to the need for there to be a body of citizens whose status as such links them to a particular state, creating unique ties of responsibilities and rights between them. Often, the people are seen to be the equivalent of a **nation**, but in reality very few states have ever existed within such a singular ethnocultural environment (and current trends in international migration now make this even less likely). For example, at Confederation in 1867 it was understood that four national cultures made up the Canadian people: English, French, Irish, and Scottish. It is now generally accepted that numerous Aboriginal peoples also existed as nations at that time, even if they were not recognized as such, while the process of immigration has produced extensive cultural diversity—or **multiculturalism**—that now gives definition to what it means to be Canadian.

> **State:** A modern form of organizing political life that is characterized by a population, territory, governing institutions, and a government that claims a monopoly of legitimate force; recognition by the international community of states (most prominently by the United Nations) may also be key.

Elsewhere, colonialism and subsequent processes of decolonization often resulted in borders being drawn in ways that created numerous multiethnic if not **multination states**, sometimes with tragic consequences. For example, while a range of economic, social, and political factors help explain the 1994 genocide in Rwanda, during which an estimated 800,000 Tutsis were killed by Hutus within a period of about 100 days, as hundreds of thousands more fled to neighbouring countries as refugees, the uneasy coexistence of these two groups both during and after the colonial period that preceded the country's independence in 1961 remains a central factor. The politics of national identity, then, have affected and continue to affect both the behaviour and forms of all states.

Second, a state also requires an established territory over which to govern. Although conflicts have probably always arisen over land, it is only relatively recently in human history that set boundaries have become such a defining feature of political organization. For example, while the ancient Chinese dynasties claimed or controlled vast territories, precise boundaries remained undefined. This was changing by the time of the *1648 Treaty of Westphalia* that brought an end to the Thirty Years' War in Europe, which was fought against the backdrop of the competing religious claims of Catholicism and Protestantism. One of the significant outcomes of the treaty was the principle that rulers could determine the religion for the territory over which each ruled. It followed that the ruler would no longer need to submit to an external religious or political authority. Thus, the **sovereignty** of the state became a legal condition, with political authority being embedded in domestic political institutions and practices. Of course, this has not eliminated disputes over where borders lie between various sovereign states of the world. Even Canada still has a number of unresolved maritime boundary disagreements with the United States (in the Beaufort Sea, at the Dixon Entrance between Alaska and British Columbia, and in the Strait of Juan de Fuca between Washington State and British Columbia, as well as around Machias Seal Island and North Rock, both of which lie between Maine and New Brunswick). More recently, the issue of Arctic sovereignty has come to the fore as Canada, the United States, Denmark, Norway, and Russia all lay claim to parts of the Arctic (see Box 2.4). While many border disputes are maintained or resolved peacefully, others can explode into violence, as occurred in 1982 when Argentina forcibly occupied the Falkland Islands (known more for sheep farming than strategic importance, although offshore oil exploitation may change that) in the South Atlantic Ocean, which had been under British control since their own forcible occupation in 1833. By the time the British subsequently retook the islands, 900 combatants on both sides were dead.

> **Sovereignty:** A legal authority over a population and territory, commonly claimed by the government of a state but ultimately sanctioned by the international system of states. In other contexts, sovereignty can be said to reside in the people or in parliament.

Third, a state requires a range of political institutions to govern the population within its territory. As noted earlier, these are often associated with the rule-making, rule-enforcing, and rule-adjudicating functions of government. For these to be undertaken in a well-ordered fashion, a capable **bureaucracy** (or civil

BOX 2.4

ARCTIC SOVEREIGNTY

As long as it remained frozen, it seemed possible to contain Canada's longstanding disagreement with the United States over who had sovereignty over the Arctic, especially the Northwest Passage. As with other border disputes between the two countries, they had, since the 1988 *Arctic Co-operation Agreement,* more or less agreed to disagree for the time being. Recently, however, other states have begun to weigh in more heavily with claims of their own. Although Canada's diplomatic dispute with Denmark over who controls tiny Hans Island (which lies between Ellesmere Island and Greenland) often generates amusement, if not bewilderment, Russia's 2007 decision to lay a flag on the seabed floor beneath the North Pole has been seen as a more assertive attempt to bolster its claims in the Arctic. The economic payoff in this sovereignty game might be quite significant. With ice sheets melting, control over the previously hidden bounty of up to one-fourth of the untapped petroleum resources in the world, along with a wealth in valuable minerals, is at stake. Thus, even as the countries involved pursue scientific and diplomatic routes to secure their control over the North, they have also been increasing their military capabilities in the region.

Source: Adapted from CBC.ca, "Arctic sees military buildup"; available at http://www.cbc.ca/canada/north/story/2010/03/25/arctic-military025.html; accessed September 29, 2010.

service) is required, that is, some form of public administration that can advise decision-makers on policy and both interpret and implement their decisions. While politics within a given country will give more precise definition to the purposes to which such activities are turned, at some general level there is an expectation that a sovereign state will possess the appropriate institutions and use them on behalf of the people. All states, however, tend to claim to have the interests of the people at heart, when clearly there are instances where this is not true. As a result, greater attention has been turned recently to the question of what responsibilities states

have to their own citizens, and whether under certain circumstances the international community can violate state sovereignty to protect a people from its own state. This debate over the international community's "responsibility to protect" was brought into sharp focus by the failure of the world to intervene in the face of the 1994 Rwandan genocide, and it arises today within the context of the human tragedy unfolding in the Darfur region of Sudan.

Fourth, a state must have, as sociologist Max Weber famously phrased it, a "monopoly of the legitimate use of physical force within a given territory."[10] Such force can be used not only to defend the country's interests but also to enforce collective decisions. This usually involves the military and police, although a small number of states only have the latter. For example, Costa Rica abolished its standing army in 1948 after a civil war that left some 2,000 dead. The country still maintains police and public security forces, however, and contributes soldiers to peacekeeping missions. The relationship between the development of the modern state and the military has been, some argue, quite close. For example, American sociologist Charles Tilly proposes that the emergence and development of European nation-states occurred as they extended their military control and their control over the military.[11] As they increasingly came to rely on standing armies to preserve and expand their political authority, large bureaucracies were created to extract the funds necessary to maintain national armies and to administer conquered territories. Moreover, with the state drawing ever more heavily on the resources of the people, Tilly suggests, over time the people came to feel that they had the right, in turn, to make increasing demands upon the state—especially with respect to some form of participation within collective decision-making. At more than $1.5 trillion (U.S.) in 2009, a 49.2 percent increase since 2000, it is worth considering whether global military expenditures and the arms trade continue to shape the nature of the state.[12] While it pales in comparison to the $100 billion spent by China or the $661 billion spent by the United States, Canada nonetheless ranked 13th in the world at $19.2 billion, an increase of 48.8 percent since 2000.

Finally, a state must be able to function within a community of states. Certainly, without international recognition an entity that possesses all the other characteristics of a state noted above will not be able to engage as an equal on the world stage, whether at the

United Nations or with respect to other international institutions. As can be seen in the case of East Timor (Box 2.5), not only can statehood result in the ability of a people to overcome oppression and determine its own future, but the status that it provides under international law can produce such tangible benefits as gaining control over local resources, and the possibility of receiving international assistance on a bilateral (i.e., country-to-country) or multilateral basis. In a sense, international recognition provides a state with the **legitimacy** to act as a sovereign state, giving a *de facto* state a *de jure* or legal status under international law. Table 2.2 lists the member states of the United Nations in 2011.

Although all states generally display these basic features, few possess all to their fullest extent. Moreover, even though some states clearly do not meet these standards, they are still considered to be states. This underscores the point that states are not all the same. At a broad level, there is a tendency today to separate states into **regimes** that are democratic and those that are authoritarian. Although each type raises definitional

> **Regime:** The whole decision-making apparatus of the state; the constitutional principles and arrangements according to which government decisions are made; the fundamental rules of the game.

difficulties—especially concerning the point at which regimes cross over from one to the other—they nonetheless possess distinguishing characteristics that are important to the study of politics.

MODERN DEMOCRATIC GOVERNMENTS

In its 2002 *Human Development Report*, the United Nations Development Program observed that an incredible burst of democratization had occurred since the 1980s: "Some 81 countries took significant steps towards democracy, and today 140 of the world's nearly 200 countries hold multiparty elections—more than ever before."[13] Notwithstanding this shift (see Figure 2.1, p. 44), the report recommended caution in considering whether this marks an irreversible turn toward democracy. Not only has the expansion of democracy been much more modest during the past decade, but the strength of democracy remains weak in a number of recently converted countries, and thus the possibility of a return to authoritarianism remains. Indeed, despite expressions of popular aspirations for more democratic rule in many countries where it does not prevail, there is evidence in both long-established

---

BOX 2.5

STATEHOOD FOR EAST TIMOR

Situated between Indonesia and Australia, East Timor has its roots as a Portuguese colony in the 16th century. When a process of decolonization that would have likely resulted in independence began to unfold in the mid-1970s, however, Indonesia invaded and annexed the territory, which subsequently resulted in the death of an estimated 150,000 of a population of 650,000 (which some label genocide). Indonesia's occupation was tacitly if not explicitly supported by the international community until the 1993 Dili Massacre, when Western journalists filmed the Indonesian military as it opened fire on and subsequently killed some 400 protesters in the capital city. By 1999, a United Nations-brokered agreement between Indonesia, Portugal, and the United States resulted in a successful referendum on independence and by the end of 2002 East Timor had become an independent state and a member of the United Nations. Although it remains heavily dependent on foreign assistance, as an independent state, East Timor now has a say over the potentially rich petroleum and natural gas resources in the Timor Sea. As Xanana Gusmao, East Timor's first president, observed on the day of his country's independence: "We wanted to be ourselves, we wanted to take pride in being ourselves—a people and a nation . . . standing on equal footing with all other people in the world."

Source: Adapted from BBC News, "E Timor independence: Gusmao's speech," accessible online at http://news.bbc.co.uk/2/hi/asia-pacific/1997437.stm

Table 2.2   The 193 Member States of the United Nations

Afghanistan	Dominica	Luxembourg	Senegal
Albania	Dominican Republic	Madagascar	Serbia
Algeria	Ecuador	Malawi	Seychelles
Andorra	Egypt	Malaysia	Sierra Leone
Angola	El Salvador	Maldives	Singapore
Antigua and Barbuda	Equatorial Guinea	Mali	Slovakia
Argentina	Eritrea	Malta	Slovenia
Armenia	Estonia	Marshall Islands	Solomon Islands
Australia	Ethiopia	Mauritania	Somalia
Austria	Fiji	Mauritius	South Africa
Azerbaijan	Finland	Mexico	South Sudan
Bahamas	France	Micronesia, Federated	Spain
Bahrain	Gabon	States of	Sri Lanka
Bangladesh	Gambia	Moldova	Sudan
Barbados	Georgia	Monaco	Suriname
Belarus	Germany	Mongolia	Swaziland
Belgium	Ghana	Montenegro	Sweden
Belize	Greece	Morocco	Switzerland
Benin	Grenada	Mozambique	Syrian Arab Republic
Bhutan	Guatemala	Myanmar	Tajikistan
Bolivia	Guinea	Namibia	Thailand
Bosnia and Herzegovina	Guinea-Bissau	Nauru	The former Yugoslav
Botswana	Guyana	Nepal	Republic of
Brazil	Haiti	Netherlands	Macedonia
Brunei Darussalam	Honduras	New Zealand	Timor-Leste
Bulgaria	Hungary	Nicaragua	Togo
Burkina Faso	Iceland	Niger	Tonga
Burundi	India	Nigeria	Trinidad and
Cambodia	Indonesia	Norway	Tobago
Cameroon	Iran, Islamic	Oman	Tunisia
Canada	Republic of Iraq	Pakistan	Turkey
Cape Verde	Ireland	Palau	Turkmenistan
Central African	Israel	Panama	Tuvalu
Republic	Italy	Papua New Guinea	Uganda
Chad	Jamaica	Paraguay	Ukraine
Chile	Japan	Peru	United Arab Emirates
China	Jordan	Philippines	United Kingdom of
Colombia	Kazakhstan	Poland	Great Britain and
Comoros	Kenya	Portugal	Northern Ireland
Congo, Republic of the	Kiribati	Qatar	United Republic of
Costa Rica	Kuwait	Republic of Korea	Tanzania
Côte d'Ivoire	Kyrgyzstan	Romania	United States of
Croatia	Lao People's	Russian Federation	America
Cuba	Democratic Republic	Rwanda	Uruguay
Cyprus	Latvia	Saint Kitts and Nevis	Uzbekistan
Czech Republic	Lebanon	Saint Lucia	Vanuatu
Democratic People's	Lesotho	Saint Vincent and the	Venezuela, Bolivarian
Republic of Korea	Liberia	Grenadines	Republic of
Democratic Republic of	Libyan Arab	Samoa	Viet Nam
the Congo	Jamahiriya	San Marino	Yemen
Denmark	Liechtenstein	Sao Tome and Principe	Zambia
Djibouti	Lithuania	Saudi Arabia	Zimbabwe

Source: United Nations, "List of Member States," available at http://www.un.org/en/members/index.shtml; accessed September 29, 2010.

Figure 2.1 **The World Is Becoming More Democratic**

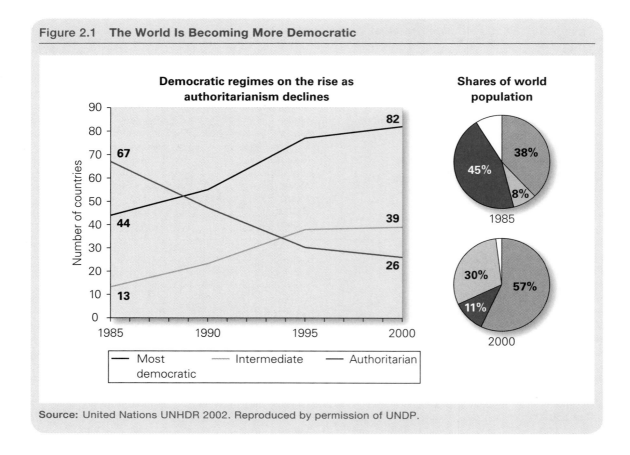

Source: United Nations UNHDR 2002. Reproduced by permission of UNDP.

and newer democracies that publics have been growing disillusioned with the seeming inability of the institutions of democratic governance to meet expectations. While this often arises in established democracies through a decline in voter turnout and trust in public institutions, in some cases it has resulted in calls for a return to more authoritarian forms of government.[14]

The need to probe in greater detail how to make democracies work is not simply a question of addressing the perception of a democratic deficit in long-standing democracies, or of testing the democratic claims of other states, although these are valuable undertakings; it has also emerged as a question of considerable international importance. In recent years, **democratization** has become a component part of the foreign policies of a number of countries, including Canada, and recent efforts to institutionalize democracy in Afghanistan and Iraq reveal how difficult this

process can be. Moreover, the language of democracy has come to permeate, if not dominate, political discourse, even in countries where it is practised least. So what do we mean when we talk about a democracy?[15]

First, as noted in Chapter 15, the government must be established, and it must be possible to replace it, through free and fair elections. It is in this way that it can be said that power resides with the citizenry. Moreover, it is through their elected representatives that the people can (indirectly) govern. The rulers, therefore, have power on loan from the people and must return it when asked to do so. For elections to be free and fair several conditions need to be met, including the possibility of competition between different political parties, accessible information on both party and candidate positions as well as the issues, and the regulation of the election itself by a nonpartisan agency whose job it is to ensure that everyone adheres to the law. Furthermore, votes should be cast through a secret ballot and people should not be intimidated or harassed at the polls. Thus, an election in and of itself is not democratic if it is not free and fair. Even established democracies can have difficulties in administering such contests, as the United States found in 2000, when the election between President George W. Bush and former Vice-President Al Gore ultimately had to be settled (and not without controversy) by the Supreme Court.

Second, the people need to constitute an active citizenry. On the one hand, they ought to be engaged politically, by participating in elections, keeping abreast of important political issues, supporting a political party, or running for office. On the other hand, they should be engaged civically, getting together with fellow citizens to volunteer or participate in a range of social organizations as members of **civil society**. Through such means—often voluntary, ideally peaceful—citizens can mobilize around issues of importance to them, scrutinize government actions, and attempt to influence state behaviour. Moreover, through the multitude of forms of participation open to citizens in a democratic system, bonds of social trust and commitment to the political system itself may be strengthened.[16]

Finally, a democracy must be based on the rule of law, through which both citizens and the state are equally subject to fair judicial proceedings. In a democratic system, the people are protected by the law, which limits the scope of state activity and provides avenues of redress against illegal state activities. For their part, the courts are to act as neutral arbiters and interpreters of the law, and must not be subject to interference from other branches of government or society. Thus, all individuals, regardless of their economic, political, or social position, are equal before the law. The rule of law must also incorporate provisions for human rights protections. Everyone must be protected from such practices as arbitrary arrest or imprisonment, inhumane treatment or torture, or summary execution. People should have the right to know any charges brought against them and defend themselves in a public trial. Thus, within a democracy every citizen possesses basic rights as a human being that cannot be taken away. Often these will be enshrined within a constitution, and they may be supported under international law as well. Of course, no country, even the most democratic, fulfils all **human rights** all the time. This can be seen with a quick look through Amnesty International's annual report, the 2010

edition of which lists human rights violations in 159 countries, many of which—such as Canada—are long-standing and established democracies.[17] Particularly noteworthy is the recent increase in counter-terror and security-related human rights issues in established democracies, which can affect both citizens and non-citizens (such as immigrants and asylum seekers) alike.

MODERN NONDEMOCRATIC GOVERNMENTS

Clearly, then, while democracy exhibits several basic institutional features, and requires a commitment on the part of the population to sustain it over time, it is no simple matter to create one. This complexity is increased by the fact that most states in the world make some kind of claim to be democratic. For example, the constitution of the People's Republic of China states that "the Chinese people of all nationalities will continue to adhere to the people's democratic dictatorship and the socialist road, steadily improve socialist institutions, develop socialist democracy, improve the socialist legal system, and work hard and self-reliantly . . . to turn China into a socialist country with a high level of culture and democracy." While China nonetheless lacks most of the core features commonly associated with a democracy, it underlines the point that many governments we call authoritarian have some element or elements we can associate with democracy. In the Islamic Republic of Iran, for example, the President is elected through a competitive process, but the Supreme Leader (who controls the military and shapes the direction of policy, among other significant powers) is elected by an Assembly of Experts (Islamic scholars), which itself is created through an electoral contest in which only government-approved candidates can compete. Thus, the democratic features of such regimes are often outweighed by characteristics that are difficult to reconcile with democracy.

Such states are often called dictatorships and are commonly divided into **authoritarian** and **totalitarian**

Authoritarian Government: A nondemocratic form of government that is not based on free and fair elections, severely curtails public participation in political life, and holds the actions of the state to be above the law; such regimes often commit gross human rights violations in order to maintain their power.

states.[18] These regime types lack several of the basic features commonly associated with democracy. Thus, while there may be elections, they are neither free nor fair as, for example, parties cannot compete freely or ballots are not accurately counted. For its part, the citizenry is often discouraged or prevented from debating and promoting issues outside official channels, and may be subject to harassment or even face execution for doing so. The state will seek to control all forms of **mass media** tightly—especially new technologies associated with the Internet that threaten the containment of political mobilization. As for the rule of law, it is generally undermined by a lack of judicial independence from the state, while the government itself often acts with impunity. As a result, such regimes feature prominently in the work of organizations such as Amnesty International and Human Rights Watch in calling attention to governments and states that sustain their power through gross violation of human rights. Moreover, corruption is often rampant in such regimes. As a result, citizens are more like the subjects of the ancient absolute monarchies, and the people are ruled with few opportunities to be rulers as well. In order to maintain their power, the leadership is often closely associated with military, police, and other security forces—indeed, they may come from the ranks of such organizations—and these often receive considerable public funding in an attempt to maintain the regime in power against any public opposition. Because so much power is centred around the leader, that role is often glorified as the interests of the country are equated with those of its leader. While the vast majority of people are likely to live in poverty in such regimes, the leadership and its supporters are rarely found wanting. Because of such personification of power, when governments do change it is often a violent process.

There are, however, important differences between authoritarian and totalitarian regimes. For example, authoritarian regimes tend to have a much less clearly defined ideological orientation and reflect, instead, a more pragmatic approach to power. Thus, they may adopt and promote discourses and policies aimed at economic development, national independence, public order, or social justice, for example. To these ends, authoritarian regimes will seek to mobilize particular segments of the population—to allow forms of political mobilization that bolster the regime. In contrast, totalitarian regimes seek to wholly control and transform the people through an all-encompassing

An Iranian veiled opposition protester flashes a victory sign during the anti-government protest in Tehran, Iran in December 2009.

ABACAPRESS.COM/The Canadian Press(Amir Sadeghi)

ideology that speaks to their cultural, economic, political, and social roots and destiny. Rather than distancing itself from society, totalitarian regimes seek to absorb it. In the 20th century, prominent totalitarian regimes include Nazism in Hitler's Germany, **fascism** in Mussolini's Italy, Soviet **communism**, especially under Stalin, and the agrarian communism in Pol Pot's Cambodia, which resulted in the death of an estimated two million civilians within half a decade. Although the number of authoritarian or totalitarian governments has

Totalitarian government: A nondemocratic form of government that seeks to wholly control and transform the people through an all-encompassing ideology that speaks to their cultural, economic, political, and social roots and destiny. Totalitarian regimes were responsible for two of the worst genocides of the 20th century, in Europe during the Second World War and in Cambodia in the 1970s.

BOX 2.6

EXAMPLES OF PRESENT-DAY AUTHORITARIAN REGIMES

China is, of course, the most populous country in the world, and—while it has experienced a slow-down during the recent global recession—it is expected to become the largest economic power in the world within a little more than a decade. Although it has embraced aspects of capitalism, China remains a one-party communist state, and among its more notorious legacies is the Tiananmen Square massacre of student dissidents in 1989. Since that time, the country has continued to be subject to criticisms for its human rights record, and in 2010, Liu Xiaobo, who was given an 11-year sentence by the Chinese government for his pro-democracy advocacy, was awarded the Nobel Peace Prize. Among various authoritarian features are government influence over the judiciary; executions of people convicted of nonviolent crimes such as tax fraud; arrest, detention, imprisonment, and even torture of labour activists, journalists, human rights defenders, and political and religious dissidents; government control of the media (including the Internet); and severe restrictions on freedom of expression and religion in Tibet and in such areas as the Xinjiang Uighur Autonomous Region.

Iran is an Islamic Republic located next to Iraq; it is a leading example of a theocratic state, which—in contrast to a secular state—institutionalizes a central role for religious authorities in political affairs. The constitution gives supreme authority to the Spiritual Leader (despite the existence of an elected President), and requires that the precepts of Islam be the basis for political, social, and economic relations. In response to anti-fraud and pro-democracy protests following the 2009 presidential elections, the Iranian state responded with violence, leaving dozens dead and thousands arrested. There is widespread evidence of the use of torture against detainees, and dozens were prosecuted in "show trials" that left many with long-term prison sentences and at least six facing the death penalty. Other authoritarian features include shutting down reformist newspapers and jailing journalists; legal limitations on the ability to criticize Islamic values, including a new category of "Internet crimes"; extensive discrimination against ethnic and religious minorities as well as women; and the use of such cruel, inhuman, and degrading punishments as judicially ordered amputations. In recent years, there has been increasing talk of the likelihood of an American or Israeli attack on Iran in response to its nuclear enrichment program, which has already resulted in UN Security Council votes in favour of economic and political sanctions.

North Korea, formally the Democratic People's Republic of Korea, is another state whose nuclear ambitions have raised concerns in recent years—especially after it conducted nuclear tests in 2006 and 2009, and as security experts and authorities such as the International Atomic Energy Agency conclude that it has joined the small list of states possessing or believed to possess nuclear weapons: the United States, Russia, Great Britain, France, China, India, Pakistan, and Israel. Like China, North Korea is a one-party state, with Kim Jong-il wielding extensive powers as the country's Supreme Leader. Having succeeded his father (Kim Il-sung) in 1998, and expected to be succeeded in turn by his son (Kim Jong-un), Kim Jong-il continues a family practice in promoting a cult of personality to bolster his hold on power. He has also continued his late father's "self-reliance" or isolationist policy, which has removed the country from the influence of the former Soviet Union and China but also (as a socialist state) has underlined its opposition to the United States and other Western powers. Nonetheless, despite widespread famines that have likely killed some two million people since the 1990s and left a third of the population—nine million—malnourished, the country relies extensively on international food aid from other countries, including the United States. Although human rights monitors are denied access, leading human rights experts report that North Korea has one of the worst human rights records in the world, routinely engaging in arbitrary detention, torture, and forced disappearances and relocations, alongside extensive suppression of freedom of speech and freedom of association, among others.

Sources: Reports from Amnesty International, Human Rights Watch, and The Europa World Year Book.

been in decline over the past 25 years, the examples provided in Box 2.6 (p. 47) show that they still have a marked presence in world politics.

Indeed, "authoritarian state" is the designation more commonly applied today to nondemocratic states, and great variation within this category can be found. Some of the new "democracies" during the past few decades, in fact, have retained attributes of their former authoritarian selves, which probably helps to explain the tenuousness of the more general turn toward democracy during the past few decades. Early hopes that the end of the Cold War would lead to democracy in Russia, for example, have been disappointed by evidence of its transformation into an authoritarian capitalist regime.[19] Moreover, the growth of legislation and policies to counter terrorist threats in recent years—which frequently involve the suspension of certain liberties that otherwise remain central to democratic political life— has opened up an increasing debate over a "creeping authoritarianism" in established democracies.

NON-STATE GOVERNMENTS

If you take a map of the world and overlay it with the 193 member states of the United Nations, some more democratic and some more authoritarian, you would not have an accurate representation of the full range of either governments or state-like entities in the world. Not only would you miss areas where it is not quite clear who is sovereign, but you would also overlook places where other types of government or state-like entities operate. To understand more fully the nature of governments and states, it is necessary to consider a few of these situations.

Traditional Governments

Human history is replete with instances of some groups dominating others, perhaps absorbing them into their own populations through conquest or maintaining them as dependencies in order to extract valued resources, for example. European colonialism from the late 15th century onwards provides countless such examples, as Western explorers, militaries, and rulers searched the globe for new trade routes, areas for settlement, and riches. As they moved through Africa, Asia, Latin America and the Caribbean, and beyond, they

often encountered—and conquered or displaced— Indigenous peoples. Some, such as the Aztecs (of present-day Mexico), had long-standing and complex political systems, based in highly developed city-states ruled by kings and tributary relations that impressed Europeans. Thus, although he sacked it in 1521, the Spaniard Hernán Cortés praised the sophistication and splendour of Tenochitlán (which was perhaps larger than any other European city aside from Paris at the time) in letters to his king. In North America, proto-typical democratic forms of government could be seen among some Aboriginal groups, such as those that made up the Iroquois Confederacy. Although nomadic peoples, such as the Maasai (now of Kenya and Tanzania) and the Bushmen (in southern Africa), had less observable political structures they nonetheless possessed complex understandings of societal norms and political relations and of religion and trade, some of which had possibly developed over centuries.

While Europeans often depended upon the knowledge of such groups for survival in unfamiliar climates and terrains, they generally held Indigenous peoples to be less "civilized" (or even "uncivilized") in comparison. In some instances an assertion of cultural and racial superiority served to justify—in their own eyes— their domination over such groups, while in others, subtle arguments were developed to show that these "new lands" could be considered *terra nullius* (empty lands), as Indigenous peoples did not utilize systems of law or property that conformed to European models of governance. In either case, it was often argued that these groups existed in a pre-political "state of nature" that called for European control. After centuries of marginalization and even outright oppression, there is now a world movement of Indigenous peoples that meets on a regular basis to discuss and recommend political actions to promote recognition of spheres of independent Indigenous political authority in many states. To this end, the *Declaration on the Rights of Indigenous Peoples*, adopted by the United Nations General Assembly in 2007, states that "Indigenous peoples have the right to maintain and strengthen their distinct political, legal, economic, social and cultural institutions, while retaining the right to participate fully, if they so choose, in the political, economic, social and cultural life of the State" (Article 5).

It is impossible to do justice here to the great variation of such arrangements that have been or might be made, as there are between 300–350 million Indigenous people in the world, constituting some 5,000 different groups in more than 70 countries. The struggles they face are diverse and are no longer simply a product of colonial times (although colonialism remains a necessary framework through which to view them). For example, the Yanomani lived in near seclusion within the Amazon rainforest until the 1970s, when the discovery of gold led to (sometimes deadly) conflicts with miners. Although land was set aside for the Yanomani in 1992, miners continue to work illegally within the territory, resulting in environmental and health threats that undermine the Yanomani way of life. In Canada, considerable progress has been made in recognizing the diverse cultural, economic, environmental, and social challenges faced by Aboriginal peoples in recent years. This has largely been due to the organization of and involvement in Canadian politics by Aboriginal peoples themselves since the 1960s, which has produced increased calls for **Aboriginal self-government**. Given that there are more than 600 different Aboriginal groups in Canada (consisting of more than one million people), with varying degrees of political organization, territorial cohesion, and self-government ambition, the models that might be developed vary greatly. A recent example was instituted with the *Nisga'a Treaty* of 2000, which recognized the authority of a Nisga'a government in British Columbia within the context of the Canadian constitutional structure.

> **Aboriginal self-government:** Diverse arrangements whereby the authority of Aboriginal or Indigenous groups to govern themselves is recognized; such authority (over various aspects of community life) would have to be consistent with the laws operating within existing sovereign states.

Other Non-state Governments

Aside from such traditional governments without states, there is also one area of the globe with neither government nor state—Antarctica, which has no permanent population but is the fifth-largest continent in the world. Although seven countries claim parts of the Antarctic, these have been laid aside for the time being under the *1959 Antarctic Treaty*, the purpose of which is to ensure that Antarctica remains demilitarized and accessible for peaceful scientific research.

There are also various entities around the world that have state-like attributes but do not possess state sovereignty. For example, numerous colonies, dependencies, and external territories are linked and in some way subordinate to an established state. Often, such relationships have grown out of particular colonial histories, while at other times they reflect geographic proximity. At present, there are more than 50 dependencies and areas of special sovereignty in the world (according to the U.S. State Department), including such well-known examples as Bermuda, the Cayman Islands, and Puerto Rico. Although they tend to be associated with western states such as Australia, the Netherlands, Norway, the United Kingdom, and the United States, two are linked to China (Hong Kong and Macau). For its part, Canada does not possess any such territories but can point to the case of the islands that make up the Territorial Collectivity of Saint Pierre and Miquelon, which lies just off the coast of Newfoundland and has been under the control of France since the 1763 *Treaty of Paris*.

There also exist what might be called *de facto* states that have not received *de jure* recognition from the United Nations. Palestine is recognized at the United Nations as a non-member entity. It maintains—like the Holy See of the Catholic Church in Vatican State—a permanent mission at UN headquarters in New York, and is allowed to participate as an observer in the General Assembly. Other cases are less clear-cut: Taiwan, for example, is claimed by China, and the Sahrawi Arab Democratic Republic effectively controls a significant amount of territory otherwise claimed by Morocco in the Western Sahara. Only a minority of states have been willing to establish diplomatic relations with either entity. Elsewhere, while the United States and many European countries support statehood for Kosovo, this is opposed both by Serbia and Russia, among others. There are also several possible *de facto* states that are not really recognized by anyone else. These include the areas of Northern Cyprus (which is recognized only by the Turkish government), Abkhazia and South Ossetia (in Georgia), Nagorno-Karabakh (in Armenia-Azerbaijan), Somaliland (in Somalia), and Transnistria (in Moldova). By challenging the authority of ruling governments from within, such state-like entities might one day become sovereign in their own right; however, they might also foster a condition of state failure.

Failed States

The issue of state failure has become particularly acute in the post-Cold War era, and even more so in the wake of September 11, 2001. Although the international system of states had seen major shakeups before, what has happened since the Cold War has been especially dramatic. For example, with the demise of the Soviet Union, 16 new states were recognized by the United Nations, while the breakup of the former Yugoslavia has resulted in six new member states and Kosovo could soon constitute a seventh. In some instances, such as the 1989 Velvet Revolution in Czechoslovakia, this process was fairly peaceful. In others, it was extremely turbulent, as in the former Yugoslavia, which was beset by violent interethnic conflict between 1991 and 2001, resulting in the death of perhaps 120,000 people and the displacement of more than two million others. The issue of state failure took on heightened resonance following September 11, when a more explicit link was proposed between such states and **terrorism**. In short, it was argued that failed or failing states could provide a safe haven for terrorists when no central authority was willing or able to confront them. For these and other reasons, the international community (along with those who study politics) has been paying increased attention to identifying the conditions of state failure and trying to determine how best to respond.

The conditions of state failure might at first seem to be fairly obvious: a state is no longer a state when it loses one or more of the five characteristics covered above. Thus, a **failed state** would be one, for example, that no longer had "a monopoly of the legitimate use of physical force within [its] given territory." This answer, however, does not take us very far because, as we saw above, very few states match the full ideal of statehood, and even states that clearly do not meet certain criteria are still considered to be states by the international community. For example, although no national government has been able to control the country's sovereign territory since 1991, the international community still recognizes the Somali Republic as a state. As opposed to stateless governments, those in power in a recognized state at least nominally have a territory over which they possess jurisdiction under international law.

Indeed, the factors at play in state failure are diverse and can combine in various ways. This has led the researchers behind the Failed States Index, a joint project

of *Foreign Policy Magazine* and the Fund for Peace, to suggest that "Just as there are many paths to success, there are many paths to failure for states on the edge."[20] In constructing the index, a variety of economic, political, and social indicators are gauged (see Box 2.7), and in 2010, the five states deemed most likely to fail were Somalia, Chad, Sudan, Zimbabwe, and the Democratic Republic of the Congo, followed by Afghanistan and Iraq. Each indicator represents a range of complex issues that defy easy understanding or solution, and to address any of them requires political will from both the state in question and the international community, which is not always easy to attain. Moreover, as can be seen in Box 2.8, a new twist has been added to the issue of state failure with global warming.

BOX 2.7

INDICATORS OF STATE FAILURE

Social Indicators

1. Mounting demographic pressures
2. Massive movement of refugees or internally displaced persons creating complex humanitarian emergencies
3. Legacy of vengeance-seeking group grievance or group paranoia
4. Chronic and sustained human flight

Economic Indicators

1. Uneven economic development along group lines
2. Sharp and/or severe economic decline

Political Indicators

1. Criminalization and/or delegitimization of the state
2. Progressive deterioration of public services
3. Suspension or arbitrary application of the rule of law and widespread violation of human rights
4. Security apparatus operates as a "state within a state"
5. Rise of factionalized elites
6. Intervention of other states or external political actors

Source: Fund for Peace. "Methodology Behind CAST"; available at http://www.fundforpeace.org/web/index.php?option=com_content&task=view&id=107&Itemid=145; accessed September 29, 2010.

CLIMATE CHANGE AND STATE FAILURE

As public recognition of the threat of global warming grows, new possibilities of state failure have been identified. Take, for example, the case of the tiny island state of Tuvalu (consisting of four reef islands and five atolls), which is the least populated and fourth-smallest member state of the United Nations. This Polynesian country, located between Australia and Hawaii, gained independence from Britain in 1978 and has survived mainly on foreign aid ever since. Although it is a fully functioning constitutional monarchy, with a democratically elected parliament, the state faces the prospect of failure due to rising sea levels as the country is—on average—just six feet above sea level. Tuvalu is one of a number of island states whose very physical existence as a territory is threatened in this way.

Source: "Tuvalu: That Sinking Feeling: Global warming, rising seas," a documentary by Elizabeth Pollock; available online at http://www.pbs.org/frontlineworld/rough/2005/12/tuvalu_that_sin_1.html; accessed on September 29, 2010.

While state failure is generally discussed in terms of countries in the developing world, the concept also extends to "pockets of state failure" that can occur in any political system. For example, when Hurricane Katrina hit New Orleans in 2005, the United States was unable to mount an effective reaction for several days; that same year, France declared a state of emergency after weeks of rioting in Paris and beyond. More generally, there have been concerns that the emergence of a pandemic, such as the outbreak of influenza that killed an estimated 50 million persons worldwide between 1918 and 1920, might produce situations of state failure if hospital systems become overloaded. By expanding the concept of state failure, of course, the point is not to equate the political situation in Canada, for example, with that of Somalia, for clearly differences in the degree, nature, and consequences of failure are significant. It does, however, remind us that every state has the potential to fail for reasons of external intervention, internal combustion, or both, and that history suggests that all states are likely to confront such challenges at some point.

Postnational States?

While questions of state failure still seem remote for the more established states of the world, there has been considerable talk of their transformation since the late 20th century, often in the context of a process of **globalization**. According to one scenario, in an era of increased international migration, the old notion of the *nation-state*, while never an accurate depiction, has become an especially inappropriate term for the increasingly diversified societies around the world today. This might, in fact, change the meaning of citizenship that lies at the heart of the definition of a state. In another scenario, states are being challenged both from within and from without, as the power generally associated with the national state is transferred upwards to international governing structures or devolved downwards to regional or municipal levels. With respect to the former, analysts often focus on institutions such as the **World Trade Organization**, which is supposed to ensure that national economic activities conform to certain shared standards of behaviour, or the **European Union**, through which a range of administrative, executive, judicial, and legislative functions have been passed from member states to a higher political authority. With respect to the latter, the focus often shifts to the rise of "global cities" such as New York, London, and Tokyo, which—while existing within sovereign states—operate through global economic and social networks that create powerful political interests and forces within national capitals. In either case, pressing and challenging questions are raised as to the nature and functions of governments and states, and it suggests that their evolution is far from over.

CONCLUSION

As will become evident as you work your way through this textbook, governments and states do not define the entire scope of the study of politics, but they are often important factors and are rarely very far removed from modern political life. Clearly, whether we live under a democratic or an authoritarian regime quite literally shapes our prospects for living—as Aristotle observed—the good life. It also affects the types of politics that surround us and in which we become engaged. It is important, therefore, that we study the governments under and the states within which we live to understand how they operate, determine whether they work well, and decide how they need to be altered. Indeed, history reminds us that no political regime is perfect, and that each might be improved. In an age of increasing globalization, moreover, it is ever more difficult to isolate ourselves from what is going on in the rest of the world, making it essential to study the nature of other governments and states, how they are similar to or different from our own and why, and what kinds of ties—whether of self-interest or shared responsibility—might bind us together.

DISCUSSION QUESTIONS

1. Is Aristotle's scheme for classifying governments only appropriate for the ancient world, or is it still relevant today? Where would you place Canada?

2. In what ways are modern democracies less democratic than they might be, and how might they become more democratic?

3. Should the international community intervene or put pressure on authoritarian states in order to effect a regime change toward democracy?

4. Should we be concerned about state failure in countries halfway around the world? If so, what should we do about it?

5. Is Aboriginal self-government compatible with state sovereignty in an increasingly globalized world? Why or why not?

FURTHER READING

Berger, Mark T., ed. *From Nation-Building to State-Building*. New York: Routledge, 2007.

Bethell, Leslie, ed. *The Cambridge History of Latin America, Volume 1, Colonial Latin America*. Cambridge: Cambridge University Press, 1984.

Diamond, Larry, Marc F. Plattner, and Philip J. Costopoulos, eds. *World Religions and Democracy*. Baltimore: The Johns Hopkins University Press, 2005.

Dunn, John. *Democracy: A History*. Toronto: Penguin Canada, 2005.

Europa World Year Book. London: Europa Publications, 2007.

Finer, S.E. *The History of Government from the Earliest Times, Vols. I–III*. Oxford: Oxford University Press, 1997.

Hawkesworth, Mary, and Maurice Kogan, eds. *Encyclopedia of Government and Politics*. New York: Routledge, 2003.

Hughes, Lotte. *The No-Nonsense Guide to Indigenous Peoples*. Toronto: Between the Lines Press, 2003.

Krieger, Joel, ed. *The Oxford Companion to Politics of the World*, 2nd ed. Oxford: Oxford University Press, 2001.

ENDNOTES

1. A comprehensive account can be found in Peter Marshall, *Demanding the Impossible: A History of Anarchism* (Oakland, CA: PM Press, 2010).

2. Alan C. Cairns, "The Embedded State: State-Society Relations in Canada," in D.E. Williams, ed., *Reconfigurations: Canadian Citizenship & Constitutional Change, Selected Essays by Alan C. Cairns* (Toronto: McClelland & Stewart Inc., 1995), pp. 31–61, 358–61.

3. Gabriel A. Almond, "A Functional Approach to Comparative Politics," in G.A. Almond and J.S. Coleman, eds., *The Politics of the Developing Areas* (Princeton: Princeton University Press, 1960), pp. 3–64.

4. "In a world-historical perspective, then, the Middle East is the cradle of organized government, and it was to retain its cultural, political, and military supremacy … for over 2,000 years." S.E. Finer, *The History of Government from the Earliest Times, Vol. I* (Oxford: Oxford University Press, 1997), p. 99.

5. See John Dunn, *Democracy: A History* (Toronto: Penguin Canada, 2005).

6. For some pre-Athenian examples, see Eric W. Robinson, *The First Democracies: Early*

Popular Government Outside Athens (Stuttgart: Steiner, 1997).

7. Aristotle, *The Politics*, trans. T.A. Sinclair, revised and re-presented by Trevor J. Saunders (London: Penguin Books, 1981 [1962]), p. 60. Aristotle viewed men to be by nature superior to women, and on this ground he justified the rule of the former over the latter, and the exclusion of women from politics.

8. *Ibid.*, p. 222.

9. John Locke, *Second Treatise of Government*, ch. 9, sec. 123, originally published in 1689 and accessible online through *Project Gutenberg,* available at http://www.gutenberg.org/etext/7370; accessed September 29, 2010.

10. Max Weber, "Politics as a Vocation," originally delivered as a speech in 1918 and accessible online through Wikisource, available at http://en.wikisource.org/wiki/Politics_as_a_Vocation; accessed September 29, 2010. He defines a state as "a human community that (successfully) claims the monopoly of the legitimate use of physical force within a given territory."

11. See Charles Tilly, *Coercion, Capital and European States, AD 900–1990* (Cambridge, Massachusetts: Basil Blackburn, 1990).

12. Sam Perlo-Freeman, Olawale Ismail, and Carina Solmirano, "Military Expenditure," in Stockholm International Peace Research Institute, *Yearbook 2010: Armaments, Disarmament and International Security* (Stockholm: SIPRI, 2010), p. 177.

13. United Nations Development Program, *2002 Human Development Report* (New York: Oxford University Press, 2002), p. 1.

14. See, for example, the regional reports on the state of popular support for democracy included in *Journal of Democracy* 18(3) (July 2007).

15. See Larry Diamond, "What Is Democracy?," lecture at Hillah University for Humanitarian, Scientific and Religious Studies, January 21, 2004, available at http://www.stanford.edu/%7Eldiamond/iraq.html; accessed September 29, 2010. Diamond advised the Coalition Provisional Authority in Baghdad in its efforts to establish a democratic political system in Iraq, and delivered this speech on the basic characteristics of a democracy to some 1,500 Iraqi leaders in 2004.

16. This is the basic thrust of Robert Putnam, *Bowling Alone: The Collapse and Revival of American Community* (New York: Simon & Schuster, 2000).

17. Amnesty International, *Amnesty International Report 2010,* available at http://thereport.amnesty.org/en; accessed September 29, 2010.

18. See James Malloy, "Contemporary Authoritarian Regimes," in M. Hawkesworth and M. Korgan, eds., *Encyclopedia of Government and Politics, Vol. I* (London: Routledge, 1992), pp. 229–46.

19. See Azar Gut, "The Return of Authoritarian Great Powers," *Foreign Policy* 86(4) (July/August 2007), pp. 59–69.

20. "The Failed State Index," *Foreign Policy,* 161 (July/August 2007), p. 56.

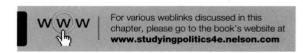

States and Nations: Cultural Pluralism, Nationalism, and Identity

Yasmeen Abu-Laban

CHAPTER OBJECTIVES

After you have completed this chapter, you should be able to:

- define the key concepts of nationalism, state, nation, multination state, genocide, ethnic cleansing, diaspora, race and racialization, globalization, dominant conformity, and cultural pluralism
- outline and evaluate different approaches to the study of nationalism
- discuss the debate over the impact of contemporary globalization on national identity
- describe some contemporary expressions of nationalism and other identity-based claims

WHY STUDY CULTURAL PLURALISM?

According to demographic statistics, only about 10 percent of countries can be said to be ethnically homogeneous.[1] The fact that cultural pluralism is a reality in most countries has important implications for politics. As noted in Chapter 2, modern government has come to rest largely with the state. Given that 90 percent of the countries of the world are characterized by having a heterogeneous population (see Table 3.1), it is easy to see why political scientists are interested in cultural and ethnic diversity. The sense of identity people have, the relations between different cultural and ethnic groups, and the possibility of different and even conflicting demands made by groups can all affect the terrain of state governance. A better understanding of these issues has considerable practical significance, affecting people's quality of life and helping decision-makers who wish to enact effective public policies.

In this way, the attempt to describe ethnic, cultural, and other forms of diversity is not merely an abstract theoretical exercise. The research findings of political and other social scientists on issues pertaining to diversity are extremely relevant. This fact has been recognized at the highest levels internationally, as exemplified by the mandate of the Management of Social Transformations (MOST) program, launched in January 1994 by the United Nations Educational, Scientific and Cultural Organization (UNESCO). MOST is an ongoing project designed to promote international comparative social science research, with the aim of transferring policy-relevant findings to governmental and nongovernmental decision-makers. A central goal of the MOST project in its first phase of operation (1994–2003) was to better understand multicultural and multiethnic societies, precisely because of

---

Table 3.1   Diversity in Selected Countries

Drawing on national census data and other statistical information, *The World Factbook* of the U.S. Central Intelligence Agency lists ethnic groups present in all countries of the world.

Afghanistan	Pashtun 42%, Tajik 27%, Hazara 9%, Uzbek 9%, Aimak 4%, Turkmen 3%, Baloch 2%, other 4%
Australia	White 92%, Asian 7%, Aboriginal and other 1%
Belgium	Fleming 58%, Walloon 31%, mixed or other 11%
Brazil	White 53.7%, mulatto (mixed white and black) 38.5%, black 6.2%, other (includes Japanese, Arab, Amerindian) 0.9%, unspecified 0.7%
China	Han Chinese 91.5%, Zhuang, Manchu, Hui, Miao, Uighur, Tujia, Yi, Mongol, Tibetan, Buyi, Dong, Yao, Korean, and other nationalities 8.5%
Finland	Finn 93.4%, Swede 5.6%, Russian 0.5%, Estonian 0.3%, Roma (Gypsy) 0.1%, Sami 0.1%
Germany	German 91.5%, Turkish 2.4%, other 6.1% (made up largely of Greek, Italian, Polish, Russian, Serbo-Croatian, Spanish)
India	Indo-Aryan 72%, Dravidian 25%, Mongoloid and other 3%
Iraq	Arab 75%–80%, Kurdish 15%–20%; Turkoman, Assyrian, or other 5%
Iran	Persian 51%, Azeri 24%, Gilaki and Mazandarani 8%, Kurd 7%, Arab 3%, Lur 2%, Baloch 2%, Turkmen 2%, other 1%
Israel	Jewish 76.4% (of which Israel-born 67.1%, Europe/America-born 22.6%, Africa-born 5.9%, Asia-born 4.2%), non-Jewish 23.6% (mostly Arab); Gaza Strip: Palestinian Arab; West Bank: Palestinian Arab and other 83%, Jewish 17%
Mexico	Mestizo (Amerindian-Spanish) 60%, Amerindian or predominantly Amerindian 30%, white 9%, other 1%
South Africa	Black African 79%, white 9.6%, coloured 8.9%, Indian/Asian 2.5%
Sudan	Black 52%, Arab 39%, Beja 6%, foreigners 2%, other 1%
Switzerland	German 65%, French 18%, Italian 10%, Romansch 1%, other 6%
United Kingdom	White 92.1% (of which English 83.6%, Scottish 8.6%, Welsh 4.9%, Northern Irish 2.9%), black 2%, Indian 1.8%, Pakistani 1.3%, mixed 1.2%, other 1.6%
United States	White 79.96%, Black 12.85%, Asian 4.43%, Amerindian and Alaska native 0.97%, native Hawaiian and other Pacific Islander 0.18%, two or more races 1.61%*

* Note: a separate listing for Hispanic is not included because the U.S. Census Bureau considers Hispanic to mean persons of Spanish/Hispanic/Latino origin including those of Mexican, Cuban, Puerto Rican, Dominican Republic, Spanish, and Central or South American origin living in the US who may be of any race or ethnic group (white, black, Asian, etc.); about 15.1% of the total US population is Hispanic.

Source: Central Intelligence Agency, *The World Factbook* 2009; available at https://www.cia.gov/library/publications/the-world-factbook/index.html; accessed November 6, 2010.

---

the potential implications for a host of policy areas. Accordingly, it was argued,

> The major challenge facing policy-makers in the fields of education, health, social welfare, and justice is to formulate policies in such a way as to promote and sustain peaceful multi-ethnic and multi-cultural co-operation and to rebuild such co-operation in societies undergoing post-war political, social and economic reconstruction.[2]

This quest continues in the second phase of operation (2004–2013) with an explicit focus on "International Migration and Multicultural Policies."

To highlight "best practices" and to facilitate effective policymaking, the MOST project has developed a series of publications and electronic databases to provide relevant information to policymakers grounded in evidence-based social science research.

This chapter examines the internal diversity of nation-states in light of a belief system that profoundly shaped politics and events in the 20th century: nationalism. For political scientists today, a major research question concerns the salience of nationalism in the 21st century, given contemporary patterns of globalization. The economic, cultural, and technological processes associated with globalization now seem to challenge both national identity as the only or main form of identity experienced by people, as well as the **nation-state** as a form of political organization. In this chapter, it is argued that while national identity is not disappearing, its primacy is being challenged by contemporary globalization.

In the first section of this chapter, key concepts pertaining to nationalism are explained. The second section contains an overview of theories of nationalism with reference to historic nationalist liberation struggles in the developing world. In the third section, the tension between nationalism and other forms of identity (especially gender) is examined in light of Apartheid and post-Apartheid South Africa. Finally, the tension between nationalism and globalization is addressed, and contemporary expressions of nationalism and identity claims that are not based on a single national identity are explored in relation to Canada.

KEY CONCEPTS IN THE STUDY OF NATIONALISM

Connotation of Nationalism

What comes to mind when you think of the word *nationalism*? Are your reactions positive or negative? No matter how you answer these questions, you will enter into a debate that has raged among analysts and historians for over two centuries. This momentous force has been viewed as the root cause of such diverse events as the emergence of the European state system, World War I, the rise of fascism in Europe, Third World anti-colonial struggles, reassertions of national identity by minorities in industrialized countries (e.g., in Scotland and in Quebec), and post-Cold War conflict in the former Soviet bloc countries (e.g., the Balkans and Central Asia).

Some consider nationalism as a positive force. It has been suggested, for example, that the existence of nations is associated with the existence of ties of love or kinship.[3] Frequently, we may speak of nations as "motherlands" and "fatherlands." Citizens form a national "family." Immigrants are said to "adopt" countries that are not their native homes. In the United States, the president and the president's spouse are referred to as the "First Family." In Canada, the first two lines of the national anthem (at least in English, as the Canadian anthem's meaning is different in French!) are "O Canada! Our home and native land! True patriot love in all thy sons command." When Nelson Mandela became the first president of post-apartheid South Africa, his wife at the time, Winnie Mandela, was honoured as South Africa's "Mother of the Nation."

Probably more often, however, nationalism has been associated with hatred. Some have viewed nationalism as the most destructive force of the 20th century—the cause of violence, atrocity, and incalculable human misery.[4] The Nazi regime in Germany and the evils of the Holocaust stood as the mid-century's horrifying example of this scourge. Responding to the tragedy of the Holocaust, Polish jurist Raphael Lemkin coined the term **genocide** (from the Greek word *genos*, meaning race, and the Latin word *caedere*, meaning to kill).[5] An international prohibition against genocide was established in 1948 when the United Nations adopted the Convention on the Prevention and Punishment of the Crime of Genocide.

> **Genocide:** The deliberate and systematic extermination of a national, ethnic, or religious group. The term was developed in response to the horrors of the Holocaust.

In the 1990s, the violence, bloodshed, and killing that occurred among rival ethnic and religious groups in the former Yugoslavia (Serbs, Croats, and Muslims) and also in Rwanda (Hutus and Tutsis) emerged as new horrors that led many to reaffirm that nationalism was one of the most destructive forces imaginable and to refocus international attention on genocide.

The 1992–1995 war in Bosnia-Herzegovina was the key segment in the dissolution of Yugoslavia, which began when the republics of Croatia and Slovenia seceded in 1991, leaving open the possibility of an independent Bosnia. There was no clear ethnic majority in Bosnia; the three constituent peoples (as defined by earlier Yugoslav constitutions) were the Muslims (most numerous at 42 percent of the population), followed by the Serbs and the Croats.[6] In this climate of uncertainty in Bosnia, President Slobodan Milosevic of Serbia used the crisis to consolidate his power by sending in his paramilitary troops bent on ethnic cleansing.[7] While the United Nations attributes violence in Bosnia-Herzegovina to all sides, the term **ethnic cleansing** was used specifically to refer to a slate of violent measures and policies designed to eliminate or dramatically reduce the Muslim and Croat populations in Serb-held territory.[8] Ethnic cleansing included the systematic rape by Serbian soldiers of Muslim and Croat women, whose captivity, torture, and forced pregnancies were designed to reproduce "Serbians."[9] The term "ethnic cleansing" is also controversial because it is seen as somewhat euphemistic (in contrast to *genocide*) and serves to mask the impact of this nationalist violence.

> **Ethnic Cleansing:** The removal of one or more ethnic groups from a society by means of expulsion, imprisonment, or killing. The term entered the political lexicon in reference to the former Yugoslavia; it was first used to describe the violent measures and policies designed to eliminate or dramatically reduce the Muslim and Croat populations in Serb-held territory.

The Rwandan genocide began on April 6, 1994, when a small group of Hutu political and military leaders targeted and began the slaughter of more than a half a million Tutsis—a group that constituted about 10 percent of the population—along with thousands of Hutus who opposed the elite in power. This genocide differed from others in its rapidity (lasting about a hundred days) and in the number of ordinary people who were mobilized by a small elite to kill.[10]

The travesties in both Rwanda and the former Yugoslavia, which clearly included both the direct and indirect involvement of governments, led to renewed calls within the international community for more effective means to prosecute such crimes. To this end, the United Nations created an International Criminal Court, whose jurisdiction includes the ability to prosecute the crime of genocide, as defined in the 1948 Convention on the Prevention and Punishment of the Crime of Genocide. These tragic events of the 1990s also had an impact on the study of nationalism. Indeed, in 1993, Michael Ignatieff wrote an international bestseller, tellingly entitled *Blood and Belonging*, in which he argues that the end of the Cold War has been replaced by a new age of violence based on nationalism and ethnic particularism.[11]

Some see the continuation of this age of violence in the 21st century through the prism of the "war on terrorism." Here, many longstanding national conflicts have come to be viewed as somehow reflecting a "clash of civilizations"—a term popularized by the late political scientist Samuel Huntington (see also Box 3.1 on Israel/Palestine). Following the end of the Cold War, as marked by the collapse of the Berlin Wall in 1990, Huntington predicted that the main characteristic of international politics would be that of a civilizational clash involving Western societies on the one hand and non-Western societies on the other.[12] Huntington's thesis enjoyed a period of renewed currency following the September 11, 2001 attacks in New York and Washington because it seemed to explain a divide between the East (specifically, Islam) and the West (specifically, Christianity). However, the "clash of civilizations" thesis has also been subjected to criticism for treating the West and the non-West as homogeneous and, therefore, not accounting for the complexity of both or for the ways "cultures" (as well as people) intermix.[13] Notably, Huntington's 2004 book dealing with America and immigration, particularly from Mexico, entitled *Who are We? The Challenges to America's National Identity*[14] drew very similar criticisms since it suggested that Catholic and/ or Spanish influences were seemingly incompatible with the British and/or Protestant settler foundation and national identity of America.[15] Such debates, whether about domestic or international politics, suggest the need for a careful definition of nationalism.

Denotation of Nationalism

While there are radically different readings of the impact of nationalism as a force, political scientists are on less contentious ground in delineating what nationalism is. At root, **nationalism** may be defined as an ideology or belief system that contains three major assumptions.[16] The first assumption is that certain identified populations contain characteristics that make them nations. The second is that the world is divided into nations. The third is that a nation should be able to establish its own institutions, laws, and government and to determine its future—this is really what lies behind the idea of self-determination. The doctrine of self-determination holds that a group of people who call themselves a nation have a right to have control over territory or domains that immediately concern them, normally through statehood. The idea of self-determination may be traced back to the emergence of the European state system in the middle of the 17th century. In the 20th century, it became enshrined in the principles of international institutions such as the United Nations, and self-determination is now considered a human right under international law.[17]

> **Nationalism:** An ideology that holds that certain populations are nations, that the world is divided into nations, and that a nation should be self-determining (i.e., able to establish its own institutions, laws, and government and to determine its future).

Other Associated Concepts: State, Nation, Multination State, Diaspora

Unpacking the ideology of nationalism requires a closer examination of several associated concepts. The first concept is that of the state. Political scientists have theorized much about the state, but there is no clear consensus about whose interests it promotes. For example, as noted in Chapters 4 and 6, the 19th-century thinker

Nationalistic Americans fear "dangerous" Arab nationalism.

Kirk Anderson/Artizans

Karl Marx (1818–1883) argued that in a capitalist society the state was a class instrument that served the interests of the owners of the means of production (the bourgeoisie) over the interests of the workers (the proletariat). For Marx, the state was central in the functioning of the capitalist system and the perpetuation of class inequality. This is why Marx called on workers to unite, overthrow the state, and usher in a more egalitarian (in this case, communist) society. More recently, radical feminists have argued that the state is central in perpetuating patriarchy (the rule of males) by privileging men in law and public policy.[18] Other (mainly liberal) theorists assert that the state operates in the interests of different individuals or groups at different times.

Although there is considerable debate about whose interests are represented by the state, most political scientists do agree on what the state is and use the definition first provided by Max Weber (1864–1920), as noted in Chapter 2. Weber argued that the "**state is a human community that (successfully) claims the monopoly of legitimate use of physical force within a given territory.**"[19] For Weber, the state is characterized by territory (existing in a given geographical boundary), by sovereignty (the state is the highest authority and can back up its claims with force), and by institutions (including the bureaucracy, the military and the police, and the legislature).

It should be noted that the way political scientists use the term *state* to refer to territory, sovereignty, and institutions is very comprehensive and precise; the term *state* is not synonymous with *country or government*. The term *country* describes geographical units of the globe. When you look at the divisions of the world in an atlas, you are looking at countries. As discussed in Chapters 1 and 2, the term *government* refers to the set of institutions and/or individuals that makes and enforces collective public decisions.

The ideology of nationalism holds that territory, sovereignty, and institutions must be allocated to people of a single nation. While belonging to a state may be a simple matter of citizenship, belonging to a **nation** rests on a subjective sense of identity and belonging, marked by distinct cultural or linguistic traditions, which is usually in turn marked by membership in a distinct ethnic group.[20] A leading theorist of nationalism, Benedict Anderson, refers to nations as "imagined communities" precisely because

the idea of a nation rests on a subjective sense of belonging to a community that is neither voluntary nor organizationally defined. Joining an organization such as an undergraduate students' association (which likely holds elections for those willing to run for president, vice-president, and the like) is not like being part of a nation. In contrast, belonging to a nation is somewhat similar to belonging to a family—it is seemingly "natural" and involuntary.[21] For this reason, according to Anderson, dying for one's nation "assumes a moral grandeur which dying for the Labour Party, the American Medical Association, or perhaps even Amnesty International cannot rival, for these are all bodies one can join or leave at easy will."[22] Undoubtedly, we could put campus student associations in this same "voluntary" category as political parties or interest groups.

> **Nation:** A community of people, normally defined by a combination of ethnicity, language, and culture, with a subjective sense of belonging together.

Although the ideology of nationalism implies that there ought to be an easily definable correspondence between territory, a single nation, and rule, this is not the case with most countries. Some states contain more than one nation; such a state is called a **multination state**. For example, Canada has been variously described as containing two nations (the French and the British), three nations (the French, the British, and Aboriginal peoples), and even numerous nations (particularly when the multiple traditions and languages among all Aboriginal peoples in Canada are considered). This is where the problems of the doctrine of self-determination become apparent. Often in real-world politics the same territory is claimed by more than one group. This is especially apparent in a country such as Canada—a settler colony with an Indigenous population and a minority francophone population located primarily in Quebec. The fact that Aboriginal peoples have land claims all over the country, including Quebec, became very apparent during the 1995 Quebec referendum on sovereignty. Although separation from the rest of Canada was rejected by a very narrow margin by Quebecers (50.6 percent to 49.4 percent), some Aboriginal groups, including the Cree and the Montagnais, held their own separate referendums on the issue of sovereignty, in which the proposal was also rejected by a much wider margin. Another international example of competing national claims to the same land is seen in the conflict zone of Israel–Palestine (see Box 3.1).

Multination state: A state that contains more than one nation.

A further complication to the doctrine of nationalism is the fact that nations may spill out across state boundaries—a feature encapsulated in the concept of

---

BOX 3.1

TWO NARRATIVES: "PALESTINE" AND "ISRAEL"

Both Palestinian Arabs (Muslims and Christians) and Israeli Jews lay claim to the territory of Palestine/Israel as their national home on the basis of long residence, history, and religion. The area known as Palestine was, until World War I, part of the Turkish Ottoman Empire. Following the war, the League of Nations (the forerunner to the United Nations) granted Britain a mandate over Palestine. Flowing from the 1917 Balfour Declaration, the British government viewed "with favour the establishment in Palestine of a national home for the Jewish people," and promised to use immigration to support this objective.

While Palestinian Arabs remained a majority in the area until the late 1940s, the goal of creating a Jewish state in Palestine was further developed in the United Nations Partition Plan in 1947. The Partition Plan sought to divide Palestine into an Arab state and a Jewish state, with the city of Jerusalem designated as an international zone. The Partition Plan was viewed as unacceptable and unfair by Palestinian Arabs, who believed it threatened the geographical integrity of Palestine and disagreed with the manner in which Palestine was divided. Hostility between Arabs and Jews mounted in Palestine, and civil war broke out. On May 14, 1948 the British mandate came to an end and an independent state of Israel was declared. As a result, open warfare between the surrounding Arab states and Israel erupted. By the end of the war, there was more land taken by Israel than had been allotted under the Partition Plan. In the meantime, Israel rapidly gained the recognition of both the world's superpowers—the United States and the Soviet Union. Israeli leaders immediately indicated that the new state belonged to all the Jewish people around the world and invited immigration from the Jewish diaspora. This is codified as the Israeli state's "law of return."

The events of 1948 are subject to very different national narratives on the parts of Palestinians and Israelis. For many Israelis, the years 1947 and 1948 are seen as a period in which the birth of a national state was made possible after the Holocaust and after what Israelis call the War of Independence of 1948. In contrast, for most Palestinians, the year 1948 represents a disaster (in Arabic the *Nakba*) characterized by half of the Arab population losing homes and property and becoming stateless refugees outside of mandatory Palestine. Today Palestinians make up the world's largest and one of the oldest refugee groups. Indeed, from 1949, the Palestinian national identity crystallized around the loss of homeland, the longing to return, and the desire for self-determination. This is symbolized in the quest for a "right of return."

A series of wars in the region (in 1956, 1967, 1973, and 1982) served to reconfigure control of the land in favour of the state of Israel. For example, after the 1967 war, the territories of the West Bank and Gaza (known as "the occupied territories") came under Israeli control. The Oslo agreement signed in 1993 by Israel and the Palestine Liberation Organization (PLO) allows for parts of these two territories to be handed over to Palestinian rule. Nonetheless, disputes over land continue, and peace has remained elusive between Israelis and Palestinians as well as in the larger region.

TWO NARRATIVES: "PALESTINE" AND "ISRAEL" (Continued)

This case provokes a number of questions of interest for studies of pluralism, nationalism, identity, and contemporary politics, including:

1. Outside the region, President Barack Obama in the United States has called for renewed peace talks between Israeli and Palestinian leaders, aimed at fostering a "two state solution" wherein it is envisioned that a Palestinian state and an Israeli state will co-exist in peace and security. However, some Palestinian and Israeli intellectuals have advanced a "one state" option based on equal rights and citizenship for all (that is, regardless of ethnicity, national origin, or religion) as well as recognition of collectivities through policies like bilingualism. Can competing claims to the same territory be adequately resolved by either of these options?

2. Since 2005, in response to a call from Palestinian civil society groups, there has been a growing international movement aimed at "boycott, divestment, and sanctions" against the state of Israel. Proponents see this movement as a means for civil society groups outside the region (for example, unions, church groups, student groups, etc. in Western countries) to challenge human rights abuses experienced by Palestinians, and to foster Israel's compliance with international law by ending the occupation and the plight of Palestinian refugees. Critics charge that this movement unfairly targets Israel, and in the process promotes a "new anti-Semitism." What factors account for the rise of this movement, and the varied interpretations of this movement?

3. Since the events of September 11, 2001 there has been a renewed interest in the "clash of civilizations" thesis forwarded by Samuel Huntington. In what ways does the thesis apply, or not apply, to the case of Israel/Palestine?

diaspora. The term was originally applied to Jewish people, but today it is used to describe any ethnic group that has experienced or currently experiences dislocation across multiple states, and yet typically nurtures narratives and political projects about a "homeland" as a place of eventual return at some opportune time.[23] In contemporary usage it has been applied to such diverse groups as Palestinians, Armenians, and Cubans.[24]

> **Diaspora:** An ethnic group that has experienced or currently experiences dislocation across multiple states, yet typically nurtures narratives and political projects about a specific "homeland" as a place of eventual return.

Racial Discrimination and the Politics of Multiculturalism

Finally, as part of understanding nationalism it should also be noted that ethnic groups can have many different political demands and points of mobilization that do not take the form of nationalism and self-determination but instead stress gaining acceptance and equality.[25] In particular, some groups may struggle against discrimination based on race (racism) as well as processes of **racialization** (the historically and contextually specific ways in which certain groups come to be seen as separate and inferior on the basis of biology and/or culture).

> **Racialization:** The historically and culturally specific processes associated with representations or assertions of superiority by one group over another on the basis of purported biological and/or cultural characteristics.

In the past, the term **race** has been used in many different ways. During the 19th century, biologists used it to refer to different "subspecies" of humans. The inspiration behind eugenics movements—which advocated the use of "scientific" breeding techniques to improve the genetic potential of humans—was the supposed existence of biological differences between different "racial" groups. In the early 20th century, the term *race* was often used as a synonym for nation and *ethnic group*. This can be seen in the metaphor of America as a "melting pot," popularized in the 1908 play *The Melting Pot* by Israel Zangwill. Zangwill spoke of different "races" (by which he meant Germans, Russians, the English, the French, and the Irish) jumping into a common melting pot and emerging as Americans.[26] By the middle of the 20th century, as a result of the atrocities of the Holocaust, the use of *race* to refer to biological differences between people was completely discredited; instead, many began to talk about "the human race" to indicate that eugenics was wrong, as all people are of the same species.

> **Race:** Historically, the term *race* was used to speak about differences between people that were supposedly biologically based. Today social scientists completely reject the idea that there are any significant biological differences between people that warrant the use of the term. While some suggest that in light of this the term should not be used at all, many contemporary social scientists put the term in quotation marks to refer to differences that are socially constructed and historically specific, but have important consequences in the form of racism. Contemporary discussions of racism assume that it involves a biological and/or cultural assertion of superiority by one group over another.

Today, social scientists use the term *race* to refer to socially constructed rather than biologically inherited differences. In other words, race is viewed as significant only because of socially created beliefs about differences between people, not because biology itself determines culture or personality. In particular, social scientists are interested in examining how the experiences and impact of racism (and processes of racialization) are manifested in practices and institutions to the detriment of particular groups in particular times and places. Some have advocated rejecting the term *race* altogether, or at least putting it in quotation marks to signify that there are no inherent differences between people.[27]

The idea that "race" and processes of racialization are socially constructed and temporally specific can be readily documented. For example, historically, the Irish were held to be a separate and inferior "race" to the British; they experienced discrimination in a host of spheres in Britain, Canada, and the United States. Today groups struggling with racial discrimination include African-Americans in the United States.

African-Americans overcame slavery in the 1800s, and through the civil rights movement in the 1950s and 1960s successfully challenged segregation in public schools and private establishments, yet discrimination against them remains a fact of life.

The continued inequality in employment and earnings between African-Americans and all other groups has led to public policy measures such as affirmative action. **Affirmative action** is designed to equalize the chances of members of minority groups or groups traditionally discriminated against, such as African-Americans, women, and people with disabilities, in accessing education and jobs by setting goals for ensuring the statistical representation of these groups. Affirmative action has become increasingly controversial in the United States. Critics charge that it is "reverse discrimination," while proponents argue that it helps put into practice the principle that all people are of equal worth. In the United States, affirmative action has tended to be supported by African-Americans more than by other groups.[28] Given the historical and contemporary social context of that country, categories such as "black" and "white" (and increasingly, "mixed race") are important politically. Indeed, the legacy of slavery has been so profound that the 2008 election of President Barack Obama, the country's first African-American President, has been widely interpreted as an "historic" moment.

Contemporary theoretical discussions of racism are further complicated by the fact that analysts have increasingly sought to identify the relationship between culture (not just biology) and processes by which groups can experience differentiation, discrimination, and disadvantage. For example, British political theorist Tariq Modood distinguishes "colour racism" (as seen in hierarchically distinguishing "black" and "white") and "cultural racism." For Modood, the primary example of cultural racism today can be seen in how Muslims in Britain face discrimination and their religion is vilified (also captured in the more popularized concept of Islamophobia).[29] Modood states as well that this tendency predates the events of September 11, 2001.

Whether looking at African-Americans in the United States or British Muslims, the projects of such groups tend to be different from groups seeking national self-determination. Political theorist Will

Kymlicka suggests that in Canada and elsewhere many minority and immigrant groups have mobilized to demand **multiculturalism**. Kymlicka points out that this pursuit of multiculturalism is geared primarily to achieve inclusion in the dominant culture, rather than to attempt to live separately from it. For Kymlicka, multicultural responses to minority and immigrant group claims might involve such diverse policies as affirmative action, guaranteed seats in legislatures, curriculum changes in schools, work schedule changes to accommodate diverse religions, flexible dress codes, literacy programs in the first language of immigrants, and bilingual education programs for the children of immigrants.[30] In this way, multiculturalism may be seen as a very different kind of demand than national self-determination.

> **Multiculturalism:** A policy sometimes adopted in a state characterized by cultural pluralism that supports ethnic and cultural groups in maintaining their customs and traditions, often with public financial assistance.

EXPLAINING NATIONALISM: NATIONAL LIBERATION MOVEMENTS AND DECOLONIZATION

So far in our discussion, two main themes have emerged. First, nationalism has been associated with many different—even opposite—phenomena in the 20th century: war, violence, hate, oppression, liberation, family, and love. Second, political scientists have defined the ideology of nationalism and related concepts in a precise way that seems to capture the essence of most, if not all, expressions of nationalism. The areas of agreement and disagreement help account for two very distinct approaches to studying nationalism that political scientists have used in explaining its emergence in very different times and locales.

Because the ideology of nationalism is fairly consistent across its various expressions, political scientists have tried to determine whether there is one primary factor that can explain the emergence of nationalism in so many different places. Those searching for this all-purpose general explanation have engaged in *universalizing comparisons*; that is, they have attempted to show how all instances of nationalism follow the same patterns. In contrast, other political scientists have postulated that, partly because of the sheer variety of phenomena associated with nationalism (from oppression to liberation), there may be many different explanations for why nationalism emerges in different locales—that is, that there is no universal explanation. Those searching to discover such differences have engaged in *individualizing comparisons*, which attempt to show the unique characteristics of a given instance of nationalism.

To evaluate these two different approaches, it is helpful to consider how each might account for the same manifestation of nationalism, namely that of 20th century Third World anti-colonial movements. During the 19th century, **imperialism**—in the form of **colonization** of other countries and the establishment of empires—led to the expansion of Western power over the rest of the world. However, during the 20th century, the formal control of Western states in different parts of the world largely came to an unexpected end in a relatively short period of time. Consider that in 1945, when the United Nations emerged as the primary international organization to promote peace and human rights, 51 states obtained membership. As can be seen in Table 3.2, out of these 51 states, only three were located in Africa (Ethiopia, Liberia, and South Africa), three in Asia (of which only China was independent of colonial rule), and seven in the Middle East. Initially, then, the great majority of member states in the United Nations were the countries of North America, the Commonwealth, and Europe, including the former Soviet Union. Notably, most observers in the 1950s did not expect European power to end in their lifetime.[31] However, by the end of 1965, 66 new states had joined the United Nations, bringing the number up to 117; in 2006 Montenegro became the 192nd member and in 2011 South Sudan made it 193.

The addition of 66 new states by 1965 symbolized a dramatic political change: the formal transfer of power from Europeans to non-Europeans and the liberation of some one billion people from colonial rule in Asia and Africa. The emergence and successes

Table 3.2	The Original 51 Member States of the United Nations, 1945			
Argentina	Czechoslovakia	Honduras	Panama	Ukraine
Australia	Denmark	India	Paraguay	United Kingdom
Belgium	Dominican	Iran	Peru	of Great Britain
Bolivia	Republic	Iraq	Philippines	and Northern
Brazil	Ecuador	Lebanon	Poland	Ireland
Belarus	Egypt	Liberia	Russian	United States
Canada	El Salvador	Luxembourg	Federation	of America
Chile	Ethiopia	Mexico	Saudi Arabia	Uruguay
China	France	Netherlands	South Africa	Venezuela
Colombia	Greece	New Zealand	Syrian Arab	Yugoslavia
Costa Rica	Guatemala	Nicaragua	Republic	
Cuba	Haiti	Norway	Turkey	

of Third World nationalist anti-colonial movements might be explained in different ways depending on the approach one uses.

Universalizing Comparisons

Traditionally, many political scientists used universalizing comparisons to try to establish that all forms of nationalism follow the same patterns or rules. This approach was widely accepted during the 1950s, 1960s, and 1970s, and there are still people who use it today. Its popularity may be related to how political science, as a discipline, has been influenced by developments in the United States. In that country, during the first two to three decades after World War II, political analysts were very much concerned with developing generalizations that could be applied to all societies at all times. This was part and parcel of developing a "science" of social and political life.[32]

The accounts that address nationalism from the vantage point of universalizing comparisons generally suggest that nationalism was rooted in the European experience, dating from the French Revolution and gaining speed with the unification of Germany and Italy in 1870. In this view, nationalism was somehow related to the processes of industrialization. What exactly is highlighted as important about industrialization varies in different accounts that make use of universalizing comparisons. Some have argued that technological developments in mass communication and the introduction of mass education made it

possible for people to communicate easily with each other across vast distances.[33] As a result, people started to identify with one another in a new way—as part of national communities. Others have proposed that capitalism accompanied industrialization, and with capitalism came uneven development, such that, when there were pockets of poverty in distinct regions, expressions of nationalism emerged.[34] Both of these scenarios that use industrialization to explain nationalism have a universalizing quality to them—a sense that the ideology of nationalism developed in Europe and was simply exported to Africa and Asia on the back of European colonialism.[35]

More recently, such universalizing explanations have been criticized for being Eurocentric—that is, focused only on the experience of Europe. Critics also argue that they are ahistorical—that is, they tend to ignore the unique historical context of different countries outside of Europe in accounting for nationalism. There is value to these criticisms, since political scientists have never been able to produce one general theory that accounts for the emergence of nationalism everywhere and for all time.

Individualizing Comparisons

Individualizing comparisons, then, take into account both historical and geographical specificity. They seek to uncover that which is unique about a given form or instance of nationalism. Broadly speaking, the suggestion that comes out of such accounts is that many expressions of Third World nationalism may be viewed as a political reaction against colonialism, as seen in Chapter 14.[36] This political reaction occurs in societies where traditional modes of social and political organization have collapsed as a result of the changes introduced by colonialism.

One way to understand how Third World expressions of nationalism were a reaction against the oppressive effects of colonial rule is to consider how colonized people were treated and depicted by colonial powers. The famous lines by British poet Rudyard Kipling on "The White Man's Burden" provide a literary example of this broader phenomenon. Kipling's poem, written in 1899, describes the need for British men—and more broadly white men—to go out to the colonial world and rule the peoples there, whom Kipling describes as "half devil and half child."[37]

Unequal power relations that rested upon the dehumanized depiction of the colonized by the colonizer are key to understanding the motivation behind Third World nationalist movements for liberation. Imperialism and colonialism worked to erode the dignity of peoples of the Third World, but nationalism formed a part in the recovery of that dignity.[38] Consequently, one of the things that tend to surface in such expressions of Third World nationalism aimed at liberation is an attempt to invert and put value on the identity of the colonized. For example, Léopold Sédar Senghor, a poet who became the first president of Senegal after it achieved independence from France in 1960, is associated with a literary and political movement known as négritude. The négritude movement, which began in the 1930s and reached its zenith in the 1960s, launched a critique of Western society for suppressing blacks and for cutting African blacks off from their roots. Négritude aimed to rediscover ancient African values so that Africans could feel pride and dignity in their heritage and culture.

Likewise, Frantz Fanon, a West Indian-born psychoanalyst and philosopher who spent time in Algeria when it was under French colonial rule, went on to write about the necessity of creating or recreating a national cultural consciousness as a means of achieving true independence. In contrast to the négritude movement Fanon saw an important, almost redemptive, role to be played by violence. He describes this idea in his famous 1963 book *The Wretched of the Earth*, which deals with the situation in Algeria. Between 1954

and 1961, there was a bitter and violent war between France and Algeria, as a result of which Algeria gained its independence in 1962. For Fanon, the lessons of the Algerian war of independence suggest the value of violent struggle as a means to empower colonized people. Violence, he argues, is a cleansing force that "frees the native from his inferiority complex and from his despair and inaction."[39] Yet ultimately, the development of a genuine national consciousness leading to real liberation is difficult to achieve, Fanon points out, because the forces of domination are internalized by indigenous elites.[40] Even after decolonization, the unequal social and economic structures inherited from colonialism might well continue. Fanon sensed very early on that the national liberation movements in countries that experienced colonization might be successful in overthrowing foreign rulers, but that this might not necessarily in and of itself lead to an egalitarian future.

The basic idea behind individualizing comparisons is that while nationalism might be a single ideology, it contains several subvarieties.[41] From the vantage point of individualizing comparisons, manifestations of nationalism in the Third World in the context of national struggles for liberation may be seen as unique because the factors that motivated nationalism were unique. Universalizing explanations, in contrast, fail to take into account the specificity of the situation in the Third World. In an attempt to fit all manifestations of nationalism into one pattern, they neglect to consider the historical effects of imperialism and colonialism in the countries of the developing world. Individualizing comparisons do not have these limitations, suggesting the general necessity of attending to context when trying to understand nationalism in the contemporary period.

THE NATION VERSUS OTHER FORMS OF IDENTITY: CONSIDERING SOUTH AFRICA

The advantages of individualizing comparisons do not completely negate the need to theorize about the nation in relation to internal forces. The warnings of Frantz Fanon about the future of liberated (postcolonial) states highlight the complexities present in any nation. Any population that calls itself a nation is inevitably internally diverse and divided along some combination of class, gender, age, and rural–urban lines. As one prominent example of the relevance of this kind of internal diversity within nations, it is useful to consider the more recent work of feminist scholars who have insisted on the importance of gender diversity in the study of national identity and relations of power. We have noted how nationalist discourses often make use of metaphors relating to kinship—motherlands, fatherlands, and the like. Such "familial" depictions of the nation have been the starting point for the work of these feminist scholars who stress that nationalist movements can act to subordinate women. For example, whether women have children, how women socialize children, and even how women dress are often extremely important to most nationalist movements.[42] In recent years, political debates in Canada and other Western countries about the appropriateness of some Muslim women wearing the *hijab* (a head cover) or the *niqab* (a head and face cover) underscore the fact that how women dress is not simply a question of individual choice, but can tap into wider issues of identity, community, and nation.

Because women frequently play a central role in transmitting and reflecting cultural traditions across generations, the argument has also been made that it is women who play the primary role as "bearers of the nation," rather than schools or forms of mass communication (as has been suggested by some accounts focusing on explaining the rise of nationalism in relation to industrialization).[43] In this way, women can become specific targets as both the "property of men" and the "embodiment of the nation," as attested to by the systematic use of rape in the name of ethnic cleansing.[44] While, typically, nationalist movements themselves are tied to gendered relations, this does not always mean that they specifically improve the position of women. Indeed, according to feminist scholars, those who assume that nationalist movements generally improve the lot of the disadvantaged often neglect to attend to specific social and political structures and belief systems that can keep women in subordinate positions.[45]

In the context of nationalist movements aimed at liberation, South Africa provides a noteworthy recent example of a country where gender equality had to be considered explicitly. The history of the African National Congress (ANC) illustrates this point. The ANC was created in 1912 as the principal organization reflecting indigenous black South African interests. Although it was outlawed in 1960, the ANC was later instrumental in ending the racist policies of apartheid (or apartness) that had supported white (European) colonial political and economic dominance.[46] Nelson Mandela, once branded a "terrorist" by the South African government, emerged from a long prison term to lead a successful anti-apartheid movement and then become the first president of post-apartheid South Africa in 1994.

The history of politics in South Africa and the reaction of black women there to the long years of resistance and hope for liberating the country from white control demonstrate that black women's relation to nationalism has undergone changes.[47] Initially, when the ANC was created, women were denied formal representation in the organization, yet gradually, as a result of women's own insistence, they were granted full participation. Nevertheless, calls for women's emancipation were generally seen as secondary to national revolution, sometimes even by women themselves. Over the late 1970s and 1980s, however, the issue of women's empowerment began to be raised as a project distinct from national, democratic, and social revolution. By the early 1990s, female ANC nationalists carried placards with the slogan "A nation will never be free until women are free."[48]

Such women's demonstrations were successful in leading to formal recognition of women's rights within the ANC, which in 1990 issued a Statement on the Emancipation of Women. The statement argued that the experience of other societies with successful national liberation struggles showed that the emancipation of women does not necessarily follow from national liberation. The statement asserted that, given this historical record, women's emancipation had to be addressed within the ANC, the mass democratic national movement, and society as a whole. It went as far as to say that all "laws, customs, traditions and practices which discriminate against women shall be held unconstitutional."[49] Indeed, under Nelson Mandela a new constitution was passed that emphasized not only formal but also substantive equality for women.[50] Formal equality refers to the idea that everyone has the same rights; substantive equality refers to the idea that everyone is able to actually access the same opportunities by holding and exercising those rights.

While it has been observed that no other country has a constitution with such progressive ideas to eliminate sexism,[51] constitutions do not in and of themselves necessarily guarantee all the rights they may proclaim. For this reason, in the context of "national liberation" and the transition to democracy in South Africa, gender equality and issues relating to women's inequality remain on the agenda for analysts as well as women's organizations.[52] Additionally, profound economic inequalities in post-Apartheid South Africa today (commonly referred to as "economic apartheid") have also drawn analytical attention to forms of inequality on the basis of class and race, as well as gender.[53] Overall then, the case of South Africa and the ANC demonstrates how nationalism still matters, how nations are internally diverse, and how national movements and even successful liberatory projects may be affected by diversity.

NATIONALISM VERSUS GLOBALIZATION

Given the internal diversity of nations and the fact that what motivates nationalism might vary depending on the time period and geography, it seems clear that the idea of a universal theory of nationalism is problematic. The limitations of universalizing explanations should be kept in mind as we turn to the grand question concerning the future of national identity and nationalism in light of contemporary globalization.

In an important way, as attested to by the examples of imperialism and colonialism, **globalization** is not a completely new phenomenon. For centuries, people, money, ideas, goods, and corporations have crossed geopolitical boundaries. But the processes associated with contemporary globalization (since 1945) have some distinct features. Globalization before the end of World War II was based on imperialism, colonialism, and coercion practised by institutions of empires (such as the British or French Empires). Contemporary globalization processes rest on a multitude of multilateral institutions (such as the World Trade Organization) and, since the collapse of the Soviet Union, the political and economic dominance of the United States.[54] As well, as noted in Chapter 17, the contemporary economic, technological, and cultural flows associated

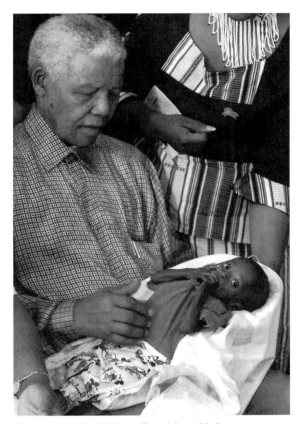

Former South African President Nelson Mandela holds a six-month-old baby infected with HIV during his visit to Beautiful Gate, a home that looks after children in Crossroads township, outside of Cape Town, South Africa; Saturday, December 1, 2001.

AP Photo/The Canadian Press(Obed Zilwa)

Globalization: The movement of goods, capital, ideas, and people across geopolitical boundaries today and in the past. Contemporary patterns of globalization involve a deepening constellation of economic, technological, and cultural changes that are worldwide in scope and that challenge the sovereignty of the state.

with globalization today are more intense than in earlier periods.[55] The unprecedented speed with which capital (in the form of cash, stocks, and shares, for example) can move around the world as a result of new information technologies illustrates how economic flows have changed in the past several decades. The speed with which information can flow across the planet as a result of the Internet, social networking (Facebook), and other developments in communications (such as the advent of CNN, which is based in Atlanta in the United States but has overseas operations and services) means that information flows are not simply national but global. As well, while people may always have moved from place to place, the flows are now much more widespread and multidirectional. Currently all regions and countries both send and receive people.[56]

The combination of all of these developments has led some political scientists to question the future viability of the state as a form of organization, because one of its key aspects is sovereignty, the assumption that it is the highest authority. But sovereignty may be eroding in the face of the contemporary worldwide reorganization of economic, technological, and cultural flows. For example, states now have much more difficulty controlling the flow of information.

Globalization and National Identity

Globalization also raises questions concerning national identity. Stuart Hall, a leading British analyst of culture, has argued that the developments associated with contemporary globalization that appear to challenge the state and its sovereignty also raise issues about the future of nationalism. Hall argues that the seemingly "natural" priority given to national culture (and identity) is in fact a historical phenomenon tied to the emergence of the nation-state. He suggests that contemporary globalization appears to have the effect of "contesting and dislocating the centred and 'closed' identities of a national culture."[57] Globalization raises many uncertainties about the future of national identity, not only because people who move across national boundaries may bring with them different cultural influences, but also because there are forms of culture (from Mickey Mouse to world music) that are not simply national but global. Furthermore, there are elements of identity (gender, for example) that may assume as much importance for some people as national identity, if not more.

According to Stuart Hall, the 21st century carries three possibilities for national identity.[58] One possibility is that national identity may actually be strengthened in response to globalization. Another possibility is that national identity may be weakened. The third possibility is that new, shifting, and even hybrid forms of identity may emerge to challenge a singular national identity.

Drawing from our discussion on the advantages of individualizing comparisons, it is probably more useful to attend to specific cases when considering these propositions rather than to attempt to make universal claims. We will therefore turn our attention to the cases of the **European Union (EU)** (see Box 3.2) and Canada to gain insight into the possibilities that contemporary globalization raises for the future primacy of national identity.

The Canadian Case

In Canada, the daily news reminds us that people of many different backgrounds reside here—that is, that Canada is a country that reflects a reality of cultural pluralism. Among a host of possible demographic statistics that might be used to illustrate this reality are those on ethnic diversity (Table 3.3, p. 70) and religious diversity (Table 3.4, p. 70). A dominant issue that structured Canada's history as a settler-colony concerned the rights of Catholics versus those of Protestants. For example, the 1774 *Québec Act* granted the freedom to practise the Catholic faith, and retained the French civil law and seigneurial landholding systems. While the *Québec Act* did not say anything about the use of the French language, the appointed council (overseen by a colonial governor) allowed for Roman Catholics to hold office. Today, this particular division between Catholics and Protestants has less obvious resonance. Instead, Canadian electoral and other political debates have often revolved around the place of the province of Quebec, and the future of the sovereignty movement, still supported by many francophones there.

BOX 3.2

A NEW "EUROPEAN" IDENTITY?

The modern nation-state system arose in Europe, so it is particularly relevant to consider developments in this region when examining the question of whether national identity is weakening. The European Union (EU) is an international organization dating back to the 1950s, created with the specific goal of weakening national rivalries (especially between France and Germany) through greater economic cooperation. Initially consisting of only Western European countries, in May 2004 the EU gained 10 new members, including for the first time former Soviet-bloc countries of Central Europe. As of 2011, membership stands at 27: Austria, Belgium, Denmark, Finland, France, Germany, Greece, Ireland, Italy, Luxembourg, Spain, Sweden, the Netherlands, Portugal and the United Kingdom were joined by Cyprus, the Czech Republic, Estonia, Hungary, Latvia, Lithuania, Malta, Poland, Slovakia, and Slovenia in 2004, and by Bulgaria and Romania in 2007.

Over the 1980s and 1990s, economic cooperation in Europe deepened significantly, also affecting the political sphere. A European flag, anthem, and parliament were created, and in 1993 the **Maastricht Treaty** introduced a citizenship of the European Union. The rights associated with EU citizenship include the right of free movement; for example, a Dutch citizen has the right to move to and work in Belgium or any other member country. EU citizens also have the right to vote and stand for elections at the local level and at the European level in any member state. Finally, EU citizenship entitles one to consular protection when abroad from any embassy of a member country.

Every citizen of an EU member state is considered to be an EU citizen. However, the rights of EU citizenship, and especially the right of free movement, were not fully implemented across all EU countries (for a period of anywhere from two to seven years) for citizens of the countries that joined in 2004 and 2007.

The EU and its citizenship raise many interesting questions. Does EU citizenship contribute to a new form of belonging or identity—that of being "European"? If so, how does that differ from national identity? Does EU citizenship really weaken national citizenship? Should EU citizenship have been automatically and fully granted to the citizens of the 12 countries that joined between 2004 and 2007, or was it reasonable to do this over time? Should full EU citizenship be granted to any person who permanently lives in Europe regardless of citizenship (including some 18.5 million legally residing migrant workers and their families who have come mainly from countries of the developing world)?

Beyond the potential secession of Quebec, other issues related to cultural identity cause heated debates. For example, what about the right of francophones outside of Quebec to speak French in public institutions? What about Aboriginal peoples and their quest for self-government and cultural preservation? What about non-French or non-British immigrants and their offspring—to what extent should the maintenance of languages other than French and English be encouraged and to what extent should Canadian institutions change to reflect and accommodate peoples of all backgrounds? And what about those who want to define themselves as simply "Canadian"—should the Canadian state foster only this kind of allegiance?

All of these questions lie at the heart of the politics of multiculturalism, national recognition, and nationalism in Canada, and there is an ebb and flow about which ones assume prominence in public debate. Since the events of September 11, 2001, and the fallout from the U.S.-led "war on terrorism," there has been a strong shift to thinking of accommodation and multiculturalism through the lens of religious difference, and to the question of accommodating religious minorities (i.e., non-Christian

Table 3.3 Top 15 Ethnic Origins in Canada, 2006

The following are the results of the 2006 census, based on the responses to the question "To which ethnic or cultural group(s) did [your] ancestors belong?" People were allowed to name more than one origin.

	Total Response	Single Responses	Multiple Responses
Total population	31,241,030	18,319,580	12,921,445
Canadian	10,066,290	5,748,725	4,317,570
English	6,570,015	1,367,125	5,202,890
French	4,941,210	1,230,535	3,710,675
Scottish	4,719,850	568,515	4,151,340
Irish	4,354,155	491,030	3,863,125
German	3,179,425	670,640	2,508,785
Italian	1,445,335	741,045	704,285
Chinese	1,346,510	1,135,365	211,145
North American Indian	1,253,615	512,150	741,470
Ukrainian	1,209,085	300,590	908,495
Dutch	1,035,965	303,400	732,560
Polish	984,565	269,375	715,190
East Indian	962,665	780,175	182,495
Russian	500,600	98,245	402,355
Welsh	440,965	27,115	413,855

Source: Statistics Canada. "Ethnic origins, 2006 counts, for Canada, provinces and territories - 20% sample data", adapted from Statistics Canada publication Ethnic Origin and Visible Minorities, 2006 Census, Catalogue 97-562-XWE2006002, http://www.statcan.gc.ca/bsolc/olc-cel/olc-cel?catno=97-562-XWE2006002&lang=eng&lang=eng

Table 3.4 Major Religious Denominations in Canada, 2001 (as % of population)

Christian Faith Communities

Roman Catholic	43.2
Protestant	29.2
Christian Orthodox	1.6
Christian, not included elsewhere	2.6

Non-Christian Faith Communities

Muslim	2.0
Jewish	1.1
Buddhist	1.0
Hindu	1.0
Sikh	0.9

No Religious Affiliation

No Religion	16.2

Source: Adapted from Statistics Canada, 2001 Census: Analysis Series Religions in Canada, Catalogue No. 96F0030XIE2001015 (2003).

faith groups, in contrast to the historic focus on Catholics versus Protestants), especially Muslims. The focus on religious minorities was in evidence in Ontario during the 2005 debate over religious-based arbitration (especially as it concerned **sharia law**) as well as the 2007 electoral discussion over faith-based schools. In Quebec in 2007, Premier Jean Charest formed a commission, headed by two prominent academics—historian Gérard Bouchard and political theorist Charles Taylor—to address the question of "reasonable accommodation" as it concerns religious minorities and practices in relation to public institutions. The Bouchard-Taylor Commission traced the growing fixation on the idea of "reasonable accommodation" found in print media coverage, and broadly set its discussion in relation to the theme of secularism, even calling for more explicit attention to be paid by the Quebec National Assembly to outlining Quebec's secular model.[59] Whether framed in relation to "secularism" or not, it can be anticipated that religion will remain a key feature of Canadian discussions in the second decade of the 2000s. Still, it is only one facet of diversity that has entailed questions of governance.

Prior to European colonization in the early 17th century, Aboriginal societies were characterized by a rich range of cultural, linguistic, social, and political practices.[60] When the French and the British established their settlements and expropriated land from Aboriginal peoples, they brought with them their own cultures and languages. Since then, there have been many waves of immigration from other European countries, and increasingly, since the late 1960s, from countries outside of Europe. For much of Canada's history, government policies reflected an emphasis on the model of **dominant conformity** and, specifically, Anglo conformity. The idea behind dominant conformity is that all groups should assimilate to the

language, culture, and values of the dominant group, and in the case of Anglo conformity in Canada, that all groups should conform to the British group.

In the last few decades, as a result of pressures from different minority groups, the Canadian state has adopted a series of public policy measures designed to deal with diversity in a different way. In 1969 a national policy of official bilingualism (French and English) was introduced. In 1971 a national policy of official multiculturalism within a bilingual framework was established, giving recognition to the multiplicity of ethnic groups represented in the country. In recent years, both the federal and provincial governments have been involved in discussions pertaining to settling Aboriginal land claims and fostering forms of Aboriginal self-government. Canadian human rights commissions and courts have also followed suit, such as by highlighting the need for employers, landlords, and public officials to make "reasonable accommodation" for a range of groups (including persons with disabilities and religious minorities) in such areas as job duties and expectations, building design, or even school rules. For instance, in March 2006 the Supreme Court of Canada ruled that a Quebec schoolboy, who is an orthodox Sikh, could wear the *kirpan* (ceremonial dagger) to school, and that refusing to allow this on the basis of a general prohibition against students carrying "weapons" was a violation of the religious freedom guaranteed by the Canadian Charter of Rights and Freedoms.[61]

Does the shift since the 1960s suggest that national identity is weakening? If that identity is defined in terms of Anglo conformity, then the answer is yes. These kinds of initiatives reflect Canada's commitment to a variant of the model of **cultural pluralism**. While the term cultural pluralism refers to the existence of diverse ethnic and cultural groups within a

---

Dominant Conformity: A model of ethnic group integration holding that all groups in a society should conform to the language and values of the dominant group. In the case of Canada, this is the idea behind historical policies emphasizing Anglo conformity, which aimed to have all groups assimilate by speaking English and holding the values of the dominant British-origin group.

Cultural Pluralism: The coexistence of many ethnic and cultural groups within a country. Such diversity is the starting point in arguing that all groups in a society can maintain their linguistic, cultural, and religious distinctiveness without being relegated to the economic or cultural margins, and is achieved through the creation of a common set of values and institutions.

country, the cultural pluralism model specifically aims at promoting peaceful cooperation and recognition among these groups. The model of cultural pluralism suggests that groups can maintain distinct features without being marginalized economically or socially. Moreover, it contends that the cultivation of differences does not necessarily produce conflict; rather, it can produce peaceful coexistence through overarching values and institutions.

The models of dominant conformity and cultural pluralism represent opposite methods of dealing with ethnic and cultural diversity within a country. While many federal policies in Canada today reflect the model of cultural pluralism, it should also be noted that these policies have been controversial. For example, members of the Conservative Party (and its precursors, the Reform Party and Canadian Alliance)

and some intellectuals have argued that multiculturalism is leading to the fragmentation of Canada and should therefore not be publicly recognized or funded. In a related way, it has been suggested that a policy emphasis on "being Canadian" would contribute to the unity of the country and the loyalty of citizens toward the Canadian state.[62] These developments illustrate that there are those who would like to see the strengthening of a singular national identity in Canada.

Finally, there is evidence that Canadians identify in many ways that are not captured completely by the idea of belonging to any one group, whether defined by gender, ethnicity, or other factors. Indeed, by the early 1990s, when the National Action Committee on the Status of Women still had a vibrant national presence in English-speaking Canada, it increasingly began to

Members of Team Canada celebrate after winning the gold medal game against the USA in the men's hockey final at the 2010 Winter Olympic Games in Vancouver: for many Canadians, the ultimate expression of their nationalism.

The Canadian Press(Jonathan Hayward)

take the position that there is a complex heterogeneity among Canadian women along racial, ethnic, class, and other lines. Likewise, we see that Canadians self-identify in complex ways. For example, in the 2006 census over 41 percent of Canadians gave multiple responses to the ethnic origin question.[63] It is clear that many Canadians describe themselves as having multiple heritages, such as writer Lawrence Hill who has referred to himself as a "zebra" to describe the hybrid experience of having a white mother and a black father.[64] It could be anticipated that such kinds of multiple and mixed identities might increase as a result of contemporary globalization, since people may migrate several times in a lifetime, and since a growing number of people appear to be at ease with multiple national attachments and fluid and shifting identities.[65]

The case of Canada therefore suggests that an argument can be made that the salience of a single national identity (particularly in the form of Anglo conformity) has lessened with time. Although there are still debates about the desirability of having one dominant national identity, there is evidence that many Canadians see themselves as having multiple origins and identities. This suggests that while national identity is not about to disappear, it may be increasingly less dominant in the 21st century. In light of this tension, this may be why the politics associated with diversity—as seen in the recent turn to looking at "reasonable accommodation" in Canada—has been so vexed.

CONCLUSION

This chapter examined key terms and concepts pertaining to the politics of cultural pluralism. It surveyed different theoretical approaches to the study of nationalism, arguing that helpful insights are gleaned by attending to specific cases and using contemporary approaches that consider issues such as gender and different forms of identity. The central question raised in this chapter concerns the future of the nation-state and the salience of national identity in the contemporary era of globalization. It was suggested that there are three possibilities: national identity may be strengthened; national identity may be eroded; or new, shifting, and even hybrid forms of identity may emerge. The chapter tested these three possibilities by examining the case of Canada. The findings suggest that while national identity is not disappearing, its primacy is indeed being challenged by contemporary globalization.

Given the internal diversity of most countries around the world today, and given the fact that contemporary globalization itself may create the conditions for new and evolving forms of identity, it seems that political scientists will have much to examine in the years ahead. As well, because the already heterogeneous national populations are increasingly (and perhaps differently) affected by the larger international context, policymakers will have to think creatively to enact effective public policies.

DISCUSSION QUESTIONS

1. Is nationalism primarily a negative or a positive force? Why?

2. It has been suggested that the gendered aspects of nationalism are particularly apparent when it comes to war, the transmission of culture, and dress. Can you provide examples supporting this idea? Can you think of other ways in which men and women are called upon differently in the name of "the nation," or ways in which they are called upon similarly?

3. Are people attached primarily to a singular national identity, or is there another form (or other forms) of identity to which people are attached?

4. Does contemporary globalization weaken or strengthen nationalism? What examples would you use to support your position?

5. Are the demands made by minority ethnic groups for policies such as affirmative action or flexible work or dress codes easier or more difficult to resolve than claims for self-determination?

FURTHER READING

Abu-Laban, Yasmeen, ed. *Gendering the Nation-State: Canadian and Comparative Perspectives.* Vancouver: University of British Columbia Press, 2008.

Banting, Keith, Thomas J. Courchene, and F. Leslie Seidle, eds. *Diversity, Recognition and Shared*

Citizenship in Canada. Montreal: Institute for Research on Public Policy, 2007.

Canadian Journal of Political Science 43, 2 (2010). (This special issue of the journal is devoted to "diversity and democratic politics").

Gagnon, Alain-G. *The Case for Multinational Federalism: Beyond the All-Encompassing Nation.* London and New York: Routledge, 2010.

Goldberg, David Theo. *The Threat of Race: Reflections on Racial Neoliberalization.* Malden, MA: Blackwell, 2009.

Green, Joyce, ed. *Making Space for Indigenous Feminism.* London: Zed Books, 2007.

Kymlicka, Will. *Multicultural Odysseys: Navigating the New International Politics of Diversity.* Oxford and New York: Oxford University Press, 2007.

Modood, Tariq. *Multicultural Politics: Racism, Ethnicity and Muslims in Britain.* Minneapolis: University of Minnesota Press, 2005.

Zureik, Elia, David Lyon, and Yasmeen Abu-Laban, eds. *Surveillance and Control in Israel/Palestine: Population, Territory and Power.* London and New York: Routledge, 2011.

ENDNOTES

1. *MOST Newsletter* 3 (June 1995): 1, available at http://www.unesco.org/most/newlet3e. htm; accessed August 22, 2001.

2. *MOST Newsletter* 1 (December 1994): 5, available at http://www.unesco.org/most/ newlet1e.htm; accessed August 22, 2001.

3. See Benedict Anderson, *Imagined Communities: Reflections on the Origin and Spread of Nationalism,* rev. ed. (London: Verso, 1991).

4. See Elie Kedourie, *Nationalism* (London: Hutchinson, 1985).

5. Danilo Türk, "Genocide," in Joel Krieger, ed., *The Oxford Companion to Politics of the World* (Oxford: Oxford University Press, 2001), p. 316.

6. Srda Trifkovic, "Bosnian War," in Krieger, *The Oxford Companion to Politics of the World,* p. 79.

7. *Ibid.*

8. Elizabeth Philipose, "Ethnic Cleansing," in Lorraine Code, ed., *Encyclopedia of Feminist Theories* (London: Routledge, 2001), pp. 192–93.

9. *Ibid.,* p. 193.

10. Allison Des Forges, "Rwandan Genocide," in Krieger, *The Oxford Companion to Politics of the World,* p. 749.

11. Michael Ignatieff, *Blood and Belonging: Journeys into the New Nationalism* (Toronto: Penguin Books, 1993).

12. Samuel Huntington, "The Clash of Civilizations," *Foreign Affairs* 72(3) (Summer, 1993): 22–49.

13. Yasmeen Abu-Laban, "Humanizing the Oriental: Edward Said and Western Scholarly Discourse," in Naseer Aruri and Muhammad A. Shuraydi, eds., *Revising Culture, Reinventing Peace: The Influence of Edward W. Said* (New York and Northampton: Interlink, 2001), pp. 85–103.

14. Samuel Huntington, *Who Are We? The Challenges to America's National Identity* (New York: Simon and Shuster, 2004).

15. Louis Menand, "Patriot Games: The New Nativism of Samuel P. Huntington," *The New Yorker* (May 17, 2004), available at http://www.newyorker.com/ archive/2004/05/17/040517crbo_ books?currentPage=all; accessed November 27, 2010.

16. E. Ellis Cashmore, *Dictionary of Race and Ethnic Relations* (London: Routledge and Kegan Paul, 1984), p. 182.

17. Pereket Hablte Selassie, "Self-Determination," in Krieger, *The Oxford Companion to Politics of the World,* pp. 760–61.

18. Janine Brodie, "State Theory," in Code, *Encyclopedia of Feminist Theories*, p. 462.

19. Quoted in Ronald H. Chilcote, *Theories of Comparative Politics: The Search for a Paradigm Reconsidered* (Boulder: Westview Press, 1994), p. 98.

20. Sometimes the term *civic nationalism* is used to refer to an inclusive form of national belonging based on participation in a shared public sphere, as contrasted with *ethnic nationalism*, which is based on a belief in shared ethnicity or blood ties. However, the utility of this dichotomy has been called into question on a number of grounds, including the claim that *civic nationalism* can serve to mask the power of the dominant ethnic group(s) in organizing public life in the first place. See Claude Couture, *Paddling with the Current: Pierre Elliott Trudeau, Etienne Parent, Liberalism and Nationalism in Canada* (Edmonton: University of Alberta Press, 1998), p. 112.

21. Walker Connor, "A Nation Is a Nation, Is a State Is an Ethnic Group Is a ….," *Ethnic and Racial Studies* 1(4) (October 1978): 381.

22. Anderson, *Imagined Communities*, p. 144.

23. James Clifford, "Diasporas," in Montserrat Guibernau and John Rex, eds., *The Ethnicity Reader: Nationalism, Multiculturalism and Migration* (Cambridge: Polity Press, 1997), pp. 283–90.

24. *Ibid.*, p. 284.

25. Tomas Hylland Eriksen, "Ethnicity, Race and Nation," in Guibernau and Rex, *The Ethnicity Reader*, pp. 33–41.

26. Yasmeen Abu-Laban and Victoria Lamont, "Crossing Borders: Interdisciplinary, Immigration and the Melting Pot in the American Cultural Imaginary," *Canadian Review of American Studies* 27(2) (1997): 33.

27. Robert Miles and Rudy Torres, "Does 'Race' Matter? Transatlantic Perspectives on Racism after 'Race Relations,'" in Vered Amit-Talai and Caroline Knowles, eds., *Re-situating Identities: The Politics of Race, Ethnicity and Culture* (Peterborough: Broadview Press, 1996), pp. 25–46.

28. Lucius J. Barker and Mack H. Jones, *African Americans and the American Political System* (Englewood Cliffs: Prentice Hall, 1994), pp. 30–49.

29. Tariq Modood, *Multicultural Politics: Racism, Ethnicity and Muslims in Britain* (Minneapolis: University of Minnesota Press, 2005).

30. Will Kymlicka, *Finding Our Way: Rethinking Ethnocultural Relations in Canada* (Don Mills: Oxford University Press, 1998), p. 42.

31. John Isbester, *Promises Not Kept: The Betrayal of Social Change in the Third World* (West Hartford: Kumarian Press, 1995), p. 109.

32. For an example, see Karl W. Deutsch, *Nationalism and Social Communication: An Inquiry into the Foundations of Nationality* (New York: John Wiley, 1953).

33. See Ernest Gellner, *Nations and Nationalism* (Oxford: Basil Blackwell, 1983) on these points, and see Anderson, *Imagined Communities*, regarding the significance of the printing press.

34. See Tom Nairn, *The Break-up of Britain* (London: NLB, 1979).

35. See especially Kedourie, *Nationalism*, p. 145.

36. Isbester, *Promises Not Kept*, p. 106.

37. *Ibid.*, p. 102.

38. *Ibid.*, pp. 105–48.

39. Frantz Fanon, "The Wretched of the Earth," in Omar Dahbour and Micheline R. Ishay, eds., *The Nationalism Reader* (New Jersey: Humanities Press, 1995), p. 283.

40. *Ibid.*, pp. 274–83.

41. Anthony D. Smith, *Theories of Nationalism*, 2nd ed. (London: Gerald Duckworth, 1983), p. 193.

42. Nira Yuval-Davis and Floya Anthias, *Woman-Nation-State* (Basingstoke, U.K.: Macmillan, 1989).

43. Nira Yuval-Davis, "Gender and Nation," in Rick Wilford and Robert L. Miller, eds., *Women, Ethnicity and Nationalism* (London: Routledge, 1998), pp. 23–35.

44. Elizabeth Philipose, "Ethnic Cleansing," in Code, *Encyclopedia of Feminist Theories*, p. 183.

45. For a discussion of these issues, see Deniz Kandiyoti, "Identity and Its Discontents: Women and the Nation," in Patrick Williams and Laura Chrisman, eds., *Colonial Discourse and Post-Colonial Theory: A Reader* (New York: Columbia University Press, 1994), pp. 376–91.

46. For an overview of apartheid, see the chapter by David Theo Goldberg on "racial southafricanization," in David Theo Goldberg, *The Threat of Race: Reflections on Racial Neoliberalization* (Malden, MA: Blackwell, 2009), pp. 245–326.

47. For an overview, see Sheila Meintjes, "Gender, Nationalism and Transformation: Difference and Commonality in South Africa's Past and Present," in Wilford and Miller, *Women, Ethnicity and Nationalism*, pp. 62–86.

48. This account of women's organizing and example of the placard is adapted from Anne McClintock, *Imperial Leather: Race, Gender and Sexuality in the Colonial Context* (New York: Routledge, 1995), pp. 379–86.

49. McClintock, *Imperial Leather*, p. 384.

50. Meintjes, "Gender, Nationalism and Transformation," pp. 82–83.

51. *Ibid.*, p. 83.

52. *Ibid.*, p. 84.

53. See David Theo Goldberg, *The Threat of Race*, pp. 245–326.

54. David Held et al., *Global Transformations: Politics, Economics and Culture* (Stanford: Stanford University Press, 1999), pp. 425–26.

55. *Ibid.*

56. *Ibid.*, p. 297.

57. Stuart Hall, "The Question of Cultural Identity," in Stuart Hall et al., eds., *Modernity: An Introduction to Modern Societies* (Cambridge: Polity Press, 1995), p. 628.

58. *Ibid.*, pp. 596–634.

59. Quebec, Commission de consultation sur les pratiques d'accommodement reliees aux differences culturelles," *Building the Future: A Time for Reconciliation Report* (2008).

60. Olive Patricia Dickason, *Canada's First Nations: A History of Founding Peoples from Earliest Times* (Toronto: McClelland and Stewart, 1992), pp. 63–83.

61. Yasmeen Abu-Laban and Baha Abu-Laban, "Reasonable Accommodation in a Global Village," *Policy Options* 28(8) (September 2007): 28–33.

62. For this position, see Rhoda Howard-Hassmann, "Canadian as an Ethnic Category: Implications for Multiculturalism and National Unity," *Canadian Public Policy* 25(4) (1999): 523–37. For a critique of this position, see Yasmeen Abu-Laban and Daiva Stasiulis, "Constructing 'Ethnic Canadians': The Implications for Public Policy and Inclusive Citizenship," *Canadian Public Policy* 26(4) (December 2000): 477–87.

63. See Table 3.3.

64. Lawrence Hill, "Zebra: Growing Up Black and White in Canada," in Carl E. James and Adrienne Shadd, eds., *Talking About Difference: Encounters in Culture, Language and Identity* (Toronto: Between the Lines, 1994), pp. 41–47.

65. See, for example, Parminder Bhachu, "The Multiple Landscapes of Transnational Asian Women in the Diaspora," in Vered Amit-Talai and Caroline Knowles, eds., *Re-situating Identities: The Politics of Race, Ethnicity and Culture* (Peterborough: Broadview Press, 1996), pp. 283–303, and Ayse S. Caglar, "Hyphenated Identities and the Limits of 'Culture,'" in Tariq Modood and Pnina Werbner, eds., *The Politics of Multiculturalism in the New Europe* (London: Zed Books, 1997), pp. 169–85.

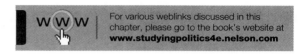

For various weblinks discussed in this chapter, please go to the book's website at **www.studyingpolitics4e.nelson.com**

States and Markets: Studying Political Economy in Political Science

Rodney Haddow

CHAPTER OBJECTIVES

After you have completed this chapter, you should be able to:

- explain what political economy is, and what it can contribute to the study of political science
- indicate how differently countries produce and redistribute wealth, and why this is the case
- illustrate what it means for political scientists to explain something in terms of "big structures, large processes, [and] huge comparisons"
- show how the development of Canada's political economy compares with what has happened in other affluent countries
- grasp the concept of globalization for understanding how the well-being of citizens may change in the future

INTRODUCTION

What do political scientists mean when they refer to themselves as *political economists* or when they characterize their scholarship as *political economy*? How can political economy deepen our understanding of politics? This chapter offers answers to these questions. The term *political economy* is used with a wide, sometimes bewildering, range of meanings in political science and a reader must examine closely how the term is being used by a particular author to determine which of these meanings is intended. In this chapter, we will argue

that one particular definition is most useful because it is most tangible and encompasses much of what is written by authors who use the term in other ways. **Political economy**, by this definition, is the study of the relationship between the **state**, as the leading authoritative actor in affluent societies, and the *economy*, the site in these societies where wealth is produced and exchanged.

> **Political Economy:** The study of the relationship between the *state*, as the leading authoritative actor in affluent societies, and the *economy*, the site in these societies where wealth is produced and exchanged.

The traditions of political economy discussed here have always stressed how much variation there is among countries in how this state–economy relationship functions. The countries covered in this chapter all have capitalist or private-market economies, that is, economies in which most production takes place in the private sector rather than under state ownership, and where the exchange of goods takes place in mostly private markets. Nevertheless, they differ fundamentally in how they organize economic life. In some cases the state is very active in guiding the private sector in a certain direction; in other cases it does little of this. Moreover, private economic interests coordinate with each other substantially in some cases, but not much elsewhere. Political economists study these variations and seek to identify what impact they have on the lives of citizens.

Political economy is also distinguished by its tendency to study this state-economy connection with reference to "big structures, large processes [and] huge comparisons."[1] Political economists may focus their attention on specific topics—the development of new bank regulations, changes over time in how training programs work, and so forth. But the concepts they use to explain these particular issues usually refer to the broadest or *macro* level of a society, rather than to features of only the particular field or sector (banking, training) where developments took place (an intermediate or *meso* approach) or of the specific individuals and organizations directly involved in events (a *micro* level method). This point is explained more fully below.[2] For reasons of length, our attention will be directed mainly to political economy as it is used in the study of the politics of particular countries—including Canada—and in comparisons between these countries. The political economy of the international system, or of relations between countries, is a very valuable topic in its own right but it is not treated here. For the same reason, we concentrate on the political economy of now-rich (or developed) countries.

The first section below discusses definitions of political economy that are the main alternatives to this one, indicating their strengths but also illustrating how relying on one of these would narrow our focus too much. The following section then expands on the definition provided above and explains the field's origins, development, and current main features. The third and fourth parts discuss in greater detail the approaches to understanding variable relations between the state and the economy that have been proposed by comparative political economists. The chapter then looks at the political economy of Canada and asks what impact globalization is having on the political economies of developed countries.

POLITICAL ECONOMY AS A METHOD

Political economy, as defined above, is a *focus* within political science—the study of the relationship between state and economy. The main alternative definitions instead treat it as a *method* or a *theory* that can be applied to a wide range of topics, sometimes well beyond this particular focus. One such method is called *rational choice*; its main alternative is *Marxian political economy*.

To understand why these different meanings emerged, it helps to refer to some history. During the 17th and 18th centuries, many European societies began to witness the extensive development of private markets in which goods were bought and sold by profit-seeking merchants that were relatively free from control by the state or by the traditional aristocracy. Such activities had existed for a long time, but now became more extensive. Ever-larger segments of society in this emerging **capitalism** consisted of people who depended on such market activities for their livelihood. Especially in England, where an industrial revolution began in the late 18th century, working people increasingly depended on earning money wages for their survival, rather than themselves producing enough food to subsist or depending on the kinds of feudal ties that were once common.

In this setting a new discipline of political economy emerged; it focused on how these market activities worked, and how they might be organized so as to maximize wealth and incomes for everybody. Adam Smith's *The Wealth of Nations*, published in 1776, was the single most prominent contribution to this new study. While focusing on wealth, these early political economists nevertheless paid close attention to how wealth-creation related to the activities of the state, and how it affected and depended upon different groups and classes in society. They also tended to examine these questions historically: what happens today can only be understood in terms of what came before. This early political economy therefore included much of what we would now call the social sciences: it touched upon what is currently included in economics, political science, sociology, and history.[3] By the late 19th and early 20th centuries, however, the study of wealth-creation was becoming narrower and more technical. The modern discipline of economics emerged, which sought to understand markets more abstractly, and without nearly as much attention to their political, social, and historical context. The separate and equally-specialized disciplines of sociology and political science also emerged at this time. In Canada, this process of specialization unfolded more slowly.[4] At the University of Toronto, the study of economics, politics, and society remained united within a Political Economy Department until well after World War II.

A department with that name was finally abolished, with its remaining Economics and Political Science components invited to go their separate ways in 1982.

Today's **rational choice** approach to political economy essentially takes the method of modern economics, rather than of its broader 18th and 19th century antecedents, and applies it to non-economic phenomena, including politics. Modern mainstream economists stress the extent to which individuals are motivated by a desire to maximize their *utility*, calculated mostly in terms of wealth and income, when they engage in market activities. A market works well, they argue, if it is structured in such a way as to offer individuals ample opportunities to pursue this goal while producing something of value to (equally utility-maximizing) consumers. Rational choice scholars may extend the idea of utility to include power, prestige, and so forth, as well as wealth. The institutions they examine may lie well outside of what we normally call politics; for example, rational choice has been used to explain why people marry and form families. But we will concentrate on its application to **government**. A pioneering study of this kind explained why the major political parties in countries often differ only modestly in their proposals. It argued that politicians' utility is maximized by winning elections. This leads all parties to move their proposals closer to those of their main opponents in order to capture the same *marginal voter*, the hypothetical single voter in the middle of the political spectrum whose support can make the difference between winning and losing an election.[5] The alleged tendency of government bureaucracies to grow over time has been explained by referring to bureaucrats' desire to maximize their utility in the form of income and organizational power.[6] The success of an interest group has been accounted for in terms of its ability to make sure that individuals who might benefit (derive utility) from the group's activities would have to help finance it as a condition for receiving these benefits.[7]

Rational Choice: An approach to political economy (and political science more generally), which is largely borrowed from economics and in which social processes, including politics, are said to reflect the outcome of interaction among individuals and organizations that each seek to maximize their own self-interest or utility, which may include power and prestige as well as wealth and income.

Karl Marx's 19th century contributions to political economy, most prominently in the first volume of his *Capital* (1867), offer the main method-based alternative to rational choice. Here the focus is on social **classes** and their interests and resources. According to **Marxian political economy**, society is made up of different classes, which consist of persons who share a common relationship to the economic property system or *means of production*. In a market-based or capitalist economy, the dominant social class is the capitalist one, which consists of those who own and control substantial amounts of property (in manufacturing, transportation, banking, and so forth). The working class consists of those who do not have access to productive property of this kind, and must sell their labour to capitalists to earn a living. The interests of these classes are opposed. In the long term the main non-economic institutions of society can be expected to favour the interests of capitalists, and to preclude the emergence of a non-capitalist alternative that would be in the interest of workers. But these institutions nevertheless can also embody some concessions to workers' interests, so as to legitimate the capitalist system as a whole. Thus, Marxian political economy was used in the 1970s to account for the large welfare states that had emerged by that time: it was depicted as a necessary concession to the working class in view of its significant (though still subordinate) power at that time.[8]

Marxian Political Economy: An approach to political economy that stresses the importance of social classes and of class conflict, and that identifies the interests of the dominant class, the capitalist one under capitalism, as the main influence on social institutions, including the state.

How popular are each of these approaches today? Rational choice is currently among the most prominent approaches to the study of political science, especially in the United States where rational choice theory is often treated as synonymous with political economy.[9] The standing of rational choice is somewhat lower elsewhere, particularly in Canada where its adherents contribute a smaller current of scholarship. The Marxian approach, on the other hand, was important during the 1970s but has since declined to a marginal presence in American political science. It remains

"Why don't we take a few days off and let the free market handle things?"

Rex May/Artizans

more significant in the United Kingdom, though.[10] While Marxian scholarship is also less prominent in the study of Canadian politics than it was a couple of decades ago, it nevertheless remains a more significant current here than in the U.S.

POLITICAL ECONOMY AS A FIELD OF STUDY

If we adopt either of the above definitions of political economy we exclude valuable research contributed by practitioners of the other. We also ignore what might be termed the "broad middle" of contemporary political economy. Most self-described political economists rely primarily on neither rational choice nor Marxism, though they may make use of both. They instead adhere to the definition given at the beginning of this chapter: they study the relationship between state and economy. The questions they address are among the most important treated in political science: What patterns of state-economy relationship and of connection among organizations and actors within the economy have been conducive to economic prosperity? Why does there seem to be a persistent variety of such patterns? German, American, and Japanese affluence had different origins and remain distinct. What are the implications of these different state-economic contexts of growth for the level of inequality and poverty in a country? It seems clear, in fact, that some patterns are consistently associated with higher inequality and poverty than are others. These are much higher in the U.S., for instance, than in Sweden. What are the implications of these differences for the economic and social situation of women? Does inequality- and poverty-reduction go further in countries with particular kinds of welfare states than in others? What were the causes of these variations?

As these questions indicate, much contemporary political economy seeks to return to the broader approaches that typified early political economy; it brings together political, economic, and social questions that the various social sciences now treat separately, and it often deals with them historically. While many political economists work in political science departments, others are sociologists, and some are management or industrial relations scholars or economists (in the latter case often dissenting from much mainstream thinking within their own discipline). As the above queries also suggest, contemporary political economy typically is *comparative:* it identifies multiple cases (usually countries) with similar or different state-economy patterns, and asks which of these cases' features are most important for explaining these similarities or differences. Again, one cannot emphasize too much the focus of comparative political economists on variety. For instance, the pattern of economic growth in the United Kingdom or the United States has usually not relied on extensive planning and intervention by the state. But we know that such a *laissez-faire* approach is not a prerequisite for prosperity because other now-affluent economies, such as Japan and France, have at times relied heavily on such intervention. Political economists will then ask: what characteristics do the Anglo-Saxon (English-speaking) cases have in common, but which are substituted by alternative features in Japan and France, that might explain why the former succeeded with a laissez-faire approach? Conversely, what features of the Japanese and French state-economy settings allowed them to benefit from intervention? The approach to explanation is not primarily the application of a particular methodological insight, but the use of comparisons between appropriate and carefully-observed cases.

As noted earlier, these comparisons are usually made at the *macro* level of the countries studied, rather than the more narrowly-defined sector (a *meso* level approach), or the *micro* level flow of day-to-day events.

For example, the forces that shape labour market training policies could be studied in different ways. At the least aggregated, or *micro*, level, one might examine the short-term factors that led to a specific program change, such as a new measure to help unemployed workers acquire the skills they need to find a new job. The beliefs and actions of individuals who can make these changes would be the focus of attention: What did the minister of education and training think? What were the opinions of his or her senior bureaucrats? Did these decision-makers have career or social ties with outside experts or interested "stakeholders" in the training system who favoured the changes? Did they simply find some of these non-governmental representatives more congenial personally? Scholarly studies often refer to factors of this kind; but primary reliance on these individual-level factors is more common in writing by journalists.[11]

A *meso* or intermediate level account looks for more enduring features of the context in which this new training initiative was discussed. But these features would be sought within the particular sector of policy-making that deals with training.[12] In a Canadian province such a study might ask: Does the ministry of education and training habitually have the autonomy from other ministries, the budget, and the expertise to pursue innovations? To what extent do non-governmental organizations with a stake in the training sector, such as the community colleges and their unionized employees, typically have an important policy role? Do they have the resources to defend their interests? In this case, do these interests (such as maximizing college budgets and protecting teachers' careers and salaries) favour or oppose reform? Is the federal government an important actor in this field, and does it encourage independent provincial initiatives? Are there non-governmental think-tanks with expertise and prestige in the training sector? Are the proposed reforms consistent with long-established views in these organizations?

Political economy scholarship may include these kinds of micro and meso level data. But its distinctive focus is at the *macro* level, on the long-term and slowly-changing features of the countries being studied as a whole, features that are relevant to understanding changes across many policy fields as well as the interconnection between these different domains. For instance, a recent comparative study found that where union movements are strong (because many workers belong to them)

and are linked to strong left-wing parties, retraining programs are pursued aggressively.[13] Retraining is seen by these organizations to be in workers' interests because it provides them with access to an alternative livelihood if they lose a job. By contrast, where unions are weaker and Catholic institutions are strong, the focus of policy has been in entirely different sectors, for example, using regulations to protect now-employed workers from lay-off and maintaining expensive unemployment insurance programs that are not closely linked to training. Where neither strong union movements nor strong Catholic traditions exist, policy instead reflects the views of business and of free market-oriented political parties. In this case, none of these policies is favoured, and there is a preference for program cuts. In each of these three scenarios the outcomes reflect broad features of each country's setting: the overall strength of unions, businesses, religious institutions, and different kinds of political parties are factors whose importance goes well beyond any one policy sector. Moreover, developments in different sectors are linked: strong labour movements prefer retraining workers, so they do not foster policy developments in other sectors, such as job protection or even some kinds of unemployment insurance. As we can see, political economy can provide more integrated and complex explanations of political life than is possible with less encompassing alternatives. Its focus on "big structures, large processes [and] huge comparisons" can have a major payoff.

STRONG VERSUS WEAK STATES AND CORPORATISM VERSUS PLURALISM

This section and the next discuss the main currents in contemporary political economy internationally; the following one treats Canada specifically. In this section, we discuss the main building-block ideas for understanding political economies that were developed during the 1970s and 1980s. The next section deals with refinements that have been introduced in recent years. While this new research has departed from the earlier work in important ways, it cannot be understood well without a clear appreciation of the ideas that came before.

Between the end of World War II and the 1970s, social scientists mostly assumed that economic development occurred similarly in different countries.

Countries that are underdeveloped now (in Africa, Asia and Latin America, for example) can achieve affluence, these social scientists argued, if they modernize in the same way as now-rich European and North American countries did during the 19th and early 20th centuries. As noted in Chapters 14 and 15, in his highly influential book, W.W. Rostow detailed the common *stages of economic growth* that he claimed countries have gone through, or will experience, en route to prosperity.[14] Mainstream theory in economics, similarly, contends that countries will converge on common "equilibrium" institutions, as they move towards the most efficient way of organizing their economies.[15]

As has been stressed already in this chapter, comparative political economy scholarship generally rejects this view. Political economists do not agree on how much capitalist countries differ, or on whether these differences will persist in the future. But they concur in saying that variation is now very important. Starting in the 1970s, two bodies of scholarship emerged to challenge the postwar consensus. One focused on the fact that the state was more active in promoting industrialization in some now-affluent countries than it had been in others, and argued that current arrangements still reflect these differences. A comparison of England and France can illustrate this point. Badie and Birnbaum argue that the transition to a market economy occurred relatively smoothly and without government guidance in England during the 16th and 17th centuries, with the result that that country could be termed a **weak state**: the state neither required nor developed a capacity to guide the economy.[16] In France, by contrast, the transition to market capitalism lagged behind England and encountered obstacles from within French society that only state intervention could overcome. As a result, France acquired a *strong* state, able and willing to intervene in the economy. Badie and Birnbaum argue that the economic roles of the British and French states continue to diverge between these weak and strong models. More recent research often agrees that this is the case, but stresses that strong states in Europe are not as interventionist as they used to be.

Weak State: The form of state that exists in countries where it did not play an important role in fostering the transition to a market and industrial economy, and in which it continues to play a modest role in guiding overall economic development.

During the two decades after World War II, for instance, France's state provided very firm guidance to the private sector, pushing it to invest in specific industries, to develop certain technologies, and so forth. Now, however, the state is likely to use a much lighter approach, such as negotiating with companies about their future plans and listening carefully to feedback that it receives from them.[17] In East Asia, on the other hand, strong state guidance still exists, although it is also more relaxed than it was a few decades ago.

The second stream of research that crystallized in the 1970s distinguished two kinds of relationship *among* the major interests within the economy, rather than *between* the economy and the state. In many Northern European countries the economy depends on close cooperation among organizations that speak for big business and other producer interests (such as farmers), on the one hand, and unionized workers on the other.[18] In these **corporatist** countries, the business, labour union, and other economic interests are highly organized: they have well-staffed national organizations and they have a certain amount of power over lower-level business and labour groups within particular firms, regions, or economic sectors. Labour unions tend to be much stronger in these countries, representing a quite high percentage of all workers. Much government policy concerning the economy and social programs is formulated after extensive discussions among the leaders of these organizations, who acquire a habit of compromising with each other. By contrast, other countries in the English-speaking world and in Southern Europe, are termed *pluralist*. In these nations, business and labour are not nearly as well organized above the level of individual companies. Labour unions typically are weaker than in corporatist countries, which is one reason why business does not bother to develop strong national organizations to respond to them. In pluralist countries, business is more likely to get what it wants without having to organize extensively. There is little coordination between these economic interests. The different interests, and even individual firms, tend to see each other as rivals in a competitive struggle for higher profits and wages. Government policy is made without the formal involvement, let alone the cooperation, of the economic interests.

The two approaches described above can combine to provide an overall account of how countries that share a market economy nevertheless organize

Figure 4.1   Variations in Political Economy Type among Advanced Countries

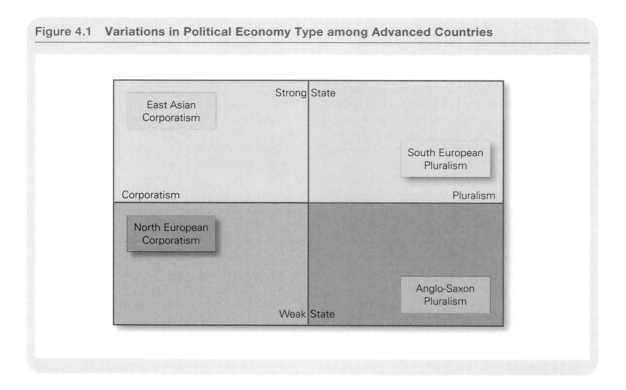

their political economies very differently. Figure 4.1 illustrates how this can be done. On the north–south (up-and-down) axis it distinguishes strong from weak states. At the bottom are those countries where the state mostly follows the **laissez-faire** path, allowing the private sector to pursue its own preferences. At the top are countries where the state still seeks to guide firms to an important extent, even if not as much as it would have a few decades ago. The east–west axis divides countries between corporatist (on the left side of the figure) and pluralist (on the right side). In the former, business and labour are well-organized, unions are generally stronger, and there is significant policy coordination among these actors. All of these features are much less present in the pluralist cases. As we can see, the richer countries of the world can be distinguished into four broad clusters, based on these distinctions. We should keep in mind, however, that these distinctions are quite general and they simplify what is, in fact, a very complex pattern of variation among the political economies of rich countries. Anglo-Saxon countries are in the lower right-hand corner of the figure, signifying that they combine a laissez-faire (weak state)

approach to the economy with pluralism. Southern European nations also have weak business and labour organizations, and are therefore pluralist, but combine this with a state that is still stronger than it is in Anglo-Saxon countries, though not as strong as it once was. On the left side of the diagram, Northern European countries combine very highly developed **corporatism** with states that are below-average in their degree of intervention (strength). Near the upper-left corner, finally, are richer East Asian countries, such as Japan, South Korea, and Taiwan, where the state remains quite strong and where there is also a considerable amount of corporatism. Table 4.1 identifies the 10 most prominent examples of corporatist and pluralist countries today, based on the most commonly-used measurement; it also sub-divides these countries into two categories with different degrees of state strength.

Corporatism: A political economy in which formal bargaining and compromises among leading societal interests, above all business and labour, are very important for social and economic outcomes.

Table 4.1 **Corporatist and Pluralist Political Economies**	
Corporatist Countries	Pluralist Countries
Northern European Variant: (with weaker state)	**Anglo-Saxon Variant: (with weak state)**
Austria	USA
Norway	Canada
Sweden	United Kingdom
Netherlands	Australia
Denmark	Ireland
Germany	**Southern European Variant: (with stronger state)**
Switzerland	France
Finland	Greece
Belgium	Italy
East Asian Variant: (with strong state)	Spain
Japan	Portugal

Source: Alan Siaroff, "Corporatism in 24 Industrial Democracies: Measurement and Meaning," *European Journal of Political Research,* 36 (3)1999), p. 198. The different variants identified in the table are this author's addition to Siaroff's categorization.[19]

Table 4.2 (p. 86) shows the degree to which the strength of labour unions varies between corporatist and pluralist countries today, indicating that these two types of market economy remain very different from each other, just as the original writers found them to be in the 1970s and 1980s. As we can seen, on average a much larger proportion of workers belong to a labour union in Northern European corporatist countries (43.7 percent), than in pluralist ones (23.4 percent in Anglo-Saxon countries; 19.8 percent in Southern Europe). Yet we can also see that the unionization figures vary substantially within each of these groups, and that the one East Asian corporatist case in the table (Japan) has a quite low unionization level. Clearly, the corporatist–pluralist and strong–weak state distinctions do not explain everything of importance about differences among affluent market economies.

Because of complications like this, comparative political economy research has developed new concepts for understanding the variety of contemporary capitalism. The desire for new ideas was also strengthened by the belief that globalization (discussed below) required a fresh look at this question. While still strongly resonating with ideas from this earlier scholarship, these new approaches seek to account more carefully for inter-country differences.

They also have much more to stay about the *consequences* of differences: how, for instance, the economies of different countries specialize in different areas, and how they produce different levels of social spending and of poverty. They are discussed in the next section.

THE NEW GENERATION OF COMPARATIVE POLITICAL ECONOMY

The leading school of comparative political economy today is called **Varieties of Capitalism (VoC)**. Here again, we start with a distinction between two models, *Coordinated Market Economies* (CMEs) and *Liberal Market Economies* (LMEs). In this discussion,

Varieties of Capitalism (VoC): The foremost contemporary political economy approach to developed countries. These are divided between Coordinated Market Economies (CMEs), where firms rely on coordination with other actors, and Liberal Market Economies (LMEs), where they do not.

Table 4.2 Unionization Levels in Advanced Political Economies

Corporatist Countries	%	Pluralist Countries	%
Northern European: (weaker state)		**Anglo-Saxon: (weak state)**	
Austria	29	USA	12
Norway	53	Canada	27
Sweden	68	United Kingdom	27
Netherlands	19	Australia	19
Denmark	68	Ireland	32
Germany	19		
Switzerland	18	**Southern European: (stronger state)**	
Finland	67	France	8
Belgium	52	Greece	24
		Italy	33
East Asian: (strong state)		Spain	14
Japan	18	Portugal	20
Average for Northern European Variant	**43.7**	*Average for Anglo-Saxon Variant*	**23.4**
		Average for Southern European Variant	**19.8**

Source: Based on data from Trade Union Density under Trade Union under Labour from *OECD.StatExtracts*, http://stats.oecd.org (February 9, 2011). Figures report the percentage of the employed workforce that belonged to labour unions in 2009.

these models will be called *Coordinated* and *Liberal*, for short. VoC scholars pay much less attention to the level of business and labour organization, or of cooperation between them, at the national level than did the corporatism–pluralism scholarship. Because of globalization, they sometimes argue that this has become less important than it once was. They focus instead on individual firms, and how much they coordinate with each other and with other economic interests. In Coordinated countries, the success of firms depends on long-term coordination with other firms to develop new products and technologies, with financial institutions to obtain financing for new projects, and with their workers regarding skills. Firms in Liberal countries instead pursue a firm-centred strategy where competition and responding to short-term price signals replace cooperation in each of these areas.[20]

Despite its different criteria for defining how political economies vary, VoC divides the world into categories that strongly resemble those previously discussed. Thus, the Coordinated category includes almost all of the countries termed *corporatist* in the earlier research,

while the Liberal one includes the Anglo-Saxon *pluralist* countries. The Southern European countries represent a "Mixed" case for VoC researchers, with more active states than the Anglo-Saxon countries, but firms that otherwise do not coordinate much.[21] The East Asian countries are considered to be Coordinated, but are recognized to be a different sub-category from the Northern European variant. We can therefore use the categories set forth in Figure 4.1 to distinguish the political economy types discussed by this new research: Northern European corporatist countries are now termed Coordinated, East Asian strong-state corporatist cases are a different variant of this category, Anglo-Saxon pluralist countries are Liberal, and the Southern European pluralist countries form a mixed cluster.

So what does this new research have to offer that was not available from the older scholarship? VoC's main contribution has been to say much more about the *consequences* of belonging to different categories. It has done this in many areas, but only three examples will be given here. First, it has explained a pattern that observers have often noticed but previously had not explained well: while Coordinated economies have remained concentrated in manufacturing industries, Liberal ones have largely shifted to the service sector. The new research has documented how these different types of economy each have a particular strength (or what is called "competitive advantage") in the sector they specialize in, which gives them an incentive to remain committed to that specialty. Coordinated behaviour is conducive to the slow improvement in procedures that is the hallmark of successful manufacturers. By contrast, service firms must often radically innovate how they do business in order to remain competitive; this is easier to do in an Anglo-Saxon setting where firms have few long-term commitments to other actors.

Second, the new research also has much to say about why some Coordinated and Mixed economies, such as those Germany and most Mediterranean countries, do not provide more economic opportunities to women: historically, manufacturing industries have mainly employed men. Because many Coordinated and mixed economies still concentrate in this sector, they have been slower than Anglo-Saxon countries to offer women opportunities to work and to achieve economic independence. Women are therefore less likely to be employed in some Coordinated economies than in Liberal ones, and often earn less when they do work. Third, because unions are stronger in the coordinated settings, governments are much more likely to use economic policies to restrain union power than is the case in Anglo-Saxon countries, where unions are much weaker. For instance, the German government will forestall excessive wage demands from unions by curtailing economic growth in the country, an action that will probably induce the unions to restrain their wage demands for fear that these demands might now cause many workers to lose their jobs. American and British governments, in contrast, are less restrained about pushing their economies to grow faster. They do not have as much reason to fear that this will result in an explosion of demands for higher wages from powerful unions.

In spite of its prominence today, not all political economists accept the VoC approach. Some critics prefer approaches that hark back to the old corporatism–pluralism or strong–weak state literatures. Nevertheless, most fruitful research in this field today is conducted by scholars using the VoC categories or by their opponents who are seeking to challenge them. If one looks through recent issues of the political science or sociology academic journals that publish articles on comparative political economy, one will therefore quickly encounter the VoC terminology.

Next to VoC, the leading current approach to comparative political economy is one introduced about 20 years ago by Gøsta Esping-Andersen.[22] Unlike VoC, this one focuses almost entirely on social policy. Esping-Andersen argues that the kind of social security system (or **welfare state regime**) that each country has—how much it designs its programs and how much it spends and reduces poverty—varies considerably. The main factor explaining this difference is the strength of organizations that represent workers and how effective the organizations were in forming alliances with other interests when the welfare state was first being developed in the late 19th and 20th centuries. While the corporatist scholars focus on labour unions in measuring the power of workers, Esping-Andersen, though not dismissing their importance, concentrates on the strength of social democratic and democratic socialist parties. Traditionally, these parties received much of their support from workers or from other voters who were friendly to workers' interests. These parties typically have supported larger **welfare states** that spend more money, that redistribute more from the rich to the poor, and that reduce poverty substantially. Their main opponents have been parties that are pro-business and that tend to oppose all of these goals, or Christian Democratic parties. The latter are strong in many European countries. While favouring larger welfare states than pro-business parties, Christian Democrats accept more inequality than do social democrats. Consistent with the Catholic social teachings that heavily influenced them, Christian Democratic parties see an important role for government to pursue collective goals on behalf of society, but also accept social hierarchy as inevitable and perhaps desirable.

Welfare State Regimes: The welfare states of affluent, capitalist countries are said to come in three variants, social democratic, Christian Democratic, and liberal (Anglo-Saxon), which originated in different political party and social coalitions. These result in different levels of poverty and inequality.

As Table 4.3 indicates, the strength of social democratic parties differs substantially across countries. In particular, they have been in power at the national level much more in the Northern European corporatist group of countries than in either variant of pluralist country,

Table 4.3	The Variable Strength of Social Democratic and Socialist Parties in Advanced Political Economies		
Total number of years that "left" parties were in power, 1946–2000			
Corporatist Countries	**Years**	**Pluralist Countries**	**Years**
Northern European: (weaker state)		**Anglo-Saxon: (weak state)**	
Austria	33	USA	0
Norway	41	Canada	0
Sweden	45	United Kingdom	20
Netherlands	14	Australia	20
Denmark	32	Ireland	6
Germany	15		
Switzerland	14	**Southern European: (stronger state)**	
Finland	23	France	16
Belgium	19	Greece	N/A
		Italy	9
East Asian: (strong state)		Spain	N/A
Japan	1	Portugal	N/A
Average for Northern European Variant	***26.2***	*Average for Anglo-Saxon Variant*	***9.2***
		Average for Southern European Variant	***12.5***

Source: LIS Employment Key Figures by Gender, http://www.lisdatacenter.org (29 June 2011). Luxembourg: LIS.

on average, though there is variation among countries within each category, especially the Anglo-Saxon one. In the Northern European corporatist countries, social democrats were in power, on average, for 26.2 of the 55 years between 1946 and 2000. In Anglo-Saxon and Southern European countries, in contrast, they averaged 9.2 and 12.5 years in power.

Esping-Andersen did not find that welfare states were always larger and that poverty was lower in countries where social democrats were often in power. Equally important, social democrats may have formed strategic alliances with other parties, for instance those representing small farmers or white collar workers, when the welfare state was developing. If they did this, as was typically the case in the Nordic countries (which include Sweden, Norway, Finland, Denmark, and Iceland), they exercised an influence that was even greater than their own electoral support would have justified. This resulted in very well-funded welfare states that also substantially reduced inequality and poverty. In Anglo-Saxon countries, on the other hand, social democratic parties have either been very weak at the national level (in the United States and Canada) or, though stronger, failed to form strong alliances with parties representing other groups in society. The latter was true, for instance, of the British and Australian Labour Parties. Both governed their countries for 20 of the 55 post-war years, but never obtained the support of a large share of middle class voters. They were therefore unable to push through the kind of more expensive and poverty-reducing programs that they might have preferred. A third kind of welfare state developed in many Continental European welfare states where Christian Democratic parties governed most of the time after World War II. Here, social spending might not be much lower than in the Scandinavian countries; however, because Christian Democrats were less interested than social democrats in promoting equality, these welfare states do not reduce poverty as much as the Scandinavian ones. Nevertheless, even the Christian Democratic cases are not all the same: social democrats tended to be stronger in Northern than in Southern Europe, so that welfare states are more egalitarian in the former than in the latter.

These patterns are illustrated in Tables 4.4 and 4.5 (p. 90). First, Table 4.4 indicates that when it comes to spending money on social programs, the main dividing line is between the Anglo-Saxon countries on the one hand, and all of the other countries on the other. The Anglo-Saxon countries, whose welfare states largely reflect the influence of business-oriented parties that oppose welfare state expansion, spend on average 17.6 percent of their Gross Domestic Product (GDP) on social security measures. In the Northern and Southern European countries, spending is much higher, respectively 25.2 percent and 24.2 percent of the GDP. The countries in these categories formed welfares states either under social democratic (Nordic countries) or Christian Democratic (all the others) dominance; either way, these welfare states are relatively expensive.

To distinguish between the Northern and Southern European cases, we need only turn to Table 4.5. As expected, poverty levels are highest in the Anglo-Saxon countries, with their small welfare states; poverty averages 13.4 percent for this group of countries, and it never falls below 12 percent for any country in this group. Despite their high spending, however, the Christian Democratic welfare states of Southern Europe, formed under particularly weak social democratic influence, also have a relatively high average rate of poverty, at 11.6 percent, though France's level is quite a bit lower. The Northern European countries, either social democratic or formed by Christian Democrats in countries where left parties and labour unions nevertheless were generally much stronger than in Southern Europe, have a much lower average level of poverty at 7.1 percent. The social democratic cases (marked with an SD in the table) in Table 4.5 average 6.3 percent, while the Northern European Christian Democratic countries have an average poverty level of 7.5 percent. If we look at statistics on overall inequality (not reproduced here) rather than poverty, we see more of a distinction between the social democratic

---

Table 4.4   Variations in the Size of Welfare States

Total social security expenditures as a % of Gross Domestic Product (GDP)

Corporatist Countries	%	Pluralist Countries	%
Northern European: (weaker state)		**Anglo-Saxon: (weak state)**	
Austria	27	USA	17
Norway	22	Canada	17
Sweden	28	United Kingdom	21
Netherlands	21	Australia	17
Denmark	26	Ireland	16
Germany	26		
Switzerland	26	**Southern European: (stronger state)**	
Finland	25	France	29
Belgium	26	Greece	21
		Italy	26
East Asian: (strong state)		Spain	22
Japan	19	Portugal	23
Average for Northern	**25.2**	*Average for Anglo-Saxon Variant*	**17.6**
European Variant		*Average for Southern European Variant*	**24.2**

Source: Based on data from Social and Welfare Statistics, from *OECD.StatExtracts,* http://stats.oecd.org (9 February 2011).

Table 4.5 Levels of Poverty in Advanced Political Economies			
Corporatist Countries	%	Pluralist Countries	%
Northern European: (weaker state)		**Anglo-Saxon: (weak state)**	
Austria	7	USA	17
Norway	7 (SD)	Canada	13
Sweden	6 (SD)	United Kingdom	12
Netherlands	6	Australia	12
Denmark	6 (SD)	Ireland	13
Germany	9	**Southern European: (stronger state)**	
Switzerland	8	France	7
Finland	7	Greece	12
Belgium	8	Italy	12
East Asian: (strong state)		Spain	14
Japan	15	Portugal	13
Average for Northern European Variant	*7.1*	*Average for Anglo-Saxon Variant*	*13.4*
		Average for Southern European Variant	*11.6*

Source: LIS Inequality and Poverty Key Figures, http://www.lisdatacenter.org (9 February 2011). Luxembourg: LIS.

cases and the Northern European Christian Democratic ones, with inequality being significantly lower in the Nordic countries. Predictably, inequality is higher in Southern Europe than in either the Nordic or Northern European Christian Democratic countries, and highest of all in the Anglo-Saxon countries.[23]

To what extent do the more expensive welfare states in non-English speaking countries hamper economic growth? Would their economies grow faster if, as some critics suggest, they cut social spending and allowed poverty to rise? Growth is, in fact, higher on average in some welfare state regimes than in others.[24] But it is not true that larger welfare states necessarily result in lower economic growth. Growth since the 1980s has been about as strong, on average, in the costly social democratic Nordic countries as in the much cheaper and less generous liberal regimes of the Anglo-Saxon world. Growth is generally lower, however, in the Southern European countries which have expensive welfares states that nevertheless do not redistribute very extensively. Financial crises in Portugal, Greece, Spain, France, and Italy in 2010–2011 precipitated heated debates and significant reform in

these countries. But the Nordic cases show that, contrary to much press coverage, it is not the cost and overall generosity of a welfare state that creates a major problem.[25]

WHAT ABOUT CANADA?

How does Canada fit into these comparative typologies? Most scholars consider that Canada belongs to the Anglo-Saxon (LME or Liberal) category of the VoC typology, and that it also has a typically Anglo-Saxon, relatively-small welfare state. The data in the tables discussed above generally seem to support this view. Yet observers also qualify this characterization, noting that some features of the Canadian case depart in important ways from what one would expect in an Anglo-Saxon setting. These unusual features of Canada's political economy have drawn the attention of a distinctive scholarly tradition. Its formative figure was Harold Innis, who argued during the 1940s and 1950s that Canada's colonial dependency upon France and then the United Kingdom caused its economy to develop along quite different lines than did the United States, or than mainstream economics would anticipate for a country that achieved affluence in the 20th century.[26] The staples theory argues that rather than moving from raw material production to manufacturing and then to services, Canada remained locked in a *staples trap*. As a result of this, its exports continued to be dominated by raw materials. These were what the European "mother countries" wanted from Canada, while manufacturing was discouraged. Canada has long since become a politically sovereign country but, for Innisians, the country remains locked into this pattern of exporting raw materials and importing higher value-added goods and services from a dominant external economy. By the mid-20th century the latter role had passed from the United Kingdom to the United States. Data on Canada's pattern of exports does, in fact, show that the country is still by a wide margin a net exporter of raw materials, such as oil, lumber, and minerals, and that it also remains a net importer of manufactured goods.

A number of important departures from the Anglo-Saxon norm of a laissez-faire, non-interventionist state are associated with this staples pattern in Canada's history. The cost of infrastructure (such as railways and electricity) needed to facilitate resource extraction in a country with a huge land mass but a small population was immense. Canadian governments therefore were much more active in promoting the economy's development than is typical in weak state settings. For instance, the trans-Canadian railway network that was built during the later 19th century, starting with the Canadian Pacific Railway (CPR), was heavily subsided by government funds; private entrepreneurs were not attracted to the idea of building it without government assistance. During the 20th century, similarly, the federal government was also responsible for the beginnings of radio and television broadcasting in Canada, and for commercial air travel. Since the 1980s the federal government has become much less involved in the economy than it once was; it has sold Air Canada and the Canadian National Railways to the private sector and reduced its regulatory role in the economy. For some observers, this shift marked an end to its earlier pattern of interventionism, making Canada much more typical of a weak state, laissez-faire economic model than it ever was before. Other observers would disagree with this view, arguing that Canada's state remains more involved in the country's economy than is typical in the Anglo-Saxon cluster of countries.

Other features of Canadian political life also were heavily marked by the country's pattern of economic development. For instance, raw materials are distributed unevenly across the Canadian landmass, and were exploitable at different points in the country's history. Moreover, when an internally-focused manufacturing sector did develop after Confederation (designed to produce manufactured goods for sale within the country but not, for the most part, for export to other countries), it was concentrated in a corridor between Windsor, Ontario, and Montreal. Resource-based provinces outside of this region came to perceive their own circumstances as representing a dependency on the central provinces that was analogous to that of Canada as a whole on its American partner.[27] For political economists, this acute economic heterogeneity accounts for the often-noticed tensions among the Canadian regions as much as, or more than, the more commonly-discussed cultural and linguistic differences. Regional sensitivity, in its turn, fostered a decentralized federalism where citizens' loyalties are divided between the country and their own province. In this setting, after 1945 provincial states embarked on *province-building*, motivated to intervene in economic and social life of their residents to counter federal encroachments.[28]

Regarding its welfare state, Canada again departs in some important ways from the Anglo-Saxon norm of limited spending and little poverty-reduction. Unlike the United States, for instance, Canada's welfare state developed an employment insurance scheme that was quite generous, especially in poorer regions. It also included important universally-available income security measures and universal public health insurance. According to the best available statistics, inequality is now much lower in Canada than in either the United States or the United Kingdom and lower even than in several European countries.[29] Working class political pressures, especially through the New Democratic Party (NDP), encouraged these developments. But until 2011 the NDP was always a minor party at the Canadian federal level. Working-class power likely cannot, therefore, account for these features. Political economists instead turn to an account of Canada's party system first developed by Frank Underhill. In his view, Canada's diverse political economy and the resulting inter-regional frictions required the main political parties (the Liberals and Conservatives) to perform a *brokerage* role, resulting in a **brokerage party system**.[30] Rather than advancing an **ideology** of either the left or the right, they sought to assemble (or broker) large enough coalitions of heterogeneous voters from different regions to win elections. The main parties, therefore, differed little overall in their attitude to redistribution, and both had the strong links to business necessary for financing and legitimacy. Yet to win, both Conservatives and Liberals needed the support of non-business, including working class, voters. It was in response to this imperative, expressed in terms of regional demands more than class ones, that Canada developed a more ample welfare state than did the U.S.[31] The fact that regional and federal–provincial sensitivities remain acute in Canada may also explain why welfare state cutbacks have been more muted here since the 1980s than in either the U.S. or the U.K.

> **Brokerage Party System:** A definition of Canada's national party system which argues that ideological polarization is less pronounced in Canadian politics than in many other countries; instead, the main political parties are said to attempt to aggregate enough diverse interests to win elections.

Canada's fragmented political economy begat a decentralized federation in which sub-national (provincial) governments have more autonomous power than elsewhere. This suggests another potentially distinctive

avenue for Canadian research: the political economy literatures reviewed in the previous sections identify sovereign countries as the level at which to study macro-level factors that shape wealth-creation and redistribution. The ample resources available to Canadian provinces and their diversity imply that we might want to adapt their cross-national typologies for use in inter-provincial comparisons. Thomas Klassen and Rodney Haddow argued that the political economies and party systems of Canada's four largest provinces differ significantly, and diverge from the national pattern for Canada.[32] Tables 4.6 and 4.7 indicate the extent of differences among the provinces in the strength of their labour movements and in the importance of their social democratic parties—two important potential causes of policy variations. For instance, the unionization rate is much higher in Quebec (at 40 percent) than in Alberta (25 percent). Alberta's figure is certainly typical of a pluralist, Anglo-Saxon country but Quebec's level is much more comparable to those in Northern European corporatist countries. Similarly, Table 4.7 indicates that social democratic parties (NDP or Parti Québécois) have been in power in some provinces far more than in others since 1970. Based on Esping-Andersen's account, we would expect welfare states to be better developed in the provinces with more frequent social democratic governments and, perhaps, those with stronger union movements.

Table 4.6   Unionization Rates in the Canadian Provinces

Province	%
Newfoundland	39
PEI	32
Nova Scotia	31
New Brunswick	29
Quebec	40
Ontario	28
Manitoba	37
Saskatchewan	36
Alberta	25
British Columbia	31

Source: *Unionization rate, by region, 2009 (percent of employed workers),* published in *Indicators of Well-being in Canada - Work - Unionization Rates,* URL: http://www4.hrsdc.gc.ca/.3ndic.1t.4r@-eng. jsp?iid=17. Human Resources and Skills Development Canada, 2010 (from Statistics Canada publication *Labour Force Historical Review 2009* (Table 078), Catalogue 71F0004XVB). Reproduced with the permission of the Minister of Public Works and Government Services Canada, 2011.

Table 4.7   Variable Strength of Social Democratic Parties in Canadian Provinces

Total number of years that social democratic parties were in power, 1971–2007

Province	Years
Newfoundland	0
PEI	0
Nova Scotia	0
New Brunswick	0
Quebec	19
Ontario	5
Manitoba	23
Saskatchewan	27
Alberta	0
British Columbia	13

Source: Compilation by the author. Figures represent the total number of years, between 1971 and 2007, when social democratic parties (NDP in English Canada, Parti Québécois in Quebec) were in power in each province.

The Klassen-Haddow study concluded that, indeed, policy-making in Quebec differed significantly from the pattern in Canada's three most populous Anglo-Saxon provinces. It included some features that resembled the more corporatist settings to be found in Europe. This was not the case in Ontario, British Columbia, or Alberta. Reflecting its weak labour movement and the absence of an effective social democratic force, Alberta's policies were particularly consistent with the laissez-faire, low-spending norm in Anglo-Saxon countries.[33] More recent research by Haddow indicates that Quebec's social programs also reduce inequality and poverty more than do those in other Canadian provinces, while Alberta's programs do less of this than is the case in almost all other provinces.[34] In light of these findings, Canadian political economy might benefit from more comparative provincial research.

As with the ideas reviewed earlier, one might ask how relevant this Canadian scholarship remains in the current era of globalization-induced change. The next section turns to this question.

GLOBALIZATION AND CHANGE

There are reasons to believe that political economies in the 21st century are altering. Foremost among these reasons is "globalization." From a political economy perspective, **globalization** has a specific meaning: since the 1970s the economies of different countries have become much more open to each other.[35] The proportion of each country's production that is exported to other countries, or imported from them, has increased substantially. Although foreign investment has always been very important in Canada, it has become much more salient around the world; there is now much more Foreign Direct Investment (FDI) than there was 30 years ago. Firms are now more likely to be multinational or **transnational corporations**, that is, to locate different parts of their production in different countries. Finally, there has been an explosion in the global flow of capital, subject to little or no restraint by national governments. The impact of these changes is reinforced by increasingly-powerful inter-governmental organizations (IGOs), such as the **World Trade Organization** (WTO), the **International Monetary Fund** (IMF) and the **G8** and G20, which encourage, or push, countries to open up their economies ever-more to international forces, as discussed in more detail in Chapter 17.

> **Globalization:** A process that is leading to ever-closer economic relations among the countries of the world, based on increased trade, foreign direct investment, activity by multinational corporations, and financial flows.

Table 4.8	How Much Has Trade Increased for Advanced Political Economies?		

Trade openness = Exports + Imports as a % of GDP

		%	
		1980	2008
Corporatist Countries			
Austria		69	113
Sweden		61	100
Netherlands		105	145
Germany		45	89
Japan		28	35
Pluralist Countries			
United States		21	30
Canada		54	69
United Kingdom		52	61
France		44	56
Italy		45	58
10-country average		**52.4**	**75.6**

Source: Based on data from Trade Union Density under Trade Union under Labour from *OECD.StatExtracts*, http://stats.oecd.org (9 February 2011).

Of all of the above, the trade and FDI changes are the most often-cited aspects of globalization. Tables 4.8 and 4.9 indicate how much more exposed countries are to these global economic currents today than they were in 1980. The most common measure of how much a country trades is its trade *openness*; this is calculated by adding together the total value of exports and imports, and measuring the total as a percentage of GDP. As Table 4.8 indicates, for the top 10 countries reported in the earlier tables in this chapter, trade openness has increased substantially since 1980—on average from about one-half of the value of a country's GDP to about three-quarters of GDP. This means that a larger share of what is produced in each country is subject to competition from goods and (less often) services produced elsewhere. Table 4.9 indicates that the share of FDI in these countries has increased even more dramatically. In 1980, on average, the value of direct investments by foreigners equalled 6.3 percent of the GDP in these countries; by 2008, this figure had risen over five-fold to 33.1 percent. In both cases, we can also see that the extent of this increase has been more modest for Canada which, as we already noted, has always been very exposed to external economic interests.

How will these changes affect national political economies? One frequent answer is that it will cause a *race to the bottom*,[36] which will eventually eliminate, or at least dramatically reduce, the variations among political economies that have been the focus of comparative political economy scholarship since the 1970s. Because firms and countries increasingly have to compete with each other to export products and to attract foreign investors who might otherwise take their capital (and the resulting jobs) somewhere else, they are now determined to cut costs. Non-Anglo-Saxon political economies, which have relied on cooperation among economic actors and which have maintained more expensive welfare states, will abandon these and move towards the less costly and less interventionist arrangements that typify, for instance, the United States. Abetted by IGOs, which often preach the virtues of laissez-faire and of low taxation and government spending, this view concludes that these globalization pressures will undermine the **sovereignty** of independent states, making them less able to constrain the rising power of big business or impede rising inequality and poverty.

Table 4.9 How Much Has Foreign Ownership Increased in Advanced Political Economies?		
Foreign Direct Investment (FDI) stocks as % of GDP		
	%	
	1980	**2009**
Corporatist Countries		
Austria	4	34
Sweden	2	55
Netherlands	11	71
Germany	4	21
Japan	> 1	2
Pluralist Countries		
United States	3	23
Canada	20	31
United Kingdom	12	32
France	5	49
Italy	2	13
10-country average	*6.3*	*33.1*

Source: United Nations Conference on Trade and Development, http://unctadstat.org/ReportFolders/ reportFolders.aspx?sCS_referer=&sCS_ChosenLang=en; accessed February 10, 2011. These figures report the percentage of assets in each country that is owned by foreign interests, as a percentage of its Gross Domestic Product. For 1980, German figures are for West Germany alone.

Most political economists disagree. For them, globalization will have a more complex impact.[37] Depending on the circumstances, it might reinforce the ability and determination of countries to defend what is distinctive about their political economies. Even if it does curtail national sovereignty in some areas, it might strengthen it in others—for instance, by enhancing the influence of states on international decision-making, and by buttressing their ability to support the new information technologies that are now so important.

Nevertheless, many political economists agree that globalization is likely to affect existing political economies *somehow*, so that approaches to political economy that appear to rule out fundamental change are highly questionable. Therefore, some recent contributions try to modify (without abandoning) the approaches reviewed earlier in this chapter to accommodate the idea that political economies might be forced to change in an era of globalization. Streeck and Thelen call for research that shows how political economies are constantly the site of conflict among organized groups and economic interests, even after they develop to a quite advanced level.[38]

They argue that political economies experience constant gradual change as different interests adjust their goals and gain or lose power in new circumstances, such as those presented by globalization. Moreover, these stimulants to constant change mean that a country may not conform to a "pure" type of the kind proposed by the theories discussed earlier in this chapter. Countries may have "hybrid" features that mix elements of one type with aspects of another. Even if a country's political economy appears to be a pure Coordinated one today, it may look different five years from now. In the face of globalization, political economy scholarship may in the future have to tolerate more "messiness," with less room for dividing the world into a few clearly distinguishable categories.

What this more change-sensitive and messy comparative political economy can look like is illustrated here with an example. By 2000 there was much criticism inside Germany—supported by business—that its political economy, which the VoC typology characterizes as Coordinated (or CME), was in trouble. It was experiencing chronically high unemployment, and rising social security taxes and expenditures. According to the critics, this was happening because Germany could not create enough high-skill, high-wage jobs to provide work for everyone. Employers were also reluctant to create more work because regulations made it hard to fire unproductive employees. The solution, for the critics, was to make it easier for employers to fire people, and to change regulations and the tax system so that low-wage jobs could be created for people who lacked high skills. Labour unions unsuccessfully opposed these changes, a sign that business had gained in power at labour's expense. In fact, the changes, commonly called the *Hartz IV reforms*, were passed by a social democratic party-led government. In the reforms' wake, unemployment declined in Germany, even after a global recession began. Many new jobs pay low wages by German standards, and are in low-skill occupations; few of these new workers are unionized. This new sector strongly resembles what one would find in an Anglo-Saxon or Liberal (LME) political economy. But Germany's Coordinated model otherwise remains in place, and the economy has rebounded. It is now experiencing an economic boom. This is based on a resurgence of exports from its very competitive manufacturing sector in which high skills, high wages, and strong unions persist. Consequently, there is little reason to believe that the main elements of Germany's core Coordinated model are currently in danger, even as a significant Liberal-type labour market emerges alongside it. The resurgence might even restore some of the unions' lost power.

This narrative includes several of the elements recommended for a more change-sensitive, if messier, comparative political economy: attentiveness to the importance of changing objectives among key societal groups (in this case, as is usual in political economy scholarship, business, and labour) and of shifts in the balance of power between them, and an appreciation that change may lead to mixed results with the outcome not corresponding clearly to one or another model but blending elements of each.

How might such an approach be applied to Canada? We saw that earlier generations of political economists were reluctant to situate Canada fully in the laissez-faire category, alongside other Anglo-Saxon countries. Have recent developments justified seeing Canada as more purely laissez-faire and low-spending than before? On the one hand, one is struck by how much Innis's **staples thesis** remains relevant. Canada continues to rely on raw materials for a large part of its exports. On the other hand, it is no longer clear that Canada's national state plays a larger role in the country's economic development than is the case in other Anglo-Saxon countries. Since the 1980s, most tariffs have been abandoned, state enterprises privatized, and many economic sectors deregulated. Trade agreements signed since that time, culminating with the WTO in 1994, now preclude many forms of intervention. Changes in Canada's welfare state have also been important. Yet in this case, the available welfare state research suggests that the transformation has been less dramatic.[39] Inequality has increased in Canada, but by less than in most Anglo-Saxon countries. Social programs also redistribute about as much today as they did during the 1980s. The elements that supported redistribution during the post-war era arguably remain in place, including a brokerage national party system, an influential NDP, and a union movement that is now much stronger than its American counterpart. This evolving pattern for redistribution could benefit from careful comparative studies of Canada and other welfare states.

> **Staples Thesis:** An interpretation of Canadian economic development, which argues that unlike most other now affluent countries, the production of raw materials for export markets has remained central for the Canadian economy. It has not been replaced by a focus on manufactured goods and then services.

CONCLUSION

Political economy has been examined in this chapter as a focus of scholarship, although alternative definitions that treat it as a method have also been explained, as these remain very important within political science. This approach draws our attention to the highly variable nature of the relationship between authority-wielding states and market-based economies in affluent countries, and to equally diverse relations among economic actors in them. Political economy treats much that is exciting and important in political science. By tackling political questions from a macro perspective, one that draws our attention to broad and fundamental features of social life, political economy addresses institutions and forces that can remain hidden to meso- and micro-level scholarship. It also permits us to deal with influences that extend beyond any one sector, and to trace to their origins influences on political change that affect various sectors simultaneously.

Examining the relationship of states and market also has an important practical value for us not just as students of politics but as citizens. The main traditions of political economy have for a long time stressed the variety of ways in which people produce and redistribute wealth. The modern world is not an "iron cage," to borrow a term from the classical sociologist Max Weber, in which we are compelled to accept as inevitable certain ways of organizing our economic lives and to acquiesce to particular levels of inequality in power and wealth. Political economy reminds us that there has always been much variation among countries in these terms. Since this variety is at least in part the result of distinctive *choices* made by different peoples throughout their histories, they are revealed to be not inevitable. And since macro-level scholarship almost always draws our attention to the uneven distribution of political power and economic wealth in society, it also forces most of us to think critically about our societies. These fall well short of achieving the equality of opportunity much cherished in modern democracies.[40]

DISCUSSION QUESTIONS

1. Is a focus on political economy more or less useful than other approaches to the study of political science that you have looked at?

2. Do you agree that the variety of political economies that exist in the developed world supports the view that the citizens of these countries have a meaningful choice in determining their political and economic futures?

3. For rational choice political economists, politics is about people and organizations pursuing what is in their own self-interest. Do you agree?

FURTHER READING

Clarkson, Stephen. *Uncle Sam and Us: Globalization, Neoconservatism and the Canadian State.* Toronto: University of Toronto Press, 2002.

Downs, Anthony. *An Economic Theory of Democracy.* New York: Harper, 1965.

Esping-Andersen, Gøsta. *The Three Worlds of Welfare Capitalism.* Princeton: Princeton University Press, 1990.

Greenspon, Edward, and Anthony Wilson-Smith. *Double Vision: The Inside Story of the Liberals in Power.* Toronto: Doubleday, 1996.

Haddow, Rodney, and Thomas Klassen. *Partisanship, Globalization, and Canadian Labour Market Policy.* Toronto: University of Toronto Press, 2006.

Ohmae, Kenichi. *The Borderless World.* New York: Harper Perennial, 1991.

Orloff, Ann. "Gender and the Social Rights of Citizenship: The Comparative Analysis of Gender Relations and Welfare States," *American Sociological Review* 58 (1993): 303–328.

Pontusson, Jonas. *Inequality and Prosperity: Social Europe vs. Liberal America.* Ithaca: Cornell University Press, 2005.

Tilly, Charles. *Big Structures, Large Processes, Huge Comparisons.* New York: Russell Sage Foundation, 1984.

Underhill, Frank. *Canadian Political Parties.* Ottawa: Canadian Historical Association, 1957.

Weiss, Linda. *The Myth of the Powerless State.* Cambridge: Polity Press, 1998.

ENDNOTES

1. Charles Tilly, *Big Structures, Large Processes, Huge Comparisons* (New York: Russell Sage Foundation, 1984.)

2. Also see Robert Alford and Roger Friedland, *Powers of Theory: Capitalism, the State, and Democracy* (Cambridge: Cambridge University Press, 1985).

3. C.B. Macpherson, "Politics: Post-liberal Democracy?," in Robin Blackburn, ed., *Ideology in Social Science* (London: Fontana, 1972).

4. Daniel Drache, "Rediscovering Canadian Political Economy," in Wallace Clement and Daniel Drache, eds., *A Practical Guide to Canadian Political Economy* (Toronto: Lorimer, 1978).

5. Anthony Downs, *An Economic Theory of Democracy* (New York: Harper, 1965).

6. William Niskanen, *Bureaucracy and Representative Government* (Chicago: Aldine, Atherton, 1971).

7. Mancur Olson, *The Logic of Collective Action* (Cambridge: Harvard University Press, 1965).

8. Ian Gough, *The Political Economy of the Welfare State* (London: MacMillan, 1979).

9. See, for instance, the recent definition of the latter term in Barry Weingast and Donald Wittman, "The Reach of Political Economy," in Weingast and Wittman, eds., *The Oxford Handbook of Political Economy* (New York: Oxford University Press, 2006), p. 3.

10. See, especially, Bob Jessop, *The Future of the Capitalist State* (Cambridge: Polity, 2002).

11. For an excellent example, see Edward Greenspon and Anthony Wilson-Smith, *Double Vision: The Inside Story of the Liberals in Power* (Toronto: Doubleday, 1996).

12. William Coleman and Grace Skogstad, "Introduction," in Coleman and Skogstad, eds., *Policy Communities and Public Policy in Canada: A Structural Approach* (Mississauga: Copp Clark Pitman, 1989).

13. Jingjing Huo, *Third Way Reforms: Social Democracy after the Golden Age* (Cambridge: Cambridge University Press, 2009).

14. W.W. Rostow, *The Stages of Economic Growth*, 2nd ed. (Cambridge: Cambridge University Press, 1971).

15. John Myles and Paul Pierson, "The Comparative Political Economy of Pension Reform," in Paul Pierson, ed., *The New Politics of the Welfare State* (Oxford: Oxford University Press, 2001), p. 312.

16. Bertrand Badie and Pierre Birnbaum, *The Sociology of the State* (Chicago: University of Chicago Press, 1983), pp. 73–76.

17. Vivien Schmidt, *The Futures of European Capitalism* (Oxford: Oxford University Press, 2002).

18. Philippe Schmitter, "Still the Century of Corporatism," *Review of Politics* 6 (1) (1974): 85–131; Peter Katzenstein, *Small States in World Markets* (Ithaca: Cornell University Press, 1985).

19. Rankings in the original source were based on a scale of 1 (pure pluralism) to 5 (pure corporatism). In this table, countries are listed as "corporatist" if their score, rounded to the nearest whole number, was 4 or 5. They are identified as "pluralist" if this number was 3 or less.

20. Peter Hall and David Soskice, "An Introduction to Varieties of Capitalism," in Hall and Soskice, eds., *Varieties of Capitalism* (Oxford: Oxford University Press, 2001).

21. Óscar Molina and Martin Rhodes, "The Political Economy of Adjustment in Mixed Market Economies: A Study of Spain and Italy," in Bob Hancké, et al., eds., *Beyond Varieties of Capitalism* (Oxford: Oxford University Press, 2007), pp. 223–252.

22. Gøsta Esping-Andersen, *The Three Worlds of Welfare Capitalism* (Princeton: Princeton University Press, 1990).

23. Inequality is usually measured with the Gini index. The higher the Gini index, the greater is the inequality in society; a score of zero would mean complete equality; a score of 1.0 would entail complete inequality, with all income being held by one person. In the real world, all national Gini indexes are between zero and one. The most recent average Gini for the four groups of countries discussed here are as follows: Nordic countries, .243; Northern European Christian democratic countries, .271; Sothern European Christian democratic countries, .315; and Anglo-Saxon countries, .332. See Luxembourg Income Study, *LIS Key Figures*, available at http://www.lisproject.org/key.figures/; accessed February 14, 2011.

24. Jonas Pontusson, *Inequality and Prosperity: Social Europe vs. Liberal America* (Ithaca: Cornell University Press, 2005).

25. The problem in the Southern European countries, more likely, is the fact that they deliver

unsustainably high benefits to certain privileged categories of citizens, impede people from entering and moving around in the job market, especially young people and women, and use inefficient forms of taxation.

26. Harold Innis, *Essays in Canadian Economic History*, edited by Mary Innis (Toronto: University of Toronto Press, 1956).

27. Vernon Fowke, *The National Policy and the Wheat Economy* (Toronto: University of Toronto Press, 1957).

28. Edwin R. Black and Allan Cairns, "A Different Perspective on Canadian Federalism," *Canadian Public Administration* 9 (1966): 27–44.

29. Luxembourg Income Study, *LIS Key Figures*, http://www.lisproject.org/key.figures/; accessed February 14, 2011.

30. Frank Underhill, *Canadian Political Parties* (Ottawa: Canadian Historical Association, 1957).

31. Jane Jenson, "Representation in Crisis: The Roots of Canada's Permeable Fordism," *Canadian Journal of Political Science* 23 (1990): 655–683.

32. Rodney Haddow and Thomas Klassen, *Partisanship, Globalization, and Canadian Labour Market Policy* (Toronto: University of Toronto Press, 2006).

33. *Ibid.*

34. These calculations were made by me in a manuscript that is not yet published.

35. See Harman Schwartz, "Round Up the Usual Suspects: Globalization, Domestic Politics and Welfare State Change," in Paul Pierson, ed., *The New Politics of the Welfare State* (Oxford: Oxford University Press, 2001).

36. Kenichi Ohmae, *The Borderless World* (New York: Harper Perennial, 1991).

37. Linda Weiss, *The Myth of the Powerless State* (Cambridge: Polity Press, 1998).

38. Wolfgang Streeck and Kathleen Thelen, "Introduction," in Streeck and Thelen, eds., *Beyond Continuity: Institutional Change in Advanced Political Economies* (Oxford: Oxford University Press, 2005). On the importance of conflict, see also Jack Knight, *Institutions and Social Conflict* (Cambridge: Cambridge University Press, 1992).

39. Marc Frenette, David Green, and Garnett Picot, "Rising Income Inequality in the 1990s," in David Green and Jonathan Kesselman, eds., *Dimensions of Inequality in Canada* (Vancouver: UBC Press, 2006).

40. Brian Barry, *Why Social Justice Matters* (Cambridge: Polity, 2005).

For various weblinks discussed in this chapter, please go to the book's website at **www.studyingpolitics4e.nelson.com**

Political Values

Photo courtesy of Wendy Lill

WENDY LILL

Wendy Lill grew up in London, Ontario and went to York University where she graduated with a B.A. in Political Science. That degree has led Wendy in two divergent yet related directions: she is a writer and a former parliamentarian.

After graduation, Wendy worked as a freelance writer in northwestern Ontario and Winnipeg, Manitoba before moving to Nova Scotia with her husband Richard Starr. She continued her writing career until she was elected as the NDP Member of Parliament for Dartmouth in 1997. She was re-elected in 2000 and decided not to run for a third time in 2004. As a Member of Parliament, Wendy was actively involved in such issues as Canadian heritage, culture, communications, children, and persons with disabilities, and also sat on the Joint Committee on the Library of Parliament.

As a playwright, Wendy has written for radio, magazines, film, and television, and much of her work has a political dimension. Her plays have been produced internationally, and across the country from coast to coast to coast. In the Atlantic region, her plays have been produced at Neptune Theatre, Eastern Front Theatre, Ships Company Theatre, and Theatre New Brunswick. Her work has resulted in two ACTRA Awards, a Golden Sheaf Award (for her film *Ikwe*), nominations for Chalmers and Gemini awards, as well as four nominations for the Governor General's Literary Award for Drama (*The Occupation of Heather Rose*, *All Fall Down*, *Glace Bay Miners' Museum*, and *Corker*). *Chimera* premiered in January 2007 at Tarragon Theatre in Toronto. Wendy was one of the founding members of Eastern Front Theatre Company in Dartmouth in 1993 along with Mary Vingoe and Gay Hauser.

In addition to her writing, Wendy remains a strong advocate for persons with disabilities, the environment, and Canadian culture. She is a member of the board of the Dartmouth Learning Network, the chair of the Community Homes Action Group advocating for more appropriate housing for persons with developmental disabilities in Nova Scotia, and Chair of the Energy Issues Committee at Ecology Action Centre. She is a past member of the board of L'Arche Halifax, Playwrights Atlantic Resource Centre, and Independent Living Nova Scotia. In 2009, her radio drama series, *Backbencher*, about a fictional MP from a fictional riding called East Nova, premiered on CBC radio. *Backbencher* returned with a second season in 2011.

Wendy is the proud daughter of Edwin Henry and Margaret Lill and lives in Dartmouth with her partner, Richard Starr, and sons, Sam and Joe.

Political Culture and Socialization: The Media and Other Mind Shapers

Andrew Heard

CHAPTER OBJECTIVES

After you have completed this chapter, you should be able to:

- outline the relationship between a society's culture and its politics
- discuss the nature of political culture
- explain the significance of identity politics
- describe how deep divisions between groups in a society may be handled
- understand the processes through which we acquire our political knowledge and beliefs

WHAT IS POLITICAL CULTURE?

Politics is all about things we value and wish to see respected and protected, whether they are specific material benefits, such as health care, or higher moral principles, such as freedom of speech. What we think about the society we live in, the government that rules over us, and the other groups of people who live alongside us are all matters of personal attitude that can have profound political effects. One will know very little indeed about politics without an appreciation of the broader cultural context within which it

occurs. Ultimately, the politics of a society is a reflection of that society's culture. The depth of differences among groups within a society and the way they are dealt with can profoundly shape the nature of political discourse and conflict. For example, the difference between a stable, harmonious society and one wracked by a bloody civil war can flow from answers to such basic cultural questions as "To which group do I most strongly identify myself as belonging?" and "How is my group treated by others in my country?" These concepts were introduced in Chapter 3.

Comparisons of Canadian political phenomena with those from around the world can provide an idea of the practical consequences of the cultural values people hold. A large number of francophones in Quebec have supported separation throughout most of the last three decades, while there is no significant separatist movement within the United States, despite its enormous ethnic diversity. Canada does not have the death penalty, while China not only executes people but often does so in public settings. Most women have had the vote in Canadian national elections since 1918, while women in Kuwait only won the right to vote in 2005.[1] In the end, the differences between Canada and the other countries mentioned in these examples stem fundamentally from different values in the cultures of those societies.

Quite clearly, the variations in cultural values in societies can have a significant effect on these societies' politics. In order to understand the politics of any state or the variations and similarities between states, one has to appreciate the framing role of cultural values in political objects, principles, and processes. To understand politics, we need to grasp the essence of political culture, realize how the predominant values of that culture come to be passed on among its members, and discover whose values come to be accepted as the norm. Political scientists are interested in how deeply individuals identify with different social groups, what enduring cleavages may exist between these groups within a given society, and how political systems accommodate, foster, and suppress conflicts between them.

We all have a sense of what culture means, but the concept of culture is highly contentious; there are literally hundreds of definitions. In a general sense, culture consists of the shared values, beliefs, practices, and symbols relating to the food, clothing, social relations, language, religion, literature, music, and so on that are practised or favoured among a particular group of people. But culture in a larger sense relates to the fundamental values of communities and their beliefs about how life should be lived, how people should behave, and how society should be organized. Political culture is essentially this social phenomenon applied to politics. Indeed, political culture is really just a particular aspect of a society's broader culture.

Political culture is the collection of the understandings, values, attitudes, and principles of a community or society that relate to its political organization, processes, disputes, and public policies. Out of a society's political culture come important beliefs and values that structure the citizens' attitudes and expectations toward such basic political concepts as legitimacy, power, authority, and obedience. These attitudes

> **Political culture:** The collection of the understandings, values, attitudes, and principles of a community or society that relate to its political organization, processes, disputes, and public policies. Out of a society's political culture come important beliefs and values that structure the citizens' attitudes and expectations toward such basic political concepts as legitimacy, power, authority, and obedience.

play an important background role in the success and effectiveness of the government in that society. The extent to which citizens acquiesce in or defer to their political leaders has a significant bearing on whether the government feels it necessary to use more force and coercion than influence in order to exercise authority and secure compliance with its decisions. As well, these attitudes can shape the informal processes through which a society manages to direct and settle disputes outside the formal political institutions.

The levels of trust and types of interactions between citizens and their governments are fundamentally shaped by cultural attitudes. Some powerful consequences can flow from as seemingly simple an attitude as "We should respect and defer to the political leaders of our country. They are the elders of our group. They know things that I do not know." One can expect a very different relationship between the citizens and their political leaders in a democracy where the culture encourages people to believe "My view is as good as the prime minister's"—an attitude more typical in Canada. A 2009 opinion poll found that only 30 percent of Canadians said that they respect politicians; that figure contrasts with the 77 percent who respect judges and 89 percent who respect teachers (see Table 5.1).[2] On the other hand, another poll revealed that 58 percent of Canadians had trust in the House of Commons.[3] This seemingly stark contradiction may be explained by contrasting the emotional baggage entailed in the word "politician" with a general confidence Canadians have in their political system as a whole, as symbolized by confidence in the House of Commons as an institution.

Cultural differences can also be clearly seen when comparing Canadian and American attitudes toward capital punishment. While strong majorities in both countries favoured the death penalty for murders in 2010 (62 percent in Canada and 84 percent in America), clear differences emerge in opinions about executing people for other crimes. Only a small minority of Canadians supported execution for those who committed rape or kidnapping, 31 and 17 percent respectively, compared to 62 and 53 percent of Americans.[4]

Political culture is not just about those things explicitly related to the political system; it is also about general social attitudes that can have political ramifications. For example, attitudes toward sexual practices are largely a matter of personal, private behaviour in Western countries, but they become political when

Table 5.1	Levels of Respect for Various Professions

An international survey asked people: "Generally speaking, do you tend to have a great deal of respect, a fair amount of respect, not much respect or very little respect for each of the following professions?" The percentages of those who said that had a great deal or a "fair amount" of respect are listed.

	Canada	UK	USA
Farmers	95	81	95
Doctors	94	92	92
Teachers	89	80	93
Police Officers	87	75	85
Military Officers	87	80	90
Judges	77	62	78
Priests	65	57	82
Building Contractors	60	43	73
Journalists	58	26	59
Lawyers	48	49	52
Business Executives	48	32	53
Bankers	47	21	58
Politicians	30	12	28
Car salespeople	23	14	31

Source: "Politicians, Car Salesmen Most Derided Professionals in Western Countries," August 31, 2009, p. 3. © Visions Critical Communications Inc. 2009

issues of government censorship of pornography arise or when debates over the promotion of gay rights come up. Whether the government should ban homosexual behaviour or allow same-sex marriages has been strongly debated at different times in many countries, and an individual's attitudes toward the role of the state in this matter are deeply connected to his or her beliefs about what types of sexual behaviour are to be prohibited, tolerated, or even celebrated. An international poll conducted in 2010 revealed very clear distinctions in national beliefs about how the law should treat gay and lesbian couples. It found that 61 percent of Canadians believed that same-sex couples should be allowed to legally marry, while only 41 percent of Britons and 36 percent of Americans agreed.[5] The positions taken by different groups on many political issues are often largely determined by their broader social beliefs and principles. The "social" becomes "political" as members of a society who hold opposing views compete over whose beliefs should be embodied in their government's laws and policies.

The values and beliefs of individuals regarding their governments and about their own sense of responsibility toward their governments can have a crucial impact on those governments' abilities to function properly. Attitudes of people in a variety of countries on questions of employment policy are one example of different values and beliefs; they are compared in Table 5.2. Another example is people's attitudes toward paying taxes. Canadians may take taxes for granted because of a high rate of compliance; there may be a certain amount of fiddling, but only a small minority of Canadians refuse to report the bulk of their earnings and pay taxes on them. People in different parts of the world have very different attitudes toward paying taxes to their governments; yet governments cannot function effectively without an adequate tax base. Without enough tax revenue, a government simply will not have the capacity to fulfil its required functions. The Swiss are the most likely to pay their taxes, with just six percent of the country's economic activity going untaxed.

Table 5.2   Attitudes Toward Employment Policies

An international survey asked people if they agree with the following questions: "When jobs are scarce ..."

Country	MEN HAVE MORE RIGHT TO A JOB THAN WOMEN		PRIORITY SHOULD BE GIVEN TO "CO-NATIONALS" OVER IMMIGRANTS	
	Agree	Disagree	Agree	Disagree
Argentina	27.7	60.0	71.9	17.4
Canada	14.3	77.9	40.9	46.1
Egypt	89.1	4.3	97.9	0.2
France	18.1	73.8	42.1	46.4
Germany	17.8	66.8	55.7	27.9
India	51.4	20.5	75.2	6.1
Italy	22.0	59.2	63.9	19.1
Japan	27.1	17.9	62.7	6.1
Mexico	25.3	67.6	74.8	11.0
Russia	36.6	43.7	81.4	9.00
South Africa	37.1	49.5	78.3	11.0
Sweden	2.1	94.1	11.8	79.9
United Kingdom	16.2	76.1	52.9	36.4
United States	6.8	66.4	55.4	20.0

Source: Data are from the European Values Study Group and World Values Survey Association, 2005–2008.

In Canada, only about 15 percent goes untaxed, in contrast to 27 percent in Italy.[6] In the United States the 16 percent of uncollected tax revenue is estimated at approximately $300 billion each year.[7] In the United Kingdom, unpaid taxes amounted to £42 billion in 2008/9.[8] This is a large sum for Britain considering that the 2010 deficit, which sparked an enormous round of service cuts, totalled £45 billion.[9] The problem is chronic in many other countries. In Kenya, for example, almost 64 percent of the workers are estimated to be employed in the informal sector, beyond state taxation.[10]

POLITICAL SUBCULTURES AND THE POWER OF ELITES TO SHAPE IDEAS

Political cultures are almost never homogeneous or monolithic; indeed, the political cultures of most societies contain many different subgroups or subcultures. Even in liberal democracies, political culture is often a majoritarian phenomenon—the majority within any group essentially gets to determine and foster the views that are taken as representative of that group. As a result, it is important to keep in mind the distinction between generalization and universalization: just because most members of a society believe something does not mean that everybody believes it. It is equally important to ask whose ideas are accepted as the "norm" in a society and why. Political culture is every bit as much a creation as it is an organic phenomenon.

> **Subculture:** A cluster of people who share the same basic political values and attributes that are distinct from those of other groups in society or from the predominant values and attributes of society as a whole.

By delving more deeply into particular aspects of a society's culture, one can often find that it is not even a majority but rather a small powerful group or **elite** that is able to dominate or even totally control the values propagated publicly in that society. This is most clearly seen in states with totalitarian regimes, where ruling elites mould most aspects of the society's public values; Nazi Germany, Stalinist Russia, and Maoist China are some examples of this phenomenon. However, one can also suggest that even in liberal democratic societies powerful cliques are able to set the tone and range of public discussion for the general community. For example, those who control the media have an enormous influence, as discussed later in this chapter. Critics of Western democracies argue that even in these supposedly free cultures, dominant socioeconomic groups not only assert their preferred values as the "ideals" but also create an attitudinal environment that leads the members of the various lower strata of society to accept their exploitation. Predominant attitudes taught to the poor thus lead them away from openly questioning the distribution of benefits within their society and toward acquiescing in the prevailing order.

> **Elite:** A small group of individuals who have significantly more power than other members of their community. They are either in a position to make authoritative decisions or have privileged access to decision-makers.

In most societies one finds significant distinctions between the values widely held among the elites and those held by the mass population. But because elites are the ones who make most of the public policies for a society, it is their values that are often embodied in government policies; furthermore, it is their values that are usually reflected in public descriptions of what their society believes in. Examples of the mass–elite division of values and beliefs are easy to find in Canada. For example, a majority of Canadian members of parliament have voted against capital punishment on three occasions: in 1967, 1976, and 1987. Opinion polls, however, showed that a majority of the general adult population consistently favoured the death penalty right up until the early 21st century. Only in 2004 did a national survey reveal that Canadian public opinion had caught up with the decisions of their elites with

only 42 percent in favour of the death penalty in Canada.[11] But by 2010, as noted, popular opinion was once again at odds with the elites, with 62 percent of Canadians favouring capital punishment for murder.

The **ideologies** favoured by a society's elites are usually reflected in the dominant political culture of a country as well. The elites' general understandings about how a country's economy and political system should be organized end up forming the basis of the public policies and political debate in the state. In a telling critique of human societies, Antonio Gramsci has developed an important notion of a hegemony of ideas that describes particular values and beliefs so ingrained in people that they not only do not question them but they consider them as pure common sense. Furthermore, Gramsci has argued that political rulers would succeed in the long run only to the extent to which the masses they ruled accepted the elite's worldview.[12] Perhaps the ultimate exercise of political power by elites in a society is the ability to structure the beliefs of those they rule in such ways that the masses neither question the elites' rule nor understand that their own interests may lie in a different political order or set of public policies.

> **Ideology:** A fairly coherent set of beliefs that not only explains what may be wrong with society, but also provides a vision of what society should be like.

Michel Foucault has also argued that elites in society are able to structure even our most basic conceptions of who we are and what actions or benefits are truly in our own interest.[13] One does not have to take these perspectives to the point of asserting some deliberate conspiracy of mind control to appreciate the enormous potential that the various agents of political socialization have in shaping and moulding members of a society into sharing a vast array of common beliefs and perspectives. Furthermore, as students of politics, we can ask ourselves what interests and values particular to women, minority groups, or even the majority of "ordinary people" are not being articulated and embraced in the general political culture of a society.

POLITICAL TRUST, EFFICACY, AND ALIENATION

Several types of personal attitudes can deeply affect a political system when they are aggregated among all the members of a society. How individual members feel about their political system and even how they think about it can have very significant effects on the political culture of groups in society.

Affective attitudes and orientations are those we hold because of the way we feel about something; they are an emotional response to issues and events. *Cognitive* attitudes and orientations are those we hold because of what we know about the issues and events, or at least what we think we know about them. (Remember here that just because we believe something to be a fact does not mean it is true.) *Evaluative* attitudes and orientations are ones that combine emotion and knowledge—that is, where we combine what we know with what we feel about something to make judgments about political phenomena and events. A subtle but important part of our personal maturation process as we grow up, as well as the political socialization process in general, lies in how we learn to think about events and issues. Our behaviour in the political world will be very different depending on whether we are guided by affective, cognitive, or evaluative attitudes.

How we think is very much influenced by how we have been taught to think, by role models as well as by implicit instruction. What we believe we know about our political system and how we feel about it greatly influence our own sense of where we personally fit into our society. If we feel that we have political representatives or other leaders who generally act honestly, in good faith, and use good judgment in furthering our collective well-being, then we may have a strong sense of **political trust** in our political elites. Figure 5.1 reveals varied degrees of trust in different Canadian political institutions. **Political efficacy** is the belief that we as individuals can have some influence upon the decisions that affect our lives. If, however, we have a low degree of trust in our political leaders and have little sense of political efficacy, then we may well feel **political alienation**.

CIVIC CULTURE AND DEMOCRACY

Two American political scientists, Gabriel A. Almond and Sidney Verba, first coined the term *civic culture* to describe the group of attitudes and beliefs needed in a political culture in order for a stable, liberal democracy to thrive.[14] Many of Almond and Verba's views have since come under severe criticism, particularly their belief that America was an example of the virtues of a civic culture. Some of their observations, however, have spawned a continuing debate over the cultural requirements for a peaceful, democratic society, now termed **civil society**. Not only is representative democracy predicated upon the general population having significant trust in their elected representatives, but citizens must also have a sense of efficacy in order to participate in many of the society's political processes. Thus, a stable democracy with a civic culture is most likely to be found in societies where the political culture reflects high levels of trust and efficacy but low levels of political alienation.

Civic culture and civil society do not *cause* stable democracy, but they do appear to be an essential precondition for a stable liberal democracy.[15] A lack of a civic culture or strong civil society might explain the significant difficulties some countries have when they try to adopt a democratic form of government after many decades of a system of government that fostered political alienation and distrust of political elites. (This issue is addressed in Chapter 15.) It is also important for the political culture to embrace a spirit of genuine compromise and an ability to lose out from time to time. After all, the essence of a democracy is that different factions are willing to reach a compromise and not remain rigidly demanding that all of their claims be met. Furthermore, a group has to be willing to lose in elections and allow another group to take office.

Willingness to compromise and an ability to lose may seem rather vague and distant attitudes, but they are essential cultural values for a democratic form of government to survive more than one party's term in office. Samuel P. Huntington described the fate of newly minted democracies in the late 20th century as follows:

> Threats to third-wave democracies are likely to come not from generals and revolutionaries who have nothing but contempt for democracy,

Figure 5.1 Canadians' Trust in Public Actors

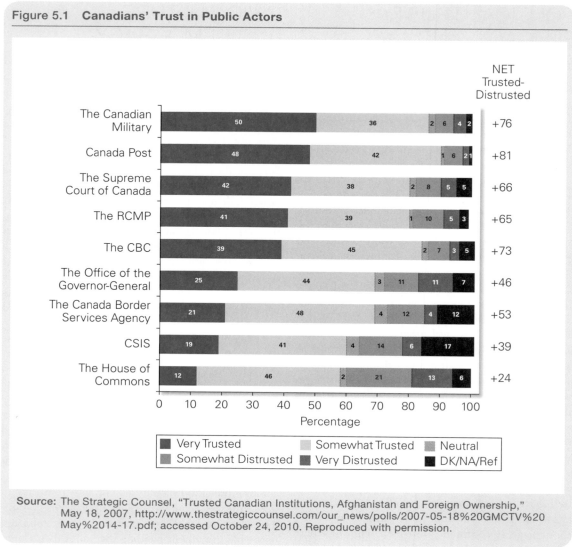

Source: The Strategic Counsel, "Trusted Canadian Institutions, Afghanistan and Foreign Ownership," May 18, 2007, http://www.thestrategiccounsel.com/our_news/polls/2007-05-18%20GMCTV%20May%2014-17.pdf; accessed October 24, 2010. Reproduced with permission.

but rather from participants in the democratic process. These are political leaders and groups who win elections, take power, and then manipulate the mechanisms of democracy to curtail or destroy democracy.[16]

What is important, however, is that Western political scientists do not simply suppose that their own perceived virtues of Western liberal democracies are necessary for other countries to adopt in their entirety or that they are readily transferable to other, ancient cultures.

IDENTITY POLITICS

An individual's self-identification is profoundly personal and yet has enormous political relevance. How we view ourselves and who we believe ourselves to be are matters of complex psychological evolution over the course of our lives. One of the strongest human inclinations we develop is to identify ourselves with some group, or several groups, to which we feel we belong. Humans are social, gregarious animals, and most of us are naturally inclined to interact with others. Speaking in general terms, we seem to have a need to be part of a group. Most of us have many sides to our personalities and a range of interests, and as a result we associate with different groups at different times to match different aspects of our character. Some of the groups we identify ourselves with have little political significance, such as a group of friends who share a love of snowboarding. But we may also identify ourselves with other groups that can at times have real political significance.

Identity politics draws attention to ways in which political power is structured around group politics in society. The term **identity politics** (or the politics of difference) describes political activity by particular groups looking for recognition of their status and identity, as introduced in Chapter 3; such groups wish to see acknowledgment of the ways their beliefs and value systems differ from others in their society. Thus, Canadian political philosopher Charles Taylor has argued that a "number of strands in contemporary politics turn on the need, sometimes demand, for *recognition.*"[17] Examples include women's rights movements, minority rights groups, Aboriginal movements, movements for the rights of disabled persons, and gay and lesbian rights movements. Another example is seen in the political debate launched in Canada when the 1987 Meech Lake Accord proposed that Quebec be recognized as a "distinct society."

Of particular importance is a group's belief about how its members are treated, as a group, by the rest of society (see Box 5.1). For many groups, a prime struggle is to create and project a positive identity to counteract negative stereotypes of them created by other groups in their society. This process may involve finding ways for individual members of the group to develop a new positive self-esteem, as well as the group acting collectively to create in others a positive, respectful image of them.

For many people, group identity and membership creates the framework for meaningful choices made by an individual: who we are, the values and goals we possess, and where we stand in society are given to us by our culture and history. Culture, therefore, is not simply the sum of individual values. Attachments such as gender, sexual orientation, class, and ethnicity define

BOX 5.1

CLASS IDENTITY AND FALSE CONSCIOUSNESS

Class is a concept that describes the hierarchical layers within a society that result from different levels of wealth, income, occupation, and social status. Social scientists distinguish between objective class levels, which are often measured based on income, and subjective class levels, which is the class people say they identify themselves as belonging to. The difference between objective class and subjective class is striking in Canada, where there are enormous disparities in income spread across the population but where the overwhelming majority of citizens identify themselves as "middle class." As a result, class conflict is largely absent from Canada's political scene. Countries such as Poland or Brazil, where a significant number of people possess **class consciousness** and identify themselves as "working class" and even "lower class," have much more polarized political systems and much higher levels of support for left-wing political parties than in North America.

Marxists talk about "false consciousness" in situations where poor people have been socialized into believing they are middle class so that they are unlikely to organize and change the existing social and economic order. The Marxist critique is that members of the objective working class falsely identify with a higher class and therefore are not aware of the "true interests" of the group to which they really belong.

The issue of false consciousness and ignorance of one's own group's true interests is a controversial one but it can be applied to most characteristics upon which identity is based. For example, does each group based on ethnicity, gender, sexual orientation, religion, and so on have an objective set of true interests that everyone who belongs to the group should be aware of and pursue? If so, who gets to decide what those interests are?

BOX 5.2

CHECK YOUR OWN IDENTITY

Think about how you think of yourself. The questions that follow, and your answers to them, should give you some idea of the importance of how you view yourself. You should also have a clearer idea of the impact on you of other people's views of who you are.

- Your parents gave you a name at birth. Do you like it, dislike it, or not care much? Why? Are you still called by that name, or do people call you by a short form of it (e.g., Jo instead of Joanne) or by a nickname? If the name you are called has changed, did you initiate the change or have you lived with what others decided to call you? Do different groups of people call you different variations of your name? What significance would there be in that?
- How many different defining characteristics do you think of yourself as having? For starters, think about religion, language, gender, sexual orientation, ethnic background(s), body size and shape, attractiveness, physical abilities, the neighbourhood or town you grew up in, how much money you have, etc.
- Have you ever felt you have received privileged treatment because of who you are? Have you been singled out for poor treatment because of a personal characteristic someone else did not like?
- What sorts of negative things that people have said about who or what you are have hurt you? How difficult has it felt to try to change other people's negative views of you?
- What things about yourself would you not change, even if it meant putting up with abuse from other people?

an individual's place in society and, as such, constitute part of one's culture (see Box 5.2). This is a very different view from the dominant liberal view of culture and groups. Liberalism separates the individual from his or her community and culture; it treats culture as an aggregate of the beliefs and values of individuals. From the perspective of liberalism, communities exist only insofar as they find expression in the values and beliefs of individuals.[18]

The politics of identity is about more than merely wanting to be valued. Achieving the respect of others is just the first step in trying to participate in the political system on a more equal basis. In many respects, identity groups are reacting against existing political structures in which a dominant culture, espousing the language of universalism, attempts to deny the importance of the particular circumstances and values—particularism—of those groups. This denial of difference is a way for the dominant culture to exercise political power and control over these groups. Identity politics and the politics of difference, in effect, represent a demand for greater political power by groups in society through the recognition of their different identities and value systems. This demand for political power is usually framed in the language of "rights."

Universalism does not recognize differences among people in the granting of rights and maintains that everyone should be treated equally and in exactly the same manner, irrespective of differences in gender, religion, sexual orientation, ethnicity, and history. The focus is on individual rights—rights that apply to all individuals equally. The purpose of these rights is to guarantee that everyone gets equal treatment in politics and in law. The particularism advocated by many identity groups, on the other hand, is based on the argument that real equality cannot be achieved without recognizing the value of differences and according differential rights on the basis of group membership. The focus here is on collective rights or group-differentiated rights. The purpose is to overcome the vulnerability and disadvantage of certain groups—to help them acquire the ability to make choices.

Historically marginalized groups such as African-Americans, people with disabilities, or Aboriginal people have not just striven for recognition and respect from the larger society—they also desire to be full participants in their society and to effectively pursue their own interests. The politics of identity involve groups seeking political goals related to fostering those things that give them a distinct identity. For example, francophone parents across Canada have sought the establishment of French-language schools so that their children may learn the language and cultural heritage of their group. These parents believe that French schools will help preserve and foster the most important things that set their group apart from the rest of society.

Thus, there is a continuing controversy in modern politics about how to balance individual equality with special treatment for particular groups. Should a group receive special benefits to foster the characteristics that give its members their identity, or should all groups be treated equally? Some advocates argue that to treat different groups in very different circumstances with absolute equality only serves to perpetuate the existing inequalities between the groups. To achieve substantive equality between groups, one has to treat them in ways that account for their differences. A current example of this dilemma in Canada relates to Aboriginal self-government. Many critics of self-government argue that it offends the principle of equality by creating a particular form of government for one "race" when all other races in Canada belong to a common political system. (Note the discussion on the contemporary and historical usage of the term *race* in Chapter 3.)

Others counter that it is race that has created the disadvantages that so many Aboriginal people face, and that a "race-based" government is actually the best solution to a cultural problem. Will Kymlicka has forcefully argued that modern liberalism can and should adapt equality to allow for special treatment that fosters a group's cultural identity.[19] This is justified on the grounds that individuals fully develop only within the context of their group memberships, and thus by providing different benefits required by the circumstances of different groups (particularly minority groups), one is fostering the development of all individuals in society. The difficulty that modern politicians face in many countries is finding a way to accommodate the claims and needs of different groups while still ensuring that the common good is furthered. As Kenneth Hoover has written, "democracy becomes an exercise in balancing particular sources of distinctiveness and individual difference against the universal needs of all citizens."[20]

Many feminist writers have argued that women can be truly free only if public policies take into account the inherent differences between the genders. The social context and basic characteristics of women are said to be so different from those of men that to treat men and women exactly the same would perpetuate the subordination of women and deny them the ability to develop. Carole Pateman puts it this way: "Women's equal standing must be accepted as an expression of the freedom of women *as women*, and not treated as an indication that women can be just like men."[21]

However, there is a lively political and academic debate over just what really are the distinguishing characteristics of women that should be accommodated. The social, economic, and political discrimination faced by women can be assessed, but it is much more difficult to determine whether there are innate attitudinal and behavioural characteristics that define women that go beyond those acquired through millennia of socialization into caregiver roles. Carol Gilligan is one feminist theorist who believes there are essential characteristics that are part of women's nature and identity.[22] Simone de Beauvoir, however, has written, "One is not born a woman, but rather becomes a woman."[23] The key point here is the enormous political significance of current debates about the identity of women.

The most potent aspect of the politics of identity and difference arises when a group believes that it is a distinct cultural nation that needs greater political control over its own affairs. Most states today are **multination states**, in that they contain more than one distinct cultural nation. A group's pride in their cultural nation—nationalism—can be a powerful force if it does not have an effective outlet within the political structures of their country. Many groups demand greater political autonomy to control matters of direct importance to them, usually because they believe their interests are continually sacrificed in favour of other, more dominant groups in their country. The drive for self-determination, and ultimately political independence, is founded on a very strong national identity and a belief that members of the nation cannot develop their group's identity, values, and needs by remaining just as one of several other groups within the existing state. Quebec nationalism is a staple of Canadian politics, and Quebec's quest for independence has become an established part of Canadian politics ever since the Parti Québécois was first elected as the provincial government in 1976. An important milestone was reached in Canadian politics of identity when the House of Commons passed a motion in 2006 that recognized the Québécois as a "nation within a united Canada." Canada is lucky that most of the politics of self-determination for Quebec has played out relatively peacefully. Many civil wars have broken out across the globe as one minority group or another struggled to establish a separate state of its own. Bangladesh and Eritrea are only two examples of states that arose from civil wars aimed at the independence of a group.

While identity politics is a potent force, it is important not to overstate the phenomenon. The difficulty is that since all individuals have many characteristics that form their identity, they may belong to a wide variety of groups. A particular issue, such as abortion or affirmative action, may incline one to identify with the group most relevant for the moment, but another issue will find most of us identifying with a different group—or none at all. Postmodernism is a perspective on society that underlines the complexity of both individuals and society taken as a whole. In this view, it is unsound to reduce political behaviour to simple, enduring categories. Since identities are multidimensional, many people are motivated to find new ways of expressing and identifying themselves over time and across issues. Whole new social movements, such as environmentalism, are spawned as a result.

POLITICAL CLEAVAGES

Some group identities endure, and the prevailing attitudes and beliefs of that group are relevant across a wide range of public policy issues. As noted in Chapters 11 and 12, political **cleavages** arise in a society when there are enduring differences between groups within a society over political values, perspectives, and objectives. Many cleavages may occur at the same time in a society, according to gender, religion, socioeconomic class, language, ethnicity, and even ideology. Depending on what causes these cleavages, how deeply entrenched they are, and how opposed they are in outlook, a country may simply have a richly diverse political culture or be destabilized into civil war. Much also depends on the reaction to the political cleavages of political leaders of both the larger society and of the groups involved. In general, there are four broadly different strategies for reacting to political cleavages in a society.

First, there may be an attempt to actively foster a single overarching culture. While subgroups may continue to exist, their members may come to identify even more strongly with the general culture. The melting pot of the United States is one example: significant cleavages exist within American society, but they are minimized by the overarching patriotism and attachment to America as a whole. A common "American" identity is layered on top of other group identities.

A second strategy may be to recognize the cleavages and try to accommodate them by fostering mutual tolerance and respect. In essence, the multicultural policies of Canadian federal governments have successfully defused the most negative resentment toward immigration by hailing as a virtue the cultural diversity brought by immigrants to the country. This approach fosters **cultural pluralism**, which means not only that are there strong subcultures within a society, but also that they are fostered and accommodated as a positive aspect of the political culture.

A third approach involves designing the country's political structures to accommodate the most significant cleavages within the institutional framework. In this way, the subgroups are more inclined to pursue their objectives within the existing state structure than to aim for independence and the breakup of the country. **Federal** systems of government are a common choice of institutional design in countries where significant cleavages coincide with geographic regions. The main idea of federations is to allow considerable variation at the regional level of the public policies most important to the different provincial or state societies. In essence, as in the case of the division of powers between the federal and provincial governments in Canada, control of issues central to the regional cultures can be given to those communities while still ensuring common national policies for other matters.

A fourth approach to political cleavages involves actively repressing the subgroups in violent or nonviolent ways, which means trying to stamp out the cleavages. This may take the form of prohibiting the use of a language or practice of a particular religion. In Canada's history, there is a shameful reminder of this approach, where for several generations Canadian governments tried to eliminate the Aboriginal cultures by teaching Native people to behave like white people. Thousands of children were taken away from their families at a young age and taught to dress, act, and speak like those of European descent. **Genocide** or **ethnic cleansing** by forcible expulsion are the most extreme forms of dealing with cultural cleavages, aimed at simply eliminating all those who belong to the subgroup.

Another important issue arising from deep political cleavages is the question of how the groups involved respond to the approaches taken by the government. If a group believes strongly that the current situation is likely to lead to its continued subordination or even extinction by dominant groups, then a country will in all likelihood face significant political turmoil.

POLITICAL SOCIALIZATION: MOULDING THE MIND

If political cultures and identities are so important, the following questions arise: How are they formed? What processes create dominant beliefs and attitudes among large groups of people? The answers lie in one of the most important social phenomena of human existence. The sharing and propagating of attitudes, knowledge, values, and other beliefs are fundamental processes that create human societies. While the net result may be measured on a collective, group-wide level, the process occurs bit by bit on each individual member of the society. Wide ranges of influences and forces are at work throughout our lives to shape us into the people we become. The sum of those forces on all of the members of a community is what eventually creates its general culture.

Most of us would like to think of ourselves as essentially self-made individuals. We might recognize and appreciate the influence of parents and perhaps of a few key teachers and friends along the way, but overall we would like to believe that we are the people we are principally because of choices we have made for ourselves. But are we really self-made? What kinds of influences, both direct and unseen, have really moulded us and structured the range of choices that we feel we have made for ourselves? How many of our individual beliefs and attitudes are actually the product of other people's choices about what we should or

should not believe? In reality, it is clear that individual members of any society are shaped by a lifelong process through which cultural, moral, and political values are shared and passed on and through which a group's culture is fostered.

Political socialization is the process through which political knowledge, attitudes, and beliefs are transmitted within a society. It is important to note that political socialization is not necessarily only about explicitly political attitudes and values, such as "Capitalism is good." It also involves broader cultural and social values, such as views of the role of women, which can also have political implications. Through this process, most of us come to share certain core values and identify ourselves as members of a larger group or community. It is also through political socialization that the preferred values of particular groups and individuals within society are acquired by or even imposed on others.

> **Political socialization:** The process through which attitudes toward and knowledge about political matters are passed on within a society.

The values of a political culture are passed on as new people enter the society, either as immigrants or as native-born children. People born and raised in Argentina, China, India, Kenya, Russia, Taiwan, and Canada likely have had a different upbringing, which results in adults with many different attitudes. The whole environment and context in which we grow up has a tremendous effect on what we believe to be right and wrong and on the principles we regard highly and value above others. This socialization has its most profound impact during childhood years, but our political values and knowledge continue to be shaped throughout the rest of our lives.

Political socialization can work through several processes, with knowledge and beliefs being either deliberately expounded or passively transmitted. The deliberate sharing of ideas might occur, for example, when a parent or teacher tells a child how to behave or what to think. The lesson might be as benign as "Share your lunch with someone who doesn't have any," or it might be a more potent one such as "Remember who your people are and that the rulers are our enemies." Knowledge and beliefs can also be spread through imitation. It is common for people to imitate, sometimes unconsciously, role models whom they admire. Charismatic political and religious leaders, or even peers, are often imitated in how they treat others and in what they have to say about society. Many people also learn ideas about gender roles simply from seeing how their parents interact over the years.

Agents of Political Socialization

There are countless ways in which political socialization occurs, but specific **agents of political socialization** can be identified as having a role to play in an individual's life. It is primarily through these that an individual acquires particular knowledge, attitudes, and beliefs about the political world. Given the potential impact on political systems, it is perhaps curious that political scientists do not undertake more serious study of the socialization process; indeed, political socialization is more usually the province of sociologists, anthropologists, and psychologists.[24] Political scientists, however, do concern themselves quite frequently with the consequences of socialization. For example, studies of voting patterns often examine whether there are correlations between the choice of political party and the specific social attributes of the voters, such as income, education, religion, or gender, as discussed in Chapters 11 and 12. A brief examination of the principal agents of political socialization, which follows, will give you an idea of the powerful forces that can mould our views of society throughout the course of our lives, and it will illustrate how relevant political socialization can be to the study of politics.

> **Agents of political socialization:** Those groups of people or institutions that convey political attitudes and values to others in society.

The Family Undoubtedly, family is one of the most fundamental influences on an individual's outlook on politics. Children learn all sorts of political lessons from their families in both direct and indirect ways. The most overt way in which families may act as agents of political socialization is through explicit training, when parents engage in active, deliberate instruction on the political values to hold, the political parties or leaders to support, and the ways to participate in the political process. From an early age, children are aware of their parents' partisan preferences, and parents who are politically active become clear role models. Such politically active parents may also take their young children along to party functions or political demonstrations. In many families, countless hours around a dining table are spent discussing views about the political leaders and events of the day.

Children also acquire important beliefs from their families about their group identities and common enemies, both of which can have profound political implications later in life. From their family upbringing, individuals may develop strong views about the place of their group in the larger society and the wrongs their group has suffered. Nationalist movements have as their basis a commonly held belief among a large collection of individuals that they form a distinctive group; this belief is usually created and instilled on the family level. It is not an exaggeration to say that many civil wars started because of what children learned from their families.

The political socialization role of families, however, is not limited to such overt political instruction. Children also learn in subtle ways an enormous amount about how decisions are made within a group. The parental figures in the family may make authoritative decisions without consulting the children, or children may learn from an early age that they are entitled to voice their opinion and participate in a "family conference," in which important decisions are reached collectively. In either case, the children are learning about decision-making. In countless ways, children learn from their families which social and moral principles they should value and uphold, and these in turn have many political dimensions. For example, some children may be actively taught to engage in acts of charity toward strangers; they may be given to understand that it is a good thing for those with more to share with those who have less. On the other hand, family members may believe and teach their children that it is only important to help one's relatives and close friends; they may feel they have no responsibility to help others in need, as those people must be responsible for themselves. These opposing views are examples of how children learn from their families about their relationship and responsibility to others in their community.

Everyday family dynamics also teach children a great deal about social hierarchy, deference to authority, obedience to rules, and acquiescence in judgments they do not support. There is a kernel of truth to the charge that all children are born into totalitarian regimes. Parents and other caregivers have total control over the lives of infants, and many only reluctantly and incompletely give up trying to exercise that degree of control as the children grow older. Just about every child cries out at some point in complaint against a parent's decision, "That's not fair!" And in doing so, children are expressing volumes about a conception of justice and fair process they have started to develop from a very tender age. Most children in Western families today are raised in an environment where they are encouraged, as they grow older, to voice their own opinions and question the views of their adult caregivers. Freedom of expression and a sense of personal autonomy are usually ingrained into Canadian children as a matter of course.

Families around the world lay the foundation for different understandings of gender roles—for example, on the question of how active and vocal females should be in their society—by the role taken by the mother in relation to the father (if present in

the family) or by the different opportunities given to the sons rather than daughters. Patriarchy has its social roots in the family, but those roots spread out in many ways into the political system. The Victorian-era family supposedly gave the father total final decision-making powers, and that reflected the predominant male view of the time that women were simply unsuited to vote in elections, let alone hold political office. As the patriarchal family model has begun to erode in Western countries, the place of women in society has also changed. The cultural gender roles learned at home can have a huge impact on people's attitudes towards the role of women in politics. For example, an international survey conducted in 2005 and 2006 found that a majority of people in China, Russia, and Turkey agreed that men make better politicians than women. In contrast, over 80 percent of Britons, Canadians, and Italians disagreed. It is interesting to note that the connection between family and political views of gender roles is underlined by the fact that 85 to 90 percent of Chinese and Turkish respondents say they disapprove of single mothers, while only a minority of Britons, Canadians, and Italians do.[25]

The life lessons that children learn in the family can flow directly into the general political culture. Table 5.3 shows quite a range in views about family life that came from international surveys conducted in 1999 and 2000. At one extreme, 90 percent of Mexicans believe that parents should be loved and respected regardless of what they do. Mexicans also placed relatively high importance on teaching children to be obedient and unselfish in the family. By contrast, 40 percent of Germans felt that parents need to earn the love and respect of their children, and they placed very little emphasis on teaching children obedience and selflessness in the family. One would expect Mexican and German political cultures, then, to reflect these differences in family life, with the Mexicans more deferential and obedient to government authority and the Germans much more individualistic. Indeed, the modern history of authoritarian politics in Mexico and hotly contested elections in Germany are consistent with these divergent sets of values. In the same surveys, 54 percent of Mexicans agreed that it was a good idea to have "a strong leader who does not have to bother with parliament and elections," while only 19 percent of Germans agreed.

"This is America, son. You can grow up to be anything I want you to be."

Mark Anderson/Artizans

Table 5.3 Attitudes Toward Families

An international survey asked people questions about the following beliefs:

Country	DUTY TO LOVE AND RESPECT PARENTS		IMPORTANT QUALITIES FOR CHILDREN TO LEARN AT HOME INCLUDE:		
	Always	If Earned	Independence	Obedience	Unselfishness
Argentina	87.9	13.2	37.0	37.0	12.7
Britain	64.6	35.4	53.4	46.8	60.3
Canada	79.2	20.8	62.0	31.1	45.6
Egypt	95.2	4.8	72.6	53.2	21.6
France	75.2	24.8	29.0	36.4	40.2
Germany	60.0	40.0	69.7	13.9	8.7
India	88.8	11.2	56.2	55.7	36.6
Italy	79.4	20.6	41.4	20.3	41.4
Japan	71.6	28.4	81.6	4.3	53.2
Mexico	90.0	10.0	44.4	58.6	48.7
Philippines	93.6	6.4	68.2	44.4	38.3
Russia	84.6	15.3	29.6	34.4	20.6
South Africa	90.8	9.2	58.4	55.4	32.2
Sweden	43.0	57.0	68.6	12.2	33.2
United States	77.3	22.7	62.0	32.3	39.1

Source: Data are from the European Values Study Group and World Values Survey Association.

Educational Institutions The next major influence on a person's development is usually the school. Educational institutions can be very powerful agents of political socialization. In the most transparent instance, schools deliver a curriculum developed by the government to deliberately indoctrinate children with a particular set of views. This is clearly seen in authoritarian countries, where the ruling party ensures that the official dogmas of the party are taught throughout the school years. Yet similar processes occur in democratic countries—even if the indoctrination is far less visible and not implemented to the same degree. State school authorities usually set the official curriculum guidelines for material taught in the main subjects offered in public schools—and often in private schools as well. This curriculum includes not just a sanctioned view of the society's history but also much material that has political implications, even if it is not directly political.

Students in Canada are exposed to many different messages during their school years that lead them to accept the importance of individual freedoms and personal autonomy. Tolerance of diverse cultures and religions is another social norm instilled in students that has significant implications for political culture in both Canada and the United States. Just as significant is what is not taught in school. For example, few American or Canadian secondary school graduates will have ever studied Marx and Engels' *The Communist Manifesto*; capitalist free enterprise is simply accepted as the norm in North American schools, and only a few students are exposed to teachings that seriously envision alternative forms of organizing society and the economy. Instead, many corporations are making inroads into schools through product placement and advertising.

Schools have important socializing effects in many informal ways as well. The structure of classroom time and the interaction between students and their teachers can both serve as political models. A class that is structured in an informal setting, with students able to get up and move around or talk to other students, provides a very different sense of liberty than does a classroom where students may never move or speak without permission. Students who use a teacher's first name will have a different notion of equality and social hierarchy than those who must call their teachers "master," "madam," or "sir." The degree to which discipline is kept in the school through verbal abuse or corporal punishment can leave strong impressions on school children about the importance of deferring to or obeying authority. For that matter, however, overly strict or cruel discipline may incline students to grow up resentful of authority and make them ready to rebel.

Something as simple as teaching students to inquire and make up their own minds, rather than simply learn by rote memorization, can have consequences for the political culture. In schools and universities in many authoritarian states, students have been taught from a single thick book that contains all they need to memorize about that subject. Learning becomes a matter of simply absorbing, accepting, and repeating the official position. Citizens in such countries have a very different starting point from which to assess their government's actions than people who have grown up learning that there are many different views and interpretations on important subjects and that their own opinion is valued.

The influence of the school is so significant that across the Western industrialized world increasing education levels correlate with greater political interest and participation, as well as with more liberal attitudes on civil rights and social welfare issues.[26] However, this raises the question of whether it is education per se that has this effect, or whether these liberal values are so common among Western educators and so consistently propagated that the longer individuals are exposed to these views, the more likely they are to absorb them. Some of the most important differences in attitudes relate to the amount (if any) of postsecondary education that individuals have had. This makes particular sense in Western democracies, where universities and colleges usually present quite a different style of learning and intellectual inquiry than students experienced in their earlier schooling.

The Media The **mass media**, in their broadest sense of "the means of mass communication," include radio, television, and newspapers, as well as books, movies, music, and the Internet. Taken together, a country's media have the power to provide an important part of the cultural glue that defines that society's culture. The media provide some of the most powerful means of reinforcing common values and beliefs that create a nation's sense of identity. The media play a central role in conveying political attitudes, beliefs, and knowledge among not just the members of one society, but also across societies around the world. Whether it is news broadcasts of political developments or debates over opposing views, much of what we come across on television, radio, and in newspapers frames what we think we know about political issues and causes. In media coverage of political issues, what is not said is just as important as what is said. An enormous amount of filtering occurs as to what issues or events are reported in the first place, as well as in the kind of coverage they receive. To understand the role of the media in modern society is to understand a lot about that society. As Marshall McLuhan (1911–1980) put it, "The medium is the message."

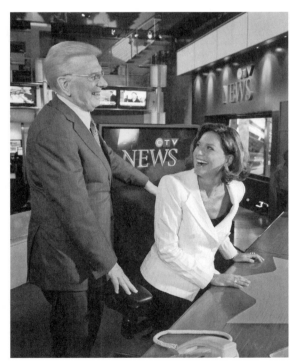

Lisa LaFlamme sits in the anchor's chair as CTV announces that she will succeed Lloyd Robertson as anchor of the CTV News.

The Canadian Press(Adrien Veczan)

Noam Chomsky is the best-known living critic of the media and their ability to shape a society's knowledge and understanding of political events. In a series of stinging commentaries, Chomsky has argued that one of the principal roles of the media is to manufacture consent among the masses for the existing social and political order and to control what people are told about the world around them.[27]

The power of the media to influence society's political views is most clearly demonstrated in different relationships between the media and the government found across the globe (see Table 5.4). In many countries of the world the state owns and controls all media organizations so that the only views and information that get publicly disseminated are those that the rulers of that society want people to know. In other countries, media corporations may be in private hands, but the government still exercises close supervision and censorship of the content, again to prevent the publication of facts and opinions that undermine

the rulers' control of their society. At the other end of the scale is the value placed in established democracies on ensuring that the state does not censor or control the media in a general way. In these countries, because of an acceptance of the media's ability to profoundly shape people's knowledge and perceptions, freedom of expression in the media is a cornerstone of the society's culture. The more sources of information and the more perspectives citizens can draw from, the better they are able to form their own opinions on political events and issues.

Events in early 2002 show that the importance of getting the right message across in the media is not lost on either autocratic or democratic governments. Zimbabwe enacted legislation barring foreign news agencies from basing reporters in that country; in addition, local journalists are required to apply each year to the Minister of Information for a permit, which can be refused if the government disapproves of their work. In the United States, the Department

---

Table 5.4 Ranking of Selected Countries on Press Freedom

Freedom House ranks the countries of the world according to the freedom under which the news media operate. The categories indicate the level of restrictions put on journalists and media companies by governments, as well as other factors, such as the concentration of ownership.

FREE (1–30)		PARTLY FREE (31–60)		NOT FREE (61–100)	
Finland	10	South Africa	32	Pakistan	61
Sweden	10	Hong Kong	33	Malaysia	64
Belgium	12	India	33	Morocco	66
Switzerland	13	Italy	33	Singapore	68
New Zealand	14	Brazil	43	Sri Lanka	72
Jamaica	16	Philippines	48	Venezuela	75
Germany	17	Tanzania	50	Afghanistan	76
United States	18	Turkey	51	Yemen	80
Canada	19	Tanzania	51	Russia	81
Britain	19	Indonesia	52	Vietnam	82
Japan	21	Ukraine	53	Saudi Arabia	83
Australia	22	Nigeria	54	China	84
Slovakia	23	Kuwait	55	Zimbabwe	84
Taiwan	24	Thailand	58	Iran	89
Ghana	26	Egypt	60	Cuba	93
South Korea	30	Mexico	60	North Korea	99

Source: Freedom House, Freedom of the Press 2010 Global Rankings, cited on November 6, 2010. Reprinted with permission from Freedom House.

of Defence was forced to close down its Office of Strategic Influence after only two months of operations, once it became clear that one of its prime missions was to provide disinformation to foreign news agencies as part of the campaign against terrorism.

Given the important role that the media have in informing people about political events and opinions, it is crucial to understand that the coverage of news and views that actually does occur is very incomplete, even within democracies. Only a relatively small number of stories can be covered in any one radio or TV broadcast. Newspaper editors have a finite number of column inches to devote to news items. On any given day, news editors must face choices about which stories to cover, which to ignore, and how much coverage to give to the stories they do choose to report on; they also have to find a balance between local, provincial or state, national, and international stories. Inevitably, many stories that do get reported are greatly simplified to fit time or space constraints. The creation of news reports is far too often a matter of producers deciding what "take" their reporters should follow on the story so that the finished report will reflect the views of those producers.

A number of studies reveal that the media consistently fail to report on certain newsworthy issues and that their coverage often favours one side of an issue over another. For example, the views of business may predominate over the views of unions. Furthermore, from time to time editors kill stories initiated by individual reporters because they cast a negative light on associates of the media corporation's owners or—more often—on those who pay for advertising. Journalists often engage in self-censorship because of a fear of repercussions, such as becoming targets of intimidation or death threats if they investigate widespread corruption in the corridors of power or the activities of organized crime. In many countries of the world, journalists are arrested, beaten, or killed by government forces if their stories become too critical of the ruling party. Self-censorship may also occur because a reporter does not want to lose important contacts and informants. Reporters who cover their local police forces are particularly vulnerable, since a negative story on some police officers' activities can quickly dry up their sources for the inside scoops they rely on when covering general criminal activity.

Canadians put a high value on a free press and impartiality in news reporting. The freedom of the press is usually seen as freedom from government control and censorship. Even where all the media organizations are not owned by the government in some countries, potential media owners or journalists must get the permission of the government. This permission is not simply the technical broadcast licensing we think of in Canada, but actually provides the real opportunity for a government to stifle those who would be critical. At various times many countries have practised official censorship, where scripts of news and even entertainment shows must be approved by government censors; material that is considered either immoral or politically controversial would not be allowed. However, freedom from government control does not mean that a newspaper or TV station will be fair and impartial in its coverage of current events. Where the media are privately owned, the companies aim first and foremost to make a profit; the editors will publish the news that sells and overlook or ignore material that would lead to a drop in public viewers or advertisers. Few media owners would allow their companies to champion for long positions that vilify the owners' personal political or economic interests. Such biases are, in a sense, inevitable, and may be balanced in a competitive media market by alternative perspectives and stories covered by different media.

In many countries, the concentration of media ownership can provide very little competition in news reporting. Where the main media sources are owned by one or two companies, the public will be presented with little range of news stories and perspectives. For example, by the late 1990s three media chains controlled two-thirds of all daily newspaper circulation in Canada,[28] and many dailies had a complete monopoly on local news in their communities. A significant shift in media ownership occurred in Canada in 2000 and again in 2010. CanWest Global transformed itself into Canada's largest owner of daily newspapers in 2000 when it bought most of the newspapers and Internet sites owned by Conrad Black's Hollinger and Southam companies. CanWest Global controlled a vast media empire, with the largest group of newspapers in Canada, as well as the Global TV system and a range of specialty cable channels. The economic recession in the next decade, however, took its toll, and CanWest Global was split and sold off in 2010. The Global TV network was bought by Shaw Communications, while the newspaper assets were bought by a newly formed company, Postmedia Network, founded by a group of

Table 5.5 Daily Newspaper Market in Canada, 2006		
Corporation	Average Weekly Circulation	Percentage of Total
CanWest (now Postmedia)	8,198,500	30.5
Quebecor/Sun Media	6,354,458	23.7
Torstar	3,181,200	11.8
Power	3,064,517	11.4
CTVGlobemedia	1,891,629	7.0
FP Canadian Newspapers	999,246	3.7
Transcontinental	650,749	2.4
Halifax Herald	751,474	2.8
Brunswick News	547,161	2.0
Continental Newspapers	332,984	1.2
Independents	310,423	1.2
Glacier Canadian	267,189	1.0
Alberta Newsgroup	210,348	0.8
Black Press	90,667	0.3
Total	26,850,545	100.0

Source: Newspapers Canada. "Circulation Data Report 2009," p. 15. Reproduced with permission.

CanWest's creditors. Postmedia kept the newspaper holdings together and, as a result, became Canada's largest publisher of newspapers. As Table 5.5 shows, CanWest accounted for 30 percent of total daily newspaper circulation in 2009.

Shaw's purchase of CanWest's television assets sparked a fresh debate about media consolidation in Canada. Shaw began as a cable company, simply carrying signals from other TV networks, but now it directly owns many channels. Bell Canada also expanded its media holdings, purchasing the CTV network in 2010. Rogers had previously bought CITY-TV in 2007. As communications moves further into handheld and wireless access in the 21st century, there is concern that wireless broadcasters may give preference to their own media, limiting the choice of wireless users.

However, consumers still retain an enormous range of choice in Canadian media, even after the latest rounds of consolidations. Unfortunately, Canadians tend to limit themselves to just a few news services. This results in one radio or TV station having a crushing lead in terms of listeners and viewers in any particular market. These few broadcast stations then end up having an enormous influence over the public, and the tangible value of the freedom of the press and multiple news outlets is eroded.

This trend may be reduced, however, by the diversification that the Internet has brought. Most North Americans now regularly include visits to Internet media sites as part of their daily routine. Indeed, as newspaper circulation has shrunk in the past decade, those newspapers have come to rely more and more on online readers to their websites for advertising income. This trend was highlighted in 2009 when the *Seattle Post-Intelligencer* stopped printing its daily newspaper and in favour of online content; this may have been a sound business choice, as the website was receiving 40 million page views per month by 2010.[29]

Surveys show that public attitudes toward the media involve a mixture of trust and wariness and that the public are more likely to believe news from some sources than from others. For example, a 2009 poll found that more Canadians trusted TV news (42 percent) than newspapers (23 percent), the radio (16 percent) or the Internet (11 percent); these trends hold up even for the 18- to 29-year-old

Table 5.6	**Attitudes Toward the Media**			
An international survey asked people how much confidence they have in the press.				
Country	A Great Deal	Quite a Lot	Not Very Much	None at All
Brazil	6.6	36.7	35.8	20.9
Britain	1.4	12.4	54.5	31.8
Canada	4.4	29.4	50.1	16.1
Egypt	11.2	53.6	25.3	9.9
France	2.1	36.4	42.1	19.3
Germany	2.2	27.2	54.9	15.8
India	36.2	39.6	18.8	5.4
Italy	1.5	23.6	59.9	15.0
Japan	7.6	67.0	23.4	2.0
Mexico	12.0	38.1	31.5	18.4
Russia	3.6	33.3	42.6	20.5
South Africa	17.4	43.5	30.8	8.3
Sweden	1.1	32.0	54.4	12.5
United States	2.4	21.5	59.9	14.8

Source: the European Values Study Group and World Values Survey Association. (revised from table 4.5 3e)

cohort.[30] The significance of this discrepancy is all the more important because Canadians rely far more heavily on TV than on newspapers as their primary news source. There are indications, however, that many people are becoming more sceptical of the media over time; Gallup surveys in the United States show a dramatic increase in the number of Americans who distrust the media to report events fairly and accurately, rising from 26 percent in 1976 to 57 percent in 2010.[31] Table 5.6 provides a comparison of attitudes toward the press in a number of countries. A comparison of Tables 5.4 and 5.6 shows that freedom from state control and censorship does not necessarily translate into public confidence that journalists are depicting events in a country fairly. It may also be that a more educated and politically aware population simply expects more from their media.

The tremendous globalization of mass communication in the late 20th century has also created a situation in which the media have a powerful role in lessening the traditional distinctiveness of some nations' cultures by spreading "alien" ideas, beliefs, and knowledge around the world. National cultures are constantly being reshaped by the adoption of ideas spread by the media. Starting in the mid-20th century, radio was deliberately used as a **propaganda** tool by both Western and communist states to beam broadcasts to each others' citizens, in hopes of providing a fresh view of the world to the other side. The later growth of television has superseded the impact of short-wave radio in reaching into the homes of people around the world. CNN now provides live TV broadcasts by satellite to every continent, and countless entertainment programs are dubbed into foreign languages to be watched by global audiences.

Propaganda: An organized attempt to spread beliefs through a communications campaign. It implies the use of exaggerated facts.

Television, however, is being supplanted in many ways by the Internet, which has a potential for global communication that can only be described as staggering. An estimated two billion people worldwide made use of the Internet by 2010, to which 77 percent of North Americans had access. The growth in Internet

Figure 5.2 Internet Usage by World Region

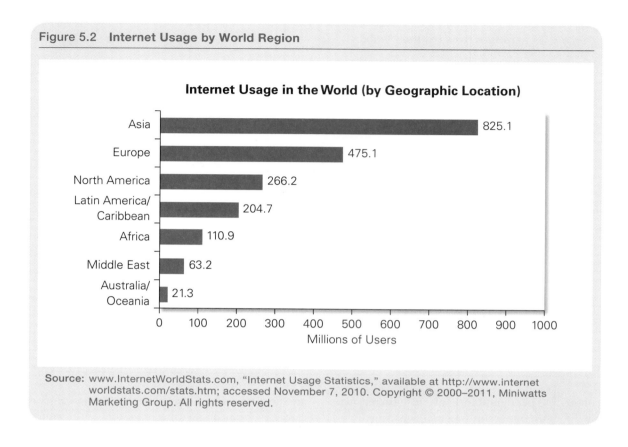

Internet Usage in the World (by Geographic Location)

Region	Millions of Users
Asia	825.1
Europe	475.1
North America	266.2
Latin America/Caribbean	204.7
Africa	110.9
Middle East	63.2
Australia/Oceania	21.3

usage has exploded in the last 10 years, with the number of people accessing it having grown by five times. By 2010, Asia and Europe counted many more Internet users than North America, and the worldwide patterns of Internet usage will continue to change significantly as the vast populations of Africa and Asia come on line in increasing numbers.[32] (See Figures 5.2 and 5.3.)

The Internet already serves as an alternative source for news and information and there is speculation that a kind of global cyber culture is emerging that may cause us to rethink basic ideas about the territorial basis of society. People's access to news used to be largely limited to their own community's media, but the Internet has created a whole wave of "citizen-journalists" who record their views for the world to read on their blogs. The rapid emergence of the "blogosphere" in the early 21st century not only multiplied, by millions, the number of viewpoints made available for all to read, but blogs have also circumvented government media restrictions around the world. During the current military engagements in Afghanistan and Iraq, for example, soldiers there from other countries have been recording their experiences and opinions on personal blogs, greatly undermining their governments' former tight control of information from battlefront areas.[33] Public blogs and more private discussion forums have created places for individuals across the globe to meet and, sometimes, collectively prepare for political action. Much of this activity has been relatively benign, but some has provided a locale for disaffected people who wish to organize violent protests or even significant acts of terrorism.

The growth of social media on the Internet has been a distinctive feature of the 21st century. Communities of friends, relatives, and like-minded strangers have erupted in both small and large scale. Although newsgroups and bulletin boards have existed since the early days of the Internet, the development of such massive communities as Facebook has radically changed how millions of people interact and share their views. Since its founding in 2004, Facebook has grown into a global phenomenon, with over 500 million users in 180 countries, interacting in more than 70 languages. The site has become much

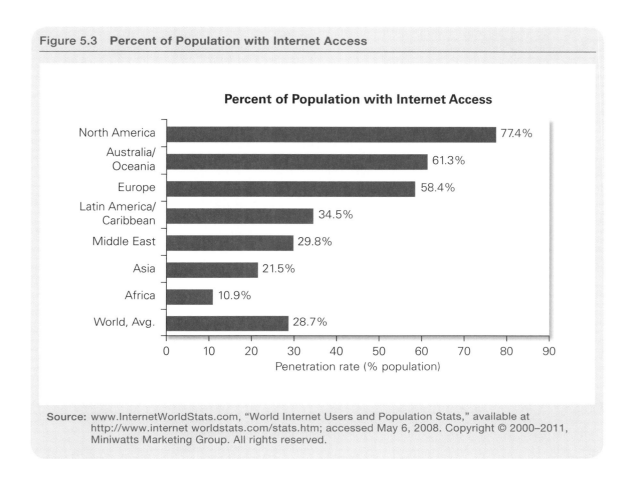

Figure 5.3   **Percent of Population with Internet Access**

Percent of Population with Internet Access

Region	Penetration rate (% population)
North America	77.4%
Australia/Oceania	61.3%
Europe	58.4%
Latin America/Caribbean	34.5%
Middle East	29.8%
Asia	21.5%
Africa	10.9%
World, Avg.	28.7%

more than simply a place to share photos and gossip.[34] People are able to meet, share views, and even organize real-world action through online groups at such sites. A milestone was reached when Canadians reacted angrily to Prime Minister Harper's prorogation of Parliament in late 2009. Over 200,000 people joined the Facebook group "Canadians Against Proroguing Parliament." Thousands protested this suspension of Parliament by attending rallies across the country on January 23, 2010 which were organized through this group.[35]

There is also a threat of an economic and cultural "digital divide" between those people who have ready access to information technology and those who do not. In contrast to the Internet access enjoyed by the majority of people in Canada and other industrialized countries, millions of impoverished people are unable to make use of the technology. In the developing world, Internet access remains, for the time being, a privilege of a very small minority.

Michael de Adder/Artizans

The powerful potential for the media to affect social change was vividly demonstrated in events in the Middle East in early 2011. Simmering discontent with authoritarian regimes in several countries reached a boiling point, and a call for collective action quickly spread through email, social media such as Facebook, and in the television reports of the Al Jazeera network. Virtual revolutions ignited mass protests that ousted the presidents of Tunisia and Egypt, as well as the uprising against the Gadhafi regime in Libya. The important role played by various media in these events was underlined by government attempts in Egypt and Libya to shut down Internet access completely. The Libyan government even jammed the satellite signal of Al Jazeera's broadcasts to North Africa in an attempt to stop the rebellion from spreading.

Religious Institutions Religious institutions may also play an important role as agents of political socialization. This idea may seem at first somewhat strange to people in Canada today, where we are used to accepting the general principle of the separation of church and state. It is widely believed in Canada that the state should not embrace one religion as the official religion of the society that is promoted above or to the exclusion of others. Furthermore, the separation of church and state means that religious institutions and leaders do not play an active role in the administration of government. Through religious teachings, however, individuals can learn about their role in society, their responsibility to others, the importance of tradition, tolerance or intolerance of other faiths, and the existence of higher duties that transcend any that secular authorities might try to impose. All of these beliefs have political implications. As well, followers of some religions acquire a very strong sense of group identity based on that religion, with strong cultural understandings of the history of that group and its place in the larger society. Perceived and actual wrongs inflicted by others in the same society on that religious group can have direct political consequences, such as providing a basis for nationalist aspirations. As Table 5.7 shows, significant numbers of people in many countries regularly partake in religious services.

Table 5.7	Attendance at Religious Services		
An international survey asked people how frequently they attend religious services.			
Country	At Least Monthly	Occasionally	Hardly Ever/Never
Brazil	65.1	29.2	5.8
Britain	23.5	30.0	46.6
Canada	34.2	31.1	34.7
Egypt	59.5	21.1	19.5
France	11.0	28.8	60.1
Germany	18.9	39.2	42.0
Ghana	88.8	7.9	3.3
India	58.7	37.2	4.2
Italy	54.2	34.1	11.7
Japan	9.8	79.4	10.8
Mexico	64.3	24.3	11.4
Russia	13.1	52.8	34.3
South Africa	69.3	17.1	13.6
Sweden	7.9	41.6	50.6
United States	48.9	25.5	25.6

Source: Data are from the European Values Study Group and World Values Survey Association.

Attending such services on a regular basis, one is much more likely to be influenced by the values espoused by one's religious leaders; after all, if one disagrees one is likely to stop attending.

Even with the formal separation of church and state in North America, we still see the interplay of religion and politics. In Canada, prayers are still part of many official functions, the Christian Lord's Prayer is still recited in some public schools, and ordained ministers and priests do occasionally hold elected office. In the United States, religion is an even bigger part of everyday politics, with many organized religious groups actively funding or campaigning for their favourite candidates and against their perceived enemies. These situations are nevertheless quite different from that in Great Britain, where the Church of England is the official church and where the queen or king, as head of state, is also the head of the church. Ironically, almost half of the British population hardly ever or never attend religious services. Nor can the North American situation compare with the one in Iran, where religious leaders have an official place in the constitution and are able to exercise political power. In some Latin American countries, social liberation theology leads many priests and their followers to expose brutal tactics of repression used by the government and wealthy landowners. As a result, some local Catholic churches become centres of political activity in ways not seen in Canada or the United States, and security forces actively target priests for intimidation or even assassination.

The power of religion has been well understood in states that try to prohibit all organized religion. Karl Marx once said religion is the opium of the people; he believed religion merely ensured that the workers of the world accepted their oppressed lot in society in anticipation of a better life after death. More practically, however, the belief in a higher divine authority may lead many devotees to disobey the laws of man. Thus, organized religions were banned in many communist countries as insidious elements that would otherwise undermine the creation of a socialist society. After all, a quest for freedom of religion might very easily snowball into demands for other freedoms, such as freedom of expression, which would have a direct bearing on the stability of the political regime.

Religious beliefs also provide a framework for people to understand and form opinions on a wide variety of controversial political issues, from abortion to same-sex marriage. For example, a 2010 poll found that gay marriage was opposed by 68 percent of Americans who attended religious services at least once a week, while it was supported by 59 percent of those who seldom or never attended.[36]

Perhaps the most vivid example of the political impact of religious values came when Islamic extremists hijacked four planes in September 2001 and crashed two of them into the World Trade Center towers in New York City and another into the Pentagon in Washington. Although the geopolitical circumstances of the Middle East were part of the motivation behind those actions, the hijackers became a new version of suicide bombers only because of their religious conviction that they were fighting a holy war and would be rewarded in the afterlife for their martyrdom. Anti-Americanism moved from being a political sentiment to a holy cause.

Peer Groups Peer groups can be very important agents of socialization even though they remain unorganized. Once children enter school, most of their experiences are shared by their friends. Throughout the rest of our lives, we share with our friends our thoughts and reactions, and their reactions, in turn, become an important framing for our assessment of what is right and wrong. By the late teenage and early adult years, peer groups come to play an increasingly important role in an individual's life. At election time, people end up having most of their discussions with their friends about political events and candidates. As a result, our peer groups become a crucial social context from which we learn new information about political events and where we debate political alternatives.

In our interactions with friends we practise important political principles, such as freedom of expression, but we also practise group conformity and exclusion of "others"; we may even defer to the unofficial leader of the group. While we may have a broad collection of different types of individuals within our circle of friends, there are strong pressures on individuals to "go with the flow" and do what is considered popular with the group. In addition, we tend to exclude or even ostracize individuals who "go too far" and stray beyond what the group tends to think of as acceptable attitudes and behaviour. These pressures are strongest and most visible in the teenage years, but carry on to some degree into later life.

The Workplace In North America, the workplace is not often thought of as being a political arena, yet there is much in our work life that has political import. Although it very much depends on the particular place of work, we can be exposed to many situations in our jobs that carry over into our political world.[37] For example, a rigidly hierarchical workplace gives people a very different sense of the importance of the individual, depending on whether they are at the top or at the bottom. If the lesson from work is to defer to the boss and acquiesce in authoritative decisions, we may carry this attitude with us into society in general. In contrast, based on experiences in a workplace where we are actively consulted and where we feel we can have meaningful input into collective decisions, we may be more inclined to become actively involved in the political affairs of our society.

An important minority of Canadians and Americans work in situations that are highly charged by adversarial union–employer dynamics. An active belief in the power of collective action through unions translates directly to the political world. Unions can be important sources of funds and volunteers for political parties that seek to change society and economic relations in ways that favour the workers. Pro-business parties and governments may inspire trade unions to actively support parties and governments that promise to implement policies favouring the country's workers instead of the country's industrialists. For example, there have been historically strong ties between organized labour in Canada and the New Democratic Party (NDP); in fact, trade unions even get to exercise formal votes in NDP conventions. A highly polarized workplace that pits rich bosses against poorly paid workers may actually have a politically energizing influence on the workers; the latter may see their poverty and exploitation as resulting from a political regime that ensures the continuing dominance of business people and corporate interests. Indeed, it was the highly exploitative setting of industries in the 19th century that provided the inspiration for Karl Marx and others after him to argue that the entire political, economic, and social orders must be swept away and replaced by ones organized on socialist or communist principles. The workplace may breed, not just political activism, but **revolution**!

State Actors State actors can act as agents of political socialization, propagating official views of the society in hopes of garnering support or acquiescence in government policies. Schools are one such state institution, as are state-owned media. All governments engage to some degree in publicity and propaganda, spreading their messages to the populace about what is good and proper in a political sense through pamphlets, media advertising, and public events. For example, successive Canadian governments since the 1970s have actively (and quite successfully) campaigned for Canadians to embrace multiculturalism as a central part of Canada's political culture.

A crucial element of most governments' mission is to foster—and sometimes even create—a distinct national identity for their country. An important part of this is the selection and promotion of symbols (such as flags and national anthems) and rituals (public holidays and celebrations) that promote a sense of pride in the country. American governments have been particularly successful in developing a strong sense of **patriotism**. The Canadian federal government took a series of measures in the 1960s and 1970s to develop a new set of Canadian symbols that distinguished Canada from its colonial past. In 1965, in a very controversial move at the time, the flag was changed from the one based on the British Union Jack to one focused on the maple leaf. Over the next few years, the government eliminated virtually all references to "Royal" in government institutions; for instance, the Royal Mail became Canada Post. One criticism of the Canadian government is that our problems with national unity may stem in part from a failure to develop an effective sense of Canadian patriotism (which some say would be rather un-Canadian anyway).

Patriotism: A sense of pride in one's country.

In some countries—democratic as well as nondemocratic—the military plays a crucial socialization role because almost every male is required to do a compulsory period of military service. In Israel, even women have to join. The military is able to indoctrinate, in both subtle and overt ways, vast numbers of citizens with views about the nature of the state, its society, and the duties of citizens to obey and defend.

Political parties also act as important agents of socialization. In authoritarian countries in particular, where only one party is allowed to exist and is made a part of everyday life, it can engage the citizens in many ways—for example, through newspapers, youth groups, neighbourhood activities, and sports clubs. In democratic countries, we do not tend to think of political parties as official state actors, and yet they are intimately tied to the political system and the process of governing. Political parties in every country can come to play central roles in the lives of those who are politically active, and these individuals acquire many beliefs and much information through party activities.

It should be clear by this point that there are many forces at work within a society that combine to mould individuals and ensure that most members of society come to accept common attitudes and beliefs. Where the same set of messages is reinforced by multiple agents—such as the family, school, friends, and the media—it is far more likely that people within a particular community will hold common attitudes and beliefs without serious questioning. Socialization may be a straightforward process of indoctrination, effectively brainwashing people to revere certain beliefs and revile others, but the socialization process that any one individual goes through usually is as much about the individual's reaction to the messages as it is about the messages themselves. This explains why members of the same family raised in much the same way and living within the same community can have very different views about political issues and principles. Nevertheless, we are all shaped by a multitude of agents of political socialization to become in some ways very much what others have wanted us to become, while still becoming in other ways what we ourselves have actually chosen to become. Political socialization is a process of absorbing information and ideas presented by others, observing role models, and internalizing our reactions to these inputs. Individuals within a group who are exposed to the same upbringing can and do react differently, but they also share many predominant views.

THE CONSEQUENCES OF POLITICAL SOCIALIZATION

Political socialization creates a political culture. A general culture is created and perpetuated through the accumulated effects on each individual in society. Cultures can and do change over time, but even that change occurs as new ideas spread through agents of political socialization. For example, women have

struggled for political and social rights for a very long time but feminism made significant headway only once agents of socialization in the late 20th century dealt with women's issues.

It is crucial to understand who is spreading what values and beliefs, and how easily new ideas can get circulated within an established society to spark new ways of thinking about politics. For example, research has shown very strong correlations between authoritarian views in a country's populace and the extent of authoritarian measures practised by their government. In short, authoritarian governments rely on state-orchestrated socialization to impart widespread support for the values that the government wishes to enforce and how they are enforced. By the same token, a population that strongly supports democratic values would not voluntarily tolerate authoritarian measures by their government.

A great deal depends on the type of values propagated through the various agents of socialization, on how deliberate the process of indoctrination is, and on the degree to which the various agents of political socialization reinforce the same messages. The political socialization process in the People's Republic of China, for example, involves massive, overt indoctrination that provides a stark contrast to the seemingly haphazard and uncoordinated process in Canada or the United States. However, it would be a mistake to conclude that the Canadian or American political socialization processes are not as effective as the Chinese in instilling widespread support for and belief in the values that the most important elites in the country wish the majority of citizens to hold. Indeed, Ralph Miliband has decried the political socialization process in Western democracies as "very largely a process of mass *indoctrination*" aimed at instilling support for the existing social order and capitalist economy.[38] The belief in diversity and freedom of expression provides a more heterogeneous political culture in Canada and the United States, but that diversity and the expression of opposing points of view do not contradict the existence of many values deeply shared by most citizens that result in mass acceptance of the existing social order.

Political socialization has many important consequences for a society and for individuals and groups within a society. Essential to any stable community is a large degree of acceptance of shared values about the structure of political institutions, about the processes used to settle political disputes and issue authoritative decisions, and about the basic parameters of social and economic policies to be pursued by those who hold political office. Socialization allows the spread of beliefs, attitudes, and knowledge needed for a widespread sharing of that acceptance. In short, political socialization underlies any stable society by ensuring that enough new members who are born into or immigrate to it come to hold many values and attitudes in common with those already present. Through socialization, a society of many different subgroups can also be melded into sharing one overarching culture. The United States is often taken as a prime example of the successful creation of a single nation despite enormous regional differences in culture and ethnic background. The *melting pot* is an expression often used to describe American cultural history and socialization.

Yet the process of political socialization may have many different outcomes. Existing divisions and tensions within a society may be perpetuated and even exacerbated over time. For example, there have always been tensions between French- and English-speaking people in Quebec, but the political socialization processes in Quebec in the past four decades have amplified the nationalist sentiments that a minority had long held. By the 1990s, a large number of francophones in Quebec were in favour of separation or "sovereignty-association," and this growth in nationalist fervour was fostered through schools and peer groups, in the arts, and in the media. The growth of Quebec nationalism can even be seen to have occurred in the workplace, through provincial legislation and policies designed to enhance the use and predominance of the French language in business.

The enduring power of political socialization is vividly highlighted in theories about the character of political cultures in societies that are largely made up of immigrant settlers. In the 1960s Louis Hartz developed a theory of political culture known as the *fragment theory*, which was also explored by Seymour Lipset.[39] Hartz argued that the contemporary political culture of an immigrant society reflects the dominant views of the different groups of immigrants who settled there. Each wave of immigrants is usually recruited from a specific place in their original country and thus represents only a fragment of the original country's political culture. Each different wave of immigrants

can establish an enduring set of beliefs and attitudes that will be reflected in the modern politics of the new society. Gad Horowitz adapted this theory to explain some of the most significant differences between Canadian and American political cultures, particularly the wider range of ideologies that have popular appeal in Canada, as opposed to the United States.[40] If true, the survival of these original fragments of political culture is a testament to the political socialization process that passed the values down from generation to generation. It should be noted, however, that the contemporary values of these groups have indeed evolved significantly over time, and are not simply time capsules of the values of bygone European cultures.

Further significance of political socialization lies in the ways in which political scientists study politics. For several decades, political behaviour has been studied by conducting surveys in an attempt to correlate the social background of individuals with their support for particular policies or political parties. It was thought that if religion, education, and occupation can have an impact on an individual's beliefs, one might be able to explain people's political behaviour by studying their social, economic, and cultural backgrounds. This approach to studying politics started out trying to concentrate on developing statistical models of political behaviour. In recent years, however, an appreciation of the complexity of human behaviour and of the strong interplay of the various forces in our lives has uncovered serious puzzles for political scientists to unravel.

CONCLUSION

Political culture—the set of beliefs, values, attitudes, and principles widely held among members of a society—may be a concept formulated by academics, but it has enormous practical implications. Political culture provides the foundation upon which any political system is created and operates. The degree of consensus on fundamental values, and what those values actually are, can have a profound effect on the stability of the political order in a particular country. Identity politics, which stems from individuals' identification with groups within a society and involves those groups' pursuit of their perceived needs, has important political ramifications. The depth and causes of political cleavages and how the political elites react to accommodate or suppress members of subgroups can lead not only to the creation of a healthy, vibrant political pluralism but also to separatist movements, civil war, and the disintegration of the state.

At the heart of understanding political culture lies our awareness of the process of political socialization, through which attitudes, knowledge, and beliefs are passed on within a society. Political socialization occurs through a variety of agents, including the family, schools, peer groups, religious institutions, the media, the workplace, and various state actors. The power of ideas is tremendous, and in every society a wide variety of groups and individuals act, sometimes in very subtle ways and at other times in strikingly forceful ways, to try to ensure that others embrace their values.

DISCUSSION QUESTIONS

1. Do you think that the courts should protect citizens' rights? Try to think of all the different sources of information that have led you to give an answer to that question. Could you name several or none? Does your answer strike you simply as common sense?

2. Think of a particular issue such as clearcut logging, strip mining, trade union rights, universal medicare, or trade between Canada and some state with an authoritarian regime. Ask yourself what your views on it are and what you think the government should do about it. Then ask yourself how you came to learn about this issue and develop an opinion. Who informed and influenced you, and how?

3. Think about the various agents of political socialization that you have read about in this chapter. How would you rank them in order of the effects you believe each has had in forming your own political beliefs and attitudes?

4. Which agent of political socialization do you think you have reacted negatively to the most? Have other agents positively reinforced your negative reactions?

5. How deeply divided by political cleavages do you think our society is? What do you think are the main causes of those cleavages? Do you think our political system tries to accommodate subgroups or meld them into a single, national culture?

FURTHER READING

Almond, Gabriel A., and Sidney Verba. *The Civic Culture: Political Attitudes in Five Democracies.* Princeton: Princeton University Press, 1963.

Herman, Edward, and Noam Chomsky. *Manufacturing Dissent.* New York: Pantheon, 1986.

Kymlicka, Will. *Multicultural Citizenship.* Oxford: Clarendon Press, 1997.

Miliband, Ralph. *The State in Capitalist Society.* London: Weidenfeld and Nicolson, 1969.

Nevitte, Neil. *The Decline of Deference.* Peterborough: Broadview Press, 1996.

Orum, Anthony, and John G. Dale, *Political Sociology: Power and Participation in the Modern World,* 5th ed. New York: Oxford University Press, 2008.

ENDNOTES

1. BBC News, "Kuwait Women Win Right to Vote,"; available at http://news.bbc.co.uk/2/hi/middle_east/4552749.stm; accessed November 6, 2007.

2. Angus Reid, "Politicians, Car Salesmen Most Derided Professionals in Western Countries," August 31, 2009, p. 3.

3. The Strategic Counsel, "Trusted Canadian Institutions, Afghanistan, and Foreign Ownership," May, 18, 2007, p. 7, available at http://www.thestrategiccounsel.com/our_news/polls/2007-05-18%20GMCTV%20May%2014-17.pdf; accessed October 24, 2010.

4. Angus Reid, "Americans, Britons and Canadians Take Harsh Stance on Crime," January 22, 2010, p.5, available at http://www.visioncritical.com/wp-content/uploads/2010/01/2010.01.22_Crime.pdf; accessed November 5, 2010.

5. Angus Reid, "Canadians and Britons Are More Open on Same-Sex Relations than Americans," July 26, 2010, pp. 4–5, available at http://www.visioncritical.com/wp-content/uploads/2010/07/2010.07.26_SameSex.pdf; accessed July 28, 2010.

6. The information for Canada and Italy is from Government of New Zealand, "Tax Compliance"; available at http://executive.govt.nz/96-99/compliance/chapter7.htm; accessed June 2, 2008.

7. US Department of the Treasury, "Update on Reducing the Federal Tax Gap and Improving Voluntary Compliance," 2009, p. 2, available at http://www.irs.gov/pub/newsroom/tax_gap_report_-final_version.pdf; accessed October 31, 2010.

8. James Chapman, "£42 Billion Missing from the Taxman's Coffers," *Daily Mail*, September 17, 2010, available at http://www.dailymail.co.uk/news/article-1312720/42bn-missing-taxmans-coffers-10-revenue-goes-uncollected.html; accessed October 31, 2010.

9. Sean O'Grady, "Britain's Deficit Constraining Public Finances, Says IMF Report," *The Independent*, September 2, 2010, available at http://www.independent.co.uk/news/business/news/britains-deficit-is-constraining-public-finances-says-imf-report-2068028.html; accessed October 31, 2010.

10. Hans Christiaan Haan, "Training for Work in the Informal Sector: New Evidence from Kenya, Tanzania and Uganda," p. 14, International Labour Organization website; available at http://www.ilo.org/public/english/employment/infeco/download/haan.pdf; accessed August 6, 2002.

11. Ipsos Reid, "How We See Each Other: Part II," December 1, 2004, available at http://www.ipsos-na.com/news/pressrelease.cfm?id=2480; accessed October 22, 2007.

12. Antonio Gramsci, *Letters from Prison* (New York: Columbia University Press, 1994).

13. Michel Foucault, *Ethics: Subjectivity and Truth* (New York: New Press, 1997).

14. Gabriel A. Almond and Sidney Verba, *The Civic Culture: Political Attitudes in Five Democracies* (Princeton: Princeton University Press, 1963). For a more recent discussion of related issues that have since been discussed in terms of civil society, see John Keane, *Civil Society and the State* (London: Verso, 1988).

15. For a discussion of the importance of civil society, as well as the limits of its political effects, in transitions from authoritarian regimes to democratic societies, see Emmanuel Gyimah-Boadi, "Civil Society in Africa," *Journal of Democracy* 7 (1996): 118.

16. Samuel P. Huntington, "Democracy for the Long Haul," *Journal of Democracy* 7(2) (April 1996): 8.

17. Charles Taylor, "The Politics of Recognition," in Amy Gutmann, ed., *Multiculturalism and the Politics of Recognition* (Princeton: Princeton University Press, 1992).

18. Iris M. Young, *Justice and the Politics of Difference* (Princeton: Princeton University Press, 1990); Will Kymlicka, *Multicultural Citizenship* (Oxford: Clarendon Press, 1997).

19. Will Kymlicka, *Liberalism, Community and Culture* (Oxford: Oxford University Press, 1989), pp. 182–205; see also Will Kymlicka, *Finding Our War: Rethinking Ethnocultural Relations in Canada* (Toronto: Oxford University Press, 1998).

20. Kenneth Hoover, *The Power of Identity: Politics in a New Key* (Chatham: Chatham House, 1997), pp. 37–38.

21. Carole Pateman, *The Sexual Contract* (Stanford: Stanford University Press, 1988), p. 231.

22. Carol Gilligan, *In a Different Voice: Psychological Theory and Women's Development* (Cambridge: Harvard University Press, 1982).

23. Simone de Beauvoir, *The Second Sex* (New York: Vintage Press, 1973), p. 301.

24. Richard G. Niemi and Mary A. Hepburn, "The Rebirth of Political Socialization," *Perspectives on Political Science* 24 (Winter 1995): 7–16.

25. Data are from the European Values Study Group and World Values Survey Association, 2005–2008.

26. Neil Nevitte, *The Decline of Deference* (Peterborough: Broadview Press, 1996).

27. See Edward Herman and Noam Chomsky, *Manufacturing Dissent* (New York: Pantheon, 1986); Noam Chomsky and David Barsamian, *Chronicles of Dissent* (Monroe, ME: Common Courage Press, 1992); and Noam Chomsky, "Media Control," available at http://www.zmag.org/zbooks/224; accessed June 2, 2008.

28. James Winter, *Democracy's Oxygen: How Corporations Control the News* (Montreal: Black Rose Books, 1997).

29. Seattle Post-Intelligencer, "About seattlepi.com," available at http://www.seattlepi.com/facts; accessed November 7, 2010.

30. Nik Nanos, "TV is Still Top and Most Trusted News Sources; Newspapers Second, and Internet Last," (2009) 30 *Policy Options*, June, p. 1.

31. Gallup, "Public Trust in Federal Government Remains High," available at http://www.gallup.com/poll/releases/apr990108.asp; accessed January 8, 1998; and Gallup, "Distrust in U.S. Media Up to Record High," available at http://www.gallup.com/poll/143267/distrust-media-edges-record-high.aspx; accessed November 7, 2010.

32. World Internet Stats, "Internet Usage Statistics," available at http://www.internetworldstats.com/stats.htm; accessed November 7, 2010.

33. See "Soldier-Reporters Rewrite the Rules," *Toronto Star*, August 11, 2007, available at http://www.thestar.com/sciencetech/Ideas/article/245204; accessed November 6, 2007.

34. Facebook, "Statistics," available at http://www.facebook.com/press/info.php?statistics; accessed November 7, 2010.

35. CBC News, "Thousands Protest Parliament's Suspension," January 23, 2010, available at http://www.cbc.ca/canada/story/2010/01/23/prorogue-protests.html; accessed November 7, 2010.

36. Pew Forum, "Support for Same Sex Marriages Edges Up," available at http://pewforum.org/Gay-Marriage-and-Homosexuality/Support-For-Same-Sex-Marriage-Edges-Upward.aspx; accessed November 7, 2010.

37. For an examination of the relationship between the workplace and political attitudes in America, see Steven A. Peterson, *Political Behaviour: Patterns in Everyday Life* (Newbury Park: Sage, 1990), ch. 8.

38. Ralph Miliband, *The State in Capitalist Society* (London: Weidenfeld and Nicolson, 1969), p. 181.

39. Louis Hartz, *The Founding of New Societies* (New York: Harcourt Brace, 1964). See also Seymour Martin Lipset, "Canada and the United States: A Comparative Review," *Canadian Review of Sociology and Anthropology* 1 (1964): 173–85.

40. Gad Horowitz, "Conservatism, Liberalism, and Socialism in Canada: An Interpretation," *Canadian Journal of Economics and Political Science* 32 (1966): 143–71.

For various weblinks discussed in this chapter, please go to the book's website at **www.studyingpolitics4e.nelson.com**

Thinking about Politics: Ideas and Ideologies

Richard Sigurdson

CHAPTER OBJECTIVES

After you have completed this chapter, you should be able to:

- discuss the ways in which one's view of human nature helps determine one's attitude toward government and politics
- outline the different views on equality put forward by conservatives, liberals, and socialists
- distinguish between negative and positive concepts of freedom, and discuss the relevant policy implications in emphasizing one view of freedom over another
- enumerate various answers to the question "Who should rule?"
- differentiate between the political left and right and define the following concepts: progressive, liberal, conservative, and reactionary
- define the term *ideology* and outline its functions in the contemporary world
- explain the notion of the far-right and discuss its significance for modern politics

INTRODUCTION

Political *theory* (or political *philosophy*) is the subfield of the discipline of political science that involves theoretical or philosophical reflection on the "big ideas" about things political: the nature and function of the state; the role, legitimacy, and proper ends of government; the relationship between the individual and society; the meaning of liberty, obligation, and rights; and the connections between law, justice, authority, and power. Political theory has been practised by thinkers in various eras and cultures—whenever and wherever people have given their collective condition and governance structures philosophical consideration. In the Western world, political philosophy dates at least

as far back as the ancient Greeks, whose philosophers debated the merits of most of the forms of government still known to us today: monarchy, aristocracy, democracy, tyranny, and oligarchy. As noted in Chapter 2, it was Aristotle (384–322 BCE) who famously classified types of government according to the number of rulers (the one, the few, or the many), as well as the ends pursued by the rulers (illegitimate rule is for the benefit of the rulers alone and legitimate for the benefit of all).[1] Political philosophers in the East struggled with similar issues related to politics and statecraft. In ancient China, Confucius (551–471 BCE), Mencius (372–289 BCE), Han Fei (280–233 BCE), and others produced vibrant philosophies during an era of political chaos and constant warfare. In ancient India, notable figures such as Kautilya (also known as Chanakya, 350–283 BCE) also pondered the philosophical issues of political life. This tradition was sustained throughout the Middle Ages when Christian thinkers, such as Augustine (354–430) and Thomas Aquinas (1225–74), and Islamic philosophers, such as al-Farabi (872–951) and Ibn Khaldun (1332–1406), studied the Hellenic writers and proposed their own philosophies and versions of the ideal state. From the early modern period to today, political thinkers around the world and in many cultures have theorized about the foundations of power, issues of social welfare and equality, and the relative merits of different forms of political authority.

Reading these classic works of political philosophy is not always easy for the modern student. Those who write political theory tend to address a scholarly rather than a popular audience. Not only are the issues they tackle challenging, but the work is not particularly accessible to the non-specialist reader. Indeed, it can be quite a struggle to decipher the texts of Cicero (106–43 BCE) or Marsilius of Padua (1275–1342), G.W.F. Hegel (1770–1831) or Giorgio Agamben (1942–). What is more, it is usually not possible to get the most out of the study of political theory without some knowledge of the long tradition of social and political ideas within a civilization or culture. In the Western tradition, for instance, the major political ideas were developed over a long period of time and through the interaction of different thinkers from various periods and countries. One way to conceptualize this tradition is as a "conversation" about the big ideas advanced over the centuries, primarily found today in a limited number of major historical texts with which almost everyone writing political theory is familiar. (See Box 6.1 for a list of important primary texts.)

BOX 6.1

THE TOP 10 TEXTS OF WESTERN POLITICAL THEORY

1. Aristotle, *The Politics* (350 BCE)
2. Plato, *The Republic* (360 BCE)
3. Augustine, *The City of God* (413–26)
4. Thomas Aquinas, *Summa Theologiae* (1265–74)
5. Niccolò Machiavelli, *The Prince* (1513)
6. Thomas Hobbes, *Leviathan* (1651)
7. John Locke, *Second Treatise on Government* (1690)
8. Jean-Jacques Rousseau, *The Social Contract* (1762)
9. Karl Marx and Friedrich Engels, *The Communist Manifesto* (1848)
10. John Stuart Mill, *On Liberty* (1859)

Knowledge of this "canon" of Western political philosophy is generally regarded as fundamental to the discipline of political science in the Anglo-American academy. Yet some contemporary students might wonder why they should have to spend the time and effort to understand philosophical texts that were written centuries ago, in obscure languages, discussing disputes long since dormant. Moreover, these writings are often very abstract and far removed from the nitty-gritty of political life. How do they provide insights into a modern world dominated by practical considerations, not idealistic theory? How exactly is the study of political theory going to help us come to grips with contemporary international relations or with the workings of domestic politics? Why, in short, should we even bother to study the history of political thought?

For one thing, the ideas of many now-dead political philosophers profoundly shaped the strategies and practices of actual political leaders, whose actions directly affect our daily lives. Thinking about big political ideas led to the ideologies that underlie all modern political systems: liberalism, conservatism, socialism, feminism, anarchism, political Islam, and so on. The Chinese thinker SunTzu (544–496 BCE), for instance, greatly influenced military strategists in many lands over many centuries. Even if our most crafty politicians have not actually read Niccolò Machiavelli's (1459–1527) *The Prince*, our reading of it helps us to comprehend political life in the modern world. The ideas of John Locke (1632–1704) and Baron de Montesquieu (1689–1755) provide the intellectual underpinnings for the liberal democratic **nation-state**, informing such founding documents as the Constitution of the United States. The writings of Adam Smith (1723–1790) helped create the modern discipline of political economy and provide the rationale for capitalism, free trade, and libertarianism. Jean-Jacques Rousseau's (1712–1778) contemplations on freedom and equality inspired the French Revolution of 1789, which had as its slogan the Rousseauian phrase: "*liberté, égalité, fraternité.*" A direct line can be drawn between the advocacy of women's equality of opportunity by Mary Astell (1666–1731) and Mary Wollstonecraft (1759–1797) and the feminist movement of the contemporary era. The radical ideas of Karl Marx (1818–1883) and Friedrich Nietzsche (1844–1900) aroused, often unwittingly, political movements—communist and fascist respectively—that had a tremendous impact on the 20th century.

Mao Zedong's (1893–1976) adaptation of Marxist notions to the Chinese context provided the blueprint for the creation of the People's Republic of China in 1949. Frantz Fanon (1925–1961) used his knowledge of psychotherapy to help provide the inspiration for anticolonial liberation movements throughout the Third World. Current attempts to reconcile rational philosophy with Islamic theology have their roots in the interpretations of both Western and Eastern traditions by philosophers such as Avicenna (980–1037). And more recently, Sayyid Qutb (1906–1966), who argued that sharia law should be the sole basis for government and who defended a broad application of jihad, can be seen as an author of the political version of Islam prominent in the 21st century among various political actors, including those in al Qaeda.

But there is more to studying political theory than linking the meaning of what philosophers said with the role their ideas have played in social or political struggles, or with identifying the historical consequences for which this or that political philosopher's ideas are commonly held responsible. The study of political ideas can also afford us the opportunity to think through, in our own mind and with our own experiences as points of reference, the big political questions that face humankind in all ages and territories. By so doing, we can come to our own conclusions about issues such as how political institutions should best be arranged and for what purpose. Our engagement with the writings of major political philosophers of the past is simply one way to help clarify in our own minds the precise meaning and utility of notions such as equality, freedom, and justice. And we can ask ourselves whether these key concepts that are still relevant today are coherent or contradictory with each other: can we have equality without limiting freedom? Is allowing everyone to be free going to lead to justice? Such questions are more than merely abstract thought experiments. They represent conflicts which are at the root of contemporary political life everywhere on the planet.

Over the past two centuries, as we will see in the second half of this chapter, it has become common to see political disputes as primarily involving clashes between competing ideologies: liberalism, conservatism, socialism, communism, fascism, and so on. Is a national government or political party on the "right" or "left"? What is the intellectual motivation behind this or that politician or reformer? What is the basis of the so-called "Tea-Party" conservatism that is altering the political landscape in contemporary America? Or what about the "clash of civilizations" that some people refer to when speaking of the major political divisions in the world today?[2] We need to try to understand these terms and ideas if we are to fully engage in the world, developing our own perspectives on the big issues of our day.

The goal of this chapter is to introduce some of the key ideas about politics and to explore their meanings and consequences. In the latter part of the chapter, we will look at how political ideas form the foundation for major world ideologies. But first we will examine some of the perennial issues and topics in political thought, organizing the material thematically in an effort to provide a broad survey of the subject. While the specific theories of individual philosophers cannot be given the space they deserve in a single chapter, it is hoped that students will take up the challenge of reading in their own words not only some of the great historical political thinkers from the distant past but also some of the most prominent political philosophers of our own day. (See Box 6.2 for a list of some of the most influential political philosophers from the past century.) Political theory is by no means a field of merely historical study. Ideas are alive today and the debates over them are as important and lively as they have ever been.

PERENNIAL ISSUES IN POLITICAL THOUGHT

Human Nature and Politics

"Knowledge of human nature," Henry Adams (1838–1918) once said, "is the beginning and end of political education."[3] Most social science theories, in fact, are founded on some concept of the nature of human beings. Indeed, political philosophy is sometimes regarded as one long meditation on the question of human nature. What does it mean to be human? What is our human essence? Are we by nature social animals, as Aristotle said? Or are we solitary and isolated creatures, as Thomas Hobbes (1588–1679) assumed? Is the desire for power intrinsic to human nature, as Nietzsche believed? Or are we by nature benign beings, capable of mutual love and cooperation, as Mencius suggested? Our answers to these questions will determine how we approach all other aspects of political philosophizing.[4]

Our thinking about human nature sets the foundation upon which our political theories are constructed.

BOX 6.2

PROMINENT POLITICAL THEORISTS OF THE PAST CENTURY

Hannah Arendt (1906–1975). Key works: *The Origins of Totalitarianism* (1951); *Eichmann in Jerusalem: A Report on the Banality of Evil* (1963)

Michel Foucault (1926–1984). Key works: *Madness and Civilization* (1961); *Discipline and Punish* (1975)

Jürgen Habermas (1929–). Key works: *Legitimation Crisis* (1973); *The Theory of Communicative Action* (1981)

Friedrich Hayek (1899–1992). Key works: *The Road to Serfdom* (1944); *The Constitution of Liberty* (1960)

Leo Strauss (1899–1973). Key works: *The City and Man* (1962); *Political Philosophy: Six Essays by Leo Strauss* (1975)

Catherine MacKinnon (1946–). Key works: *Towards a Feminist Theory of the State* (1989); *Only Words* (1993)

Herbert Marcuse (1898–1979). Key works: *Eros and Civilization* (1955); *One-Dimensional Man* (1964)

Robert Nozick (1938–2002). Key works: *Anarchy, State, and Utopia* (1974); *Philosophical Explanations* (1981)

John Rawls (1921–2002). Key works: *A Theory of Justice* (1971); *Political Liberalism* (1993)

Charles Taylor (1931–). Key works: *Hegel* (1975); *The Politics of Recognition* (1992)

For instance, Hobbes famously asserted that humans are isolated, selfish creatures, driven by their "desires" and "aversions." Two basic postulates about human nature provide the basis for all his political theorizing: first, that humans are inescapably engaged in a perpetual struggle for power over others that ends only in death; and second, that our strongest aversion is to violent death, which we will seek to avoid at all costs. Hobbes comes to these conclusions about human nature by imagining what people would be like if they lived in a "state of nature"—that is, in a condition free of any government or rule-making authority. Hobbes concludes that a natural condition without authority or rules would be one of constant war "of every man against every man." Life in the state of nature, as Hobbes succinctly declares, would be "solitary, poor, nasty, brutish, and short."[5] Thus, the only rational thing for humans to do in order to avoid perpetual violence or the fear of it is to quit the state of nature, agreeing mutually to abdicate to a sovereign power all of one's natural rights to govern oneself. **Civil society**, the result of this covenant between rational human beings, is to Hobbes but an expedient. He says that while it is not natural for humans to live in society,

their self-interest will compel them to bind together for the purposes of mutual security and benefit.

Aristotle presents an entirely opposite point of view. For him, it is living in society that is natural—humans are *by nature* social and political animals. Only a beast or a god (the subhuman or the superhuman) could live without being a member of a political community. For us humans, it is in our nature to commune with our fellow citizens. More than that, political life is to Aristotle the highest form of self-actuality. We are most alive, most true to our nature, when we are participating in political activity, especially when we are governing in a good state. Because *polis* life is natural, the best states are ones in which the interests of one person are the same as the interests of all. Hence, a person who acts for his or her own good must also act for the good of all fellow citizens.

But if we are by nature social and political beings, and we want to live in concert with others, what accounts for the fact that there is so much strife and political violence in the world? Is it "natural" for humans to fight with each other? For Thomas Hobbes, the answer is yes. Humans, in his mind, are avaricious and selfish by nature. Conflict is natural. It is also potentially destructive of the conditions needed for a productive and peaceful life. Uncontrolled, the competition between individuals will undermine any chance of social cooperation, which is a requirement of civil society. A similar perspective on human nature was advanced two thousand years earlier by Xun Zi, who contradicted leading Confucian scholars such as Mencius by insisting that human beings are innately selfish and contentious. Left uncurbed, what Xun Zi calls man's "detestable disposition" will lead to anarchy and the impossibility of an amenable life. Like Hobbes, he envisioned civil society not as a natural state for humankind but as an artificial construct devised to channel and control the natural impulse to be diffident.

An alternative, more optimistic perspective is found in the thought of Jean-Jacques Rousseau. He believed that humans are essentially decent beings but that they have been gradually led away from their natural, congenial condition toward one that is corrupt, unjust, and divisive. This misfortune occurred, Rousseau theorizes, because humans introduced into their lives private property, which led to inequality, selfishness, distrust, and the concentration of power in the hands of a few. Rousseau's thesis, put very simply, is that humans are basically good but have been corrupted by their sociopolitical environment: bad institutions have distorted the natural goodness of humankind. Rousseau offers us hope that human goodness can be rediscovered if social conditions are put right, specifically if an enlightened leader governs in a manner that reflects the will of all. This reasoning, which goes back at least as far as the philosophy of Mencius in the 4th century BCE, has struck a positive chord with a variety of thinkers and political actors over the years. For instance, most modern liberals believe that by reforming social and political institutions we can help develop the moral character of the individual members of society. T.H. Green (1836–1882) believed that humans are not only naturally inclined to advance their own welfare but those of others as well. Utopian socialists also stress the inherent human capacity for consensus and cooperation and imagine strategies for creating a world of peace and harmony. Marx's doctrine of historical materialism rests on a faith in inexorable historical progress toward the highest phase of communist society, in which there will be no social classes and therefore no destructive political conflict.

More will be said in a subsequent section about the concepts of the political left and right, but it can be noted at this stage that Western thinkers on the so-called left (liberals, socialists, communists) are more likely than those on the right (conservatives, Christian democrats, fascists) to hold the belief that human nature is good, or inherently perfectible, and that political ills stem from societal influences rather than any essential human flaws. Thus, the goal of leftist or liberal political action is to create the sorts of institutions that would be most likely to provide the necessary positive influences to benefit humanity. Thinkers on the political right tend to share a belief in the imperfection of human nature, seeing in the individual varying degrees of weakness, irrationality, perfidy, and immorality. Indeed, conservatives think that humankind is not only morally imperfect but intellectually imperfect as well. Thus, they hold that humans simply cannot know enough to be sure that their radical social experimentation or tinkering with the institutions of government will actually lead to positive change rather than to more sociopolitical problems.[6]

In the Western world, the conviction that humankind is morally imperfect is rooted in the Christian doctrine of original sin. According to this teaching, human beings are fallen creatures, alienated from the goodness of their Creator and divided against each other by selfishness. Most instructive on this topic is the work of St. Augustine, who regarded humans as invariably corrupt and helpless, driven by their most base passions to commit grievous wrongs and to suffer dearly for doing so. In contrast to the Platonic Socrates, Augustine regarded as naïve the idea that people will do what is right and good if they only know the truth. According to Augustine, human beings are from conception wicked and dangerous creatures driven by lust, including the lust for power. No amount of proper education or wisdom will reverse their fallen state. Not surprisingly, he believed that people need to be coerced and restrained by harsh laws, a strict code of behaviour, and brutal punishment for transgression. Augustine accepted that temporal institutions, as creations of a sinful humanity, would always be inherently flawed and could never bring true happiness. Yet he concluded that secular political institutions, no matter how oppressive, must be respected, since they constitute the only earthly bulwark against disorder.

Another point of view on the issue of human nature is found in Islam, which does not presuppose any inherent wickedness of human nature. Instead, the Qur'an teaches that human beings are born in a state of *fitrah*, which denotes the inherent disposition toward goodness and virtue in humankind that is manifest in peaceful submission to the will of Allah. Thus, there is no concept of original sin in Islam. People are not per-fect, to be sure, and must struggle to remain on the right path. But any deviation from one's original virtuous state is due to external factors, suggests the Qur'an, and true repentance of sin can return a person to the original sinless state. According to Muslim theology, humankind's chief failing is pride and rebellion. In their pride, humans attempt to become equals of Allah, and this runs counter to the primary theological concept of Islam, the belief that there is only one God. Thus, pride is a cardinal sin. The chief virtue, again, is submission to divine will. In Islam, *sharia* is the expression of divine will and it forms a system of obligations and duties that are incumbent upon all Muslims. Politically, this is at the root of the Islamic adherence to a strict legal frame-work within which both public and private aspects of life are regulated for those living under **sharia law**. It is often pointed out that in political Islam there is no inherent separation between matters for the state and those for the church as there is in **liberal democracy**.

> **Liberal democracy:** A form of government com-mon to Western political systems in which there is a combination of the "liberal" right to individual freedom and the "democratic" right to representative govern-ment. Hence, the ability of the elected representa-tives to exercise decision-making power is subject to the rule of law as established by a constitutional system that recognizes fundamental rights and freedoms (e.g., free speech, freedom of the press and religion, and the right to free association) along with certain legal rights to property, privacy, equality under the law, etc. Liberal democracies also include protection for minorities against possible encroach-ment on their rights by the majority, such institutional structures of representative government as open and free elections with multiple party systems, civil-ian rule, separation of powers between the executive and legislative branches, an independent judiciary, and a political culture of tolerance and pluralism.

Equality and Social Justice

Along with the larger question about the essence of humankind, political philosophers, especially in the modern era, have been intensely focused on the issue of equality. Again, there are religious roots to the doctrine of **egalitarianism**. The Christian belief that all humans are equally created in the image of God provides the foundation for the more robust moral concept that all

human beings are equal in worth and status, which can be found in various forms of Western secular thought. Islam is also based on the fundamental notion that each human being is spiritually equal to every other human being in the eyes of God. As with Christianity, moreover, this spiritual egalitarianism in Islam does not always translate into an ethos of social egalitarianism. Social distinctions, such as the relegation of homosexuals to the realm of unnatural beings, and subordination, such as the subordination of women to men, are seen by many religious thinkers as necessary to the maintenance of society, order, and morality. Politically, therefore, the struggle to achieve a greater measure of social equality for all individuals and groups, which has become almost a hallmark of modernity, is often waged against the well-entrenched interests of religious and societal prejudice.

> **Egalitarianism:** The doctrine that advocates that people should be treated as equals regardless of differences of wealth, income, class, sex, religion, ethnicity, physical ability, and so on. At minimum, egalitarianism promotes the equality of social and political rights for all citizens. At maximum, egalitari-anism calls for a much greater equality of wealth and income for all persons across all divisions in soci-ety. Reform-oriented liberals emphasize the former, postulating a need for an equality of opportunity, which guarantees to all the equal chance to com-pete for the social, economic, and political benefits available in society. Socialists emphasize the lat-ter, interpreting egalitarianism to require an equality of condition, so that all goods and resources in a society would be distributed equally.

For political philosophy, the initial question is whether human beings are in essence equal or unequal. Clearly, our modern bias is toward the view that humans are in essence equal (although our societies are still rife with social and economic inequalities). Yet the majority of political thinkers throughout history take the opposite view. Ancient Indian political philosophy gives kingship a central place in political life, which is not uncommon, but it also sets out an elaborate system of social strati-fication. For ancient philosophers and legislators in this tradition, such as the authors of the *Manu-Smrti* (written between 200 BCE and 200 CE), the king was a key figure in a social order based on a caste system. Caste divided society into distinct classes, with individ-uals assigned their positions and occupational roles by birth: the *Brahmans* were responsible for education and priestly duties, and were said to have divine powers; the *Ksatriyas* were the rulers and warriors; the *Vaisyas* cultivators, manufacturers, and businesspeople; and the *Sudras* were the lowest rank within society, performing the manual jobs and existing essentially in servitude. Below these groups yet are those with *Dalit* status—often called "untouchables" or "outcastes"—who were regarded as literally outside of society and who served in the most subservient positions. Natural law or *Dharma* depended on the observance of these class divisions.

Ancient Greeks also presupposed a rank order of humankind, in this case according to one's capacity for reason. On this basis, Aristotle excluded from citizenship whole categories of humanity—for example, artisans, workers, women, and slaves—because they allegedly lacked the ability to reason for themselves. Plato was more willing to regard women as equal to men, but he was by no means an egalitarian. He designed an elaborate theory of government to justify the rule of the naturally superior individual, the philosopher-king. Throughout the Middle Ages and well into the modern era European political philosophers simply assumed that humans were unequal in essence, and did not even question political arrangements which distributed power and resources unequally. It was not until Thomas Hobbes employed the "state of nature" metaphor in *Leviathan* (1651) that one finds the presumption that in nature all men are indeed equal—at least in their equal ability to do harm to one another in their quest to satisfy their own desires. And even so, this observation led Hobbes to the non-egalitarian conclusion that the best possible arrangement was for the people to hand over all of their sovereign authority to a king who would enjoy unfettered power over all citizens.

More recently, and in contradiction to the growing egalitarianism of his contemporaries, Friedrich Nietzsche maintained that humans are radically unequal in virtually every way that matters. Nietzsche was frustrated by the fact that philosophers and politicians in the modern age were increasingly promoting what he called the "slave" doctrine of equality and the values of the inferior "herd" over what he dubbed "master morality" and the noble doctrine of aristocracy. Writing near the end of the 19th century, when most leading thinkers and political actors were on the side of egalitarianism of some sort or another, Nietzsche—author of the *Untimely Meditations* (1873–1876)—was clearly out of step with the ethos of his society. In his more fanciful moments, he looked forward to the rise to power of a new breed of "supermen" who would reflect the highest potential for human creativity and vitality. Nietzsche's ideas about a new master race were subsequently misappropriated by apologists for Nazism and used to justify Hitler's racist and nationalist doctrine (in spite of the fact that Nietzsche specifically denounced racism and nationalism as perverted ideologies).[7]

In Anglo-American and European thought of the past 250 years, attitudes toward equality have been especially instructive of the divide between conservatives and liberals. The traditional conservative position is nicely represented by the English thinker and statesman Edmund Burke (1729–1797), who argued that humanity is naturally and hierarchically ordered. Like many conservatives, Burke valued order, stability, and the preservation of the existing social structure. He very much feared that the egalitarian ethos arising from the French Revolution was undermining the preconditions for order and stability, including the right to property ownership among the traditional elite and the recognition of the social obligations that go with such entitlement. Burke held that the best government is an **aristocracy**, in which the privileged orders, the high-born and well-bred, would rule wisely and for the good of the whole.

> **Aristocracy:** Government by an elite or privileged class or by a minority regarded as those best fit to rule. For the Ancients, the term is reserved for the rule by the few "best" (aristos in Greek). Indeed, aristocracy was regarded by the Ancient philosophers as the very highest form of government, since it implied that the most educated, wise, brave, and selfless people would rule in the interests of the whole society rather than their own. According to this understanding, membership in the aristocracy was based on character and achievement, not just heredity. But during the Middle Ages in Europe the term became associated with a particular social class, otherwise known as the "nobility." Members are born into this class (or are allowed to purchase their way into it by the monarch), and they can automatically pass on their titles and privileges to their descendants. While some might argue that superiority still inheres with the upper classes, and thus aristocrats deserve a disproportionate role in decision-making, the term aristocracy has generally lost its original positive connotation and it is now common for it to carry a pejorative meaning in liberal democratic societies.

In contrast to Burke's aristocratic conservatism, the liberal opinion is that humans are by nature free and equal creatures, equally in possession of their own natural rights (primarily, the right to preserve oneself, but also the right to individual freedom and the enjoyment of private property). Such a philosophy provides the intellectual foundations for the liberal democratic nation-states epitomized by the great republics arising out of the 18th century revolutions in France and America. The public philosophies of these liberal republics are heavily influenced by thinkers such as Hobbes, Locke, and Montesquieu. The substance of this liberal perspective is nicely summed up by Thomas Jefferson (1743–1826) in the *Declaration of Independence*: "We hold these truths to be self-evident: that all men are created equal; that they are endowed by their Creator with certain inalienable Rights: that among these are Life, Liberty and the pursuit of Happiness."

As a statement of political ideals, the *Declaration* stakes out an inspiring egalitarian position that is rightfully revered by patriots as symbolic of America's democratic roots. Indeed, many a noble reformer—in America and elsewhere—has found motivation and strength in these powerful words. Yet reflection on Jefferson's text reminds us of the huge disparity between the ideals it expresses so clearly and the stubborn persistence of social and political inequality in the republic Jefferson helped create. When the *Declaration* was penned in 1776, and for almost a century thereafter, slavery was legal in the country. Indeed, the American Constitution, ratified in 1791, legitimated and codified the institution of slavery. Many signatories of the *Declaration*, including Jefferson himself, and many representatives to the Constitutional Convention, including George Washington (who once denounced slavery as "repugnant"), owned slaves. It was not until the Emancipation Proclamation and the passage of the 13th, 14th, and 15th Amendments in the wake of the Civil War that American constitutional law entrenched racial equality—and even then the courts were largely unwilling to enforce any of its provisions on state governments wishing to continue various forms of racial segregation and discrimination.

Nor should it escape our attention that the *Declaration* and the rights it champions were limited to "all men" and not to the female half of the population. American women did not receive equal political rights until the 19th Amendment was passed in 1920, and even today women in America are without the protections that would have been extended to them had the proposed Equal Rights Amendment (ERA) been passed. Neither were the rights that were claimed by the male American colonists extended to the Indigenous peoples of America, who were largely regarded as savages unfit for citizenship and equal treatment under the law. Finally, full political rights were not even enjoyed by all white men in the Thirteen Colonies, since those who did not own sufficient property were excluded. In spite of the Founders' lofty rhetoric, therefore, the notion that all human beings should be regarded as equal and treated so by law was not a reality in America at its inception. Indeed, even the formal achievement of equal rights in America, to the extent that this has been achieved at all, must be regarded as a very recent phenomenon.

Of course, America is by no means alone in this regard. A history of inequality and exclusion—of Native peoples, religious and ethnic minorities, etc.—is clearly evident in Canada, as it is in other "settler societies." Most striking, of course, is the history of discrimination and dispossession of First Nations peoples. In Canada, to take one example, thousands of Indian children were removed from their families and placed in residential schools where they were to be educated into the superior ways of the white, Christian majority. Not only did these schools disrespect the languages and cultures of the students, but they subjected them to psychological, physical, and often sexual abuse. The legacy of this system is an impediment to achieving justice and good relations today. Hence, as part of a comprehensive claim against the Canadian government by the survivors, a Truth and Reconciliation Commission has been established, somewhat along the lines of the one created by President Nelson Mandela in post-apartheid South Africa, to reveal past injustice as a means of resolving conflict in the present.

While attempts to provide restitution for past injustice is hardly uncontroversial, very few citizens in liberal democracies today would justify the crimes against equality that are epitomized by slavery or discrimination against Aboriginal peoples. There is today a widespread acceptance of the values of the 1948 United Nations Declaration of Human Rights, with its affirmation of the "inherent dignity and of the equal and inalienable rights of all members of the human family." Indeed, most liberal democratic states have formally eradicated any official obstacles to equality before and under the law. It is no longer legal to deny services to people based solely on their gender or race. But does the adoption of formal rules providing for legal equality create an egalitarian society? Now that virtually all of the formal and legal obstacles to equal participation have been dismantled in places such as the United States and Canada, have women, visible minorities, Indigenous peoples, immigrants, and the poor achieved full equality?

To be sure, social inequality persists in many forms even in the most advanced Western societies. Statistics indicate that women and minorities suffer inequalities of income, political power, and social status. Moreover, there are significant disparities along **class** lines in all advanced capitalist societies. How can we justify such inequalities in societies that are avowedly egalitarian? How much inequality is permissible, and of what sort? What, if anything, should society or the state do to address the problem of persistent social inequality? Here one finds diverging views, even among those who regard themselves as egalitarians. For some, including contemporary conservative thinkers and politicians, the answer is typically that we should guarantee formal or legal equality and then rely on the free market to produce an equilibrium of societal benefits. That is, we should make sure that there is no legal or official discrimination allowed and then accept that a fair system of competition will eventually produce equitable results. Beyond ensuring impartiality and nondiscrimination, however, the state should not be used to provide specific advantages for historically disadvantaged groups, which is the project typically associated with various forms of **affirmative action** programs. The use of the state's power to intervene in the economic or social arena, even

for the laudable goal of reducing societal inequality, is regarded by many critics as itself a crime against equality, since it ends up treating some people differently from others on the basis of race or sex or ethnicity.

For the most part, opponents of affirmative action are often adherents to some version of **conservatism**. The proponents of contemporary **liberalism** often tend to support affirmative action, usually on the principle of equality of opportunity. That is, they believe that for freedom and equality to be meaningful, everyone must have an equal chance to compete fairly, on a level playing field with all others, for a share of the social and economic benefits that society has to offer. Judged by the results, contemporary liberals say, the playing field is not at all level; it is still tilted very much in favour of members of certain groups (such as middle-class white men). So in the name of equality, the power of the state must be used to ensure fair chances for all citizens (e.g., through affirmative action programs for hiring minorities).

Conservatism: The ideology defending the status quo against major social, economic, and political change. The classic statement of this philosophy can be found in the speeches and writing of the English statesman Edmund Burke. He argued that political order and stability will be maintained only if change is gradual and evolutionary rather than rapid and revolutionary. Today conservatism is often used to label anyone on the political right, especially those who want to conserve the free-market capitalist system against radical demands for progressive reforms.

Affirmative action: The giving of preferential treatment to targeted groups in such areas as employment, promotion, housing, or education to redress the effects of past discrimination. Affirmative action began in America in the 1960s, focusing mainly on increasing opportunities for African-Americans. In the 1970s, it began to be used to increase the number of women in professional and managerial positions. Affirmative action is also used to promote hiring of ethnic minorities and Aboriginal people. While the bulk of reform-oriented liberals, feminists, and minorities support it, many contemporary conservatives claim that affirmative action amounts to reverse discrimination.

Liberalism: The ideology based on the paramount value of individual liberty. Liberals regard the individual as a rational creature who can use his or her intelligence to decide how best to live life and to maximize individual well-being. Liberalism assumes that all humans are free and equal by nature, and that society is a vehicle for the protection and enhancement of our natural rights. In its earlier form, often called classical liberalism, this ideology assumed a limited role for the state. In later years, liberals tended to advocate a larger role for the state to guarantee equality and to help foster the full development of the individual. There are many forms of liberalism, and it has become a widely held political position across the Western world.

In this fashion, no one will be excluded from, nor unduly disadvantaged when engaging in, societal competition. Yet liberals fully expect that once equality of opportunity is assured—once there is an even playing field—the most talented or industrious individual should still be able to reap the rewards of his or her own competitive efforts. As long as the competition between individuals is free and fair, the liberal will not deny that some should have more and others less. Social or "conventional inequality" will exist in a liberal society, since some individuals will gain more because they will work harder or have more ability than others. However, this conventional inequality is justifiable, from the liberal point of view, so long as no one is denied a meaningful opportunity to compete and to be successful, especially on the basis of attributes or identifiers over which they have no control, such as race or gender.

It is at this point that **socialism** breaks with liberalism and insists that true egalitarianism demands more than equal opportunity or equal social and political rights. Socialists are most concerned with material inequality and the equal access to the resources of the community. It is often said, then, that while liberals are content with an equality of opportunity, socialist justice requires an actual equality of condition. For those on the moderate left (e.g., social democrats), the equality of condition is more of an ideal than a practical goal. That is, the objective is to narrow the gap

as much as possible between rich and poor, gradually levelling out society's social and economic inequalities by raising the floor for those at the bottom and lowering the ceiling for those at the top. Socialists argue that the free market system, left unchecked, allows for the accumulation of enormous wealth by the very few at the expense of the majority of citizens. In the name of equality, social democrats want the state to intervene in the economy, adjusting the effects of the disparities between winners and losers that inevitably arise from market competition. Likewise, they support the rights of organized labour as a bulwark against unfettered capitalist exploitation of workers. The stronger the unions, the less power will employers have to increase profits and drive down wages. In effect, social democrats want to see a redistribution of wealth and income, and so they promote such measures as steeply graduated income taxes, whereby the rich are taxed at a higher rate than the less affluent; extensive social welfare programs, which use public funds to provide services and benefits to those who cannot otherwise pay for them; and full employment or job guarantee policies, whereby all those willing and able to work can do so.

For radical socialists and **communists**, however, these social democratic strategies are insufficient, since they can never provide for an absolute equality of condition. For justice to be achieved, it is argued, the fundamental inequality of classes—most importantly, the gap between the **bourgeoisie** and the workers—must be addressed at its root. Redistributive economic policies and trade unionism will not, in themselves, bring about full equality. Indeed, they might even forestall it by improving conditions that would otherwise lead to the overthrow of capitalism. Vladimir Ilyich Lenin (1870–1924), the leader of the Bolshevik Revolution, insisted that social democratic parties and their trade union partners could

---

Socialism: The doctrine advocating economic equality of the classes and the use of government to serve the collective good of the whole society. Socialists value the collective good over the private interests of individuals, and thus emphasize cooperation over competition. Socialists support a positive role for government in the economy. They advocate public ownership of key industries, regulation of the market, redistribution of resources, and protection of fundamental social rights and freedoms. Although general agreement about the goals of socialism exists, there is a wide variety of opinion on how best to achieve them. Social democrats insist on working within the parliamentary system and achieving socialism through democratic and evolutionary change. Communists and other, more radical socialists believe in the need for total, revolutionary change, often through the violent overthrow of the existing regime.

Bourgeoisie: In Marxist theory, the ruling class in capitalist society consisting of those who own the means of production, such as factories or mines. This capitalist class rules over the proletariat, or working people. In contemporary society, the term "bourgeois" has come to refer simply to the middle classes, those between the very wealthy and the working classes on the social scale. The term is often used in a derogatory fashion to refer to anything conventional and middle-of-the-road, as in "bourgeois values."

not be vehicles for truly revolutionary change. What was needed was not a redistribution of wealth and income through higher wage settlements for workers but the complete abolition of **capitalism** and its replacement with full public ownership of all of the means of production. In order for there to be real equality, he and other communists would say, the capitalist system must be replaced with a planned economy, one in which central authority decides what is to be produced and to whom it will be distributed. Communists envision a society organized around the principle: "From each according to his ability, to each according to his need."

Capitalism: An economic system in which the means of production (land, factories, technology, etc.) are privately owned and operated according to the profit motive. Decisions about production, investment, and distribution of resources are determined according to market forces (i.e., whether a profit can be made producing and marketing a product), rather than collective or community priorities. In capitalism, workers do not collectively own the means of production and perform their work in exchange for wages or salary. Although it is often called the "free enterprise system," capitalism can exist in certain variants even where the state controls the system and directs the economy according to capitalist principles.

Of course, disparities in wealth and income are not the only forms of inequality that are of critical political importance. In the North American context, the most contentious and historically significant debates regarding equality and social justice have involved **race**, gender, and sexuality. More than anything, slavery and the legacy of racial discrimination against African-Americans dominate the thinking about the politics of equality in America. Can there ever be racial equality in a country built on the enslavement of tens of millions of people? For many observers the election in 2008 of Barack Obama—the first African-American President—marked a symbolic victory for racial equality in America. Yet as Cornell West puts it, race still matters in America.[8] For political theorists, as noted in Chapter 3, race is regarded as a "socially constructed" phenomenon, not a natural or even biological one. Still, it is a social construct with powerful political implications. By racializing a population, as a new book on race and political philosophy argues,[9] political rulers produce and then make

use of racial categories to divide and rule their citizens. Members of the privileged racial group will come to see the racialized one as unruly, uncontrolled, and dangerous; thus they will acquiesce in the state's racist tactics of management and control. Seen in this fashion, racial inequality is not only ubiquitous in a liberal state like America, but it is necessary as a means of maintaining the status quo. While this argument is obviously compelling with regard to the history of discrimination against African-Americans, it is also relevant that "Muslims" have become a specifically racialized group since 9/11.

Sex inequality has also received a good deal of attention from theorists in recent years. Political philosophers in the past did not always spend much time debating the matter, since they assumed that men and women were by nature different and that their dissimilarities justified unequal gender roles. Aristotle epitomized this view when he said that "the relation of male to female is naturally that of the superior to the inferior—of the ruling to the ruled."[10] Women are justifiably excluded from politics, in Aristotle's estimation, since they are naturally unfit for rulership. In various renderings, Aristotle's position held sway among political thinkers for centuries. Mary Astell and Mary Wollstonecraft were among the first female authors who challenged this view, arguing that women and men are equally capable by nature. They regarded the exclusion of women from proper education as the main source of perceived inequity between the sexes. Another notable early proponent of women's rights was John Stuart Mill (1806–1873), who advocated for the full political equality of women and denied that there were any politically relevant differences between men and women. It is not due to nature, he said, but to social convention hardened by centuries of oppression that women are kept inferior to men. The *Subjection of Women*, published in 1869, was thought to be extremely radical in Mill's time but is now seen as a classic statement of democratic and liberal feminism.

Most theorists today, in the West at least, agree that women should have the same legal and political rights as men. There are still theoretical disputes, however, regarding the significance of observable gender differences between men and women. For instance, Carol Gilligan, who became known as the founder of "difference feminism," asserted that women have differing moral and psychological tendencies than men. According to Gilligan, men think in terms of rules

"Wait a minute — you want freedom *and* justice?"

Rex May/Artizans

and justice and women are more inclined to think in terms of caring and relationships. Unlike those who might wish to denigrate women as a result of gender differences, however, Gilligan insisted that Western liberal democracies must value both sexes equally.[11] This position has not been uncontroversial. Although she denied that sex differences were a matter of biology, and instead located the sources of differing psychological orientations between men and women in the socialization process, Gilligan's work is still often criticized for its political implications. If women are seen as somehow different from men in essence, then this can provide a justification for excluding them from certain roles in society. Moreover, some fear that Gilligan's findings can be used to reinforce the sexist presumption that women are prone to emotional and irrational decision-making, and thus cannot be fully trusted in key political positions. This is a significant matter, given that there are still many fields in which women are underrepresented, even if they are not officially excluded.

Authority and Liberty

Political theory over the centuries has been preoccupied with finding the right balance between authority and liberty. For most of this history, the assumption has been that authority from above was necessary. Order had to be imposed from above by philosopher-kings, as Plato suggested; by divinely inspired kings, as the medieval philosophers presumed; by religious experts who

know the will of God; by a spirited and ruthless prince, in the manner described by Machiavelli; or by the well-bred and naturally superior **elite**. Liberalism emerged as a reaction against this will to impose power from above. It theorized a broad, bottom-up notion of authority according to which the government is empowered by the people to protect their freedom and rights. Indeed, liberals have always harboured a degree of uneasiness with the power of the state or with large social institutions, since they can provide an opportunity for tyranny—a base for power-hungry individuals to usurp the rights of others. This is the reason for their belief in a limited government and in **checks and balances**. It was a liberal thinker, Lord Acton (1834–1902), who famously said that "Power tends to corrupt, and absolute power corrupts absolutely." But he and other liberals do not conclude from this that there should be no state authority—that each individual should be entirely free to do as he or she pleases. On the contrary, the liberal message is that one needs a properly working constitutional democracy. Arbitrary power and tyranny are the likely consequences of regimes without sufficient constitutional checks and balances. According to this logic, the power of one individual or group needs to be held in check by countervailing powers of other individuals and groups. In addition, individuals need to be protected, as much as possible, from arbitrary authority and from pressures to conform to the majority viewpoint.

Liberals tend to conceive of freedom essentially as the absence of coercive authority. One is free to the extent that one can live as one chooses, seeking one's own happiness, pursuing one's own self-interest, striving to fulfil one's own goals and aspirations. In economics, this translates into the principle of **laissez-faire**, the idea that the economic system works best when there is no interference from government. The virtues of this doctrine were first elaborated by the Scottish writer

Laissez-faire: A French phrase meaning literally "Let do"; this economic theory provides the intellectual foundation for the system of free-market capitalism. Following the principles of Adam Smith, proponents of *laissez-faire* believe that the economy works best when there is no government intervention. Thus, the theory rejects state ownership or control, advocates a free market, values individualism, and promotes free trade.

Adam Smith, who argued that if government abandoned its regulatory function, leaving individuals to enter or leave economic relations as they see fit, the "invisible hand" of the market would maximize individual well-being and ensure public welfare. This concept of *laissez-faire* became the distinguishing feature of modern capitalism and remains its most sacred principle.

Again, even free-market liberals recognize some need for government authority. There is always a threat that unscrupulous individuals will pursue their selfish interests in ways that impinge upon the freedom of others. Consequently, the very freedoms that liberals hold most dear (i.e., the right to "life, liberty, and property") can survive only when people are defended against the violent, coercive, or fraudulent behaviour of others. Protecting people's lives and possessions by maintaining law and order is therefore a fundamental job of government. But is this all that government should do? For some, the answer is yes. The only legitimate role for the state is to be a guarantor of security and a protector of private property. Anything beyond this limited role for government becomes a threat to liberty. Such a minimalist government is often referred to as the "night-watchman state." It tends to be promoted by libertarians and neo-liberals. But others doubt that such a state can serve the interests of all people. For them, freedom requires more than simply being left alone to do as you please, since one needs a certain amount of social and economic power to exercise freedom. As you can see, the issue is not as simple as choosing between liberty *or* authority.

To help us clarify this issue, it is worthwhile to turn to Sir Isaiah Berlin (1909–1997), who distinguished between negative and positive concepts of freedom.[12] The former is stressed by classical liberals and was discussed above—namely, freedom consists in the lack of external (usually governmental) restraints imposed on the individual. The greatest threat to personal freedom, from this point of view, comes from the unwanted interference from other people, including governments acting on behalf of the people. Representative writers in this tradition would include Locke and Mill, as well as the more recent theorist Robert Nozick (1938–2002), who took as his first principle that people have natural rights, and that any interference in one's activities on the part of the state is, prima facie, a violation of those rights. The latter, the concept of positive liberty, consists in there being sufficient conditions for each individual to develop to his or her full potential. From this

perspective, the greatest threat to personal freedom comes not from other people per se, but from an insufficiency of resources, wealth, or the opportunity to act freely. Representative writers in this tradition include Rousseau and Marx, as well as the more recent theorist John Rawls (1921–2002), who took as his first principle that "justice is fairness," which means that the goods necessary to freedom—resources, wealth, and the opportunity to fulfil one's life plans—should be distributed equally unless an unequal distribution is to the advantage of the least favoured in society.

A common way to express Berlin's distinction is to say that negative liberty is freedom *from*, while positive liberty is freedom *to*. Examples of negative liberty are the "fundamental freedoms" protected in liberal democracies through such measures as the Canadian Charter of Rights and Freedoms. Among others, negative freedoms include the freedom of religion, speech, association, and assembly, as well as such legal rights as the freedom from cruel and unusual punishment or the freedom from unlawful search and seizure. In these cases, we are free *from* the unwanted interventions by external authorities. For instance, we are free *from* government restrictions on what we might be able to write in a newspaper article; we are free *from* rules that instruct us on when and where we must worship; and we are free *from* the unwarranted harassment by police officers as we walk or drive down a public street. On the other hand, positive liberty involves the power *to* develop to the fullest of one's potential, the capacity *to* take charge of one's own life and direct one's actions, and the freedom *to* enjoy all opportunities for self-realization and self-fulfilment that might be available. Positive freedom implies not just the existence of certain opportunities (e.g., freedom to pursue higher education) but also the means necessary to take advantage of them (e.g., the motivation to seek such an education and the funds for tuition). Since the achievement of positive liberty involves the removal of concrete obstacles to individual participation and human development, there is an implication that some persons (or more likely, some social institutions) must take responsibility for providing the conditions necessary for its realization. If one takes seriously the right to positive liberty, therefore, one has to accept that it imposes on the collective the obligation to provide meaningful opportunities for self-determination in concert with others. Perhaps the best articulation of this concept of freedom is Rousseau's vision of a society in which all individuals find their freedom through participation in the process of self-government according to the general will.

Not surprisingly, use of the state in the name of positive freedom is often viewed as a potentially dangerous interference in private affairs. Even Berlin himself was wary of the possibilities for authoritarianism that might flow from attempts to implement a strategy of positive liberty. It may be fine, critics say, to encourage everyone to realize his or her own goals and to achieve self-actualization, but not if this comes at an unreasonable cost to others who might have to give up their freedom or some of their resources in order to provide the means necessary for the realization of someone else's life plans. The obvious concern here is that the pursuit of the equal right to self-realization will come at the expense of traditional individual liberties. In particular, it is likely to come at the expense of the individual right to do what one wants with one's own property, since the public goods necessary to produce adequate conditions for all to enjoy equally the opportunities for self-determination will have to be paid for in some fashion—through either taxation or the collective ownership of key resources. In liberal democratic states, those whom we today call fiscal conservatives will point to the deleterious consequences of high taxes, and will argue that efforts at dramatic income or wealth redistribution are an offence to individual liberty. Indeed, many will also argue that the pursuit of public solutions to what are essentially private problems (lack of self-respect, failure to succeed economically, and so on) is simply wrongheaded. Individuals, the argument goes, must take responsibility for their own choices and the satisfactory pursuit of their own life plans, and should not rely upon social institutions to solve their problems for them. For the most part, this is the view from the contemporary political right, and it stems from the presumption that the individual's liberty to do what he or she desires should almost always prevail over the state's authority to force individuals to do what they do not want to do—even if this activity will benefit the greater good of a majority of the people.

When it comes to social or moral issues, the political right and left tend to disagree on the amount of freedom that should be allowed, say, in matters such as euthanasia, drug use, flag-burning, pornography, civil disobedience, and so on. Contemporary liberals often take their cue on matters such as these from John Stuart Mill. In his famous essay "On Liberty," Mill defended the thesis that only self-protection can justify either the state's tampering with the liberty of the individual or any personal interference with another's freedom—particularly with respect to freedom of thought and discussion. According to Mill's famous "harm principle," only conduct that might do harm to others (and not action that might do harm only to oneself) is susceptible to the authority of the state or society. "In the part which merely concerns himself," Mill emphatically stated, "his independence is, of right, absolute. Over himself, over his own body and mind, the individual is sovereign."[13] Mill used as an example the case of liquor prohibition, which he saw as an unwarranted infringement on liberty. In our day, we might use Mill's arguments to advocate for the decriminalization of marijuana possession. Even if smoking marijuana might do harm to oneself, the liberal would say, it is not conduct that is harmful to others. Hence, the state should not legislate against its use.

John Stuart Mill also raised the issue of the **tyranny of the majority**—a phrase that originated with the French writer Alexis de Tocqueville (1805–1859), author of the famous study *Democracy in America*. Tocqueville found in America an impressive commitment to equality, but he was troubled by the evidence that individual liberty was often damaged by the suffocating force of public opinion. Mill, too, was alarmed that the majority in modern society was

Tyranny of the majority: Abuse of the minority by the majority through excessive use of power. Many liberals believe that we have as much to fear from the oppression at the hands of unconstrained majorities as we do from the despotic rule of an all-powerful ruler. Majority tyranny was a special concern for 19th-century liberals, who distrusted the masses and feared that universal suffrage would lead to class rule of the poor over the wealthy and the more refined citizens. Today majority tyranny is evident in the social and cultural realms, where the conformity of popular opinion runs counter to individual freedom and the right to be different. As well, ethnic and other minorities feel oppressed by the actions of majorities, who can rule through the sheer force of superior numbers.

able to impose its views on the minority. The typical check against this tendency is the constitutional protection for individuals, such as those written in a bill or charter of rights. But even then, the power of a tyrannical majority—or of politicians acting on behalf of what they believe to be majority opinion—is very real. It is a troubling fact that societies founded upon political tolerance can often become incredibly intolerant of alien or non-mainstream views and values. A popular historical example of this phenomenon comes from the Cold War period in America. Swept up in "Red scare" politics, the public became increasingly fearful of a communist threat to American liberty. Republican Senator Joseph McCarthy capitalized on this fear, becoming famous as the chair of a congressional committee investigating "un-American activities." McCarthy used unscrupulous techniques and questionable evidence to attack anyone he deemed to be a communist sympathizer or a subversive. So notorious was he that the term *McCarthyism* is now used generically to refer to the phenomenon of the political witch hunt. What is important to note about this event is that for the most part the American public acquiesced in the vilification of various left-of-centre politicians, bureaucrats, journalists, writers, and performers on the basis that even if they were not

John Stuart Mill (1806–1873), one of the most important philosophers of liberalism.

Library of Congress/LC-USZ62-2939

members of any communist organization and had not broken any laws they were, by virtue of their opinions alone, guilty of being "fellow travellers" in an unpatriotic cause.

Today there is no longer any Cold War, but the so-called "war on terror" has produced new concerns about the rise of state authority and the loss of freedom for individuals and groups. Since the terrorist attacks of 9/11, for instance, Americans have been increasingly asked to accept restrictions on long-cherished individual freedoms in the name of preserving democracy or maintaining national security. Given that the enemy is often racialized and depicted as dangerous to the very values of the state, many citizens (from the core or "normal" ethnic groups) come to believe that their interests cohere with practices such as racial profiling at airports or, worse, the detention of suspected terrorists without trial at Guantanamo Bay prison. At the same time, rights and liberties in America are routinely withheld from racial minorities via state management of political membership (e.g., naturalization, the right to vote, access to benefits and services).

Fear of the racialized "other" and the curtailment of individual liberty in the name of a normalizing state are also evident in the majority backlash against minorities, especially Muslims, throughout Western Europe. A case in point is the minaret controversy in Switzerland. Fearing further Islamization of Swiss society, right-wing politicians in the Swiss People's Party launched a campaign in 2009 that resulted in a referendum that approved, with a 57 percent majority, a constitutional ban on the construction of minarets— the spire-like structures of Muslim mosques. (At the time of the referendum there were only four such structures in the whole country.) Meanwhile, in France, where the politics of headscarves worn by Muslim women and girls has been in hot debate for over a decade,[14] the government passed a bill in 2010 banning veils, including *burqas* and *niqabs*, in all public places. These measures were supported by a vast majority of French citizens, since they are seen as upholding the republic's tradition of **secularism**. As we have seen in these cases, the majority in a liberal democratic society can find it quite acceptable to use the power of the state to curtail individual practices or behaviours that are regarded as outside of the mainstream culture and as possibly injurious to the solidarity of the whole.

Power, Democracy, and Order

Clearly, it can be difficult to get the balance right between the protection of individual liberty and the use of authority. In all polities, even liberal democratic ones, the exercise of authority involves the exercise of power, usually the power of those in state authority over individual members of the community. When is it justifiable to exert **power** over others? Questions about power and its benefits have always been at the centre of political thinking. For the ancients, power was recognized as indispensable to the good life. Aristotle regarded the active exercise of political power, in common with one's fellow citizens, as the highest human activity. Plato justified power as necessary for justice, which he understood as the establishment of the proper order, both for society and for the individual. For Christian thinkers, such as Thomas Aquinas, all political authority derives from divine law. Political power is sanctioned by God so that there may be peace and justice on Earth. Humans use natural law (i.e., reason) to establish governments and to rule them according to their own laws. This is why the divine law is eternal and unchanging but human laws can vary and change. Likewise, Islam holds that all power is derived from Allah, whose revelations form the basis for the comprehensive code known as sharia law.

Probably the most celebrated theorist of power is Niccolò Machiavelli, generally regarded as the key spokesperson for a new and distinctively modern approach to questions of civil society and humankind. His best-known work, *The Prince*, explains in delightful detail how a ruler might seize and maintain power, justifying all sorts of misdeeds according to their political ends. The best ruler, in Machiavelli's presentation, is a ruthless yet skilful practitioner of the art of politics, one who is willing to put aside conventional morality for the sake of noble political objectives. Hence, it has become common to use the term *Machiavellianism* as a synonym for amoral political calculation and as a justification of sheer power. However, Machiavelli did not justify power for its own sake. His message was that the power of the talented ruler could serve to elevate the populace as a whole, bringing nobility and glory to the collective political enterprise. Machiavelli was a patriot who thought that bringing glory and honour to one's homeland was a noble end that justified almost any means of achieving it. He was thus an early exponent of the justification of power based on specific national units rather than holy empires. Roughly a half a century later, the French political philosopher Jean Bodin (1530–1596) would also argue in favour of a state possessing a single, unified, and absolute power. Bodin was one of the first to develop the doctrine of national sovereignty as the source of all legal legitimacy.

In these two thinkers we can see that the question of power in the modern world involves both the matter of who should rule and in what sort of state. Both are old questions in political science. Box 6.3 lists a number of definitions of power as held by different individuals or groups. In the West, we have become accustomed to assume that only secular rule is legitimate. We tend to accept the notion that church and state should be separate, and that individuals should be granted the right to believe and to worship in whatever way they choose. Yet these are relatively recent ideas in the history of political philosophy and run up against a powerful tradition of thinking, from both the West

---

BOX 6.3

WHO RULES? WHAT'S IN A NAME?

Rule by one: autocracy

Rule by the few: oligarchy

Rule by the hereditary king or queen: monarchy

Rule by the usurper of legal authority: tyranny

Rule by the best or the elite: aristocracy

Rule by the people: democracy

Rule by the most honourable: timocracy

Rule by the wealthy: plutocracy

Rule by thieves: kleptocracy

Rule by the masses: ochlocracy

Rule by the clerics: theocracy

Rule by men: patriarchy

Rule by women: matriarchy

Rule by technical experts: technocracy

Rule by administrators: bureaucracy

and East, that holds that power in the state should be harnessed for the realization of divine purposes. In this regard, both Christianity and Islam are at odds with the modern notion that political power should be directed primarily toward satisfying the mere material needs of the people. Instead, religious thinkers say, power should serve a spiritual purpose, power holders should be at the service of God, and politics should follow the direction established in revealed truth. Wise legislators are still needed, of course, since holy books do not explicitly state all the social rules necessary for every time and place. Yet good rulers do not have to rely solely upon their art or skill, the way Machiavelli suggests, since religious law provides the general framework for the derivation of regulations necessary for changing conditions of time and place.

Viewed from the outside, many states in the world today appear to be based on an illegitimate exercise of power by a strong leader or small group. But what is illegitimate? For the ancients, tyranny is the unlawful and arbitrary exercise of power for one's own advantage, often by means of cruel measures against one's own people. By these standards, one might reasonably regard the heavy-handed rule by Robert Mugabe in Zimbabwe as a modern form of tyranny. Indeed, the rule by so-called "strong men," invariably backed by the military, is commonplace throughout the Global South. For the most part, this sort of rule can be characterized as "authoritarian," by which we mean that power is centralized or concentrated, usually in the hands of unelected leaders, who insist on widespread submission to authority and provide little scope for dissent. This form of government can prove unstable. Without a democratic means for regime change, the usual method of replacing an authoritarian leader is through violent overthrow or internal military coup. The popular uprisings in Egypt and elsewhere in the Middle East and North Africa in 2011 demonstrate that in some instances it is possible for citizens of countries ruled by authoritarian leaders to exert sufficient pressure through civil disobedience to effect positive change.

Democrats of various stripes tend to hold that "the people" should rule, either directly or through their elected representatives. An entire branch of political philosophy focuses on what democracy means and how it is best institutionalized in law and in political practice. Debates rage among democratic theorists about, first, the mechanisms or procedures that are most efficacious for ensuring that the will of the people prevails and, second,

what the substance of political life in a society must be in order to be deemed truly democratic. That is, some democratic theorists are concerned primarily with analyzing processes for translating the will of the people into political action. Locke and other early liberal thinkers set the groundwork for the theory that government is legitimate only if the people consent to be ruled. It is now largely assumed that full consent implies majority rule in a system of free and fair elections. Of course, many questions arise about the best systems of election, as well as about the larger questions about representation and responsiveness. These latter issues move us somewhat beyond the strictly procedural conception of democracy and into the realm of substance. How representative of all of its constituent parts must a government be before it can be called democratic? How responsive must the legislators be to the wishes of the people, and how will this be manifest? Indeed, these and other questions are taken up in a variety of ways by democratic theorists who examine the substance or content of political life from the normative point of view of democracy.

While liberal theorists laid most of the foundations for democratic theory, non-liberal thinkers have also contributed to the critical conceptualization of popular rule. For instance, followers of Karl Marx offer an alternative view of democracy. They conclude that the self-description of liberal capitalist societies as democracies is a sham, since class inequality renders political competition meaningless. In spite of the introduction of supposedly democratic electoral systems, the same rules prevail in capitalist liberal democracies as they have for centuries: namely, that those who control the wealth of society get to monopolize power. Politics through the ages, Marxists observe, involves the rule of one class over others. In modern liberal democracies, where the bourgeoisie or capitalists own all of the means of production (the factories, mines, and so on), the working class (the proletariat) is necessarily dominated and ruled against its interests. Since the mechanism for historical change of class rule is revolution, there must be a violent overthrow of the bourgeoisie by the proletariat in order to bring about a situation that would be democratic, in the sense that the people will rule in their own interest. An obstacle for some observers who seek to appreciate the democratic intention of Marx is his insistence that the transition to communism would necessarily involve a period which he called the **dictatorship of the proletariat**, whereby a government would rule in a tyrannical fashion in order to implement proletarian rule and guard against the re-emergence of bourgeois interests. The notion of dictatorship simply does not fit with most people's views of democracy. Still, the concept has to be understood within the larger whole of Marxist-Leninist thought. Actually, it was Lenin more than Marx who emphasized the practical need for a heavy-handed government during the immediate post-revolutionary period. As we have seen, Lenin feared that the working classes, left to themselves, would never become true agents of **revolution**. Therefore, the communist party, as the "vanguard of the proletariat," must rule autocratically, but in the name of the proletariat as a whole. The legacy of Lenin's theorizing is the one-party communist state, which is today only in operation in China, North Korea, Cuba, Laos, and Vietnam. While it has lost much force as a socio-political movement since the fall of the Soviet Union in 1991, communism as an ideology and Marxism as an academic study remain influential.

> **Dictatorship of the proletariat:** A Marxist concept that refers to the interim period immediately after the proletariat (the working class) has triumphed in revolutionary class war over the bourgeoisie (capitalists). Lenin explained that even after taking power in one country, the proletariat will have to remain on guard against the power of the capitalists. He used this concept to justify the class rule of the communists in a one-party state. In theory, the rule of the proletariat was expected to give way to the classless society in the final stage of history, when full communism was realized.

POLITICAL IDEOLOGIES
The Nature and Function of Ideology

Throughout this chapter we have been discussing ideas about politics and the issues and debates to which they give rise. It has been impossible to avoid touching upon various ideologies—conservatism, liberalism, socialism—in our discussion. But what exactly is ideology as a social scientific concept? What does an ideology do? Put broadly, an **ideology** is a reasonably consistent system of political beliefs that aspires to explain the world, to justify certain power relationships, and to maintain or transform existing institutions. An ideology is a system of thought according to which we can orient ourselves politically and act accordingly. Political ideologies provide a link between the world of ideas and the concrete realm of political action—for example, political parties, interest groups, mass movements, and constitutional systems.

In its philosophical aspects, the function of an ideology is to explain the key problems facing a society and to interpret key events. In this way, an ideology provides meaning for human life and history. In its policy-oriented aspects, ideology shapes the objectives and priorities of political action—it encourages the identification of specific social problems and influences the selection of the most desirable and feasible solutions. An ideology thus operates as a perceptual screen that accepts some alternatives but filters out others. Furthermore, ideology helps those persons holding power to gain acceptance for their deeds. For instance, Italian Marxist

Brant Parker and Johnny Hart, *The King Is a Fink.*

By permission of John L. Hart FLP and Creators Syndicate, Inc.

Antonio Gramsci (1891–1937) argued that power is maintained through "hegemonic strategies," which are political-economic measures used to "manufacture consent" among the population in capitalist societies. Of course, ideology is also used by activists and opposition politicians who do not exercise governmental power. Ideology can challenge established authority, criticize existing policies, and offer proposals for change. Indeed, a primary function of an ideology is to mobilize human efforts behind a cause, such as ecological preservation (environmentalism) or freedom from government regulation of individual activity (libertarianism).

Ideologies are espoused by intellectuals concerned with politics—writers, teachers, politicians, journalists, lawyers, and so on. But they are necessarily mass belief systems. An ideology must be accepted by a large number of people in order to be effective. Ideological messages are formulated in a manner that can be readily understood by potential followers who do not have the ability, the interest, or the inclination to become political experts. Ideological discourse therefore seeks to simplify the inherent complexity of the world, imposing on apparent disorder a more or less systematic body of concepts and moral beliefs that can be called upon to help people make sense of the political world. In this way, ideology helps people determine how to act appropriately, and how to distinguish right from wrong in political circumstances.

To a certain extent, ideology is a necessary ingredient of modern political life; it helps individuals make their way in a complex world. In this regard, many experts follow Sigmund Freud in emphasizing the psychological function of ideology as a means of equipping individuals with an appropriate set of reactions to social and political demands, allowing them to cope with personal strain or anxiety. This sort of analysis would suggest that ideology is an ever-present element in political life, essential as it is to humankind's social and mental requirements.

Ideological Thought

Ideology can also be understood as a *style* of thought. Persons who think in terms of ideology tend to perceive and interpret events in the light of broad and abstract ideas, such as gender equality (feminism) or faith in the common people (populism). When we say that a particular viewpoint or line of argument is "ideological," we mean to suggest that it is based upon a general or abstract set of political principles or doctrines, rather than unique, specific, or concrete conditions. Used in this fashion,

ideology refers to a specific manner or style of thinking. Sometimes this will apply to patterns of thought characteristic of a whole class or group of individuals. We might say, for example, that pride in one's consumer possessions is an attribute of "bourgeois ideology," since it is characteristic of the predominant ideas, values, and attitudes of the middle class in capitalist societies. Conversely, the principled refusal to live a life geared toward the accumulation of material wealth, on the basis that the production of unnecessary consumer goods does ecological harm, is an element of environmentalism as an ideological style.

The word "ideologue" is used to describe an advocate of a particular ideology, or perhaps to refer to the official exponent of an ideological party line (e.g., the ideologue for the Communist Party of China). Someone who always appears to be propagandizing in favour of a single sociopolitical program will often be called an ideologue. This term, in contemporary society, has an unmistakably derogatory connotation and is often freely batted back and forth between political opponents. It implies that someone is narrow-minded, unduly attached to a single way of seeing the world, and given to overly simplistic explanations for complex social and political phenomena. The term is also commonly used to refer to those who voice their ideas in an uncompromising, doctrinaire manner. Political activists and people advocating fundamental changes in the existing political situation are often accused of being ideologues.

What is often ignored by those who resort to using the term "ideologue" as a rhetorical device to undermine an opponent's intellectual or moral position is that the accusers necessarily base their own political views on grounds that are every bit as "ideological" as those they dislike. Yet so long as our political language attaches a negative connotation to the term, it will be employed as a weapon but seldom as a designation of one's own position. Few people proudly declare themselves ideologues. Yet most people are motivated by ideology when they react, either positively or negatively, to political issues or events. Moreover, the claim that one is nonideological is sometimes advanced in a positive context, as if it is a morally superior position to that of the ideologue. Again, the connotation is most likely that one who is nonideological is more likely to be open and objective about political matters, rather than biased or prejudiced toward one conclusion or the other.

Political language is not unlike other political resources—those who control it (e.g., those who own and operate major outlets of the mass media) will use

Karl Marx (1818–1883), the most famous philosopher of socialism.

this resource to their own advantage, in this case by branding their opponents ideologues and painting themselves and their supporters as nonideological pragmatists. The irony here is that a primary source of ideology's bad name comes from the writings of Karl Marx, the intellectual founder of revolutionary communism. To Marx, ideas and values (including ideologies) are determined by concrete material relations within society, especially class relations. When we study ideologies, we are focusing on the distorted and usually misleading reflections of real class interests. Marx also added to the debate the notion of false consciousness, which occurs when a group or class accepts an ideology that in reality is contrary to its "true" or objective interests. Marxists use this concept to explain the fact that so many working-class individuals reject communism and instead share the ideological views of the capitalists. In this way, the workers are said to be duping themselves and helping to prop up an economic and political system that keeps them subservient.

Many commentators in the West, especially during the Cold War, were prone to regard Communism and other non-liberal ideologies as nothing more than sources of lies and deception designed by manipulative leaders to exploit the people. There is a tendency, in other words, to identify ideology with systems of social control, political mobilization, and manipulation common in such political systems as the former USSR, Nazi Germany, and Afghanistan under the Taliban.

Again, the basis for this presumption is the view that ideology is a phenomenon that somehow hinders or obscures our ability to see the truth. Ideology is also associated with mass movements and with the mobilization of large numbers of people, who cannot seem to resist being swept up into an ideological frenzy. The image that might stick in one's mind when thinking about ideology is from the propaganda film, *Triumph of the Will*, showing Adolf Hitler addressing the 1934 Nazi Party Congress in Nuremberg. In this film, produced by Leni Riefenstahl, mass crowd shots are interspersed with footage of party followers, including members of the Nazi Youth, preparing for the big event. These images were meant to demonstrate the power and popularity of the Nazi ideology, but today they reinforce the notion that ideology is a dangerous and illiberal force. According to this critique, ideology encourages people to abandon their reliance on individual judgment and rational choice, and leads to a group mentality that is driven more by emotion than reason. Instead of thinking for themselves, critics suggest, ideologically influenced people turn to a preordained and comprehensive vision of total societal conformity—as presented in Marxist-Leninist doctrine, the fascist leadership principle, or fundamentalist religion.

Indeed, one finds in Western public opinion and political discourse an almost blanket condemnation of states with an "official" ideology, since it is taken for granted that such an ideology must be repugnant to individual rights and freedoms. Officially sanctioned ideologies such as communism, it is said, foster an atmosphere in which individuals are discouraged from thinking freely and acting for themselves because they are indoctrinated into systems of belief rather than provided with the skills and opportunities necessary to choose freely and for themselves. Examples easily come to mind. Chinese youth were "brainwashed" during the Cultural Revolution of 1966–1976, when the Maoist government sought to restore ideological purity and combat creeping capitalism. Likewise, as we have seen above, citizens of Islamic states are now portrayed in the Western media as "fanatics" whose passions are whipped up in a frenzy of anti-Western hysteria. As valid as these concerns may be in specific circumstances, it is equally important to note the extent to which Western liberal states can privilege one ideological system over others, rendering marginal any political position that is outside the accepted liberal democratic mainstream. Political scientists refer to **political socialization** as the process by which individuals learn about politics, establishing their individual attitudes, values, and ideals. As discussed in Chapter 5, the agents of socialization include the family, schools, religious institutions, peers, and the media—all of which serve to inculcate in the individual a given worldview or political culture that helps establish the parameters of acceptable political thinking.

The Political Spectrum: Right, Left, and Centre

As our discussion so far has served to demonstrate, there can be many different political views stretching across a wide range of possible ideological positions (see Figure 6.1). At this stage, therefore, it might be useful to clarify some of the key concepts often used in debates about political ideas and ideologies. First, it is conventional to use the terms **right** and **left** to refer to the orientation of a person or group according to a spectrum of political positions. It is important to note, however, that these terms can be used only to designate ideas and ideologies in the modern era; they make little sense when applied to periods prior to the dawn of industrial capitalism and the rise of liberal democratic politics. It is not useful to speak of Plato as being on the right, for example, although it makes perfect sense to refer to Marx as a leftist thinker. And while there is some debate about the issue, many believe that these terms do not have much relevance to the political divisions in many non-Western societies either, especially those with the most traditional economic, social, and political institutions or systems.

Many of the ideological terms we use today are firmly rooted in European political experience and actually date from the time of the French Revolution and immediately thereafter, when people's reaction to the events of 1789 was indicative of their basic political orientation. Conservatives, like Edmund Burke, were generally opposed to the ethos of the revolution, while liberals and socialists, in varying degrees, generally approved of the spirit of the revolutionary movement. In fact, the terms *right* and *left*, in reference to political positions, come to us from the seating arrangements in the French National Assembly of 1789, where members of the nobility, who supported the retention of substantial powers for the monarchy, were seated on the right side of the presiding officer. Seated on the left were those who wished to reduce dramatically or eliminate entirely the powers of the monarch, favouring instead a pure republic in which the elected representatives of the people would be sovereign. Today we still say that the more conservative individuals, or those who desire the least radical change to the status quo, are on the right, in contrast to the progressives or radicals on the left, who seek far-reaching and often revolutionary change.

Following the collapse of the Soviet Union and the decline of Marxism as a powerful world ideology, however, many commentators claimed that we had reached the end of ideology and that the concepts left and right were no longer relevant. Most widely known among these pundits is Francis Fukuyama, whose book *The End of History* declared that the Western capitalist ideal has proved victorious and that ideological conflict as we have known it for the past two centuries is henceforth over.[15] Italian political scientist Norberto Bobbio challenged this view, arguing in an equally influential book that the fundamental left/right political distinction is still very much relevant today.[16] Bobbio holds that the political left is committed to equality whereas the right is committed to inequality. He further distinguishes between moderates and extremists. Put simply, moderates favour tolerant and democratic methods, whereas extremists prefer militaristic, authoritarian means. Moderates and extremists can be found on both the political left and the right.

One way to understand the continuing differences between those on the political left and right is to

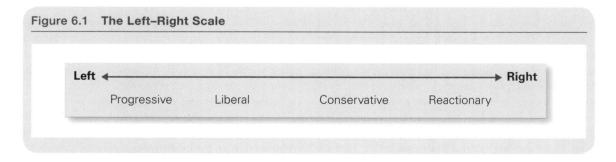

Figure 6.1   The Left–Right Scale

Left ←——————————————————————→ Right

Progressive   Liberal   Conservative   Reactionary ask what their views are on important issues or policies. Table 6.1 helps illustrate some of the key themes that differentiate leftists (e.g., Democrats in America, Liberals and Social Democrats in Europe) from rightists (e.g., Republicans in America, Christian Democrats in Europe). Some of the issues are more relevant to North American politics than European politics. It should also be remembered that these are generalizations not meant to capture all of the views of left- or right-wing people and parties. Moreover, practical political positions will change over time and according to specific circumstances.

One virtue of the left/right terminology is that it helps us visualize the relationships between and among ideological perspectives. The notion of a spectrum or a continuum also helps us realize that there are overlapping values and ideals, and that being on the left or the right is very much a matter of degree. While there is more than one set of measures that can be used to place thinkers or parties along the spectrum, a popular measure of placement is attitude toward societal change, including both the degree of change deemed necessary and the direction of the change that is preferred. On the left, progressives (anarchists, communists, socialists) tend to be discontented with the status quo and demand rapid and extensive change. The term *progressive* indicates that the political change desired tends to be forward-looking and inclusive, intended to improve the general lot of all people in society, especially the poor and disadvantaged. Sometimes, these individuals are called "radicals." The word *radical* comes from a word for root, and so

Table 6.1   Left/Right Political Differences

	Left (Liberal/Social Democrat)	Right (Conservative/Christian Democrat)
Role of Government	Positive role in providing for needs of majority through activist policies	Negative role, limited to protecting citizens and enforcing laws
Business	Mix of public and private enterprise, with strict regulations	Free enterprise with little or no public corporations; minimal regulation
Labour	Pro-union, more worker protection	Pro-employer, fewer worker entitlements
Taxes	Maintain or increase, as needed	Decrease or eliminate, as possible
Trade	Fair trade	Free trade
Minimum wage	Government-mandated, as high as practicable	Non-binding, as low as practicable
Family values	Progressive	Traditional
Affirmative action	Promote	Oppose
Abortion	Pro-choice	Pro-life
Same-sex marriage	Support legalization	Oppose legalization
Law and order	Focus on social causes of crime; protect rights of accused	Tough punishment for criminals; protect rights of victims
Death penalty	Oppose	Support
Gun control	Support	Oppose
Religion	Separation of Church and State; no faith-based government initiatives	Allow religion in schools and support other faith-based government initiatives
Freedom	Freedom from inequality	Freedom from intrusive government
Equality	Level playing field for all groups, free of systemic discrimination	Individual opportunity to achieve or fail, depending on skills and effort
International relations	Diplomacy, pacifism, internationalism	Might, militancy, patriotism
Immigration	Open and inclusive; multiculturalism; support amnesty for illegal aliens,	Closed and exclusive; assimilationist; oppose amnesty for illegal aliens,
Highest value	Justice	Order

in political circumstances what the radicals want to do is to get to the roots of societal injustice and, if need be, to uproot the entire economic and political system in order to remake society along more egalitarian lines. For example, radicals in capitalist societies see the private ownership of the means of production as the root source of injustice. Hence, they wish to eradicate capitalism itself and replace it with some version of communal property ownership. Radicals often believe that only through violent revolutionary upheaval will society be changed in total. But not all progressives are committed to the use of revolutionary tactics and most do not condone violence as a strategic option for realizing their political goals. There is a range of progressive beliefs depending on the extent of change desired and the means deemed appropriate to achieve it. Hence, anarchists and communists are considered to be farther to the left than socialists, and social democrats and reform liberals closer to the centre than others in the progressive range. Since the late 1990s *progressive* has become a more popular term to refer to left or left-liberal positions in American politics. Progressive has replaced "liberal" in campaign literature and political discourse because politicians and activists on the left of the American political spectrum feel that "liberal" has become a negative term.

It is customary to label as "liberal" the moderate range that fits somewhat between the socialist/communist left on the one hand and the conservative/reactionary right on the other. Here again, one must be sensitive to the extent of the subtle range of different viewpoints captured within this middle category. On the left of this range one finds reform-oriented or left-liberals who, like social democrats, favour progressive social change that can be seen as quite radical. They share the view that government should be used to improve social and political life through various types of social planning and policy experimentation. Left-liberals champion freedom from inequality in all its forms, and are willing to use the state to achieve the goal of improving the lives of the less advantaged. Historically, reform liberalism was associated in the United States with proponents of President Franklin Roosevelt's New Deal legislation in the 1930s and with the civil rights movement and the "war on poverty" in the 1960s. In Canada and elsewhere outside of the United States, reform liberalism brings to mind the use of a mixed economy (private ownership along with some public corporations), a Keynesian approach to fiscal policy (the use of public funds to "prime the pump" of economic development),

and a far-reaching **welfare state** system (characterized by old age pensions, universal medical coverage, unemployment insurance, social assistance programs, and the like). Indeed, one will still find the term *welfare liberal* used to designate these left-of-centre liberals and to distinguish them from more business-oriented liberals. More often, however, they are simply called left-liberals, since they support extensive reforms or changes to existing institutions or practices in a manner similar to social democrats and other leftists.

> **Welfare state:** A concept that stresses the role of government as a provider and protector of individual security and well-being through the implementation of interventionist economic policies and social programs. This positive role for government stands in contrast to the minimalist government (or "night-watchman state") that has as its only function the protection of personal property and individual security. The welfare state is regarded as having a positive role in promoting human welfare and in shielding the individual against the economic and social consequences of unemployment, poverty, sickness, old age, disability, and so on.

On the right within the liberal range are those who might be dubbed classical liberals or business liberals (and now more often "neoliberals"). These people are concerned, first and foremost, with the right to private property and with the protection of individual liberty against intrusive government action. As is often noted, there is not much of a difference on economic matters between the classical liberal position and the views of those we would today call conservatives, including members of Conservative parties in the United Kingdom or Canada or the Republican Party in the United States. This overlap between classical liberalism and contemporary conservatism can cause confusion, especially in those places where a liberal is clearly someone on the left of the political spectrum and not one who, like a classical liberal, promotes a limited state and a *laissez-faire* style of capitalism. To make matters even more confusing, the term **neoconservatism** is widely used to refer not just to those who were socially conservative but also to free-market champions of the 1980s. In many ways, the term **neoliberalism** is the much more accurate term to identify the ideology of contemporary political philosophers and politicians who support *laissez-faire* capitalism and global free trade. In terms of global economic policy, in particular, neoliberalism is an important term for those associated with such organizations as the International Monetary Fund (IMF) and the World Bank.

The assumption that liberals are somehow in the moderate middle can often be a self-serving idea promoted by liberals themselves. Most people like to consider themselves as moderates and would place themselves in the middle between the extremes of left or right. But it is important to probe more deeply to determine whether the so-called moderate liberal position is not in fact slanted one way or the other. Moreover, the placement of individuals or political parities along the continuum will depend upon the political culture and type of political party system that has developed in any given polity. In countries like the United States, where there is a firm two-party system dividing Democrats (liberals) from Republicans (conservatives), there is often not much middle ground. Without a history of socialism, moreover, there is no legitimate leftist ideological position against which liberals might be judged as more moderate or centrist.

Conservatism is usually understood to be on the right of the political spectrum. But again, there are many sorts of conservatives. Typically conservatives place order and authority above liberty and equality in their hierarchy of values, stressing the duties of citizenship and not just the rights or entitlements of citizens. Conservatives tend to be traditionalists who venerate the beliefs and moral values that have been passed down from generation to generation within a culture. The conservative predisposition is to be relatively content with the status quo, though some of the more romantic conservatives will pine for the way things used to be. Conservatives instinctively defend existing institutions against challenges from reformers on the basis that it took a long time and a lot of commonsense wisdom to create what we now have. Change should be measured, incremental, and respectful of the values of the past. Indeed, conservatives are largely skeptical about the human ability to improve life through social engineering on a grand scale. Hence, they prefer the tried and true to the new and experimental. Conservatism today is especially evident among those who decry the many "progressive" social changes that are associated with such movements as feminism, gay and lesbian rights, multiculturalism, and so on. We often refer to these people as social conservatives, since they are most concerned with preserving traditional cultural or social values and virtues. In contrast, fiscal conservatives are worried mainly about progressive changes to the economy. They fear growth of government and rising taxation rates. Again, they share many traits with classical liberals or what are now called "neoliberals" (see Box 6.4).

Most conservative persons are relatively moderate in politics. They realize that some change is inevitable,

---

BOX 6.4

NEOLIBERALISM AND NEOCONSERVATISM

The terms *neoliberalism* and *neoconservatism* are regularly used today to refer to related but slightly different trends within global politics. Neoliberalism is an economic philosophy that holds that a system of free markets, free trade, and the free flow of capital is the best way to ensure the greatest social, political, and economic good. It argues for reduced taxation, reduced government regulation, and minimal state involvement in the economy. Neoliberals support the privatization of health and welfare benefits, the weakening or dismantling of trade unions, and the general opening up of the economy to foreign competition. The term itself is not normally used by proponents of such policies; rather, it is widely employed in a pejorative sense by heterodox university professors and by leftist politicians. Neoconservatism, a somewhat older term, is applied to politicians on the political right in Anglo-American democracies who combine neoliberal economic policies (low taxes, smaller government, limited social spending) with conservative social policies (opposition to abortion, gay rights, feminism) and a "hawkish" foreign policy (increased military spending, pro-nuclear weapons, vigilant "war on terror"). While they denote distinct ideological phenomena, the two terms are often used interchangeably, which is especially understandable since the original neoconservatives, U.S. President Ronald Reagan and British Prime Minister Margaret Thatcher, are also widely regarded as among the most prominent and influential neoliberals.

but they prefer change to be evolutionary and organic rather than revolutionary and experimental. They prefer democratic methods to militaristic or authoritarian rule. To their extreme right along the ideological continuum, however, one finds various sorts of radical political ideas that are often referred to as "far-right" or "reactionary." Unlike traditional conservatives, the far-right reactionary is not content with the way things are but wants to effect dramatic change—even if it is intended as a return to the ideals of some bygone day, real or imagined, when things were better. The level of discontent and frustration is very high among reactionaries, and they are usually willing to go to extreme lengths to change things. In this regard, they resemble radicals on the extreme of the political left. But unlike leftists, who regard themselves as progressives, reactionaries seek retrogressive social change. For the most part, the reactionary wants to turn back the tide of social change, including the ideals of egalitarianism and inclusiveness characteristic of the contemporary era. Hence, there is an anti-democratic core to reactionary politics. Indeed, reactionaries will often say that many contemporary problems stem from an excess of democracy, an overabundance of choices and options that lead people away from the proper values of society. Hence, reactionaries tend to favour stern government that is unafraid to enforce strict rules. For many reactionaries, not surprisingly, the best government is found in authoritarian military rule.

The ideology of the far-right is intimately linked to the history of European fascism and totalitarianism. The Nazi and fascist movements of the 1920s and 1930s in Germany and Italy were exemplars of far-right politics. Fascism takes the right-wing assumption that people are unequal to the extreme by supporting racial supremacy and rejecting social or political equality. Historically, fascists capitalized on the fear people had of outsiders and aliens, especially at a time of economic crisis. By championing the values of the dominant race and the virtues of the ancestral nation, fascists built a positive image of a pure and healthy ethnonational group that needed protection against infiltration by impure and alien elements. Nazism in particular was founded on an extreme philosophy of racial hatred, focused primarily (though not exclusively) on hatred of Jews. Nazi anti-Semitism was combined with a totalitarian ideology intent on controlling all aspects of social life. When Hitler and his National Socialist government came to power in Germany, as is now so well known, they implemented a well-orchestrated confiscation of Jewish rights and property, followed by the most horrific extermination program in history. The murder of six million Jews in the Holocaust is the primary legacy of the far-right in power in the 20th century.

As appalling as it is, there are those today who turn to Nazism as a model to be emulated. In Europe, far-right and anti-immigration movements have gained strength in recent decades, often promoting an openly neo-fascist agenda. In many instances, the far-right is not very well organized and represents a marginalized faction within the larger society. In this regard, one might think of the "skinheads" of the 1990s in Germany who adopted a counterculture youth style from the United Kingdom, including short hair and big boots. They became notorious for violent attacks on immigrants and refugees, primarily Turks. Although their violent actions were almost uniformly condemned, the anti-immigrant sentiment behind skinhead violence was shared by a significant minority in Germany and elsewhere. Far-right political parties and ultranationalists give voice to a growing discomfort among majority populations with the large numbers of ethnically-different residents in Western European countries. Prominent parties of the reactionary right include:

- the National Front in France, whose leader came second in the presidential election of 2002 and fourth in 2007;
- the Freedom Party of the Netherlands, which won a significant following (placing third in parliamentary elections in 2010) by denouncing Muslim immigration;
- Belgium's Flemish Bloc, which stands for both Flemish nationalism and anti-immigration policies;
- the Swiss People's Party, which won 29 percent of the vote (the highest of any party) in the 2007 parliamentary election; and
- Jobbik, Hungary's far-right party which has capitalized on popular resentment of the country's Roma population.

In North America, the electoral system is not very conducive to the creation of small, fringe parties. The anti-immigrant and ultranationalist minority is more marginalized and must find room within the larger national party of the political right, the Republicans. Still, there is often concern that within the Republican Party too much influence is wielded by spokespersons for the so-called "religious right." These individuals oppose many social policies that might contradict what they refer to as "family values," including abortion rights and same-sex marriage; they argue for a return to more traditional gender roles in society and oppose state funding for daycare; they are generally skeptical about the role of the Supreme Court and object to judicial activism; they do not believe that the Constitution mandates the separation of church and state, and support school prayers and the teaching of Creationism; and they oppose the service of gays in the military.

Many people on the right do not share the social conservative principles of the Christian right. They are instead primarily concerned with economic issues, and wish to see a smaller government levying fewer taxes. Hence, a popular way to conceive of the left/right split is to use a scale charting attitudes toward the use of the state as an instrument for effecting social and political policy (see Figure 6.2). On the whole, representatives of the political right are less comfortable with the use of state power to promote collective political purposes than are people on the left. Free-market capitalists would therefore be regarded as right-wingers, while socialists and communists would be leftists. Still, as we have already seen, there are differences of degree on each end of the spectrum. On the right, more ideologically driven fiscal conservatives will oppose almost all government regulation and intervention, while more traditional conservatives will allow for a considerable degree of state control or direction in order to ensure order and stability for the community as a whole. On the political left, social democrats, with their faith in a mixed economy, will be closer to the moderate centre than those adhering to various brands of hard-line communism, which calls for total public ownership and full state control of the economy.

Moreover, if we use attitude toward the role of the state as the only means of determining the left/right split, we have to deal with certain anomalies (see Figure 6.3, p. 158). First, fascists and communists are both in principle willing to use a strong state to impose their philosophical views throughout the entire society. If we used a "freedom/authority" scale, they would both be on the side of strong authority. Yet these ideologies are clearly on opposite ends of the spectrum in terms of the goals they wish to achieve. Historically, fascists and communists have been mortal enemies. In fact, **fascism** first arose as an extreme

Fascism: The political system of the extreme right, based on the principles of the strong leader (dictator), a one-party state, nationalism, total control of social and economic activity, and arbitrary power, rather than constitutionalism. In 1922 in Italy, Benito Mussolini created the first fascist regime, emulated by Adolf Hitler in Germany. Fascist regimes also held power in Spain and Argentina. Today there are numerous neofascist movements advocating ultranationalist, racist, and anti-immigrant political positions.

Figure 6.2 The Ideological Continuum

Left ←——————————————————————————————→ Right

Socialism   Classical liberalism

Communism   Social democracy   Fascism

Anarchism   Reform liberalism   Conservatism

Feminism?
Environmentalism?
Nationalism?
Populism?

Figure 6.3   Attitude Toward the State

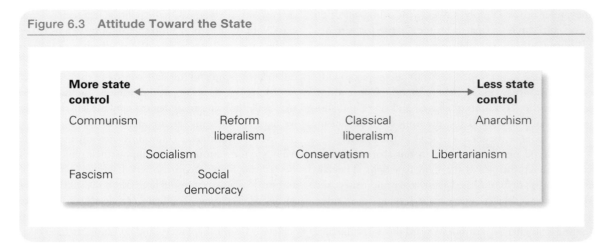

reaction against socialism and communism. Much of the initial fascist violence was directed at trade unions and other progressive organizations in society. Likewise, economic libertarianism and anarchism could appear to fit on the same side of the scale, since they both stand for the maximization of individual freedom and the absence of a coercive state. Yet, if one turns to the motivation for opposing state power, these ideologies clearly belong on the opposite ends of the left/right scale. Libertarianism defends the unfettered individual right to acquire and enjoy personal property without interference from the community. In this regard, it is quite similar to classical liberalism or fiscal conservatism, ideologies of the political right. **Anarchism**, on the other hand, shares many of the general values of radical socialism and communism. Many leading anarchists, such as Mikhail Bakunin (1814–1876) or Emma Goldman (1849–1940), began their political lives as communists and later broke with their comrades over the latter's insistence on the heavy use of state power.

Finally, we should note that there are several "isms" that do not fit comfortably on the left/right spectrum, including nationalism, populism, environmentalism, and feminism. While these ideologies can be either leftist or rightist in orientation, it is probably most accurate to suggest that the former two—nationalism and populism—are today more associated with conservative or right-wing politics, while the latter— environmentalism and feminism—are more often seen as progressive, left-wing movements.

Take **nationalism**, which is explored in greater detail in Chapter 3 of this book. As we have seen, the Nazis and their precursors were proponents of a vehement nationalism. That is, they promoted the interests and values of their own ethnocultural nation (or race) above all others, and regarded the autonomy of their national unit as a primary political good. The far-right political parties spreading throughout Europe today take a similar stance. When Jobbik party members chant "Hungary belongs to the Hungarians," they are expressing a patriotism that is motivated by animosity towards the non-ethnic Hungarian population, specifically Jews and Roma. This is clearly a right-wing ultranationalism in action. Yet nationalist convictions can be exhibited by various groups, many of whom see national independence or autonomy as a means by which to construct a progressive society organized around the principle of equality for all members of the political community, regardless of ethnicity, race, or religion. The national liberation movements that arose in the mid-20th century to fight against Western colonialism and create independent states in Africa or Asia were often led by communists. The nation-states that emerged once colonial rule was thrown off were comprised of vastly multicultural citizens who seldom shared a common language, but did share a colonial heritage of racial and imperial exploitation. The states constructed out of the national liberation struggle were almost invariably leftist in economics and finance. Still, a survey of nationalist movements today would more likely result in a list dominated by right-of-centre leaders and parties, intent not on creating a socialist state in their homelands but ethnically pure ones.

Populism—the faith in the wisdom of the common people—is regarded as being neither inherently right-wing nor left-wing. Populists tend to struggle against the elites and the big interests in the name of the people. This can take either a left- or right-wing slant. In Canada, left-wing populism was a major influence in the first major social democratic party in Canada—the Co-operative Commonwealth Federation (CCF), forerunner to today's New Democratic Party. Populism of the political right expressed itself in the Alberta Social Credit Party in the 1930s, and more recently it inspired the founders of the federal Reform Party in the 1990s. Populism has been an even more essential feature of American political culture, playing an explicit role in party politics in the late 19th and early 20th centuries in parties such as the People's Party (popularly known as the "Populists") and Theodore Roosevelt's "Bull Moose" or Progressive Party, each of which espoused reform-minded, anti-establishment ideals in opposition to established economic interests. Today, populism in the United States is most often recognized as being conservative and libertarian. For instance, the Tea Party Movement is proud of its grassroots or populist character. It has no centralized leadership and is not an official political party, though it does have clear alliances with the Republican Party and such politicians as Sarah Palin and Michele Bachman. Tea Party activists stand for a reduction in the size of government, lower taxation, reduction of the national debt and deficit, and a repeal of President Obama's healthcare legislation. In general, these measures are fiscally conservative or libertarian in their ideological orientation.

One of the fastest-growing and most truly global ideological movements in the 21st century is environmentalism, which holds that the main goal of sociopolitical action should be to preserve the natural environment. It is also difficult to locate environmentalism on the traditional left/right scale, though most observers would put it on the left side due to its generally progressive policy orientation. Proponents of environmentalism, however, often proudly claim to be "neither left nor right, but green." Environmentalists suggest that their ideology is unique in that it is the only one that repudiates the idea that humans should dominate and subdue nature. Although they may disagree about the ways to distribute the goods derived from the human exploitation of the environment, ideological conservatives, liberals, socialists, and communists all encourage the idea of humanity

mastering nature for its own purposes. Environmentalists alone challenge this "human-centred" approach and promote an alternative "Earth-centred" philosophy. As we have seen in other ideologies, there is a range of opinion, or of political positioning, among adherents to environmentalism. On the more moderate wing, one would find proponents of policy change aimed at gradually reducing the effects of pollution, conserving more of our natural resources, and generally lowering the overall harm done to the natural environment by human activity. On the more radical side, one finds those who call for more drastic measures to reverse humankind's damage to the environment, as well as adherents to the animal rights or "Deep Ecology" movements. As we have found in other movements, then, environmentalism includes both a "reformist" brand and a more "revolutionary" version, with many self-described ecological followers fitting in at various locations between these poles.

The ideology of **feminism** is also somewhat independent of the traditional ideologies, although it is by definition a progressive ideology calling for a change to the status quo of male domination. Feminism affirms the equality of the sexes and decries the subjugation of women in all of its forms. Again, there is a continuum of sorts along which one can imagine placing feminist individuals and groups according to their degree of radicalism, especially involving the practical issues of what is to be done to realize greater equality. In its less radical form (often called liberal feminism), the feminist program calls for various concrete measures aimed at producing an equality of opportunity for women—for instance, by advocating affirmative action plans or pay equity legislation. In its more radical variants, feminism regards the systematic oppression of women by men through violent patriarchy as the most fundamental moral problem. From this point of view, all of the traditional ideologies are implicated, since they are inherently male-centred and hence illegitimate. Like other major ideologies, feminism is based on a presumption that its core principles are applicable universally and not just to members of certain societies. Accordingly, feminism comes into conflict with those who argue that each culture or society or religious group should be able to determine its own values, including those regarding the relative status of women. Probably in no case does this matter get greater attention today than in the case of women and Islam. Feminists by and large oppose the social inequality prevalent in Muslim-majority societies, and urge a broadening of women's rights under Islam. Defenders of Islamic tradition complain that Western feminists are imposing an alien ideology on a unique culture, and suggest that there is a systematic misinterpretation in the West of Muslim women and their rights in the Islamic state.

CONCLUSION

As this survey of key political theories and ideologies should have demonstrated, ideas continue to play a large role in politics. Our understanding of political events and our orientation toward the political world are informed by a long tradition of political thinking, stretching back in the West at least as far as the ancient Greeks. The types of laws we live under, and the sorts of governments we support, were developed under the influence of leading political thinkers. By examining the works of the great thinkers of the past, we can better comprehend our own societies as well as equip ourselves to participate as active citizens in our own communities. And ideology plays a continued role in our lives as students and citizens. Even if we do not see ourselves as ideologues, most of us have strongly held political beliefs about who should rule and what should be done by those in positions of political power. Moreover, contemporary political elites—government officials, politicians, media representatives, interest group leaders, and others active in the political process—represent ideological points of view, in spite of their frequent reluctance to be seen to do so. Conflicting ideologies offer us a means of understanding our society, situating ourselves in the political world, and participating in actions intended to advance our interests and those of our communities.

DISCUSSION QUESTIONS

1. Given the nature of human beings, is it possible for all people to be united in a conflict-free society?

2. If human beings are equal in essence, what explains the fact that there are inequalities of rank, status, power, and wealth in virtually every society? Are these inequalities justifiable?

3. Is it sufficient to provide equality of opportunity to all citizens in a society, or should there be an effort to create a greater equality of condition?

4. In what cases are you willing to see the state interfere in society, in particular by limiting the right of individuals to live as they choose? Consider issues such as euthanasia, abortion, and pornography.

5. Are the terms *right* and *left* still relevant today? Do they help explain such ideologies as environmentalism or feminism?

6. How is the far-right different from traditional conservatism?

7. Define the terms *neoconservative* and *neoliberal* and discuss their significance in contemporary Western liberal democracies.

8. Is it accurate to say that only radical regimes, such as those in Nazi Germany or the communist USSR, govern ideologically?

FURTHER READING

In its *Very Short Introductions Series*, Oxford University Press publishes small books on a variety of topics, including the following on issues related to this chapter:

MARX: A Very Short Introduction, by Peter Singer (2000)

MACHIAVELLI: A Very Short Introduction, by Quentin Skinner (2000)

DEMOCRACY: A Very Short Introduction, by Bernard Crick (2002)

HOBBES: A Very Short Introduction, by Richard Tuck (2002)

IDEOLOGY: A Very Short Introduction, by Michael Freeden (2003)

POLITICAL PHILOSOPHY: A Very Short Introduction, by David Miller (2003)

ANARCHISM: A Very Short Introduction, by Colin Ward (2004)

SOCIALISM: A Very Short Introduction, by Michael Newman (2005)

FREE SPEECH: A Very Short Introduction, by Nigel Warburton (2009)

Other general books of interest on political ideas and ideologies include:

Ball, Terrence, and Richard Dagger. *Political*

Ideologies and the Democratic Idea, 6th ed. New York: Longman, 2005.

Baradat, Leaon P., *Political Ideologies*, 11th ed. New York: Longman, 2011.

Bird, Colin. *An Introduction to Political Philosophy.* Cambridge: Cambridge University Press, 2006.

Eagleton, Terry, *Ideology.* New York: Verso Press, 2007.

Harvey, David. *A Brief History of Neoliberalism.* New York: Oxford University Press, 2006.

Kymlicka, Will. *Contemporary Political Philosophy: An Introduction*, 2nd ed. Toronto: Oxford University Press, 2003.

Mackenzie, Iain. *Politics: Key Concepts in Philosophy.* London: Continuum International Publishing, 2009.

ENDNOTES

1. Aristotle, *The Politics*, trans. Ernest Barker (London: Oxford University Press, 1958), bk. III, chs. 6–7.

2. This phrase was popularized by Samuel P. Huntington, "The Clash of Civilizations?," *Foreign Affairs*, 72(3) (Summer 1993): 22–49.

3. *The Education of Henry Adams: An Autobiography* (New York: Oxford World Classics, 1999), p. 180.

4. In formulating the key questions this way I owe a debt to an old textbook, Glenn Tinder's *Political Thinking: The Perennial Questions*, 6th ed. (New York: Harper Colllins, 1995).

5. Hobbes, *Leviathan,* ed. C.B. Macpherson (Harmondsworth: Penguin English Library, 1981), ch. 13, pp. 185–86.

6. See Anthony Quinton, *The Politics of Imperfection: The Religious and Secular Traditions of Conservative Thought in England from Hooker to Oakshott* (London: Faber & Faber, 1978).

7. See Jacob Golomb and Robert S. Wistrich, eds., *Nietzsche, Godfather of Fascism? On the Uses and Abuses of Philosophy* (Princeton: Princeton University Press, 2002).

8. Cornell West, *Race Matters* (New York: Vintage, 1994).

9. Falguni A. Sheth, *Toward a Political Philosophy of Race* (Albany: State University of New York Press, 2009).

10. Aristotle, *The Politics*, bk. I, ch. 5, para. 6.

11. See Carol Gilligan, *In a Different Voice: Psychological Theory and Women's Development* (Cambridge: Harvard University Press, 1982).

12. Isaiah Berlin, "Two Concepts of Liberty," in *Four Essays on Liberty* (New York: Oxford University Press, 1969).

13. John Stuart Mill, *On Liberty* (New York: Bobbs-Merrill, 1956), p. 13.

14. See John R. Bowen, *Why the French Don't Like Headscarves: Islam, the State, and Public Space* (Princeton: Princeton University Press, 2006).

15. Francis Fukuyama, *The End of History and the Last Man* (New York: Penguin, 1992).

16. Norbert Bobbio, *Left and Right: The Significance of a Political Distinction*, trans. and introduced by Allan Cameron (Chicago: University of Chicago Press, 1996).

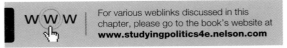

For various weblinks discussed in this chapter, please go to the book's website at **www.studyingpolitics4e.nelson.com**

Courtesy of Kathryn Royal

KATHRYN ROYAL

Kathryn Royal graduated with an Honours B.A. in political science from the University of Western Ontario in London in 2003. She subsequently pursued an M.A. in political science at McMaster University in Hamilton, with a particular focus on policy and international relations.

As a student at Western, Kathryn was involved in several clubs, on one of which she was an executive member. She also worked on initiatives to raise awareness of environmental issues and subjects related to poverty in the developing world. Although her major area of study was political science throughout her studies at Western and McMaster, she also took classes in business, economics, statistics, and political economy to focus on the interaction between these areas.

In 2005 Kathryn applied to the Ontario Ministry of Finance through a posting on the Government of Ontario website. She began her career as an Economist for the Treasury Board Office at the Ministry of Finance, where she worked with a team to undertake fiscal and financial policy analysis for the government. As part of this team, Kathryn was responsible for producing and coordinating major portions of the provincial budget and quarterly financial updates, as well as providing strategic analysis and policy advice to the Minister of Finance and senior government officials.

After spending several years working on policy relating to government expenditures, Kathryn took on a secondment as an Executive Assistant and Special Policy Adviser with the Associate Deputy Minister of Finance in charge of taxation and revenue-raising matters. Kathryn's tenure in this role exposed her to developments in pension policy and significant reforms to Ontario's tax policy, including the introduction of the Harmonized Sales Tax (HST).

Most recently, Kathryn has taken on a new challenge as a Team Leader with the Results-based Planning and Performance Management team in the Treasury Board Office. In concert with other central government agencies, her team develops and coordinates the expenditure-planning process for the Government of Ontario and is responsible for the management of expenditures, the identification of risks, and the analysis of performance measures.

Kathryn's experience at Western and McMaster, including her studies in political science, have laid the groundwork for an exciting and rewarding career in the public service. Moreover, in a world where business, global issues, and public administration intersect, Kathryn's complementary studies in economics and business have helped her take a well-rounded approach to the analysis and development of public policy.

Designing and Limiting Governments by Constitutions

Stephen Phillips

INTRODUCTION

Until recently constitutions were a neglected topic of research by political scientists. This is not altogether surprising given the fact that in most states the constitution itself is rarely at the centre of political debates. After all, while constitutions allocate political power to core institutions of government, such as executives, legislatures, and judiciaries, they do not state with precision the political ends to which such power is to be applied. Thus, while a constitution may assign wide powers of taxation to the national government, it does not specify how the proceeds of such taxation must be spent. Should the government provide free university tuition for qualified students or allocate more funds to municipalities for public transport? Should it spend more money on

its armed forces or increase old age pensions? In most states, it is questions such as these, rather than those of constitutional authority, that chiefly engage the attention of governments, political parties, pressure groups, politically attentive citizens, and the media.

Moreover, for many years constitutions were thought to have no obvious effect on the policy choices of governments. Rather, such choices were presumed to hinge primarily on socioeconomic factors such as class, political culture and ideology, and the influence of organized interest groups.[1] Consequently, it was these subjects that became the principal focus of political studies, especially in the United States, while the study of constitutions was left to legal scholars.

Today there is a new interest in constitutions among political scientists, generated by two major developments. The first is a growing recognition that the design of state institutions can have an important bearing on political outcomes and on political behaviour itself. In other words, what governments do, or fail to do, may be shaped to a considerable extent by their constitutional structure. This insight is part of an approach to studying politics known as neo-institutionalism.[2] In recent years there has been a growing interest among scholars in the design of political institutions and the special challenges of governing multinational states.[3]

The second development sparking interest in the study of constitutions has to do with the drafting of new constitutions in many states in the past two decades, such as the post-communist states of Eastern Europe and post-apartheid South Africa. Established democracies, such as France, the United Kingdom, and Australia, have also undergone or debated important constitutional reforms since the late 1990s. In addition, the continuing redesign of the European Union (EU) and its governing institutions is an ongoing exercise in constitution-making. That project, in turn, is shaping the politics of the EU's 27 member states in important ways. In short, there are sound reasons for students of politics to take a closer look at the once-neglected subject of constitutions.

WHAT IS A CONSTITUTION?

The term **constitution** has two generally accepted meanings. In its broader sense, the constitution of a state is that body of fundamental laws, rules, and practices that defines the basic structures of government, allocates power among governmental institutions, and regulates the political relationship between citizens and the state.[4] In this sense, all states have an identifiable constitution, whether they be established liberal democracies (such as Canada and the United Kingdom), communist states (such as North Korea and the People's Republic of China), or authoritarian states of various kinds (such as Nigeria, Myanmar, and Iran). In its second, narrower sense, the term constitution refers to a specific document or collection of documents that embody the legal rules of the constitution. Examples of such constitutional documents include the Constitution of the United States, the Basic Law of Germany, and Canada's Constitution Acts, 1867 and 1982.

> **Constitution:** The body of fundamental laws, rules, and practices that defines the basic structures of government, allocates power among governmental institutions, and regulates the relationship between citizens and the state.

In either case, constitutional rules are binding on political actors, taking precedence over non-constitutional rules. This is made clear in Section 52 of Canada's Constitution Act, 1982, which declares the Constitution to be "the supreme law of Canada" such that any law that is inconsistent with its provisions "is, to the extent of the inconsistency, of no force or effect." Constitutions also embody norms and understandings about the appropriate exercise of political power. For example, if Canada's governor general were to refuse to sign a bill duly passed by Parliament, he would assuredly be accused of acting unconstitutionally, even though, in theory, he possesses the legal authority to withhold giving assent to bills.

EMERGENCE OF MODERN CONSTITUTIONS

The idea that constitutions should limit the exercise of governmental power is relatively new, having been established in England in 1688, when parliament achieved supremacy over the King, an event known as the Glorious Revolution. The principle of **constitutionalism** holds that political leaders, no matter how exalted, are bound to follow the constitution. Constitutional laws, in turn, limit government in several ways. First, by allocating power to various institutions of government, the constitution avoids an undue concentration of power in the hands of a single person or group of officeholders. After 1688, the English Constitution transferred lawmaking authority from the king alone to the "King-in-Parliament," meaning that laws were to be enacted with the advice and consent of the two houses of parliament, the House of Commons and the House of Lords. Meanwhile, the power to execute laws was left to the king and his ministers, while the power to resolve disputes about the law was to be exercised by an independent judiciary.

> **Constitutionalism:** The idea that the constitution should limit the state by separating powers among different branches and levels of government and protecting the rights of individuals and minorities through a bill of rights.

England's constitution was lauded by the French political philosopher Montesquieu, who saw in its partial separation of executive, legislative, and judicial powers an effective safeguard against tyranny. His most important work, *The Spirit of the Laws* (1748), elaborated a theory of the separation of powers that profoundly influenced the framers of the U.S. Constitution of 1787.

Constitutions may further limit government by requiring that certain procedures be followed in the making and implementing of decisions. For example, police in Canada may not ordinarily enter a private residence without a judge's warrant. Constitutions may also limit government by imposing restrictions on the content of prospective laws or executive actions through a constitutional bill of rights. Such substantive limits include the First Amendment of the U.S. Constitution, which prohibits Congress from passing laws to establish a state religion or to abridge freedom of speech. Such guarantees are designed to protect the **civil rights** and **liberties** of citizens.

It must be acknowledged that while all states today have a recognizable constitution, not all of them adhere to the principle of constitutionalism. Here it is useful to distinguish between two kinds that do not: nominal and façade constitutions. A nominal constitution, rather than limiting the power of the state, simply describes and legitimizes "a system of limitless, unchecked power."[5] Such a constitution would not embody the principle of constitutionalism because even the most capricious and oppressive measures of the state would always be in accordance with the constitution. From this point of view, a constitution that vested all executive, legislative, and judicial powers in an elected assembly would violate the principle of constitutionalism no less than one that vested all political power in an absolute monarch. A façade constitution, in contrast, is one whose provisions are routinely ignored. The arbitrary arrest, torture, and extrajudicial execution of civilians carried out by certain regimes professing to respect the rule of law attests to the sham nature of their constitutions. The real purpose of such constitutions is to serve as window dressing for the international community. Nevertheless, even if the constitution of a state does not accurately describe how political power is actually used in all circumstances, it may perform other functions that reveal something about the political character of the state.

FUNCTIONS OF CONSTITUTIONS

Constitutions perform a variety of functions. The most common of these functions, and the constitutional provisions associated with them, are as follows:

1. To define the structure of major institutions of government. Constitutions typically identify the principal offices and institutions of the state, specify who is eligible to hold office, and indicate how officeholders are to be selected—for example, by election or appointment—and for what term.

2. To divide powers and responsibilities among the various institutions of government. The constitutions of most states divide powers and responsibilities horizontally among the executive, legislative, and judicial branches of government. The constitutions of federal and confederal states (discussed later) also specify how powers and responsibilities are to be allocated vertically between two levels of government.

3. To regulate relations between the citizen and the state. Constitutions often contain rules regulating how power will be exercised by the state in relation to individual citizens or members of minority groups. These rules are usually characterized as rights and codified in a constitutional charter or bill of rights. Such rights fall into two broad categories: negative rights and positive rights. Negative rights are designed to protect the interests of individuals and minorities by restricting the scope of allowable government action. Many constitutions guarantee freedom of religion, thereby limiting the power of the state to ban or unduly restrict religious worship. Positive rights, in contrast, impose a duty on the state to provide certain benefits to citizens. For example, Canada's constitution requires the federal government to deliver its services to citizens in English and French.

4. To serve as a political symbol. A constitution is normally expected to vest legitimacy in the state and may even serve as a focus for the allegiance of its citizens. To this end, many constitutions expressly invoke values and touchstones embedded in the history of a nation or people; other constitutions may seek to produce a break with the past and to proclaim the advent of a new political era. For example, the preamble of the constitution of the Republic of Ireland, adopted in 1937, pays tribute to past generations for "their heroic and unremitting struggle to regain the rightful independence of our nation."[6] The preamble of the 1954 constitution of the People's Republic of China declared that the Communist Revolution of 1949 marked the end of "imperialism, feudalism, and bureaucratic capitalism" and the beginning of

a process of social transformation leading "to the attainment of a socialist society."[7] Other constitutions emphasize order and continuity; for example, the Canadian constitution, in its most memorable phrase, authorizes Parliament "to make laws for the Peace, Order, and Good Government of Canada."

5. To specify a method for amending the constitution. The procedure for amending most constitutions is more onerous than that for amending ordinary laws. Among other things, the relative difficulty of amending constitutions is designed to maintain the stability and continuity of the political order and to prevent transitory democratic majorities from abolishing too easily the constitutional rights of minorities.

ORIGINS OF CONSTITUTIONS

The introduction of a new constitution or the significant amendment of an existing one often follows tumultuous and sometimes bloody events. Among the circumstances that give rise to new constitutions, we may count the following:

1. Revolution. **Revolutions** bring about extensive political, social, and/or economic change. The American Revolution of 1774, the French Revolution of 1789, and the Bolshevik Revolution of 1917 overthrew the existing political order and ultimately produced new constitutions. More recent events include the revolutions in Eastern and Central Europe in 1989 that brought an end to communist rule.

2. Decolonization. Most of the states in existence today came into being after 1945 as colonies in Asia, Africa, the Caribbean, and elsewhere gained their independence from European powers. In many cases, as in French Algeria and Portuguese Angola, independence was achieved after bloody wars of national liberation.

3. Aftermath of war. The defeat of a state in war may so discredit the political regime that the old constitution is scrapped and a new one adopted. In some cases, such action is driven by a new balance of domestic political forces, as occurred in 1870 when France's imminent defeat in the Franco-Prussian War led to the downfall of the Second Empire and the establishment of the Third Republic. Similarly, Germany's defeat in World War I brought an end to the authoritarian Prussian-dominated Second Reich and led to the founding of the Weimar Republic in 1919, based on a liberal democratic constitution. In other cases, such as in Japan and in Germany following World War II, a new constitution was adopted by the defeated state at the behest of foreign military occupiers. The partitioning of Germany in 1945 into separate zones of occupation led in 1949 to the founding of two states: the Federal Republic (West Germany) under a liberal democratic constitution, and the German Democratic Republic (East Germany) under a Soviet-style communist constitution. Following the collapse of Soviet power in Eastern Europe in 1989–1990, the two Germanys were reunited under the constitution of the Federal Republic.

4. Secession. Another occasion for the drafting of new constitutions is the breakup of a state following the secession of one or more of its constituent regions. In 1971, an uprising in East Pakistan against rule by West Pakistan led ultimately to East Pakistan's secession and the founding of the new state of Bangladesh. A more peaceable breakup occurred in Czechoslovakia in 1993, resulting in the establishment of two new states, the Czech Republic and Slovakia. Attempted secessions may also give rise to constitutional change. A case in point is the defeat in the U.S. Civil War of the Confederate States of America, which had attempted to secede from the United States. The postwar (or Reconstruction) period saw passage of the so-called Civil War amendments to the U.S. Constitution, which outlawed slavery and extended to the state governments the provisions of the U.S. Bill of Rights. In Canada, secessionist pressures in Quebec have generated several rounds of intensive constitutional debate. When Quebec voters rejected secession in a referendum held in May 1980, the federal government sought to weaken the appeal of separatism by implementing a controversial package of amendments to the Canadian constitution, key elements of which included the Charter of Rights and Freedoms and a domestic amending formula.

Not surprisingly, the circumstances in which new constitutions are adopted have a major influence on their content. The United States Constitution, for example, affirms the ideals of liberal constitutionalism that were beginning to gain ground in Europe in the late 18th century. However, so thorough was their repudiation of monarchy that the drafters went much further in restricting and diffusing governmental power than most other liberal democracies have thought necessary or desirable. As Harold Laski observed, "The American system, in its ultimate foundations, is built on a belief in weak government."[8]

Many national constitutions reflect an intention to remedy the perceived defects of past constitutions. Examples of such reactive constitutions include the West German constitution of 1949 and the French constitution of 1958. West Germany's constitution, known as the Basic Law, was drafted with a view to addressing the shortcomings of the Weimar Constitution of 1919 and preventing a recurrence of the political extremism that had preceded the rise to power of the Nazis. It was thought, for example, that one source of political instability in Weimar Germany was the ease with which parliament could defeat a government on a vote of non-confidence. Under the Basic Law, therefore, the Bundestag (German Parliament) may remove the chancellor only on a constructive vote of non-confidence. This requires the opposition parties simultaneously to remove the chancellor and to install his or her successor, a more difficult undertaking than merely bringing down the government. The Basic Law also authorizes the Federal Constitutional Court to ban political parties that seek to undermine democratic institutions.[9]

France's constitution of 1958 reflects the accumulated experience of the many constitutions adopted and discarded since the French Revolution. The constitution of the Fifth Republic established a mixed presidential—parliamentary system in which executive power is divided between a directly elected president and a prime minister and cabinet (who are responsible to parliament). It is designed to avoid an excessive concentration of executive power in one person (a tendency known in France as "Bonapartism") and an excessive diffusion of power among political parties and factions in the National Assembly.

TYPES OF CONSTITUTIONS

Written Versus Unwritten Constitutions

A traditional basis of classifying constitutions is to distinguish between **written** and **unwritten constitutions**.

A written constitution is one whose fundamental rules have been reduced to a single document or limited set of documents. An unwritten constitution, in contrast, is one whose subject matter is dispersed across a variety of statutes, court rulings, and unwritten political practices known as constitutional conventions. Though widely used, this terminology is unsatisfactory for at least two reasons. First, since the United Kingdom, New Zealand, and Israel are the only states in the world having an unwritten constitution, the overwhelming majority of constitutions cannot usefully be classified under this scheme. Second, the term unwritten constitution wrongly implies that most if not all of the constitutional rules of the state exist in the form of conventions. Yet much of the "unwritten" British constitution exists in written form, chiefly in leading common law cases and in various acts of parliament, such as the Bill of Rights (1689), the Act of Settlement (1701), and the Parliament Acts of 1911 and 1949. At the same time, it must be said that many of the constitutional rules of states having a written constitution exist in unwritten form.[10] It is perhaps more appropriate to distinguish between codified and uncodified constitutions. In each case, the constitution consists of both written and unwritten rules.

> **Written constitution:** A constitution whose fundamental provisions have been reduced to a single document or set of documents.

> **Unwritten constitution:** A constitution whose subject matter is dispersed across a variety of statutes, court rulings, and unwritten political practices known as constitutional conventions.

As noted above, conventions are an important element of all constitutions. A **constitutional convention**, according to K.C. Wheare, is "a binding rule, a rule of behaviour accepted as obligatory by those concerned with the working of the Constitution."[11] Because conventions are not entrenched in a constitutional document or enacted in statutory form, they

> **Constitutional convention:** An unwritten rule of constitutional behaviour that fills in gaps in the written constitution and conditions the exercise of legal powers under the constitution. While considered obligatory, such rules are not legally enforceable.

lack legal status and are not enforceable by the courts. Nevertheless, they are indispensable to the operation of modern constitutions, providing "the flesh which clothes the dry bones of the law."[12] Conventions not only provide guidance where the written constitution is silent, but also specify how the legal powers set out in the written constitution are to be exercised.

For example, many of the principles of parliamentary government in Canada are defined by convention rather than by the Constitution Act, 1867. The role of the prime minister and cabinet in Canada is nowhere spelled out in the written constitution. Similarly, the Act is silent on one of the central features of parliamentary government: the obligation of the government to resign or to seek a dissolution of Parliament if it is defeated in the House of Commons on a vote of confidence. These institutions and practices were well-established conventions of British parliamentary government by the late 1700s and were well known to the Canadian politicians who drafted the British North America Act (later called the Constitution Act, 1867) between 1864 and 1866. Accordingly, it was felt sufficient to declare in the preamble of the BNA Act Canada's desire to adopt a constitution "similar in principle to that of the United Kingdom." In this way, Canada's written constitution acknowledged and continued in force a large body of British conventions which had been adhered to for at least 20 years by the pre-Confederation governments of Britain's North American colonies.

In addition to filling in gaps in the written constitution, conventions indicate how its legal powers are to be exercised. For example, Section 50 of the Constitution Act, 1867 refers to the power of the governor general to dissolve the House of Commons for a general election. By convention, however, it is understood that this power is to be exercised only on the advice of the prime minister. In Westminster systems, the power of prime ministers to determine the timing of general elections (within the five-year maximum term of a Parliament) is one of the most formidable powers they have at their disposal.[13] In the case of Canada, this conventional power of the PM was ostensibly curtailed in 2007 when Parliament passed a law providing for fixed election dates. Under the terms of the new law, general elections are to be held every four years; accordingly, the PM may only request an early dissolution if the government loses a vote of confidence. Ignoring the intent, if not the strict letter, of his government's fixed election date law, Prime Minister

Stephen Harper requested, and was granted, a dissolution in September 2008, two years ahead of schedule.[14]

It should be noted that not all established political practices constitute conventions. Practices that are not generally thought to embody important constitutional principles are known as usages. Although neither conventions nor usages are legally enforceable, "there is a stronger moral obligation to follow a convention than a usage," and the breach of a convention is liable to attract louder criticism.[15] For example, in naming a chief justice of the U.S. Supreme Court, it is customary for presidents to appoint someone who has previous judicial experience. When President Eisenhower departed from this practice in 1953 by nominating Earl Warren, former governor of California, the nomination was mildly criticized but ultimately ratified by the Senate.[16] Breach of a convention is viewed more gravely, as proved to be the case when Franklin D. Roosevelt broke a U.S. convention limiting presidents to two terms of office by seeking (and winning) an unprecedented fourth term in 1944. Controversy about Roosevelt's breach of the term-limit convention led to its being entrenched in the U.S. Constitution in 1951 as the Twenty-Second Amendment.

Vertical and Horizontal Divisions of Power

Another way of classifying constitutions turns on the allocation of governmental authority within the state. Constitutions allocate governmental authority both vertically and horizontally among the leading institutions of the state. When referring to the vertical division of power, we are concerned with the allocation of sovereign or supreme lawmaking authority between the national government and various subnational governments. Depending on the way in which sovereignty is divided between different levels of government, we may identify three major types of constitution: confederal, federal, and unitary.

Constitutions may also be classified on the basis of the horizontal division of governmental authority between the executive and legislative branches. Here we may identify three principal forms of government: parliamentary, presidential, and semi-presidential systems. We will consider these latter forms of government in Chapter 8. For now, we will discuss confederal, federal, and unitary systems, as illustrated in Figure 7.1.

Figure 7.1   **Confederal, Federal, and Unitary Constitutions**

Central government

Member states — **Confederal system**

Citizens

Central government

Provincial/state governments — **Federal system**

Citizens

Central government

Regional/local governments — **Unitary system**

Citizens

→ Laws passed by sovereign or semi-sovereign body
⇢ Authority delegated by sovereign body

Confederal States

A confederal state (or confederation) is one in which sovereignty is retained by numerous existing states that agree to cooperate in order to achieve certain common purposes.[17] Under a confederal constitution, the central government exercises only such powers as are delegated to it by the constituent states. That is to say, any powers transferred to the central government may be modified or revoked at any time by the subnational governments. Typically, the powers of the central government are limited in number and scope. For example, the central government usually lacks the power to levy taxes and relies instead on periodic financial contributions from the constituent states. Moreover, the states may exercise a power of veto over certain decisions taken by the central government or else reserve the right to opt out of decisions with which they are unwilling to comply. Finally, states belonging to a confederation retain the right of secession.[18]

Relatively few examples can be cited of functioning confederations today. In North America, the oldest confederal form of government is the Iroquois Confederacy, an association of six Iroquoian First Nations.[19] Some confederations evolve into federations, as in the case of the 13 American states that established a confederal association under the Articles of Confederation in 1781. The chronic inability of the central government to take action in the common interests of the states led to the drafting of a new federal constitution in 1787.

The **European Union**, an association of 27 sovereign states, embodies many of the characteristics of a confederation. So, too, does the Commonwealth of Independent States, an association of former Soviet republics established in 1991 to promote cooperation in areas of mutual interest. The confederal nature of the EU is reflected in the fact that any member state may opt out of key decisions agreed to by the others. For example, Britain, Sweden, and Denmark chose to retain their national currencies and to refrain from participating in the launching of the common EU currency, the Euro, in 2002. Similarly, in 1989, Britain's Conservative government, alone among the then 12 members of the European Community, chose to opt out of the Social Charter, a set of social and employment rights addressing such matters as the right to social assistance and equitable wages

and the right to join a union. Britain reversed its position in 1997 following the election of a Labour Government.[20]

Also consistent with the confederal principle is the fact that the EU does not directly tax the citizens of its member states but relies instead on revenues transferred to it by national governments. The sources and extent of these revenues are determined in multi-year agreements reached by the EU's Council of Ministers, a confederal body on which each member state has one representative.[21]

The structure of the EU and its governing bodies is defined by a series of treaties that have been signed by each of the member states. The earliest treaty, the Treaty of Rome, established the European Economic Community (EEC) in 1957. The Treaty, drafted by the EEC's six founding members,[22] has been supplemented and amended many times over the years, most notably by the Single European Act of 1986, the Treaty on European Union of 1992 (better known as the **Maastricht Treaty**), the Amsterdam Treaty of 1997, the Treaty of Nice of 2001, and, most recently, the Treaty of Lisbon of 2007. Each new treaty must be ratified by every member state before it can take effect.[23]

Federal States

Under a federal constitution, sovereignty is formally divided between two levels of government: a national (or central) government and a number of subnational governments. Both levels of government exercise legislative authority over the territorial units that make up the federation, such that neither level is subordinate to the other. These territories are known variously as provinces, states, cantons (in Switzerland), or Länder (in Germany).[24]

While unitary constitutions outnumber federal constitutions by a ratio of nine to one, federalism is a significant form of government nonetheless. Approximately one-half of the world's population lives in federal states, and **federalism** tends to be the constitutional system of choice for geographically

> **Federalism:** A form of government in which the sovereign powers of the state are formally divided under a constitution between two levels of government, neither of which is subordinate to the other.

BOX 7.1

THE ELUSIVE GOAL OF AN EU CONSTITUTION

In order to consolidate the European Union's various treaties into a single document, and to simplify its increasingly cumbersome decision-making rules, the EU resolved in 2002 to draft a unified constitution. The task of writing such a document was given to a committee headed by former French president Valéry Giscard d'Estaing. The final text of the constitution was approved by the European Council in June 2004 and signed by all 25 EU heads of government in October of that year. Among other things, the constitution proposed new powers for the EU executive (the European Commission), the European Parliament, and the European Court of Justice. It also proposed to remove national vetoes in certain areas.

However, the EU constitution was still subject to ratification by each country in accordance with its own laws. While some countries submitted it to their national parliaments, others held national referendums. By early 2005, nine countries had ratified it; however, the process came to a halt in May of that year when voters in France and the Netherlands rejected it in separate referendums. Many opponents of the constitution saw it as a stepping stone to European federalism, a form of association that would entail a transfer of sovereignty from national parliaments to the EU. Others objected to the enshrinement of neoliberal economic doctrines that they felt posed a threat to the future of the European social market model of capitalism.[25]

In 2007, EU leaders resolved to resume the project of institutional reform. But instead of resurrecting the failed constitution, they sought to achieve most of their objectives by amending, rather than replacing, existing EU treaties. To that end, a new "amending treaty" was signed at Lisbon in December 2007. According to its proponents, the Treaty of Lisbon was not a constitution and thus did not need to be ratified by politically risky national referendums. In accepting this view, the British and Danish governments announced amid much controversy that they would scrap plans for a referendum and proceed instead with parliamentary votes on the new treaty. Other EU countries declared similar intentions, with the exception of the Irish Republic, which held a national referendum on the Lisbon Treaty in June 2008.

When Irish voters rejected the Treaty, EU leaders were obliged to agree to a number of amendments to satisfy opponents in Ireland and elsewhere. An amended version of the Treaty was approved in a second Irish referendum held on October 2, 2009. Following ratification by the Czech Republic the following month, the Treaty came into effect on December 1, 2009.[26]

President Mary McAleese and her husband cast their ballots in the second Irish referendum on the Lisbon Treaty, held on October 2, 2009.

European Photopress Agency/Landov

Table 7.1	**Federations of the World**	
Argentina	Germany	South Africa
Australia	India	Switzerland
Austria	Malaysia	Tanzania
Belgium	Mexico	United Arab Emirates
Brazil	Nigeria	United States of America
Canada	Pakistan	Venezuela
Comoros	Russia	

Source: Barry Turner, ed., *The Stateman's Yearbook, 2008* (New York: Palgrave Macmillan, 2007). Reproduced with permission of Palgrave Macmillan.

large countries such as Canada, Australia, Brazil, India, Russia, and the United States, as can be seen in Table 7.1.

Federal unions are formed for a variety of purposes. For small states, membership in a federation may offer the advantage of a common military defence against external threats. It may also offer economic advantages in the form of a larger internal market for trade and the building of national economic infrastructure by a central government that has superior financial resources. Both of these factors had a bearing on the decision of several of Britain's North American colonies to establish a federal union in 1867 and on that of the Australian colonies to do likewise in 1901. At the same time, federalism allows the territorial units to retain their separate identity and to continue to exercise decision-making authority over a range of local matters. Canada's adoption of a federal constitution in 1867 was, in large part, a concession made to French-Canadian political leaders anxious to retain authority at the provincial level over matters vital to the preservation of their culture, religion, and language.

Intergovernmental Division of Powers Under a federal form of government, the written constitution allocates authority to each level of government to pass laws in relation to particular subjects. This division of powers may be effected by enumerating separate heads of authority for the national and subnational governments. For example, the Canadian constitution assigns to the federal parliament the authority to pass laws in relation to such matters as national defence and marriage and divorce. It goes on to assign to the provincial legislatures, in their

list of **enumerated powers**, authority over such matters as hospitals and municipal government. Other constitutions, such as those of the United States and Australia, allocate lawmaking power over certain subjects to the national government and declare all non-enumerated subjects to be the responsibility of the subnational governments. In either case, the constitution grants to one level of government or the other the power to deal with matters not clearly assigned to either level of government. These **residual powers** belong to the federal government in Canada and India and to the state governments in Germany and Switzerland.

Most of the fields of legislative authority listed in federal constitutions are to be occupied exclusively by one level of government or the other. In other words, if banking is assigned to the federal government, a provincial government may not pass laws in relation to banks. However, federal constitutions may also grant **concurrent powers**—that is, designate certain areas of jurisdiction in which both levels of government may pass laws. Where there is a conflict between a federal and a provincial law in a jointly occupied field, the constitution specifies which law shall prevail or have paramountcy.

Responsibility for administering, enforcing, and interpreting laws does not necessarily follow the intergovernmental division of legislative powers. For example, most civil servants in Germany are employed by the Länd governments and are responsible for implementing both Länd and federal laws. In Canada, the power to enact criminal law is a federal responsibility; the provinces, however, are responsible for the administration of justice in their provinces, which includes the provision of police services, the handling of most criminal prosecutions, and the administration of a unitary system of courts that adjudicates disputes falling under provincial and federal jurisdiction. In the United States, in contrast, the federal principle is reflected in a dual system of state and federal courts, each of which is restricted to adjudicating cases of state law and federal law respectively.

Judicial Review As a practical matter, no constitution divides legislative powers between the two levels of government with absolute precision. Inevitably, there is considerable functional overlap between the broad categories of federal and provincial jurisdiction. For example, in Canada, the Constitution Act, 1867, assigns responsibility for unemployment insurance to the federal parliament (Section 91[2A]) and responsibility for education to the provincial legislatures (Section 93). Who, then, has jurisdiction to establish job training programs, involving classroom instruction, for recipients of federal Employment Insurance benefits? Similarly, does a province's jurisdiction over health and welfare allow it to apply occupational health and safety standards to industries such as national airlines, railways, and broadcasting, which are otherwise subject to federal regulation under Ottawa's power over interprovincial transportation and communications?

In federal systems, disputes of this kind typically are resolved by the courts, which are armed with the power of **judicial review** over law and executive action. If the courts find a particular law to be in violation of the constitutional division of powers, or in conflict with some other aspect of the written constitution, such as a bill of rights, they have the authority to declare it invalid. Germany's Basic Law explicitly establishes a Constitutional Court with the power of judicial review. In other federations, such as Canada and the United States, judicial review is not provided for in the written constitution but has come to be accepted as a legitimate power to be exercised by each country's Supreme Court.[27]

Evolution of Federal Systems As noted above, a literal reading of the written constitution paints an incomplete and often inaccurate portrait of the real constitution of a state. This is especially true of federations, in which power may be considerably more centralized or decentralized than the written constitution

would lead one to suppose. How, then, do federal constitutions evolve over time, if not by formal amendment? Three agents of change may be identified.

First, through judicial review, the courts may interpret particular fields of jurisdiction narrowly or expansively. For example, the Judicial Committee of the British Privy Council, which served as Canada's final court of appeal between 1867 and 1949, tended to give a restrictive reading to powers assigned to the federal parliament and a comparatively wide reading to powers assigned to the provinces. In contrast, the United States Supreme Court enlarged many areas of federal jurisdiction, especially in cases decided after 1937. These divergent judicial legacies explain in part why American federalism is decidedly more centralized today than its Canadian counterpart, contrary to the intentions of each country's founders.

A second factor shaping the nature of federalism is the political legitimacy attached to the exercise of certain federal and provincial powers. In other words, is the vigorous use of certain legal powers held by one level of government or the other widely accepted as appropriate? In Canada, strong regional and provincial loyalties, overlaid by a robust defence of provincial autonomy by successive Quebec governments, has inhibited federal governments from exercising the full range of their legal powers. For example, the federal cabinet has the unrestricted legal authority to disallow any provincial law within a year of its passage.[28] However, owing to strenuous objections by the provincial premiers to the use of the disallowance power, it has long since fallen into disuse.[29] In Australia and the United States, in contrast, there is a broader acceptance of political initiatives by the federal government.[30]

A third agent of change in federations has to do with social and economic developments and their impact on financial relations between the national and subnational governments. Federations established in the 19th century tended to assign constitutional responsibility for health and social welfare to the subnational governments. These subjects were not considered to be matters of national importance in an era in which hospitals and welfare services were largely provided by religious and private charitable institutions. By the 20th century, with the rise of the welfare state, governments began to assume responsibility for the provision of a wide array of public services and benefits. In federations, these burgeoning responsibilities often exceeded the revenue-raising capacity of the provincial or state governments, creating a problem of **fiscal imbalance**.

> **Fiscal imbalance:** In federal states, the constitutional responsibilities of the provincial or state governments to deliver a wide range of public services often greatly exceed the financial capacity of such governments. This gulf between public expenditures and public finances usually requires the central government to provide cash and other transfers to the provinces.

In most federations, the central government's financial resources are superior to those of the subnational governments; the national government, after all, has a broader tax base than that of any single province or state and typically has access to a wider range of tax instruments (such as customs duties, excise taxes, and corporation taxes). As a result, the problem of fiscal imbalance in federations is usually addressed through the transfer of federal funds to the subnational governments (see

Table 7.2). Such transfers give the central government the potential to influence the content and administration of laws falling outside its jurisdiction. This is most obviously the case where the central government attaches conditions to funds transferred to the subnational governments. The use of such conditional grants has had the effect of centralizing power in many federations by giving the federal government leverage over the policies and programs of the subnational governments. Such grants are used extensively in the United States to ensure the compliance of state and local governments with a variety of federal laws, from civil rights legislation to environmental regulations.

Strictly speaking, conditional grants do not impair the constitutional authority of the provinces because the latter are free to decline them. Politically, however, it is difficult for the government of a province or state to refuse federal largesse; after all, its citizens have contributed to these funds through their federal taxes. Less intrusive federal fiscal transfers include unconditional grants and federal tax abatement agreements, whereby the federal government partially vacates a field of

---

Table 7.2 Conditional Grants as a Percentage of Federal Transfers to Subnational Governments in Selected Federations, 2004

Federation	Percentage
United States	100.0
Austria	78.9
Switzerland	73.1
Spain	66.1
Canada	64.9*
Germany	64.5
Mexico	55.5
Australia	40.9
India	40.7
Malaysia	39.3
Brazil	25.0
South Africa	11.5
Russia	9.0
Belgium	5.7

*The CHT/CST transfer is included here as conditional. If deemed to be unconditional, because of the general nature of the conditions, the adjusted figure for Canada would be 26.8 percent.

Source: Ronald L. Watts, "Autonomy or Dependence: Intergovernmental Financial Relations in Eleven Countries." Working Paper 2005 (5). Institute of Intergovernmental Relations, Queen's University," p. 54.

taxation jointly occupied by both levels of government in order to create additional "tax room" for the provincial or state governments. The reliance of subnational governments on fiscal transfers from the federal government is a useful benchmark for measuring the effective degree of centralization of a federation.

Intrastate Federalism So far we have been discussing the intergovernmental division of powers. This aspect of federalism is known as interstate federalism. Another feature of federal systems has to do with the representation of the subnational units within the institutions of the central government. This aspect of federalism, known as intrastate federalism, is typically reflected in the formal representation of states or provinces in the upper house of the national legislature. For example, in the United States Senate, each of the 50 states has two senators, who are elected to a six-year term. In Germany, the governments of each of the 16 Länder appoint between three and six members to the Bundesrat (or Federal Council), who act as delegates of the Länd governments. The Länder are also represented in Germany's central bank, the Bundesbank.

Other forms of intrastate federalism may form part of the unwritten constitution or of established political practice. For example, in Canada, it is customary for prime ministers to ensure that their cabinet contains members of parliament representing each of the 10 provinces. Similarly, when appointing judges to the Supreme Court of Canada, prime ministers strive to maintain territorial balance.[31]

The Case for and Against Federalism Leading arguments in favour of federalism include the liberal idea that federalism provides an institutional safeguard for individual liberty and minority rights by ensuring that political power is not concentrated exclusively in the hands of the central government. Indeed, by dividing political authority between two levels of government, federalism arguably acts as a second check on the potential abuse of power, along with the constitutional separation of powers within each level of government. James Madison expressed this idea in *The Federalist Papers* as follows:

"In the compound republic of America, the power surrendered by the people is first divided between two distinct governments, and then the portion allotted to each subdivided among distinct and separate departments. Hence a double security arises to the rights of the people. The different governments will control each other, at the same time that each will be controlled by itself."[32]

The interests of a national minority group are best served under a federal constitution where its members are concentrated in a particular region of the country. In that way, they may hope to have effective political influence and may even constitute a majority in the legislature and government of that region. This is the case in Canada with regard to francophones, 85 percent of whom live in the province of Quebec. Likewise, the Sikh and Muslim populations of India constitute majorities in the states of Punjab and Kashmir respectively, while being heavily outnumbered at the national level by the majority Hindu population.

A related strength of federalism is that it permits subnational governments to adopt policies that reflect the preferences of local populations, whereas the central government may tend to reflect the interests of a dominant section of the national electorate. For example, governments of regions of the country in which conservative social values are prevalent might choose to maintain stricter liquor licensing and Sunday trading laws than those of regions in which more liberal values hold sway. Similarly, federalism would allow states or provinces whose populations attach a high priority to the environment to implement more stringent measures to combat pollution and global warming. In the United States, for example, California has long taken the lead in enacting strict controls on automobile emissions.

By allowing for a diversity of policies across the country in areas assigned to the subnational government, federalism may foster policy innovation. As the provinces take different approaches to addressing problems common to them all, they serve as laboratories of policy experimentation. Policies that prove to be successful and popular in one jurisdiction may then be emulated by others. For example, Saskatchewan's CCF–NDP government pioneered Canada's first comprehensive public health insurance program in 1962 in the face of fierce opposition from the province's doctors and the Saskatchewan Liberal Party. Yet the program, once implemented, proved to be such a success that it was soon embraced by the federal government and adopted by every other province.

There are, of course, potential drawbacks to federalism. Federalism does not necessarily serve the interests of minorities that are geographically dispersed. In fact, it may be inimical to their interests by making them vulnerable to hostile local majorities. Despite the abolition of slavery in the United States in 1865, African-Americans remained subject to many forms of discrimination for decades to come. In numerous southern states, this discrimination was institutionalized in the form of racial segregation of schools and other public services and systematic efforts by state officials to thwart the registration of black voters. In these circumstances, African-Americans applied to the national government, including the federal courts, to challenge oppressive measures in their home states.

This aspect of federalism remains contentious today in the United States, where the states have jurisdiction over the conduct of national elections. Both the 2000 and 2004 U.S. presidential elections were marred by charges of political partisanship and racism in several states, including the states of Florida and Ohio, states in which leading Republican Party officials were in charge of the state's electoral process. In Canada, by contrast, responsibility for the conduct of federal elections lies with an independent, nonpartisan national body, Elections Canada.

Federalism may also give rise to intergovernmental conflicts over jurisdiction and may obstruct or delay decisions requiring joint action by both levels of government. In this regard, federalism has been a factor impeding the development of social security programs.[33] On the other hand, federalism may make it equally difficult to curtail programs over which both levels of government have some say. In an era of incessant cuts to public programs in many countries, this feature of federalism is not insignificant.[34] For example, in Canada contributory public pensions are an area of concurrent jurisdiction. As a result, the federal government may not make changes to the Canada Pension Plan without the consent of two-thirds of the provinces representing at least two-thirds of the population.

Finally, as an institutional response to the challenge of governing a large, culturally heterogeneous state, federalism may be a double-edged sword. Rather than merely accommodating existing territorial differences in the country, it may reinforce and even magnify them as provincial governments compete with the central government for power and prestige. In short, "province-building" may strengthen the parochial identities of citizens at the expense of their attachment to the national political community.[35] In extreme cases, this tendency may give rise to secessionist movements.

Unitary States

Under a unitary form of government, sovereignty is vested in the central government alone. Other levels of government, such as regional, county, or municipal governments, exercise only those powers that have been delegated to them by the national government. Consequently, such powers may be modified or withdrawn as the national government sees fit. Britain, France, Japan, and New Zealand are all examples of unitary states.

By centralizing constitutional authority, a unitary state enables the national government to make decisions on a full range of matters of importance to the nation as a whole, unimpeded by the jurisdictional conflicts to which federations so often are susceptible. This capacity for decision-making at the centre offers the potential for uniformity and consistency in the design of social and economic policies. Over time, the leading role taken by the national government in public affairs may promote national unity by fostering among citizens a stronger sense of allegiance to the national political community. This was a principal aim of the Jacobin leaders of the French Revolution, and their heirs, who set about establishing in Paris a strong central government that would enact laws for all of France. So centralized became the French state that under the Third Republic (1870–1940) it was said that at any minute of any hour of the school day, the French Minister of Education knew the exact page of the national curriculum that a student in any grade should be reading!

On the other hand, an excessive centralization of authority may have undesirable consequences. The national government may be insensitive to regional differences arising from diverse local conditions. The imposition of uniform national policies may provoke resentment and undermine the legitimacy of the national government and, ultimately, that of the constitution itself. In practice, all unitary states delegate at least some authority to subnational governments. This delegation of authority, known as **devolution**, may be broad or narrow in scope. Under administrative devolution, local authorities are responsible for delivering services and implementing policies made by the central government. Legislative devolution, sometimes known as home rule, involves a partial transfer of lawmaking authority to regional governments.[36]

Unless the terms of devolution are entrenched in the written constitution, the central government may alter them by ordinary legislation. As a result, the vertical distribution of power in a unitary state may shift back and forth between periods of relative centralization and decentralization, depending on changing political conditions both locally and nationally. This point may be illustrated by reference to the politics of devolution in the United Kingdom in the past 30 years. In the 1980s the British Conservative government of Margaret Thatcher imposed severe restrictions on local government authorities in furtherance of its program of reducing government expenditure and privatizing public services. For example, local governments were required to offer for sale government-owned council houses to their renter-occupiers and were prohibited from using the proceeds of such sales to build new public housing units. Legal restrictions were also placed on local rate (or property tax) increases in order to prevent local councils from avoiding cuts to public services made necessary by reductions in central government grants. When the Greater London Council (GLC) openly campaigned against the government's policies, the government responded by passing legislation abolishing the GLC itself.[37]

At the same time, the Conservative government was steadfastly opposed to devolving power to regional assemblies for Scotland and Wales, a long-standing demand of Scottish and Welsh nationalists and of sections of the British Labour Party. The Conservatives feared that regional devolution would open the door to a "dis-United Kingdom."

In 1997, the Labour Party, led by Tony Blair, was elected to office on a platform that included support for regional devolution and enhanced authority for local governments. After the new government's devolution proposals were approved by voters in separate referendums held in Scotland and Wales in 1997 and in Northern Ireland in 1998, it proceeded to establish regional assemblies, each structured differently to reflect the unique conditions in each of the three regions. The Scottish parliament is an example of home rule, since it has lawmaking powers in designated fields, including a limited power of taxation. The Welsh Assembly exemplifies administrative devolution, since it lacks the authority to pass primary legislation.[38]

The Northern Ireland Assembly was established as part of a larger agreement addressing many aspects of the 30-year political conflict in Ulster. However, continuing conflict between the Protestant Unionist and Roman Catholic Nationalist parties made it impossible to form a stable power-sharing executive. As a result, the Assembly was suspended in late 2002 by the British secretary of state for Northern Ireland and direct rule from London restored. By early 2007, an agreement on outstanding issues was brokered by the British and Irish governments. Following fresh Assembly elections held in March 2007, a new Executive was formed and the Assembly's powers were restored.

CONSTITUTIONAL CHANGE

How does a constitution change over time, short of being replaced by an entirely new constitution? Under conditions of relative political stability, there are three principal mechanisms of constitutional change: evolving usages and conventions, judicial review, and formal amendment.

Usages and Conventions

Since all constitutions consist of both written and unwritten components, changes in the latter may transform a constitution in significant ways. For example, the role and powers of the president under France's Fifth Republic were powerfully shaped by the two longest-serving occupants of the office, Charles de Gaulle (in office from 1958 to 1969) and François Mitterrand (in office from 1981 to 1995). As president, de Gaulle established the pre-eminence of the presidency, even in areas that the written constitution appeared to assign to the prime minister and government. De Gaulle was able to enlarge the scope of presidential power as long as his political allies in parliament commanded majority support and he was free to appoint prime ministers who would defer to him. In 1986, a Socialist president, François Mitterrand, was forced to appoint a Conservative prime minister and government when the Left lost its majority in the National Assembly. It was unclear whether the constitution could accommodate such a bifurcation of political authority; some even speculated that Mitterrand would resign and force early presidential elections. Instead, a *modus vivendi* was reached between the president and prime minister, under which the former retained paramount responsibility for foreign affairs while the latter took responsibility for most aspects of domestic policy. This pattern, once established, guided subsequent "cohabitations" in the 1990s.[39]

Judicial Review

Another means by which constitutions may evolve is judicial review. Through judicial review, the words of the written constitution may be reinterpreted by the courts to reflect changing times and circumstances. This function of judicial review was memorably captured in 1930 by Britain's Lord Chancellor, Viscount Sankey, who described Canada's constitution as "a living tree, capable of growth and expansion within its natural limits."[40] The particular case before the court had to do with whether women were "qualified persons" within the meaning of the British North America Act and thereby eligible for appointment to the Canadian Senate. The Supreme Court of Canada had ruled that women were not qualified persons for this purpose since the act, drafted in 1867—decades before women acquired the right to vote—refers to members of parliament in masculine terms only. In overruling that judgment, the Judicial Committee

"Do you ever have one of those days when every-thing seems unconstitutional?"

Joseph Mirachi/www.cartoonbank.com

of the British Privy Council said that constitutions should be interpreted in the light of contemporary circumstances rather than being frozen in time. This view is not universally accepted. For example, in the United States some conservative jurists contend that the courts should interpret the constitution strictly in accordance with the "original intent" of its 18th-century drafters. A more widely held concern, addressed with humour in the cartoon below, is that unchecked powers of judicial review may invite judges to substitute their own views for those of elected legislators.

Constitutional Limits in an Age of Terrorism In recent years, governments throughout the world have been invoking the war against terrorism as a justification for the enactment of stringent new security measures, many of which infringe civil liberties and other constitutionally protected interests. For example, special counter-terrorism laws were passed in the United States, Britain, and Canada following the September 11, 2001 attacks on the United States. Some of these measures restricted or suspended altogether rights of due process for terrorism suspects, including the right of habeas corpus and the right to counsel. The surveillance powers of police and security services were also widened at the expense of privacy rights.

In many cases, courts have upheld the constitutionality of such laws and sanctioned restrictions on civil liberties. In other cases, however, the courts have declared such measures to be unlawful, in whole or in part. Examples of the latter include the ruling of the Supreme Court of Canada in February 2007 declaring security certificates to be a violation of certain provisions of the Charter of Rights and Freedoms. Such certificates empowered the state to conduct secret trials of noncitizens accused of having ties to terrorism and to impose indefinite prison terms.[41]

Likewise, in June 2006 the Supreme Court of the United States struck down an executive order pursuant to which President Bush had sought to establish special military commissions to try detainees at the notorious facility at Guantanamo Bay, Cuba. Invoking the constitutional principle of the rule of law, the Court found that the commissions were not authorized by federal law and that they violated the Geneva Conventions.[42] The Court went on to say that the President might put the commissions on a lawful footing by obtaining the necessary authority from Congress. Weeks before the U.S.

mid-term elections, Congress obliged the President by passing the Military Commissions Act of 2006.

On taking office in January 2009 President Barack Obama ordered a halt to military commissions pending a review of their future use. He also announced that the Guantanamo Bay detention centre would be closed by January 2010, although it did not happen. Instead, the Obama Administration proposed amendments to the procedures governing military commissions and provided for certain detainees to be tried in the U.S. in federal criminal courts. Some, though not all, of the Administration's proposals were approved by Congress in the Military Commissions Act of 2009.[43]

Constitutional Amendment

If the constitution is a framework of fundamental laws of the state, it follows that it should not be easily amendable. After all, it would be disruptive and upsetting if the rules of a hockey game could be amended by the home team in the middle of the third period, or if the bylaws of a students' council were fundamentally changed every couple of weeks. Nevertheless, there are occasions when a constitutional amendment is thought to be necessary. In most states, the constitution prescribes a special procedure for its own amendment, a procedure that requires a higher threshold of support than is required for amendments to ordinary laws. Even so, not all **amending formulas** are equally onerous; some are relatively flexible while others are relatively rigid.

Not surprisingly, the most **flexible** amending procedures are found in those states that have unwritten constitutions; in such cases the constitution may be amended through ordinary legislation. Unitary states having a written constitution usually specify the need for an extraordinary parliamentary majority for constitutional amendments. For example, Finland's constitution provides that proposed amendments shall be approved by at least two-thirds of the membership of the country's unicameral parliament. In 2008 France's parliament, by the required three-fifths majority of both houses, ratified a package of constitutional reforms sponsored by President Nicolas Sarkozy. One of the amendments restricts the President of the Republic to serving a maximum of two terms.

Amending formulas employed in federal systems are among the most **rigid** because of the requirement to secure agreement both at the national level of government and among some combination of the states or provinces. For example, the United States Constitution requires that constitutional amendments be approved by two-thirds majorities of both houses of Congress and ratified by three-quarters of the states. Since the ratification of the first 10 amendments to the U.S. Constitution in 1791 (known collectively as the Bill of Rights), only 17 amendments have been ratified.

Until 1982, the principal component of Canada's written constitution was the British North America Act. Since it was a British statute, most parts of it could be amended only by the U.K. parliament; in practice, however, the British willingly enacted amendments requested by the Canadian federal government. Within Canada, a constitutional convention developed to the effect that the consent of a substantial number of provinces was required before the federal government could legitimately request amendments affecting the fundamental interests of the provinces. In 1982, with the patriation of its constitution, Canada acquired a revised constitution, which included a domestic amending formula that codified the requirement for provincial ratification of key amendments (see Box 7.2).

A feature of the constitutional amending formula of some states is the requirement that amendments be ratified by citizens in a national referendum. For

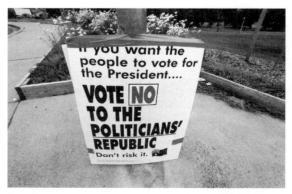

Political banners outside a polling booth for the Republic Referendum, Canberra, 1999 by Loui Seselja.

Political banners outside a polling booth for the Republic Referendum, Canberra, 1999 by Loui Seselja, Call Number: PIC NL38605 (B) Frame 25 LOC NL38605 Photographic collection shelves. Reprinted by permission of the National Library of Australia.

BOX 7.2

AMENDING CANADA'S CONSTITUTION

Canada's amending formula is found in Part V of the Constitution Act, 1982. Strictly speaking, the amending formula consists of five different formulas. The formula that applies to a particular amendment depends on the subject matter of the amendment.

General Amending Formula

The general amending formula (Section 38) applies to most types of constitutional amendments, including the federal—provincial division of powers. It requires that an amendment be approved by Parliament and by the legislatures of at least two-thirds (or seven out of 10) of the provinces whose combined population is equal to at least 50 percent of the population of all the provinces.

As worded, this means that Ontario or Quebec must give their consent. After all, if neither of them does, then the remaining eight provinces would only have a combined population of about 38 percent of the population and thus fail the second part of the '7 + 50' requirement.

Note too that Section 38 contains an opting-out clause designed to protect the interests of individual provinces. Under subsection (3), if a majority of provinces agree to an amendment transferring a certain category of provincial jurisdiction to Parliament, up to three provinces may opt out of the transfer. Suppose, for example, that all of the provinces except Saskatchewan and Quebec agreed to an amendment transferring to Ottawa responsibility for colleges and universities. By opting out of the amendment, the two dissenting provinces would retain jurisdiction over postsecondary education while Ottawa would assume responsibility for it in the rest of the country.

Unanimity Formula

Certain matters are considered to be so important as to require the unanimous consent of Parliament and all 10 of the provinces. These matters, listed in Section 41, include amendments affecting the monarchy and changes to the amending formula itself.

Amendments to Provincial Constitutions

Section 45 gives each provincial legislature the power to amend the constitution of the province. Pursuant to this authority, a province may increase (or decrease) the number of seats in the provincial legislature. It might even use this power to create a bicameral legislature—a legislature consisting of two chambers. Canada's provincial legislatures are unicameral (single-chamber) assemblies, unlike their counterparts in the United States and Australia.

Amendments to Central Government Institutions

Section 44 gives Parliament a parallel power to amend central government institutions that form part of "the Constitution of Canada" (narrowly defined). The Conservative Government of Stephen Harper has proposed to use this section to establish a limited term for newly appointed senators. However, a number of provinces have contended that Section 38 properly governs such an amendment; as such, the consent of at least two-thirds of the provinces would be required.[44]

Province-Specific Amending Formula

Pursuant to Section 43, amendments that would only affect one or two provinces may be made with the consent of Parliament and the province (or provinces) affected. Among the amendments made in the 1990s pursuant to this section were changes to the constitutional basis of the school systems in Newfoundland and Quebec.

example, one of the two methods of amendment set out in France's constitution of 1958 states that a proposed amendment, having been approved by a simple majority of both houses of parliament, must be ratified by referendum. This procedure was employed most recently in September 2000 to reduce the term of the president from seven years to five.[45]

Australia's constitution requires amendments that have been approved by parliament to be ratified by a national majority of voters; that national majority, in turn, must consist of majority votes in at least four of the six Australian states. In November 1999, a proposal was submitted to Australian voters to establish a **republic** by replacing the Queen with an Australian head of state. The amendment was rejected by 55 percent of voters on a national basis and defeated in all six states.[46] Many Australians who favoured a republic nevertheless voted to retain the status quo because they disapproved of the particular republican model on offer. That model proposed the election of a president by members of the Australian parliament, whereas most supporters of a republic favoured a popularly elected president.

Referendums are sometimes used to establish the **legitimacy** of controversial constitutional proposals, even where there is no constitutional requirement for a referendum. As discussed earlier, the devolution measures implemented in the United Kingdom in 1998 were enacted by parliament only after they had been approved by voters in separate referendums held in Scotland, Wales, and Northern Ireland. Though not legally binding, the national referendum held in Canada in October 1992 on a package of constitutional amendments known as the Charlottetown Accord effectively sealed its fate when the Accord was decisively rejected by voters.

THE POLITICS OF CONSTITUTIONAL AMENDMENT

Formal constitutional amendment in most states is not as significant an agent of constitutional change as judicial review or evolving constitutional conventions. In many states this has to do, at least in part, with the rigidity of the amending formula. A mere fraction of the thousands of proposed amendments

to the U.S. Constitution has made it past the first hurdle—that of approval by Congress—while less than 20 percent of the amendments approved by the Australian parliament since 1906 have been ratified in national referendums.[47] However, the difficulty of amending a constitution in democratic states also has to do with the fiercely contested nature of constitutional politics. After all, the stakes involved in constitutional change are often higher than those involved in the passage of ordinary legislation. Whereas a controversial law may be repealed, or an unpopular government defeated at the polls, a constitutional amendment, once adopted, is considerably more difficult to undo.

Constitutional politics also tend to arouse passions when a proposed amendment seeks to enshrine values in the constitution that are not firmly embedded or widely held within the national political culture. This was evident in Canada in the 1980s and early 1990s, when Quebec's desire for constitutional recognition as a "distinct society" was fiercely resisted by many English-speaking Canadians. Antipathy to the "distinct society" clause in the Charlottetown Accord was one of the factors contributing to the accord's defeat in the 1992 constitutional referendum. Conflicting constitutional visions also doomed the European Union Constitution in the French and Dutch referendums of 2005.

Sometimes governments seek to entrench particular social or economic policies in the constitution so as to put such policies beyond the reach of governments of a different political stripe that may be elected in the future. For example, following the Portuguese Revolution of 1974, the left-wing provisional government proceeded to nationalize key industries and large land holdings. A new constitution, adopted in 1976, declared Portugal to be in "transition to socialism" and referred to the property nationalized since the revolution as "irreversible conquests of the working classes."[48] In the 1980s, a centre-right majority government was elected on a program that included the privatization of some state-owned industries. However, lacking the two-thirds majority in parliament necessary to amend the constitution, the government was unable to implement these promises. It was finally able to act in 1989, when the opposition Socialist Party agreed to the necessary constitutional amendments.

Of course, conservative parties also seek the constitutional entrenchment of elements of their social and economic programs. For example, right-wing Republicans in the United States have long favoured an amendment to the constitution that would require the federal government to maintain a balanced budget. More recently, Republicans have responded to court decisions mandating same-sex marriage by proposing a constitutional amendment that would enshrine the traditional (heterosexual) definition of marriage. In Canada in 1980–1981, Progressive Conservative MPs advocated the entrenchment of a property rights provision in the proposed Canadian Charter of Rights and Freedoms (see Box 7.3), to better protect the economic interests of private property owners. The Liberal government ultimately rejected inclusion of such a provision in response to opposition from New Democrat MPs, who feared that a property rights clause would be used by corporations to challenge legitimate forms of economic regulation.[49]

BOX 7.3

THE POLITICS OF THE CANADIAN CONSTITUTION

An essential starting point from which to understand the nature of the constitutional debate in Canada today is the tortuous process that led to the patriation of the Constitution in 1982. Prime Minister Pierre Trudeau considered patriation to be the crowning achievement of his premiership. Others suggest that the country paid too high a price for it. Whatever history's ultimate verdict, there is no question that Canada is still living with the legacy of patriation.

The Road to Patriation (1968–1982)
When Canada effectively acquired its independence from Britain in 1931 with the passage of the Statute of Westminster, it was presumed that the federal and provincial governments would shortly agree on a new constitution to replace the British North America (BNA) Act, an act of the British parliament. Such a constitution would require a domestic amending formula. However, various attempts to reach agreement on these matters between Ottawa and the provinces ended in failure.

By the 1960s, the emergence of a powerful nationalist movement in Quebec raised the constitutional stakes for Canada. Unless relations between English and French Canada could be put on a more stable foundation, it was widely feared that Quebec's separation from Canada would just be a matter of time. The federal government took a major step toward accommodating the French fact by designating English and French official languages of Canada in 1969.

The Liberal government of Pierre Trudeau then set out to achieve the constitutional entrenchment of bilingualism, including guarantees of access to minority-language education in the provinces. Despite numerous attempts, however, intergovernmental agreement proved elusive.

The first Parti Québécois (PQ) government was elected to office in 1976. Committed to the founding of a sovereign Quebec state, the PQ called a referendum on independence for May 1980. Toward the end of the referendum campaign, Prime Minister Trudeau pledged that if Quebeckers voted No, his government would seek to renew Canadian federalism. When the ballots were counted, 60 percent of Quebeckers had voted No to independence, as against 40 percent on the Yes side.

The referendum results gave a fresh impetus to Trudeau's quest for constitutional reform. So once again the federal government made overtures to the provinces. When talks with the provinces reached another impasse, Trudeau stunned everyone by declaring his government's intention to go to London unilaterally—without the consent of the provinces—to request the constitutional changes it deemed necessary. The federal government's position was staunchly opposed by eight of the ten provinces; only Ontario and New Brunswick lent their support.

(Continued)

THE POLITICS OF THE CANADIAN CONSTITUTION (CONTINUED)

The standoff ultimately reached the Supreme Court of Canada, which was asked to rule on the constitutionality of the federal government's unilateral action. In a split decision, the judges ruled that while the federal government's action was legally valid, it violated a constitutional convention requiring the consent of a "substantial number" of provinces to major constitutional amendments.

The decision enabled both Ottawa and the provinces to claim at least a partial victory; it also allowed both sides to submit to a compromise solution without losing face—always an important consideration in politics.

The major players reassembled in Ottawa in November 1981 in a last-ditch effort to resolve their differences. By the end of the conference, agreement was reached between Mr. Trudeau and nine of the premiers. The provinces would accept the proposed Charter of Rights and Freedoms, provided it contained a "notwithstanding clause" that would allow legislatures to override certain sections of it. For its part, the federal government agreed to substitute the provinces' draft amending formula for its own.

Quebec Premier René Lévesque not only refused to sign the agreement but also angrily denounced his fellow premiers for having struck a deal behind his back. In Lévesque's view—and that of many Quebeckers—the new constitution eroded Quebec's jurisdiction over language and education in the province while failing to grant Quebec the right to veto constitutional amendments to which it objected. Lévesque accused English Canada of nothing short of betrayal!

Aftermath of Patriation

With the proclamation of the Canada Act (UK) on April 17, 1982, the Canadian constitution ceased to be a British statute and became whole with the addition of a domestic amending formula and a Charter of Rights.

On the other hand, patriation had been achieved at a high price: Quebec's estrangement from the rest of the country. In the mid-1980s, the Progressive Conservative Government of Brian Mulroney attempted to achieve a rapprochement with Quebec in two further rounds of constitutional negotiations. Both the Meech Lake Accord of 1987 and the Charlottetown Accord of 1992 proposed, among other things, to give formal constitutional recognition to Quebec as a "distinct society." However, these proposals aroused considerable opposition across the country, and neither agreement was implemented.

The Meech Lake Accord expired in June 1990 when it failed to secure the unanimous provincial consent required for ratification. Many Quebeckers took the failure of Meech Lake to signify the futility of efforts to achieve a constitutional agreement between Quebec and the rest of Canada. This sentiment produced a dramatic upsurge of support in Quebec for political independence and led to the founding of the separatist Bloc Québécois.

Two years later, at Charlottetown, Prime Minister Mulroney reached agreement with the premiers on a new package of constitutional proposals. The Charlottetown Accord of 1992 largely replicated the Meech Lake proposals, but also embraced a wide range of new issues, from Senate reform to **Aboriginal self-government**, in an effort to address many of the criticisms that had been levelled at Meech. Nevertheless, the Charlottetown Accord was soundly defeated in a national referendum held in October 1992. Interestingly, while many Canadians rejected the Accord because they believed that it gave too much power to Quebec, most Quebeckers were of the view that it gave Quebec too little!

The constitutional roller-coaster ride was not yet over. In 1994, the PQ returned to power in Quebec, promising to call another referendum on independence within a year of taking office. The results of the referendum of October 1995 were much closer than before; indeed, only a thin majority of Quebeckers voted against separation—50.6 percent to 49.4 percent.

BOX 7.3

THE POLITICS OF THE CANADIAN CONSTITUTION (CONTINUED)

Following the defeat of the Charlottetown Accord and the uncomfortably close results of the second Quebec referendum, federal politicians were unwilling to reopen the Pandora's Box of constitutional reform. The preferred approach now was to pursue common objectives through political rather than constitutional means. For example, in 1999 Prime Minister Jean Chrétien signed an agreement with the provinces undertaking not to finance new social programs in areas of provincial jurisdiction—such as child care or prescription drugs—without first obtaining the consent of the provinces. In November 2006, acting in a similar non-constitutional vein, Prime Minister Stephen Harper introduced a resolution into Parliament affirming that "the Québécois form a nation within a united Canada." While the precise meaning of this declaration was far from clear, reaction across the country was remarkably muted. Most critics were evidently reassured by the fact that it did not form part of the Constitution.

Nowadays, private property rights increasingly are codified in international trade and investment agreements, such as the **North American Free Trade Agreement (NAFTA)** and the General Agreement on Trade in Services (GATS), and in the rulings of international bodies such as the **World Trade Organization (WTO)**. Through such agreements, states undertake to refrain from enacting laws that may be construed as interfering with international trade and investment. Many observers consider the constraints imposed on governments by these agreements to be analogous to constitutional limitations. However, while modern constitutions are largely concerned with conferring rights on citizens, both as individuals and as members of minority groups, trade agreements confer rights on corporations. Since governments may not infringe the corporate rights enshrined in trade agreements, some observers fear that such agreements may seriously weaken the ability of governments to act in defence of the public interest.[50]

CONCLUSION

This chapter discussed the origins of modern constitutions, outlined their major political functions, and examined the relationship between written and unwritten elements of constitutions. It then described and assessed the principal types of constitutions—confederal, federal, and unitary—which allocate power on a territorial basis. The chapter concluded with an examination of the major processes of constitutional change. It demonstrated that constitutions, as well as the government institutions they authorize, are an indispensable part of the larger subject of politics. In the next three chapters, we take a closer look at the core institutions of government.

DISCUSSION QUESTIONS

1. In what circumstances is federalism likely to preserve the unity of a territorially diverse state? In what circumstances is it likely to exacerbate territorial differences?

2. What is the best method for amending a constitution? Should the method used to amend the constitution of a unitary state differ from that used to amend the constitution of a federal state? Explain.

3. How much detail should a written constitution provide with regard to each of the following matters?

   a) the structure of government institutions
   b) the values and principles on which the state is based
   c) the rights of citizens vis-à-vis the state
   d) social and economic policies

4. Are the interests of minorities better protected under federalism (or a decentralized unitary system) than under a centralized unitary state? Does the existence of a constitutionally entrenched bill of rights make a difference to your answer?

5. Which pose a greater threat to the freedom, security, and well-being of citizens today: governments or global corporations? Should constitutions in the 21st century be as preoccupied as those of the 19th and 20th centuries with restricting the power of governments?

FURTHER READING

Bagehot, Walter. *The English Constitution*. Cornell: Cornell University Press, 1966.

Butler, David, Vernon Bogdanor, and Robert Summers, eds. *The Law, Politics, and the Constitution: Essays in Honour of Geoffrey Marshall*. Oxford: Oxford University Press, 1999.

Elster, Jon, et al. *Institutional Design in Post-Communist Societies: Rebuilding the Ship at Sea*. Cambridge: Cambridge University Press, 1998.

Heard, Andrew. *Canadian Constitutional Conventions: The Marriage of Law and Politics*. Toronto: Oxford University Press, 1991.

Hyden, Goran, and Denis Venter. *Constitution-Making and Democratisation in Africa*. Pretoria: Africa Institute of South Africa, 2001.

Reynolds, Andrew, ed. *The Architecture of Democracy: Constitutional Design, Conflict Management, and Democracy*. Oxford: Oxford University Press, 2002.

Vile, M.J.C. *Constitutionalism and the Separation of Powers*. Oxford: Clarendon Press, 1967.

Watts, Ronald L. *Comparing Federal Systems*, 3rd ed. Montreal and Kingston: McGill-Queen's University Press, 2008.

ENDNOTES

1. Vernon Bogdanor, "Introduction," in Vernon Bogdanor, ed., *Constitutions in Democratic Politics* (Aldershot: Gower, 1988).

2. See Peter B. Evans, Dietrich Rueschmeyer, and Theda Skocpol, eds., *Bringing the State Back In* (Cambridge: Cambridge University Press, 1985); James G. March and Johan P. Olsen, *Rediscovering Institutions* (New York: Free Press, 1989); and R. Kent Weaver and Bert A. Rockman, *Do Institutions Matter? Government Capabilities in the United States and Abroad* (Washington, DC: Brookings Institution, 1993).

3. See Sujit Choudhry, *Constitutional Design for Divided Societies: Integration or Accommodation?* (New York: Oxford University Press, 2008).

4. S.E. Finer, ed., *Five Constitutions* (Harmondsworth: Penguin, 1979), p. 15.

5. Giovanni Sartori, "Constitutionalism: A Preliminary Discussion," *American Political Science Review* 56 (December 1962): 853–64.

6. Quoted in Ivo D. Duchacek, *Power Maps: Comparative Politics of Constitutions* (Santa Barbara: American Bibliographical Center, 1973), p. 18.

7. *Ibid.*, p. 23.

8. Harold Laski, *The American Presidency: An Interpretation* (New York and London: Harper and Brothers, 1940).

9. This power was used in the 1950s to ban a neo-Nazi party and the West German Communist Party.

10. K.C. Wheare, *Modern Constitutions*, 2nd ed. (London: Oxford University Press, 1966), p. 15.

11. *Ibid.*, p. 122.

12. W. Ivor Jennings, *The Law and the Constitution*, 5th ed. (London: University of London Press, 1959), p. 81.

13. Ordinarily, the governor general may not refuse a prime minister's request for a dissolution. That is not to say that in appropriate circumstances the governor general would not be justified in exercising his or her prerogative to deny such a request. See Eugene Forsey, *Freedom and Order: Collected Essays* (Toronto: McClelland and Stewart, 1974).

14. The legality of the 2008 dissolution was challenged in court by Democracy Watch, a public

interest advocacy group. In September 2009, the Federal Court of Canada rejected the claim on the grounds that the law did not restrict the governor general's legal prerogative to dissolve Parliament (*Conacher* v. *Canada (Prime Minister)* 2009 FC 920). This ruling was upheld in May 2010 by the Federal Court of Appeal.

15. Peter W. Hogg, *Constitutional Law of Canada*, Student Edition (Scarborough: Thomson Carswell, 2006), p. 25.

16. The most sustained criticism of the appointment in the Senate Judiciary Committee came from southern Democrats displeased with what they took to be Warren's excessively liberal views and from a North Dakota senator who insisted that the appointment be filled by someone from his home state. Henry J. Abraham, *Justices and Presidents* (New York: Oxford University Press, 1992), pp. 257–58.

17. While Canada styles itself as a confederation, it is more accurately classified as a federation. The error stems from the fact that in the 19th century the terms confederation and federation were often used interchangeably. For example, Switzerland continued to style itself as a confederation after adopting a federal constitution in 1848.

18. Karl W. Deutsch, *Politics and Government: How People Decide Their Fate* (Boston: Houghton Mifflin, 1970), pp. 181–82.

19. Donald S. Lutz, "The Iroquois Confederation Constitution: An Analysis," *Publius* 28 (1998): 99–127.

20. Duncan Watts and Colin Pilkington, *Britain in the European Union Today*, 3rd ed. (Manchester: Manchester University Press, 2005), pp. 179–182.

21. Ronald L. Watts, *The Spending Power in Federal Systems: A Comparative Study* (Kingston: Institute of Intergovernmental Relations, Queen's University, 1999), pp. 40–46.

22. France, the Federal Republic of Germany, Italy, Belgium, the Netherlands, and Luxembourg.

23. Neill Nugent, *The Government and Politics of the European Union*, 6th ed. (Durham, NC: Duke University Press, 2006).

24. Part of the land base of the federation may be under the exclusive authority of the central government. Examples include the Canadian federal government's authority over the country's three northern territories (Yukon, the Northwest Territories, and Nunavut) and the Australian Commonwealth government's authority over the Northern Territory, the Australian Capital Territory of Canberra, and the various island territories.

25. Katrin Bennhold, "France rejects EU constitution," *New York Times*, May 29, 2005.

26. For information on the Lisbon Treaty, including the full text, see the EU's official website: http://europa.eu/lisbon_treaty/take/index_ en.htm; accessed October 8, 2010.

27. The U.S. Supreme Court asserted its authority to review the constitutionality of acts of the federal executive in 1800 in the case of Marbury v. Madison, [1805] 5 U.S. 137 (1 Cranch). On the origins of judicial review in Canada, see B.L. Strayer, *The Canadian Constitution and the Courts*, 3rd ed. (Toronto: Butterworths, 1988).

28. See Sections 56 and 90 of the *Constitution Act, 1867*.

29. The last time the disallowance power was used was in 1943, when the federal cabinet disallowed legislation relating to banking and currency passed by the Social Credit government of Alberta.

30. See Peter H. Russell, "The Supreme Court and Federal-Provincial Relations: The Political Use of Legal Resources," in R.D. Olling and M.W. Westmacott, eds., *Perspectives on Canadian Federalism* (Scarborough: Prentice-Hall, 1988).

31. The *Supreme Court Act* stipulates that at least one-third of the nine-person Court must be members of the Bar of Quebec. This requirement ensures that there are a sufficient number of judges who are qualified to hear appeals

arising from Quebec's Civil Code, a system of private law that differs materially from the common law legal system in force in the other provinces and territories. In practice, the remaining seats are allocated as follows: three to Ontario, two to the Western provinces, and one to the Atlantic provinces.

32. Clinton Rossiter, ed., *The Federalist Papers* (New York: Mentor, 1961), p. 323.

33. Keith G. Banting, *The Welfare State and Canadian Federalism*, 2nd ed. (Montreal and Kingston: McGill-Queen's University Press, 1987), p. 41.

34. For example, in the 1990s, the Christian Democrat government of Helmut Kohl was stymied in its efforts to curtail pension benefits because of opposition from state governments represented in the upper house of the German parliament.

35. The term province-building was coined by Edwin R. Black and Alan C. Cairns in "A Different Perspective on Canadian Federalism," *Canadian Public Administration* 9 (March 1966): 27–44.

36. Andrew Heywood, *Politics*, 2nd ed. (Basingstoke, UK: Palgrave, 2002), p. 167.

37. Eric J. Evans, *Thatcher and Thatcherism*, 2nd ed. (London: Routledge, 2004), pp. 58–64.

38. Bill Jones, "Devolution," in Bill Jones et al., *Politics UK*, 4th ed. (Harlow: Pearson Education, 2001). See also Russell Deacon, *Devolution in Britain Today.* (Manchester: Manchester University Press, 2006).

39. David S. Bell, *Presidential Power in Fifth Republic France* (Oxford: Berg, 2000).

40. *Edwards v. A.-G. Can.,* [1930] A.C. 114.

41. Kirk Makin, "A Big Thumbs-Up for Civil Libertarians," *Globe and Mail,* February 24, 2007, p. A4.

42. Charles Lane, "High Court Rejects Detainee Tribunals," *The Washington Post,* June 30, 2006, p. A1.

43. Jennifer K. Elsea, *The Military Commissions Act of 2009: Overview and Legal Issues* (Washington, D.C.: Congressional Research Service, April 6, 2010).

44. Campbell Clark, "Harper to revive Senate reform plan," *Globe and Mail,* January 5, 2010.

45. The reduced term took effect at the beginning of the presidential mandate in 2002.

46. John Warnhurst and Malcolm Mackerras, eds., *Constitutional Politics: The Republic Referendum and the Future* (St. Lucia: University of Queensland Press, 2002); Ian McAllister, "Elections Without a Cue: The 1999 Australian Republic Referendum," *Australian Journal of Political Science* 36 (2) (July 2001): 247–69.

47. Gwyneth Singleton et al., *Australian Political Institutions*, 8th ed. (Frenchs Forest, NSW: Pearson Education Australia, 2006), p. 57.

48. Kenneth Maxwell, *The Making of Portuguese Democracy* (Cambridge: Cambridge University Press, 1995), p. 159.

49. The proposed property rights clause was also opposed by a majority of the premiers, who feared it would encroach on the legislative authority of the provinces. Alexander Alvaro, "Why Property Rights Were Excluded from the Canadian Charter of Rights and Freedoms," *Canadian Journal of Political Science* 24 (2) (June 1991): 309–29.

50. Stephen Clarkson and Stepan Wood. *A Perilous Imbalance: The Globalization of Canadian Law and Governance* (Vancouver: UBC Press, 2010); Stephen McBride, *Paradigm Shift: Globalization and the Canadian State*, 2nd ed. (Halifax: Fernwood, 2005).

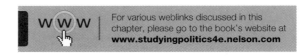

WWW For various weblinks discussed in this chapter, please go to the book's website at **www.studyingpolitics4e.nelson.com**

The Political Executive and Bureaucracy: On Top and On Tap

Stephen Phillips

CHAPTER OBJECTIVES

After you have completed this chapter, you should be able to:

- identify the main functions of the executive branch
- distinguish the role of head of state from head of government
- compare parliamentary, presidential, and semi-presidential executives
- describe the political role of the bureaucracy
- recognize the various means by which the executive is held accountable.

INTRODUCTION

The main functions of modern states are carried out by the three great branches of government: the executive, the legislature, and the judiciary. Of the three, the executive is unquestionably the least specialized. In fact, the broad range and sheer number of tasks to which the executive sets its hand are truly remarkable. Consider the many circumstances that routinely bring citizens into direct contact with the state. Every year, millions of Canadians post (or send electronically)

their income tax returns to the Canada Revenue Agency. If they are lucky enough to qualify for a refund, it will be delivered to them by an employee of Canada Post. Workers who lose their jobs must pay a visit to the local office of Human Resources and Skills Development to apply for unemployment benefits. Business owners must file a host of forms with various government agencies as well as ensuring their compliance with regulations having to do with such matters as land use, product safety, and employment standards. In each of these cases, citizens interact directly with the executive branch of government.

By way of contrast, citizens rarely, if ever, come into contact with the judiciary. Few citizens have occasion to attend the local courthouse to appear before a judge or to be called upon to do jury duty. A larger number of citizens—albeit still a minority—may have direct dealings with their member of parliament or their member of the provincial legislature. Citizens may write to their MP to seek assistance with a local problem or to convey their views on a political issue of concern to them. However, many citizens would be hard pressed even to name their MP.

The importance of the executive branch goes beyond its extensive reach into the daily lives of citizens. The executive is first and foremost the nerve centre of the state, having responsibility both for proposing and implementing a full spectrum of public policies, from national defence and foreign policy to budgetary decisions on taxation and public spending to the regulation of TV broadcasting and agricultural pesticides. In other words, the executive is both on top and on tap: it is on top by providing political leadership and direction, and on tap by supplying the state with the wherewithal to accomplish its aims. For this reason, the study of executives is a central preoccupation of political scientists.

In this chapter, we shall discuss the main types of executive found in modern democratic states and raise a number of questions about the exercise of executive power. A key issue to be addressed is the appropriate balance to be struck between the goals of effective governance and democratic accountability.

THE EXECUTIVE DEFINED

The term **executive** is rather broad and imprecise. Strictly speaking, the executive branch is concerned with the implementation and enforcement of laws and other authoritative decisions of the state. However, the executive also plays a leading role in formulating **public policy** and providing political leadership. It is customary, therefore, to distinguish between the political executive and the administrative (or bureaucratic) executive. The political executive consists of those public officeholders who have political responsibility for making public policy. Presidents, prime ministers, and cabinet ministers constitute the core of the political executive. In ordinary parlance, the political executive is synonymous with the government of the day.[1] In democratic states, the political executive may undergo a wholesale change of personnel following a general election.

> **Executive:** The branch of government concerned with the implementation and enforcement of laws and other authoritative decisions of the state. The executive also formulates public policy and provides political leadership.

The administrative executive comprises a vast array of bureaucratic institutions that support the work of the political executive and ensure the smooth operation of the machinery of government. The administrative arm of the state assumes a variety of organizational forms. However, most public servants (or bureaucrats) have certain common characteristics. Unlike politicians, public servants are nonpartisan and enjoy security of tenure. That is to say, they are obliged to carry out their duties impartially and are not liable to lose their jobs if a general election produces a change of government. In other words, bureaucrats, like judges, form part of the permanent apparatus of the state.

It should be noted that the term *bureaucrat* ordinarily denotes a public official who works in a government department headed by a minister (a member of the political executive). Beyond this bureaucratic tier, a host of other public institutions operate with more autonomy from the government on a day-to-day basis. Such institutions include state-owned corporations and regulatory agencies. Collectively, these institutions are often referred to as the *public sector*. Other distinctive components of the executive branch include the military and the police. Operating at a further remove from the political direction of ministers is the wider *para-public sector*, which includes public hospitals, public schools and postsecondary institutions, and a range of social service agencies. While these institutions derive the bulk of their financing from the state, they typically have wide discretion to manage their internal affairs (See Figure 8.1).

THE EMERGENCE OF MODERN EXECUTIVES

The executive is the oldest branch of government. Before the rise of legislative assemblies and independent courts, all of the functions of government were discharged by, or in the name of, absolute monarchs. Before the rise of constitutional government, kings made law by issuing decrees, edicts, and other proclamations, which they enforced through a network of officials. As servants of the Crown, these officials held office at the pleasure of the sovereign and could be dismissed at will. Meanwhile, justice was dispensed through the King's Courts. Most routine cases were decided by local customary law or, in medieval England, by a uniform body of common

Figure 8.1   **The Principal Components of the Executive**

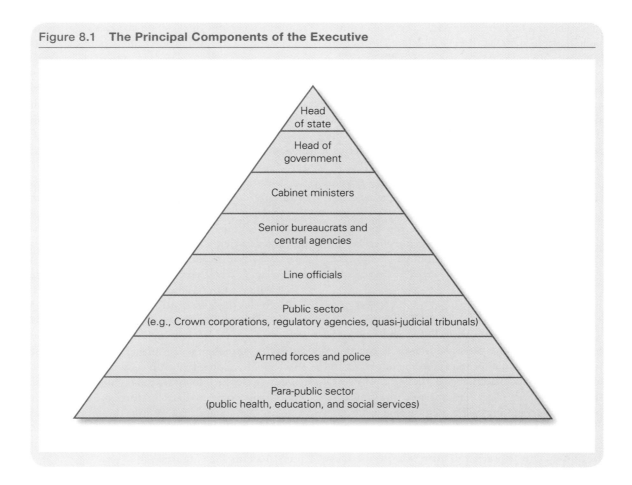

law applicable throughout the realm.[2] Nevertheless, the sovereign retained wide prerogatives, including the power to grant pardons in criminal cases and to dismiss (and even to arrest) judges whose rulings displeased him!

The struggle for constitutional government was a struggle to limit the power of the Crown. As noted in Chapter 7, the prerogatives of English monarchs were narrowed considerably after the Glorious Revolution of 1688, in which parliament established its supremacy over the Crown. In the decades that followed, constitutional safeguards were put in place to protect the judiciary from improper interference by the executive branch. By the middle of the 19th century, the British monarchy had been transformed; it now belonged to the "dignified part of the constitution." According to Walter Bagehot, the "efficient secret" of the British Constitution was the fusion of executive and legislative power in the cabinet, which he described as a

> board of control chosen by the legislature, out of persons whom it trusts and knows, to rule the nation. . . . A Cabinet is a combining committee—a hyphen which joins, a buckle which fastens, the legislative part of the State to the executive part of the State.[3]

In an influential commentary on Bagehot's classic work, *The English Constitution*, Richard Crossman observed that with the rise of disciplined political parties in the late 19th century, the cabinet came to dominate parliament. Crossman and others went on to describe a significant centralization of power within the executive branch itself since the end of World War II. In their view, prime ministers and senior bureaucrats exercise such wide-ranging powers nowadays that, in many respects, the cabinet has joined parliament and the Crown in forming part of the dignified (or decorative) part of the constitution.

FUNCTIONS OF THE EXECUTIVE

Today the main functions of the executive may be stated as follows:

- *To provide political leadership to the nation.* It is to the executive branch that citizens look to take the initiative to address political problems. Most of those problems are of a routine, ongoing nature, but citizens also expect the political executive to respond swiftly, decisively, and competently to national crises, both domestic and foreign. Note that while the approval of parliament (or the legislature) is often required in order to give formal, legal effect to the policies of the government, the initiative for most legislation lies with the executive.
- *To implement laws formally approved by the legislature.* The political executive dominates the early stages of the policy process, at which policy is formulated, as well as the latter stages, at which policy is implemented. In regard to the latter function, executive agencies of the state (chiefly, the bureaucracy) are responsible for ensuring that taxes are collected, that public services are delivered, and that a host of regulatory laws are enforced. In Canada, the prime minister and his or her government have ultimate political responsibility for the efficiency, effectiveness, and fairness with which such functions of the state are carried out.
- *To make rules and regulations.* In modern democratic states, the government needs legal authority from the legislature to carry out most of its operations. Legislative grants of authority to the executive tend to vest wide powers in the government to draw up detailed regulations that flesh out the often skeletal framework of legislation. In Canada, for example, the *Firearms Act* authorizes the federal government to establish a national registry for firearms and to determine the procedures to be followed (and the fees to be paid) to register a gun. Other statutes give the Minister of Immigration the authority to establish a procedure to process claims for refugee status and the Minister of Agriculture—or agencies that the ministry sets up—wide powers to set production quotas for dairy and poultry farmers.
- *To administer government departments and other agencies.* As in any large organization, governments need to be organized into specialized units that are responsible for performing particular functions. A key task of the political executive is to organize the apparatus of the state, including its personnel, which may number in the hundreds of thousands. In carrying out this managerial role, the political executive relies heavily on the advice of high-ranking public officials within the bureaucracy.

HEAD OF STATE VERSUS HEAD OF GOVERNMENT

The political executive sits at the apex of the executive branch. On closer examination, we may distinguish between two leading offices of state: the **head of state** and the **head of government**. In parliamentary and semi-parliamentary systems, these posts are filled by separate officeholders. This arrangement is known as a **dual executive**. In presidential systems, the two positions are combined and held by a single office-holder, an arrangement known as a **single executive**. For now, let us take a closer look at the respective roles of the head of state and the head of government under a parliamentary system of government.

Dual executive: A form of executive in which the posts of head of state and head of government are divided, and each is held by a separate officeholder. In parliamentary systems, the head of state is a constitutional monarch or an elected president and the head of government is the prime minister.

Single executive: A form of executive in which the posts of head of state and head of government are combined and held by a single officeholder. This arrangement is characteristic of presidential systems, such as those of Argentina, Mexico, and the United States.

German Chancellor Angela Merkel congratulates Christian Wulff, the newly and narrowly elected President of the Federal Republic, July 2010.

European Photopress Agency/Landov

In parliamentary systems, the office of head of state is held either by a constitutional monarch or an elected president. Spain, Japan, and the Netherlands are examples of parliamentary democracies having a monarchical head of state. Heredity is the principle governing succession to the throne, although the rules of succession vary somewhat among national monarchies. For example, in Norway the eldest child of the reigning monarch is deemed the heir apparent, whether male or female, whereas in Japan only males may accede to the throne. In Britain, the line of succession privileges male heirs; under the law of primogeniture, women may accede to the throne only in the absence of a male heir. Moreover, the 1701 *Act of Settlement* bars Roman Catholics from acceding to the British throne. Not surprisingly, there has been much debate about repealing these laws, neither of which can easily be reconciled with contemporary views about equality.

Interestingly, Queen Elizabeth II is head of state not only of the United Kingdom but also of some 15 other countries belonging to the Commonwealth, including Canada, New Zealand, and Jamaica.[4] However, with the exception of the United Kingdom, the Queen's duties in each of these countries are carried out by her representative, known as the Governor General (GG). In federal states, such as Australia and Canada, the Queen also has representatives at the state or provincial level of government. They are known as Governors or Lieutenant Governors. These officials are appointed by the Queen or GG, on the advice of the Prime Minister—or the State Premier, as the case may be—and usually serve a five-year term.[5]

A parliamentary **republic** is headed by an elected president, but despite the use of this latter title, we should not confuse it with a presidential system such as that of the United States. In a parliamentary republic, the president may be directly elected by the people, as in Portugal, Austria, and the Republic of Ireland. In other states, including Greece and Italy, the president is chosen by members of the national parliament. In Germany the President is chosen by an electoral college (called the Federal Convention) comprising all members of the lower house of the federal parliament and an equal number of delegates elected by the state parliaments.

The second part of the parliamentary dual executive is headed by a prime minister or premier (known in Austria and Germany as the chancellor). The prime minister (PM) is appointed by the head of state, usually following a general election, and is invited to form a government by naming a cabinet. In most cases, the prime minister is the leader of the party having the largest number of seats in parliament. As head of government, the prime minister advises the head of state on the exercise of the legal powers held by the latter, and, except in highly unusual circumstances, the head of state is obliged to comply with the prime minister's advice.

What then is the point of having a head of state separate from the head of government? There are three generally accepted roles for the head of state.

1. *To carry out ceremonial duties.* Part of the role of a head of state consists in dedicating new bridges and hospital wings, conferring awards and other honours, formally receiving and accrediting new ambassadors to the country, and hosting state banquets for visiting heads of state. By performing these duties, the head of state lightens the burden of the PM, allowing him or her to concentrate on government business.
2. *To serve as the nonpartisan representative of the state.* Unlike the prime minister, the head of state is expected to represent the nation as a whole, even if, as in many parliamentary republics, he or she was elected to office as the official candidate of

a political party. Being above the partisan fray, the head of state has the potential to represent all shades of political opinion and to serve as a focus for national unity. To this end the head of state, in public pronouncements, tends to address broad, unifying themes and can even act as a kind of moral compass for the nation. As president of the Federal Republic of Germany from 1999 to 2004, Johannes Rau made a series of speeches reflecting on the nation's Nazi past and warning of a recurrence of political extremism in Germany.

3. *To act as guardian of the constitution.* If the PM seeks to undermine the constitution, the head of state may take corrective action by using the wide legal powers at his or her disposal. This is the so-called "fire extinguisher" function of the head of state.[6] For example, if the PM were to ignore a parliamentary vote of non-confidence, the head of state would be within his or her rights to dismiss the PM. In an even rarer and more extreme situation—a temporary vacuum of governmental authority—the head of state could assume effective control of the state pending the formation of a new government. Such an event occurred in the Caribbean island nation of Grenada in 1983 when the Governor General, Sir Paul Scoon, assumed the reins of government following the murder of Prime Minister Maurice Bishop in an attempted *coup d'état*. The coup was thwarted, controversially, by a U.S. military invasion of the island.[7]

In the normal course of events, the head of state exercises his or her formal powers only on the advice of the prime minister or the cabinet as a whole. Nevertheless, there are certain situations in which the head of state has some discretion and is not bound to follow the advice of the ministry. In such cases, the head of state may exercise what are known as reserve or prerogative powers. These are residual powers of the crown that have not been abolished by parliament or the written constitution. However, the head of state does not have an entirely free hand in exercising such powers; rather, he or she is expected to follow any applicable constitutional conventions. In many states that adopted new constitutions after 1945, some of these conventions have been spelled out in the constitution.

Two of the main prerogative powers held by the head of state in a parliamentary system are the power to appoint or dismiss the prime minister and the power to dissolve parliament for a general election.

Appointment and Dismissal of the PM

In appointing a prime minister, the head of state is guided in most cases by well-known constitutional conventions. For example, if an incumbent government is re-elected in a general election, the current PM stays on and is invited to form a new government. If the ruling party is decisively defeated, the outgoing PM tenders his or her resignation to the head of state, who then appoints as the new PM the leader of the party that won a majority of parliamentary seats. Sometimes, however, it may not be immediately apparent which party leader is in a position to form a government following a general election. In such cases, the head of state may have to hold discussions with parliamentary leaders and to exercise his or her own judgment in naming a prime minister, subject to any applicable conventions. Situations of this kind arise in European democracies from time to time, in which multiple parties are represented in parliament and coalition governments are the norm.

Another well-established convention arises when a prime minister chooses to resign before the government is obliged to go to the polls. Given the reality of party government, prime ministers who wish to retire before the next election will usually announce that their resignation is to take effect as soon as the party has elected a successor—a process that may take days or months, depending on the procedure by which the governing party selects its leader. In Canada, governing parties elect their leaders in large national leadership conventions or by way of a balloting of the entire membership of the party. By either of these methods it can take months to select the successor to a retiring PM; in the meantime, the incumbent typically remains in office until the party has made its choice.[8]

A more controversial power of the head of state is the power to dismiss the head of government. This power is to be used only in the most extraordinary circumstances, if at all. In democratic states the general rule is that a prime minister and cabinet are responsible to parliament and ultimately accountable to the electorate. In 1975, the governor general of Australia created a firestorm of controversy when he dismissed the prime minister, who headed a majority government at the time (see Box 8.1).

BOX 8.1

THE DAY A GOVERNOR GENERAL FIRED A PRIME MINISTER

On November 11, 1975 Australians were shocked to learn that the Governor General, Sir John Kerr, had fired the Prime Minister, Mr. Gough Whitlam, despite the fact that Whitlam's Labor Government held a majority of seats in the House of Representatives, the lower house of the Australian parliament. The ostensible reason for this unprecedented use of the reserve powers of the Crown was the government's inability to secure passage in the Senate of its supply bills—bills giving the government legal authority to spend public money. For three weeks, the Liberal and National Country parties in the Senate had refused to approve supply unless Whitlam agreed to call early elections for the House of Representatives. This Whitlam refused to do on the grounds that in blocking supply the Senate was violating a long-standing convention of British parliamentary government. Adding fuel to the fire was the fact that the Opposition parties had recently gained control of the Senate by flouting another constitutional convention.*

Whitlam resolved to break the deadlock between the two houses by advising the Governor General to call early Senate elections. When the Prime Minister arrived at Government House, the Governor General's official residence, he was unaware that Sir John had already summoned the Opposition leader, Mr. Malcolm Fraser. While Fraser waited in an adjacent room, out of view of the Prime Minister, Sir John abruptly informed Whitlam of his dismissal from office. He then invited Fraser to form a new government on condition that Fraser ensure the immediate passage of supply and that he advise a double dissolution of Parliament—the simultaneous election of both houses. Fraser agreed to these terms.

Later that afternoon, Fraser entered the House of Representatives to inform members that the Governor General had just appointed him the new Prime Minister. In response, Labor members, who were still in the majority, passed a motion of non-confidence in Fraser and called on the Governor General to reappoint Whitlam! By this time, the Governor General had already despatched his secretary to the steps of Parliament House to read the proclamation dissolving Parliament and fixing the date of the general election. The proclamation ended with the words, "God Save the Queen." Taking his cue from those words, an indignant Gough Whitlam famously declared: "Well may we say God save the Queen because nothing will save the Governor General!"

Most Australians had disapproved of the Opposition's obstructionist tactics and were stunned by Kerr's response. Some even accused him of staging a *coup d'état*. Indeed, as news of Whitlam's dismissal spread, thousands of workers walked off the job in protest. Nevertheless, once the election campaign was under way public attention began to focus on other issues— notably the parlous state of the economy—and on polling day Fraser's Liberals won sizeable majorities in both Houses.

Kerr considered the election results to be a vindication of his actions. However, most political analysts fault the Governor General for having resorted to such a drastic measure as the dismissal of an elected government. On this view, Kerr should have confided in his prime minister and helped to broker a political solution to the impasse. Others, however, applaud Kerr's conduct, including Sir Garfield Barwick, then Chief Justice of the Australian High Court and a former (Liberal Party) Attorney General.[9]

The events of 1975 left a bitter legacy and remain a *cause célèbre* to this day, more than 30 years later. Today "the Dismissal" serves as a reminder of the vast reserve powers of the Crown in many parliamentary democracies. It also underscores the importance of conventions that preclude the use of such powers in all but the most extraordinary circumstances. Finally, it sounds a cautionary

BOX 8.1

THE DAY A GOVERNOR GENERAL FIRED A PRIME MINISTER (CONTINUED)

note about the difficulty of combining an all-powerful elected senate—one capable of blocking a budget—with a parliamentary system of responsible government.

* When two Labor-held seats in the Senate had become vacant several months earlier, convention dictated that the vacancies be filled by nominees of the Australian Labor Party (ALP); that way, party standings in the Senate, as of the previous election, would be maintained. Instead, the state governments of New South Wales and Queensland, both ruled by opposition parties, appointed opponents of the ALP. As a result of these breaches of constitutional convention, the Opposition gained effective control of the Senate.

The Dissolution Power

The other main prerogative power is the power of dissolution—the power to dissolve parliament and call a general election. As a general rule, the head of state exercises this power on the advice of the prime minister in one of two circumstances: when the prime minister (still having the confidence of parliament) sees the need for an early election or when the government has been defeated in parliament on a confidence motion. However, the head of state is not bound to dissolve parliament in either of these cases: he or she retains some discretion.

In 1926, the refusal of Canada's governor general, Lord Byng, to grant a dissolution requested by the prime minister, William Lyon Mackenzie King, created a political uproar that came to be known as the King–Byng Affair. In that case, King had sought a dissolution in order to pre-empt an imminent vote in Parliament on a motion of censure against his minority government—a motion that, if passed, would have constituted a vote of non-confidence. Following the denial of his request, King resigned as PM and Lord Byng invited the Leader of the Opposition, Arthur Meighen, to form a new government. Meighen's government took office but was defeated days later on a confidence vote. In the ensuing election campaign, Mackenzie King openly criticized the actions of the Governor General. When the Liberals were returned to office—albeit with another minority government—many took the result to be a vindication of King's position.

But is the lesson of the King–Byng Affair that the Governor General may never again refuse the request of a PM for a dissolution? That view is certainly wrong. Constitutional experts agree that there are still circumstances in which the GG would be perfectly entitled to refuse a dissolution request.[10] What if a PM insisted on calling a series of elections merely because he was dissatisfied with the results?[11] As such a course of conduct would constitute an abuse of parliament, the governor general arguably would be duty-bound to put a stop to it.

Such arguments were advanced more recently in Canada when, on December 4, 2008, Conservative Prime Minister Stephen Harper stunned the nation by asking the Governor General to prorogue the First Session of the 40th Parliament, a mere 16 days after the session had begun following the general election of October 14, 2008. As in the King–Byng Affair, the government was anxious to avoid imminent defeat in Parliament on a non-confidence motion. Meanwhile, the Liberal and New Democratic parties announced their intention, following the government's defeat, to form a coalition government with support in Parliament from the Bloc Québécois (which support the BQ undertook to provide for a minimum of 18 months). Amid much controversy, Governor General Michaëlle Jean agreed to prorogue Parliament until January 26, 2009.

Prorogation is a routine procedure used by prime ministers to end a session of parliament when the government, having carried out the bulk of its legislative agenda, wishes to begin a fresh session with a new set of legislative priorities. However, Mr. Harper's use of prorogation in this case was far from routine. In the view of many observers, it was an improper, even unconstitutional, move by the PM to prevent Parliament from exercising its right to defeat the government. On this view, the Governor General should have refused the

PM's request.[12] Others contend that it would have been improper, and unconstitutional, of the Governor General to have refused the request of a PM who still (technically) had the confidence of Parliament. On this view, parliament's privileges would not have been infringed since the Opposition parties would still have had an opportunity to defeat the government when the new session opened in January.[13] By that time, however, the Liberals had chosen a new leader, Michael Ignatieff, who was no longer intent on defeating the government.

Twelve months later, Prime Minister Harper abruptly prorogued the Second Session of the 40th Parliament and delayed its return for a period of six weeks beyond the scheduled Christmas break. This time the PM was apparently intent on shutting down a parliamentary committee that was inquiring into the government's policies and actions in Afghanistan regarding the transfer of detainees by Canadian forces to Afghan authorities. Again, the prime minister was accused by many of evading accountability to Parliament and of undermining responsible government.[14] Nevertheless, Governor General Jean granted the prorogation, the request for which the PM had communicated by telephone instead of the customary personal visit.

PARLIAMENTARY, PRESIDENTIAL, AND SEMI-PRESIDENTIAL SYSTEMS

As discussed in Chapter 7, the distinction between confederal, federal, and unitary states has to do with the vertical distribution of power between national and subnational governments. But what about the horizontal distribution of power within one level of government or the other? Here we may distinguish between parliamentary, presidential, and semi-presidential systems.

Parliamentary Systems

The parliamentary form of government, in its modern form, originated in Great Britain in the 18th century and has been widely imitated throughout the world. Countries having a parliamentary system include Canada, Australia, Germany, Japan, and Sweden.

While there are important national variations in the form and function of parliamentary systems, certain essential features may be identified. First, parliamentary systems have a dual executive consisting of a separate head of state and head of government. A second feature of parliamentary systems has to do with the relationship between the executive and the legislative branches of government. In parliamentary systems based on the British (Westminster) model, there is an overlapping of powers and personnel between the two branches, which arises from the fact that the PM and members of the cabinet simultaneously hold office in both. As elected members of the legislature, the PM and cabinet are intimately involved in parliamentary affairs, from introducing government bills to responding to questions from opposition MPs. Indeed, the prime minister and cabinet dominate the parliamentary agenda, starting with the **Speech from the Throne**, an outline of what the government hopes to achieve in any given session of parliament. At the same time, the PM and cabinet are responsible for discharging the executive functions of the state. As such, their duties include administering the daily operations of government departments and exercising a host of executive powers, from conducting foreign relations with other states to appointing hundreds of public officeholders, such as judges, ambassadors, senior civil servants, and the heads of various agencies, boards, and commissions. This intersection of the two branches of government in the PM and cabinet is known as the **fusion of powers**.

> **Fusion of powers:** In parliamentary systems, the joint exercise of legislative and executive powers by the prime minister and members of the cabinet, who simultaneously hold office in the legislative and executive branches of government.

A third feature of parliamentary systems is the doctrine of **responsible government**, according to which the government may hold office only as long

> **Responsible government:** A defining principle of Westminster-style parliamentary government, which states that the cabinet may only hold office as long as it has majority support in the legislature (or lower house in a bicameral parliament) on votes of confidence.

as it maintains majority support in the legislature. If the government is defeated on a vote of confidence, it must resign or seek early elections. In Westminster systems, the prime minister also has the discretion to call an early general election, even if the government retains the confidence of parliament. This point is discussed further below.

Parliamentary systems based on the Westminster model entail an enormous concentration of power in the hands of the PM and cabinet. This is especially so in cases where the governing party has an absolute majority of seats in parliament; that is, a **majority government**. Moreover, political parties tend to be highly disciplined and cohesive in parliament; after all, the governing party cannot afford to lose a vote of confidence. As a result, it is customary for MPs belonging to the same party to vote as a bloc on bills and resolutions before parliament.

Advantages of Parliamentary Government

Parliamentary constitutions have many advantages. First, a government with a stable parliamentary majority is able to act decisively to implement its legislative program. This is equally true whether the government is formed by a single party or by a durable multiparty coalition. More specifically, parliamentary governments are well equipped to adopt measures designed to serve the national interest, even if such measures be opposed by powerful sectional groups in the country. Indeed, disciplined parties, while disparaged by many Canadians, provide individual MPs with some degree of protection against the efforts of powerful lobby groups to influence the votes they cast in parliament.[15] Second, by concentrating political power in the PM and cabinet, parliamentary systems clarify political responsibility. The opposition parties in parliament hold the government to account both for its policies and its administrative competence. Equally, general elections in parliamentary systems tend to offer electors a choice between parties campaigning on national issues, rather than being a series of contests among individual candidates on local issues.

Third, the mechanism of the **non-confidence vote** allows for the removal of a government that has lost support in parliament. Such was the case in Britain in March 1979, when the Labour government of James Callaghan was defeated in the House of Commons—by a single vote—and was obliged to call an early election. In Canada a similar fate befell the Liberal Government of Paul Martin in November 2005 and the Harper government in early 2011, although the latter was soon re-elected.

Disadvantages of Parliamentary Government

A leading criticism of parliamentary systems is that they vest excessive power in the hands of the government. According to Lord Hailsham, a former British politician, a majority government constitutes an "elective dictatorship," since it faces no effective check on its power in parliament. This is especially true of parliamentary systems such as those of Canada and Great Britain, in which the electoral system tends to give one party an absolute majority of seats and in which the upper house of parliament lacks effective power.

Another criticism of parliamentary systems is that by engendering disciplined national parties, they leave MPs less free to represent local interests, particularly where those interests conflict with the policy of the party to which an MP belongs. MPs affiliated with the governing party are especially constrained in this regard.[16]

Finally, parliamentary government can be unstable if no party is able to secure majority support in parliament. This has been the experience of Italy, where there have been over 50 changes of government since 1945. Governments in France under the Fourth Republic (1946–1958) were also notoriously short-lived. On the other hand, as many commentators have noted, postwar governments in Italy and Fourth-Republic France were less unstable than they appeared. Typically, the same coalition partners remained in office following a change of government, key ministers were reappointed to the same portfolios, and major government policies continued in force.

Presidential Systems

The presidential (or congressional) form of government originated in the United States in the 1780s. Although not as widely practised as its parliamentary counterpart, it has been adopted by most Central and South American states. The U.S. presidential system was designed with a view to avoiding an undue concentration of political power in any single branch of government. Consequently, there is a strict **separation of powers** among the executive, the legislature, and the judiciary.

> **Separation of powers:** A principle of constitutional government that is usually taken to mean that the legislative, executive, and judicial functions of the state should be carried out by separate branches of government. No one may hold office in more than one branch at the same time.

Under a presidential system, executive functions are consolidated in the president, who is both head of state and head of government (known as the *administration*). Legislative powers are assigned to the bicameral Congress, which comprises the Senate and the House of Representatives. On the relationship between the legislature and the executive, it is more accurate to say that there is a separation of personnel and a sharing, rather than a separation, of powers. For one, the president and all members of the cabinet are barred from sitting in Congress while holding executive office.[17] In addition, presidential elections are held independently from congressional elections. Thus, while the president is elected every four years, elections for the House of Representatives are held every two years; senators, meanwhile, serve six-year terms, with one-third of the Senate being up for election every two years.

The exercise of executive and legislative powers is subject to a complex system of **checks and balances**. Bills passed by both houses of Congress may be vetoed by the president. Congress, in turn, may override a presidential **veto** by a two-thirds majority vote of both houses. This sharing of legislative power by the two branches is also reflected in the joint exercise of certain executive powers. For example, key presidential appointments, from cabinet secretaries to federal judges to the heads of key executive agencies, must be formally confirmed by the Senate. Similarly, treaties negotiated by the president must be ratified by a minimum two-thirds majority vote of the Senate.

Since both branches have fixed terms of office, the president may not dissolve Congress to hold early elections; by the same token, Congress may not remove a president in whom it no longer has confidence, except by the extraordinary procedure of impeachment. Under Article II (Section 4) of the U.S. Constitution, the president may be impeached for "Treason, Bribery, or other high Crimes and Misdemeanours." If articles of impeachment are approved by the House of Representatives, the matter proceeds to the Senate, where the president can be removed from office on a two-thirds majority vote. No U.S. president has been successfully impeached, although Richard Nixon resigned the presidency in 1974 after articles of impeachment were passed by the House Judiciary Committee.[18] The most recent attempt at impeachment, brought against Democratic President Bill Clinton by the Republican-controlled Congress in 1998, fell well short of the two-thirds majority required in the Senate. The political, as opposed to judicial, nature of impeachment was clearly revealed in that case as members of Congress voted strictly along party lines.[19]

The Case for and Against Presidential Government Proponents of presidentialism cite various points in its favour. Among other things, it is argued that presidential executives are stable owing to their constitutionally fixed terms and to the provision made for the automatic installation of the vice-president in case the president is unable to complete his or her term. At minimum, these features of presidentialism help to avoid the frequent changes of government to which parliamentary systems may be susceptible. It has also been observed that presidents have a larger pool of talent from which to make cabinet appointments than do prime ministers in Westminster systems. Not being restricted to persons who have been elected to parliament, presidents may appoint cabinet secretaries from the ranks of business, academia, or other institutions.

Presidentialism also gives the legislature a more meaningful role as a lawmaking body by allowing members of the congress to defeat, or substantially amend, a bill sponsored by the president without automatically removing the president from office. Parliamentary executives, in contrast, too often hold the latter prospect like a hammer over the heads of MPs to cow them into supporting the government's measures. Congressional legislators therefore enjoy greater freedom from party discipline and have more scope to represent local interests. But the leading argument made in support of presidentialism is that the diffusion of political authority safeguards individual liberty against unreasonable encroachment by the state.[20]

Critics of presidentialism deplore its tendency to produce deadlock between the two branches of government. This feature of presidential systems arises from the diffusion of decision-making authority and the reciprocal vetoes held by the executive and legislative branches. Moreover, being separately elected, each branch can claim to have a mandate from the people and, for that reason, may be unwilling to reach a compromise with the other branch. And since the president lacks the power to dissolve Congress, there is no effective means to end the impasse. In the United States, the fragmentation of political authority arguably has helped well-funded lobby groups to block or significantly water down such measures as effective gun control and universal public health insurance. A related shortcoming of presidentialism is the difficulty that voters face in assigning responsibility for political decisions (or political inaction) under a system of dispersed decision-making authority. This difficulty is compounded by the organizational looseness of national parties and by the tendency for congressional candidates to campaign for election on local rather than national issues.[21]

Proponents of presidential government reply to these points by noting the capacity of a strong president to unify the nation and to command considerable political authority. As the only officeholder to be elected by the nation as a whole, the president can claim to have a truly national mandate. In addition, presidents derive much authority from their dual status as head of state and head of government, not to mention their role as commander-in-chief of the armed forces. Indeed, the prestige of the presidency can bestow on even a mediocre occupant of the office considerable stature and gravitas, at least in the eyes of many ordinary citizens. In times of national crisis, this symbolic resource can be a significant asset for presidents as they seek to mobilize support from Congress and the nation. On the other hand, critics are quick to note the vulnerability of presidential systems when the chief executive brings the office into disrepute. When U.S. President Richard Nixon was implicated in criminal behaviour in the Watergate affair of 1972–1974, his status as head of state created a crisis of legitimacy in the institution of the presidency. Presidentialism can also exhibit antidemocratic features, as when presidents (and their supporters) equate legitimate political opposition to the head of state with disloyalty to the

state itself.[22] To critics of presidentialism, such as Juan Linz, it is no coincidence "that most of the countries with presidential constitutions have been unstable democracies or authoritarian regimes."[23]

Another point of contention between advocates of parliamentary and presidential government concerns the question of prior political experience. In parliamentary systems, prime ministers usually come into office after many years of service in parliament and in senior cabinet positions. As such, they bring to the office direct knowledge of national politics and the inner workings of cabinet government. In presidential systems, the chief executive is more likely to take office with little or no prior experience in national government. In the U.S. three of the last five presidents—George W. Bush, Bill Clinton, and Ronald Reagan—were state governors prior to their election to the White House. While presidential candidates often seek to make a virtue of their status as Washington "outsiders," it is debatable whether inexperience in national government is a desirable quality for the leader of a major democracy, let alone a world superpower.

Semi-presidential Systems

A halfway house between parliamentary and presidential systems is the so-called semi-presidential form of government. Semi-presidential systems combine elements of parliamentary and presidential government; broadly speaking, they combine a popularly elected president with a parliamentary prime minister.[24] Unlike the head of state of a parliamentary republic, the president has real power and the authority to use it. The quintessential example of a semi-presidential system is France under the Fifth Republic, especially since 1962 when the presidency became a popularly elected office. Other examples of semi-presidential systems include Finland, Russia, and several of the new democracies of Eastern Europe, including Poland, Romania, and Bulgaria (see Table 8.1).[25]

Sometimes the label "semi-presidential" is applied to any parliamentary system having a directly elected president. By this broad definition, countries such as Austria and the Republic of Ireland would be classified as semi-presidential systems. But as Lijphart points out, the real test of a semi-presidential system is whether the president, rather than the prime minister,

Table 8.1 Selected Parliamentary, Presidential, and Semi-presidential States		
Parliamentary	Presidential	Semi-presidential
Australia	Argentina	Belarus
Belgium	Brazil	Bulgaria
Canada	Chile	Finland
India	Costa Rica	France
Italy	Indonesia	Lithuania
Jamaica	Mexico	Poland
Japan	Nigeria	Romania
Norway	Philippines	Russia
Spain	United States	South Korea
United Kingdom	Venezuela	Ukraine

Source: Based, *inter alia,* on Robert Elgie, "The Classification of Democratic Regime Types: Conceptual Ambiguity and Contestable Assumptions," *European Journal of Political Research* 33(2) (1998): 228

is the pre-eminent head of government.[26] In states such as Russia and France, the president is usually in charge. While leaving the day-to-day business of government in the hands of the prime minister, the president reserves the right to intervene in matters of policy and administration. The president may even sack a prime minister who still has the confidence of parliament.[27]

France is an interesting case because the president's wide powers, which are largely unwritten, are significantly curtailed when parties opposed to the president win control of the National Assembly. In that case, the president is obliged to appoint a prime minister acceptable to the new parliament. In such periods of cohabitation, France functions much like a parliamentary republic, with the notable exception that the president retains responsibility for foreign affairs and can dissolve the National Assembly on his own initiative before the expiration of its five-year term.

THE CHIEF EXECUTIVE: PRIME MINISTERS VERSUS PRESIDENTS

Prime ministers and presidents sit at the apex of power in parliamentary and presidential systems of government. As chief executives, they are widely seen to have ultimate responsibility for the executive branch as a whole, even though much of their decision-making authority is formally shared with other political actors. This point was famously made by U.S. President Harry S. Truman: a sign on Truman's desk proclaimed, "The buck stops here." Let us examine the vastly different institutional settings in which prime ministers and presidents operate, their status and powers, and the political institutions that enhance and constrain the exercise of power.

The Prime Minister

In parliamentary systems, the political executive consists of the **prime minister** and **cabinet**. In fact, parliamentary government is sometimes called **cabinet government**, a phrase that denotes the fact that the cabinet is the decision-making centre. More specifically, government policy is formally set by the cabinet through a collective and collegial process of decision-making. According to this theory of cabinet government, the prime minister is *primus inter pares* (first among equals) at the cabinet table.

The office of prime minister originated in Great Britain in the 18th century. Sir Robert Walpole is generally considered Britain's first prime minister. During Walpole's long premiership (1721–1742) certain conventions of cabinet government began to take form. Nevertheless, well into the 19th century, monarchs continued to exert personal influence over affairs of state because of their capacity to buy the allegiance of members of parliament elected from "pocket boroughs" (parliamentary districts containing small numbers of eligible voters). The *Reform Act* of 1832 abolished most of the pocket boroughs, thereby requiring MPs to reflect more faithfully the views of their constituents. Henceforth, the king would be obliged to appoint a prime minister who was Parliament's first choice, if not necessarily the king's.[28] As a result of these developments, the prime minister emerged as the effective head of government. According to Bagehot, the rights of the monarch in relation to the prime minister could now be summed up as follows: "the right to be consulted, the right to encourage, and the right to warn."[29] The monarch no longer had the right to refuse the advice of a prime minister having the confidence of the cabinet and of parliament.[30]

If the 19th century saw political power shift decisively from the crown to parliament, the 20th century saw a comparable power shift from parliament to the political executive. Meanwhile, within the executive itself in recent years, more and more power has become concentrated in the hands of the prime minister at the expense of the cabinet as a whole. Before exploring this question, let us identify the principles of cabinet government and discuss the formal role of the PM.

Principles of Cabinet Government The following are three core principles of cabinet government in Westminster systems such as Canada's:

- **Collective responsibility**. The principle of **collective responsibility** means that all members of the government ("the ministry") are collectively responsible to parliament for government policy and for the overall performance of the government. Thus, when a minister introduces a bill into parliament on behalf of his or her ministry, that bill is taken to be a statement of government policy. The

Collective responsibility: In Westminster parliamentary systems, members of the political executive are collectively responsible to parliament for government policy and for the overall administrative performance of the government.

defeat in parliament of a bill introduced by a particular minister is therefore treated as a repudiation of the policy of the government as a whole. As noted earlier, the defeat of an important government bill is treated as a vote of non-confidence and has the effect of bringing down the government.

- **Cabinet solidarity**. The principle of **cabinet solidarity** refers to the constitutional obligation of all ministers publicly to support the policy of the government. Cabinet meetings are held behind closed doors and are subject to strict rules of cabinet secrecy. Ministers may speak candidly about proposed government policies and actions; however, once cabinet has reached a decision, all ministers are obliged to explain and defend it in public. This practice enables parliament to identify the policy of the government and thus to hold the cabinet collectively responsible for it.

Cabinet solidarity: The constitutional duty of ministers to publicly support the policy of the government. Ministers who openly dissent from government policy must resign from the government.

Any minister who is unable to support the decisions of his or her colleagues must resign from the cabinet. In Britain, it is not uncommon for ministers to resign from the cabinet on matters of principle. For example, in 2003, Robin Cook and Clare Short, two members of Tony Blair's government, resigned from the ministry to protest the government's decision to participate in the U.S.-led invasion of Iraq. In 1990, Geoffrey Howe, a senior minister in Margaret Thatcher's government, resigned in protest against the Prime Minister's policy toward Europe and her autocratic style of leadership. In Britain, resigning ministers tend to make a big splash when they depart the government by giving a resignation speech in the House of Commons—delivered while the PM sits a few yards away trying to look nonchalant!

In Canada, ministers rarely resign because of philosophical or policy differences with their colleagues. An exception to that rule occurred in November 2006 when Michael Chong resigned from the Cabinet of Stephen Harper to protest the Government's decision to designate the Québécois as a nation (see Chapter 7). However, it is more common for ministers to resign as a result of their being caught up in political scandals.

- **Ministerial responsibility**. The principle of **ministerial responsibility** refers to the responsibility of individual ministers to parliament. Under this doctrine, a minister is responsible not only for his or her own actions and decisions, but also for those of officials in the department—whether or not the minister was aware of them. In other words, the minister is the public face of the department and must take *political* responsibility for it.

> **Ministerial responsibility:** The responsibility of individual ministers to answer to parliament for the administration of their departments, including the actions of public officials employed in such departments.

Holding Government to Account In formal terms, there are various mechanisms for holding the executive accountable for its conduct in parliamentary systems. The oldest form of parliamentary control of the executive is the power of the purse—that is to say, the requirement that parliament authorize public spending and the imposition of new taxes by the executive. Parliament also has the opportunity to scrutinize public expenditures after the fact when ministries prepare detailed public accounts; in Canada, these records are examined by an independent officer, the Auditor General, whose annual report is then submitted to Parliament. Shortly before Jean Chrétien stepped down as prime minister in 2003, Auditor General Sheila Fraser delivered a scathing indictment of the way in which federal advertising and sponsorship contracts had been tendered by the Department of Public Works in the years following the 1995 Quebec referendum on independence. The political outcry that ensued led Chrétien's successor, Paul Martin, to appoint a judicial enquiry into the so-called sponsorship scandal.

On a day-to-day basis, ministers are obliged to explain and defend government policy and executive actions through the oral question period as well as through routine debates in parliament. Ministers and senior civil servants are also expected to appear before parliamentary committees.

From time to time, opposition parties demand the resignation of a minister for maladministration. While such demands are rarely complied with, ministers are more likely to resign if they are deemed to be personally responsible for a questionable action than if the fault lies with subordinates in the minister's department. In either case, the minister is obliged to answer to parliament. This dilution of the doctrine of ministerial responsibility has led some to identify a new doctrine of ministerial answerability.[31] The general rule nowadays appears to be that the prime minister decides whether to request the minister's resignation, on the basis of an assessment of the minister's overall usefulness to the government.

Beyond the formal institutions of parliament, the news media can act as an important agent of government accountability. While the media are usually drawn to the more sensational and melodramatic aspects of political life, investigative journalists nevertheless can expose serious cases of executive misconduct or bring to light the consequences of ill-conceived government policies. Adverse news coverage, in turn, can act as a spur to corrective action.

Prime Ministerial Government The prime minister occupies a position of preeminent power in Westminster systems. As noted above, many observers have detected a long-term trend toward the growing concentration of decision-making power in the hands of the PM at the expense of the cabinet. On this view, cabinet government has been superseded by **prime ministerial government**.[32] An early cartoon depicting this phenomenon is reproduced on the next page.

> **Prime ministerial government:** The notion that the prime minister is now so pre-eminent that the label "Cabinet government" no longer accurately describes how decisions are made in the political executive in Westminster model systems, especially that of Canada.

Others dispute this dire assessment; in their view, there remain significant checks on the powers of prime ministers. Nevertheless, it cannot be doubted that prime ministers have wide decision-making powers. Some of these powers are based on written or unwritten rules of the constitution while other powers have a legal basis in collective decisions of the cabinet to delegate certain heads of authority directly to the PM.

'And now that we're reshuffled — onwards and upwards!'

This 1967 cartoon depicts the governing style of British Prime Minister Harold Wilson.

Copyright Guardian News & Media Ltd 1967. William Papas; The British Cartoon Archive, University of Kent, catalogue record 10434 at www.cartoons.ac.uk.

Among the most important powers that are wielded by the prime minister we may count the following:

- *To make appointments to cabinet.* The prime minister names the members of the cabinet, who are then sworn into office by the head of state. In Westminster systems, the only constitutional requirement to be met is the need for ministers to have a seat in parliament (normally the lower house of a bicameral legislature). The prime minister also has the power to remove ministers from the cabinet or to reassign them to other portfolios (called a cabinet shuffle).
- *To determine the organization of cabinet and of government departments.* Every prime minister has the discretion to determine how large the cabinet

shall be. In a small cabinet, some ministers will have responsibility for two or more departments of government. Alternatively, the PM may choose to merge separate departments into a smaller number of large departments. In such cases, cabinet ministers may be assisted by one or more junior ministers (ministers without cabinet rank), under-secretaries or parliamentary secretaries.

- *To call a general election.* By convention, the prime minister has sole authority to advise the head of state on the timing of a general election, within the normal lifespan of a parliament. As noted, this advice is almost invariably followed. Armed with this power, the PM may choose an election date that maximizes the governing party's chances of re-election. As the opposition parties are not privy to the PM's intentions, it is difficult for them to prepare their election campaigns with certainty.

Some have argued that the PM should not be able to play games with election timing in this way. They contend that elections should be held at fixed intervals, as in the United States. In Canada, several provinces have passed laws establishing fixed election dates. As noted in Chapter 7, a similar law governing federal elections was adopted by Parliament in 2007. In all of these cases, an early election may still be triggered by the defeat of the government on a confidence vote.

- *To make appointments to various posts within the government.* In addition to appointing cabinet ministers, the prime minister also chooses a host of other public officials, such as high-ranking civil servants, senior members of the judiciary, ambassadors, and the heads of state-owned enterprises. Some of these appointments are made on the basis of patronage—i.e., the appointee's main qualification being his or her past political services to the governing party.
- *To convene and chair cabinet meetings.* The prime minister can call cabinet meetings at any time, and has various means of influencing its decisions. First, through control of the agenda, prime ministers can ensure that no item of business can come before cabinet without their approval. Thus, if prime ministers are unsure that an important issue will go their way in cabinet, they can keep it off the agenda until they have mobilized sufficient support for their preferred outcome. Second, the prime minister controls the establishment of cabinet committees and determines their membership. The recommendations of these committees go to the full cabinet, where they are usually ratified. Third, instead of calling a vote within cabinet—where the PM might not prevail—the prime minister sums up discussion by articulating the predominant mood of cabinet—as the PM sees it. Even if the prime minister's definition of consensus does not reflect the majority view, the PM's summation becomes the official position of the government and is recorded as such in the minutes. At that point, the doctrine of cabinet solidarity obliges all ministers to defend the policy of the government or to resign from cabinet.

- *To act as chief spokesperson for the government.* Occasionally, when journalists pose questions to ministers about the pressing issues of the day, a minister will go out on a limb and state a position that is inconsistent with that of the PM. In that case, the PM will usually make a statement purporting to explain what the errant minister really intended to say! In such cases, the minister invariably endorses the PM's view; as a result, all members of the government are once again in the happy position of singing from the same hymnbook. In the case of a fundamental disagreement between the prime minister and a senior minister, it is understood that the minister must give way. Shortly after the election of the Socialist–Green coalition government in Germany in 1998, a serious disagreement about economic policy broke out between Chancellor Gerhard Schroeder and his finance minister, Oskar Lafontaine. As a consequence of this breach, Lafontaine resigned his post in March 1999.

Limits on Prime Ministerial Power Despite their undoubted power, prime ministers cannot act with impunity. To be a successful leader, the prime minister needs to be aware of important political constraints and to exercise power with discretion. The nature of such constraints varies from one state to another and can even vary over time within a single state.

In the matter of cabinet formation, the PM may wish to appoint all of his or her closest political allies, but there are other considerations that cannot be ignored. For example, in most European countries national elections are conducted using some form of proportional representation (PR). One of the characteristics of PR-based elections is that single-party majority governments are rarely formed; instead, one of the major parties is obliged to enter into a coalition with one or more of the other parties represented in parliament. In such cases, prime ministers must reach agreement with their coalition partners on the allocation of cabinet posts. Even if the government is formed by a single party, the prime minister must be mindful of certain political realities. If the governing party contains distinctive ideological camps, party unity may demand that major currents of opinion be adequately represented in cabinet.

In other countries, the importance of ideology may be overshadowed by the need to ensure that major social groups and regional populations are represented in the cabinet. In Canada, the prime minister is expected to ensure that at least one MP from each province has a seat at the cabinet table. Canadian prime ministers must also maintain an appropriate balance of anglophone and francophone ministers. It should be added that in all Western democracies today, prime ministers are expected to provide at least some representation for women in the cabinet (see Box 8.2).

BOX 8.2

WHAT ABOUT EXPERTISE?

Odd as it may seem, prime ministers are not unduly concerned, when forming a cabinet, that a minister possess expertise in the subject matter of his or her portfolio. Thus, it is not thought necessary to appoint a physician minister of health or a retired general minister of defence. The role of the minister is to act as political head of the department; accordingly, he or she is expected to defend its interests at the cabinet table, to explain and promote government policy in parliament and the country, and to ensure that the department is soundly administered. To fulfil these functions, the minister requires *political* skills, which are usually honed as a result of years of parliamentary experience.

To the extent that ministers need to acquire specialized knowledge to perform their tasks, they rely on the expertise of permanent officials in the department. Critics contend that this reliance on senior bureaucrats is a recipe for ministers to become captive to the interests of their departments.

Interestingly, the internal rules of the governing party may also curtail the power of the prime minister. For example, under the constitution of the Australian Labor Party (ALP), members of the cabinet are to be elected by members of the Labor caucus in parliament. A Labor prime minister may, however, assign cabinet members to specific portfolios. Party constitutions also determine the procedure by which a party leader may be removed. If the party is in power, removal of the leader entails a change of prime minister. In some parties, the leader can be removed by his or her parliamentary colleagues with remarkable dispatch. In this way, Margaret Thatcher was forced to step down as British Conservative Party leader and prime minister in 1990. Likewise, Australian prime minister Kevin Rudd was ousted by his Labor colleagues in 2010, shortly before a scheduled general election that the Party was expected to lose. Rudd's successor, Julia Gillard, led Labor to a narrow victory in the general election of August 21, 2010. In other parties, the leader is elected by a vote of the party's rank-and-file or by a vote of elected delegates at a party convention. These extra-parliamentary methods of selecting and deselecting leaders are said to promote internal party democracy and to make party leaders more accountable to their members. Paradoxically, leaders who are elected outside parliament appear to have a more secure grip on power.[33]

While there has undoubtedly been a long-term trend toward the concentration of power in the hands of prime ministers, not all first ministers are able or willing to centralize power to the same degree. The balance of power between the prime minister and the cabinet is conditioned by such factors as the PM's personality and governing style. While some prime ministers choose to centralize power in their office, others prefer a more collegial style of governance in which the advice of cabinet is both sought and heeded. The prime minister's ability to dominate cabinet is also conditioned by the calibre of the ministers. If there are strong personalities around the table, prime ministers are less likely to be successful in bending the cabinet to their will. The PM's authority also hinges on the government's position in parliament. Other things being equal, a prime minister must be more conciliatory toward cabinet (and caucus) colleagues when the government is in a minority position in parliament; in such cases, the PM must also exercise more tact in dealing with the opposition parties. On the other hand, prime ministers who have just led their party to a resounding election victory are in a strong position to assert their authority in cabinet, in caucus, and in parliament.

The President

In certain respects, presidents command wider authority than prime ministers. Article II of the U.S. Constitution vests executive power in the president alone. Accordingly, "[t]he president is not first among equals; he is explicitly 'number one,' the person in charge."[34] The cabinet is not, therefore, a body for collective decision-making. While the president may consult individual members of the cabinet (called "cabinet secretaries" in the U.S.), he is under no obligation to do so. In other words, the policy of the administration on all matters is ultimately that of the president. The president also derives considerable political authority from the fact that he is directly elected by the people, unlike a prime minister.[35]

On the other hand, as noted earlier, presidents are subject to a host of formal checks and balances. For example, in the U.S. only Congress can create new departments and agencies and authorize the funds necessary to run them. Moreover, the president must formally submit cabinet nominees to the Senate for confirmation. This requirement also applies to other senior executive appointments, including ambassadorships and the heads of major federal agencies such as the FBI, the CIA, the Federal Communications Commission, and the Supreme Court bench. Senate confirmation hearings are not a mere formality; indeed, it is not unheard of for the Senate to reject presidential nominees. In 2005, President George W. Bush was forced to withdraw his nomination of Harriet Miers for the Supreme Court in the face of strong opposition from members of the Senate Judiciary Committee. The President's substitute nominee, Samuel Alito, met with the approval of most senators and was duly confirmed.

One striking difference between presidential and parliamentary executives lies in the field of foreign affairs. In Westminster parliamentary systems, the political executive has exclusive authority over foreign relations, including the power to conclude treaties, to commit troops overseas, and even to declare war. The formal approval of parliament is not required in these cases; it must be said, however, that governments will often allow parliament to vote on such matters in order to lend greater legitimacy to the decisions taken by the prime minister and cabinet. For example, the parliament of Canada formally approved a resolution declaring war on Germany in September 1939. In 2003, British Prime Minister Tony Blair yielded to pressure from backbench MPs on both sides of the House to hold a debate in Parliament on the impending deployment of British troops in Iraq.[36]

In presidential systems, the president must submit treaties to the legislature for ratification, and in the United States, they must be approved by at least two-thirds of the Senate. Ratification is not guaranteed in all cases, and in 1979 President Carter withdrew a major arms control treaty (SALT II) he had negotiated with the Soviet Union because it lacked sufficient support in the Senate. Article I (Section 8) of the U.S. Constitution gives Congress, not the president, the power to declare war. In practice, this formal limitation has not significantly hampered the ability of presidents to send troops into combat. During the Vietnam War, the Johnson and Nixon administrations committed tens of thousands of troops to Indochina without a formal declaration of war. Instead, following an attack on U.S. ships in the Gulf of Tonkin in 1964, Johnson sought, and obtained, broad congressional approval for combat operations in Southeast Asia. The Gulf of Tonkin resolution authorized the president "to take all necessary measures to repel any armed attack against the forces of the United States and to prevent further aggression."[37]

In 1973 Congress attempted to curtail the president's power to send U.S. troops into combat with the passage of the War Powers Resolution. It requires the president to consult with Congress prior to the start of hostilities and to remove U.S. troops from theatres of combat within 60 days if Congress has not declared war or passed a resolution authorizing the use of force. In practice, this limitation on the power of presidents to wage war has proven to be ineffective. As chief executive and commander-in-chief of the armed forces, the president is in a powerful position to define threats to the security interests of the state. Among other things, the president has access to intelligence information to which most members of Congress are not privy. Moreover, the president in most cases can appeal successfully to the patriotism (if not jingoism) of citizens when embarking on military operations abroad. This point is illustrated by the U.S. Senate's 77–23 vote in October 2002 authorizing the president to use military force against the regime of Saddam Hussein. At that time, the White House insisted that Iraq possessed "weapons of mass destruction" and thereby posed a clear and present danger to the stability of the Middle East, a claim later proven false.[38] Equally unfounded were administration claims that Iraq was behind the September 11 attacks on the World Trade Center and the Pentagon. Figure 8.2 is an organization chart of the whole U.S. government apparatus.

Figure 8.2 Organization of the U.S. Government

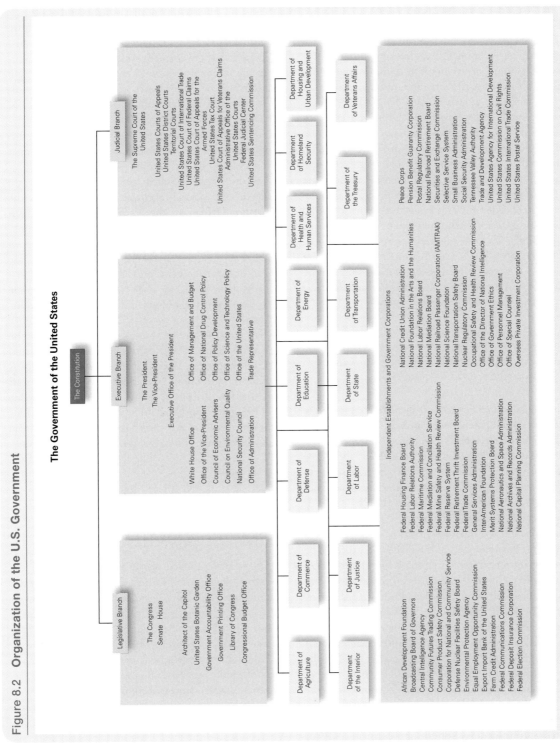

The Government of the United States

The Constitution

Legislative Branch

The Congress
Senate   House

Architect of the Capitol
United States Botanic Garden
Government Accountability Office
Government Printing Office
Library of Congress
Congressional Budget Office

Executive Branch

The President
The Vice-President

Executive Office of the President

White House Office
Office of the Vice-President
Council of Economic Advisers
Council on Environmental Quality
National Security Council
Office of Administration

Office of Management and Budget
Office of National Drug Control Policy
Office of Policy Development
Office of Science and Technology Policy
Office of the United States
Trade Representative

Judicial Branch

The Supreme Court of the
United States

United States Courts of Appeals
United States District Courts
Territorial Courts
United States Court of International Trade
United States Court of Federal Claims
United States Court of Appeals for the
Armed Forces
United States Tax Court
United States Court of Appeals for Veterans Claims
Administrative Office of the
United States Courts
Federal Judicial Center
United States Sentencing Commission

Department of Agriculture

Department of the Interior

Department of Commerce

Department of Justice

Department of Defense

Department of Labor

Department of Education

Department of State

Department of Energy

Department of Transportation

Department of Health and Human Services

Department of the Treasury

Department of Homeland Security

Department of Housing and Urban Development

Department of Veterans Affairs

Independent Establishments and Government Corporations

African Development Foundation
Broadcasting Board of Governors
Central Intelligence Agency
Community Futures Trading Commission
Consumer Product Safety Commission
Corporation for National and Community Service
Defense Nuclear Facilities Safety Board
Environmental Protection Agency
Equal Employment Opportunity Commission
Export-Import Bank of the United States
Farm Credit Administration
Federal Communications Commission
Federal Deposit Insurance Corporation
Federal Election Commission

Federal Housing Finance Board
Federal Labor Relations Authority
Federal Maritime Commission
Federal Mediation and Conciliation Service
Federal Mine Safety and Health Review Commission
Federal Reserve System
Federal Retirement Thrift Investment Board
Federal Trade Commission
General Services Administration
Inter-American Foundation
Merit Systems Protection Board
National Aeronautics and Space Administration
National Archives and Records Administration
National Capital Planning Commission

National Credit Union Administration
National Foundation in the Arts and the Humanities
National Labor Relations Board
National Mediation Board
National Railroad Passenger Corporation (AMTRAK)
National Science Foundation
National Transportation Safety Board
Nuclear Regulatory Commission
Occupational Safety and Health Review Commission
Office of the Director of National Intelligence
Office of Government Ethics
Office of Personnel Management
Office of Special Counsel
Overseas Private Investment Corporation

Peace Corps
Pension Benefit Guaranty Corporation
Postal Regulatory Commission
National Railroad Retirement Board
Securities and Exchange Commission
Selective Service System
Small Business Administration
Social Security Administration
Tennessee Valley Authority
Trade and Development Agency
United States Agency for International Development
United States Commission on Civil Rights
United States International Trade Commission
United States Postal Service

Source: *The United States Government Manual, 2009–2010* (Washington, DC: Office of the Federal Register, National Archives and Records Administration, 2009), found at http://frwebgate.access.gpo.gov/cgi-bin/getdoc.cgi?dbname=2009_government_manual&docid= 217558tx_xxx-2.pdf, p. 21

CENTRAL AGENCIES

Political executives face a formidable challenge in developing public policy and managing the multifaceted operations of the modern state. In an attempt to establish a more efficient and rational system of decision-making, governments have increasingly come to rely on **central agencies**. Unlike government departments, central agencies do not, in the main, have regulatory or program responsibilities. Rather, their mandate is to support the work of the political executive. Three key functions of central agencies are to prepare strategic plans for government, to develop and integrate economic and budgetary policies, and to allocate and manage the human and other resources of government.[39] Central agencies assumed a larger role in Canada and other Western democracies beginning in the 1970s as governments sought to fashion a more coordinated approach to policy-making and to exert more effective control over public spending.

> **Central agencies:** Those agencies of the state that assist the political executive to coordinate and control overall government operations. They provide both policy advice and administrative support.

In Canada three key central agencies are the **Prime Minister's Office**, the **Privy Council Office**, and the **Department of Finance**.[40] The Prime Minister's Office (PMO) is staffed by political appointees of the prime minister. Its task is to provide partisan political advice to the PM—advice that civil servants are precluded from giving. Among other things, it assists the PM in developing overarching goals for the government as well as writing speeches and organizing the PM's busy schedule. Not surprisingly, members of the PMO can expect to be replaced when a new prime minister is sworn into office.

The Privy Council Office (PCO) is staffed by civil servants seconded from various government departments. The PCO is headed by the Clerk of the Privy Council and Secretary to the Cabinet, who is the highest-ranking civil servant in Ottawa. Being a non-partisan agency, the PCO serves the government of the day, regardless of its political stripe. The main roles of the PCO are to coordinate the flow of information to the PM and cabinet and to provide analysis of major policy proposals. The PCO also advises the PM on the organization of government and on the appointment of senior civil servants in government departments and of officials who serve on various agencies, boards, and commissions.

The Department of Finance provides economic expertise to the government. It is responsible for managing the national economy, raising revenue through taxation and other measures, fixing public expenditures, and making economic forecasts. In the 1990s, the Department of Finance had a large say in determining the fate of a wide range of public programs as governments sought to reduce the federal budget deficit through public spending cuts.

In the United States, the president relies on a myriad of central agencies. These include the **Executive Office of the President** (EOP), which employs over 2,000 officials and serves as the functional equivalent of the PMO. Other executive agencies that report directly to the president include the Office of Management and Budget, the National Security Council, and the Council of Economic Advisers. Given the unitary nature of the U.S. political executive, cabinet secretaries, advisors, and other officials constantly seek the ear of the president. The president's Chief of Staff therefore occupies a position of great importance since it is his or her role to act as gatekeeper to the president. Ideally, the Chief of Staff and other key officials in the White House Office keep the president's workload to manageable proportions while ensuring that he or she keeps abreast of crucial issues across the full range of government operations.

THE BUREAUCRACY: THE ADMINISTRATIVE ARM OF GOVERNMENT

So far, we have looked at the upper echelons of the executive branch—the formal executive, the political executive, and the central agencies that support the work of the latter. In numerical terms, these institutions make up but a small fraction of the total membership of the executive branch of government. On a day-to-day basis, the functions of government are carried out by thousands of public servants, commonly called bureaucrats (or functionaries). In this section, we consider some of the functions carried out by bureaucrats and distinguish the role of senior officials from that of line officials. We also identify the organizing principles of the public service and the main structural forms through which bureaucratic authority is exercised. Finally, we address the question of political control of the bureaucracy.

To many people, the term **bureaucracy** carries a negative connotation. It is popularly associated with a rigid adherence to routine, a lack of imagination and compassion in dealing with ordinary citizens, and an obsessive preoccupation with arcane rules and procedures ("red tape"). In North America in particular, disparaging references to the public service are regularly featured in the popular press, where examples of bureaucratic rigidity or incompetence are portrayed as the norm rather than the exception. The rise of neoconservative parties in Western democracies in the 1980s gave added momentum to this unflattering view of the public service.[41] As part of their larger critique of Big Government, neoconservatives routinely denounce the inefficiency of the public sector while extolling what they take to be the inherent superiority of private enterprise. Building on these assumptions, many critics of the public sector insist that government should be run like a business. To others, it is far from clear that the application of business principles to government is either appropriate or desirable.

The German sociologist Max Weber considered bureaucracy to be the most rational form of organization for modern states. He identified the following essential characteristics of a well-ordered bureaucracy:[42]

- hierarchical organization of public offices
- specialization of labour
- decisions based on the application of impersonal rules
- a clear demarcation of legal authority between public offices
- recruitment to the public service on the basis of technical qualifications
- promotion based on seniority or achievement (or both)

On the relationship between bureaucrats and political leaders, Weber did not doubt that the former should be subordinate to the latter. In that respect, he agreed with Woodrow Wilson, a professional political scientist prior to becoming president of the United States. Wilson contended that there should be a clear division between politics and administration—politics being the concern of elected politicians and administration the purview of bureaucrats.[43] In practice, the line between politics and administration is not so clear. Politicians rely heavily on the expertise and advice of senior bureaucrats in formulating public policy. At the same time, bureaucrats must exercise discretion in executing their duties.

Senior Bureaucrats versus Line Officials

It is useful to distinguish the role of senior bureaucrats from that of subordinate officials. In Canada, the highest-ranking officials in government departments are called **deputy ministers**. In Britain, such officials are called permanent secretaries. They, along with a cadre of senior administrators, have a dual role—they are responsible both for developing policy advice for ministers and for overseeing the administration of government departments. Such officials are sometimes called *mandarins*, a term originally used to denote the senior bureaucrats of Imperial China. Line officials, on the other hand, are concerned with the delivery of government programs and the enforcement of regulations.

Deputy Ministers In Westminster systems, deputy ministers are appointed directly by the prime minister. While they are usually career public servants with a wealth of experience in government service, they may, on occasion, be recruited from outside the public service, usually from academia, nongovernmental organizations, or the corporate world. Some of the leading functions of senior officials include the following:[44]

- *Policy initiation.* A key role of deputy ministers is to advise the political head of the department (the minister) on policy matters. Having expertise in the subject matter of their respective departments, deputy ministers identify issues that need to be addressed and then present their minister with various options for addressing those issues. In cases where the minister himself or herself takes an active interest in policy, it is the responsibility of the deputy minister to provide expert advice on the ways and means by which the minister's goals can be realized.
- *Channel for inputs.* Senior officials serve as a channel for transmitting information, advice, and political demands from pressure groups (and civil society in general) to the minister. Since most government policy originates in departments, it makes sense for organized groups wishing to influence public policy to seek access to senior departmental personnel. In

fact, it is usually more fruitful for pressure groups to intervene at this pre-legislative stage of the policy process than to lobby for legislative changes at the parliamentary stage.

- *Rule-making.* After a law has been enacted by parliament, it falls to senior bureaucrats to draft detailed rules and regulations to flesh out the broad strokes of legislation. This post-legislative function is highly significant and is often conducted in close consultation with interested groups. While the minister has final authority to give legal effect to draft regulations, he or she relies heavily on the advice of departmental officials.

- *Management.* Deputy ministers manage government departments on a day-to-day basis. While the minister has political responsibility for the department, it is the deputy minister who manages departmental budgets and personnel and ensures the efficient delivery of public programs and services.

Line Officials Line officials are those bureaucrats who interact with the public in the course of delivering government services and enforcing rules and regulations. Two of their leading functions include:

- *Implementation and enforcement.* Most public servants are engaged, directly or indirectly, in the delivery of public programs and services and in the implementation and enforcement of rules and regulations. This is true of tax collectors, customs officers, food safety inspectors, and a host of other functionaries.

- *Interpretation and adjudication.* In the process of implementing public policies and enforcing regulations, bureaucrats necessarily must exercise some discretion. Does a claimed expense qualify for a tax deduction? Does a disability pension application meet the eligibility criteria? Has a prison inmate satisfied the conditions for parole? In all of these cases, bureaucrats must exercise their judgment in applying rules of general application to specific fact situations.

Organizing Principles

As with other aspects of its parliamentary system of government, bureaucracy in Canada is closely modelled on the British civil service. Key defining principles of the Anglo-Canadian administrative state are set out below.

Merit The **merit principle** governs recruitment to, and promotion within, the bureaucracy. It stipulates that positions within the public service should be filled by the best-qualified persons on the basis of competitive entry requirements. This principle is to be distinguished from the earlier spoils system, under which most public offices were filled by **political patronage** appointments. Political patronage worked reasonably well as long as the role of government was fairly limited. However, by the early 20th century the nature and scope of governmental activity in many countries began to undergo a radical change, with the development of public health measures, the establishment of government-run research labs, the introduction of social security programs, and the growing need for government regulation of various kinds. These new responsibilities required the state to recruit public officials with specialized knowledge and expertise. Competence, not party affiliation, became the new imperative for recruitment.

In Canada the merit principle was formally enshrined in legislation with the establishment of the Civil Service Commission (CSC) in 1918. In the decades that followed, well-defined procedures were laid down for recruitment to the civil service and for promotion within its ranks. Senior managers are responsible for hiring and promotion within the public service, subject to the procedures laid down by the Public Service Commission, or PSC (successor to the CSC). Any breach of the rules can be appealed to the PSC.

This is not to say that patronage has been, or arguably should be, banished entirely from government service. There remain a number of exempt positions within government departments that may be filled at the discretion of ministers.

Security of Tenure Public servants are protected from arbitrary dismissal by governments. The principle of security of tenure reinforces the idea that the public service is a professional corps of men and women pledged to execute faithfully the functions of the state. In this context, security of tenure does not mean that public servants can never be dismissed. On the contrary, public servants who are found to be negligent, incompetent, or corrupt are subject to a range of disciplinary sanctions, including dismissal. However, discipline is meted out not by the minister but by disciplinary bodies within the public service that operate at arm's length from government in order to ensure their impartiality.

It should also be noted that governments have wide powers to lay off public servants for budgetary reasons or as part of a reorganization of government departments. However, in reducing the number of public servants, the government may not single out a particular individual for dismissal in a deliberate and punitive way.

Political Neutrality The modern era demands strict political neutrality on the part of public servants. This principle goes hand in hand with the previous points about merit and security of tenure. Public servants are expected to serve the government of the day, whether or not they personally support the party in power or are in accord with its policies. It is the politicians, after all, who must answer for the wisdom and effectiveness, or lack thereof, of the government's policies.

Anonymity Public servants work in relative obscurity. Indeed, when political controversy envelops a government department, it is the minister who answers for the department, pursuant to the doctrine of ministerial responsibility. In such cases, the identity of particular public servants is generally not disclosed; as a result, they avoid being drawn into the political crossfire in parliament and the press. If instead beleaguered ministers were to point the finger of blame at their officials, then ministers, and the government as a whole, would cease to carry political responsibility. Such finger-pointing would also tend to prejudice any internal disciplinary proceedings against the officials in question. All the same, the veil of anonymity is lifted from time to time. This chiefly occurs when public officials are called to testify before parliamentary committees and public inquiries.

Representative Bureaucracy While merit remains the paramount guiding principle of the public service, it has been complemented in recent years by the goal of creating a more representative bureaucracy. The idea here is to foster the development of a public service that more accurately reflects the demographic composition of society. In Canada, the Official Languages Act (1969) was designed in part to promote the recruitment of francophones into the federal public service at a time when its higher levels were almost exclusively populated by anglophones. In more recent years, the federal government has striven to promote the recruitment of various groups that are underrepresented in the public service, particularly at managerial levels. Four groups have been targeted since the mid-1980s: women, Aboriginals, people with disabilities, and visible minorities.[45]

Bureaucratic Structures

Government bureaucracies are organized into a bewildering variety of institutions. Three of the organizational forms through which bureaucratic authority is exercised are government departments, regulatory agencies, and state-owned corporations. A key distinction among them has to do with the extent to which each of them is subject to ministerial control and direction. The extent of ministerial direction runs along a continuum; it is highest in the case of departments and lowest in the case of state-owned industries.

Government Departments Government departments are formally headed by a minister, who is responsible both for policy and administration. In reality, ministers rely heavily on their deputy minister in discharging both functions. As political head of the department, the minister takes the department's policy proposals to cabinet while explaining and defending its existing policies in parliament and the country. The deputy minister, as noted, assumes responsibility for the day-to-day administration of the department, a task for which most ministers have neither the time nor the skill.

In Westminster systems departments are required to draw up detailed spending plans for the year (known as Estimates) which are tabled in parliament. The Estimates are then sent to parliamentary committees, where MPs have an opportunity to grill the minister, and sometimes the deputy minister, not only about the department's spending plans but also about the operations of programs and services delivered by the department. The Estimates must be formally approved by Parliament before the government may appropriate and spend public money. At the end of the financial year, departments must report to Parliament on how they spent their budgets.

Because the minister is the political head of the department, departmental affairs frequently become the target of opposition party attacks in parliament. For example, in the years when the post office was a government department, the Postmaster General would always be bombarded by opposition questions in Parliament during a national postal strike. In the early 1980s, the post office was converted into a Crown corporation. This change of organizational form gave the managers of Canada Post more freedom from ministerial control to manage the postal service. At the same time, by establishing a more arm's-length relationship between the government and the post office, the government became somewhat more insulated from the political flak that greeted unpopular decisions taken by Canada Post—such as the closure of rural post offices and continual increases in the price of stamps!

Regulatory Agencies The term *regulatory agency* or **administrative tribunal** embraces a wide range of agencies, boards, and commissions. A task common to all of them is the interpretation and application of regulations under various statutes (acts of parliament). To the extent that this role involves court-like functions, certain regulatory agencies are referred to as quasi-judicial bodies. For example, the Immigration and Refugee Board acts like a court in determining whether an applicant for landed immigrant status or refugee protection has met the relevant statutory and regulatory requirements and has been dealt with properly by the bureaucracy.

Members of regulatory agencies are appointed by the PM, the relevant minister, or the cabinet as a whole, depending on the enabling legislation. Given the quasi-judicial nature of many regulatory bodies, however, they must be free from ministerial interference to decide individual cases. It is improper, therefore, for a minister to direct, or even to lobby, a regulatory agency as to how it should decide a particular application that is before it. On the other hand, it is permissible for the cabinet to issue policy directives to regulatory agencies. The purpose of such directives is to clarify the policy purposes underpinning a particular body of regulations. Legislation may provide a right to appeal the decision of an agency to the minister or the full cabinet. In any event, regulatory agencies are subject to less searching scrutiny by parliament than government departments.

State-Owned Corporations State-owned corporations (known in Canada as **Crown corporations**) are established by government to fulfil a variety of public policy purposes, such as the promotion of regional economic development, the advancement of arts and culture, or the provision of transportation services. Such corporations are subject to the least ministerial control. The cabinet appoints a board of directors, which in turn appoints a president and other senior executives to manage the corporation. Unlike a publicly traded company owned by shareholders, a crown corporation is wholly owned by the government.

Compared to their counterparts in government departments, the managers of crown corporations have a freer hand in personnel matters, such as hiring and promotion. While some crown corporations are directed to act like a commercial corporation and to turn a profit, many of them require subsidies from the public treasury. For example, every year the CBC receives a subsidy, formally approved by Parliament, to carry out its mandate.

Political Control of the Bureaucracy

According to constitutional theory, the bureaucracy is subject to control by the government, which in turn is responsible to parliament. Many observers contend that this theory does not always correspond to reality. In particular, it underestimates the inherent power of the bureaucracy. Table 8.2 sets out the respective characteristics of senior bureaucrats and ministers.

The relationship between senior bureaucrats and their ministers can sometimes be highly unequal. Ministers come to office knowing little or nothing about the workings of their department or the subject matter of their portfolio. Being novices, they must rely on the experience and expertise of their officials. Moreover, because of their relatively short tenure, most ministers are not in a position to pursue far-reaching policy changes. Innovation also carries political risks. While ministers can expect to be blamed for any teething problems a new initiative may experience in its early stages, they may not receive credit for its success in the long run. It may take years for a new

Table 8.2	Comparison of Characteristics of Bureaucrats and Ministers	
Bureaucrats	**Ministers**
Expert knowledge	General knowledge
Long tenure	Short tenure
Anonymity	Political responsibility

program or policy to bear fruit, by which time the minister will likely be in another portfolio or back on the opposition benches.

Winston Churchill once remarked that experts should be "on tap, not on top."[46] Yet many students of bureaucracy—and some former politicians—contend that it is all too easy for ministers to be captured by their senior officials.

Countervailing Power Recognizing the danger that ministers, and the government as a whole, may become unduly influenced by the interests and preferences of the bureaucracy, governments have attempted to enhance their political control of the bureaucracy. Steps toward this end include the following:

- *Turnover of senior officials by a new government.* A new prime minister—particularly one who has just led his or her party to victory at the polls after a long spell in opposition—can signal an intention to pursue a new agenda by replacing some of the top-ranking bureaucrats. While it is inadvisable for a new government to dispense with too many experienced hands at the top, a certain amount of turnover can reinvigorate the bureaucracy as a whole. This practice is more characteristic of changes in administrations in the United States than at the federal level in Canada.
- *Use of political staff.* Nowadays, all governments make use of political advisors to provide them with advice that is independent of that generated by the bureaucracy. Such advisors are called "exempt staff" because they are hired outside the normal rules that govern recruitment to the public service. This practice is highly developed in France, where ministers have their own "ministerial cabinet," a body of appointed advisors who serve the minister's political interests and monitor the activities of departmental officials.[47]
- *Enhanced role of central agencies.* One of the functions of central agencies is to counteract the influence of individual departments on the formulation of government policy. In Canada, the enlarged role of the PCO, the Department of Finance, and other central agencies reflects, in part, a strategy of using bureaucrats to check the power of other bureaucrats.

- *Election of a party with clear policy aims.* Other things being equal, a government will be better able to overcome bureaucratic inertia if it comes to office with a clear idea of what it intends to accomplish. This point is well illustrated by the records of reform-minded governments across Canada over the years. Provincial examples include the Saskatchewan government of T.C. Douglas (1944–1961), the Quebec government of Jean Lesage (1960–1966), and the Ontario government of Mike Harris (1995–2002). Likewise, the British governments of Clement Attlee (1945–1951) and Margaret Thatcher (1979–1990) and the New Zealand government of David Lange (1984–1989) instituted sweeping (and controversial) changes in economic policy and the delivery of government services.

New Public Management: Running Government as a Business

The downsizing of government in many countries in the 1990s did much to mitigate concerns about all-powerful bureaucracies. This development formed part of a larger reconfiguration of the role of government that saw the dismantling of certain elements of the postwar **welfare state**, the **privatization** of many state-owned industries, and the diffusion of **neoliberal**, anti-statist norms embodied in global trade agreements. In English-speaking countries in particular, a renewed faith in the efficacy of the capitalist marketplace in recent decades had important effects on the organization and functioning of the executive branch of government. Increasingly, government services have been outsourced to private contractors, public–private partnerships, or other forms of alternative service delivery. The expectation is that public services can be delivered more efficiently by the private sector or by the application of business principles. The advent of this philosophy, known loosely as the **New Public Management**, has brought in a new emphasis on the use of quantifiable measures of performance, the expansion of public choice, and the achievement of efficiency gains, usually expressed in terms of financial cost savings.[48]

The New Public Management (NPM) is more advanced in some countries, such as Britain and Australia, than in others, including Canada. Proponents of NPM point out that the goal of using public resources with maximum efficiency is shared by conservative and social democratic governments alike. They also reassert the view that politics should be separated from the technical business of administration.[49]

Critics reply that politics and administration cannot be neatly compartmentalized. Democratic governments must accommodate many different, and often conflicting, political demands. Such demands have to do not only with the ends of public policy but also with the means of realizing them. In choosing among alternative courses of action, efficiency is just one consideration among many.[50] As one observer aptly put it, "one person's red tape is another's due process."[51]

In any case, it may be difficult to measure quantitatively the performance of public bodies. For example, the benefit of health and safety regulations lies in the harm that is avoided, even if the financial costs of regulation can easily be measured. Conversely, the costs of deregulation may only become evident in the long run. This point was powerfully underscored by the global financial crisis that unfolded in late 2008, a consequence in large part of the deregulation of capital markets that began in the United States in the 1980s and was emulated by other countries. Today western governments are busily imposing new regulations on the financial industry.[52]

CONCLUSION

The executive branch of government is powerful and pervasive. It provides political leadership for the nation while also having responsibility for the day-to-day administration of government operations. The executive assumes a wide variety of institutional forms, even among states having a shared commitment to democratic values. In this chapter, we considered three main types of executive: parliamentary, presidential, and semi-presidential. In evaluating these different forms of government, it is useful to consider the relative weight each assigns to the goal of firm and effective government and the need for the legislature to hold the executive to account. We should also be mindful of the capacity of the political executive to assert control over the administrative executive.

DISCUSSION QUESTIONS

1. Where does power lie in a parliamentary system?

2. Where does power lie in a presidential system?

3. Discuss the advantages and disadvantages of separating the head of state from the head of government.

4. Are prime ministers too powerful? If so, how should their powers be curtailed?

5. Are the traditional governing principles of Anglo-Canadian bureaucracy still relevant today?

6. Should governments be run like a business?

FURTHER READING

Elgie, Robert, and Sophia Moestrup, eds. *Semi-presidentialism Outside Europe: A Comparative Study*. London: Routledge, 2007.

Jones, Charles O. *The Presidency in a Separated System*, 2nd ed. Washington, DC: The Brookings Institution, 2005.

Kelly, Paul. *November* 1975: *The Inside Story of Australia's Greatest Political Crisis*. St. Leonard's, NSW: Allen and Unwin, 1995.

Lijphart, Arend, ed. *Parliamentary Versus Presidential Government*. Oxford: Oxford University Press, 1992.

Linz, Juan J., and Arturo Valenzuela, eds. *The Failure of Presidential Democracy: Comparative Perspectives*. Vol. 2. Baltimore: Johns Hopkins University Press, 1994.

Peters, B. Guy. *The Politics of Bureaucracy: An Introduction to Comparative Public Administration*, 6th ed. New York: Routledge, 2009.

Savoie, Donald J. *Court Government and the Collapse of Accountability in Canada and the United Kingdom*. Toronto: University of Toronto Press, 2008.

ENDNOTES

1. Andrew Heywood, *Politics*, 2nd ed. (Basingstoke, UK: Palgrave, 2002), p. 334.

2. J.H. Baker, *An Introduction to English Legal History*, 4th ed. (London: Butterworths, 2002), chs. 1–2.

3. Walter Bagehot, *The English Constitution*, Introduction by R.H.S. Crossman (Ithaca, NY: Cornell University Press, 1966), pp. 67–68. Originally published in 1867.

4. The Commonwealth is a voluntary association of 53 states that were once colonies of the United Kingdom. After achieving political independence, many chose to retain the Queen as their head of state, although the majority, including India and all of the African members, chose to become republics.

5. In Canada Lieutenant Governors are appointed by the Governor General on the advice of the Prime Minister. In Australia Governors are appointed by the Queen on the advice of the state premier. See David Butler and D.A. Low, eds., *Sovereigns and Surrogates: Constitutional Heads of State in the Commonwealth* (Basingstoke, U.K.: Macmillan, 1991) and Peter Boyce, *The Queen's Other Realms: The Crown and Its Legacy in Australia, Canada, and New Zealand* (Annandale, NSW: Federation Press, 2008).

6. Frank MacKinnon, *The Crown in Canada* (Calgary: McClelland and Stewart, 1976).

7. Peter Fraser, "A Revolutionary Governor General? The Grenada Crisis of 1983," in D.A. Low, ed., *Constitutional Heads and Political Crises: Commonwealth Episodes, 1945–1985* (New York: St. Martin's Press, 1988).

8. On the other hand, if the PM is in a hurry to step down, the government caucus may select an interim leader to hold the reins of office pending the holding of a leadership convention.

9. Paul Kelly, *November 1975: The Inside Story of Australia's Greatest Political Crisis* (St. Leonards, NSW: Allen and Unwin, 1995); Colin Howard and Cheryl Saunders, "The Blocking of the Budget and Dismissal of the Government," in Gareth Evans, ed., *Labor and the Constitution, 1972–1975: Essays and Commentaries on the Constitutional Controversies of the Whitlam Years in Australian Government* (Melbourne: Heinemann, 1977); Garfield Barwick, *Sir John Did His Duty* (Wahroonga, NSW: Serendip, 1983).

10. Peter W. Hogg, *Constitutional Law of Canada*, Student Edition (Scarborough: Thomson Carswell, 2006), pp. 290–91.

11. J.R. Mallory, "Crises That Didn't Happen: Canada 1945–1985," in D.A. Low, ed., *Constitutional Heads and Political Crises*, pp. 229–31. The situation in Ontario after the 1985 provincial election is generally regarded as a instance in which the Lieutenant Governor would have been justified a refusing a dissolution had the premier, Frank Miller, requested one. Instead, following the defeat of his Conservative government in the Legislature, Miller tendered his resignation and the Lieutenant Governor invited the Leader of the Opposition, David Peterson, to form a minority government. Peterson's Liberal Government remained in office for two years with the support of the New Democratic Party.

12. Andrew Heard, "The Governor General's Suspension of Parliament: Duty Done or a Perilous Precedent?," in Peter H. Russell and Lorne Sossin, eds., *Parliamentary Democracy in Crisis* (Toronto: University of Toronto Press, 2009); Gary Levy, "Confidence Game," *Inroads* 25 (Summer 2009): 48–59.

13. C.E.S. Franks, "To Prorogue or Not to Prorogue: Did the Governor General Make the Right Decision?," in Russell and Sossin, *Parliamentary Democracy*; Peter Neary, "Confidence: How Much is Enough?," *Constitutional Forum* 18 (2) (September 22, 2009).

14. "The Americas: Halted in mid-debate; Canada without Parliament," *The Economist*, January 9, 2010, p. 39.

15. C.E.S. Franks, *The Parliament of Canada* (Toronto: University of Toronto Press, 1987), p. 96.

16. See generally Christopher J. Kam, *Party Discipline and Parliamentary Politics.* (Cambridge: Cambridge University Press, 2009).

17. An exception to that rule in the U.S. concerns the Vice-President, who presides over the Senate and casts the deciding vote in case of a tie.

18. In 1868, impeachment proceedings against President Andrew Johnson failed by a single vote to meet the two-thirds threshold in the Senate.

19. See generally William B. Perkins, "The Political Nature of Presidential Impeachment in the United States," in Jody C. Baumgartner and Naoko Kada, ed., *Checking Executive Power: Presidential Impeachment in Comparative Perspective* (Westport, CT: Praeger, 2003).

20. See Matthew Soberg Shugart and John M. Carey, *Presidents and Assemblies: Constitutional Design and Electoral Dynamics* (Cambridge: Cambridge University Press, 1992).

21. See Juan J. Linz, "Presidential or Parliamentary Democracy: Does It Make a Difference?," in Juan J. Linz and Arturo Valenzuela, eds., *The Failure of Presidential Democracy: Comparative Perspectives*, Vol. 2 (Baltimore: Johns Hopkins University Press, 1994).

22. U.S. President George W. Bush arguably strode down this path in his address to a joint session of Congress on September 20, 2001 when he said: "Every nation, in every region, now has a decision to make. Either you are with us, or you are with the terrorists."

23. Juan J. Linz, "Presidential or Parliamentary Democracy," p. 4. See also John Gerring, Strom C. Thacker, and Carola Moreno, "Are Parliamentary Systems Better?," *Comparative Political Studies* 42 (3) (March 2009): 327–59.

24. Maurice Duverger, "A New Political System Model: Semi-presidential Government," *European Journal of Political Research* 8 (June 1980).

25. Karen Henderson and Neil Robinson, *Post-communist Politics: An Introduction* (Hemel Hempstead: Prentice Hall, 1997), p. 168.

26. Arend Lijphart, *Patterns of Democracy: Government Forms and Performance in Thirty-Six Countries* (New Haven, CT: Yale University Press, 1999), p. 121.

27. Robert Elgie, ed., *Semi-presidentialism in Europe* (Oxford: Oxford University Press, 1999).

28. John P. Mackintosh, *The British Cabinet*, 2nd ed. (London: Methuen, 1968), ch. 3.

29. Bagehot, *The English Constitution*, p. 111.

30. Mackintosh, *The British Cabinet*, p. 118.

31. Paul G. Thomas, "The Changing Nature of Accountability," in B. Guy Peters and Donald J. Savoie, eds., *Taking Stock: Assessing Public Sector Reforms* (Montreal and Kingston: McGill-Queen's University Press, 1998). See also Donald J. Savoie, *Court Government and the Collapse of Accountability in Canada and the United Kingdom* (Toronto: University of Toronto Press, 2008).

32. For a good overview of this debate, see Patrick Weller, *First Among Equals: Prime Ministers in Westminster Systems* (London: Allen and Unwin, 1985). For a Canadian perspective, see Donald J. Savoie, *Governing from the Centre: The Concentration of Power in Canadian Politics* (Toronto: University of Toronto Press, 1999), ch. 4.

33. Thomas M.J. Bateman, "Party Democracy Increases the Leader's Power," *Policy Options* (September 2001): 20–23; and Christopher Moore, "Backbenchers Fight Back," *National Post*, February 13, 2001, p. A16.

34. Norman C. Thomas and Joseph A. Pika, *The Politics of the Presidency*, 4th ed. (Washington, DC: Congressional Quarterly Press, 1997), p. 259.

35. Strictly speaking, U.S. presidents are indirectly elected by the Electoral College, a body of men and women, elected in each state, who are pledged to cast their votes for the presidential candidate who wins the most votes in their state. Ordinarily, the candidate who wins the most votes nationwide also wins a majority of Electoral College votes. However, this was not

the case in the presidential election of 2000, when Democratic candidate Al Gore won half a million more votes than Republican candidate George W. Bush. Bush nevertheless won a majority of votes in the Electoral College. See Chapter 11.

36. Andrew Grice and Ben Russell, "Parliament to be Recalled after Blair Bows to Pressure for Debate," *The Independent*, September 11, 2002.

37. Walter LaFeber, *America, Russia, and the Cold War, 1945–2006*, 10th ed. (New York: McGraw-Hill, 2008), pp. 250–52.

38. Neither UN nor subsequent U.S. weapons inspectors were able to find evidence of WMDs in Iraq.

39. Colin Campbell, *Governments Under Stress* (Toronto: University of Toronto Press, 1983).

40. Gregory J. Inwood, *Understanding Canadian Public Administration: An Introduction to Theory and Practice* (Toronto: Pearson Education, 2009), pp. 138–42.

41. Donald J. Savoie, *Thatcher, Reagan, Mulroney: In Search of a New Bureaucracy* (Toronto: University of Toronto Press, 1994), pp. 88–94.

42. Max Weber, *The Theory of Social and Economic Organization* (New York: Oxford University Press, 1947). Originally published in 1922.

43. Woodrow Wilson, "The Study of Administration," *Political Science Quarterly* 2 (2) (June 1887).

44. Inwood, *Understanding Canadian Public Administration*, pp. 145–49.

45. *Ibid.*, pp. 282–93.

46. Randolph S. Churchill, *Twenty-One Years* (Boston: Houghton Mifflin, 1965), p. 140.

47. Alistair Cole, *French Politics and Society* (London: Prentice-Hall, 1998), pp. 110–11.

48. Allan Tupper, "New Public Management and Canadian Politics," in Janine Brodie and Linda Trimble, eds., *Reinventing Canada: Politics of the 21st Century* (Toronto: Pearson Education, 2003); Peter Aucoin, "New Public Management and New Public Governance: Finding the Balance" in David Siegel and Ken Rasmussen, ed., *Power, Professionalism, and Public Service: Essays in Honour of Kenneth Kernaghan* (Toronto: University of Toronto Press, Institute of Public Administration of Canada, 2006).

49. David Osborne and Ted Gaebler, *Reinventing Government* (Reading, MA: Addison-Wesley, 1992).

50. Janice Gross Stein, *The Cult of Efficiency* (Toronto: Anansi, 2001).

51. Donald J. Savoie, "What Is Wrong with the New Public Management?," *Canadian Public Administration* 38 (1) (Spring 1995): 116.

52. Justin Baer, "Wall Street: From Recession to Regulation," *Financial Times*, September 24, 2010.

W W W For various weblinks discussed in this chapter, please go to the book's website at **www.studyingpolitics4e.nelson.com**

Legislatures: Centre Stage But Not Top Billing

Andrew Heard

CHAPTER OBJECTIVES

After you have completed this chapter, you should be able to:

- understand the potential roles of a legislature in a political system
- discuss the range of actors that undermine the effectiveness of legislatures
- outline how laws are made
- differentiate among the different kinds of representation that legislators can undertake
- discuss ideas for the reform of legislatures.

WHAT ARE LEGISLATURES?

Legislatures are at once the centrepiece of democratic countries and yet at the same time are often viewed as the most visible failures of those very democracies. An elected legislature holds the promise of the people's representatives assembling together to debate, deliberate, and decide upon the nation's business. In a multiparty democracy, one would expect that

> **Legislature:** An institution with primary responsibility to enact laws.

significant differences of opinion would be expressed as members of the different parties listen to and weigh competing views of how best to deal with the issues of **public policy** under consideration. Perhaps even some visible compromises and changes of heart might be made among the parties as they try to forge a consensus on what is best for their society. The members of the legislature would be able to identify the most serious weaknesses in a proposed law, make the necessary changes, and reject any measures that proved to be profoundly unpopular with the people they represent. Unfortunately, reality often falls disappointingly short of these expectations.

This chapter explores the potential roles that legislatures might fill in any political system and then examines the practical factors that can limit that potential. The emphasis here is on balancing idealism with a fuller understanding of the limitations under which legislators do their work. It is equally important to resist the temptation to slip into cynicism and view legislatures as simply rubber stamps that blindly approve policies proposed by the executive. There are indeed a number of important and substantive functions that legislatures can undertake, and an appreciation of these can lead to useful suggestions for legislative reform. This chapter reviews legislatures generically, but also provides

THE STRUCTURE OF LEGISLATURES

A **unicameral legislature** has only one chamber, and all members of the legislature belong to and participate in that chamber. All the provincial legislatures in Canada are unicameral.

Example of a unicameral legislature: China

National People's Congress: 2,987 members

A **bicameral legislature** has two separate chambers (often called houses), and members of the legislature belong only to one of those chambers and have a right to participate in only their chamber's proceedings. Almost all federal systems have bicameral legislatures at the national level.

Example of a bicameral legislature: Canada

Upper house: Senate 105 appointed members

Lower house: House of Commons 308 elected members

branch of government—the power to make law is not restricted to just the legislative branch.

All political systems grant some legislative power to the executive branch of government, of which there are several possible forms. First, the constitution of a state may explicitly provide some lawmaking powers to the executive. For example, the president of the country may be able to make some laws by decree. Second, every political system also provides in some fashion that laws may be made by the ministers or cabinet who head up the executive departments of government; these laws can be variously called regulations, ordinances, or orders in council. This lawmaking power of the executive is often actually delegated to the executive by the legislature. Third, in every political system, the judiciary also exercises some lawmaking power in the course of interpreting and enforcing the legal rules enacted by the legislature or executive. So we find that the legislative power can be spread across all three branches of government.

However, the exercise of lawmaking by other institutions or officials in the political system does not mean that they constitute legislatures. Constitutions usually vest the prime lawmaking power in one particular institution, the legislature, while only limited lawmaking power belongs to the executive. And the lawmaking power of the judiciary is only an implicit power that is exercised in the course of its principal task, which is interpreting and enforcing the law.

Legislatures appear to have important symbolic cachet, judging by their proliferation over the 20th century. The vast majority of states today have a formal legislative body: 189 all told in 2007.[1] Many authoritarian regimes have legislatures in order to create a façade of democracy by holding elections and letting the people's "representatives" pass laws. In these instances, legislatures are truly rubber stamps and any laws proposed by the rulers are dutifully passed with no criticism of the government. Only a few countries do without a legislature, reserving principal lawmaking power for the executive.[2] In a few of these countries, an absolute monarch still exercises the lawmaking power. In Saudi Arabia, for example, the king is the sole source of formal legislative power. Others are ruled by a dictator who issues laws by personal decree.

an opportunity to understand Canadian and other legislatures around the world. In order to assess our own legislatures, it is essential that we have a global view that allows us to appreciate what can and does occur elsewhere; as in other chapters, a comparative perspective can help us better understand what might be done to improve our own political institutions (see Box 9.1).

The first task is to identify just what a legislature is. For a political institution to be called a legislature, that institution must be centrally involved in the lawmaking process. Moreover, the legislature must actually make law; it is not simply a consultative body that provides advice to another lawmaking official or institution. For example, the Shura Council in Saudi Arabia cannot be described as a legislature, since its only formal power is to offer advice on public policy to the council of ministers. On the other hand, legislatures are not the only institutions or political actors in a political system that make law. It is important to distinguish between the legislative power and the legislative

POTENTIAL FUNCTIONS OF LEGISLATURES

In studying legislatures, political scientists have a number of concerns and interests. First and foremost, we are concerned with identifying what specific roles legislatures may fill in a political system and what factors have an impact on how effectively the legislatures carry them out. Legislatures can play vital informal roles in a political system, on top of the formal ones detailed in their countries' constitutions, and a deeper understanding of the functioning of any particular legislature may well arise from an appreciation of the broader contexts in which all legislatures operate in general.

One can easily identify a few key roles that legislatures perform, such as making **laws**, representing the people, and debating public issues. A simple reason for most legislatures' failure to fulfil these roles can be just as readily identified: many legislatures are effectively controlled by the executive or by the leaders of a dominating party or coalition of parties. In either case, strict discipline of the members of the legislature prevents them from taking independent positions on matters under debate and consideration. Examined in such stark terms, most legislatures around the world, whether they are part of democratic or authoritarian systems,

would have to be written off as failures; they would be nothing better than symbolic ornaments in contrast to the executive's total control of the policy process. One could also argue that even in legislatures where individual members have considerable personal discretion to decide what position to take on a matter under debate, such as in the U.S. Congress, the realities are that the legislators simply choose the positions demanded by those who provide them with the financial support needed to get re-elected. On closer examination, however, such views of legislatures may prove to be more cynical than accurate.

Perhaps the best starting point for examining legislatures is to review briefly all the possible roles that legislatures can play in a political system. The great variety of functions can be surprising to many, and they give a clue to the potential value of a legislature that works well. The lawmaking role of legislatures is the most visible, but there are many other functions that are equally important—and sometimes even more so.

The following are the potential roles of legislatures:

- to legislate
- to represent
- to debate
- to educate
- to institutionalize opposition
- to investigate issues and events
- to suggest or initiate new policies
- to scrutinize executive activities
- to legitimate the policies of the executive
- to ratify or veto executive decisions and actions
- to refine and improve policies suggested by the executive
- to decide who holds executive offices (in parliamentary systems)
- to provide alternative governments or political leaders
- to provide an ombudsman service for citizens
- to adjudicate in a judicial or quasi-judicial role

In the process of passing new laws, legislators can actively engage in several other general functions as well. In a fully democratic system, members of the legislature debate the wisdom of any proposed law (or **bill**) and consider a variety of suggested improvements. Inevitably, such debates over

Stephen Harper uses the clapper to turn parliament on and off.

Graeme MacKay/Artizans

the preferred policy and form in which to enact it involve a subtle but important educational role. Through listening to these debates, it is possible for those in power to learn about different perspectives on their policy proposals, and at the same time others may see the weaknesses in their own initial positions. Perhaps the most crucial part of this educational function occurs when the media effectively report on events in the legislature and influence the views held by the general public.

> **Bill:** The formal text of a proposed law before it has been enacted into law. When the bill has completed all stages of the legislative process, it becomes law and is known as a statute or an act.

In the course of these debates, members also engage in representing the interests of a wide range of groups in the general population. Depending upon the number of political parties present in the legislature and the discipline imposed on members of those parties, a wide range of views may be raised. This can have

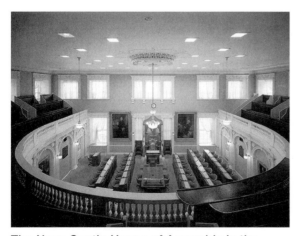

The Nova Scotia House of Assembly is the oldest legislative building in Canada, with deliberations held here since 1819. In 1848, it was the site of the first successful passage of a non-confidence motion in any colonial legislature in the British Empire. This marked the start of responsible government in Canada.

Courtesy of the Nova Scotia House of Assembly; photo by Chris Reardon

an important symbolic function in providing citizens with a direct and visible display of views they personally support being expressed in the legislature. As a result of these "talking" functions, legislative assemblies serve as a crucial institutional channel through which disputes get aired publicly and settled in an authoritative fashion by a majority vote.

One of the important functions of legislatures can be to institutionalize **opposition**. While we may take this for granted in a democratic society, we would soon miss the opposition if it were to be suppressed. On a broad level, people are less likely to take to the streets in violent demonstrations or start a civil war if they believe that opposition to the ruling party's policies plays some role in the legislature. Indeed, a hallmark of how democratic a country is can be seen in how free members of the legislature feel to openly criticize the government. An illustration of the importance of institutionalizing opposition came after the Liberal Party won every seat in New Brunswick's 1987 elections for the provincial legislature. Although they had no obligation to do so, the Liberals invited the leader of the Progressive Conservative Party to appear in the assembly on a regular basis to participate in Question Period, when cabinet ministers are questioned about their conduct of public affairs.

Legislatures also have the potential to conduct investigations into issues and events of political importance. Committees most effectively carry out these investigations, but sometimes a series of questions on the main floor of the legislature can reveal the facts of some controversial happening. When an inquiry is held into an event, it is usually conducted as part of the legislature's role of overseeing the work of the executive branch of government, essentially to discover what government officials did or did not know or do. A committee can also hold hearings on a matter of public policy in order to make suggestions about how the policy can be improved; these can range from very focused issues, such as policies dealing with juvenile offenders, to much broader questions, such as the nation's basic foreign or defence policy. Hearings into matters of public policy are also often held as part of the process of considering legislation.

Many important functions of legislatures relate to their relationship with the executive branch of government. Briefly stated, the legislature has two sorts of functions to perform with respect to the executive. The first relates to processing and legitimating the executive's decisions concerning new policies it wants enacted into law, and the second involves performing an overseeing function to scrutinize how the executive has carried out its responsibilities. Particularly in parliamentary systems, where the cabinet controls most of the policy process and proposes virtually all the bills that eventually become laws, the legislature has an important symbolic role in performing at least a ritual public debate and examination of these proposals.

Many legislatures perform a role not found in Canada, with the requirement that the legislature review and ratify any international agreements the executive has signed; for example, the U.S. Senate must ratify treaties. Some legislatures allow individuals and groups from the public to make presentations to the committees that study the cabinet's proposed laws and international treaties, and this public input adds another layer of democratic legitimation to the legislation. But in order for this legitimation to have substance, the scrutiny of bills must be more than just a ritual. If legislation is to be legitimate, there must be a meaningful debate of the merits and flaws of the proposals and a real possibility of amending the bills and forcing the government to withdraw the most unpopular proposals.

Similarly, legislatures can have a significant function to perform when they oversee the executive. This oversight can involve two types of activity: one is to ensure that the government is acting acceptably and properly, in the legislature's view; the other is to ensure that the executive complies with the policies previously approved by the legislature. These oversight functions, when done well, can provide a significant check on a government that might otherwise try to cover up its misdeeds and abuses. In parliamentary systems, the legislature wields an ultimate threat over the executive: the power to cast a vote of **non-confidence** in the cabinet and force it to either resign or call an election. This is a powerful sanction that may be rarely exercised in countries such as Canada, where the party forming the cabinet usually controls a majority of the legislature's members in

Confidence (or Non-Confidence) Vote: Alternatively, an explicitly worded motion indicating that the legislature either has or does not have confidence in the government; a vote on a matter that the government has previously declared to be a matter of confidence; or a vote on important measures that are central to the government's plans, such as the budget.

a **majority government** situation. But it is a real sanction that has brought down governments in Canada and in many other countries as well; six Canadian federal governments have either resigned or called an election as a result of a vote of non-confidence, but they were all instances of **minority governments**. The Americans' presidential system does not provide their legislatures with the power to vote non-confidence in the political executive, but Congress still has the capacity to expose and informally censure executive wrongdoing and mismanagement. Semi-presidential systems such as those in France and Russia put the president out of normal reach, but the prime minister and cabinet can be subject to non-confidence motions.

Majority government: A government in which one party holds all the seats in the cabinet as well as the majority of seats in the legislature (or lower house in bicameral legislatures).

Minority government: A government in which one party holds all the seats in the cabinet but has fewer than 50 percent of the members in the legislature.

The most visible difference in executive oversight between the U.S. system and parliamentary government lies in the **Question Period** that just about every parliament holds. On regular occasions, members of the legislature may put direct questions to the prime minister and other cabinet ministers about their policies and the actions of their officials. While substantive answers are rare indeed, Question Periods do provide the opportunity to highlight government bungling and misdeeds, which every now and again can blow up into real political crises that eventually force the resignation of a cabinet minister or the downfall of the whole cabinet. Question Period also forces individual cabinet ministers to account publicly for their actions. The media play a crucial role in this regard by publicizing and focusing attention among the electorate on the events in the legislature; indeed, media coverage is important to many dimensions of the legislature's effectiveness.

An important function for legislatures in many countries involves selecting or confirming senior executive officials. One review of constitutions found at least 19 states where members of the legislature directly

Contentious Canadian parliament turned into boxing ring.

Malcolm Mayes/Artizans

choose the head of state.[3] In some cases, such as India and Germany, members of the lower house meet in a joint session with representatives of the state legislatures and collectively elect the president. In the United States and the Philippines, the legislature selects the president in the event of a tie after the general population has voted. This role is only a formal one for the U.S. House of Representatives, whose members vote to choose the president if no candidate wins a majority of votes in the electoral college convened after the general election; in almost all circumstances, the House vote simply confirms the candidate who won the most electoral college votes.

Legislatures in parliamentary systems have several roles that are not applicable to the U.S. congressional system because of the principle of **responsible government** that gives parliamentary systems their essential character. A cabinet must have the formal confidence of a majority in the legislature in order to govern; in legislatures with two houses, this principle usually applies just to a majority in the lower house. In a broad sense, a parliament ultimately decides whether a cabinet can stay in office; the head of state may appoint a new prime

> **Responsible government:** A defining principle of Westminster-style parliamentary governments, which states that the cabinet may only hold office as long as it has majority support in the legislature (or lower house in a bicameral parliament) for votes of confidence.

minister and cabinet, but they have to obtain and maintain the confidence of the legislature in order to govern for any period of time. Parliaments are usually organized in an adversarial fashion, in which government MPs square off against the opposition. One theoretical role of the opposition is to provide an alternative government. Should the legislature force the resignation of the government, the head of state must be able to count on the opposition to step in and act as the new government, at least until new elections are held. But in a broader political sense, the opposition party or parties continuously act in the legislature to portray themselves to the public as an alternative to the ruling party, in some cases as a **coalition government**.

> **Coalition government:** A government that occurs when two or more parties hold seats in cabinet supported by a combination of parties that forms a majority in the legislature.

The U.S. system, however, gives the legislature another role in deciding who holds executive positions. The Senate must approve the president's nomination of individuals to the cabinet, senior levels of the civil service, the judiciary, and the armed forces. In the first year of the 111th Congress, which sat in 2009 (the first year of President Obama's term in office), the Senate considered a total of 24,951 nominations; 1,901 of which were either unconfirmed or not approved for one reason or another.[4] The most visible of these nomination reviews involve hearings to scrutinize individuals who have been nominated to sit on the Supreme Court, a task sometimes suggested as a useful innovation for the Canadian parliament to consider.

Loosely related to the executive oversight function, and an important part of many legislatures, is an ombudsman role. In this role, a legislator acts on behalf of citizens and tries to sort out troubles they may be having with the bureaucracy. This is usually known as **constituency** work (or service), and the vast bulk of it occurs outside the legislative chamber, with legislators or their staff phoning or writing to civil servants or cabinet ministers on behalf of the person involved. In a parliamentary system, MPs can raise questions during Question Period or in committee hearings about specific cases they are handling, but the sheer volume of constituency work means that only a fraction of cases are dealt with in a public forum in this manner. Despite the "invisible" nature of constituency work, it has come to be the most time-consuming task of legislators in many countries.

Two studies in the 1990s revealed that Canadian MPs devote on average over 42 percent of their time to constituency work.[5] A 1996 survey of British MPs found they spent a similar amount of time on constituency work, about 40 percent.[6] However, there is a great disparity between the Canadian public's general perception of the importance of this function compared to that of their MPs. In a 1993 Gallup poll, the public rated this the least important part of an MP's work, but when MPs were asked the same question, they rated it as their number one priority.[7] The difference might be explained by the personal satisfaction MPs feel in helping individuals, in a job that has few direct personal rewards; on the other hand, only a very small segment of the population ever turn to their MP for help, and so this work is of little consequence to most of the general public.

A limited exercise of judicial power can also be one of the functions that legislatures are expected to fill. The most important examples involve the impeachment of senior public officials. When the U.S. House of Representatives charged President Clinton in impeachment proceedings in 1998, the Senate acted as a jury of a court chaired by the chief justice—and found Clinton not guilty. Brazil, India, and the Philippines are other countries whose legislatures conduct impeachment hearings of not just the president but of senior judges and other officials. In 2001 the Indonesian parliament impeached President Abdurrahman Wahid on charges of extensive corruption. Sometimes a President will resign when it becomes clear that the legislature will almost certainly vote for impeachment; this was the case with U.S. President Richard Nixon in 1974 and Brazil's President Fernando Collor in 1992. Another common exercise of judicial power is seen in the 24 countries whose legislatures act as courts to hear charges of disputed or corrupt elections; this function is a power of parliaments historically descended from the British model, but most are like Canada in delegating this function to the courts.

The British parliament appears unique in the world because the highest court in the land has for centuries been a committee of the House of Lords, the Appellate Committee. The specially appointed Law Lords heard cases in five-judge panels; when they pronounced judgment, they delivered a report to a full meeting of the House of Lords. However, the *Constitutional Reform Act*, passed in 2005, replaced the Law Lords with an independent Supreme Court in 2009.

The historic British model involved the principle of the High Court of Parliament, reflecting its early origins as a council that dispensed justice. However, Westminster-model legislatures today continue to retain one aspect of this principle, in acting as a court to try charges of "contempt of Parliament" that can still result in imprisonment for the guilty. In 1992, for example, the Quebec National Assembly ordered imprisonment for someone who was found to be in contempt.[8]

FACTORS LIMITING THE EFFECTIVENESS OF LEGISLATURES

Legislatures have many functions, but just how effectively these are performed depends upon a wide range of factors. Many of them are interrelated, and attempts to reform the legislature by trying to deal with one aspect alone may not succeed; they may even exacerbate the situation, since other limiting factors are at play.

Two factors that go hand in hand in limiting a legislature's ability to fulfil its functions effectively are party discipline and the domination of the legislature by the executive. These are almost inherent problems in modern parliamentary systems, but they can play a key role in presidential systems as well. Fairly strict party discipline is needed in a parliamentary system for a variety of reasons: the cabinet must have the support of a majority in the legislature in order to remain in office; the cabinet is supposed to be the focus of the policy process and secure the passage of most of its legislation; and cohesive party blocs are the organizational foundation of most of parliament's daily work. Indeed, parliamentary government in the modern context is really *party* government.

The following are the factors limiting the effectiveness of legislatures:

- executive dominance
- party discipline
- size
- frequency of meetings
- amount and complexity of legislation
- number, size, and membership of committees

- research and support staff
- legislators' pay
- procedural rules
- informal rewards and penalties
- electoral system
- media attention
- political culture

Canada is typical of other parliamentary systems, with the prime minister and cabinet managing to direct almost everything that transpires. The cabinet is able to do this because of strict **party discipline**, which is the

> **Party discipline:** The practice that all members in a legislature belonging to the same political party should normally vote the same way, in accordance with their party's stand on the issue at hand.

requirement that all members of a legislature belonging to the same party should normally vote according to the party's position on an issue. Each party selects one of its members of the legislature to act as an official called a *whip*, whose primary functions are to assign members to particular duties in the legislature and to make sure that they vote the way the party requires them to. Whips rely mainly on peer pressure and persuasion, but they also have a range of informal rewards and punishments at their disposal. In addition to the whip's rewards and penalties, the parliamentary party as a whole known as the *caucus* (see Box 9.2) can impose even more severe punishments, such as temporary exile or permanent expulsion from that caucus. Expulsion is the ultimate punishment, since most Canadian voters—like many voters elsewhere—decide for whom to vote on the basis of a candidate's party or the party's leader. Surveys of recent federal elections show that few Canadian voters

---

BOX 9.2

CAUCUS: THE LEGISLATURE'S SECRET CHAMBER?

Some of the most tangible work of legislatures occurs behind closed doors in caucus meetings. A **caucus** is a group of legislators united in a common cause. The most common kind of caucus is the party caucus, in which the members of a legislature who belong to the same party gather on a regular basis to discuss party affairs, in particular, what position the party should take on issues coming up in the legislature. These meetings are invariably confidential, although leaks to the media often occur. Some of the most heated debates in Canadian legislatures take place not in the public arena of the formal chamber itself but in the party caucuses. Here, legislators can make their most forceful arguments on behalf of the interests and constituents they represent. Once the caucus debate is over and the party's position is established, however, members are supposed to fall into line and defend that position publicly. As a result, much of the real representational function of the legislature occurs out of the public eye and usually goes unreported in the media.

Government caucuses in parliamentary systems can also serve an important function in the legislative process. In many parties, caucus committees are established to look at policy issues and suggest new laws or even changes to bills already before the legislature. Some but not all of these suggestions are taken up by the cabinet and included in the measures that are presented publicly in the legislature. In addition, it is possible in many government caucus meetings for ordinary members to question cabinet ministers about their policies and conduct. Again, some of these exchanges are extremely frank and are important parts of actual oversight of the executive.

Other types of caucus meetings are organized for the members of parties from particular regions of the country or even for members of different parties who share a common interest. Each party in the Canadian parliament has regional or provincial caucus meetings prior to its general caucus meeting, for example, while the U.S. Congress also has bipartisan caucuses that include members from all the parties; examples include the Congressional Caucus for Women's Issues, the Congressional Black Caucus, and the Congressional Corn Caucus.

make their voting choice primarily on the basis of the individual candidates. In the 2000 election, for example, less than half of Canadian voters had any preference for individual candidates, and the individual candidate was decisive in the voting decision for only five percent of voters.[9] Members expelled from their party may sit as an independent or "cross the floor" to join another party.

Party discipline is something of a mixed blessing in legislatures. While disciplined party blocs make the legislative process more efficient and clarify voters' choices, party discipline also seriously impedes the legislature's ability to perform many of its functions. In particular, the ruling party or coalition of parties is able to keep tight control over the outcome of most decisions in the legislative chamber and in committees. This means that the Cabinet will almost never lose a vote on a bill or have to face a committee report criticizing the government's policies. So long as discipline holds for a Cabinet with a majority of seats, the legislature will not cast a vote of non-confidence in the government.[10] Party discipline is taken to its extreme in the Labor parties in Australia and New Zealand, which both require their MPs to sign a pledge that they will always vote according to the party position.[11] In contrast, parties in the British parliament display a much looser discipline; one study of voting patterns in the British House of Commons found dissident votes in 20 to 28 percent of recorded votes in the three parliaments that sat in the 1970s.[12] At both the federal and provincial levels in Canada, party discipline is very strict. For example, during the life of the two parliaments which lasted between 2004 and 2008, the lowest level of party cohesion was found among Liberal MPs voting in the House of Commons, at 95 percent for 2004–2006 and 98 percent for 2006–2008.[13] It should be noted that Canada's upper chamber, the Senate, has a tradition of much more relaxed party discipline than does the lower house. For example, a study of votes held in the Senate from 2001–2005 found that over a third of all votes involved at least one Senator voting against his or her party's position; a third of all senators had voted against their party's position in at least five per cent of the votes they cast.[14]

The American presidential system is a very different type of government, and members of Congress demonstrate a freedom to vote as they choose that would be the envy of many legislators in parliamentary systems. However, it is a mistake to equate the relative freedom in the United States with a lack of party cohesion. There has, in fact, been a trend to much stronger caucus unity in the 21st century, and more votes are split down party lines. In the House of Representatives, the Republicans on average voted with a majority of their caucus in 91 percent of major votes in 2003, while Democrats did so 87 percent of the time; these numbers contrast with 60 percent and 58 percent respectively in 1970. Even the Senate, which has traditionally been a bastion of independent-minded members, has seen a similar change. In 2003, Republican senators voted with the majority of their caucus in 94 percent of votes and Democrats did so 85 percent of the time; the same figures for 1970 were 56 percent and 55 percent.[15]

The combination of party discipline and executive dominance has a significant effect on a legislature's ability to perform a range of its potential functions. Lawmaking may get boiled down simply to a public debate prior to approving most of whatever the cabinet has proposed. Figure 9.1 shows that even during the minority government headed by Stephen Harper, bills sponsored by cabinet ministers have been much more likely to pass than those proposed by private members; during minority governments, opposition parties could combine to pass bills introduced by private members but in practice do not often do so. When a government has a majority in the legislature, party discipline can seriously weaken the examination of cabinet proposals and oversight of executive, and committees are often unable to produce innovative policy suggestions that run counter to the cabinet's policy agenda.

Other variables can also limit a legislature's effectiveness. Factors as basic as the size of the legislature, the number of days in the year it sits to conduct business, the research and support staff working for individual legislators, and the internal procedural rules of the legislature all can leave a legislature quite hamstrung. The number of issues that can be dealt with effectively is heavily impacted by how long and often a legislature meets. While many national legislatures meet throughout the year, the number of actual sitting days can vary considerably. For example, in 2009 the U.S. House of Representatives met for a total of 159 days in 2009; the Canadian House of Commons met for 128 days; and Ontario's legislature sat for 96 days. Some

Figure 9.1   Treatment of Government and Private Members' Bills: Canadian House of Commons, 2006–2008

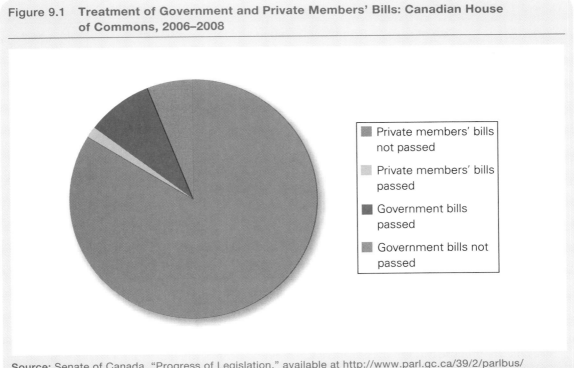

- Private members' bills not passed
- Private members' bills passed
- Government bills passed
- Government bills not passed

Source: Senate of Canada, "Progress of Legislation," available at http://www.parl.gc.ca/39/2/parlbus/ chambus/Senate/deb-e/prog-e.htm and http://www.parl.gc.ca/39/1/parlbus/chambus/Senate/deb-e/ prog-e.htm, accessed November 12, 2010; "Status of House Business: 39th Parliament 1st Session," available at http://www2.parl.gc.ca/HousePublications/Publication.aspx?Language=E&Mode=1&Parl= 39&Pub=status&Ses=1, accessed November 12, 2010.

legislative assemblies meet even less: the BC provincial legislature met for 62 days in 2009, PEI's for 39. But even these infrequent sessions are more substantive than those of some other legislatures. The Chinese National People's Congress only meets for two weeks each year. Curiously for the advanced democracy one expects in America, five state legislatures in the U.S. (Montana, Nevada, North Dakota, Oregon, and Texas) only meet on a biennial basis—every other year.

Very different dynamics occur within a legislature's membership depending upon its size. As Table 9.1 on p. 230 illustrates, Canadian provinces have legislatures ranging in size from 27 to 125 members, with an average size of 70 and a cabinet of about 22 ministers. Provincial cabinets, therefore, form a significant portion of the legislature's total membership and an even higher proportion of the governing party's caucus. In 2010 provincial cabinets filled, on average, 30 percent of their legislature's

seats, and 43 percent of the ruling party's membership in the legislature. This simple fact of size alone provides a significant explanation for the high level of executive dominance of the legislative process in Canadian provincial government and weakens the legislature's ability to effectively fill several other of its potential roles. In comparison, the House of Commons in Ottawa has 308 members, and the Harper cabinet in 2010 constituted only about 12 percent of the total membership of the House. With the cabinet's presence diluted by the size of the chamber, the federal parliament is not as strongly controlled by the cabinet as are provincial legislatures. Even the size of the Canadian House of Commons stands in stark contrast to the lower houses of Britain, with 650 members; France, with 577; Germany, with 622; and the United States, with 435. With large national legislatures, it is more difficult for party leaders to keep all their members voting according to the party line. Many members

	Table 9.1	Dominant Presence of Canadian Cabinets in their Legislatures				
Legislature	Size of Legislature	Size of Cabinet	Cabinet as % Legislature	Size of Govt Caucus	Cabinet as % Govt Caucus
Canada	308	36	11.7	142	25.4
BC	85	24	28.2	49	49.0
AB	83	24	28.9	68	35.3
SK	58	18	31.0	38	47.4
MB	57	19	33.3	36	52.8
ON	107	28	26.2	72	38.9
QC	125	26	20.8	65	40.0
NB	55	16	29.1	42	38.1
PEI	27	11	40.7	23	47.8
NS	52	12	23.1	31	38.7
NL	48	19	39.6	42	45.2

Source: All data verified at the websites of the respective legislatures and governments on Nov 11, 2010.

realize that there just are not enough party favours to be distributed around large caucuses, and they become much more independent minded.

The differences in size between the provincial legislatures and the federal House of Commons also mean that, in comparison to most provincial legislatures, the House of Commons can have many more functioning committees at work, because there are more than enough MPs to sit on them. Those Commons committees can be free of Cabinet ministers, while many provincial legislatures may need to have Cabinet ministers sitting on committees, if only because there are not enough competent government **backbenchers** to do the work. As a result, committees in Ottawa can have relatively more independence from the executive than most provincial committees.

Another practical consideration is how much business a legislature is expected to do in a certain period of time. For example, in 2009 the Prince Edward Island legislature considered 138 government bills in just 36 sitting days, while performing many other tasks at the same time. In contrast, the British Columbia legislature sat for 62 days that year and only had 33 government bills to consider. The PEI legislature could devote only a fraction of the time to each bill compared to that available to the British Columbian MLAs.

A related issue is how much legislators get paid. If they are paid a relatively low wage, then one cannot expect the legislature to sit year-round, as many members will need to supplement their income. Furthermore, many competent professional people will not want to take a significant cut in pay in order to leave their normal jobs and run for political office. Canadian reluctance to pay much for politicians was plainly evident when the Saskatchewan government decided in 1993 to reduce the size of the provincial legislature by eight members, and Ontario in 1995 by 27 members, as part of a general cost-cutting drive. Savings continue with the research and support staff available to Canadian legislators. Many provincial legislators make do with just one or two staff members, and even MPs in Ottawa have allowances for only four staff members to serve them in Parliament and in their constituency offices. Their U.S. counterparts in Washington have dozens of staffers, and committee chairs can have up to 200 people working for them. This is not just a matter of stinginess; it has a direct impact on the kind of job legislators can do. They are simply not able to perform serious reviews of public policy without sufficient staff to provide the technical expertise needed to formulate independent policy appraisals and initiatives.

The procedural rules of a legislature can also limit its effectiveness. Whoever controls the timetable in the legislature controls what business will be considered and how much time is to be devoted to any particular measure. In most parliamentary systems, the government is able to exercise this level of control through a cabinet minister known as the House Leader. **Closure**, or time allocation, is one procedural tool available to control the amount of time spent debating any particular item on parliament's agenda. With closure, the government can cut off debate and force a vote to be held. Between 1993 and early 2002, the Chrétien government used closure or time allocation in the House of Commons 75 times. It is the counterpart to the opposition's use of extended debates, or a **filibuster**.

> **Closure:** A term used to describe procedural rules that permit the majority to put an end to debate on a motion and require that a vote on the matter be held; also known as cloture, the guillotine, or time allocation in various countries.

> **Filibuster:** A device used by a member or group of members who take advantage of the procedural rules of a legislature that allow members to speak for extended periods of time in order to stall proceedings.

While one theory of parliamentary government is that the cabinet is held "continuously" accountable to the legislature, the procedural rules may allow only limited opportunities for this to occur. In the Canadian House of Commons, there is a 45-minute Question Period every day, but British Columbia has Question Periods that last only 15 minutes. In the United Kingdom, members can ask the prime minister questions only once a week. With only these differences in the rules, one sees a significant difference in the ability of legislators to hold cabinet ministers to account.

No legislature allows business to unfold in a haphazard fashion, and someone has to decide what will be considered when. In Canadian legislatures, the government house leaders are in total control. They consult with house leaders from the opposition parties, but this consultation may not have any influence on what the government decides to do. Other jurisdictions avoid this problem by providing in their rules that the Speaker of the assembly can decide whether important measures should be brought forward for a vote; the Speaker of the British House of Commons, for example, has broad personal discretion to select the issues that are debated and voted upon.

Other crucial procedural rules deal with who can introduce what. In presidential systems, a great deal can change in the functioning of the legislature if the president is able to directly introduce bills into the legislature, as is the case in Mexico. In the United States, on the other hand, the president is unable to introduce bills and must negotiate with individual members of Congress to find someone who will "sponsor" the bill and introduce it.

The number, size, and membership of committees can also influence a legislature's ability to perform its roles effectively in assessing and amending bills, as well as in conducting investigations into events and issues. Small legislatures, such as most Canadian provincial legislatures, have few committees and make little use of even those they have. Some legislatures funnel most proposed legislation through Committee of the Whole, which is all the members of the legislature simply sitting as one large committee. This is a highly inefficient process, since bills can be dealt with only one at a time, and no other business can be conducted in the legislative chamber while this goes on. Legislatures that have a well-developed committee system are able to process much more business and do so in greater depth. Greater efficiency and scrutiny can occur because work can proceed in parallel in many committees at the same time, and the members of these committees can develop more expertise if these are set up to deal with specific policy areas such as transportation, health, or banking. Another related factor is whether committees are created on an ad hoc as opposed to a standing basis. A permanent committee with stable membership is able to consider issues with considerably more expertise.

An important question that arises in this connection is whether cabinet ministers should sit on or chair parliamentary committees. Nova Scotia and Quebec are two provinces that regularly allow both, but such a suggestion would cause outrage in the Canadian and British parliaments. As mentioned earlier in this chapter, the presence of cabinet ministers undermines the legislature's ability to form independent judgments of the policies proposed by the executive and reduces its capacity to act as a check against the executive's power. However, the active participation of cabinet ministers in parliamentary committees can have positive effects. Since cabinet is usually the ultimate body that decides whether its caucus members should vote for an amendment, there is something to be said for cabinet ministers being present and engaged in the committee discussions so they can learn at first hand about the merits of proposed amendments.

Constitutional rules relating to the work of the legislature can also significantly undermine its ability to function. For example, the Canadian Governor General has the legal power to suspend or dissolve Parliament at any time. Normally, important constitutional conventions restraining the use of these powers are faithfully observed by the Governor General, and the cabinet. However, events in late 2008 illustrated the serious damage that can be done if the executive exercises its legal power over the legislature in an unrestrained manner. Prime Minister Harper's minority government faced almost certain defeat in a non-confidence motion which all three opposition parties had vowed to pass. He first used the government's powers under the House of Commons procedural rules to delay this vote by a full week. But during that time, the opposition parties reached and signed an agreement to form a coalition government if their motion to defeat the Conservative government succeeded. Faced with this situation, Harper advised the Governor General to suspend Parliament for almost two months (officially known as prorogation). Governor General Michaëlle Jean agreed, the opposition coalition collapsed over the break, and the Harper government survived a vote of confidence when the House of Commons resumed. There is considerable controversy over this prorogation of Parliament. While there is disagreement over whether Jean should have refused to prorogue Parliament, there is near universal agreement among constitutional scholars that the Prime Minister's request was wrong. The House of Commons was prevented from performing its most important function in a parliamentary system: the legislature's granting or withholding of confidence in the government of the day is the very basis of any government's legitimacy to hold office.[16] The Harper government also used the occasion to discredit the concept of a coalition government, as seen in Box 9.3.

Several sets of factors external to legislatures can also have an impact on their effectiveness. The first is the electoral system, which may produce legislative

assemblies that bear little resemblance to the choices made by the voters, as noted in Chapter 11. This is a particular problem in countries such as Canada with the **first-past-the-post** system. In this system, the person who gets the most votes in a riding wins the seat; as a result, candidates who have wide support but do not manage to come in first place do not get to represent the people who voted for them. The worst example of this system's potential to distort the citizens' choices was seen in the 1987 New Brunswick election, where the Liberals won about 60 percent of the votes but gained every seat in the legislature; this meant that the 40 percent of the electorate who voted for other parties were left with no one to represent them. The British Columbia Liberal Party won 97.5 percent of the legislature's seats in 2000 with only 58 percent of the overall vote. Some countries have electoral laws that ban certain parties, or ensure that there is only one official party for all elections; again, this limits the legislature's ability to represent the people and assess policy proposals. For example, legislatures in communist countries are usually filled in uncompetitive elections in which only communist party candidates are allowed to run. Informal domination by a single ruling party can also stifle effective opposition in some apparently democratic countries. Singapore may have a capitalist economy and the framework of Western democracy, but it has been tightly ruled by the People's Action party through largely uncompetitive elections; 55 of the 84 elected seats in Singapore's parliament were filled by acclamation in the 2001 elections. With few opposition members in a legislature, the executive is able to command at will, and the representative and executive oversight functions of the legislature are very poorly fulfilled.

Another external factor is the role of the media in conveying to the public what transpires in the legislature and in covering the public's reaction. The media are known as the "Fourth Estate" precisely because of their crucial role as a link between political institutions and actors on the one hand and the general public on the other. In countries that control the media or where media are concentrated in a few hands, the coverage of both legislative events and public reaction can be distorted, to say the least. Chapter 5 showed that even in societies with a vibrant media, problems arise due to only a few items being selected for coverage

BOX 9.3

COALITION GOVERNMENTS

During Canada's constitutional crisis of late 2008, the three opposition parties in Canada's House of Commons signed an agreement that would have seen a coalition government formed with Liberal and NDP cabinet ministers supported in all confidence votes by the Bloc Québécois for at least 18 months. This group of parties had been supported by 54 percent of Canadian voters and had won a majority of seats in the national election held less than two months earlier. Even so, the incumbent Conservative government, which had won only 38 percent of the vote and 46 percent of the seats, was able to raise a serious question mark in many Canadians' minds about the legitimacy of such a coalition.

Some hesitancy can be explained by such concerns of the moment as the perceived weakness of Liberal leader Stéphane Dion and the role of the Bloc. However, the deeper reasons lie in Canada's political culture, which has seen a strong preference for minority governments over formal coalitions. Many believe that the legitimate right to govern is mandated to the party which wins the most seats in an election, even if it has not won a majority of seats.

Such a view, however, is based on a misunderstanding of how democratic legitimacy arises in parliamentary governments. In all parliamentary systems, the people are unable to elect an entire government—they can only elect individual representatives. Whoever can command a majority of those representatives governs through the will of the people. When one party wins a majority of seats, there is no doubt as to their legitimate right to govern. But the situation is more complicated when no party wins a majority of seats.

Some concern was raised in 2008 because the members of the proposed coalition had not run on a coalition platform in the preceding election. It was said that they were trying to 'steal the election' by hoping to form a coalition afterwards. The experience in other parliamentary systems is very different. A great many routinely, even permanently, depend on coalition governments. The political values in these cultures hold that it is reasonable for minor parties to give their support to a government only if they have a seat at the cabinet table to help decide those government measures. In some countries possible coalition partners are identified before or during the election campaign. In other countries, the composition of potential coalitions is deliberately left open until after the realities created by the election results are known.

Coalition governments, by their nature, appear to offer two important strengths: they ensure that cross-party consensus and compromise underlie every government decision, and the formal agreements between coalition partners can create a more stable platform than minority governments who may have to play one party against another on every vote. As a counterpoint, coalition critics point to Italy's history of notoriously unstable coalitions. But that example is contradicted by many other countries' experiences. In the Netherlands, for example, coalition governments formed around the same core group ruled from 1946 right through to 1994—a record unmatched by any majority government in parliamentary systems around the world. In a quest for stability, two countries with political cultures similar to Canada's—Britain and Australia—moved to coalition governments after unclear election results in 2010, while in 2011, Canadians elected a majority Conservative government.

because of space and time constraints, the policy preferences of the media owners, or the public's lack of interest. Furthermore, effective coverage of legislatures requires considerable knowledge of the political system and issues, and poor coverage can often result from reporters' inexperience. Ironically, the success of legislatures that work effectively and efficiently through an extensive committee system may become a barrier to full media coverage. The U.S. Congress, for instance, has about 300 committees and subcommittees, and it is impossible for the media to cover the work of more than a select few.

The largest and most intangible of the external factors is the general political culture of a society. The most visible manifestation of this factor is the poor representation of women in all legislatures, since political cultures around the world continue to favour males in many subtle and not-so-subtle ways. The same absence from the legislature applies to minority groups in many societies. This underrepresentation of groups in the legislature not only undermines the representation function, but can also have an impact on the specific policies considered and on how they are treated. Other general cultural values come into play in the legislature as well. Whether the general public wants or tolerates very strong leadership by the executive or prefers individual members of the legislature who act independently will have an effect on the strength of party discipline in the legislature. Dozens of national parliaments across the globe are modelled on the British system, yet each performs its potential functions to varying degrees.

Several countries have presidential systems modelled on that of the United States, but in practice none is very similar to the U.S. system. Certain differences among parliamentary and congressional legislatures can be explained by procedural rules or other specific details of the legislature, but unique political cultures remain the most important cause. The impact of political culture, at least at the elite level, is seen in quite another context in Mexico. The legal framework of its constitution is fairly similar to that of the American, with a presidential system of government. But a range of cultural factors have led to a much tighter party discipline in the ruling party, which allows the president to direct the work of the legislature to such an extent that the practical workings of the Mexican legislative process bear little resemblance to those of its U.S. counterpart.

LAWMAKING

Lawmaking is one of the most important roles of legislatures, and it is this function that sets them apart from the other branches of government. The process through which proposals must pass before they become law can give ample opportunity for them to be amended or even scrapped entirely. There is definitely the potential for new public policy proposals to be significantly improved and for unpopular or impractical ones to be abandoned as a result of scrutiny in the legislature and subsequent public reaction. In authoritarian regimes, the legislature plays little more than a formal, ritual role in enacting into law the policies already decided upon by the political executive or ruling party. In democratic parliamentary systems, the legislature has a substantive role to play in making laws, even if the cabinet is the main source of legislative initiatives and directs much of the process in the legislature. For the most part, however, MPs focus on reviewing the cabinet's proposals rather than developing new initiatives of their own. In democratic presidential systems, the legislature can have a truly independent role to play in developing and initiating new legislation, as well as in scrutinizing proposals developed by the executive.

The lawmaking procedure in the legislature is only part of the whole on-going public-policy process. Ideas for new laws are generated throughout the political system by individuals, groups, and corporations, as well as by political parties, civil servants, the cabinet, individual legislators, and committees of the legislature. The ideas are then reviewed and drafted into legal language suitable for a future law; at this point, they are ready to be introduced into the legislature. It considers the proposed laws, makes any changes that the majority thinks necessary, and decides whether to enact these proposals into law. Most modern statutes passed by the legislature cannot contain all the detail necessary for their implementation, so they delegate to the executive branch the power to pass regulations filling in the details; this is known as delegated or subordinate legislation. The law and its regulations are then ready to be implemented and administered by the executive. The new policies, in turn, generate a reaction among those in the public who are affected, which can eventually lead to ideas and demands for yet new laws. In this whole process, the legislature can potentially provide the most important public stage for formal debate and improvement of public policies.

In parliamentary systems such as Canada's, cabinet ministers propose most of the measures that are eventually enacted into law. When cabinet ministers decide to change a public policy that needs to be achieved through legislation, they consult the civil servants in their department for advice on the best means to achieve that policy. The ideas are then presented to the cabinet or a cabinet committee and, if approved, are drafted into a legal document. The cabinet then reviews the matter again and makes a final decision on whether to present the measure to the legislature. When there is an opening in the work schedule in the legislature, the sponsoring cabinet minister introduces the measure as a bill.

The Canadian parliament follows a legislative process that is similar to that in most legislatures patterned after the British model, although each legislature has its own particular variations in detail. In Canada, as illustrated in Figure 9.2, the bill goes through three readings, or particular stages, each of which serves a specific purpose. First Reading occurs when the bill is first introduced. It is only a formality; the first reading gives everyone notice that the bill has entered the pipeline but no debate occurs at this time. The next stage, Second Reading, is the consideration of the main principles of the bill; considerable debate can occur at this time. After Second Reading, the bill

Figure 9.2 Legislative Process in the Canadian Parliament

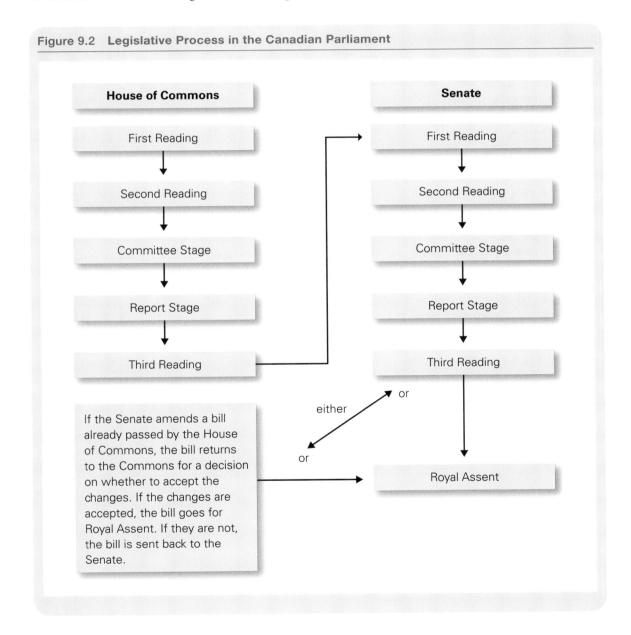

usually enters the committee stage, where detailed examination occurs. In the Canadian parliament, the committee usually invites interested members of the public to present their views of how the bill can be improved. While there is great potential for this public input, the sheer volume of people wanting to have their say on controversial bills means that a very deliberate and partisan process occurs within the committee to decide who will actually be allowed to give testimony. Depending on the controversy engendered by the bill and on subsequent media coverage, significant changes can be made when the governing party's members of the committee believe that it is in their best interests to do so. Often, they check informally with the minister who sponsored the bill to see if he or she agrees to the changes, but sometimes the minister appears as a formal witness to defend the proposal and discuss potential amendments. The committee then reports back to the legislature, and all the members can debate and vote on any changes the committee proposed. After that, a debate on Third Reading is held, and members have a final opportunity to consider the bill as a whole.

Once a bill has passed Third Reading, it is sent to the other house and goes through the same stages all over again. The Canadian parliament contains two chambers or houses, the House of Commons and the Senate, and a bill must be approved in identical form by both before it can become a law. The vast majority of bills are introduced first in the House of Commons, because the lower house is elected, while the Senate is appointed. The Senate does sometimes make changes to bills that have already been passed by the House of Commons, and then the Commons must decide whether to accept the Senate amendments or reject

them. Occasionally, a bill goes back and forth several times between the Senate and House of Commons before one of them compromises, but since the Senate is an appointed body, it normally should be the one that eventually gives way.[17] Only on rare occasions does the Senate actually defeat a bill.

Once a bill has been agreed to by both the House of Commons and the Senate, it is ready for Royal Assent by the Governor General and it becomes an act of Parliament. No Canadian provincial legislature has the equivalent of the Senate, so a bill goes through the three readings in the assembly and then gets Royal Assent from the Lieutenant Governor. The whole process of considering and passing legislation in Parliament usually takes several months, but can often go on for a year or more; public reaction to the bill becomes crucial during such an extended period and often induces the cabinet minister responsible for the bill to accept or propose important amendments. On rare occasions, however, a bill can go through all stages in the House of Commons in a day; such speedy consideration usually occurs only if all the political parties in the House agree.

Perhaps the most important question that emerges from a review of the legislative process is how effective the legislature actually is. Table 9.2 gives a summary of the treatment of government bills in several Canadian legislatures, as well as in the British parliament, for comparison, and demonstrates that legislatures do have a substantial role to play in reviewing the bills proposed by the cabinet. One obvious measure is that the government never gets all its bills through the legislature. Although some provincial governments come very close to complete adoption on occasion, many government bills fail to pass the legislature simply

Table 9.2 Success of Government Bills in Selected Parliamentary Systems				
Legislature	Period	Number of Government Bills Introduced	Percent of Bills Amended	Percent of Bills Enacted
UK parliament	2008–2010	50	72.0	96.0
Canadian parliament	2006–2008	117	31.6	56.4
British Columbia	2008–2009	80	21.3	95.0
Ontario	2007–2010	65	66.2	96.9
Note: These figures include only government public bills.				

because the members run out of time before the end of the session.[18] A more useful measure of the practical importance of legislatures is the percentage of government bills that get amended. Table 9.2 reveals that a significant number do. Despite the tight party discipline, governments often accept significant changes to their proposals once these are considered by their legislatures. For example, in Ontario, the governing Liberals controlled about two-thirds of the seats, but saw two-thirds of their government bills amended in 2007–2010. However, the dynamics of a legislature not only vary greatly from one jurisdiction to another but also from one period of time to another. In British Columbia, the governing Liberals controlled just under 60 percent of the seats but managed to limit amendments to only 21 percent of their bills; curiously, when the same party held over 95 percent of the seats between 2000 and 2004, 35 percent of government bills were amended. The opportunities for debate on government proposals, both in the legislature and in the media, allow the interested public and the government caucus to think about the issues and to exert pressure for changes to be made. There certainly are times when a government manages to ram a measure through the legislature, whipping its troops into line to pass a bill untouched. But most democratic governments cannot do this consistently and have to relent on many occasions, allowing some changes to be made to its bills and deciding to drop other bills altogether.

The legislative process in the U.S. Congress is quite different from that described above. First of all, the president and his cabinet cannot directly introduce bills into Congress; as a result, individual members sponsor all bills. The executive still has a strong influence on the legislative process, but this is done entirely through lobbying and negotiating with members of both the Republican and Democratic parties in both houses of Congress. Second, the vast bulk of time and attention is given to legislation in committee hearings. The only opportunity for substantial debate by all members of a house comes up at the end of the process. Third, virtually every bill is significantly altered along the way. Competing bills dealing with similar issues can be introduced by different members of both houses and are often eventually consolidated into one. Because there is much looser party discipline in the U.S. Congress, the passage of a bill depends upon a tremendous amount of negotiating among individual legislators and their staff.

Table 9.3 illustrates the enormous filtering of legislative proposals that occurs in Congress, with thousands

Table 9.3   Passage of Legislation in the 106th and 111th U.S. Congresses, 1999–2000 and 2009–2010

	House of Representatives		Senate	
	2009–2010	1999–2000	2009–2010	1999–2000
Bills introduced	6,098	4,872	3,754	2,658
Senate bills passed	56	198	120	363
House bills passed	603	708	179	402
Bills vetoed by President	0	12*	—	—
Vetoes overridden by Congress	0	1*	—	—
Bills enacted into law	237	604	—	—

* The categories bills vetoed, vetoes overridden, and bills enacted apply jointly to both houses, since bills have been approved in identical form by both. The 2009–2010 data covers the period ending August 31, 2010.

Source: "Résumé of Congressional Activity: 109th Congress, 2nd Session"; cited on November 12, 2007; available at http://www.senate.gov/reference/resources/pdf/109-2res.pdf; "Résumé of Congressional Activity: 109th Congress, 1st Session"; cited on May 1, 2005; available at http://www.senate.gov/reference/resources/pdf/109-1res.pdf; "Résumé of Congressional Activity: 106th Congress"; cited on May 1, 2005; available at http://thomas.loc.gov/home/resume/106res.html

of bills that are introduced being reduced to a few hundred that pass into law; this table compares the activities of Congress 10 years apart, to illustrate how the U.S. lawmaking process has functioned in recent years. An individual senator or representative often gives support only in exchange for an amendment that deals with one of his or her pet projects. Thus, a bill that ostensibly deals with transportation can include sections that provide meal vouchers for schoolchildren and money for pig farmers. Another major difference is that the two houses of Congress are both elected and have equal political power. As a result, an important part of the legislative process is securing eventual agreement between the two houses on identical terms for a bill; there is a joint conference committee specially charged with reconciling two versions of the same bill.

The other important difference between the U.S. and parliamentary systems arises because the president has a real **veto** over measures passed by Congress, while the official sanction by the head of state in a parliamentary system is always automatic. If a president opposes a bill passed by Congress, he or she can veto the legislation. Between 1789 and 2010, presidents vetoed 1494 bills passed by Congress. Between 2000 and 2004, George W. Bush became the first president not to veto a single measure passed by Congress in a whole term in office since James Garfield, in 1881. Bush may have avoided the veto for several reasons during his first term in office, including Republican control of both houses, strong party cohesion in Congress, and the backdrop of the "war on terror" freezing out opposition to many measures. After the Democrats gained control of both houses of Congress in the 2006 elections, Bush resorted to vetoing 10 bills by mid-2008; three of those vetoes were overridden by Congress. President Obama did not veto any bills during his first two years in office when his Democratic Party controlled both Houses of Congress. The Constitution gives Congress the ability to override a formal presidential veto, but an override requires a two-thirds vote in both houses; as a result, only 109 vetoes have been overridden. Another technique is known as the "pocket veto," in which the bill dies if the president does not sign it within 10 days of the adjournment of Congress. The pocket veto has been a favourite of many presidents, with 1,066 such vetoes recorded.[19] Many presidential vetoes came not because the president objected to the whole bill, but because he wanted to reject one of the particular items unrelated to the main purpose that had been added into a bill to secure its passage in Congress. In order to prevent so many "babies being thrown out with the bathwater," an act of Congress was passed in 1996 to give the president what is called a *line-item veto*. This procedure allowed the President to sign a bill into law while vetoing particular items within the bill. However, the U.S. Supreme Court struck down the line-item veto as unconstitutional in 1998.[20]

REPRESENTATION

A very important function of all democratic legislatures is to represent the citizenry in the heart of government institutions. Representation lies at the core of the democratic mandate of a legislature to manage the affairs of a society; because of it, members of the legislature are able to perform all the other functions of the legislature. While it is easy to state this as a vital role, it is surprisingly difficult to define what representation actually entails. The difficulties emerge because there are crosscutting views about *whom* members of the legislature should represent and how they should represent them. Unfortunately, no legislature is ever a mirror reflection of all the diverse segments and groups in society; in countries that use the first-past-the-post electoral system, the members of the legislature are seldom even a proper reflection of the electorate's support for the different political parties.

Someone recently elected to a seat in the legislature soon finds himself or herself torn in different directions by a wide range of groups and interests demanding that the legislator act or speak on their behalf. First, there are territorial community interests, which can be as large as the whole constituency in which the legislator ran for election or as small as a town, village, or neighbourhood. In this role, a legislator is representing all the members of the community as a collective whole. Second, there are non-territorial sectional interests or groups that may be represented. One of the first tugs on legislators' attention is the call for special attention to be paid to those people who actually voted for them. This is a reasonable demand, since these people chose the candidate because of the policies he or she promised to pursue. However, legislators can quickly realize that the demands of the whole community can run counter to the demands of the segment of that community who voted for them. This tension is heightened in the many constituencies where someone is declared elected with less than a majority of votes; such legislators start from a position where a majority of their constituents are opposed to their policy positions.

Members of an elected legislature also wrestle with a separate responsibility to represent the political party on whose platform they ran and got elected. Another non-territorial set of interests that legislators can represent are those relating to economic sectors or enterprises that are particularly important in the region they represent; thus, MPs can work hard on behalf of grain growers, vehicle manufacturers, a paper mill, fishers, or the high-tech service sector in their region. Finally, legislators can represent the particular social groups to which they personally belong, be they gender, linguistic, religious, ethnic, and so on. This can be an important form of representation, given the domination of most legislatures by only one social group: males from a narrow range of professional backgrounds. The ultimate goal of this aspect of representation is that the legislature should be a microcosm or mirror of society, with members of all the significant groups present in roughly proportional numbers. When we take all these potential subjects of representation together, it should be evident that a legislator often faces competing expectations to represent groups with very different (and even opposing) interests when it comes to any specific matter of public policy under consideration.

Even if it becomes clear whom a legislator should try to represent on a particular issue, there is still controversy about how that representation should be practised. Two basic approaches can be distinguished: the delegate and the trustee. The delegate perspective requires a legislator to discern the will of the group to be represented and then to voice and pursue those interests; the delegate essentially acts in the place of those he or she represents. The delegate's own views are supposed to be set aside in favour of representing the views of the group. This perspective is based on powerful arguments of democratic theory, coming from classical liberalism, that legislative activity should always reflect the will of the people and particularly of the specific group to be affected by a piece of legislation. The difficulties with this view arise both from democratic theory and from the complicated nature of society and public policy.

Modern liberal democratic theory does not support the unflinching reign of the majority—indeed, this is sometimes called the **tyranny of the majority**. Political decision-makers are supposed to accommodate and protect minority interests as well as those of the majority. So which group's delegate should the legislator be? Should it be the community's majority or the minority group whose interests may be significantly compromised? Furthermore, do all groups affected by legislation deserve to be represented equally? After all, a change to the criminal law involves the interests of both the victims of crime and the alleged criminals themselves. Even if a legislator decides which particular group he or she should speak for, it can still be difficult to discover what the preponderant view of that group really is—short of conducting ongoing opinion polls. Legislators do rely heavily on the letters and phone calls they receive, but these are always from a tiny, self-selecting group among their constituents. Sometimes petitions that are circulated in a community garner thousands of signatures, but these are not necessarily definitive of the group's position either.

The trustee view of representation, on the other hand, suggests a very different role for legislators in acting on behalf of the groups they represent. In this view, legislators should understand the opinions and wishes of those they represent, but in the end they must use their own best judgment of what position to take on an issue. The earliest proponent of this view was Edmund Burke, a Whig politician in 18th-century Britain, but his views on this subject in particular are regarded as typical of classical Tory conservatism. An excerpt from Burke's famous speech to his voters in 1774 is reproduced in Box 9.4. An interesting footnote to this speech is that Burke lost the election in which he made it!

There are several justifications for this approach, and they reveal a different notion of the role of the representative and of public policy than that found in arguments for the delegate model. The first principle is that people entrust their representative to act in the best interests of their overall welfare. Just what specific measures may favour their long-term welfare may not be immediately clear to the people, who can be motivated by individual self-interest and by the passions of the moment. It is the job of the elected representative, in this view, to ascertain all the facts and listen to the range of opinions expressed during debates in the legislature, and then come to his or her own conclusion about what should be done. In all of this, too, the legislator is viewed not simply as a representative of a

---

BOX 9.4

EXCERPT FROM EDMUND BURKE'S "SPEECH TO THE ELECTORS OF BRISTOL," 1774

Certainly, gentlemen, it ought to be the happiness and glory of a representative to live in the strictest union, the closest correspondence, and the most unreserved communication with his constituents. Their wishes ought to have great weight with him; their opinion, high respect; their business, unremitted attention. . . . But his unbiased opinion, his mature judgment, his enlightened conscience, he ought not to sacrifice to you, to any man, or to any set of men living. These he does not derive from your pleasure; no, nor from the law and the constitution. They are a trust from Providence, for the abuse of which he is deeply answerable. Your representative owes you, not his industry only, but his judgment; and he betrays, instead of serving you, if he sacrifices it to your opinion.

---

particular group or community who pursues nothing but their parochial interests. The legislator is also a national (or provincial) decision-maker who must also be concerned with the welfare and interests of the whole society. Legislators have to find a balance in the conflicts of interest between what may be good for the whole nation or province against the welfare of their own constituency. Box 9.5 discusses the issue of a representative facing the even more difficult question of changing parties.

BOX 9.5

CROSSING THE FLOOR

When representatives have been elected to a legislature as candidates for a particular party, should they be able to change their party whenever they want, or should they have to resign their seat and face an election as a candidate for the new party? The problem of "floor-crossing" is an ongoing controversy in many countries. The most recent storm of debate in Canada arose after the 2006 federal election when David Emerson agreed to sit as a Conservative MP and member of Stephen Harper's cabinet, only days after he had been elected in the Vancouver-Kingsway riding as a Liberal candidate. Great howls of protest erupted in his riding, with many people arguing that Emerson had betrayed the citizens' electoral choice in Vancouver-Kingsway. The voters there had relegated the Conservative candidate to third place in the election that Emerson had won as a Liberal. The Ethics Commissioner of the House of Commons conducted a brief inquiry and concluded that the current code of conduct had not been breached by Mr. Emerson. Another famous instance of floor-crossing happened when Belinda Stronach switched from the Conservatives to the Liberals shortly before a confidence vote in May 2005; without her move, Paul Martin's Liberal government would have lost the vote and then would have resigned or called an election.

There are two sides to the debate, with those influenced by Edmund Burke's view of representation arguing that elected members of the legislature should be able to take any course of action they believe best serves the interests of their constituency, including a change of party. Others, however, assert that modern voters essentially decide to vote on the basis of their choice of parties, and that their votes are undermined if their elected representative switches to a different party. Both South Africa and New Zealand have enacted legislation to require those who switch parties to resign and face an election if they wish to belong to a new party. These laws were subsequently challenged in court with quite different results. The South African Constitutional Court struck down the law in 2002, on the grounds that it interfered with a representative's freedom of action, while the New Zealand Supreme Court upheld the law in 2004, noting the centrality of political parties to elections and to the work of parliament.

Representation is an abstract concept that carries enormous moral and philosophical weight. However, it is also something that has to operate within the real world of everyday politics. In fact, legislators usually end up living out all the different types of representation reviewed above at different times and on different issues. The real-world setting of modern legislatures also means that the fundamental principle guiding a legislator's public actions is that of party discipline. Usually the most vociferous representation of community or group interests occurs in parliamentary settings within a party's caucus, where individual legislators try to convince their colleagues that the party's policy should reflect these interests. Despite party discipline, however, individual legislators speak out in public from time to time in order to fully represent interests that are even more important to them than party loyalty. Breaking party ranks can occur for two reasons: legislators realize that the local groups feel so strongly about an issue that they may well face defeat in the next election if they do not speak out publicly,

and individual legislators do from time to time simply hold extremely strong personal beliefs that a group's interests must be represented publicly regardless of the consequences.

A serious representational issue in many countries is the fact that their legislatures are so dominated by males and members of the largest ethnic group (see Figure 9.3 and Table 9.4). One of the issues to emerge from the microcosm or mirror view of representation is that legislatures do not currently reflect the composition of their societies as a whole. There are important practical and symbolic problems with systemic under-representation, and these are compounded when important social groups are completely lacking from the legislature. Not only may groups feel excluded from the political process if they are not visible participants in the main political institutions, but their interests may be only weakly represented by the others present—if represented at all. A continued lack of participation in the legislature, and continued losing out in the decisions made there,

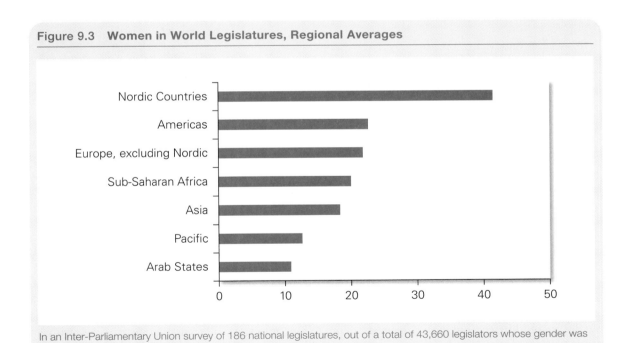

Figure 9.3 Women in World Legislatures, Regional Averages

In an Inter-Parliamentary Union survey of 186 national legislatures, out of a total of 43,660 legislators whose gender was known, women constituted only 19.1 percent as of September 30, 2010.

Source: Adapted from Inter-Parliamentary Union, "Women in Parliaments: World and Regional Averages," available at http://www.ipu.org/wmn-e/world.htm; accessed November 12, 2010.

Table 9.4	Women in Selected National Legislatures Around the World	

The 186 countries with legislatures are ranked 1 to 135 (because of a number of ties) according to the percentage of women members they included (in lower houses only for bicameral legislatures).

Rank	Country	Percentage of Women
1	Rwanda	56.3
2	Sweden	45.0
3	South Africa	44.5
6	Netherlands	40.7
10	Mozambique	39.2
16	New Zealand	33.6
18	Germany	32.8
34	Mexico	26.2
51	Canada	22.1
52	United Kingdom	22.0
56	Italy	21.3
64	France	18.9
73	United States	16.8
83	Russia	14.0
94	Japan	11.3
96	India	10.8
113	Nigeria	7.0
132	Egypt	1.8
135	Saudi Arabia	0.0

Women MPs in the Canadian House of Commons increased to 25 percent in the 2011 election.

Source: Inter-Parliamentary Union, "Women in Parliaments: World and Regional Averages"; available at http://www.ipu.org/wmn-e/classif.htm; accessed November 12, 2010.

can contribute to political alienation and eventually lead to political violence. There are many socioeconomic reasons deeply embedded in a society's political culture that combine to create conditions where women and members of minority groups do not or cannot run for office and get elected. The social groups that do participate in the legislature can make a practical difference in the legislative process. A number of studies of the American Congress and Canadian legislatures have suggested that there may be slight but discernible differences in the way members of different ethnic groups and genders vote on issues—even when other factors such as party affiliation and ideological leanings are accounted for.[21] Some researchers have even argued that women should be represented by women and ethnic minorities represented by

members of their own groups, but this is a highly contested idea.[22]

UPPER HOUSES

Although a majority of the world's legislatures are unicameral, some 63 national legislatures are bicameral. In Canada, all the provincial and territorial legislatures have a single chamber, while the national Parliament in Ottawa has two. Since unicameral legislatures are inherently more efficient, with all business conducted in a single process, it may seem strange that so many countries would set up bicameral legislatures. Indeed, many Canadians have become cynical about our upper house, the Senate, and would rather scrap it than reform it. A 2010 opinion poll found that 59 percent of Canadians favoured electing the Senate, 27 percent preferred to abolish it, and only 10 percent wanted to keep it as it is.[23] These views, however, are probably based partly on a lack of appreciation of both what the Senate actually does and the significant roles that it might play in the political system. There are two main functions for upper houses that are appealing: these houses can act as an additional check and balance in the political process and they may provide a forum for special representation of sectional (usually based on geographic regions) interests in the country.

Perhaps the most common function is to provide "sober second thought" about measures passed without proper consideration in the lower house. This can be a very useful process in states where one party or a coalition controls a majority of members in the lower house and where party discipline can ensure that this majority approves measures without much debate or against the wishes of the general public. A second chamber can act as a brake on the legislative process, give bills closer scrutiny, and hold up approval while public reaction is gauged. The Fathers of Confederation, who designed Canada's national political institutions, reflected 19th-century British thought in choosing an appointed second chamber to act as a restraint on the "passions of the moment" to which the elected MPs in the lower house could be susceptible. Our Senate, whose members are appointed and now sit until the age of 75, was modelled on the House of Lords in Britain, whose members were hereditary and appointed aristocrats. Box 9.6 addresses the different ways in which members of an upper house can be selected.

Just how effective a second chamber can be is related to its powers in the legislative process and how it uses them. Essentially, it depends upon whether the consent of the upper house is actually needed before a proposal can become law or whether the upper house can merely delay the approval process. A number of upper houses possess a "suspensive veto" only. This means that if the members of the upper house vote down a measure already approved by the lower house or fail to approve it within a set period of time, the members of the lower house can pass a motion restating their approval of the bill; the bill then becomes law, regardless of its treatment in the upper house. The House of Lords in Britain has only a suspensive veto, but it serves as a useful check and balance by forcing the government to slow down and gauge public opinion before the proposals are finally enacted into law. If the House of Lords rejects a bill, the government can reintroduce it into the House of Commons a year later and pass it without the need of sending it to the House of Lords again. The waiting period forces the government to reconsider the original measure, and the government often decides to compromise by either making important changes to the bill or by scrapping it entirely.

An upper house can be even more effective if the constitution provides it with an absolute veto. In that case, the upper house has the power to defeat

---

BOX 9.6

THE MANY DIFFERENT WAYS TO BECOME A MEMBER OF AN UPPER HOUSE

Members of upper chambers acquire the right to sit in the house in a variety of ways, and some chambers use more than one method. In Canada, all senators are chosen by the prime minister and appointed by the governor general, and they serve until the age of 75. In the United States and Australia, all senators are directly elected by the people. In India, most members of the upper house are indirectly elected, which means they are chosen by the legislatures of each state. In Russia, each state's governor and the speaker of the state legislature are ex-officio members of the country's upper house. Ireland reserves three Senate seats to be filled by elections at each of the country's two main universities. Of Pakistan's 100 indirectly-elected Senate seats, 17 are reserved for women and another 17 for clerics and technocrats. Britain's House of Lords is composed of about 750 members, with 630 peers appointed for life, 92 hereditary peers chosen either by their fellow heredity peers or by their political group, and 26 bishops of the Church of England.

a bill, and both houses must pass a bill in identical form before it can become law. In countries such as Canada, the United States, Australia, India, and Japan, the upper house has an absolute veto over all legislation.[24] In other countries, the upper house has a veto only over certain types of legislation. In Germany, for example, the upper house can veto only legislation that would affect the equivalent of provincial governments. Armed with an absolute veto, the sober second thought offered by the upper house can indeed force the government or lower house to reflect seriously on its proposals. This absolute veto is seen as an important part of the checks and balances involved in some political systems' legislative process. For this reason, almost all the American and Australian states have a bicameral legislature. An upper house may also simply amend the bill rather than veto it outright; in that case, the two houses eventually have to reach an agreement on the final form of the bill. Even in countries where the upper house has only a suspensive veto, amendments made to legislation are often voluntarily adopted by the lower house; this may be done out of expediency to pass the bill as quickly as possible or because the amendments relate to some uncontroversial technical improvements.

An important consideration, however, is whether informal constitutional principles prevent an upper house from freely exercising its absolute veto or even from amending legislation. The Canadian Senate, for instance, is constrained by constitutional conventions from using its powers to their full extent. Still, the Senate plays a role of some substance in the legislative process in amending legislation and forcing the government to reconsider its proposals before asking the House of Commons to reaffirm its policies; occasionally, the government even agrees to amendments proposed by the Senate.[25]

The other principal function of an upper house is to provide special representation in the legislature for territorial or non-territorial populations and interests that would otherwise go under-represented or completely unrepresented. Territorial representation is very common in upper houses; for example, the French Senate's members are chosen by the city, town, and county (*département*) councils. All federal countries have bicameral legislatures in order to provide the provinces or states with a more equal or more effective

representation than they have in the lower houses; this increased representation can come either through a more equitable distribution of seats among the regions or provinces or by having representatives of the state or provincial governments sit as members of the upper house. Seats in the lower house are usually distributed roughly according to population, which allows large provinces or states to swamp the smaller ones; in the United States, for example, California has 52 members in the House of Representatives, while a small state such as Rhode Island has only two. A great imbalance like this is rectified in some countries by providing each state or province equal representation in the upper house; in the United States, each state has two seats in the Senate regardless of size, and in Australia each state has 12.

Other federations do not have strict equality in the share of seats the states or provinces have in the upper house, but they do provide a more equitable distribution of seats. For instance, each of Germany's 16 states has between three and six seats in the Bundesrat, depending on its size. A few federations still have very significant disparities. Eight of India's states have only one seat in the upper house, the Rajya Sabha, while Uttar Pradesh has 34. Canada is rather odd, with a Senate that was originally designed to provide equal shares of seats for regions, not the provinces per se. The Maritime provinces, Quebec, Ontario, and the four Western provinces count as regions, each having 24 seats.[26]

But the question remains: Is the representation of territorial interests in an upper house aimed at representing the population of the provinces or states, or is it meant to provide representation for the interests of their governments? Some countries such as Australia and the United States choose to elect their upper-house representatives in order to give the citizens a direct voice. Others provide representation for the state or provincial governments rather than the people; for example, in Germany, Russia, and South Africa, political leaders from the state or provincial governments are members of the nation's upper house and, in a sense, these chambers function like a permanent federal–provincial conference. Canada is an oddity in providing neither form of representation, since the federal government appoints all the members of the Senate; as a result, neither the provincial population nor provincial governments are directly represented.

Upper houses can also provide representation of non-territorial sections of the population. Several countries allocate some of the seats in the upper house to representatives of particular professions. In Ireland, for instance, two universities each elect three senators, and 43 other senators are elected from five occupational groups.[27] Rwanda also reserves two Senate seats to be elected by academics. Various professional and trade groups elect members of the National Council in Slovenia. And in Pakistan, five members of each delegation chosen by the provincial legislatures to represent them in the national Senate must be members of certain religious or occupational groups.

REFORM OF LEGISLATURES

There are as many ways to reform legislatures as there are limitations on their effectiveness. Some reforms involve the internal structure and procedures of the legislature, while other changes might occur if only factors external to the legislature change, such as the electoral system, media coverage, or something as amorphous as the society's political culture. In parliamentary systems, most reforms centre on finding ways to reduce the cabinet's dominance of the legislature and on loosening party discipline. One of the most frequent suggestions is that legislatures make greater use of "free votes." Occasionally, votes in a legislature are held where the parties agree that they will not formally require their members to maintain party loyalty; the members are free to vote according to their own personal judgment. These votes usually involve matters of deep personal conscience, such as capital punishment or abortion, and the suggestion is that free votes could also be extended to matters that do not imply a vote of confidence in the government.

Another suggestion in Canada is that the political parties could adopt the British practice of notifying members of where a vote fits on a sliding scale of the degree of party cohesion expected. For example, a "three-line whip" means "You'd better get out of your hospital bed and vote for the party's position"; such

votes are normally matters of confidence. This scale for votes also includes two-line and one-line whips, with decreasing requirements for party cohesion. In fact, Paul Martin introduced a form of this procedure in 2004 after he became prime minister, and was fairly lenient on some measures, such as the same-sex marriage bill. But in the 2005 minority government position, the budget would not have passed without a three-line vote for Liberal MPs, the support of the NDP, the postponement of Independent MP Chuck Cadman's cancer treatments, the crossing of the floor by Belinda Stronach, and the tie-breaking vote of the Speaker. Extensive use of free votes, however, would mean that MPs need to use their own personal judgment more often; in the long run, more free votes require a much greater support and research staff for individual MPs, so that they can hold an informed assessment of the issues involved.

Other suggestions for parliaments centre on the degree of independence that legislative committees have to investigate policy issues on their own initiative, rather than requiring a cabinet-sanctioned motion in the legislature to begin the hearings. Considerable attention has also been focused in many parliamentary systems on changing the procedural rules dealing with bills introduced by private (non-cabinet) members, in order to give them a better chance of getting passed into law. Another reform that has significant potential—but a very low political profile—is to strengthen a legislature's ability to review delegated legislation and annul the regulations passed by the executive that go beyond the policies originally envisaged by the legislature when it passed the act authorizing the delegated legislation in the first place.

The upper houses of parliament in both Canada and the United Kingdom have come under increasing criticism for their non-elected membership; critics argue that legislatures must be elected in order to enjoy basic legitimacy in modern democracies. The British government has embarked on a series of reforms to transform the House of Lords over the past 20 years, but the government's latest legislation in 2010 fell short of proposing an entirely elected body. Instead the government's report noted the broad support in cross-party proposals for retaining an appointed element of experts and decided it would ultimately prefer to see the House of Lords as a hybrid body, with one-half elected and one-half appointed by an independent commission.[28] In Canada, the most vocal proponents of Senate reform argue that the body should be completely elected. This proposal was embodied in the "Triple-E" model first proposed in the 1980s in Alberta. These senators would be elected on a province-wide basis, and the Senate would fully exercise its legislative powers to amend or defeat legislation. The scheme would also see an equal number of senators for each province, as there are in Australia and the United States. The difficulty with this proposal is twofold. First, Ontario and Quebec reject the suggestion because their level of representation would be severely reduced. Second, the result of electing senators could possibly import into that house all the problems of tight party discipline that lie at the root of many of the problems in the House of Commons, leading to deadlock between the two chambers. Several times since first being elected in 2006, the Harper government has proposed legislation to reform the Senate by both limiting new senators to an eight-year term and by allowing general elections for any future vacancies. While there is strong support for reform, there are serious constitutional limits to what the federal government can achieve without formal amendments to the Constitution, formal amendments that seem unlikely because of strong resistance by the Quebec and Ontario governments.[29] Several countries have seen debates over redressing the under-representation or exclusion of women and Indigenous peoples. One shortcut solution that is sometimes discussed is to set aside a certain number of seats in the legislature to ensure that at least some groups have a physical presence. For example, New Zealand has long had separate seats for the Indigenous Maori population, and a Royal Commission on Electoral Reform proposed in 1991 that Canada set aside some seats in Parliament for Aboriginal representatives.[30] So far, such ideas have not met with widespread support. In some countries, the idea of setting aside a specific number of seats for a group results in fierce controversy. For instance, fist fights broke out in the Indian parliament in 1998 when it debated an amendment to the constitution that would have required that one-third of the seats be reserved for women in the lower house of parliament and in all the state legislatures.[31] In Canada, residents of what was to become Nunavut voted down a 1998 referendum proposal to require equal representation for women and men in the new territorial legislature. Other ways to remedy these problems of underrepresentation within the legislature involve reforms outside of the legislature itself. For example, some political parties around the world voluntarily adopt policies requiring an equal number of male and female candidates and a certain number of candidates from particular ethnic groups. Other suggestions include adopting a proportional representation system with party lists that can be deliberately constructed to provide representatives from the social groups in question.

CONCLUSION

This chapter has provided an examination of a range of issues related to the legislative branch of government. Legislatures are institutions with complex structures and processes, and their relationship with the rest of the political system involves many interconnected threads. Their many possible functions are all limited by a range of real-world constraints, some of which are integral to a particular system of government; executive dominance and party discipline remain both cornerstones and millstones of parliamentary government, for instance. However, this review of legislatures should open your horizons to the important contributions that most democratic legislatures do make to their political systems. These contributions can indeed be improved, but the interrelation between the structure and procedural rules on the one hand, and political culture on the other, mean that there are few quick fixes.

DISCUSSION QUESTIONS

1. Which form of representation do you find yourself favouring: the delegate or the trustee approach?

2. What range of social groups do you feel you belong to? If you were an MP, on what sorts of

issues would you believe that you should "represent" one of those groups rather than the others?

3. Imagine that you are a member of the governing party's caucus in the Canadian House of Commons who is not in Cabinet. Think of what you would say in a caucus meeting about the need to loosen party discipline. Then picture yourself as the Prime Minister and think of what you would say in response.

4. What do you think is the single most important constraint on Canadian legislatures that stems from our political culture? Can you see any way in which the cultural values involved may change?

FURTHER READING

Docherty, David C. *Legislatures.* Vancouver: UBC Press, 2005.

———. *Mr. Smith Goes to Ottawa.* Vancouver: UBC Press, 1997.

Franks, C.E.S. *The Parliament of Canada.* Toronto: University of Toronto Press, 1987.

Heard, Andrew. *Canadian Constitutional Conventions: The Marriage of Law and Politics.* Toronto: Oxford University Press, 1991.

Inter-Parliamentary Union. *World Directory of Parliaments.* Geneva: IPU, 1998.

Peter H. Russell and Lorne Sossin, eds. *Parliamentary Democracy in Crisis.* Toronto: University of Toronto Press, 2009.

Smith, Jennifer. *The Democratic Dilemma: Reforming the Canadian Senate.* Montreal and Kingston: McGill-Queen's University Press, 2009.

ENDNOTES

1. Inter-Parliamentary Union, "Women in Parliaments: World Classification," available at: http://www.ipu.org/wmn-e/classif.htm; accessed November 12, 2007.

2. It should be noted that even in countries without a legislature, the judiciary still exercises a certain amount of legislative power by interpreting and enforcing the laws passed by the executive.

3. Inter-Parliamentary *Union, Parliaments of the World: A Comparative Reference Compendium,* 3rd ed., vol. 2 (Aldershot: IPU, 1986), p. 1125.

4. Calculated from "Interim Résumé of Congressional Activity: 1st Session of the 111th Congress," available at http://www.Senate.gov/reference/resources/pdf/Resumes/111_1.pdf; accessed November 11, 2010.

5. David C. Docherty, *Mr. Smith Goes to Ottawa* (Vancouver: UBC Press, 1997), p. 129.

6. Philip Norton, "The United Kingdom: Restoring Confidence," *Parliamentary Affairs* 50 (1997): 360.

7. Docherty, *Mr. Smith Goes to Ottawa,* pp. 190–91.

8. J.P. Joseph Maignot, *Parliamentary Privilege in Canada,* 2nd ed. (Montreal and Kingston: McGill-Queen's University Press, 1997), p. 335.

9. André Blais, et al., "Does the Local Candidate Matter?," available at http://ces-eec.mcgill.ca/publications2000.html#10; accessed June 2, 2008. In the 2011 election, several NDP candidates in Quebec did not even campaign, yet were elected as MPs.

10. Louis Massicotte, "Party Cohesion in the Ontario Legislative Assembly, 1867–1990," paper presented at the annual meeting of the Canadian Political Science Association, Calgary, June 1994.

11. Keith Jackson, "Caucus: The Anti-Parliament System?," *Parliamentarian* 59 (3) (July 1978): 160.

12. Philip Norton, *The Commons in Perspective* (Oxford: Martin Robertson, 1981), p. 227.

13. Jean-François Godbout and Bjorn Hoyland, "Voting Coalitions and Minority Governments

in Canada," Paper presented to the American Political Science Association Meetings, Toronto, September 5, 2009, available at http://papers.ssrn.com/sol3/Delivery. cfm/SSRN_ID1466977_code1321124. pdf?abstractid=1450654&mirid=5; accessed November 11, 2010.

14. Andrew Heard, "Assessing Senate Reform through Bill C-19: The Effects of Limited Terms for Senators," in Jennifer Smith, *The Democratic Dilemma: Reforming the Canadian Senate* (Kingston: McGill-Queen's University Press, 2009), pp. 128–31.

15. *Congressional Quarterly Almanac Plus 2003* (Washington, DC: CQ Press, 2004), p. B14.

16. For different points of view, see: Peter H. Russell and Lorne Sossin, eds., *Parliamentary Democracy in Crisis* (Toronto: University of Toronto Press, 2009).

17. Andrew Heard, *Canadian Constitutional Conventions: The Marriage of Law and Politics* (Toronto: Oxford University Press, 1991), pp. 87–98.

18. Ontario Legislative Library Legislative Research Service, "The Ontario Legislature: An Overview," available at http://www.lirico.ca/ipac20/ipac.jsp?s ession=U20935I05W592.96415&profile= lirico-eng&uri=link=3100007~!429006~!310000 1~!3100002&aspect=subtab101&menu=search& ri=1&source=~!horizon&term=Ontario.+Legisla tive +Library.+Legislative+Research+Service.&in dex=#focus; accessed June 2, 2008.

19. These figures are calculated from informa- tion at "Presidential Vetoes, 1798–2010," available at http://www.infoplease.com/ipa/ A0801767.html; accessed November 12, 2010; and "House Overrides Bush Veto of Farm Bill," available at http://news.yahoo.com/s/ nm/20080522/pl_nm/bush_farmbill_dc_7; accessed May 21, 2008.

20. *Clinton v. City of New York*, [1998] 118 S. Ct. 2091.

21. For example, see Jane Arscott and Linda Trimble, eds., *In the Presence of Women* (Toronto: Harcourt Brace, 1997); and Julie Dolan, "Support for Women's Interests in the 103rd Congress: The Distinct Impact of Congressional Women," *Women in Politics* 18 (4) (1997): 88. Note, however, that contrary conclusions have been found with respect to African-American mem- bers of the American Congress; see Carol M. Swain, Black Faces, Black Interests: *The Representation of African Americans in Congress* (Cambridge: Harvard University Press, 1993).

22. Jane Mansbridge, "Should Blacks Represent Blacks and Women Represent Women? A Contingent 'Yes,'" *Journal of Politics* 61 (1999): 628. This article contains a good review of the arguments for and against mirror or descriptive representation.

23. Harris Decima, "Canadians Prefer Senate Reform or Even Abolishment to Status Quo"; available at http://www.harrisdecima.com/sites/default/files/ releases/2010/02/08/hd-2010-02-08-en466.pdf; accessed February 9, 2010.

24. Except that the Canadian Senate does not have an absolute veto over constitutional amendments, as mentioned in Chapter 7.

25. Heard, *Canadian Constitutional Conventions*, pp. 87–98.

26. Quebec and Ontario each have 24 seats. The Maritime provinces' 24 seats are divided into 10 seats each for Nova Scotia and New Brunswick and four seats for PEI. The four Western provinces each have six seats. When Newfoundland entered Confederation, it was given six seats. Each of the three territories has one senator, for a grand total of 105.

27. These five occupational groups are Culture and Education, Agriculture, Labour, Industry and Commerce, and Public Administration.

28. "The House of Lords: Reform," February 2007, available at: http://www.officialdocuments.gov.uk/document/cm70/7027/7027.pdf; accessed November 13, 2007.

29. See Jennifer Smith, *The Democratic Dilemma: Reforming the Canadian Senate.*

30. Royal Commission on Electoral Reform and Party Financing, *Final Report*, vol. 1 (Ottawa: 1991).

31. Shri G.C. Malhotra, "Parliamentary Pandemonium: Taking Opposition Too Far," *Parliamentarian* 80 (2) (April 1999).

For various weblinks discussed in this chapter, please go to the book's website at **www.studyingpolitics4e.nelson.com**

The Judiciary: Politics, Law, and the Courts

Andrew Heard

CHAPTER OBJECTIVES

After you have completed this chapter, you should be able to:

- understand the role of law and the courts in a political system
- evaluate the strengths and weaknesses of different methods of appointing judges
- discuss the issues involved in judicial independence and impartiality
- outline how access to the courts is restricted.

THE ROLE OF LAW AND THE JUDICIAL FUNCTION

In stable societies, law and judges play crucial roles that are not always seen or widely appreciated. **Law** sets the most basic rules of behaviour for all citizens and can impose fundamental limits on the power of government officials. The judicial power is an essential part of the power of governments, and through it authoritative decisions are made on disputes covering a wide range of matters. The courts have become so much a part of the fabric of our political system that they are often simply taken for granted. Yet they are in some ways "the power behind the throne." The courts perform many vital functions and have an enormous cumulative impact, not only through the policies they enforce on behalf of the elected government but also through those they develop and implement themselves. Perhaps ironically, the power of the judiciary may be most appreciated in countries where the courts are weak, corrupt, or simply subservient to the whims of the political or military leaders of the day. There, many people long for the day when the courts will become independent developers and protectors of constitutional limits on the rulers and provide effective punishments for those who undermine basic law and order or openly terrorize people through brute force.

If you stop to think about your life, you will find that much of it depends upon laws that tell you what to do and not do, help you have what you are entitled to, protect you from false accusations, and provide you with a peaceful way to resolve disputes that arise. You also probably do many things the law requires you to do, whether you like it or not, because you believe that, in general, it is right and proper to obey the law. While we all probably break some laws some of the time, most of us still believe that we should obey most laws most of the time. In democratic countries such as Canada, obedience to the law and respect for the courts are ingrained in the general political culture (see Figure 10.1).

The existence of courts to adjudicate disputes ensures that conflicts are decided by rules of law and not through the rule of might. If you have a dispute with your neighbour or a store clerk, you do not have to resort to rounding up the biggest of your friends to go and sort it out. Moreover, the courts ensure that a mere accusation is not sufficient for someone to be

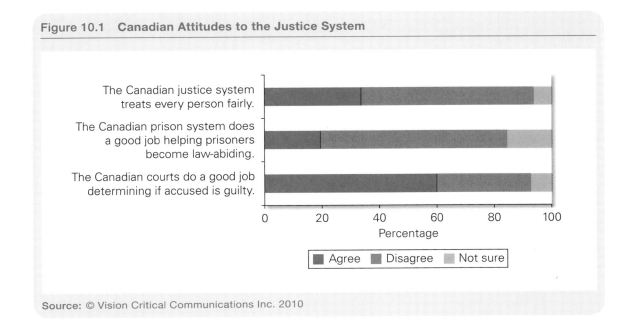

Figure 10.1 Canadian Attitudes to the Justice System

The Canadian justice system treats every person fairly.

The Canadian prison system does a good job helping prisoners become law-abiding.

The Canadian courts do a good job determining if accused is guilty.

Percentage

■ Agree ■ Disagree ■ Not sure

Source: © Vision Critical Communications Inc. 2010

punished—guilt or innocence must be carefully and objectively determined. Finally, the courts can ensure that the rule of law is observed and that the government does not act outside its powers or fail to perform duties required under law.

Unfortunately, the costs of judicial proceedings raise serious questions about the equal access of all to the courts. There are also deep controversies over the extent to which judges can, or should, exercise their own discretion in interpreting the law to reflect their own personal values. Furthermore, there are important questions about how judges are appointed and removed from office, as well as about the extent to which elected politicians should be involved in those decisions.

Connections Among Law, Morality, and Politics

Law is not an independent force in a society, nor is it simply a set of rules of procedure. Law gives life to the policies of the government. Law may be either an instrument of justice, as is the ideal in a democratic society, or an instrument of oppression. What matters in the end is the content of the law and how it is applied and enforced.

Law may be the embodiment of the noblest principles of a free democracy, or it may be the instrument used to implement torture and mass murder. Canada's legal history provides examples of the best and worst of the content of law. The law provides Canadians with free schooling, minimum wages, workplace safety, universal health care, and unemployment insurance; the *Charter of Rights* protects many rights, such as our freedom of speech and the right to vote. However, Canadian laws have also prohibited women, Chinese Canadians, and Aboriginal people from voting. Canadian laws also provided the basis for interning Canadian citizens of Japanese descent during World War II and for the complete seizure of their property and businesses.[1] There were even laws in British Columbia, Saskatchewan, Manitoba, and Ontario that prohibited white women from working for Chinese or Japanese males.

The content of law is very much a reflection of the prevailing mores and values of a society at any given time. More to the point, the law in any society embodies the prevailing moral values of the dominant elite. As times and attitudes change, so do the moral beliefs enacted into law and enforced by the courts. In Canada, homosexual activity was once illegal, but

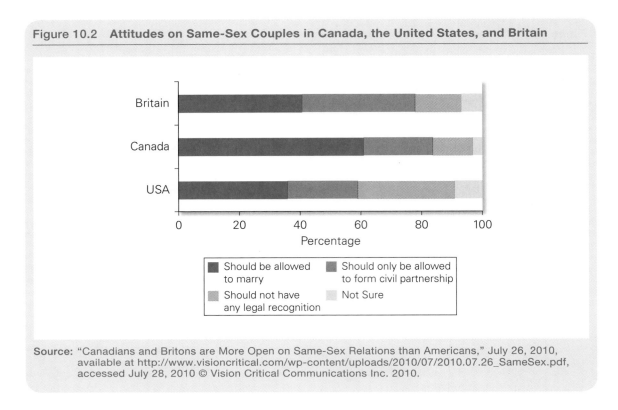

Figure 10.2   **Attitudes on Same-Sex Couples in Canada, the United States, and Britain**

recently the courts have required Canadian governments to extend spousal benefits to same-sex couples. Indeed, marriage itself has been extended to same-sex couples after a series of court rulings confirmed the equal rights of gays. Figure 10.2 shows very different attitudes among Americans, Britons, and Canadians on whether the law should allow or prohibit same-sex marriage. The content of law and the morality enforced by the law can change over time and vary from one country to another. While adultery was once illegal in the United States, it is no longer a crime enforced by the courts; on the other hand, it is still an offence for which people are executed in Saudi Arabia and Iran. Given the intimate connection between law and politics, intense political conflicts are involved in what gets written into law and how that law is interpreted.

Different Types of Law

There are different types of law to regulate different types of activity and disputes. The major division in law is public versus private. **Public law** includes constitutional law, criminal law, and many aspects of international law. Public law involves the rules of how government is structured and the powers and relations between various government bodies and officials and between the government and the public. Criminal law, part of public law, is largely concerned with matters of public safety, health, and morality. Thus, it is a crime to beat or murder somebody; it is a crime to sell dangerous drugs; and it is a crime for an adult to have sex with a child. **Private law** can be described as being principally concerned with regulating disputes between members of the public, be they individuals, groups of people, or corporations. The many different areas of private law govern contracts, corporations, inheritance, real estate, and employment.

While one might think that law is just something created by each government within a country, there is also an important body of international law. **International law** is created in many ways: formal treaties or conventions signed by the governments of the states that wish to be bound by it, declarations of the United Nations, and even the historical practice and custom of states over time. International law covers not only how the governments of different countries deal with each other, but also how businesses and individuals from one country are dealt with by other countries. International trade could not exist at today's levels without a strong collection of legal rules to regulate trade and settle disputes. There are even some international courts set up to deal with aspects of international law, such as the International Court of Justice, the International Criminal Court, and the European Court of Justice.

> **International law:** A complex body of rules, derived principally from the treaties, covenants, and declarations signed by the governments of various countries. The resolutions of international organizations, the writings of academics, and rulings of domestic and international courts can also be sources of international law when the rules are not otherwise clear.

A number of very different legal systems exist around the world; the most frequently encountered ones are based on common law, a civil code, or Islamic law. The **common law** system is practised in many countries that emerged from the British Empire. Countries as diverse as Canada, India, Jamaica, and Nigeria all base their national legal systems on the common law tradition of Britain. In this system, the fundamental principle is that like cases should be decided alike and that courts are bound by the precedents of previous decisions that dealt with similar points of law and fact—the principle known as **stare decisis**. Historically, the common law also described a set of judge-made rules that British judges developed in the late Middle Ages in the absence of extensive formal legislation by parliament. Only a small subset of these common law rules survives today; in Canada and Britain, they relate mainly to private law and some aspects of the power of the executive branch of government.

> **Common law:** A system of law in which precedents from relevant cases in the past are applied to current ones. Judges are bound by precedent and should decide like cases alike.

> **Stare decisis:** A principle of common law systems by which courts are bound to follow prior decisions that involved similar issues of law. A judgment by one member of a court binds other members, and lower courts are bound to follow the decisions of higher courts.

The civil code systems of law are found mainly in Western Europe and in newer states that emerged from the French Empire. In this system, the law is organized as a set of principles that, in theory, are applied freshly to each case. In practice, however, judges pay close attention to past decisions on the particular sections of the code involved in a case. This family of legal systems has an ancient lineage. While there are separate French, German, Dutch, and Swiss origins of the modern systems, in the French case dating from a code enacted under Napoleon Bonaparte in 1804, many principles can be traced back to the laws of the Roman Empire. It should be noted that Quebec has continued to use an updated version of the Napoleonic Code for private law matters, while the other provinces have systems based on British common law.

The most strikingly different system of law in fairly wide use today is the Islamic system of law, known as the *sharia* or **sharia law**. This system is based on a collection of ancient Islamic teachings on how people should behave and what punishments are appropriate for particular transgressions. Essentially, the Islamic holy scriptures, the Qur'an, and the later writings of scholars form the basis of the sharia. Because the sharia is based on a collection of writings, it can operate in somewhat different ways in the countries that use it, as different aspects are emphasized. Its strictest implementation is found in states such as Saudi Arabia and Iran, where punishments are meted out that seem cruel by Western standards: floggings, the severing of a hand for theft, and execution for adultery, either by beheading or stoning. The sharia also entrenches different standards for the sexes, with a prohibition against convicting a

> **Sharia law:** The Muslim or Islamic system of law, both civil and criminal, based on a collection of ancient teachings, the Islamic holy scriptures, the Qur'an, and later scholarly writing, prescribing how people should behave and what punishments are appropriate for particular transgressions.

man on the evidence of one woman while a woman may be convicted on the word of one man. The adoption of Islamic law in the late 1990s by 12 of Nigeria's 36 states caused significant controversy in that country, and was unsuccessfully challenged under the constitution in 2002 by activists who claim that it violates Nigeria's constitutional guarantees of equality by subjecting citizens in some parts of the country to significantly harsher penalties. The potential for the conflict between values enforced under the sharia and the values of other Nigerians was seen in 2010 when a sharia court ordered an end to criticisms on Facebook and other online media of amputations under Islamic law; critics of this order claimed that their constitutional right to free expression had been subjugated to the sharia.[2] Other states, such as Egypt, have adapted Islamic law and implemented more moderate aspects of the code.

In general, Islamic marital law is patriarchal, with significantly more rights for men than women, especially with respect to matrimonial property. Canadian courts have at times refused to apply foreign court judgments that enforced Islamic matrimonial law. For example, Justice Burchell of the Nova Scotia Supreme Court said in 1987: "To put it simply, I will not give effect to Iranian matrimonial law because it is archaic and repugnant to ideas of substantial justice in this province."[3] This backdrop highlights the controversy in recent years in Ontario, where the provincial government considered permitting family law cases to be settled through alternative dispute resolution settings, including a couple's religious institutions. This would have meant that disputes between Islamic spouses in Ontario could be settled according to Islamic law if both parties agreed; critics argued, however, that this meant Islamic women would be pressured into using a system inherently unfair to women. The government later abandoned this policy proposal.

The Judicial Function

With laws comes a need to interpret and enforce them. Judicial power is exercised by those institutions and officials authorized to interpret and enforce the law. Here it is important to distinguish between judicial power and the courts. Although courts are usually the primary focus of judicial power, most political systems also include other officials or institutions that have an important role to play in interpreting and enforcing

laws. Where judicial power is exercised by officials or bodies other than judges and the courts, it is usually known as quasi-judicial power. In all industrialized democracies and in most other states, the executive branch of government exercises a considerable amount of such power. For example, if you had a dispute with your landlord, you would go to a residential tenancies tribunal, where it would be heard and settled according to the laws governing apartment and house rentals. Or if you felt you had been unfairly denied unemployment insurance or welfare benefits, you would first argue your case before tribunals composed of civil servants. Refugees in Canada have their cases initially decided by a panel of officials whose job it is to determine whether someone qualifies as a refugee and may remain in the country. Thus, important issues about whether people can stay in their apartments, have enough money to live on, or remain in the country are decided according to the relevant laws by **administrative tribunals**, which are not actual courts. However, the decisions of these tribunals can usually be appealed to the courts for a final decision.

> **Administrative tribunals:** Boards or commissions established by the government to adjudicate certain disputes by applying laws to the facts; also called quasi-judicial tribunals or regulatory agencies. These tribunals are not proper courts presided over by judges.

The judicial function can also be carried out by very different types of courts, and the legitimacy or effectiveness of judicial powers may depend on which courts deal with which matters. When political scientists and lawyers refer to "the courts," we normally mean what are properly called civil courts, which are presided over by civilian judges with some degree of independence from the other branches of government and political authorities. Military courts, in contrast, are presided over by serving members of the military; depending upon the country, the presiding officers may or may not have legal training. In Canada and Britain, for example, the lowest level of military tribunals, known as *summary trials*, are presided over by the normal officer commanding the unit, who might be an engineer, a pilot, or an infantry officer. Nevertheless, some courts-martial have presiding officers who are trained lawyers.

Military courts are usually characterized by expedited processes, fewer legal protections for the accused, and harsher penalties. While most democracies restrict the jurisdiction of military courts to members of the armed forces, some countries may try the most serious offences against the state in military courts and leave more minor cases to the civil courts. And, of course, countries run by military dictators may rely exclusively on military tribunals. The use of military courts has become a political issue in the United States, as President Bush announced in 2001 that alleged terrorists captured during the war in Afghanistan would be held at the U.S. naval base in Guantanamo, Cuba and tried before military commissions. The Bush administration deliberately decided to hold their terrorist suspects there in an attempt to keep them off U.S. soil and out of the regular court system. The concern of many is that those to be tried by these offshore tribunals lack the constitutional rights that they would normally have if tried before the civil courts within American territory. However, the U.S. Supreme Court ruled in 2008 that constitutional protection did extend to these detainees.[4]

Some countries also have religious courts that may operate alongside civil courts or instead of them. Countries that fully implement the Islamic sharia, such as Saudi Arabia and Iran, are most likely to empower religious courts to try cases dealing with public offences. Religious courts usually provide few, if any, opportunities for an accused to be properly represented by legal counsel, and the laws they enforce are interpretations of religious doctrines and decrees by religious authorities rather than individual laws passed by the legislature. Perhaps the most famous example in recent times were the religious courts that dished out a brutal justice under the Taliban rule of Afghanistan in the 1990s. However, much of Western Europe also experienced religious courts in the Middle Ages, when tribunals of the Roman Catholic church exercised considerable authority; the trials of the Inquisition are the most notorious examples, with thousands put to death.

THE ROLE OF COURTS

The primary function performed by the **judiciary** is the interpretation and enforcement of the law. Laws are necessarily worded in general terms and cannot foresee all the future circumstances to which they must be applied. Thus, the judges must fill in the blanks and flesh out the wording of legal rules; they interpret what the laws mean. The judiciary also enforces the law by determining the guilt or innocence of those charged with an offence and by punishing those who do not obey the law. The courts do not go out and look for wrongdoers; they deal only with those who are brought before them. This role of enforcing the law ensures that there is general obedience to the rules of society and that peaceful people can be protected from wrongdoers.

Judiciary: The term used to refer to all the judges collectively in a country. It can also mean the whole judicial branch of government, including juries and the courts' administrative staff.

In the criminal context, the judiciary comes into play after the police or some other executive agency has discovered evidence of wrongdoing. The courts also have an important role in helping to settle private disputes (often called civil disputes) between individuals, groups, or companies. When we have a dispute over what someone has done to our property and want compensation to pay for the damages, we can go to the courts. In business, if a company does not live up to its contractual agreements or provides faulty or damaged goods, the dispute can be settled in the courts. Many disputes in our private lives can be settled in courts according to laws that apply to everybody. Judges decide who is to blame and who violated the law; they then determine what penalty is appropriate, and what compensation is due to the person or group that was wronged. Because of this, we do not have to rely on violence or vengeance to get what is owed to us. This function of the judiciary allows us to live in a peaceful society.

The courts can also act as referees that decide whether government officials are acting within their powers. The power of judicial review is the power of the courts to decide whether law authorized an action taken by a government official or body and whether a law is actually constitutional.

Courts settle disputes primarily through adjudication, which is the settling of a dispute by applying rules (laws) to the facts of a case. Adjudication is quite different from arbitration and mediation, in which one tries to find an equitable resolution to a dispute that ideally provides the best possible solution for all parties involved. Courts face a conundrum in adjudicating disputes. Although judges are supposed to apply the law to the facts of the case, the law is often ambiguous or even plagued by gaps and loopholes; there is not always a clear, existing law to apply. As a result, judges have an important role to play in interpreting the existing law. In the process of interpreting the law, judges sometimes have to make new law, and are often involved in a substantial way in policymaking, a role that is seen most clearly in dealing with constitutional rights but is involved in virtually all aspects of judicial interpretation.

The courts also have an important role to play in enforcing legal limits on the powers of politicians. While this role is almost taken for granted in established democracies, it is vital in transitional democracies, where political leaders are tempted to ignore constitutional limits in trying to implement their policies. For example, judges in Zimbabwe tried for many years to restrain President Mugabe's tightening grip on that country and steer his government into respecting the country's constitution. However, they lost their fight in 2001, when the majority of the top court resigned after the chief justice decided that he could no longer guarantee the safety of the members of that court who had stood up to Mugabe. After their resignations, Mugabe appointed new judges loyal to his policies, and they quickly went about giving the court's stamp of approval to his government's actions.[5] President Musharraf managed a similar purge of the Pakistani judiciary in 2007, as he attempted to sustain his military rule. At least the Zimbabwean and Pakistani judges fared better than those in Uganda in the 1970s, some of whom were assassinated by President Idi Amin's security forces.

In enforcing limits on the powers of politicians, the courts are enforcing the principle of the rule of law. Although this principle is open to many interpretations, key aspects can be identified to reinforce the idea that law should govern all actions of governments. Laws must emanate from a known, formal institution authorized by the constitution to exercise legislative power. Citizens must be able to find out what the laws are that they are bound to obey. The law should apply to everyone in the society, including all government officials. This does not mean that the law cannot make distinctions or exceptions, just that those exceptions must be included in the law itself. And finally, the law must ultimately be enforced by proper courts of law. These aspects of the rule of law do not in themselves mean that a government is going to be democratic or benevolent; after all, even the apartheid regime in South Africa used proper laws and courts to enforce white supremacy and the brutal oppression of the nonwhite majority. However, one can say that no democratic government can function without respecting the rule of law. Thus the rule of law is a necessary but not sufficient condition for democracy.

The rule of law is most severely tested during times of war or major threat. A government or its officials may be tempted to bend the rules in order to achieve a greater good. Or they may introduce draconian laws, all in the name of defending the values they cherish. The courts have a vital role to play in such times to ensure that the government adheres to what the law and the constitution requires. Special challenges have arisen in the U.S. "war on terror" since 9/11. An example of this is discussed in Box 10.1, which is a report about a court case trying to lift a hunt and kill order for a U.S. citizen, who is a senior al-Qaeda leader in Yemen.

In fulfilling their general roles, the courts may at times play a very active part in highly charged political disputes. For example, the Canadian Supreme Court has twice been asked to settle high-profile political controversies. In 1981, it had to rule on the constitutionality of Prime Minister Trudeau's plans to patriate the Canadian constitution and introduce the *Charter of Rights* without gaining the consent of the provincial governments. In the *Patriation Reference* case, the Supreme Court ruled that the federal government's proposed unilateral actions were legal but contravened the informal constitutional conventions that required substantial provincial consent to such significant constitutional amendments. Then in the 1998 *Quebec Secession Reference* case, the Court was asked to declare whether Quebec had a right to secede from Canada under either domestic constitutional law or international law. It ruled that Quebec did not have this right at all, but that the rest of Canada would be under a moral obligation to negotiate the terms of separation if a clear majority voted in favour on a clear question to pursue independence. In both

---

BOX 10.1

US TARGETED KILLING ORDER GOES TO COURT

WASHINGTON—Attorneys for the father of a cleric trying to inspire Muslims to kill Americans argued in court Monday to keep his son from being targeted for death by President Barack Obama.

U.S. District Judge John Bates heard arguments in the case of Anwar al-Awlaki on the same day that the American cleric made a renewed call for jihad against U.S. citizens in a video posted on extremist websites.

Al-Awlaki, believed to be hiding in Yemen, was linked to last year's shooting at Fort Hood, Texas, and the attempted bombing of a U.S.-bound flight last Christmas. In the latest video, he said all Americans are the enemy and Muslims should kill any of them at will without consulting anyone.

Al-Awlaki's father, Nasser al-Awlaki of Yemen, says in a lawsuit that international law and the Constitution prevent the Obama administration from unilaterally targeting his son for death unless he presents a specific imminent threat to life or physical safety and there are no other means to stop him. The suit also seeks to force the government to disclose standards for determining whether U.S. citizens like his son, born in New Mexico, can be targeted for death.

"What the government is doing is imposing the death penalty without trial," said Jameel Jaffer, a lawyer for the American Civil Liberties Union, which along with the Center for Constitutional Rights has taken al-Awlaki's case.

Administration officials have confirmed to The Associated Press that al-Awlaki is on a capture or kill list, although Justice Department attorney Douglas Letter said in court that he would neither confirm nor deny it. But Letter said if al-Awlaki turns himself over to authorities, he's in no danger of the United States using lethal force against him.

Letter told Bates the court has no legal authority to be "looking over the shoulder" of the president as he makes military decisions to protect Americans against terrorist attacks.

'We're going to the very core powers of the president as commander in chief," Letter said.

Bates, an appointee of President George W. Bush, challenged both sides on their arguments, which were moved to the largest hearing room at the courthouse to accommodate the hundreds of people who turned out to listen.

For instance, Bates questioned the Justice Department on why the courts have authority to approve surveillance of Americans overseas but not their killing. And he pressed al-Awlaki's attorneys on why they think the cleric would want his father to take up the case when he has denounced the authority of the U.S. judicial system.

Jaffer said the father and son are not in contact because of the threat of death against the son. But he said the prospect that Anwar al-Awlaki could face indefinite detention without charge is enough to keep him from taking up the case himself, so his father is trying to act in his best interest.

Jaffer acknowledged that Anwar al-Awlaki said some "nasty" things about the United States and said he is not suggesting that Obama is acting in bad faith. But he said putting al-Awlaki on the targeted kill list without review would give the president carte blanche to assassinate any American accused of being involved in terrorism.

Source: Nedra Pickler, "Judge Hears Arguments in Targeted Killing Case," Associated Press, November 8, 2010, available at: http://news.yahoo.com/s/ap/20101109/ap_on_go_ot/us_cleric_lawsuit; accessed November 16, 2010.

---

the *Patriation Reference* case and the *Quebec Secession Reference*, the court appeared to carefully craft a decision that went beyond the strict law and to provide answers that played to both sides of the political disputes at hand.[6] The structure of the Canadian court system is outlined in Figure 10.3.

Figure 10.3   **Canada's Court System**

Decades earlier, the U.S. Supreme Court accelerated profound social and political changes in ordering that the racially segregated school systems be integrated, leading to a system of court-monitored busing of millions of school children.[7] In December 2000, the U.S. Supreme Court became embroiled in the fallout from the unclear presidential election results that depended entirely on the outcome of voting in Florida. In a decision that generated much heated debate in the United States, the Court ruled that recounts of the votes cast in certain counties of Florida should not proceed—effectively declaring George Bush the winner and new president.[8] This decision was one of the most controversial made by the Supreme Court in years, with many critics declaring that the court's split along partisan lines showed that Republican-appointed judges came to the rescue of their party's presidential candidate.[9] The Ukraine Supreme Court played a pivotal role in 2004 and 2005 by annulling corrupted presidential elections, ordering a new round of voting, and upholding the results of the later ballot. The court's decisions ended the authoritarian rule of President Leonid Kuchma and his intended successor Viktor Yanukovych. It came as a relief and surprise to many—considering how little confidence Ukrainians have had in their judicial system (see Figure 10.4). And, in 2006 the Constitutional Court of Thailand annulled the general parliamentary elections and ordered a fresh round of voting for the nation.

Judicial Review

In democratic countries, as discussed in Chapter 7, the court's powers of **judicial review** are very important to ensuring that the principles of limited government and the rule of law are respected by government actors. If there are to be legal limits on the powers of state actors, then somebody has to review their actions to ensure that

Judicial review: A function of the courts in which judges examine actions of the government to determine whether they are authorized by law. This may also include a determination of whether statutes and regulations are contrary to the constitution.

Figure 10.4   Public Confidence in the Judicial System

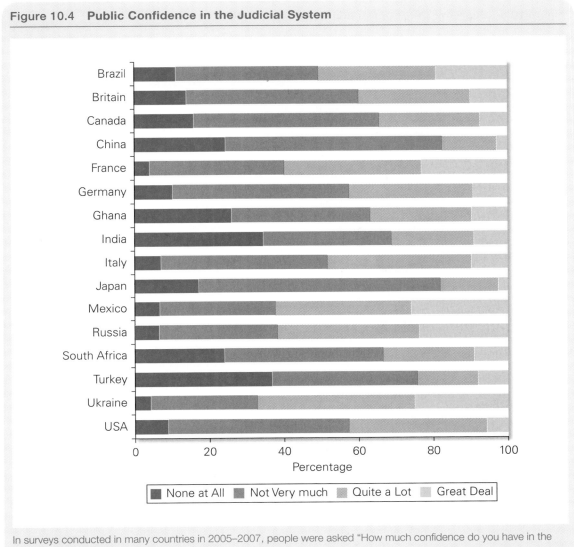

In surveys conducted in many countries in 2005–2007, people were asked "How much confidence do you have in the justice system?"

Source: Canadian data are from Léger Marketing, "Canadians and the Judicial System," April 8, 2002, p. 4; cited on April 27, 2005; available at http://legermarketing.com/documents/SPCLM/020408ENG.pdf. All other data are from the European Value Study Group and World Values Survey Association.

they are legal. The courts conduct several different types of judicial review with varying degrees of controversy (see Figure 10.5, p. 260), but they all involve the same basic role: the review of other state actors to ensure they fulfil their duties and do not act beyond their powers.

One type of judicial review is without controversy in countries that practise the rule of law: to make sure

that government officials respect the ordinary statutory provisions that govern their powers. Officials can do only what the law empowers them to do, and they must perform what the law requires them to do. Thus, teachers cannot carry guns in the classroom or beat their students with whips. School board officials must allow parents to register their children to

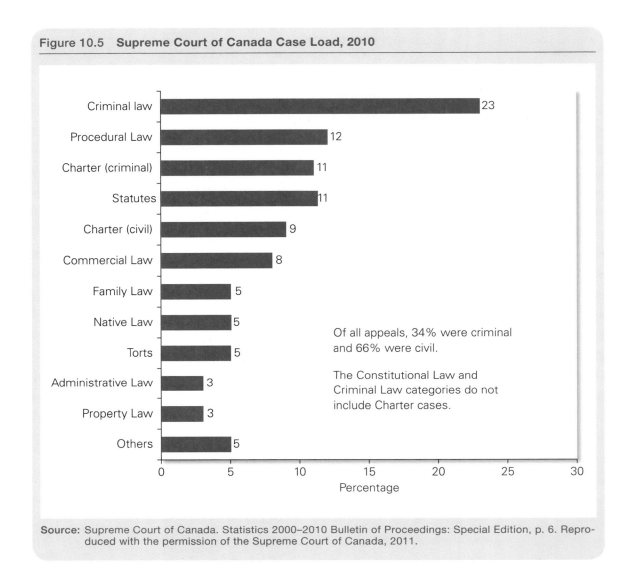

Figure 10.5 **Supreme Court of Canada Case Load, 2010**

Of all appeals, 34% were criminal and 66% were civil.

The Constitutional Law and Criminal Law categories do not include Charter cases.

Source: Supreme Court of Canada. Statistics 2000–2010 Bulletin of Proceedings: Special Edition, p. 6. Reproduced with the permission of the Supreme Court of Canada, 2011.

attend school if they meet the normal requirements of age and residency. And no one can be refused a new driver's licence just because of the colour of their skin; everyone must be issued a licence having completed all the forms, passed the test, and paid the fee. One example of judges conducting this type of judicial review is the writ of *habeas corpus*; in this process, lawyers can ask the court to determine whether their client is being lawfully held in custody. The police have to establish that the detention is justified under the law.

Judicial review of the lawfulness of officials' actions can involve both ordinary statute law as well as constitutional issues, such as the rights of citizens. The essence of this form of judicial review is to determine how officials exercise their discretion in acting one way or another.

The second broad type of judicial review involves the courts' scrutiny of the other branches of government to ensure that the laws they create are within the bounds set by the constitution. As mentioned in Chapter 7, constitutions can limit government powers either by dividing power between different levels of government or by protecting citizens' rights. Judicial review on these grounds involves the review of legislation passed by municipal, provincial, or national legislatures; it can also examine the rules passed by other administrative bodies which exercise government authority, such as administrative tribunals. It should be noted that this type of judicial review can occur only in countries having formal constitutional documents that set limits on government bodies and officials. Some countries have no equivalent of the *Charter of Rights* or a federal system, so there is little basis for this form of judicial review.

The review of legislation on the basis of a division of powers is not inherently controversial. If there is to be a real federal system in which the national and regional governments are each given jurisdiction over specific areas of public policy, the courts have to play the role of referee. Ever since Canada was founded, the courts have had the power to declare laws unconstitutional on federalism grounds. Someone has to make sure that one level of government does not try to pass laws on matters that are really in the jurisdiction of the other level of government, and the courts have that job. Controversy can occur, however, if suspicions are aroused that the courts are somehow biased in favour of one level of government. For example, Quebec nationalists have long argued that the Supreme Court of Canada has been biased because the federal government appoints all its members, although academic studies have not found any actual bias in the Court's decisions.

In the process of interpreting the division of powers, the courts can profoundly transform the character of the federal system by either centralizing power in the national government or decentralizing power in the regional governments. For example, Canada's federal system has been significantly decentralized since 1867, thanks in large part to key decisions of the **Judicial Committee of the Privy Council (JCPC)**, a British body that served as Canada's final court of appeal until 1949, when the **Supreme Court of Canada** finally did become "supreme." As noted in Chapter 7, several key decisions of the JCPC limited the federal government's power on the one hand and expanded the authority of the provinces on the other. For one, the federal government's jurisdiction over trade and commerce has been restricted to interprovincial and international

The Supreme Court of Canada building in Ottawa, a site of increasing significance in the Canadian political system.

The Canadian Press(Tom Hanson)

trade, while the provinces' power over property and civil rights has been interpreted to give them broad powers over trade within the province. The power of judicial review becomes an important engine of constitutional change in federal systems, as the courts continue to give fresh interpretations to what each level of government can or cannot do.

Judicial review based on a constitutionally protected set of rights can be even more controversial because of the social and economic policies that judges get to decide (see Box 10.2, p. 262). In essence, this type of judicial review identifies policy choices that no government may enact into law. A basic problem with this type of judicial review is the enormous range of discretion judges have in interpreting very broad wording in

---

BOX 10.2

SELECTED SUPREME COURT OF CANADA DECISIONS ON RIGHTS ISSUES

Big M Drug Mart [1985] struck down Sunday closing mandated under the *Lord's Day Act*.

R. v. Oakes [1986] set out the guidelines for interpreting Section 1 and determining the "reasonable limits" that may be placed on Charter rights.

Labour Trilogy [1987] decided that freedom of association does not include a right for unions to strike.

Ford v. Quebec [1988] ruled that aspects of the Quebec laws related to language used on signs were unconstitutional.

R. v. Morgentaler [1988] struck down the Criminal Code restrictions on abortions.

Andrews v. Law Society of B.C. [1989] ruled that equality should be determined among groups that are "similarly situated" and that prohibited discrimination may involve unintentional, systemic discrimination.

McKinney v. University of Guelph [1990] ruled that mandatory retirement was acceptable age discrimination.

R. v. Askov [1990] gave some limits to the "reasonable delay" allowed in bringing a matter to trial. This decision led to thousands of charges being dropped. The Court revisited the issue and gave more flexible guidelines in *R. v. Morin* [1992].

R. v. Sparrow [1990] set out important principles about the constitutional status of Aboriginal treaty rights.

Electoral Boundaries Reference [1991] decided that "the right to vote" included the right to

"effective representation," and so constituencies could vary in size only according to set limits.

Delgamuukw v. British Columbia [1997] laid down principles about the nature of Aboriginal title to land, particularly in the absence of a treaty.

Vriend v. Alberta [1998] declared that the Alberta *Individual Rights Protection Act* must be read to extend protection against discrimination to cover sexual orientation.

M. v. H. [1999] ruled that the statutory definition of "spouse" must allow for same-sex couples.

R. v. Sharpe [2001] ruled that while possession of child pornography is a crime, it could in some cases be allowed under the defence of "artistic merit."

Same-Sex Marriage Reference [2004] upheld the federal government's proposed law to allow same-sex marriage while refusing to answer whether the *Charter* required it.

Chaoulli v. Quebec [2005] declared that Quebec's prohibition against private health insurance violated the right to security of the person in Section 7 of the *Charter*.

Health Services and Support-Facilities Subsector Bargaining Association v. British Columbia [2007] overturned the 1997 Labour Trilogy and ruled that collective bargaining is indeed part of the freedom of association.

R. v. Willier [2010] decided in a 5–4 split that the right to counsel does not include the right to have a lawyer present during police questioning.

---

constitutional bills of rights. Over the years judges in various countries have given very different interpretations of what exactly is protected by phrases such as "the freedom of expression" or the "right to equality." The first instance of judges conducting such constitutional

review came in the 1803 case *Marbury v. Madison*, when the U.S. Supreme Court under Chief Justice Marshall declared a law unconstitutional.[10] This case marked a watershed in judicial power, as it was the first time a court anywhere successfully claimed the power to invalidate laws passed by the legislature; it is all the more remarkable since this power is found nowhere in the text of the American constitution. This vision of judicial review had been presaged by Lord Coke, chief justice of England's Court of Common Pleas, as early as 1610. In the famous *Dr. Bonham's Case*, Coke argued that the parliament's lawmaking power should be governed by the common law to be enforced by judges: "when an act of parliament is against common right and reason, or repugnant, or impossible to be performed, the common law will controul[sic] it, and adjudge such act to be void."[11] While this task of the courts seems logical and necessary if constitutional rights are to have practical substance, critics argue that judges end up acting as policymakers. This debate is worth looking at, since important issues are raised about the powers of the different branches of government and the rights of citizens. The task of constitutional review is viewed as sufficiently specialized in some countries (e.g., France and Germany) that they have a separate constitutional court to rule on the constitutionality of laws.

Those who defend judicial review on the grounds of protecting constitutional rights raise strong arguments. Just as judges must act as the referees of a federal–provincial division of powers, they also have to act as referees to sort out citizens' complaints that the government has infringed their rights in some fashion. While democratic governments do respect their citizens' rights most of the time through self-restraint, many people argue that the courts are still needed to protect the rights of individuals and minority groups which might be sacrificed by the will of the majority. To find a Canadian example of a group who suffered at the hands of the majority, one has only to think of the thousands of Japanese-Canadians rounded up during World War II and stripped of all their businesses and property. Little to no evidence has ever surfaced to show that any of these individuals would have posed any danger to Canada by siding with Japan during the war; indeed, the vast majority were people who had lived in Canada for years, for generations in many cases, and were ready to help Canada's war effort.

The courts provide impartial referees to determine the limits of government power and to protect rights. Judges are free from the electoral pressures that politicians face to placate their supporters and can therefore act as a brake upon hasty or oppressive actions by the government. The courtroom provides a forum for the different arguments to be made and weighed and for reasoned judgments to be delivered—judgments that either uphold the government's actions or strike them down in order to defend the rights of citizens. The surveys noted below have shown that Canadians would much rather have the courts than elected politicians decide on their rights.

Those who oppose judicial review of constitutional rights, however, also have substantial arguments on their side. First of all, some people have argued that a measure of a truly free society is that the people do not need to be protected from their government. Democracy means not just the rule of the majority, but also an accommodation of minority and individual interests along with those of the majority. The balance between the powers of government and the liberties of citizens swings over the course of time as circumstances and public opinion change. Ideally, the politicians who make the choice of this balance are not only elected but are accountable at future elections for their actions. A mature, established democracy such as Canada's learns from its experience and will draw a better balance over time.

But perhaps the most telling argument is that judges are simply not the impartial referees that the public believes them to be. Moreover, their judgments do not merely set the limits of government power— they legislate on crucial areas of such public policy as abortion, mandatory retirement, sexual behaviour, pornography, and union rights. Worse still, in this view, unelected judges sit in judgment on the decisions of the elected government, and those judges enforce their own personal policy preferences in ways for which the public can never hold them accountable. Several studies have shown that individual judges develop very different patterns of support for constitutional rights, with some judges characterized as more liberal (more likely to accept rights claims) and others more conservative (less likely to accept rights claims).[12] Indeed, one study of the Supreme Court of Canada in the 1980s found that the most liberal judge, Bertha Wilson, was more than twice as likely to accept a rights claim than the most conservative judge, William McIntyre. Furthermore, the outcomes of cases in which someone claimed their rights had been infringed were directly related to which group of judges heard the case.[13]

When the personal dispositions of judges come to bear in decisions on important social questions, it is argued, judges clearly are no longer simply interpreters of constitutional texts but active policymakers substituting their policy preferences for those of elected politicians.

In the end, the debate may really be one about the degree to which judges make social policy framed by their personal views rather than over whether it should be done. Indeed, a policymaking role is essentially unavoidable in interpreting constitutional rights. In order to define the practical application of the constitutional right to the freedom of expression, for example, judges have to decide whether sexually explicit material is protected in general and whether certain kinds (such as violent pornography or material involving children) can be prohibited. In deciding those kinds of questions, judges have to set the bounds of social policy. However, the question is how "activist" judges become in imposing their own preferences, as opposed to deferring to some degree to the policy choices made by elected politicians. The debate over **judicial activism** is not just an academic one; it gets to the heart of the relative powers of the judiciary, the legislature, and the executive. It is an issue of who sets limits on the powers of government and how accountable to the electorate those with political power should be in a democracy. One perspective on the matter is to view the relationship as a dialogue between the legislature and courts, with each taking turns to express their views on the proper balance of policy goals and civil rights.

Overall, Canadians seem quite aware of the power of the judiciary to set public policy priorities for the country. Most are content with the work of the courts, although their attitudes have evolved over recent years. An Ipsos-Reid poll in 2001 found that 60 percent of Canadians could name a particular Supreme Court case in the past year that stuck in their mind, and 70 percent approved of the court's work.[14] However, the Court has raised some controversies, which were revealed in a COMPAS poll in 2000. In that survey of public opinion, 43 percent of Canadians said they felt that the courts had taken too little power away from the elected politicians, while 28 percent said the courts had taken too much power.[15] These results are not surprising, given the high levels of trust that Canadians have in the judiciary. In a 2007 Léger poll, 74 percent of those surveyed said that they trust judges, while only 15 percent felt the same way about politicians.[16]

Such a wide disparity in reported levels of trust, however, may depend on the actual questions asked in the survey. When Canadians were asked a different question in another 2007 poll by Strategic Counsel, only 47 percent said they trusted the courts more than Parliament to serve their interests, while 37 percent trusted Parliament more.[17] Figure 10.6 shows 2010 poll results on how much power Canadians think major government institutions have and should have.

JUDICIAL APPOINTMENTS

Individuals come to judicial office in very different ways across the world. Judges can be appointed by the executive, nominated by the executive and confirmed by the legislature, chosen by other judges, or even elected (see Box 10.3).

In Canada, the provincial and federal governments appoint judges. Traditionally, **political patronage** played an enormous role in the choice of new judges. A government was most likely to appoint lawyers who were known supporters of the political party in power. The next largest pool of candidates was drawn from lawyers who worked for the government. Lawyers who were known to be active supporters of other political parties were almost never appointed. Patronage had several negative effects because it sometimes resulted in unsuitable or even incompetent individuals being appointed simply because the party in power owed them a favour. Highly qualified candidates might be completely overlooked simply because they supported opposition parties. Furthermore, there is the worry that candidates appointed because of their political connections might rule in favour of the ruling party in later cases that come before them.

> **Political patronage:** The awarding of benefits to individuals or companies based on their support for the governing political party.

Increasing resistance to political patronage grew in the early 1980s, and most governments in Canada have since revised their methods of selecting judges. While political patronage continues to a certain extent, it has been considerably reduced. Governments have been more focused on trying to appoint women and people

Figure 10.6 Canadian Views on Relative Power of Institutions

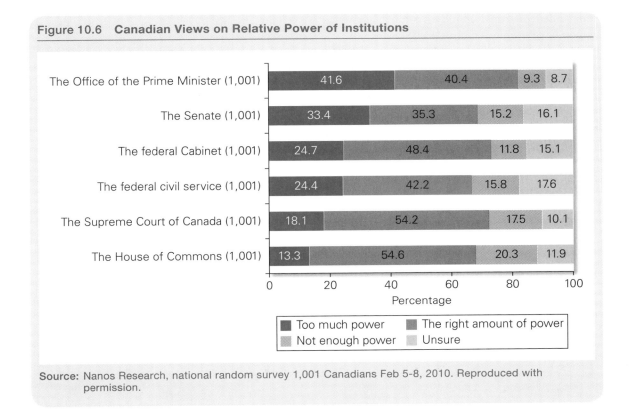

Source: Nanos Research, national random survey 1,001 Canadians Feb 5-8, 2010. Reproduced with permission.

WORLD EXAMPLES OF PROCESSES FOR SUPREME COURT APPOINTMENTS

A brief look around the world reveals many different ways to appoint judges to a country's highest court. A few are listed below with some examples of states that use the process.

- Some judges are appointed by the head of state and remain "at their pleasure," meaning judges can be fired for any reason: Guinea-Bissau.
- A number of states share the British process of appointment by the head of state, with the actual choice being made by the cabinet: Australia, Canada, Jamaica, and New Zealand.
- Judges may also be appointed by the head of state (usually the president) from a list of nominees approved by the national legislature: Indonesia.
- Some countries follow the American process where a legislative committee must approve the president's choice: Argentina, Brazil, and Mexico.
- The national legislature elects judges in some countries: Cuba, Nicaragua, and Switzerland.
- The judiciary can be responsible for selecting new judges, although the formal appointment may be by the head of state: France, Namibia, Philippines, and Romania.

from underrepresented ethnic or cultural groups, as support has grown for a more socially diverse judiciary. In many provinces, independent committees interview candidates and present the government with a ranked shortlist of candidates from which the government makes the appointment. In some cases, the Cabinet routinely selects only the top choice from that short list. A patronage scandal erupted in Quebec in 2010, with allegations by a former justice minister that a provincial Liberal Party fundraiser routinely interfered in choices for the bench. Premier Charest denied these charges and appointed a commission of inquiry which heard conflicting testimony from the premier and other officials. Even after the commission exonerated the premier, the Quebec public failed to believe Charest's refutations, and their disenchantment was reflected in a poll that revealed 68 percent of Quebecois supported electing judges instead.[18]

Although the federal government was one of the first in Canada to institute independent committees to screen candidates, it has stopped far short of the provincial reforms. The committees could only classify potential candidates into three broad groups: highly recommended, recommended, and "unable to recommend." The government uses the results of the committee work as guidance, but it is free to select individuals from any of these groups. As a result, patronage continues to flourish in federal judicial appointments. For example, among the first 30 individuals federal Justice Minister Irwin Cotler chose to appoint to the bench in 2004–2005, one-third had contributed to the Liberal Party or its candidates in the two years before

A government can steer the direction of a court by appointing judges with ideological preferences.

Michael de Adder/Artizans

their appointments. This number is more alarming when one considers that a third of those appointed were in professions where political donations could not normally be made (judges and senior civil servants). Thus, one-half of those eligible to make donations had donated to the Liberals, while none had donated to any other party.[19] The Conservative government was also accused of making patronage appointments after taking office in 2006. They abandoned the distinction between highly recommended and recommended and changed the composition of regional judicial appointment committees to include police representatives, which opponents argue is meant to inject a law-and-order bias into the screening process that would help propel conservatively minded candidates to the top. Since executive discretion still leads to patronage in federal judicial appointments, it is highly desirable to adopt a merit-based system like those in place in many Canadian provinces.

Supreme Court of Canada judges are singular exceptions in the federal government's patronage appointments. While known partisans have been appointed, they have been the exception over the past 50 years. The federal government consults widely with bar societies and other individuals, organizations, and governments in the provinces when vacancies for the Supreme Court occur. See Box 10.4 on p. 268 for a review of the processes followed for selecting Supreme Court judges since 2005.

There are some important differences in the way in which judges come to office in the United States.[20] Federally appointed judges are nominated by the president but have to be approved by the Senate. Potential members of the Supreme Court even have to face days of questioning in a Senate committee before it decides whether to confirm their appointment, and in a number of high-profile cases the Senate refused to confirm the President's choice. The general political and legal philosophy of the nominees is one of the prime considerations in the appointment of Supreme Court justices, as Americans use the appointment process to try to steer the policy direction of the Supreme Court. Over a period of time, a court that has been dominated by more liberal judges can be reshaped with the deliberate appointment of more conservative individuals to the court, and vice versa. This process is known as *stacking the court.*

It is important to note that judges are elected in many of the individual U.S. states. Supporters of judicial elections believe modern democracy requires important public decision-makers, including judges, to be elected. This method of selecting judges bears some discussion, since an increasing number of Canadians think judges should be elected; 48 percent of Canadians surveyed felt judges should be elected in 2002, but by 2007 judicial elections were supported by 63 percent.[21] Judges in the U.S. usually run under party banners and campaign on their general ideas about how justice should be served. In some jurisdictions, judges cannot run for re-election, but in many they can. The election of judges makes quite explicit the notion discussed earlier in this chapter that judges have to enforce values that reflect the dominant beliefs in their society. While elections do provide a direct democratic mandate for judicial power, they present troubling challenges to judicial impartiality. Judges may be tempted to settle cases in a particular way in order to carry out their general election promises, and justice in individual cases may be sacrificed to the judge's determination to demonstrate a consistent pattern of sentencing. Especially where judges can run for re-election, they need to be able to tell the voters that they acted according to the promises they made in the previous election. Furthermore, there is a potential problem with the degree to which individual judges owe favours to those who financed or worked on their election campaigns. Box 10.5 on p. 268 provides a report of the issues that arise when special-interest groups provide election funds to judges competing in an election.

Most countries in Western Europe take quite a different approach to the recruitment of judges. Essentially, being a judge is a professional career. Individuals interested in becoming judges go to special training institutes or universities and take years of courses related to law and the work of judges. The actual selection of new judges from these candidates is done by the judiciary itself. In addition, the judiciary is considered to be a career of advancement, in which people start on the most junior-level tribunal. In theory, the most competent are selected by senior judges to be promoted through levels of increasingly important courts. This model of appointment and promotion certainly avoids the problems of political patronage seen in Canada and the potential for popularity-seeking judges in American judicial elections. However, the European model is criticized for

BOX 10.4

SUPREME COURT OF CANADA APPOINTMENTS

For decades, political actors have debated ways to reform the way in which judges are appointed to the Supreme Court of Canada. Historically, the federal justice minister and prime minister chose individuals after informal, private consultations. The ill-fated Charlottetown Accord proposals for constitutional change would have been the first substantial reform of the appointment process. The Accord would have required the federal government to choose new appointees from a shortlist of candidates submitted by the provincial governments when a vacancy opened up on the Court. The focus of debate was to include the provincial governments formally in the process of selection.

In recent years, the debate has shifted more to the "democratization" of the appointment process, to include some meaningful role for elected members of parliament to consider potential appointments. With the growing political role of the Supreme Court, many feel that appointments should no longer be made in secret by the executive. Some believe that a parliamentary committee should interview nominees before their appointment, although perhaps not with the veto power of their American counterparts. Others, including sitting and retired Supreme Court judges, have argued that this invites a political spectacle and would discourage suitable individuals from accepting the position.

In April 2005, then federal Justice Minister Irwin Cotler announced a new process that included formal participation by parliamentarians as well as representatives of the provincial governments, while still retaining the final choice for the federal executive. In the new process, the justice minister would consult privately to produce a list of five to eight nominees whose files would be reviewed by an advisory committee. This committee would consist of an MP from every official party in the House of Commons, a retired judge, a nominee of the provincial governments where a vacancy is occurring, a representative from the local bar society, and two "eminent lay people" chosen by the federal justice minister. The committee would narrow the list of nominees down to three, from whom the federal cabinet would choose the actual appointee. After making the choice, the justice minister would appear before the House of Commons Justice Committee to explain and defend his or her choice of new judge.

The process to replace Justice John Major was interrupted by the 2006 federal election, after which the new Conservative government finalized the appointment. On that occasion, the justice minister appeared before an ad hoc committee of parliamentarians to explain his choice of candidate for the court, since Parliament was officially dissolved at the time. The chosen candidate, Marshall Rothstein, also appeared before the committee in a nationally televised hearing chaired by Peter Hogg, Professor Emeritus of Osgoode Hall Law School. While unprecedented, this appearance was criticized by many because the ad hoc committee was severely constrained in the kind of questions that could be put to Mr. Rothstein, and the appointment was to proceed regardless of the outcome of the hearing.

This process was not followed in December 2008, when the Prime Minister announced the appointment of Thomas Cromwell. He did so while Parliament was prorogued for two months. But Mr. Harper announced that he had consulted with the Leader of the Opposition prior to deciding that the vacancy required immediate filling. He declared that he intended to return to the process of holding parliamentary hearings in the future. In 2011, the Conservative government announced yet another selection process for two simultaneous Supreme Court appointments. After the Minister of Justice engaged in widespread confidential consultations, he assembled an ad hoc committee of five MPs to select an initial short-list of six candidates. The government then chose two candidates to be publicly interviewed by a parliamentary committee before being officially appointed by the prime minister.

BOX 10.5

JUDICIAL ELECTIONS AND SPECIAL-INTEREST FUNDING

NEW YORK, NY—Although pro-business special interest groups out-spent progressive interest groups by more than nine to one on television advertising in Supreme Court elections this year, progressive groups had a higher electoral success rate than did their political foes, said two national watchdog groups. All five candidates who benefited from television advertising by progressive groups won election, but only 71 percent of candidates for whom pro-business groups sponsored ads won a seat on the bench.

The highest spending interest group, the Safety and Prosperity Coalition—a Georgia group that received the majority of its funding from the American Justice Partnership, an arm of the National Association of Manufacturers—spent more than $1.3 million on advertisements that supported Mike Wiggins and attacked his opponent, incumbent Justice Carol Hunstein. The Republican Party spent an additional $550,000 to support Mr. Wiggins. Justice Hunstein sponsored her own advertising, spending $960,000. Despite being outspent almost two to one on the air, she defeated her opponent with 63 percent of the vote.

"When special interest groups become so heavily involved in judicial races, citizens conclude that judges answer to constituencies rather than the law," said James Sample, counsel at the Brennan Center for Justice at NYU School of Law. "It is heartening to see, however, that this year many voters were not swayed by special interest advertisements."

In Washington State, where special interest groups sponsored 100 percent of the 2006 advertising in the state's supreme court races, two pro-business groups outspent the opposition almost four to one, but the candidate they supported, John Groen, lost by almost 10 percentage points to incumbent Chief Justice Gerry Alexander.

Pro-business groups did succeed in helping their chosen candidates win in Michigan, Ohio, and Alabama. In Michigan incumbent Justice Maura Corrigan won with the assistance of an ad sponsored by the Michigan Chamber of Commerce. The Partnership for Ohio's Future—which shares a mailing address and has key overlapping staff members with the Ohio Chamber of Commerce—successfully assisted incumbent Justice Terrence O'Donnell and Robert Cupp in election to the state's highest court.

In Alabama, the American Taxpayers Alliance—a group that receives at least some of its funding from the U.S. Chamber of Commerce and electric utility companies—spent $721,236 to support incumbent Chief Justice Drayton Nabers and $271,844 to support incumbent Justice Lyn Stuart in their primary battles. Nabers won his primary, but lost to Sue Bell Cobb in the general election, in which he received no special interest assistance with television advertisements.

"As hardball TV ads infect more judicial campaigns around the country, it's time for every state that elects judges to take steps to reduce special interest pressure on the courts," said Bert Brandenburg, executive director of Justice at Stake.

Source: Brennan Center, "Despite High Spending, Special Interest Groups Not Entirely Successful in Supreme Court Elections." Accessed <http://www.brennancenter.org/content/resource/despite_high_spending_special_interest_groups_not_entirely_successful_in_su> (4 August 2011). Reprinted under Creative Commons Attribution-No Derivs-NonCommercial license.

creating an insular and self-perpetuating elite. And it is interesting to note that Figure 10.4 on p. 270 shows public confidence in the judicial system is stunningly low in France, which has a typically European self-recruiting judiciary.

As each of the systems has its strengths and weaknesses, a central concern is trying to balance the selection of suitable, competent individuals on the one hand with the means to ensure that judges reflect a society's diversity and prevailing mores on the other.

Another issue is the degree to which a country's elected politicians should steer the policymaking function of the courts by deliberately choosing new judges who are sympathetic to the politicians' preferred direction of public policy. Those against such intentional policy steering through appointments argue that it can severely undermine judicial impartiality. In this view, one should simply seek intelligent, competent individuals and leave them to develop their own judicial personalities over time, settling specific cases as they think best. Those who support a more deliberate, ideological selection of new judges argue that the public must recognize the enormous role the judges have in shaping **public policy**. The foundation of democracy is that the will of the people should be the guiding principle of all government power. Thus, the public's elected representatives have a responsibility to choose new judges who reflect the policy directions that the public prefers.

JUDICIAL INDEPENDENCE AND IMPARTIALITY

An independent and impartial judiciary is essential to the proper functioning of a democracy. Without independence from other branches of government, judges simply become a tool for enforcing the policies of the government of the day. Judges must be impartial in order for the public to have confidence that they will decide cases on the basis of the facts of the case and the relevant law.

Judicial independence refers to the relationship of the judiciary to the legislature and the executive and means that judges can do their work without interference from politicians, bureaucrats, and other government officials, such as the police or the military. Judicial independence in the sense discussed here is unknown in authoritarian political systems, where judges work under the supremacy of the government party and are "subject to constant party control, supervision, and accountability."[22] Old ways die hard, and some of the post-communist states in Eastern Europe, such as Moldava, have returned to what the International Commission of Jurists calls "telephone justice," with judges routinely expecting and receiving phone calls from cabinet ministers giving directions on how to decide a case of particular interest to the government.[23] The fundamental difficulty is that some governments view the courts as just another government department rather than an independent institution. As such, they expect judges to do what the government wants them to do. Unfortunately, this can mean that judges become active participants in repressing dissent or facilitating corruption.

> **Judicial independence:** A relationship between the courts and the other branches of government that allows judges to function without interference from other government officials.

The Supreme Court of Canada has laid down some important aspects of the relationship between the courts and the other branches of government that underlie judicial independence. In *R. v. Valente* the court said that judges must have security of tenure, financial independence, and administrative independence.[24] Security of tenure means that judges cannot be removed from office simply because the government does not approve of their decisions; they should hold office until retirement or for a set period of time and should be removed only for major misbehaviour, incompetence, or incapacity. It is imperative for judges not to be able to be fired if they try to enforce constitutional limits on the government. In a brazen attack on judicial independence, Fiji's President Ratu Josefa Iloilo dismissed the country's top judges in 2009, a day after they ruled that his regime had illegitimately assumed office after a coup in 2006. As a result, the Fijian government ended up hiring lawyers from Sri Lanka to fill their judicial benches. Financial independence requires that judges need not fear having their pay cut if the government does not like their decisions and that judges have no incentive to try to curry favour by siding with the government in the hopes that their pay will be increased. Administrative independence means that the scheduling of cases and assignment of individual judges to particular cases is done by the judiciary itself; this prevents the government from ensuring a favourable outcome to a case by arranging for a "friendly" judge to hear it. These considerations are not just limited to Canada; the Indian government took an important step in 2004 by handing over financial and administrative control of the lower courts from the Ministry of Justice and Human Rights to the Supreme Court.

Judicial impartiality refers to a state of mind in which judges settle cases without applying their pre-existing biases in favour of or against the people or issues involved. While impartiality is difficult to define, its essence implies that judges maintain an open mind to arguments about the facts and the proper interpretation of the law before deciding the outcome of the case. It is important to bear in mind that impartiality cannot mean a total absence of pre-conceived ideas or predispositions, something that is not only humanly impossible but also probably undesirable. There would be little public confidence in the judiciary if judges did not express or act on established biases against the horrors of murder and rape or the outrage of con men who defraud senior citizens of all their savings.

> **Judicial impartiality:** A state of mind in which judges preside over and decide cases with an open mind toward the parties and issues involved.

Concerns about judicial independence and impartiality extend well beyond the relationship between the courts and the other branches of government. Judges must also be protected from pressures from the general public, interest groups, unions, and business. If judges bow to pressures not to decide a case the "wrong" way, or anticipate rewards if they decide a case the "right" way, there can be no assurance that judges will act impartially. At the same time, the requirements of judicial impartiality also place restrictions on how judges behave on and off the bench. Canadian judges have been forced to resign because they openly socialized with figures known in organized crime circles, because they have donated money to support the election of particular politicians or political parties, or because they have been convicted of a criminal offence. In these instances, the public could not have confidence that the judges would be free from major biases.

Threats to judicial impartiality and independence come in many forms. Controversy has been stirred several times by cabinet ministers talking to judges about cases the judges have under consideration.

For example, Jean Charest resigned from Brian Mulroney's government in 1990 after it became known that he had telephoned a judge. As serious as such direct attempts to influence judges may be in Canada, they pale in comparison to other examples from around the world. Judges in Colombia and Italy live with constant police escorts because of threats to their lives from organized crime. And Italian judges fought an ongoing battle with Prime Minister Silvio Berlusconi, who has been investigated and convicted on corruption charges several times, only to have his convictions overturned on appeal. Berlusconi has claimed that left-wing judges are persecuting him and declared he would remove police protection for judges. Hundreds of Italy's judges went on a brief strike in late 2001 to protest against a move they believed was intended to bully them into leaving Berlusconi and his associates alone. A more graphic example of intimidation of judges occurred in Indonesia, where former President Suharto's son, Tommy, was sentenced in 2001—a couple of years after his father was forced from office—to 18 months in jail on corruption charges. Shortly afterward, the judge who upheld the sentence was gunned down; unsurprisingly, perhaps, the Indonesian supreme court acquitted Tommy Suharto of the original charges three months after the murder. However, Suharto was charged in early 2002 with contracting the judge's murder, in a move that was widely seen as a test of the success of new President Megawati Sukarnoputri's ability to restore confidence in the country's judicial system.

Judicial impartiality and independence also require judges to distance themselves from becoming involved in political debates and activities outside the courtroom. In a famous case in Canada, the Canadian Judicial Council reprimanded Judge Thomas Berger for having made a public speech criticizing Prime Minister Trudeau's constitutional reform package that led to the *Constitution Act*, 1982. Berger had complained that the constitutional reforms were put together without consultation with the Aboriginal leaders and without any attempt to redress their many grievances. Judges have to walk a fine line in commenting on issues of public interest without compromising the public's perception that they can still rule impartially on related issues, should these end up in their own courtroom.

As important as judicial independence and impartiality are, however, these principles still operate within limits. Although an important aspect of judicial independence and impartiality holds that judges should be able to decide cases without fear that they may lose their jobs, it is also clear that there are limits on what the public and the government will tolerate in judicial decisions. Judge Raymond Bartlett was removed from the Nova Scotia Family Court in 1987 because he frequently quoted the Bible in court and told women appearing before him that they should be subservient to their husbands. Neither of these actions would have been all that remarkable a hundred years ago, but they were considered to be unacceptable in the late 20th century. While judges are supposedly free to behave and decide cases as they think best, they cannot simply follow their personal views regardless of how out-of-step they are with prevailing values in their society. In the end, judges may lead or lag behind public opinion to a certain extent, but they will face pressures to resign or be removed if they act too far beyond prevailing mores—even in democratic countries that espouse judicial independence and impartiality.

The Personal Values of Judges Can Shape Their Decisions

While good judges can deliberately set aside many of their personal views in any particular decision, it is all but impossible not to be influenced by some of their basic beliefs on an ongoing basis. As a result, judges tend to develop distinctive patterns in their handling of cases that reflect their own underlying personal values. Like everybody else, judges are products of the socialization processes in their own upbringing. While the settled aspects of the law provide boundaries in many cases, judges have to exercise their personal discretion in many ways as they hear and decide a case before them. Questions of credibility—whose story a judge believes—are entirely discretionary and can be influenced in many subconscious ways by each judge's personal beliefs, likes, and dislikes. Judges often have considerable leeway in deciding what penalty or settlement to impose, and inevitably these decisions hinge to some extent on a judge's personal belief in what is right and appropriate. Box 10.6 provides a hypothetical example and asks you to judge the judge's decision.

BOX 10.6

YOU JUDGE THE JUDGES

What limits would you place on judicial impartiality and the ability of judges to settle cases as they see best? In theory, judges should feel free to express themselves and decide cases without fearing that they will lose their jobs simply because their decisions are unpopular. However, consider the following hypothetical case and ask yourself if you believe the judge should be removed from office.

Judge Smith hears a case in which a person is accused under Canada's *Anti-Terrorism Act* of having plotted to blow up the pipeline carrying oil to the United States; the man was arrested before the attack was carried out. At his trial, the accused states that he was motivated to do this because U.S. corporations are pillaging the environment around the world all for the sake of profits for their shareholders. He wanted to strike a blow against U.S. capitalism by trying to cut off some of their oil.

The judge acquits the man on the grounds that he was exercising his rights under the *Charter* to the freedom of conscience and expression. The judge notes that no actual attack had occurred. And Judge Smith then goes on to say that the accused had been justified in highlighting the fact that the U.S. economy is dripping with the blood of poor people around the world, whose virtual slavery is essential to providing cheap goods for voracious American consumers.

Because of the potential for personal background to play a role in judicial decision-making, concern has arisen about the social composition of the judiciary. The historical pattern in all countries has been for males of the dominant social classes and ethnic groups to fill the bench. Academics and social activists have long been concerned that this leads to an institution that embodies and enforces the values of the predominant group or groups. As a result, there have been strong calls in recent decades for the judiciary to become more socially diverse. In established liberal democracies such as Canada there has been a deliberate policy in the past two decades to try and appoint more women and people of underrepresented social groups to the bench. Even so, critics argue that the underrepresentation of women and ethnic minorities in Canadian courts creates a **democratic deficit**.[25]

> **Democratic deficit:** The perceived gap between the theoretical principles of democracy and the actual practice of ostensibly democratic institutions, including national governments and international organizations.

Social and gender diversity among judges is important, at least symbolically, in a modern democracy that espouses women's equality and multiculturalism. But does or should this diversity make a practical difference to the kinds of decisions made by the courts and the values they enforce? There are many who say that a socially diverse judiciary does act differently from an exclusively white middle-class one, and they would add that this is a good thing. Modern democratic societies should not have paternalistic and ethnocentric values perpetuated by the courts, as they had in the past. Cultural sensitivity must be embodied in judicial decisions, and what better way for that to occur than to have members from different cultural groups both deciding cases directly and acting as an educational influence on their fellow judges? Furthermore, the diverse groups within a society will have more confidence in the quality of justice delivered by the courts if members of their own groups are judges too. In fact, a number of academic studies reveal measurable differences, although not large ones, between male and female judges, and between African-American and Caucasian judges.

However, the degree to which individual judges may decide cases differently because of their sex and cultural or social background poses a challenge for those who believe that law should be interpreted and enforced as impartially as possible. In theory at least, justice can be properly served only if there is a general uniformity in the ways in which judges apply the law to similar cases.

An important point related to the personal discretion of judges is their fallibility—they can make wrong decisions. In Canada, at least a dozen people in recent decades have been finally exonerated after spending many years in jail for rapes or murders they did not commit. For example, William Mullins-Johnson was awarded $4.5 million in compensation in 2010 after having spent 12 years in jail for the murder of his niece; he had been convicted largely because of faulty testimony by a pathologist. In the United States the consequences of wrongful convictions can be much more serious; 139 people have been freed from death row since 1973, 17 of them after DNA evidence played a crucial role in establishing their innocence.[26] The police occasionally mismanage an investigation, discriminate, lie, or encourage other witnesses to lie, but judges ultimately have to decide for themselves who is telling the truth. Sometimes judges simply believe a liar's testimony. For this reason, the judicial system has to be sensitive to the possibility of convicting innocent people. As Sir William Blackstone wrote in 1765, "it is better that ten guilty persons escape than that one innocent suffer."[27]

Discipline and Removal of Judges

The discipline and removal of judges from office raises a number of complex issues. While there can be no independence for judges if they can be fired simply for offending other political actors, there also has to be some way to remove judges who engage in criminal acts or otherwise bring the administration of justice into fundamental disrepute. Both the grounds for removal and the process to be followed can have a profound impact on the independence of the judiciary and the quality of justice in a society.

Who gets to remove judges from office, and for what reasons, varies a great deal around the world. In military regimes, where the military command or president can remove a judge for almost any reason, there is no protection for judges who displease powerful authorities on policy grounds. At the other end of the spectrum is France, where all matters of judicial discipline are handled within the judiciary and there is no role for either the executive or the legislature to play at all. Many countries fall somewhere in the middle, with a mixture of involvement by the three branches of government.

Historically in Britain, the monarchs could remove judges from office whenever they felt offended by what a judge said or did. To protect the judges from such arbitrary removal by the monarch, the British parliament passed the *Act of Settlement* in 1701; after this date, judges could be removed from office only after a parliamentary resolution. The *Act* established the principle, since followed in most common law systems founded on the British model, that judges hold office during "good behaviour," which actually means that judges can be removed for "misbehaviour." It also ensured the supremacy of parliament over the other branches of government and protected judges from being removed on the whim of the executive. The specific grounds for removal, however, are open to considerable interpretation. In general, judges can be removed for failing to perform their duties or behaving in a way that fundamentally undermines the public's confidence in their ability to perform their duties. Those judges who frequently fail to appear for their court sessions or behave completely irrationally in the courtroom can be removed. But there are also wide grounds for removal for behaving in ways that are incompatible with being a judge. For example, Robert Flahiff was forced to resign from the Quebec Superior Court after being convicted of money laundering, and Ronald MacDonald had to resign from the Nova Scotia Provincial Court after being convicted of assaulting his wife.

Canada inherited the British process, and federally appointed judges can be removed from office only by the Governor General after the passage of a joint address by both houses of Parliament.[28] A trend has emerged in recent decades to distance elected politicians from both the formulation of codes of judicial conduct and the actual removal process. The tendency has been to give judges increasing control over the discipline of their colleagues. This distancing is based on a concern for the independence of judges and the belief that politics should not play a role in the disciplinary process. In all Canadian jurisdictions, complaints about judges are first dealt with either by the normal courts or by an independent judicial council. While this may be viewed as a positive development in general, it does raise the possible problem of a public perception that judges might either "protect their own" or enforce a set of values that are not in step with the prevailing public beliefs. In stark terms, the judges' "old boys' club" might protect its members from the outside world. For this reason, several provinces have included lay members from the public on their judicial councils. However, the Canadian Judicial Council that oversees federally appointed judges is composed entirely of judges.

The United States has moved away from the involvement of the legislature in judicial removal proceedings as well. Although the U.S. Constitution states that Congress can impeach judges, a new process was developed in 1980 to provide for a judicial commission to investigate and rule on judicial misbehaviour. This model is also widespread at the state level in the United States. These judicial commissions have been quite active, with New York's removing 60 of its 3,500 state judges between 1979 and 1985.[29]

While there is no controversy in removing judges who commit criminal offences, much more debate arises when judges make controversial statements that enrage or offend the public. For example, the Canadian Judicial Council recommended the removal of Justice Jean Bienvenue in 1996 when it found that the "judge's remarks about women and his deep-seated ideas behind those remarks legitimately cast doubt on his impartiality in the execution of his judicial office."[30] However, seven of the 29 members of the council voted against removal on the grounds that Bienvenue's comments were simply reflective of a bygone era and that sensitivity training would be a more appropriate remedy. A central issue is whether judicial independence should protect judges from being removed because they offend contemporary social mores.

In the end, the limits on judicial behaviour are as difficult to define as they are important to a healthy system of government. The crucial role that judges play is founded upon the general authority they have in the public eye, which in turn is based on the belief that judges act impartially to enforce the values of their society. Failure to remove individual judges can erode the public's deference to the courts' authority. In some respects, there is real merit in the elected representatives of the public having a substantive role to play in at least establishing the grounds for removing judges, as the limits on judicial behaviour are then set by people who are both representative of and accountable to the general public. In Canada, a compromise has been reached on the removal process of superior court judges. The Canadian Judicial Council, composed of senior judges across the country, must first investigate complaints about judicial behaviour. If it deems the situation serious enough, it can recommend to Parliament that a judge be removed. As judges play a more visible policymaking role, however, they have come under increasing pressures to be held accountable for their judgments and speeches. There is a danger that the discipline process is used to remove or pressure judges simply because their actions or words are politically unpalatable. And the essence of judicial independence is that judges should be free to make the decision they feel is best without fear of recriminations as a result of its unpopularity.

ACCESS TO THE COURTS

The effectiveness of the courts in their various roles can depend to a large degree on how courts function and who has access to them in practice. Several ongoing weaknesses can be identified in the courts that undermine the potential they have in a society. First and foremost, the courts are essentially passive institutions. As mentioned, judges do not go out and seek legal problems to solve or disputes to settle. Instead, they have to wait for someone to decide to take an issue to the courts. Significant disputes may go unresolved because those involved either cannot or do not want to go to court. This inability or unwillingness to take a dispute to court may arise from the prohibitive costs of a court case, or may be based on a belief that disputes should be settled outside the formal court setting. Just how equal the access to the courts is for all segments of a society has a great bearing on the kind of justice the courts can provide.

The cost barrier is a central weakness of courts as social and political institutions. The legal system and judicial processes are complex, and anyone involved

in a court case should really have a professional lawyer to conduct his or her case. In Canada, a relatively short and simple criminal case can cost several hundred to several thousand dollars, so it may cost less to plead guilty than to fight the charges through a full trial. Parties who fail to win their case in the first instance have to decide whether to appeal. But the cost of taking a case before a provincial court of appeal starts at around $25,000 to $50,000. Parties determined to take their case to the Supreme Court of Canada for final resolution can expect to spend at least $150,000 on the simplest case, but more complex cases will cost well over $1 million. Indeed recent complex criminal trials have involved enormous expenses, so huge that governments have sometimes had to pay for defence costs. For example, the BC government paid almost $12 million to the lawyers defending serial killer Robert Pickton.[31] Clearly these are costs that cannot be afforded by the average person. Governments in most liberal democracies have legal aid programs in place to help pay for the cases of the poorest members of their society. However, the limited budgets and personnel available significantly undermine the quality of representation a person can expect. Only some people benefit from paid legal counsel, and a lucky few have their cases appealed to the final court. The rich, of course, can afford to hire the most expensive legal teams and carry their cases up to the top court. In the middle are many people who either have to use up their savings or decide that, while they can finance the first court hearing, they cannot afford to appeal if they lose. A question then arises about how many innocent people are jailed simply because they could not afford a good lawyer or enough of the lawyer's time to mount a proper defence, or because they were not able to appeal an initial verdict that found them guilty.

The problem is even worse outside of the criminal law. Private cases are notorious for lengthy delays and high costs; the time and costs involved in suing a neighbour, a relative, or a business may be prohibitive. This is a particular issue in countries where losers in a private court case have to pay for the legal fees of the person they sued, in addition to their own. The quality of legal services to people of poor and modest incomes is a special concern in family law cases. When couples part or divorce, they need to divide the matrimonial property and decide on their access to and financial obligations for child and spousal support. High-quality legal representation is crucial in these proceedings, as the outcomes of these cases can have repercussions for years. One strong criticism of the cost of court access is that it unfairly affects women in family law disputes. Usually the men involved have higher incomes and more assets at the time of the marital breakup and can therefore afford better lawyers and more of the lawyer's time than women. As a result, men generally have much higher living standards several years after a divorce than do women, who more often than not have to care for their children. In 2002, British Columbia's attorney general, Geoff Plant, was formally censured by the Law Society of British Columbia because of dramatic cutbacks to legal aid services. Earlier in the year, he had announced that legal aid would no longer be available for most family law disputes, including divorce. Legal aid can now be used only if there is a question of physical danger or in cases wherein children are taken into protective custody.

Justice is supposed to be blind to the participants: the rich and poor are supposed to have equal consideration in the courts. However, the reality of the judicial process is that justice often falls very short of the mark. As legal aid programs are squeezed by government cutbacks and as court costs escalate, many people are left without fully prepared lawyers to argue their cases. Legal aid is seldom available for serious civil cases beyond family matters.

CONCLUSION

All states rely on law to structure their societies, with the policies and mores of the dominant elite groups embodied within them. The courts have a crucial role to play, particularly in democratic countries, in interpreting and enforcing the law. Democratic regimes require independent and impartial courts to act as fair adjudicators of disputes and gain public support and deference. In practice, however, both the institutional independence and personal impartiality of judges are limited. The selection and appointment of judges can be done in several different ways, and a country's choice of a particular process can provide the elected politicians with an opportunity to steer the general policy direction of the courts. Control over the discipline and removal of judges provide firm limits on the behaviour of judges, and there is controversy over the role that politicians should play both in setting the rules for judges and in effecting their removal. Judges inevitably have an important policymaking role to play in interpreting laws and in their exercise of the powers of judicial review.

DISCUSSION QUESTIONS

1. Do you believe that it is important to have all the major social and ethnic groups represented in a country's judiciary? If so, do you believe it is because members of these groups will decide cases differently?

2. Do you trust judges to enforce your rights more than you trust politicians to respect them? What is the basis for your answer—is it just a gut feeling, or do you have specific reasons?

3. What limits, if any, would you place on the independence and impartiality of judges?

4. Do you think judges should be elected so that they have a democratic mandate to conduct their work?

5. Would you be prepared to sell everything you own in order to afford a lawyer to defend you against a criminal charge that of which you know you are not guilty? Does the severity of the charge matter?

FURTHER READING

Devlin, Patrick. *Judges.* Oxford: Oxford University Press, 1988.

Gall, Gerald L. *The Canadian Legal System,* 4th ed. Toronto: Carswell, 1995.

Green, Ian. *The Courts.* Vancouver: UBC Press, 2006.

Hiebert, Janet. *Charter Conflicts: What Is Parliament's Role?* Kingston, ON: McGill-Queen's University Press, 2002.

MacIvor, Heather. *Canadian Politics and Government in the Charter Era.* Toronto: Thomson Nelson, 2006.

Manfredi, Christopher P. *Judicial Power and the Charter: Canada and the Paradox of Liberal Constitutionalism*, 2nd ed. Don Mills: Oxford University Press, 2001.

Morton, F.L. *Law, Politics and the Judicial Process in Canada*, 3rd ed. Calgary: University of Calgary Press, 2002.

Russell, Peter H. *The Judiciary in Canada: The Third Branch of Government.* Toronto: McGraw-Hill Ryerson, 1987.

Waddams, S.M. *Introduction to the Study of Law*, 7th ed. Scarborough: Carswell, 2010.

ENDNOTES

1. During World War II, all Japanese Canadians were interned and had their property disposed of; many German and Italian Canadians were also interned, as were German and Ukrainian Canadians during World War I.

2. Konye Obaji Ori, "Nigeria: Sharia Law Takes Precedence Over Freedom of speech," *Afrik-News*, March 25, 2010, available at http://www.afrik-news.com/article17221.html; accessed November 15, 2010.

3. *Vladi v. Vladi*, (1987) 79 N.S.R. (2d) 356 at para. 31 (N.S.S.C.T.D.).

4. *Boumediene v. Bush*, 553 U.S. 723 (2008).

5. Peta Thornycroft, "Pro-Mugabe Judges Rule Land Grabs Are Legal," *National Post*, October 2001, p. A15. For more background, see also Angus Shaw, "Zimbabwe Court Allows Seizures of White Farmland," *The Independent*, October 3, 2001, available at http://www.independent.co.uk/news/world/africa/zimbabwe-court-allows-seizures-of-white-farmland-630067.html, accessed June 13, 2008; Andrew Meldrum, "Supreme Court Justice Defies Mugabe Threat," *The*

Guardian, February 10, 2001, available at http://www.guardian.co.uk/international/story/0,3604,436086,00.html, accessed June 13, 2008; and British Broadcasting Corporation, "Mugabe Challenges Supreme Court," February 8, 1999, available at http://news.bbc.co.uk/hi/english/world/africa/newsid_274000/274262.stm, accessed June 13, 2008.

6. *Reference re Resolution to Amend the Constitution*, [1981] 1 S.C.R. 753; *Reference re Secession of Quebec*, [1998] 2 S.C.R. 217.

7. *Brown v. Board of Education*, [1954] 347 U.S. 493; *Baker v. Carr*, [1962] 369 U.S. 186.

8. *Bush v. Gore*, [2000] 531 U.S. 98.

9. For example, see Alan M. Dershowitz, *Supreme Injustice: How the High Court Hijacked Election* 2000 (New York: Oxford University Press, 2001); David K. Ryden, ed., *The U.S. Supreme Court and the Electoral Process*, 2nd ed. (Washington: Georgetown University Press, 2002).

10. This case is discussed in Henry J. Abraham, *The Judiciary: The Supreme Court in the Governmental Process*, 8th ed. (Dubuque, IA: Wm. C. Brown, 1991), pp. 59–62.

11. 8 Co. Rep. 107a, 114a C.P. 1610; available at http://press-pubs.uchicago.edu/founders/documents/amendV_due_processs1.html; accessed June 13, 2008. Lord Coke's notion was never acted upon by British judges.

12. For example, see F.L. Morton, Peter H. Russell, and Troy Riddell, "The Canadian Charter of Rights and Freedoms: A Descriptive Analysis of the First Decade, 1982–1992," *National Journal of Constitutional Law* 5 (1994): 1.

13. Andrew Heard, "The Charter in the Supreme Court of Canada: The Importance of Which Judges Hear an Appeal," *Canadian Journal of Political Science* 24 (1991): 289.

14. Ipsos-Reid, "Canadian Supreme Decisions: Public's View of the Supreme Court," July 4, 2001; available at http://www.ipsos-na.com/ news/pressrelease.cfm?id=1257; accessed June 13, 2008.

15. COMPAS, "The Power of Judges," February 18, 2000, available at http://www.compas.ca/html/ archives/powerjudges_surv.html;accessed July 1, 2001.

16. Léger Marketing, "Profession Barometer," May 15, 2007, p. 3, available at http://www. legermarketing.com/documents/spclm/ 070522ENG.pdf; accessed June 13, 2008.

17. Strategic Counsel, "Canadian Charter of Rights and Freedoms," March 21, 2007, p. 10, available at http://www.thestrategiccounsel.com/ our_news/polls/2007-03-21%20GMCTV%20 CharterofRights%20Mar%2010-13.pdf, accessed June 13, 2008.

18. Angus Reid, "A Majority of Quebecers Continue to Believe Bellemare, Not Charest," September 27, 2010, p. 8, available at http://www.visioncritical.com/wp-content/ uploads/2010/09/2010.09.27_Quebec_EN.pdf; accessed November 14, 2010.

19. Calculated from information available from Elections Canada, "Financial Reports"; available at http://www.elections.ca/scripts/webpep/fin/ welcome.aspx?lang=e; accessed June 13, 2008.

20. For a discussion of the American system, see Henry J. Abraham, *Justices and Presidents: A Political History of Appointments to the Supreme Court*, 3rd ed. (New York: Oxford University Press, 1992).

21. Léger Marketing, "Canadians and the Judicial System," April 8, 2002, p. 5, available at http://www.legermarketing.com/documents/ SPCLM/020408ENG.pdf, accessed June 13, 2008; Strategic Counsel, "Canadian Charter of Rights and Freedoms," March 21, 2007, p. 12, available at http://www.thestrategiccounsel.com/ our_news/polls/2007-03-21%20GMCTV%20-

CharterofRights%20Mar%2010-13.pdf, accessed June 13, 2008.

22. Konrad Zweigert and Hien Kotz, *Introduction to Comparative Law*, vol. 1 (Oxford: Clarendon Press, 1987), p. 324.

23. See the Centre for the Independence of Judges and Lawyers, "Moldava: The Rule of Law in 2004," International Commission of Jurists, 2004, available at http://www.icjcanada.org/en/ news/news_2004-11-30.pdf; accessed June 13, 2008.

24. *R. v. Valente,* [1985] 2 S.C.R. 673.

25. R. Devlin, A. Wayne MacKay, and Natasha Kim, "Reducing the Democractic Deficit: Representation, Diversity and the Canadian Judiciary, or Towards a 'Triple P' Judiciary," *Alberta Law Review* 38 (2000): 752.

26. Death Penalty Information Center, "Innocence: List of Those Freed from Death Row"; available at http://www.deathpenaltyinfo.org/innocence- list-those-freed-death-row; accessed November 16, 2010.

27. Sir William Blackstone, *Commentaries on the Laws of England*, Book IV, Ch. 27, available at http://avalon.law.yale.edu/18th_century/ blackstone_bk4ch27.asp; accessed November 17, 2010.

28. No judge has actually been removed by a vote of the two houses of Parliament, although several have resigned when it became apparent that removal procedures would have been undertaken.

29. Martin L. Friedland, *A Place Apart: Judicial Independence and Accountability in Canada* (Ottawa: Canadian Judicial Council, 1995), p. 123.

30. Canadian Judicial Council, *Annual Report* 1996–1997, App. G (Ottawa: CJC,1997), p. 70. This document is also avail- able at http://www.cjc-ccm.gc.ca/english/

annual_reports/1996–1997_append.htm;
accessed June 13, 2008.

31. CTV News, "Serial Killer's Trial Cost $102
Million," available at http://edmonton.ctv.ca/
servlet/an/local/CTVNews/20101116/pickton-
trial-cost-101116/20101116/?hub=Edmonton
Home; accessed November 16, 2010.

W W W   For various weblinks discussed in this chapter, please go to the book's website at **www.studyingpolitics4e.nelson.com**

PART

5

Political Participation

Courtesy of Keith Hutchings

KEITH HUTCHINGS, MHA

Keith was born the youngest of six children and grew up in the small community of Mobile on the southern shore of Newfoundland. He graduated from Memorial University with a Bachelor of Arts, majoring in Political Science, and later obtained a Certificate in Public Administration from Memorial, as well as completing an Occupational Health and Safety Program from Ryerson University in Toronto. He is active in the sporting community: he participates in many sports including hockey, running, ball hockey, and golf, he is involved in coaching, acts as a volunteer, and serves on various sporting executives, as well as chairing various fundraising events. Keith is married with two children.

Building on his degree in Political Science, Keith's professional career included 11 years with the Workplace Health Safety and Compensation Commission. He also served as Chief of Staff and Executive Assistant to then Leader of the Official Opposition in the Provincial House of Assembly (1996–1998) and successfully ran his own consulting business.

Keith was elected as the Member of the House of Assembly for the District of Ferryland in a by-election in 2007. Keith was re-elected in the general election later that year, and then appointed Parliamentary Secretary to the Minister of Human Resources, Labour and Employment. In November 2009 he was appointed Parliamentary Secretary to the Minister of Health and Community Services.

Keith has chaired province-wide provincial government reviews of Newfoundland and Labrador's minimum wage and, as well, the development of a long-term care and community support strategy. He has also served as Chair of the Provincial Budget Estimates Committee for the Social Services Committee for the last three years.

CHAPTER 11

Democracy in Action: Elections, Political Participation, and Citizens' Power

Brenda O'Neill

CHAPTER OBJECTIVES

After you have completed this chapter, you should be able to:

- describe the difference between direct democracy and representative democracy
- describe the functions of elections
- compare the plurality, majoritarian, and proportional representation electoral systems
- understand why voters vote the way they do
- describe the many forms of political participation and explain what influences one's decision to participate in politics
- explain the use of tools of direct democracy for increasing citizens' political power.

MODERN DEMOCRACY

In the fall of 2008 the first African-American president was elected into office, a historic milestone and clear evidence perhaps that the American myth that "anyone can become president" had become a reality. Part of this *new* reality, however, included the fact that the Obama election machine raised close to $750 million in private funds to finance his primary nomination and general election campaigns.[1] Modern election campaigns have become expensive, sophisticated enterprises that would seem completely foreign to presidential candidates from an earlier era. An ability to fundraise successfully is a minimal requirement for any would-be American president.

More than the cost of presidential campaigns, however, has changed. The arrival of the Internet as a mode of communication and interaction is slowly changing modern election campaigns. Some claim that Barack Obama's win stemmed partly from a sophisticated use of social networking tools such as text messaging, Facebook, YouTube, and Twitter to recruit volunteers, to fundraise, and to establish relationships with supporters. One estimate suggests that viewers logged 14.5 million hours watching official Obama videos on YouTube, a communication medium that is significantly cheaper and far more efficient than TV commercials.[2] The strategy was particularly successful with younger Americans—the Facebook generation—because Obama's campaign team fundamentally understood and harnessed the social networking capacity of the Internet. Success requires more than simply using the medium; John McCain also had a

Facebook page but his pastimes (fishing) and favourite movies (*Letters from Iwo Jima*) did little to help him connect with younger Americans.

Elections are often seen as the key mechanism for granting citizens a measure of power in modern democracies, but elections alone are insufficient for guaranteeing democratic legitimacy. The fact that the 2008 American presidential election generated significant interest and increased turnout levels, particularly among the young, was hailed by many as an important step for American democracy. Why is electoral turnout so important for democratic legitimacy? Why is it a concern that a modern election campaign can require close to three-quarters of a billion dollars in funding? What additional concerns are raised by modern democracy?

This chapter hopes to help answer these questions and more. Many of us employ the word *democracy* in everyday conversation, but the term is often ill defined or misunderstood. Few citizens in Western states are fully aware of the underlying assumptions, goals, and mechanisms required for the successful adoption and implementation of democracy.

Although there exist many academic definitions of the term, most agree that democracy is something close to "the rule of the people." The main principle is that political power should originate with the people rather than with those who rule. Modern democracy argues that the government's authority rests on the free and fair participation of all who are subject to its rule. Respect for the rule of law also ensures that political leaders do not govern arbitrarily, but rather follow the rules as laid out in the laws and the constitution. An independent judiciary ensures that governments respect the rule of law.

Western states and their citizens rarely challenge the normative superiority of democracies. Democracy is without question the *best* form of government. Unlike authoritarian systems, democracies provide opportunities for citizens to make decisions about the state, its citizens, and its relationship with other states because, ultimately, those very citizens will have to live with the consequences of those decisions. In other words, citizens are politically powerful. Citizen participation is assumed to lead to *better* decisions than any alternative system.

The study of politics requires us to challenge popular perceptions in an effort to better understand the use and distribution of political power. Important questions include: What are the requirements of a democratic political system? Do democracies actually provide citizens with such opportunities? Are modern democracies successful? Answering such questions requires a basic understanding of the structures, procedures, and requirements adopted by modern democratic states in an attempt to meet the "democratic ideal." It is not an ideal easily met by regimes—sometimes called *fledgling democracies*—that have only recently adopted the democratic system. But established democracies, while undoubtedly more successful at meeting the democratic challenge, are not without their own weaknesses. Few offer many opportunities for direct rule. Citizens get to vote in regular elections to select representatives in a number of legislative and executive bodies. Citizens might have an opportunity to vote in referendums on whether they support specific pieces of legislation or constitutional changes. They may also be given the opportunity to initiate their own pieces of legislation. But most democratic opportunities provide little by way of direct control over the day-to-day workings of the state. Instead of citizen rule, we have something closer to citizen choice over who will rule. For some, this is an unacceptable alternative; for others, the opportunities afforded by democracies for citizen decision-making are quite sufficient. One goal in this chapter is to explore the basis for such contradictory conclusions.

Senator Barack Obama speaks at a fundraiser in 2008. He successfully exploited the use of the Internet in raising hundreds of millions of dollars.

AP Photo/The Canadian Press(Jae C. Hong)

CITIZEN POWER

In a majority of the world's states, citizens are granted a measure of power to make public decisions. The ideal of democratic governance is to ensure that citizens "enjoy an equal ability to participate meaningfully in the decisions that closely affect their common lives as individuals in communities."[3] In other words, democracy advocates that the ultimate source of political power is the people, and that the best method for deciding upon questions that affect the community is to allow its members to debate alternatives freely and openly and to select the option that receives support from more than half of those affected.

The ideal of democratic governance, however, is rarely met. Modern democracies provide citizens with only an indirect ability to influence public decisions, and not all citizens enjoy equal ability to participate effectively in politics. The lack of formal restrictions on participation is very different from the existence of equal means and skills for participation purposes. What sets democracies apart is the belief that vesting political power in citizens is a laudable goal.

In the 5th century BCE in the city-state of Athens in ancient Greece, citizens were more intimately involved in the day-to-day decision-making required for the community.[4] Given a marked commitment to civic virtue, politics played a part in everyday life. In this version of democracy, called **direct democracy**, citizen power came from participation in popular assemblies—the equivalent of modern-day legislatures. Citizens, not politicians, were responsible for making key political decisions. Consensus was preferred, but the support of a majority of those assembled could also decide on the alternatives. A key difference from today's legislatures is that all citizens were meant to participate in these assemblies, not only a smaller number of elected representatives. Democracy, rule of the people, was direct: the people sitting in the assemblies debated and ruled on community questions. And the debate that took place in these assemblies was crucial: if citizens were made aware of alternatives, were allowed to voice their own concerns, and could hear the concerns of others then the outcome of the deliberation was believed to be *better* than that offered by some smaller, select group of individuals. Moreover, in the Athenian system, appointment to offices and executives occurred by lot, in an effort to avoid the problems that accompanied direct election.

Before concluding that this is a system on which to pattern modern democracy, take note of the fact that the ability to meet in assembly requires a limited number of citizens. Gathering thousands of people together anywhere to debate and render decisions is unlikely to be easy or successful; indeed, think about how hard it is to get even a small group of friends to agree on which restaurant to choose for a dinner out. Direct democracy in ancient Greece worked because the city-state was small (an average of 2,000 to 3,000 of the approximately 50,000 citizens would attend an assembly) and citizenship was not extended to slaves, women, and children. These exclusions meant that the men sitting in these assemblies constituted a minority of the population so that a minority imposed its will on the majority. It also worked because slavery provided Athenian citizens with plenty of free time. While this application of direct democracy is likely to leave us uncomfortable, the ideal of all citizens having an equal and direct say in public decisions remains an important standard by which to judge modern democracies.

Few modern democracies are able to employ the model of direct democracy of ancient Greece. Indeed, even among ancient political systems, the Athenian model was atypical. Democracy has evolved in response to the requirements of modern living and representative assemblies have replaced Athenian popular assemblies. Instead of making public decisions directly on a regular basis, citizens vote for individuals who will act as their representatives in these assemblies. In some modern systems, elements of direct democracy are nonetheless incorporated into the system in an effort to increase citizen participation in decision-making, as we will see later.

Representative democracies retain the important deliberative element of earlier assemblies—decision-makers must be able to gather and debate options

Direct democracy: A political system in which citizens hold power directly rather than through elected or appointed representatives.

Representative democracy: A political system in which citizens hold power indirectly by selecting representatives who render public decisions on their behalf in popular assemblies.

before coming to any conclusions—but not the popular basis for filling these assemblies. The considerable time requirement imposed by politics on Athenian citizens is made today only of citizens who choose to stand for public office. The compromise works, however, only if representatives are conscious of the needs, desires, and concerns of the people they are elected to represent; that is, citizens are powerful only if their representatives act in ways that correspond with the desires of the represented. Most modern democracies attempt to ensure this consciousness by requiring periodic elections. Elections mean that representatives must present themselves regularly before those who selected them to defend their actions and to receive the privilege of continuing on in their role. What is often overlooked in this process is each citizen's personal responsibility. To keep modern democracies from degenerating into **elite** rule, citizens must stay informed, active, and committed to the public project to ensure the accountability of elected representatives. Thus, elections assume a crucial role in the maintenance of modern democracies. According to Joseph Schumpeter, democracy is the "competitive struggle for the people's vote."[5] Because elections have degenerated to some extent into negative ad campaigns, leader image contests, and fundraising competitions, many challenge the degree to which the democratic ideal is currently being met in modern democracies. Although few formal restrictions exist on those wishing to run for political office, the reality is such that the opportunity is available only to those with sufficient economic resources at their disposal. A black man may have become president of the United States but it is highly unlikely that a poor black man could do the same.

Technology and Democracy

Technological innovation provides the potential for allowing modern democracies to incorporate the popular participation found in direct democracy and perhaps to counter the excesses of elections. E-democracy and **digital democracy** have been championed by

> **Digital democracy:** A broad term meant to encompass the application of technological innovations to politics and political participation; also called *e-democracy* or *e-politics*.

many who consider communications technology the perfect vehicle for allowing citizens to regain some of the direct political power lost under representative systems. One estimate suggests that, as of 2010, over two billion users around the world were connected to the Internet: approximately 29 percent of the world's population.[6] Given the ease of access to, and the wealth of information available on, the Internet, this medium provides the potential for citizens to become proactive democratic participants. Citizens can be tremendously empowered by communicating directly and instantly with each other, with elected representatives, and with the government. Local government in Bristol, England, for example, launched a website designed specifically to allow young people to upload text, MP3 files, and images in an effort to encourage them to participate more in local politics. The site includes a number of e-petitions launched by youth on such issues as the funding of school kitchens and public swimming pools.[7] Another option rests in the possibility for completing political transactions online, for example by e-voting. Experiments with tele-voting have been conducted in a number of party leadership races in Canada.[8] And as the 2008 American presidential election made clear, information communication technologies (ICTs) offer a whole range of options for getting many more citizens to discuss, become informed about, and participate in politics.

The potential that exists in digital democracy is mitigated, however, by a number of difficulties. Tele-voting experiments have had their share of technological problems: lost PINs (personal identification numbers), software and computer incompatibilities, site crashes, software glitches, and security breaches. Such concerns are at least as troubling as the problems encountered with the traditional technology of the "butterfly ballot" employed in the 2000 American elections. The ballot used in Palm Beach, Florida, had two vertical columns listing candidates and parties (resembling the wings of the butterfly), and voters punched a hole in the centre to indicate their preference. Unfortunately, the holes were not well aligned with the party and candidate names, and the resulting confusion has been argued by some to have cost the Democrats the presidency.

Yet there are bigger issues than simply getting e-democracy to work properly and securely. There is a "digital divide"—that is, a vast gulf separating the rich and the poor with respect to accessing this technology. Remember for a moment that the democratic ideal is to allow citizens *equal ability* to participate meaningfully in public decision-making. There is little doubt that if democracy embraces technology, a number of citizens will be left behind. Democracies such as Denmark, the United States, Sweden, and Canada boast that over 75 percent of their populations have Internet access.[9] Read differently, this means that about 25 percent do not. And those without access are disproportionately made up of the poor, the less educated and illiterate, and ethnic minorities. Estimates suggest that less than 30 percent of the population in the Middle East and less than nine percent in Africa have access to the Internet.[10] Unequal access translates into unequal ability. Greater access alone, however, is not enough to breach the divide. Broadband access in every city may help, but it cannot guarantee ability—citizens must possess the requisite skills to employ this technology successfully. If this fact is overlooked, our democracies might eventually consist of two groups: the powerful and the increasingly powerless.[11] As some point out, however, this would not be very different from the current state of affairs.

One difficulty with which modern democracies grapple is the conflicting desire to increase citizen power while at the same time ensuring that those very citizens respect the rights and obligations of others.[12] Historically, majorities have sometimes voted to remove the freedoms of minorities. While citizens in modern democracies are quick to assert the rights owed them by virtue of their citizenship, fewer acknowledge the obligations involved for greater responsibility for public decision-making. Increasing citizens' political power might result in greater rates of participation, but only if the citizens have both the capacity and the desire to participate. Creating civic capacity by increasing skills and means is partly the responsibility of government, and governments might increase the desire to participate if political systems, structures, and processes were modified to create more effective citizen power. Technology may well provide one potential mechanism for increasing this power; what is less clear is how an understanding of citizen responsibilities and obligations can be learned. Freedom of expression is fundamental in democratic systems; invoking this freedom to defend burning copies of the Qur'an is irresponsible, as was done by a U.S. clergyman.

A further challenge for modern democracy is **globalization**,[13] which has served to erode state sovereignty in such a way that modern democratic institutions may no longer be effective. If important political decisions are being made by nongovernmental organizations (NGOs) or by international political organizations, rather than by democratically elected governments, then increasing citizen political power might ultimately be in vain. Democracy is meant to provide a mechanism by which a community can render decisions on how it will be governed. If institutions and groups outside the community are making such decisions, existing democratic structures are inadequate, as discussed in Chapter 17.

ELECTIONS

One of the key democratic instruments is the **election**. Elections are the primary mechanism through which citizens in democratic states participate in the political system. And in terms of citizen power, citizen political decision-making takes place mainly through elections. Elections can provide much information about the condition of democracy in a country. When Canadians went to the polls in the 2011 general election, only 61.1 percent of registered voters bothered to take advantage of their civic right (see Figure 11.1).[14] The turnout rate has been steadily declining in Canada, although it did rebound slightly in the 2006 general election, and many take this decline to indicate that Canadians are dissatisfied with—rather than merely apathetic about—their governments, politics, and democracy.

Election: A mechanism by which the expressed preferences of citizens in democratic states are aggregated into a decision regarding who will govern.

Elections provide the prime mechanism in representative democracies for holding governments accountable. Governments are made up of representatives belonging to various political parties who are often selected on the basis of territory. Voters are provided an opportunity for retrospective evaluation—they can render a decision on whether they believe the government has done a good job while in office and whether it should be returned to power. At the same time, voters have an opportunity

Figure 11.1   **Turnout in Federal Elections, 1968–2011**

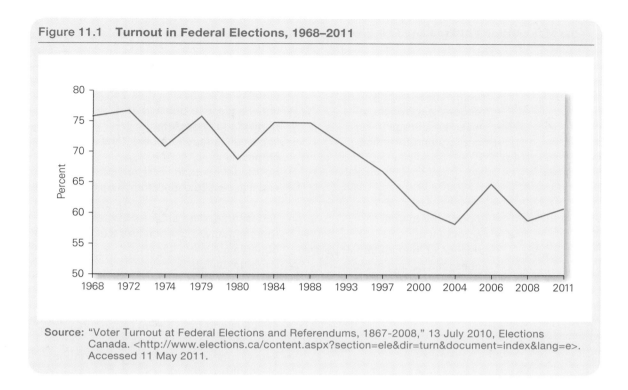

Source: "Voter Turnout at Federal Elections and Referendums, 1867-2008," 13 July 2010, Elections Canada. <http://www.elections.ca/content.aspx?section=ele&dir=turn&document=index&lang=e>. Accessed 11 May 2011.

to assess the alternative parties and their promises to see whether another party might deserve a shot at governing on the basis of the platform it puts forward. Elections should occur on a regular basis to ensure that representatives and governments are aware of the need to "face the voters." Competitive or effective elections, then, determine—either directly or indirectly—the composition of the government and attempt to ensure government accountability to citizens.[15] Competitive elections have a number of requirements.[16] Elections should not unnecessarily restrict citizens' right to vote—called the **franchise**—and most modern democracies have relatively few limitations on this right. The removal of property qualifications, the extension of the vote to women and Aboriginal people, and the lowering of the voting age greatly increased the number of voters in Canada. Free and fair elections require at the very least that political parties be relatively free to assemble and put forward candidates, as noted in Table 11.1 on p. 288. Citizens

must be presented with alternatives at elections; if they are not, the process is devoid of meaning. Not all groups, however, are given the freedom to associate and contest elections. In the Federal Republic of Germany, for example, "parties which, by reason of their aims or the behaviour of their adherents, seek to impair or destroy the free democratic basic order or to endanger the existence of the Federal Republic of Germany" are deemed unconstitutional, with the Federal Constitutional Court having the ultimate authority to decide on the question of unconstitutionality.[17] German history helps us to understand why such restrictions are in place.

Intimidation, violence, threats, and bribes should occur neither during election campaigns nor at the polls. The use of the secret ballot was adopted in part to curtail such practices. Finally, the administration of elections must be fair; the counting and reporting of votes cast, for example, should occur in an honest and consistent manner. The 2007 election ballot reform adopted in Florida came in response to the difficulties encountered in the closely fought 2000 presidential election race. Optical scan ballots (similar to the bubble sheets often used for multiple

Franchise: The right to vote in public elections.

Table 11.1	**Criteria of Free and Fair Elections**	
	Free	Fair
Campaign Period	• freedom of expression • freedom of assembly • freedom of association • universal suffrage • right to stand for office	• transparent election process • equality of political parties and groups • equal access to public media by parties and candidates • impartial, independent electoral commission • no impediments to voter registration • equal access to party information by voters
Election Day	• opportunity to vote • secret ballot • absence of intimidation of voters • accessible polling stations	• access to polling stations for party representatives, media, and election observers • impartial ballots • tamper-resistant ballot boxes • effective and transparent ballot counting procedures • effective and transparent procedures for determining invalid ballots • security measures for the transportation of ballot boxes • protection of polling stations
After Election Day	• ability to legally contest election results	• impartial and prompt treatment of election complaints • official and timely announcement of election results • unbiased media reporting of results • acceptance of results by all involved • installation in office of winners of the election

Source: Adapted from Richard Rose, ed., *The International Encyclopedia of Elections* (Washington, D.C.: CQ Press, 2000), p. 133. Copyright © 2000 CQ Press, a division of SAGE Publications, Inc.

choice exams) replaced the butterfly ballot punch card system in the hope of preventing a repeat of the election fiasco; counting votes fairly should not require that vote counters attempt to "guess" voter intent according to the depth of a dimpled chad on a punch card. Elsewhere, 13 centres served as pilot projects in e-voting during local elections in Britain in May 2007, but the results suggested that security concerns and vote-counting problems continue to plague this modern twist on an ancient act.[18]

Function of Elections

What are the effects of competitive elections, and what exactly do elections do?[19] There are two contradictory views on the main function of elections in competitive democracies. The first, called the bottom-up view, suggests that elections are mechanisms for allowing citizens to select their governments, to influence public policies, and to be represented. The alternative top-down view emphasizes the controlling elements

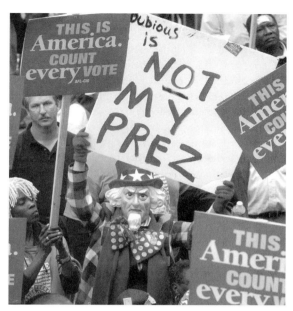

A demonstrator dressed as Uncle Sam holds up a sign rejecting Governor George W. Bush as president during a rally in support of Vice-President Al Gore in Tallahassee, Florida, in December 2000.

The Canadian Press(Dave Martin)

of elections. According to this view, competitive elections provide mechanisms for governments to control the democratic process—by focusing dissent, by limiting political participation primarily to elections, and by legitimizing a system in which citizens have little effective power. Most people accept a middle ground between these two positions: elections provide opportunities, albeit limited ones, for exchange between governments and citizens. This conclusion sets the stage for assessing how well elections perform their purported functions.

Choosing a Government

A key function of elections is to decide who will govern. In many liberal democracies, however, this is true only to a degree. Elections normally allow citizens to choose members of the legislature, but legislatures rarely govern, the American Congress being an exception (see Chapters 7, 8, and 9). Moreover, the formation of a government in parliamentary systems often results from bargaining among the

parties represented in the legislature (known as coalition governments) or from some long-standing convention, rather than from direct election. When one party wins a majority of seats in the legislature, it is normally asked to form government (known as a *majority government*). If, on the other hand, a party with the greatest number of seats in the legislature holds only a plurality but is deemed capable of governing, it can nonetheless be asked to form a government (known as a *minority government*). It is also the case that parliamentary governments can change between elections. A majority of presidential systems, on the other hand, allow for direct election of the president.[20] Yet the American president, contrary to popular belief, is not directly elected. When American voters cast a vote for president, they are actually voting for a slate of electors called the Electoral College; these electors pledge to vote for the winning candidate in their state when they formally elect the president roughly a month later. Electoral College votes are distributed on a state-by-state basis, equal to the number of members sent from the state to the two houses of Congress, making them roughly proportional to each state's population. Because most states' college electors vote as a block, it is possible for the college to elect a candidate who lost the nationwide popular vote, as was the case in the 2000 American presidential election: Al Gore won 48.4 percent of the popular vote but only 267 of the 537 Electoral College votes. George W. Bush, on the other hand, won only 47.9 percent of the popular vote but captured 271 Electoral College votes to win the presidency.[21] Finally, the public service, courts, and military play an important role in helping the executive to govern, although executive appointment rather than election is normally the rule employed to fill the vast majority of these positions. Accordingly, "competitive elections play an important part in government formation but the relationship is less tight, less strict, than many people imagine."[22]

Mechanism of Accountability

Elections are also mechanisms designed to ensure government accountability. This claim may seem suspect, given the fact that elections do not always directly determine the government. They can, however, force a change in government, particularly if the people are especially unhappy with decisions made during the government's tenure and if a clear alternative party exists. Democratic governments understand that at some point they must face the electorate, a knowledge that can constrain their behaviour to some degree. It cannot guarantee, however, that all government decisions will be popular: the Mulroney government, for example, imposed the Goods and Services Tax (GST) on Canadians in the late 1980s despite widespread public opposition.

Selection of Representatives

Elections allow citizens to choose their political representatives; they necessarily determine who serves as the representative or representatives of individual territorial districts. But the concept of representation is a difficult one to pin down, as mentioned in Chapter 9. What does it mean to represent others politically? One common interpretation proposes three styles of electoral representation: trustee, party, and constituency.[23] The trustee model emphasizes that although representatives take the interests and concerns of their electors into account, decisions are ultimately made according to the representatives' own judgment. Citizens should, the argument goes, trust their representatives' judgment. Such an argument might seem immediately unacceptable, but democracy does value the importance of debate and the articulation of alternative viewpoints for political decision-making—and this is exactly what is supposed to take place in the legislature. Only a minority of ordinary citizens have the information, expertise, and awareness of consequences that would allow them to render equally valid judgments on many current political questions.

The party model, on the other hand, emphasizes that legislators are chosen on the basis of their party membership—few independents get elected—and as a result, their responsibility is to support the party position in the legislature. This argument focuses on the fact that many people vote according to party rather than individual candidate; once elected, legislators should be bound to support that party's platform. Such an argument is often heard in Canada to criticize MPs who "cross the floor" to join another political party, a recent example being that of Belinda Stronach, who left the Conservative Party to become a Liberal Party cabinet minister in May 2005.

Finally, the constituency model emphasizes the role that representatives play in supporting the interests of their constituents by helping them to deal with the large government bureaucracy, promoting government spending in the constituency, and, in some cases, generating employment opportunities. For many Canadian backbench MPs, this casework can take up a significant portion of their time.

Political representation is particularly important in democracies given that legislators are elected to "represent" the interests of citizens. Political scientists have engaged in a continuing debate on the nature of the concept, making a distinction between substantive and descriptive representation. Is it more important to have political representatives, regardless of who they are, who will make decisions that are in the best interests of a particular constituency (substantive), or to have political representatives whose physical characteristics, such as gender, ethnicity, and age, mirror those of their constituency (descriptive)? In the latter argument, it is often assumed that if a group of legislators physically resemble those they are meant to represent then their decisions are likely to mirror the decisions that would have been made by their very constituents themselves. Although the descriptive versus substantive representation dichotomy is to some extent a false one, it has nevertheless generated significant discussion in some areas, such as **feminist** political theory where the question of who can "best" represent the interests of women has been raised (see Box 11.1).[24]

Conferral of Legitimacy

Elections are also the mechanism through which governments are granted a measure of **legitimacy**. As a key element of democratic systems, fair and free elections provide a chance for citizens to participate in politics and to decide who will hold political power. With this opportunity, however, comes the expectation that the people will comply with government decisions. The opportunity to choose rulers in a fair and legitimate manner obliges citizens to obey the decisions of that popularly elected government. The legitimacy of the electoral process provides the government with political authority, but an obligation to obey does not remove the right of political dissent and the opportunity to change such policies.

BOX 11.1

HOW THE CANADIAN ELECTORAL SYSTEM DISCOURAGES WOMEN'S PARTICIPATION

The Royal Commission on Electoral Reform and Party Financing reported in 1991 its findings concerning the principles and processes governing elections to the House of Commons. In setting out the objectives of Canadian electoral democracy, the study suggested the importance of ensuring equitable access to candidacy. And while few formal restrictions exist, the commission noted that women were greatly underrepresented among those running as candidates for and those elected to the House. For example, in 1988 women made up only 19 percent of candidates and only 13 percent of those elected. This virtual exclusion of women, it argued, was no longer acceptable. According to the report, "It is not merely a matter of political symbolism; elected representatives will not and cannot effectively represent the full range of Canada's interests if they do not reasonably reflect its society. To this extent, the electoral system fails to secure the best persons to sit in the House of Commons" (p. 8). The rationale employed by the Commission for increasing the number of women elected to the House of Commons was based on the concept of descriptive representation.

Two of the key barriers for women's entry into the House of Commons that were identified were the nomination process and the inattention of political parties. The nomination process posed a particular financial barrier to women, whose earnings were less than those of men. First, women were more likely to find themselves in expensive contested nominations rather than in acclamations to run as the party's candidate. And second, they received fewer and smaller donations than men, in part due to their different social and professional contacts.

To deal with these problems, the report recommended the imposition of spending limits on nomination contest campaigns and the issuing of tax credit receipts to those who donate money toward nomination contests. The report also highlighted the role played by political parties in increasing the representation of women in the House. Although it noted that the major parties at the federal level had measures designed to assist prospective women candidates (especially the New Democratic Party), progress had been slow. Women continued to be underrepresented in "safe" ridings, which decreased their chances of getting elected. They also continued to work in "pink-collar" positions within party organizations (e.g., as constituency association secretaries), rarely stepping stones to political office. The report recommended that "the by-laws and constitutions of registered political parties require the establishment of formal search committees and commit the parties to processes that demonstrably promote the identification and nomination of broadly representative candidates" (p. 121).

Have we made any progress in the years since the report came out? In the 2011 federal election, women made up 31 percent of all candidates and 25 percent of those elected to the House of Commons. Should there have been greater progress than this since 1988? Does it matter whether more women get elected? What do you think?

Source: How the Canadian Electoral System Discourages Women's Participation. Pages 8 and 121. Reproduced with the permission of the Minister of Public Works and Government Services, 2011, and Courtesy of the Privy Council Office.

Establishing a Policy Mandate

Elections are also meant to supply governments with a specific policy mandate for their tenure in office. Understanding the nature of elections provides insight into why this function is rarely fulfilled. Political parties offer specific campaign platforms, filled with a number of policy prescriptions. One might, then, conclude that the winning party has been given a vote of support for its specific policy proposals. In order for this to occur, however, voters must be voting for the party *because* of its policy positions and for no other reason, which is not often the case. A majority of the electorate must also support the party and its platform, which is not always true either. Although Brian Mulroney claimed that the election of the Progressive Conservative Party in 1988 indicated that Canadians wished to go forward with the Canada–U.S. Free Trade Agreement, the party had won only 43 percent of the popular vote. One cannot make the claim that elections determine public policy if more people vote against than for the positions ultimately adopted. In addition, once parties have formed the government, they can drop key elements of their electoral platforms without major repercussions. This seriously weakens the argument that elections shape public policy. In 2003, for example, Ontario Premier Dalton McGuinty broke an election promise not to raise taxes while in government. The need for the increased taxes notwithstanding, such reversals make it difficult to claim that elections constrain policy choices in government.

Mechanism for Political Education, Mobilization, and Socialization

Finally, elections provide opportunities for political education, mobilization, and socialization. Elections allow for the political education of both voters and members of political parties. Voters can learn about political campaigns, candidates, and party leaders, and the major issues facing the government. Parties and candidates have an opportunity to find out what the people are thinking and also to shape their opinions. Such education can provide an incentive for people to get out and vote and possibly become politically involved in additional ways. Elections can also socialize citizens regarding the requirements of democracy and the importance assigned to politics within a particular country.

The process of cognitive mobilization—that is, increases in education and access to political information—has led to a general rise in political sophistication and interest over time.[25] The appearance of television, and then the Internet, have significantly increased citizen access to political information for those who seek it out and elections are times when interest in politics is high. There remain, however, limits on the amount of information that can be processed, concerns regarding the quality of information that is available, and debates over the actual level of citizen sophistication. Elections nevertheless remain a time when attention to politics and, as a result, political learning, is heightened.

ELECTIONS AND THE MEDIA

Any discussion of elections in modern democracies must address the role played by the **mass media**. Television, radio, and newspapers provide an important source of information for voters, a point not lost on politicians and campaign managers. More often than not, the media present the electoral contest as a "horse race." The focus is on which party and leader are ahead on a particular day, rather than on more substantive policy issues or the parties' platforms. This sensational treatment makes for entertaining viewing, listening, or reading; it does little, however, to advance the political education of voters or the message that politics and elections are more than games. Party leaders and candidates have also had to learn to speak in sound bites, since the media like answers in the form of 10-second clips. Not all political questions, however, can be reasonably answered in so short a time.

Conservative leader Stephen Harper attending the Calgary Stampede in a cowboy outfit.

Calgary Herald/The Canadian Press(Mikael Kjellstrom)

Style Over Substance?

This focus on style, often over substance, leads politicians to hire professional image consultants and speech specialists. Selecting the proper media image is not always easy. The media's preoccupation with the hair style and colour of Australia's first female Prime Minister, Julia Gillard, has been difficult to explain. Closer to home, Canadian Prime Minister Stephen Harper has been similarly scrutinized by the media. In 2005 he was photographed at the Calgary Stampede in a too-small leather vest and odd-looking cowboy hat; in 2006 he was criticized on an official visit to Mexico for wearing what appeared to be a fishing vest compared to the starched crisp white shirts worn by Presidents Fox and Bush; and attention has been devoted to changes in his weight over time. And although none of this ought to matter for the quality of governance in democracies, the prominence of media coverage has increased the degree to which it does. Citizens need to feel that their leaders are competent, honest, able, and trustworthy. The image that they portray through the media directly determines these attitudes.

Tighter regulation might be the solution to ensuring more realistic, informative, and substance-driven media coverage of politics but the media's portrayal of politics and politicians would be extremely difficult to control. Although public broadcasters exist (CBC radio and television in Canada, for example), much of the industry is dominated by commercial (private) broadcasters and publishers, whose bottom line is either circulation numbers or size of the audience. Maximizing paper sales and viewing audience would prove difficult if the media were forced to provide in-depth and substantial coverage of politics and elections (especially given the low level of interest that Canadians have in politics and elections). And while regulation might prove successful in altering coverage, the cost to political freedom, namely freedom of expression, would certainly prove too high.

Media Concentration

A further concern is the growing concentration of mass media ownership and its increased commercialization. In the United States, giants such as Time Warner and Viacom increasingly dominate all forms of mass communication, driven by a set of values not always in line with journalistic ones. The rise in commercialization has meant a simultaneous decrease in the importance of public broadcasting based on a greater sense of public purpose and responsibility. Public broadcasters offer more current affairs and political news programs than commercial broadcasters, and help to produce a politically informed and aware citizenry. Increased concentration also raises concerns about the responsiveness of media empires to local political issues, as exemplified by CanWest Global's decisions to adopt common editorials for various newspapers across the country and to refocus journalists' stories that were at odds with the views of the owners (see Chapter 5). A challenge to media ownership concentration comes from citizen journalism, made possible by the expansion of the Internet. Blogs, wikis, and websites provide almost unlimited alternative sources of information.

ELECTORAL RULES

In each country, the conduct of elections is governed by a set of rules and regulations which detail the offices that will be filled by the election; financial, nomination, and reporting requirements for candidates and parties that wish to run in the contest; voting eligibility requirements; regulations concerning the drawing of electoral boundaries; and even the requirements for the ballot, such as the order of candidates' names.

Campaign Finance

Key among these rules are those concerning matters of party and election finance. These include the amount and sources of party funds, party and candidate spending, and *third-party advertising*—a term encompassing spending by organizations other than political parties during elections.[26] The need for financial regulation stems from a concern for equity and fairness among those contesting elections; control over how money is raised and spent can help "level the playing field" and limit the degree to which money influences electoral outcomes and ultimately government decisions. Restricting party spending during campaigns diminishes their need for raising funds, makes elections more equitable, and reduces candidates' and parties' obligations to those donating the funds.

In 2000, the government of Manitoba adopted legislation designed to address concerns regarding the perception that money unduly influences politics and elections. This legislation bans contributions from corporations and unions to political parties, limits individual contributions to $3,000 per year, limits third-party spending during election periods to $5,000, and reinstates limits on political party advertising during elections. Similar legislation has existed in Quebec since 1977. The National Citizens' Coalition, a right-wing nonprofit organization in Canada, fought hard against restrictions on third-party election advertising, which it calls "gag laws." On three separate occasions, Alberta courts agreed with the organization's argument that the rules represented an unreasonable violation of the right of freedom of expression. In the 2004 case *Harper v. Canada*, however, the Supreme Court ruled in favour of the restrictions imposed on third-party spending in the Canada Elections Act. The challenge is to balance the desire for a level playing field with the desire for ensuring free and open debate during elections.

Similar campaign finance legislation was adopted for Canadian general elections by the Chrétien Liberal government in 2003 in Bill C-24.[27] Designed to enhance the fairness and transparency of the electoral system, that bill together with the Harper government's 2006 *Federal Accountability Act* brought the *Canada Elections Act* in line with elections regulation in Manitoba and Quebec by restricting contributions to individuals, imposing spending limits on parties and candidates, enhancing financial reporting requirements, and increasing the regulation of political broadcasting. In an effort to level the political playing field and to reduce the perception of undue influence in politics, the system of public financing of election expenses was also further enhanced. The overall impact of these reforms on parties, elections, and participation, however, has been less than straightforward and the majority Harper government has embarked on the elimination of the per-vote subsidy.[28]

Similar legislation was adopted in 2002 at the federal level in the United States. The key element of the *Bipartisan Campaign Reform Act* was the regulation of "soft money" and "issue advocacy," the former involving donations to parties not specifically directed toward the support or opposition of a candidate and the latter involving campaign communications that do not expressly advocate for the election or defeat of candidates. Spending in both has skyrocketed as a result of the dramatic increases in the costs of campaigns (mass media and technology costs) and the need to overcome the limits on "hard money" and "express advocacy."[29] Unlike in Canada, however, the U.S. Supreme Court has been less willing to accept that campaign finance regulation be employed to "level the playing field" across political parties and in January 2010 overturned part of the 2002 Reform Act that limited corporate funding of independent political broadcasts in candidate elections.

Electoral Districting and Apportionment

Another key set of electoral rules governs electoral districting and apportionment, particularly in electoral systems based on territorial representation, such as those of Canada and the United States. *Districting* (or *redistribution*, as it is called in Canada) refers to the drawing of electoral boundaries in order to establish territorial districts or constituencies from which one or more representatives will be sent to the legislature. The manipulation of district boundary lines to advantage a particular group (or to disadvantage another) is referred to as *gerrymandering*. In an effort to reduce the likelihood of such manipulation, the responsibility for the drawing of electoral boundaries has been placed in the hands of independent bodies, rather than those of the sitting government.

The principle of **representation by population** ("rep by pop") advocates that electoral districts should be roughly equal in population in order to ensure that individuals receive a proportionate share of representation in government, so that each vote is of equal weight. *Apportionment*—the determination of representative seats according to population—should occur regularly, normally after a census, to account for shifting population bases. The rep by pop principle, however, recognizes that other considerations can come into play in drawing boundaries, including a desire to keep the geographic expanse of a district to a manageable size and to ensure minority groups

Representation by population: The principle suggesting that the allocation of seats in assemblies should occur in a manner that encourages an equal division of the population across electoral districts, so that each vote is of equal weight.

are not scattered across several districts, which would minimize their electoral influence. In federal states, such as Canada and the United States, rep by pop is adopted for the lower house at the national level but not for the upper house. In the United States, representation in the Senate occurs on a state basis (two representatives per state). In Canada's Senate, representation occurs on a more complicated regional basis. In both instances, however, population size is not a consideration in apportioning seats to the upper house.

ELECTORAL SYSTEMS

The rules employed to translate votes into seats have been the subject of great debate in many countries.[30] New Zealand, Japan, and Italy have recently changed their electoral systems in an attempt to address various concerns. Such changes reflect the importance of electoral systems—systems that set the rules for determining how individual votes are translated into legislative seats. Electoral systems shape electoral strategies, electoral outcomes, and voter behaviour. Because of this, students of politics require a basic understanding of the various electoral systems in use in today's democracies.

One common method for distinguishing electoral systems focuses on the electoral formula employed—that is, the rule for determining how many votes are required to earn a seat. Two main types of electoral systems are proportional and nonproportional systems (see Table 11.2, p. 296). Nonproportional systems (such as in Canada, the United States, and Britain) are defended for their tendency to produce majority governments, for encouraging the development of two-party systems, and for encouraging strong territorially defined links between representatives and their constituents. Proportional systems, on the other hand, are defended for the greater fairness in awarding seats that are roughly proportional to the share of votes obtained by each party. Electoral systems are not merely of academic concern; three Canadian provinces (British Columbia, Ontario, and Prince Edward Island) have held referendums on the question of reforming the electoral system, while Quebec and New Brunswick commissioned reports examining the issue of electoral system reform.

Nonproportional Systems

Nonproportional type electoral systems are constituency-based (the country is divided into geographically defined constituencies represented by one elected representative) and voters select a candidate on the ballot rather than a party. This group of electoral systems includes the one most familiar to North Americans: the plurality system. The requirement for winning in a plurality system *is to earn more votes than any other candidate but not necessarily a majority*—hence its more common name, **first-past-the-post (FPTP)**. In elections to the Canadian House of Commons, for example, the country is divided into single-member districts: one representative is selected from each territorially defined district. Since a number of political parties nominate a single candidate to run in each district, the winner rarely earns a majority of the votes cast. The cumulative effect of this "wasting of votes" can lead to serious distortions in the vote-share-to-seat-share ratio at the national level (see Table 11.3 on p. 297 for the distortion in Canada's 2008 federal election).[31] Such distortions have fuelled efforts to change Canada's electoral system at both the federal and provincial levels. Since the governing parties often achieve power as a direct result of this distortion, however, one can understand why they might be hesitant to change the system.

> **First-past-the-post (FPTP):** An electoral system that requires the winning candidate to receive more votes than any other in order to win the seat—that is, to receive a plurality of votes. The majority of first-past-the-post systems employ single-member electoral districts.

An additional but less common nonproportional electoral system is the **majoritarian system**. The distinction between such systems and FPTP is that the winning candidate is required to earn a majority of votes in order to be declared the winner (a majority being 50 percent + 1). This requirement means that

> **Majoritarian system:** An electoral system that requires the winning candidate to receive a majority of votes to win the seat. The majority is normally achieved through a second ballot or by an alternative voting system.

Table 11.2 Electoral Systems

Nonproportional Systems	Proportional Systems (all in multimember districts)
(a) Plurality (first-past-the-post) Candidate who wins more votes than any other (i.e., wins the plurality of votes) is awarded the seat. This method is used most often in combination with single-member districts. *Examples*: Canada (House of Commons); United States (House of Representatives). **(b) Majority** Candidate must win a majority of votes (50% + 1) in order to win the seat. Majority is achieved by employing one of three methods: *Runoff*: The second ballot lists only the top two candidates from the first ballot round. This method is used most often in combination with single-member districts. *Example*: French presidential elections. *Plurality*: A second ballot is also employed, but the winner needs to obtain only a plurality of votes. There is no significant reduction in the number of candidates on the second ballot, although a threshold may be imposed. *Example*: French legislative elections. *Alternative*: A single election occurs, but voters rank the candidates in order of preference. Winner must obtain a majority of first preferences. If no candidate earns a majority of first preferences, the second preferences of the last-place candidate are transferred to the remaining candidates until one candidate achieves a majority. *Example*: Australia (House of Representatives).	**(a) List System** Seats are awarded to parties that meet or exceed an electoral quota. In a closed-list system, voters cast a single ballot for a party, and candidates from that party's list are elected in the order in which they appear on the list. In the more common open-list system, in addition to choosing to award their votes to a single party, voters can instead choose to award their votes individually to specific candidates on the party lists. *Examples*: Israel; Switzerland. **(b) Single Transferable Vote (STV)** Voters rank their candidate choices across parties. Candidates meeting a quota are awarded a seat. Initial counting looks at first preferences only; any candidate meeting the quota is elected. Second preferences of any surplus votes (in excess of the quota) are then transferred to any remaining candidates. Again, the candidates who meet the quota after the second preferences have been transferred are elected. If seats are still vacant, the weakest candidate is eliminated and the second preferences from those ballots are allocated to the remaining candidates until the quota is met and all seats are allocated. *Examples*: Ireland; Australia (Senate).

MIXED SYSTEMS

Mixed systems combine elements of nonproportional and proportional electoral systems. The mixed member proportional (MPP) system is an example. Voters have two votes: one for the constituency representative and a second for a party. A share of seats is allocated through single-member districts, while the remaining seats are allocated in order to bring each party's seat share in line with the party's popular vote share. *Examples*: Germany (Bundestag); New Zealand.

Source: Adapted from André Blais and Louis Massicotte, "Electoral Systems," in Lawrence LeDuc, Richard G. Niemi, and Pippa Norris, eds., *Comparing Democracies: Elections and Voting in Global Perspective* (Thousand Oaks: Sage, 1996). Copyright 1996 by Sage Publications Inc Books. Reproduced by permission of SAGE.

Table 11.3	Distorting Effects of the Canadian Electoral System, 2008				
Party	Seats	Seat Share (percent)	Vote Share (percent)	Seat-to-Vote (ratio)	Perfect PR Seat Share*
Conservative Party	143	46.4	37.7	1.23	116
Liberal Party	77	25.0	26.3	0.95	81
Bloc Québécois	49	15.9	10.0	1.59	31
New Democratic Party	37	12.0	18.2	0.66	56
Total seats	308**				

Note: If the seat-to-vote ratio is greater than one, the party has been awarded more seats than it deserved on the basis of its vote share. If the ratio is less than one, the party has been underrewarded.
*The perfect PR seat share indicates the number of seats a party would obtain under a perfectly proportional electoral system, that is, a seat share equal to the party's vote share. Note that under such a system, the Green Party would have received 21 seats (instead of 0) for having earned 6.8 percent of the vote share in 2008.
**Two seats were won by candidates running as independents.

Source: Elections Canada, "Percentage of Valid Votes, by Political Affiliation" and "Distribution of Seats, by Political Affiliation and Sex"; cited on November 13, 2007; available at http://www.elections.ca/scripts/OVR2006/25/table7.html and http://www.elections.ca/scripts/OVR2006/25/table9.html

one election will often not produce a winner, since elections normally involve more than two candidates. As a result, majoritarian systems employ one of three mechanisms for producing a winner. Two of these systems require a second election in the event that no candidate earns a majority of votes in the first. Majority runoff systems include only the top two finishers from the first race in the second election. Limiting the subsequent election to only two candidates virtually ensures that a majority winner will be produced. In majority plurality systems, on the other hand, a second election is held without any reduction in the number of candidates (although some countries adopt a threshold to eliminate candidates who earned a small share of the vote). The winner in the second election is the candidate who obtains a plurality of votes—that is, more votes than any other candidate.

The third mechanism, the alternative vote, requires only one election, which many see as its advantage: voters are asked to rank the candidates listed on the ballot in order of preference (e.g., putting a "1" next to the candidate who is their first choice, a "2" next to their second choice, and so on). The winner is the candidate earning a majority of first preferences, or "1"s. If no such majority is achieved, the second preferences of the candidate with the fewest number of first preferences are then transferred to the remaining candidates. If a majority is still not achieved, the process continues until transferred preferences provide a majority of votes to a candidate. In a 2011 referendum, British voters rejected the adoption of this system.

Proportional Systems

In **proportional representation (PR)** systems, the priority lies in awarding seats to parties in rough proportion to the share of votes earned rather than in awarding the seat to a single candidate from each district. One key to understanding PR systems is that they use multimember districts rather than single-member districts; the allocation of seats according to the proportion of votes earned is only possible if there is more than one seat available. The higher the number of members to be elected per district, the more proportional the system is likely to be. In Israel, the entire country serves as a single constituency,

Proportional representation (PR): An electoral system that attempts to award seats to parties in proportion to the share of votes earned. Such systems must be combined with multimember constituencies.

allowing for a large degree of proportionality in seat allocation. The other key to understanding PR systems is that seats are generally allocated to parties rather than to candidates; although there is significant variation across PR systems, political parties are considered to be more powerful in PR than non-PR systems, in part because they often have a greater say than voters in determining which party members get elected to the legislature.

Two specific PR systems are the list system and the single transferable vote. Most PR systems use the **list system**, which requires voters to choose

> **List system:** The most commonly adopted form of proportional representation, employing relatively large multimember electoral districts and a ballot that requires voters to choose from among party lists or candidates on party lists.

from among lists of candidates prepared by the parties. In a *closed-list system*, voters are presented with a ballot that lists each of the parties contesting the election and the rank-ordering of the candidates each party has selected as their representatives if they win seats in the legislature. Voters cannot indicate preferences for individual candidates on a party's list, but instead select one party's list as their choice. The share of votes the party receives in the constituency determines the number of candidates who will sit in the legislature. Parties derive tremendous power in this system through their ability to set candidate lists. An *open-list system*, on the other hand, allows voters to choose and rank as many specific candidates from among the different party lists as there are seats to be allocated, thereby weakening the power of party officials to determine who gets elected to the legislature. While the power of parties is stronger in closed-list than open-list systems, the former more easily allow for the adoption of measures by parties for targeting certain demographics for increased representation. For instance, "zippering" party lists—making every second candidate on the closed list a woman—has been shown to be a particularly effective mechanism for increasing their numbers in legislatures.

The procedure employed for allocating seats in proportional systems varies, but it normally involves dividing the number of votes cast for the party or candidate by a quota or divisor. Seats are allocated to the parties according to the resulting figure. As an example, the "droop quota" is calculated in the following manner:

$$\frac{\text{total number of votes}}{\text{number seats to be filled} + 1} + 1$$

Each party's total votes earned are then divided by the quota to determine the number of seats they are awarded; any unallocated seats are awarded to the parties with the highest remainders (i.e., the number of votes "left over" after dividing by the quota). The end result is that the "cost" for each seat (in terms of votes) is roughly equal. Some PR systems also adopt thresholds that deny seats to parties that receive very small shares of the vote, normally around 5 to 6 percent. The argument for adopting thresholds is that it keeps extremist parties from gaining a measure of legitimacy, at least that afforded by a legislative seat. Such thresholds necessarily introduce distortion in the seat-to-vote ratio, however, a criticism often aimed at nonproportional systems.

Israel's electoral system provides a simple example of the application of a PR electoral system. As previously mentioned, Israel consists of a single electoral district with a district magnitude of 120 (the number of seats to be filled in the Knesset, Israel's legislature). A closed-list system is in place; more than a month before election day, political parties are required to submit their ordered candidate lists to the Central Elections Committee and voters are provided with a ballot that allows them to allocate a single vote to one of the party lists (rather than to individual candidates). After all the votes have been counted, parties that do not meet the existing threshold (currently two percent of all votes cast) are not awarded a seat in the legislature. *The d'Hondt formula* is then employed to allocate seats among the remaining parties. That is, the total votes earned by each party is divided by a set of numbers (1, 2, 3, 4, 5, etc.) and the result (the quotient or average votes per seat earned) determines the allocation of seats; the first seat is awarded to the party with the highest quotient or average, the second seat to the party with the next highest average, and so on until all seats are awarded.

An alternative to the list system, the **single transferable vote (STV)**, used in both Australia and Ireland, allows voters to rank their candidate preferences on the ballot. As in the alternative vote system, voters can rank as many candidates as there are seats to be allocated in the constituency. This

> **Single transferable vote (STV):** A proportional electoral system that elects candidates in multi-member ridings and provides voters with significant freedom by allowing them to rank-order their choices within and across party lists.

ballot structure provides voters rather than parties with a greater measure of power than many other PR systems. The increased choice offered to voters, and the associated decrease in the power of parties to choose the representatives to send to the legislature, was one of the rationales offered by B.C.'s Citizens' Assembly in 2004 for their selection of STV as the recommended alternative to FPTP.[32] The procedure for determining which candidates are elected involves the use of the droop quota. Each candidate's first preference votes are counted, and those whose total number of first preference votes received meets the required quota are each awarded a seat. Any surplus or remaining votes over the quota for these elected candidates are then transferred to the second-preference candidates on the winning candidates' ballots. If a candidate earned 40 percent of the winning candidate's overall second preferences, then that candidate receives 40 percent of the winning candidate's surplus votes. Candidates who meet the quota with the addition of these transferred votes are then awarded a seat. If seats remain unallocated at this point, the candidate with the fewest first preferences is eliminated, and the second preferences listed on those ballots are transferred proportionately to the remaining candidates. The process (which, given its complexity, can be very lengthy) continues until all seats are allocated.

Mixed Systems

Several countries have adopted an electoral system that combines elements of the proportional and nonproportional electoral systems into a mixed system. Japan, for example, elects 300 members of

its house of representatives using a first-past-the-post system with single-member constituencies. An additional 200 members are independently elected from 11 regional multimember constituencies through a PR system. New Zealand's **mixed member proportional system (MMP)** also creates two sets of elected members: those elected under the traditional FPTP system in 65 single-member districts and another 55 elected under a PR closed-list system. The difference, however, is that the 55 PR members are awarded to the parties in order to "top up" the seat shares awarded by the single-member districts to ensure proportionality of all seats with party vote shares cast under the list system. Since FPTP over-rewards larger parties, the PR seat allocation corrects this distortion. Most mixed electoral systems hope to maintain the territorial link between the representative and his or her constituents while injecting greater proportionality between each party's vote and seat shares in the legislature.

> **Mixed member proportional electoral system (MMP):** An electoral system that seeks to balance geographical representation with proportionality of party support by combining single-member electoral districts with other seats in the legislature distributed on the basis of the proportion of votes each party wins.

Electoral reform has recently become a key issue on the political agenda in Canada in light of growing concerns over citizen disengagement and increased political cynicism. The most common criticism directed at FPTP relates to the system's distorting effects when vote shares are translated into seat shares. Because it is a "winner take all" system, votes for parties with anything less than a plurality are essentially wasted. This distortion leads to overrepresentation for parties that win a plurality of the vote (creating "artificial majorities" in the legislature) and underrepresentation for most other parties, as seen in Table 11.3. This distortion can at times be extreme. In 2001, the Liberals came to power in British Columbia with 97 percent of the seats in the legislature, having earned only 57.6 percent of the popular vote. The New Democratic Party, on the other hand, won only two of 79 seats despite having earned 21.6 percent of the provincial vote share.

An additional criticism of FPTP relates to the fact that parties whose support is concentrated in a particular region are likely to be overrepresented in the legislature, while parties with weak but more broadly dispersed support are likely to be underrepresented. In Canada, from 1993 to 2011, the Bloc Québécois received an inflated share of seats in the House of Commons because it received a plurality of votes in a limited number of regionally concentrated ridings. The NDP, on the other hand, at least until 2011, was significantly underrepresented despite receiving a fairly consistent level of support across the country, because it failed to achieve a plurality in many ridings, leading to many votes being effectively wasted. Proponents of electoral reform have argued that this regionalizing effect has exacerbated regional tensions in Canada. The underrepresentation of women, Aboriginal peoples, and other ethnic minorities has also been identified as a weakness of FPTP. Alternatively, supporters of FPTP point to its tendency to produce majority governments capable of implementing electoral mandates, its encouragement of a territorial link between elected representative and constituents, and its overall simplicity.[33]

Although several Canadian provinces have examined the question of electoral reform, and in some cases held referendums on the question, FPTP remains in place at both the provincial and federal level in Canada. As noted above, the B.C. Citizens' Assembly on Electoral Reform recommended STV as an alternative to FPTP in 2004; a similar assembly in Ontario recommended MMP as the preferred alternative in 2007. Both recommendations were subsequently defeated in provincial referendums. We can nevertheless identify a number of potential consequences resulting from the move to a more proportional electoral system. First, the incentives for voting (fewer wasted votes) and for voting for smaller parties (because they would be more likely to gain seats in proportion to the votes they earn) would likely increase. Accordingly, turnout would likely improve and the **party system** might become more fractionalized (see Chapter 12). Second, electoral results would likely become proportional; political parties would likely earn seat shares that more closely reflect the share of votes earned. At the federal level, this might help parties such as the NDP and the Green Party, who have been underrewarded historically in seat shares. Third, the representation of minorities and women in legislatures could improve; a move to an electoral system

that allowed political parties to more directly determine which of their candidates earned legislative seats might result in more representative chambers. Fourth, some PR systems would allow voters, rather than parties, more say in determining which candidates get elected. Fifth, greater proportionality would likely translate into fewer majority governments and more coalition and minority governments. Without the representational "boost" afforded to winning parties in FPTP, governments are more likely to be formed from the merger of two or more parties than from only one.

VOTING

Elections are the primary mechanism for engaging the people in democracies. The study of voting behaviour and the way voters decide have preoccupied political scientists for quite some time, especially since the advent of public opinion polling in the 1940s. Why do people vote as they do? Three theories can be identified that together provide a fairly complete answer to this rather complex question.[34]

Sociological Model

The first theory, the sociological model, explains voting by identifying the social forces that determine individual values and beliefs. People make their decisions on the basis of such things as place of residence, the religious group to which they belong (if any), ethnic background, social class, age, and gender. These important factors work their influence indirectly. For example, gender might affect how one votes by increasing the value one places on publicly funded child care, which in turn would increase the likelihood of voting for parties that endorse such policies. An explanation like this takes us only so far, however, as people belong to many groups, often with conflicting interests; and although group memberships are fairly stable, voters often switch parties from one election to another.

Socio-psychological Model

The second theory, the socio-psychological model, casts a wider net in search of an explanation of vote decisions. The focus in this model is on the psychological process of voting—how people come to make their individual choices. The result is a much more complex model of the various factors. One group of

Like Canadians, the British keep electing people they don't like.

Bruce MacKinnon/Halifax Herald/Artizans

Rational voting: A model that seeks to explain voting decisions by emphasizing the rational evaluation of alternatives (parties and candidates) and the retrospective assessment of the governing party.

influences mirrors the social group factors identified in the sociological model. Friends and family, ethnic groups, and social **cleavages** are likely to shape the interests and values that voters bring to their vote decisions. But more important are the personal and political factors that often occur closer in time to the decision itself. Key among these is **party identification**—the longstanding psychological attachment or loyalty to a party that can directly influence where one is likely to put one's X on the ballot. Party identification acts as a filter through which individuals interpret election issues, candidates, parties, and leaders; it can serve as a shortcut in what can be the daunting process of gathering the information necessary to make a rational voting choice. But if the explanation for why a person voted for the Liberal Party, for example, is "because I always vote that way," the result is that we really have not explained very much. Moreover, evidence suggests that the importance of party identification is decreasing; younger and more educated voters are less likely to defer to partisan loyalties at the ballot box.

Rational Voting Model

The third model of voting stresses the actual calculus that voters employ. According to this model, voting is a rational decision rather than one based on social ties or partisan identification. The **rational voting** model assumes that, in deciding how to cast their ballot, voters

employ a process of evaluation, involving the important issues in the campaign, their assessment of the candidates and the parties' platforms, and their evaluations of the party leaders. This process might compare the alternatives in the search for the "right" choice or it might simply involve an evaluation of the sitting government in an attempt to determine whether a change is needed. This retrospective approach to voting is assumed in campaign slogans that emphasize "a time for change" and helps to explain why voters often punish governments in periods of economic downturn that are at least partly beyond their control. Research suggests, however, that campaigns and campaign strategies set the stage or frame the evaluations that individuals undertake in elections.[35] A party's ability to remain in government is not, then, completely outside its control. An opposition party's ability to become the government is similarly dependent on its ability to shape the electoral agenda. The rational model also helps explain the current preoccupation with party image and the attention directed to leaders.

The important part played by **public opinion polling** in modern elections should also not be overlooked.[36] Modern polling techniques allow parties to quickly and accurately gauge public opinion and potential reaction. Such information has implications for the timing of elections, the selection of leaders, and campaign strategies, tactics, and slogans. Published polls can also influence voter behaviour by deterring them from voting for "lost causes" or by providing them with the information necessary for casting a strategic vote. The importance of polls in elections is underscored by the adoption of restrictions on their publication at certain times during election campaigns. The degree to which such restrictions unnecessarily restrict freedom of expression continues to be debated.

Public opinion polling: The use of survey interviews, often conducted over the telephone, with a representative, randomly selected sample of people, providing an accurate description of the attitudes, beliefs, and behaviour of the population from which the sample was drawn.

POLITICAL PARTICIPATION

A young mother joins a parent–teacher organization to try to change school policy. A university student jumps on a bus to attend a rally in another city to protest against increasing corporate power. A senior citizen attends a political party's constituency meeting to help select the party's candidate in the next election. Each of these is an example of **political participation**, and each provides a measure of political power to the citizens who employ it. If democracy is supposed to afford political power to the people, one could make the claim that healthy democracies are those with high rates of political participation among their citizens.

> **Political participation:** Actions taken by individuals and groups in an attempt to influence political decisions and political decision-makers.

The avenues available to citizens in liberal democracies for influencing political decisions are many, ranging from the simple act of voting to more involved acts such as running for political office or organizing a petition-signing campaign. Participation can occur on several different levels: individual (voting or attending a rally), organizational (volunteering time to an interest or community group or donating money to a political candidate's campaign), and professional (working as a paid lobbyist or a political appointee). More often than not, such action is undertaken to bring about some kind of political change (including a return to the status quo), directly by influencing decision-makers, or indirectly by gaining sympathetic media coverage or public support for the cause. Participation can also occur for purely expressive rather than instrumental reasons; that is, one may participate to feel a sense of belonging with the community as much as to influence political decisions.[37]

Most liberal democracies make participation voluntary, except for the few that legally require citizens to vote, such as Australia. Note that while a failure to vote in Australia may be illegal, the penalty is minor: only about $20.[38] The objective of such laws is to instil a belief in the importance of political participation, which can result in higher rates of participation than one finds in countries such as Canada and the United States. Some have suggested that a similar law should be adopted in Canada in order to increase the rate of participation in elections—a rate that has been steadily dropping. While

the adoption of such a law would no doubt increase the number of Canadians who vote, it would do little to change the underlying causes of low voter turnout.

The vast majority of political acts in liberal democracies are legal, but some actors choose other means to affect political decisions. Civil disobedience—that is, breaking laws in a nonviolent fashion to increase public awareness of their injustice—can often be successful. Recent examples in Canada include blockades of logging roads by environmentalists and of public highways by Native groups. The emphasis on nonviolent protest and on accepting punishment willingly helps to generate support for the cause. **Terrorism**, on the other hand, is a more violent but less effective technique sometimes employed by marginal groups in an effort to dramatically focus attention on their cause. The Front de Libération du Québec (FLQ) kidnapped British trade commissioner James Cross in Montreal in 1970 to pressure the federal government to release 23 members of the group imprisoned for terrorist acts. The group, committed to Quebec independence, resorted to murdering Quebec cabinet minister Pierre Laporte in response to the invoking of the *War Measures Act* by Prime Minister Pierre Trudeau. While dramatic, the events did little to increase public support for the group's cause. The terrorist acts committed on September 11, 2001 in the United States are a vivid reminder that the use of illegal and violent acts for political purposes continues.

Early studies of political participation constructed a hierarchy of political activity in the shape of a triangle, with simple activities such as voting at the base and more demanding activities such as running for office at its peak. The width of the base of the hierarchy meant that a good portion of the population was engaged in the simple activities; the narrowness of the top of the hierarchy meant that relatively few were involved in the more demanding ones. Early researchers also assumed that citizens in democracies naturally progressed from simple activities to more demanding ones—from voting to canvassing for a political party to running for office, for example.[39] Reflecting the traditional domination of male thinking in the study of politics, the most active participants were labelled "gladiators," the less active "spectators," and the uninvolved "apathetics." The general conclusion was that many democracies did not meet the level of participation one would expect.

Early research also suggested that those who could afford to participate and those who had the time to participate made up the largest share of the politically active.[40] This included men and those from historically dominant groups, such as the British and to a lesser extent the French in Canada.[41] More recent studies point to the importance of the definition of politics one employs in determining whether certain groups can be considered to be politically active. Immigrant women, for example, have organized immigrant and ethnocultural associations in response to the lack of attention from the women's movement and minority organizations.[42] Such associations have not traditionally been defined as political, however, and as such, immigrant women's level of political participation has been underestimated. More recent studies have also abandoned the conclusion that citizens progress from simple to more demanding political activities. Data suggests that people's political activity tends to cluster into types, the three most common being voting, campaign activity, and communal activity.[43] People select a political activity partly on the basis of the amount of effort required, the degree of cooperation needed among a number of people, the degree of potential conflict involved, and the nature of the issue addressed.

One of the most striking findings regarding political participation is how few people actually participate in traditional activities. A comparison of average turnout rates between 1961 and 1999 in free elections in 40 democracies suggests that where you live determines in large measure the likelihood that you vote; while only 50 percent of eligible voters cast their ballots in Lithuania, 95 percent do in Australia.[44] The rates of participation are much lower for activities that require greater time commitments and resources. Evidence from Great Britain gives a sense of how dramatically the rates drop as the demands of the activity increase; while voting turnout in the 1990s was 72 percent, only four percent of the population belonged to a political party, and only two percent had canvassed for a candidate.[45]

The rate of participation in various political activities varies by country depending on whether the culture encourages participation and whether the institutional structure makes it easy. Electoral turnout in the United States is relatively low, partly due to the fact that electoral registration depends on individual effort. Some estimates suggest that the rate could increase by several percentage points if a centralized and less demanding system of registration was adopted.[46]

Participation also varies according to the characteristics of individuals, regardless of geography. If those who participate are not drawn equally from all groups in society, government decision-making may not accurately reflect the desires of the population. If age is an important predictor of political activity (see Box 11.2), so too

---

BOX 11.2

WHY DON'T YOUNG CANADIANS PARTICIPATE MORE IN POLITICS?

How closely do you follow politics? Have you voted every time the opportunity was available to you? You have much in common with your peers if your answers are "not very closely" and "not always." Research tells us that young Canadians are less likely to vote than older Canadians. It also reveals that they are less interested in politics but are also happier with democracy and government (see Table 11.4).

Life cycle explanations for this pattern suggest that young people are not participating at high rates because their interests are such that politics is not a priority. Once they start paying taxes, acquire a mortgage, and think about public school for their children, however, they will naturally become more involved. Evidence from a Canadian poll taken in the spring of 2000 by the Institute for Research on Public Policy suggests that the life cycle explanation can help us understand this pattern in opinion and behaviour. Today's young Canadians will be participating at higher rates in 10 years' time. The study also reveals, however, that if we compare the participation rates of today's young Canadians to those of Canadians of the same group in 1990, youth are now participating at lower levels than they were only 15 years ago. Although they will become more politically active as they age, they are unlikely to catch up to the rates exhibited by the previous generation. Can you think of an explanation for why today's young people are less politically active than in previous generations?

Source: IRPP, *Policy Matters* 2(5) (October 2001). Reprinted by permission of IRPP.

Table 11.4 Generational Patterns in Canadian Political Opinion and Behaviour, 2000					
	18–27 (percent)	28–37 (percent)	38–47 (percent)	48–57 (percent)	Over 57 (percent)
Attention to Politics					
Not very closely or not at all	59	41	42	36	32
Voted in the 1997 election	66	69	85	92	91
Very or fairly satisfied with democracy	82	75	74	70	65
Total number of respondents	271	268	281	224	211

Source: Brenda O'Neill, "Generational Patterns in Political Opinions and Behaviour of Canadians," *Policy Matters* 2(5) (October 2001), pp. 11–12, 16. Reprinted by permission of IRPP.

are gender, class, and attitudes. Women are significantly underrepresented in elite political activity, constituting only 19.2 percent of members of national parliaments around the world.[47] The poor and those of lower social classes are less likely to engage in political activity than those with greater access to resources. Political dissatisfaction, political apathy, and political cynicism are likely to turn people away from the political system.

Another striking finding is the degree of change taking place in the kind of political activity which citizens are willing to undertake. Evidence suggests that there has been a rise in the numbers willing to engage in protest behaviour in democracies, both lawful (signing petitions and joining a boycott) and unlawful (attending unlawful demonstrations and occupying buildings), especially among younger citizens.[48] Protest activity can be explained by deprivation—political alienation and frustration with the system can lead individuals to pursue unconventional modes of political activity. Alternatively, the resource model stresses that protest behaviour is merely an alternative mechanism for drawing attention to a cause; those with the political skills and resources are more likely to undertake such activity.

Explanations for the changing nature of political participation in modern democracies point to the changing nature of **civil society** or of overall patterns of social interaction (sometimes called *social capital*) and the increasing dissatisfaction with politics and governments. Robert Putnam suggests that citizens in the United States are less engaged at the civic level than they were previously and that this has important implications for the health of that democracy.[49] Community activities, ranging from bowling leagues to parent–teacher associations, provide opportunities for community members to build the social trust and social capital necessary for democratic government. There is debate, however, over whether social capital has indeed declined, or whether it may simply be manifesting itself in different ways, such as recycling (a community-minded event), and in different forums, such as the Internet (through discussion lists and "zines"—noncommercial publications of small circulation).

Neil Nevitte suggests that participation rates have changed due to a process of cognitive mobilization grounded in increased education, the expansion of mass communications, and the rise of a knowledge-based economy. People are smarter and can access information much more easily today than previous generations. Combine this with a loss of confidence in traditional political institutions and the result is a shift from traditional to non-traditional forms of participation, including protest (see Figure 11.2).[50]

Is there such a thing as too much democratic participation?[51] Some argue that effective political decision-making requires that leaders enjoy a degree of freedom from democratic demands. Decision-makers are better informed than ordinary citizens and are more likely to be able to make decisions in the general public interest. Individual citizens are more likely to think about the costs and benefits to their own neighbourhoods and groups, for example, and are less likely to have as much information or expertise as political elites. Besides, the argument goes, people are generally politically apathetic. The participation of apathetic citizens leads to uninformed decision-making. To this way of thinking, too much democracy is definitely a bad thing.

Figure 11.2   Confidence in Government Institutions, 1981–1990

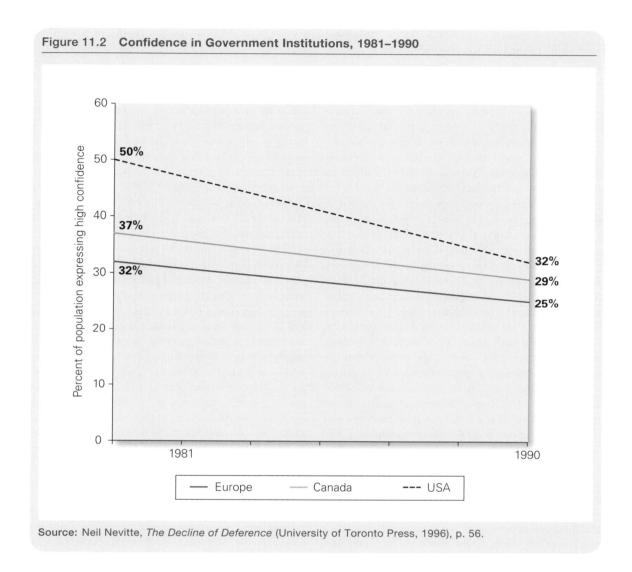

Source: Neil Nevitte, *The Decline of Deference* (University of Toronto Press, 1996), p. 56.

For others, however, full participation by an informed and rational citizenry is a necessary and crucial condition for democracy. Such an argument rests on the assumption that the pursuit of individual truths—a goal of liberalism—can and will lead to conflicting interests. The mechanism for controlling such disputes is to establish laws on the basis of popular consent. Popular consent, the argument continues, can be established only through full political participation, and without it the legitimacy of political authority is in doubt. Participation also helps citizens learn greater

tolerance, achieve greater rationality, and develop an appreciation for civic activism.

TOOLS OF DIRECT DEMOCRACY

A number of devices have the potential for increasing direct citizen political power in representative democracies, which some would regard as means of reducing the **democratic deficit**. Populist movements and parties in the western United States and Canada have successfully pushed for the adoption of these mechanisms to return a measure of power to citizens to balance that enjoyed by governments. The three most common are the referendum, the initiative, and the recall. Despite their potential, they are not immune from manipulation by governments and powerful groups of citizens alike. The result is that few governments have adopted such mechanisms wholeheartedly; most employ them on occasion, sometimes in an attempt to manipulate the political outcome.

Referendums provide opportunities for citizens to vote directly on pieces of legislation or on constitutional questions. The *binding* referendum requires that the government act on the result of the referendum, and thus provides the greatest potential for citizen power. Such referendums are employed in Australia for constitutional change. *Nonbinding* referendums (sometimes referred to as *plebiscites*) do not tie a government's hands in the same manner as binding referendums. In democracies with politically interested, informed, and active populations, however, the reality is that the results of nonbinding referendums would be hard for any government to ignore. In 1992 Canada employed a referendum to determine whether citizens accepted the constitutional changes that the prime minister and premiers had set out in the Charlottetown Accord. The results of that vote were surprising: a majority of citizens voted to defeat a constitutional package that had been the result of intense and protracted negotiations between the federal and provincial governments and leaders of Aboriginal communities in Canada. While this was only the third referendum used at the national level, thousands have been used at the municipal level and over 60 at the provincial level, most notably within Quebec regarding secession[52] and in British Columbia, Prince Edward Island, and Ontario on electoral reform.[53]

> **Referendum:** A mechanism that provides citizens with the ability to vote directly on pieces of legislation or constitutional changes.

Referendums have both advantages and disadvantages. One advantage is that public decisions are arrived at in a public manner—through free and open public debate.[54] Such debate leads to political education: people are more likely to inform themselves about issues if they have a direct say in the outcome. A second advantage lies in allowing the people to voice their own interests rather than having those interests filtered through political representatives and political parties. This empowering mechanism provides a potential counter to the increased apathy and growing cynicism occurring in many democratic states; the knowledge that one has an ability to take part in deciding fundamental public questions is likely to increase satisfaction with democracy and the political system. Perhaps most importantly, the use of referendums, especially on divisive issues, can provide a measure of legitimacy to the outcome, since it can be said that "the people have spoken." But such a result is likely only if the public believes that the process was conducted fairly.

The use of referendums can also be problematic. Opponents highlight the fact that referendums can be employed strategically by the political elite for purposes other than to solicit the people's views on the issue. Such concerns were raised in the referendums on sovereignty held in Quebec because the way the question is phrased can encourage, although rarely guarantee, a particular outcome. Second, referendums do not provide the public with a mechanism for shaping the policy agenda; instead, the people are provided with an opportunity merely to veto a government's proposal.[55] Some observers have also questioned the capacity of the general public to deal with complex issues. Finally, referendums can be highly divisive when the issue is a salient one and if it engenders strong opposing positions in various groups in society.

The **initiative**, on the other hand, is a device that allows registered voters to use petitions to propose the introduction of new laws or change existing ones. Initiatives are meant to complement representative democracy by providing citizens with a populist mechanism for introducing laws the government might be avoiding for whatever reason. One possibility is that a successful petition can force a referendum on the proposed bill, and, if sufficient support is achieved, the bill automatically becomes law. Alternatively, a successful petition can result in the bill being introduced into the legislature, where it follows the normal legislative process.

> **Initiative:** A mechanism that allows citizens to petition the government to introduce or adopt specific pieces of legislation or force a referendum on an issue.

A successful initiative process should set the requirements fairly high to ensure that minority interests do not hijack the democratic process. In 23 of the 50 U.S. states, on the other hand, initiatives appear on the election ballot if a previously circulated petition receives only a small proportion of the population's signatures; voters then have the opportunity to agree or disagree with the initiative. The process can also be taken over by wealthy interest groups and industries that hire professional signature gatherers to collect the signatures at $1.50 each.[56] Once on the ballot, many of these initiatives pass even though a majority of the state's population opposes the measure. If only a small proportion of the population actually votes a minority of dedicated voters can wield tremendous but unrepresentative influence. In some cases the proposed legislation is even inconsistent with existing laws or constitutional requirements. In others, it dangerously ties the legislature's hands. Proposition 13, for example, which passed in California in 1978, prohibited the state's government from ever increasing property taxes (one imagines it was not too difficult to gather support for the measure!). The result, however unintended, is one of the worst public school systems in the nation given the freeze on public funding. Minority interests do not always correspond with those of the greater public good.

The third mechanism of direct democracy employed in representative democracies is the **recall**, which allows registered voters to petition to remove a member of the representative assembly between elections. The mechanism is intended to increase representative accountability by providing a direct means for unhappy electors to "de-elect" their representative without having to wait for the next general election. The same concerns about the initiative exist with the use of the recall. The number of signatures required on the petition to trigger the recall of an elected member should not be so low that the process can be hijacked by a small group of disgruntled voters, for elections are costly affairs in terms of both time and money; but neither should the number be so high as to render the recall process meaningless.

Recall: A mechanism that allows citizens to petition to remove their political representative before the next election period.

The recall provides an important mechanism for ensuring that representatives keep the interests of their constituents in mind. At the same time, however, the parliamentary system makes it particularly difficult for representatives to always act according to the wishes of constituencies (assuming for the moment that such wishes are easily determined). Party discipline, for instance, requires that the interests of the party determine the actions of each representative, given the constraints of responsible government. In addition, representatives may be provided with information that makes it clear that constituents' interests may be best served in a manner that contradicts their own wishes.

British Columbia's *Recall and Initiative Act,* which came into effect in 1996, sets relatively high requirements that have only recently been met.[57] The B.C. government's decision to implement a harmonized sales tax (HST), after explicitly campaigning against such a move in the 2009 election, created sufficient unhappiness that a petition begun in the summer of 2010 to eliminate the tax became the first to pass since the law was enacted. The organizers of the petition collected signatures from 10 percent of registered voters in each of the province's 85 ridings, about 700,000 in total, thereby prompting a provincial legislative committee to call for a provincewide referendum in the fall of 2011. The new Christy Clark government made changes to the HST, but it was rejected by a 55%-45% margin in a mail-in referendum.

This decision initiated a series of recall petitions, a second element of the Act. For a recall to be successful, the signatures of 40 percent of voters within the MLA's riding would have to be collected within a 60-day period. The anger over the HST ultimately led to the resignation of the premier, Liberal leader Gordon Campbell, only 17 months into his four-year term. The BC experience provides a most interesting example of democracy in action.

CONCLUSION

Democracy is based on putting a certain measure of political power in the hands of the people. Modern representative democracies provide only a few mechanisms by which citizens are able to influence government policy. Encouraging the use of the referendum, the initiative, and the recall for increasing citizen power rests on the presumption that the citizenry desires to participate more fully in democratic decision-making. Declining voter turnout in Western nations and increased political cynicism suggest that attention should be focused on problems other than simply the lack of opportunity for political participation. Successful democracy requires above all else that citizen participation is effective—citizens must believe that legitimate political action will result in clear and understandable initiatives that respond to that action. The most fundamental of democratic institutions, the election, provides the clearest mechanism for instilling that belief. In too many instances, however, electoral results are ambiguous, do not directly reflect the choices made by the voters, and appear to shut out a number of groups and interests whose chances are directly dependent on achieving electoral success. The democratic ideal will remain an elusive goal until citizens believe they are powerful, regardless of whether they choose to act on that power.

DISCUSSION QUESTIONS

1. What factors do you consciously consider when deciding how to cast a vote in a general election? Can you think of any factors that might affect your decision unconsciously?

2. When should referendums be used? For what issues? Can you think of any occasions or reasons when the use of a referendum might be ill advised?

3. Explain why students' participation in university politics is so low. Does your answer help explain participation in politics more broadly?

4. Should a more proportional electoral system be adopted at the federal and/or provincial level in Canada? Why or why not?

5. What do you consider the greatest challenge facing modern democracies? Why?

FURTHER READING

Butler, David, and Austin Ranney, eds. *Referendums Around the World: The Growing Use of Direct Democracy*. Washington, DC: American Enterprise Institute, 1994.

Courtney, John C. *Elections*. Vancouver: UBC Press, 2004.

Dalton, Russell J. *Citizen Politics: Public Opinion and Political Parties in Advanced Industrial*

Democracies, 5th ed. Washington, DC: CQ Press, 2008.

Eijk, Cees van der, and Mark Franklin. *Elections and Voters*. Basingtoke, NY: Palgrave Macmillan, 2009.

Everitt, Joanna, and Brenda O'Neill, eds. *Citizen Politics: Research and Theory in Canadian Political Behaviour*. Don Mills, ON: Oxford University Press, 2002.

Gidengil, Elisabeth, André Blais, Neil Nevitte, and Richard Nadeau. *Citizens*. Vancouver: UBC Press, 2004.

LeDuc, Lawrence, Richard G. Niemi, and Pippa Norris, eds. *Comparing Democracies 2: New Challenges in the Study of Elections and Voting*. Thousand Oaks, CA: Sage, 2002.

O'Neill, Brenda. "Indifferent or Just Different? The Political and Civic Engagement of Young People in Canada," prepared for Canadian Policy Research Networks (CPRN) research series *Charting the Course for Youth Democratic and Civic Participation*, September 2007, 48 pp. Available at http://www.cprn.org/doc. cfm?doc1/41751&l1/4en (Document Number 48504); accessed June 13, 2008.

ENDNOTES

1. Federal Election Commission, "2008 Presidential Campaign Financial Activity Summarized," News Release, June 8, 2009, available at http://www. fed.gov./press/press2009/20090608PresStat. shtml; accessed September 2, 2010.

2. Mitch Wagner, "Obama Election Ushering in First Internet Presidency," *Information Week*, November 5, 2008, available at http://www.informationweek. com/story/showArticle.jhtml?articleID=212000815; accessed August 25, 2010.

3. Darin Barney, *Prometheus Wired: The Hope for Democracy in the Age of Network Technology* (Chicago: University of Chicago Press, 2000), p. 22.

4. This section relies heavily on David Held, *Models of Democracy*, 2nd ed. (Stanford: Stanford University Press, 1996), ch. 1.

5. Joseph Schumpeter, *Capitalism, Socialism and Democracy* (New York: Harper, 1942), p. 265.

6. The percentages vary dramatically around the world, from a high of 77 percent in North America to a low of 11 percent in Africa. See Internet World Stats, "Internet Usage Statistics: The Internet Big Picture," available at http://www.internetworldstats.com/stats.htm; accessed August 25, 2010.

7. See the Ask Bristol website at http://www.viewfinder.public-i.tv/askbristol.php; accessed June 13, 2008.

8. See David Stewart and Keith Archer, *Quasi-Democracy? Parties and Leaders in Alberta* (Vancouver: UBC Press, 2000).

9. See Internet World Stats, "Internet Usage Statistics."

10. *Ibid.*

11. For an excellent review of the interplay between democracy and information and communications technology, see Darin Barney, *Communication Technology* (Vancouver: UBC Press, 2005).

12. Held, *Models of Democracy*, p. 317.

13. *Ibid.*, pp. 353–60.

14. See the Elections Canada website at http://www.elections.ca for information on the 2011 and previous general elections.

15. In most parliamentary systems, voters choose the members of the legislature, and the share of seats held by parties within that body determines the government. Hence, voters only indirectly determine which party forms the government.

16. These requirements follow those set out by David Butler, Howard Penniman, and Austin Ranney, eds., *Democracy at the Polls: A Comparative Study of Competitive National Elections* (Washington, DC: American Enterprise Institute, 1981), p. 4.

17. See "The Basic Law for the Federal Republic of Germany," September 23, 1990, available at http://www.psr.keele.ac.uk/docs/german.htm; accessed June 13, 2008.

18. "Halt E-voting Says Election Body," BBC News International online, August 2, 2007, available at http://news.bbc.co.uk/2/hi/uk_news/politics/6926625.stm; accessed June 13, 2008.

19. See Martin Harrop and William L. Miller, *Elections and Voters: A Comparative Introduction* (Basingstoke, UK: Macmillan, 1987), ch. 9.

20. André Blais, Louis Massicotte, and Agnieszka Dobrzynska, "Direct Presidential Elections: A World Summary," *Electoral Studies* 16 (1997): 441–55.

21. See "2000 Presidential Electoral and Popular Vote," U.S. Federal Election Commission, available at http://www.fec.gov/pubrec/fe2000/elecpop.htm; accessed June 13, 2008.

22. Harrop and Miller, *Elections and Voters*, p. 251.

23. Hanna Pitkin, *The Concept of Representation* (Los Angeles: University of California Press, 1967).

24. See, for example, Anne Phillips, "Democracy and Representation: Or, Why Should It Matter Who Our Representatives Are?," in Anne Phillips, ed., *Feminism and Politics* (New York: Oxford, 1998), pp. 161–92.

25. See Russell J. Dalton, *Citizen Politics: Public Opinion and Political Parties in Advanced Industrial Democracies*, 5th edition (Washington, DC: CQ Press, 2008).

26. See Donald Blake, "Electoral Democracy in the Provinces," *Choices: Strengthening Canadian Democracy* 7 (2) (2001).

27. James Robertson, "Bill C-24: An Act to Amend the Canada Elections Act and the Income Tax Act," February 5, 2004, Parliamentary Research Branch, Library of Parliament, available at http://www.parl.gc.ca/37/2/parlbus/chambus/

house/bills/summaries/c24-e.pdf; accessed June 13, 2008.

28. See Ian Stewart, "Bill C-24: Replacing the Market with the State?," *Electoral Insight* 7 (1) (January 2005): 32–36, available at http://www.elections.ca/res/eim/pdf/insight_2005_01_e.pdf, accessed September 7, 2010; and Peter John Loewen and André Blais, "Did Bill C-24 affect Voter Turnout? Evidence from the 2000 and 2004 Elections," *Canadian Journal of Political Science*, 39 (4) (December 2006): 935–43.

29. Richard Briffault, "Soft Money, Issue Advocacy and the US Campaign Finance Law," *Electoral Insight* 4 (1) (May 2002): 9–14.

30. This section closely follows André Blais and Louis Massicotte, "Electoral Systems," in Lawrence LeDuc, Richard G. Niemi, and Pippa Norris, eds., *Comparing Democracies 2: New Challenges in the Study of Elections and Voting* (Thousand Oaks, CA: Sage, 2002), pp. 40–69.

31. The equivalent distortions in the 2004 election were as follows: Liberal, 1.19; Conservative, 1.08; Bloc Québécois, 1.41; and NDP, 0.39.

32. See http://www.citizensassembly.bc.ca/public, accessed June 13, 2008, for an overview of the mandate of the Assembly, and for its procedures and reports.

33. A number of the arguments for and against the FPTP can be found in Law Commission of Canada, *Voting Counts: Electoral Reform for Canada* (Ottawa: Public Works and Government Services, 2004) and in Louis Massicotte, "Changing the Canadian Electoral System," in Paul Howe, Richard Johnston and André Blais, eds., *Strengthening Canadian Democracy* (Montreal: IRPP, 2005), pp. 65–98.

34. See Mebs Kanji and Keith Archer, "The Theories of Voting and Their Applicability in Canada," in Joanna Everitt and Brenda O'Neill, eds., *Citizen*

Politics: Research and Theory in Canadian Political Behaviour (Don Mills: Oxford University Press, 2002), pp. 160–83.

35. Richard Johnston, André Blais, Henry Brady, and Jean Crête, *Letting the People Decide: Dynamics of a Canadian Election* (Montreal and Kingston: McGill-Queen's University Press, 1992).

36. See David Butler, "Polls and Elections," in LeDuc, Niemi, and Norris, *Comparing Democracies 2*, pp. 236–53.

37. Sandra Burt, "The Concept of Political Participation," in Everitt and O'Neill, *Citizen Politics*, pp. 232–46.

38. Australian Electoral Commission, available at http://www.aec.gov.au/Elections/australian_electoral_system/electoral_procedures/Electoral_Offences.htm; accessed June 13, 2008.

39. Lester Milbraith, *Political Participation: How and Why Do People Get Involved in Politics?* (Chicago: Rand McNally, 1965).

40. Sidney Verba and Norman H. Nie, *Participation in America: Democracy and Social Equality* (New York: Harper & Row, 1972).

41. John Porter, *The Vertical Mosaic: An Analysis of Class and Power in Canada* (Toronto: University of Toronto Press, 1965).

42. Yasmeen Abu-Laban, "Challenging the Gendered Vertical Mosaic: Immigrants, Ethnic Minorities, Gender and Political Participation," in Everitt and O'Neill, *Citizen Politics,* pp. 268–83.

43. Russell J. Dalton, *Citizen Politics: Public Opinion and Political Parties in Advanced Industrial Democracies*, 4th ed. (Washington, DC: CQ Press, 2006), p. 38.

44. Mark Franklin, "Electoral Participation," in LeDuc, Niemi, and Norris, *Comparing Democracies 2*, pp. 148–68.

45. Dalton, *Citizen Politics*, ch. 3.

46. *Ibid.*, p. 41.

47. Inter-Parliamentary Union, "Women in National Parliaments," available at http://www.ipu.org/wmn-e/world.htm; accessed September 8, 2010.

48. Russell J. Dalton, *The Good Citizen: How a Younger Generation is Reshaping American Politics* (Washington, DC: CQ Press, 2008).

49. Robert Putnam, "Bowling Alone: America's Declining Social Capital," *Journal of Democracy* 6 (1995): 65–78.

50. Nevitte, *The Decline of Deference* (Peterborough, ON: Broadview Press, 1996).

51. See the discussion in William Mishler, *Participation in Canada* (Toronto: Macmillan, 1979).

52. Patrick Boyer, *Direct Democracy in Canada: The History and Future of Referendums* (Toronto: Dundurn Press, 1992).

53. See Elections BC at http://www.elections.bc.ca/elections/ge2005/referendum.htm; accessed June 13, 2008.

54. This section relies heavily on David Butler and Austin Ranney, eds., *Referendums: A Comparative Study of Practice and Theory* (Washington, DC: American Enterprise Institute for Public Policy Research, 1978) and Patrick Boyer, *The People's Mandate: Referendums and a More Democratic Canada* (Toronto: Dundurn Press, 1992).

55. Mendelsohn and Parkin, "Introducing Direct Democracy in Canada," *Choices: Strengthening Canadian Democracy* 7 (5) 2001: 7.

56. Doug Sanders, "Practical Pitfalls of the Plebiscite," *The Globe and Mail*, October 24, 2000, p. A3.

57. *The BC Recall and Initiative Act* is available online at http://www.bclaws.ca/EPLibraries/bclaws_new/document/ID/freeside/96398_00.

For various weblinks discussed in this chapter, please go to the book's website at **www.studyingpolitics4e.nelson.com**

Political Parties: Imperfect but Essential

David Stewart

CHAPTER OBJECTIVES

After you have completed this chapter, you should be able to:

- understand some of the classic literature on political parties
- discuss the functions of political parties and how these have evolved
- describe the roles of party members
- evaluate the various methods of choosing candidates and leaders
- describe the various types of parties
- classify different party systems

INTRODUCTION

Political parties are lauded in theory, but critiqued and ignored in practice. There is widespread agreement that parties are an essential part of democracy and indeed, that democracy—particularly parliamentary democracy—is impossible without them. As British Prime Minister Benjamin Disraeli put

Political party: An organized group of people with at least roughly similar political aims and opinions that seeks to influence public policy by getting its candidates elected to public office.

it in the 1800s, "Without parties, parliamentary government is impossible." This is not simply the view of a 19th century politician; in the middle of the 20th century American political scientist E.E. Schattschneider proclaimed that "political parties created democracy and that modern democracy is unthinkable save in terms of the parties."[1] Later in the 20th century, in a magisterial analysis of parties and party systems, Giovanni Sartori argued persuasively that "parties are the central intermediate and intermediary structure between society and government."[2] At the beginning of this century, Dalton and Wattenberg noted that "political parties have created political identities, framed electoral choices, recruited candidates, organized elections, defined the structure of legislative politics, and determined the outputs of government. Indeed, to most of us, democracy without political parties is unthinkable."[3] Finally, Lawson and Merkl launched a recent analysis of parties by suggesting that "vital, resilient democracies are not possible without strong, prosperous parties."[4]

On the other hand, it is increasingly clear that neither political scientists nor citizens feel that parties are performing as expected and desired. In an examination of public opinion and political parties in established democracies, Russell Dalton finds "growing indications that the citizens . . . were becoming more critical of the politicians, political parties and political institutions that form the basis of the democratic process."[5] Indeed, following a review of the world values surveys, he shows that "across the twenty-two advanced industrial democracies included in this survey, majorities express confidence in the legislature in only four nations . . . Perceptions of political parties are even more critical. . . . The 2004 Eurobarometer study found that confidence in political parties averages only 18% across the European Union."[6] Diamond and Gunther concur, maintaining that "there is substantial and growing disaffection with many of the specific institutions of democracy, and no single institution is held in greater disrepute than the political party" and that "citizens are cynical about their representative institutions, political parties, and, most of all, their politicians."[7]

While political parties are both imperfect but essential in contemporary democracy, what exactly are they? Sartori starts with the classic definition of parties provided by British philosopher and politician Edmund Burke: a "party is a body of men united, for promoting by their joint endeavours the national interest, upon some particular point in which they are all agreed."[8] Aside from the obvious privileging of males in this 18th century definition, it underplays both the nature of organization and the electoral component. Sartori himself focuses more on the role parties play in democracy and suggests that a party is "any political group that presents at elections and is capable of placing through elections, candidates for public office."[9] Important to Sartori's definition is the capability of successfully placing individuals in public office. This is most helpful in distinguishing parties from organizations that contest elections without any hope of success. The relevance of this criterion becomes particularly crucial in descriptions of party systems because there are many more parties and candidates contesting elections than there are parties that elect members. At a more practical level, the ACE Electoral Knowledge Network offers the following definition: "a political party is defined as an organized group of people with at least roughly similar political aims and opinions, that seeks to influence **public policy** by getting its candidates elected to public office."[10]

Tory attack ads sully Canadian Parliament.

Malcolm Mayes/Artizans

PARTY FUNCTIONS

These definitions lead us into a discussion of the functions that parties are expected to perform in democracies and then to an examination of how well these functions are in fact performed. Writing in the Canadian context, Meisel and Mendelsohn provide a useful summary of these functions as follows:[11]

- integrating and mobilizing citizens by providing linkages between citizens and the state
- setting the policy agenda and formulating policy
- recruiting elites
- organizing the operation of government
- structuring the vote and elections
- organizing public opinion
- aggregating interests so that various communities have a say in decisions, compromises can be forged, and interests can be organized and heard[12]

Emerging from their discussion of party functions is what can be termed the **decline-of-party thesis**.

Decline of party thesis: A theory that many of the traditional functions performed by parties are in decline or have been taken over by other actors.

They argue that a number of factors have contributed to a decline in the role of parties. These include the rise of the bureaucratic state, the emerging strength of "interest group politics," and the shift of political discussion from legislatures to federal–provincial diplomacy. In addition, the changing role of the media, the emergence of public opinion polling, and the increasing volatility among voters mark the more challenging world in which parties find themselves.

Integration and Mobilization

Parties once provided a connection between citizens and the state and helped to forge national cohesion, but the role parties play in integrating and mobilizing citizens has diminished. Clear examples of this include diminishing rates of participation in parties, and even more importantly, declining turnout in general elections. Throughout the democratic world fewer citizens seem to be voting in elections and parties have not been able to stem this tide. In Dalton's formulation, "advanced industrial democracies are experiencing a new period of partisan dealignment, which means that a significant proportion of the public is failing to develop party attachments or is becoming openly critical of political parties as institutions of government."[13] He goes on to explain that "an analysis of the 19 advanced industrial democracies for which long-term survey data exist shows that the percentage of partisans has decreased in seventeen cases" and that "weakened partisanship is also increasing the fluidity of voting patterns."[14] Traditionally, support for different parties could be distinguished on the basis of social cleavages. Lipset and Rokkan, for instance, identified class and religion as two of the key cleavages around which party support was based.[15] Other differences based on geography, such as region or urban/rural location have also been important, as have those based on gender and age. It appears that the strength of these cleavages has declined although it remains rare to have parties receiving support evenly across all of these characteristics.

Broader changes in campaign technology and fund raising also reduce the ability of parties to integrate and mobilize citizens as members of the party directly.[16] Essentially, because parties have moved away from dependence on members and workers for the conduct of campaigns, the incentives for party involvement are somewhat reduced.

Making Policy

To some degree parties still set the policy agenda by virtue of the issues they emphasize in elections and the policies they pursue in government. Where this is so, such functions are largely in the hands of the party leaders, and ordinary party members have little say in policy formulation. But political parties generally play a limited role in policymaking; most government policy stems from the executive branch and is prepared by people in the civil service or advisors who may not even belong to the party. Moreover, government, let alone party policy, may not reflect grass roots beliefs and can rarely be traced to specific internal policy debates and resolutions.

Regarding the limited role of parties in policy formation in Canada, Ken Carty explains: "Though Canadian parties have regular policy conventions, filled with delegates from local associations, the products of these meeting do little more than indicate the general tenor of a party's ambition. The leadership has always felt free to adopt or mold them as it sees fit, in parliamentary manoeuvering or in writing electoral manifestos."[17] The decline in the social cleavages noted above has some spill-over for the policy agenda as it has led to "the growth of short-term factors, such as issues and candidate images, as a basis of electoral choice…. Parties will be judged more often by their leadership and the policies they advocate."[18] This not only enhances the importance of issue selection in connection to the policy agenda but it further emphasizes the importance of elite recruitment.

Elite Recruitment

Parties remain central players in the recruitment of political **elites**, at least as it relates to the nomination of candidates for public office and the designation of party leaders. Boss Tweed, a 19th century Democratic

Elite: A small group of individuals who have significantly more power than other members of their community. They are either in a position to make authoritative decisions or have privileged access to decision-makers.

party boss in New York (graphically portrayed by Jim Broadbent in the Hollywood movie *The Gangs of New York*) noted the importance of this role when he reputedly remarked, "I don't care who does the electing as long as I can do the nominating." Obtaining a party nomination or endorsement remains almost a necessary condition for election to public office and, in some cases, may be a sufficient condition. As William Cross explains, in some situations "the general election is little more than a formality."[19] Voters in general elections are largely restricted to choosing their representatives and Prime Ministers or Presidents from a short-list provided by the major political parties.

In 2008 Americans essentially chose between Barack Obama and John McCain, the winners of the major party primaries. The rules which parties establish help to determine the nominees, even when the selection is broadened to general voters. More than 35 million Americans voted in the Democratic party primaries of 2008, but the rules for the scheduling of these primaries and caucuses, and the number and apportionment of delegates selected by these events, were governed by the Democratic party.[20] When state parties in Michigan and Florida attempted to circumvent these rules, the party reduced their representation. Parties continue to play a major role in candidate endorsement and make important decisions about the way in which candidates will be chosen. As Gallagher wrote almost a quarter of a century ago: "the selection of candidates is the only area of party activity where ordinary members can expect to have a decisive voice."[21]

The regular election of independents[22] may diminish the importance of party nominations. The 2010 election in Australia, at first blush, provides hints of these limits of party nominations. The determination of whether Labor or the Liberals would form the federal government came down to the decisions of a handful of independent members. But in reality these members were able to choose only which of the two major parties would govern and, even more significantly, all of the independents who were elected had previously sought a party nomination or contested elections as a party candidate. Without their prior history in political parties, these individuals might never have been elected. Cross notes that in six recent Canadian elections, "there has been a cumulative total of one successful candidate who was first elected as an

Independent. Essentially, the only path to election in Canada passes through a major party nomination."[23]

Organizing Governments and Structuring Votes and Elections

The activities in Australia point out the important role played by political parties in organizing governments. The independent MPs had to negotiate with the parties and it was the decisions the parties made through their leadership that proved to be crucial. In elections where a single party obtains a majority of seats, the role of parties in organizing the government is even more evident. Questions regarding who holds what positions in government are answered by the party leadership. This is also the case in formal coalitions such as followed the 2010 British election. Negotiations among the Labour, Conservative, and Liberal Democratic parties eventually concluded in a power-sharing arrangement between the two latter parties.

With party representatives generally monopolizing positions in government and holding all but a handful of legislative seats, the role of parties in structuring the vote and **elections** is crucial. Parties provide a short-hand for voters who may not wish to inform themselves about individual candidates, since knowing something about the party greatly simplifies the voting process. Lawson notes the increasing power of party leaders, suggesting that "personalistic politics have been encouraged in order to win elections, and in the process the party's active members and elected representatives have been given a greatly reduced role in the determination of their party's candidates and policies. The pattern is found without respect for continent or history."[24]

> **Election:** A mechanism by which the expressed preferences of citizens in democratic states are aggregated into a decision regarding who will govern.

Organizing Public Opinion and Interest Aggregation

The role of parties in organizing public opinion and aggregating interests is less impressive. Elections, to some degree, follow the issues emphasized by parties, but the role played by the media and indeed interest groups in this area may well be of more importance.

Conservative leader David Cameron and Liberal Democrat leader Nick Clegg forge a coalition government after the May 2010 British election.

Rex Features/The Canadian Press(Nils Jorgensen)

However, parties have tended to promote policies that are somewhat responsive to public opinion. Lawson has criticized parties for this, suggesting that "moving toward a program more centrist than a party's members support in order to wage a more successful campaign has clear antidemocratic implications."[25]

The ability of parties to aggregate interests is complicated by the ability of interest or advocacy groups to present issues without the need for compromise that parties must make to put together their campaigns. As Dalton explains, there has been an "explosion of citizen interest groups, social movements, and other social groups in recent decades."[26] He goes on to suggest that, not surprisingly given the emergence of more groups, "there has been a dramatic increase in interest articulation over the past generation but an erosion of interest aggregation within the polity."[27] The ability to participate in policy debates and discussions is certainly available in interest groups. Canadian citizens, by a three-to-one margin, feel that interest groups are a better way to get their issues considered.[28] Fewer citizens feel that party participation is necessary for their views to be heard and considered.

Performance of Functions

The ability of parties to perform most of the roles ascribed to them has obviously weakened. The functions that parties continue to do well relate to the organization of governments, elite recruitment, and vote structuring. While the discussion above suggests that these functions have increasingly devolved to leaders, this phenomenon is not entirely new. Duverger's mid-20th century analysis noted two dominant trends, namely: "the increase in the authority of party leaders and the tendency towards personal forms of authority."[29] Leaders provide the face of the party in elections, play a role in candidate selection, and exercise great influence over the prioritization of issues. As such, perhaps the most important role parties play today is that of designating the leader.

Policy debates within parties have partially shifted to decisions regarding the selection of leaders. As Carty explains, "party members . . . know that changing party policy or electoral direction is not done by getting resolutions passed in party conventions, or promises inserted into election manifestos. Significant change is best brought about by engineering a change in personnel, especially in the party leadership."[30] That is, leaders are proxies for new policy directions. In the Canadian context this is not new. Writing in the early 20th century, André Seigfried observed that "it is of the first importance to the success of a party that it should be led by someone who inspires confidence and whose mere name is a program in itself. . . . Canadians attach themselves rather to the concrete reality than to the abstract principle. They vote as much for the man who symbolizes the policy as the policy itself."[31] More recently, Reginald Whitaker drew attention to the emergence of what he termed the 'virtual' party in Canada. As he explains, "virtual parties form around politicians seeking the leadership of parties. . . . The party, as such, serves as little more than a convenient franchise with brand recognition, marketing 'location,' and ready sources of campaign funding."[32]

THE ROLE OF PARTY MEMBERS

When one reflects on the activities that parties and their members might directly perform, it is possible to identify at least four quite distinctive endeavours.

Election Campaigns

First, party members can campaign. But the conduct of campaigns has become professionalized and parties no longer need to rely on their own members to perform these tasks. William Cross's audit of Canadian political parties points out that "the national campaigns are dominated by long-time party insiders and political professionals, with essentially no role provided for grassroots activists."[33] Local candidate campaigns, on the other hand, still have room for individual party members and volunteers.

Party Policy

Party members can also make and attempt to implement policy. However, as discussed earlier, in few parties, if any, does ordinary membership provide much of a policy voice. Nonetheless, policy views clearly relate to decisions about party membership. In the Canadian context, Cross and Young have shown that almost all party members (98 percent) identified a belief in the party's policies as a reason for joining, and over half (56 percent) indicated that a desire to influence party policy was important to the membership decision.[34] Cross and Young suggest, however, that excluding party members from a direct connection with government policy is not indefensible. As they point out, "it is elected members who are accountable to voters, not the parties' activists. The data . . . describing the socio-demographic makeup of party members also speak against allowing them a direct role in the making of public policy. They are not representative of the total population."[35]

Party Finance

Another potential role for members relates to party finance and donations. Again, this is not terribly important today because parties have developed highly sophisticated fund-raising structures or can count on some form of state support. Cross raises serious concerns about this in Canada, arguing that the system of public funding "makes political parties wards of the state and diminishes the incentive to communicate with partisans between elections and involve them in party affairs."[36]

The 2008 American presidential election outlined some of the limits to state financing. Barack Obama's effectiveness in raising money directly through social media techniques enabled his campaign to refuse matching funds in the general election. As Boatright suggests, "public financing was killed by the party that

created it, and there are few prospects that it will be resuscitated anytime soon."[37]

The funding of the parties has become a political issue in Canada. Major reforms were initiated in 1974 that provided for limitations on campaign spending and required disclosure of contributions and spending. As well, the state became involved by providing funding to parties both in the form of reimbursements of election expenses and in tax credits for contributions. The purpose was to make party financing more transparent, while also decreasing the dependence of parties on corporations for their financial well-being.[38] With the possible exception of the NDP, including individual and union funding, Canadian parties did not have a tradition of depending on their members for funds. Nor were ordinary members much used for fundraising activities.

The next series of major reforms took place almost 30 years later under Prime Minister Jean Chrétien. These changes were highly controversial, even within Liberal ranks with the party's president calling the reforms "dumb as a bag of hammers."[39] These new changes restricted the ability to make contributions to political parties largely to individuals while also cutting the amount any one person could give. Corporations and unions were shut out of the party financing business. In partial compensation for this change, direct public subsidies were provided to the parties. These subsidies were based on the vote the party received in the preceding election and began at $1.75 per vote.

The goal of such changes was to reduce the dependence of parties on the willingness of donors to support them. After the changes were implemented, donations could still be collected from individual Canadians and the parties began actively courting such contributions. Young and her colleagues argue that it remains necessary to raise funds and that the connection with donors in Canada is not fully consistent with the "cartel model," as noted below.[40]

The new Conservative party proved much better at raising money from individual donors and it began to distance itself from other parties in terms of money. Once the Harper Conservatives formed a government, they reduced the amount any individual could donate to a party from $5,000 to $1,000 in what has been described as a "calculated move" to hamper the Liberals.[41] The Conservatives now enjoy a huge advantage in funding and can almost run a "permanent campaign."[42]

A quick look at the figures on fundraising makes clear the nature of the Conservative advantage. In 2008 the Conservatives raised over $21 million from 112,184 contributors. In contrast, the Liberals managed to garner less than $6 million and only 30,890 people contributed to their coffers. The Conservatives raised more money and had more donors than the Liberals, New Democrats, Bloc, and Green parties combined. Moreover, this was no one-year fluke as the 2009 results show similar results.[43]

Young and her colleagues suggest that changes in party financing in Canada have created "three classes of parties: smaller parties that are heavily reliant on state funds (the Bloc and the Greens), parties with some reliance on the state (the Liberals and the NDP), and parties that are substantially self-supporting (the Conservatives)."[44] The ability of the Greens and the Bloc to conduct well-financed, professional campaigns without the need to raise funds has helped to change the nature of Canadian elections. After the Harper Conservatives gained a majority in 2011, however, they announced that the current $2-per-vote subsidy would be phased out over three years.

Choosing Candidates and Leaders

Finally, there is the party members' opportunity to choose the party's standard-bearers. This role involves the selection of candidates and leaders. Voters can choose only from formally nominated candidates and, in most democratic systems, candidates who do not represent parties have virtually no chance of winning. As Rahat explains, "in order to be selected to parliament, one needs first, (in almost all cases) to be selected as a candidate of a specific party. . . . Candidate selection takes place almost entirely within particular parties."[45]

In their selection of candidates, and particularly leaders, parties provide a gate-keeping role for the political system. This is the key role of party members. As Duverger explains, "membership of the party enables one to participate in the appointment of candidates for the elections. In fact the only real element of membership to be found in American parties consists in participation in the closed primaries."[46]

Table 12.1	Variations in Candidate Nomination Selectorate[50]

Designation by Leader
Choice of Small Nominating Committee
Delegate Selection
Party Members in Open Vote

Source: Gideon Rahat, "Which Candidate Selection Method is the Most Democratic?" *Government and Opposition*, Vol. 44, No. 1, p. 68.

The selection of candidates is increasingly open to more and more party members, a trend described as "the democratization of candidate selection methods."[47] Hazan notes the advantages and disadvantages of different methods of selection and suggests that caution is needed in viewing open votes by party members as an advance because it can "expand the influence of well-organized groups" and increase "even further the power of incumbents."[48]

The manner in which candidates are chosen varies substantially among political parties (see Table 12.1). At times designations are made by centralized committees while in other parties local meetings of members are decisive. In still other parties, a formal vote of all party members is necessary. The method affects the outcome and the nature of a party's candidate roster. Some parties use quotas to ensure that their roster provides a somewhat proportionate mix of men and women or in some cases ethnic minorities. Such balances are easier to insure in multi-member constituencies, and research has shown that selection by committees has resulted in a more equitable candidate mix.[49]

In Canada, the control over nominations rests largely with local members and "the right of the local association to designate their candidate is longstanding and jealously guarded. Sitting MPs must be re-nominated by their association and every election sees some incumbents unseated by riding partisans for what are usually local, idiosyncratic reasons. The party leadership . . . for the most part accepts the right of its members to choose a candidate who will represent local interests."[51]

Nonetheless, it is also important to keep in mind that parties may not simply use a single method of nomination. While the power to select candidates is generally left to local party members, there remains a key role for leaders in this process. An analysis of candidate nomination in Canada in 2006 revealed that leaders were able to protect incumbents, approve the timing of contests, exercise a final veto over who was selected, and, in the case of the Liberal party, in some cases directly appoint a candidate. Moreover, parties are requiring potential candidates to fill out extensive disclosure forms prior to be approved as a candidate for a nomination. Cross suggests that the "reality is that in no instances are the local members able to select a candidate completely free from the interference of central party dictates."[52] This is not without benefits; it is most important for parties to retain some control over who their potential candidates are, and a filtering of prospective candidates can help in this regard.[53]

Maintaining a role for the party leadership is needed since party members may not choose their candidates with the best electoral interests of the party in mind. As Dalton notes, "previous research also suggests that polarization along a policy dimension tends to be greater at the elite level than among voter blocs.[54] If party members are more ideologically oriented than voters in general, then the candidates chosen by political parties might not be those the electorate would prefer. The number and commitment of those involved in the selection process can thus be important.

In the 2010 American mid-term election, much was made of the influence of the so-called Tea Party movement within the Republican party. As the BBC reported, "in one of the biggest upsets, Tea Party-backed candidate Christine O'Donnell beat a veteran congressman for the Senate nomination in Delaware. A Tea Party candidate also won the race to stand for New York governor. Republican strategists fear that these candidates will not appeal to the wider electorate in November mid-term polls."[55] These fears proved accurate, as both candidates suffered defeats in what had been seen as winnable races.

The openness of the primary process in the United States allows relatively easy penetration and weakens the ability of party elites to affect the outcome. Incumbent members have sometimes lost their party designation as a result of such contests. For example, former Democratic vice-presidential candidate Joseph Liebermann lost the Democratic senatorial primary in Connecticut. Rather than accept the outcome, Senator

Liebermann ran as an Independent and voters in the general election returned him to office.

Such outcomes are not restricted to American primaries. In Canada, a number of MPs have faced challenges and been unseated in nomination battles. One of the more famous of these resulted in the defeat of Alliance/Conservative MP Chuck Cadman prior to the 2004 election. Mr. Cadman also refused to accept his loss and not only went on to win re-election as an Independent, but also to play a major role in extending the life of the minority Liberal government.

What applies to candidates is even more important for leaders, particularly when one considers the way in which the role and authority of leaders have increased.[56] Prospective leaders must go through the mechanisms and processes selected by parties before they reach the general population. There is immense variation in the processes parties use to choose their leaders (see Figure 12.1, p. 320). For example, we earlier mentioned the extensive primary system in the United States whereby millions of Americans cast secret ballots in state-organized intra-party elections.

Many parties use conventions at which elected or appointed party members vote for the leaders. The convention system is very different from the membership ballot since, as Duverger argued, "indirect representation is an admirable means of banishing democracy while pretending to apply it ...; the mentality of the delegates is never the same as that of those who delegate them, with the result that every additional stage of delegation increases a little more the gap between the will of the base and the decision of the apex. The election of the leaders of a party by a small group of delegates is not the same in character as their direct election by the mass of the members."[57]

LeDuc makes a similar point in discussing the democratization of party leadership selection. His depiction of the selection continuum is presented in Figure 12.1. As he puts it, "moving further along the continuum towards more inclusive institutions . . . the selectorate begins to resemble the electorate as a whole, and the leadership selection process begins to take on many of the characteristics of elections. . . . Different selectorates might reasonably be expected to choose different types of leaders."[58]

At the other end of the spectrum is the selection of leaders by elected members of legislatures

Figure 12.1   **Categorizing Party Leadership Selectorates**[59]

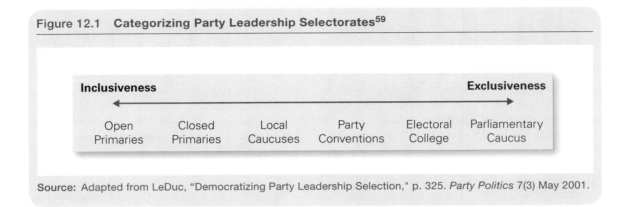

Inclusiveness   Exclusiveness

| Open Primaries | Closed Primaries | Local Caucuses | Party Conventions | Electoral College | Parliamentary Caucus |

Source: Adapted from LeDuc, "Democratizing Party Leadership Selection," p. 325. *Party Politics* 7(3) May 2001.

(parliamentary caucuses). Australia provides a clear example of this and the importance of these elected members has been demonstrated by the unseating of incumbent prime ministers. Shortly before the 2010 election, the Australian Labor party's parliamentary caucus unseated Kevin Rudd, replacing him with Julia Gillard, who went on to win a narrow victory in the general election. This process unfolded quickly and dramatically and did not involve the general party membership. Driving this process were party concerns about Rudd's re-electability, suggesting that the parliamentary decision was focused on responding to public opinion.

It is important to keep in mind that, as with candidate selection, it is possible to combine different methods. The British parties provide excellent examples of systems that combine party member primaries with a degree of influence for the parliamentary caucus. Each of the major parties gives the elected members of parliament a decisive voice in deciding the short-list from which the ordinary members can choose.[60] For instance, in the 2010 Labour party leadership election in Britain, in order to be a candidate one had to secure nominations from at least one-sixth of the party's parliamentary caucus. The final decision was made by an Electoral College in which Labour MPs and MEPs had one-third of the votes, ordinary members of the party had another one-third, with the final one-third going to affiliated organizations. These rules helped shape the outcome; if voting had been restricted to either the parliamentarians or even the regular party members, David Miliband would have become leader. Instead, his brother Ed's lead among

affiliated members was wide enough for him to eke out the win.[61]

Party Democracy

Duverger again provides a useful perspective on the degree of democracy in party operations. In his view, "democracy requires that parliamentary representatives should take precedence over party leaders and the members of the electorate over the members of the party."[62] This stands in contrast to what he observed in many parties where "there can be seen a tendency of party leaders to give orders to the parliamentary representatives in the name of the militant members. This domination of the party over its elected representatives constitutes a form of oligarchy."[63] In short, Duverger implies that democracy is weakened when the preferences of party militants take precedence over those of elected representatives and thus indirectly the general electorate.

This raises the intriguing issue of whose views in the party should predominate. If the best interests of the party, or even the polity, are the goal, then whose views should the party emphasize? For instance, should the party focus and present the views of its leaders, or should it give more weight to its wider legislative caucus? Or in contrast, should more weight be given to the party executive or those who attend party assemblies? Another option is to give more weight to the general membership and volunteers. Yet another option is for the party to be focused on the aggregation of broader societal viewpoints. Such considerations affect not only the kind of internal mechanisms that parties develop for leadership, candidate, and policy selection, but they also affect the general approaches of the parties in election campaigns and government.

Duverger presented a model of party democracy suggesting that "democratic principles demand that leadership at all levels be elective, that it be frequently reviewed, collective in character, and weak in authority."[64] Such a model is rare in the real world. Given the expertise and more rigid ideological perspectives of party activists, the notion that they control the party's agenda and its choice of candidates, leaders, and policies might not only disadvantage the party in elections, but also be far from the best interests of society in general. The mechanisms by which parties choose candidates and leaders are thus a matter of grave importance for both intra-party democracy and democracy generally.

PARTY LEADERSHIP SELECTION IN CANADA

With all this in mind, we shall now take a quick look at leadership selection in Canada. We have already seen from several authorities that the leader is perhaps even more paramount in Canada than in other democratic systems. One would be hard-pressed to overestimate the influence of leaders in election campaigns and the organization of government and, as discussed above, Canadian leaders are able to veto individual candidacies. This particular power flows from the financial reforms of 1974 discussed earlier.

The Liberal party historically dominated Canadian politics[65] and from 1993 to 2004 it was really unchallenged. Obviously, then, the selection of a Liberal leader was critical. Jean Chrétien was elected in 1990 in a traditional convention—a gathering of delegates from constituencies across the country with each constituency given equal weighting.[66] The dynamics of the convention process led the major candidates to attempt to influence the delegate selection at the constituency level. In short, supporters of the candidates would show up at the delegate selection meetings and try to elect as many delegates as possible who were willing to support their candidate. Jean Chrétien and Paul Martin were the most successful at this, but Chrétien proved more effective and was able to win a comfortable first-ballot victory.

The leadership was decided before the convention was held. In essence, the only way Chrétien could have lost was if delegates who were elected to support him voted for another candidate. This marked at least a temporary end to what can be called the deliberative convention, in which the convention itself was the key moment for leadership choice and elected delegates exercised independence as the convention moved from ballot to ballot. Instead, as the system evolved, the front runner wins easily and decision-making is displaced from the convention itself to delegate-selection meetings, where the candidates engage in trench warfare. As part of this local warfare, candidate organizations are active in recruiting instant members who will come to the delegate-selection meetings to vote for a candidate's slate of delegates. Instant members "are simply recruited into local associations by individual candidates who want their vote in a party contest."[67] Candidate organizations find it tempting to engage in organizational shortcuts, such as the involvement of interest groups or the mobilization of ethnic or religious groups.[68] The views of long-time party members are likely to be bypassed, given the exigencies of this system. Pre-convention activities became the key to victory, and party competition extended to delegate-selection meetings and even prior efforts to attract money, support, and organization.

The relations between Chrétien and Martin deteriorated over time and the pro-Martin wing of the party eventually forced Chrétien into announcing his resignation.[69] This move set up a new leadership race in 2003, but with a different set of rules. Once again there would be a convention, but instead of winner-take-all ballots for selecting delegates, voters at delegate-selection meeting would express a preference for a leadership candidate, and the delegates would be apportioned accordingly. So if 40 percent of the voters at a local delegate-selection meeting preferred Martin as leader, 40 percent of the delegates from that constituency would go to the convention pledged to vote for Martin. In the 2003 race, Martin had such a huge organizational and financial advantage that he was able to dominate the delegate-selection process and went to the convention with the vast majority of delegates pledged to support him. More than 60,000 Liberal members voted in these selection meetings and Martin's dominance was overwhelming. He secured the election of more than 3,000 delegates while his competitor elected fewer than 500.

Following the Martin government's defeat in the 2006 federal election, the party used a similar set of rules to choose a new leader, but the race was quite different. Funding changes made it more difficult to organize and no single candidate was able to dominate the delegate-selection process.[70] In the end, Stéphane Dion became Liberal leader in December 2006, as seen in Box 12.1.

Dion led the Liberals to a rather disastrous finish in the 2008 election and a new leadership selection was scheduled. However, controversy surrounding a government economic update and a potential coalition between the Liberals and the NDP helped create a situation in which Dion was pressured to resign immediately, and his successor, Michael Ignatieff, was chosen by a select group including the caucus, defeated candidates, and party executive.[73] Subsequently, the Liberals decided to move away from a convention model, and at the 2009 convention, determined that their next leader will be chosen by a direct vote of all party members.

The model adopted by the Liberals in 2009 takes us back to the Conservative party, as the Liberals basically copied the Conservative model. The method for selecting the leader was an important part of the merger that created the Conservative party in 2004; indeed, "the biggest issue was the formula for choosing the leader of the new party."[74] While both the Alliance and the Progressive Conservative parties allowed all members to vote for the leader, they used different models. The Alliance had a simple vote of all members, while the Conservatives had used different models. In 1998 they employed a direct vote, but in a nod to the brokerage nature of the country, gave each riding 100 points to distribute, regardless of how many party members were in the constituency.[75] The Alliance party had far more members than the PCs, and the PCs wanted a model that would preserve considerable influence for them. The 1998 PC model proved to be the compromise.

This method assigns the 100 points for each riding in accordance with the votes cast by the party members in the riding. The number of people voting in the riding is irrelevant; it is simply the percentage of votes cast for each candidate that matters. Almost

---

BOX 12.1

LIBERAL LEADERSHIP, 2006–2008

Under the modified Liberal rules, the 184,555 members of the party could gather in their constituencies and vote directly for a leader as well as for delegates. This vote would take place on a single "Super Weekend."[71] As in the 2003 contest, constituency equality was the norm and delegates from each constituency were apportioned in accordance with member preferences. However, unlike 2003, the votes cast by ordinary members did not prove decisive as no candidate's delegate total reached 30 percent. As a result of the votes, the delegate distribution was as follows: Michael Ignatieff, 29.3 percent; Bob Rae, 20.1 percent; Gerard Kennedy, 17.5 percent; Stéphane Dion, 16 percent; Ken Dryden, 5.1 percent; Joe Volpe, 4.8 percent; Scott Brison, 3.9 percent; Martha Hall-Findlay, 1.0 percent; and Undeclared, 2.4 percent.

The delegates selected in this manner were pledged to vote for their candidate on the first ballot at the convention, but thereafter could vote as they chose, while the "super delegates," who were not locally elected, could always vote as they wished. The votes cast by super delegates at the convention essentially moved Dion past Kennedy on the first ballot. With no decision on that ballot, the convention reverted to a deliberative model and delegates made a series of choices on subsequent ballots as to whom they wished to see become leader. On the second ballot, after receiving an endorsement from last-place and eliminated candidate, Hall-Findlay, Dion maintained his lead over Kennedy. Eventually, Kennedy dropped out and, in line with an earlier agreement, endorsed Dion who then managed to defeat Ignatieff on the fourth ballot.[72] Thus, a candidate who finished fourth in the preference vote by all members and who had very little caucus support became the Liberal leader.

100,000 members voted in the contest and Stephen Harper won an easy victory. He took 56.2 percent of the points to 34.5 percent for his main competitor, Belinda Stronach. Harper's victory was even more overwhelming if one looks at the actual vote. He out-polled Stronach 67,143 to 25,345, but the points race was closer because Stronach did better in ridings where there were fewer Conservatives voting.[76]

The debates over these models reflect somewhat different perspectives on the nature of leadership choice and the importance of members versus con-stituencies. The Conservative decision to accept riding equality was symbolic of a return to a more accom-modative approach to politics. The party reiterated its support for this leadership selection system at its 2011 convention.

All-member votes have been used by the other par-ties represented in the House of Commons, too, and the New Democratic Party and Bloc leaders were also put in place by membership votes. In the case of the Bloc, Gilles Duceppe was elected in 1997 by a mail vote of almost 50,000 members. Jack Layton secured the NDP leadership in 2003 in an all-member vote involving about 45,000 members. The model adopted by the NDP combined a mail ballot, an Internet vote, and on-site voting, and like the Labour party in Britain, provided special representation for affiliated organizations. The NDP model reserved 25 percent of the votes for affiliated organizations, largely unions.

Leadership selection methods remain in flux in Canada, but each of the major parties now has some form of party membership vote in place to choose its leader. This has not been without controversy, and concerns about 'instant members' and the devaluing of long-time service have been raised.[77] All members of the party can vote directly for their choice to lead the party and he or she will go on to set its policy direction and provide its electoral face. For most party members, their most important job is over until the next leadership election.

DIFFERENCES IN PARTY TYPE

Thus far, political parties have been discussed as if they were all the same. However, in order to under-stand parties' role in the democratic process, it is

Table 12.2	Different Types of Parties	
Cadre	Electoral-Professional	Ideological
Mass	Brokerage	Interest
Catch-all	Cartel	Franchise

crucial to discuss the differences which exist among them. Indeed, substantial debates surround different types of political parties, including those listed in Table 12.2.

One of the most influential distinctions among different types of parties was made by Maurice Duverger in his classic book, *Political Parties.* Duverger focused on party organization and dis-tinguished between mass and cadre parties.[78] *Cadre parties* were essentially groupings of notables for the purposes of election. Parties with this type of organization made little effort to recruit members, had tiny memberships whose admission was epi-sodic, were not financed by membership dues, and gave members virtually no policy voice. Such a party was dominated by the parliamentary **caucus** and its leadership. In contrast, **mass parties** had large mem-berships and engaged in the active recruitment of members. Joining the party often involved a kind of formal pledge to observe party regulations and sup-port party policies; moreover, the party generally derived a large measure of financial support from its members. Such parties were supposedly demo-cratic in policy-making, such that party conventions decided on policy and guided the elected legislative leadership. Duverger's typology focused largely on party organization, and those using this approach generally favoured the mass model for its member-ship involvement.

Mass party: A political party with a large, involved membership and a central set of principles that it promotes at the same time as it seeks electoral support.

Writing somewhat later, Kircheimer talked about the evolution of parties and especially changes to some mass parties.[79] He placed greater emphasis on the nature of the election campaigns waged by parties.

He introduced the notion of **catch-all parties** and noted the incentives pushing mass parties to move in this direction. Catch-all parties downplayed ideological perspectives, placed more emphasis on the party leadership, and offered fewer opportunities for ordinary members. Kircheimer's analysis suggested that many mass parties were moving away from their base and that "conversion to catch-all parties constitutes a competitive phenomenon. A party is apt to accommodate to its competitor's successful style because of hope of benefits or fear of losses on election day."[80]

> **Catch-all party:** A political party that takes a pragmatic approach to elections and focuses its agenda on securing electoral victory. See also electoral-professional party.

Angelo Panebianco expanded on this concept with his notion of the **electoral-professional party** that seemed to characterize parties and electoral competition in the late 20th century. The electoral-professional model resonates with the description of the way in which parties perform their basic functions.[81] Under this model, greater weight is given to professionals in the conduct of campaigns; leaders and issues are prioritized; campaigns are aimed at the general electorate rather than the traditional base; and the dependence of parties on members for funding is substantially reduced.

> **Electoral-professional party:** A political party whose primary goal is to form a government rather than to advance a particular ideology. It is characterized by a small membership, a reliance on corporate donors, and capital-intensive campaign techniques. See also catch-all party.

Katz and Mair build on the independence of parties from members and indeed the general electorate in their construction of the *cartel party* type.[82] Such parties, following the increasing disconnection between parties and their electorates, co-operated to reduce the likelihood of the volatile electorate shifting to new parties by providing advantages, particularly in financing, to the existing parties. For instance, state subventions not only reduced the dependence of parties on their ability to raise funds, but also placed a huge financial barrier in front of the formation of new parties by basing their reimbursement on previous electoral support.

Underlying these differences among parties is the way they approach and contest elections.[83] Pragmatic parties, such as catch-all[84] and electoral-professional parties,[85] generally present a non-doctrinaire approach to policy and a strategic approach to electoral competition. Such parties largely reflect the public image and priorities of their leaders and are probably the most common of western parties. They were once thought to be the general model towards which all parties were evolving. However, such an evolution was not regarded by most analysts as a positive development. Pragmatic parties are concerned with practicality, with winning elections, and indeed the key focus is electoral victory. Campaigns are geared towards victory rather than based on doctrinal beliefs. Competition between parties of this type is often marked by overlapping proposals and borrowed ideas. Conflict between such parties can be derided as lacking principles and being simply a contest between the ins and the outs. Defenders of such parties maintain that seeking to maximize their votes does not mean that they do not have any principles—just that they cannot realize their principles without winning. Similarly, it could be argued that it is not the case that such parties lack a particular viewpoint but that they are selective in emphasizing their views and indeed are highly responsive to public opinion. Parties of this type can be charged with the possession of a *hidden agenda*.

Some other parties take a more ideological or doctrinal approach. These parties make an effort to fit policies into rational value-oriented schemes and place more emphasis on ideological purity than on attaining government office. These parties want to win elections but **ideology** is more important than winning. Competing parties of this type would follow what has been described as the *manifesto model* of competition. In theory, voters are attracted to such commitment, but in reality these parties find it difficult to compete with their pragmatic counterparts. *Ideological parties* can be criticized for inflexibility and placing their own priorities ahead of those of the electorate. Party ideologies were discussed in Chapter 6.

Still other parties approach elections and campaigns as an opportunity to advance a particular interest. Such parties represent a specific issue or interest within society, be it ethnic, religious, or regional, and although they contest elections vigorously, they are not focused on winning control of government. Indeed, the narrowness of their focus effectively precludes the full acquisition of power, although they at times participate in coalitions. The parties are focused on the particular group or issue they represent and are concerned with seeing that their concerns are taken into consideration by the other parties. *Interest parties* cannot become serious contenders for power unless they broaden either their issue appeal or clientele; however, when they do so they move beyond the interest category. Ethnicity-based parties or environment-oriented parties can be placed in this category.

Research on Canadian parties has resulted in another type of party entering the mix, namely the **brokerage party**, a category in which the Liberals and Conservatives often place themselves. As Cross notes, these parties take an accommodative approach to managing **cleavages** based on language, geography, and region.[86] They are generally seen as playing a 'brokerage' role in attempting "to resolve the persistent problems of national unity in Canada," and even critics agree that "Canadian society is complex in its social divisions."[87] Carty notes that "conventional wisdom says the classic Canadian party acts as a broker, presenting policy packages that accommodate the competing claims of different regions, communities, and groups. In a word, national parties are to succeed by aggregating, rather than articulating, interests. This, of course, sets them off from the cleavage-based parties of most other democracies."[88]

Brokerage party system: A definition of Canada's national party system which argues that ideological polarization is less pronounced in Canadian politics than in many other countries; instead, the main parties are said to attempt to aggregate enough diverse interests to win elections.

Cleavage: A persistent division among two groups of voters, based on long-term demographic or economic characteristics. Examples include language, religion, class, and region. Groups on either side of the cleavage may be mobilized into a subculture which shapes the voting patterns and political perceptions of its members.

The need to accommodate and aggregate means that "Canadian parties must find ways to encompass a large, diverse, and shifting coalition of supporters who are animated by the often conflicting interests and demands of their distinctive communities, regions, and cultural groups." Carty suggests that to help us understand the way this operates, "we should think about Canadian parties as *franchise systems*,"[89] somewhat akin to Tim Hortons or McDonald's.

Thinking of parties in this manner gives us an image of an organization with an overall national brand that nonetheless adjusts to local circumstances. This model is the "franchise contract that defines the parties and can be characterized simply as local autonomy for national discipline. The parliamentary party provides the leadership who effectively set public policy; the constituency associations provide the forum for members' political participation with the power to control riding activity and the right to support party candidates that they choose."[90] In parties of this type, the important policy decisions are made at the centre, and the local organizations and members content themselves with controlling the local dimensions of politics including the selection of candidates.

PARTY SYSTEMS

Noting differences in the approaches and focus of political parties is important but it is equally vital to understand the way in which parties in the same country relate to each other. As the discussion of party types suggest, parties are affected by their competition. Political scientists use the term **party system** to describe the number of parties and the way they relate to each other.

Party system: The interaction among relevant parties that shapes political competition and the nature of government formation.

A simple way to describe the party system is to count the number of parties contesting elections. Indeed, Sartori noted in his classic work on parties and party systems that "for a long time party systems have been classified by counting the number of parties— whether one, 2 or more than 2."[91] The historical debate about party systems revolved around two-party systems versus multi-party systems, with the former often supported by a majoritarian or plurality electoral system and found largely in Anglo-American democracies. However, simply counting parties can create confusion. A visit to the Elections Canada website reveals that over a dozen political parties submitted election expenses following the 2008 election,[92] and 18 parties contested the 2011 election. Describing the Canadian party system as, say, a 15-party system would be both confusing and inaccurate.

It is useful to return to the definition of parties supplied by Sartori with its emphasis on capability. He noted that parties are "capable of placing through elections, candidates for public office."[93] This reduces the number of parties in the Canadian party system dramatically, as it is unlikely, for instance, that the Marijuana party or the Rhinoceros party can place candidates in public office. Rather, such a party is a device for attracting attention and spreading a message. A more interesting question is the nature of the Green party, which reached a height of seven percent of the vote in the 2008 election, but was still not able to elect a member to the federal parliament.

Sartori talks about the relevance criterion with respect to parties, suggesting that the parties involved in the party system must affect the competition in terms of tactics and policy.[94] By this criterion one might argue that the Green party has indeed met the definition of a party in Canada. Certainly, the number of votes secured by a party is not always a strong portent of the number of its legislative seats. In many political systems, the seven percent of the vote won by the Greens would provide them with substantial legislative representation, but the **first-past-the-post** or single member plurality system used in Canada has actually kept them from the legislature. In 2011, however, the party put most of its effort in a single riding and managed to get its leader elected. Similarly, the 38 percent of the vote won by the Conservatives in the 2008 election would in many countries using some form of proportional representation have required a coalition government. In Canada, the Conservatives were able to form a single-party government, albeit with only a minority of the seats in the legislature, until they gained a majority in 2011.[95] In short, the nature of the electoral system has a tremendous effect on party competition and election outcomes as well as party

organization.[96] (See Chapter 11 for more discussion of electoral systems.)

> **First-past-the-post:** An electoral system that requires the winning candidate to receive more votes than any other in order to win the seat—that is, to receive a plurality of votes. The majority of first-past-the-post systems employ single-member electoral districts.

The two-party system is in danger of running out of cases as in Britain, Australia, Canada, and New Zealand more than two parties are able to secure electoral representation and even become part of government. The United States thus supplies the best example of a two-party system with only the Republicans and Democrats competing realistically for the Presidency and almost all of the Congressional seats.[97] A two-party system can be readily recognized as containing only two parties capable of government participation and holding the vast majority of seats. Other parties serve more as spoilers than competitors for office.

Descriptions of multi-party systems are more complex. To use the Canadian example again, at least until 2011 only two parties had real prospects of government formation and they obtained far more seats than the other parties which elected members. Jean Blondel described a modified two-party system which he called a two and a half party system.[98] This system contains two dominant and competitive parties which alternate in power but another party (or parties) exists alongside and

Men debate the merits of the U.S. two-party system.

Richard Bartholomew/Artizans

at times their support is necessary for stable majority governments to exist. The current British party system fits this mold with the large Conservative and Labour parties competing for power and the somewhat smaller Liberal Democratic party able to determine which of these parties actually formed the government. The price of Liberal Democratic support for the Conservatives following the 2010 election was a coalition government and a referendum on electoral reform.

Most party systems fall into what can be described as a multi-party system with more than three parties securing substantial legislative representation and making single-party governments rare. Some of the debate around the classifications within this system relate not only to the number of parties, but also the nature of the competition. Sartori's classification scheme, for instance, distinguished between what he termed moderate and polarized pluralism and focused on the presence of more extreme parties and the unsuitability of some parties for inclusion in coalitions.[99]

Wolinetz provides an insightful overview of the various classification schemes used to understand party systems, and notes that "Sartori's has had the longest shelf-life and most widespread acceptance."[100] But he also shows that most liberal democracies now fall into the moderate pluralist category, making distinctions within this category essential. Siaroff's work moved in this direction by looking at such systems according to whether there is one dominant party within them, two main parties, or a balance among a larger number of parties.[101] Thus, the counting of parties is modified by focusing attention on the relative size of their support and this becomes a key feature in describing the system and distinguishing among many systems where the party count appears similar.

Sartori provided one other category that should be discussed: the predominant party system.[102] This is sometimes termed a one-party dominant system and is identified by the ongoing control of government by a single party and a large advantage for that party in the popular vote. Post-apartheid South Africa provides a good example of this as the African National Congress party has won each of the elections since 1994, securing more than three-fifths of the vote in each election and winning well over half of the legislative seats. Many other parties exist and indeed secure legislative representation, but they are not competitive with respect to government formation.

Typologies of party systems are complex and none of the existing schemes is perfect. It is nonetheless valuable to examine the differences in party systems in different countries and ensure that the classification enhances understanding of the parties and the way they relate to each other in elections and governments. Party strategy and organization are often heavily influenced by their competitors and the competitive system in which they are found. An ability to effectively characterize the party system enhances understanding of the parties themselves.

PARTY COMPETITION IN CANADA

Canada has not had a two-party system for some time. In 1921 the Liberal–Conservative duopoly of seats disappeared forever with a variety of smaller parties securing legislative representation in every subsequent election. Although at times these parties have held the balance of power, only the Liberals and Conservatives have formed governments, and the Liberals had a huge historic advantage on this dimension. Most of the time, one of the two large parties was able to form a majority government, that is, a government based on a single-party majority in the House of Commons. These majorities were almost always manufactured by the electoral system, as it is rare for a party to win 50 percent of the votes cast. Indeed, following the 1997 election, the Liberal party was actually able to form a majority government even though 62 percent of the vote went to other parties.

The Liberal party's dominance from 1993 to 2004 was owed partially to a division on the political right. Two parties, the Progressive Conservatives and either the Reform or Alliance party essentially split the vote on the right, enabling the Liberals to win relatively easy election victories. The parties on the right had to decide whether they were going to continue their split and allow the Liberals to win election after election, or compromise, merge, and perhaps be able to compete for power. In a move that took most political pundits by surprise, the two right-wing parties agreed to join forces in 2004. Internal referendums on the merger were conducted, and it was eventually endorsed by majorities in both parties, resulting in the creation of the new Conservative Party of Canada.[103] This 'new'

Figure 12.2 **Party Support in Canadian Elections**

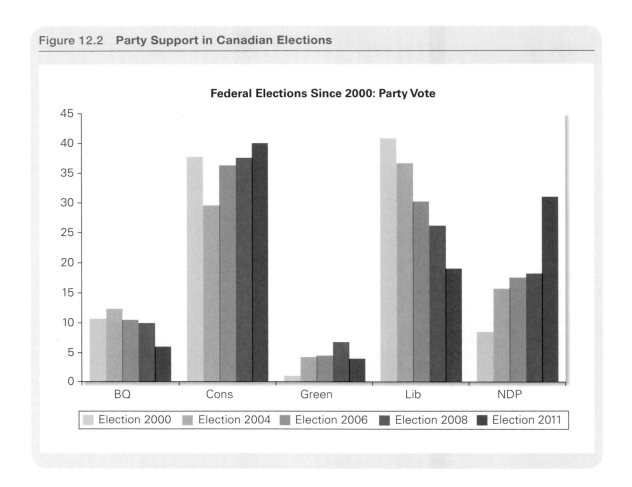

Federal Elections Since 2000: Party Vote

Legend: Election 2000, Election 2004, Election 2006, Election 2008, Election 2011

party was able to form minority governments following elections in 2006 and 2008, and a majority government in 2011. Support for various parties since 2000 is shown in Figure 12.2.

After 2004, it was generally felt that **majority governments** were difficult to achieve in Canada. Between 1993 and 2011, the separatist Bloc Québécois was able to win at least half the seats in the House of Commons from the province of Quebec. The mathematics made the acquisition of a majority, with so many seats essentially unavailable and with the

> **Majority government:** A government in which one party holds all the seats in the cabinet as well as the majority of seats in the legislature (or lower house in bicameral legislatures).

Liberals no longer able to capitalize on the division on the right, more difficult than ever before. The growing support for the Green party complicated the party competition even more.

The support for the Bloc Québécois and the Green party are in part a product of the financing reforms discussed above. Neither party attracts much money in the form of individual donations, but the state subsidies they receive not only encourage voters to support them, but also enable them to conduct better campaigns.[104]

In the aftermath of the 2008 election and the economic crisis that engulfed much of the world, the Conservative government presented an economic plan in late 2008 that included a number of controversial measures including major changes to the party-funding regime. Such changes would have left the Conservatives considerably better off than the other parties by getting rid of the vote-based subsidy. The reaction of the other parties was swift and unprecedented in Canadian politics:[105] the Liberals and New Democrats agreed to form a **coalition government**. However, between them the two parties could not outvote the Conservatives so their ability to force the Conservatives from power and form a stable government was dependent on support from the Bloc Québécois. The Bloc indicated its willingness to keep the Liberal–NDP coalition in power for an agreed period of time.

> **Coalition government:** A government that occurs when two or more parties hold seats in cabinet supported by a combination of parties that forms a majority in the legislature.

Canadian party politics appeared in crisis for a few weeks as the Conservatives obtained a controversial prorogation from the governor general and were able to survive in power. The Conservatives won the public opinion battle by focusing on the notion of 'separatists' controlling the Canadian government and the prospect of a coalition for which no one had voted.[106] The Conservatives remained in power, but they were forced to keep funding for their opponents intact.

The coalition idea demonstrates the changed world in Canadian party politics, with the New Democrats possessing 'coalition' potential and the Liberals willing to countenance a power-sharing arrangement. Although different from the union of the right-wing parties, the potential now exists for cooperation on the 'left.' An element of such cooperation could actually be seen in the 2008 election when the Liberal leader Stéphane Dion decided not to run a Liberal candidate in the riding where the Green leader was seeking election and the Greens reciprocating by not challenging the Liberal leader.[107]

What is curious is that despite the prospect of minority or coalition governments between 2004 and 2011, there was no real discussion of electoral system change at the federal level. Although there has been much discussion in the provinces, no electoral reform has taken place, and in the three provinces where the issue has been put to the voters in a referendum, the reforms were rejected.

The May 2011 federal election witnessed a massive transformation of the Canadian party system and in the competition among the main parties. The Conservatives gained a majority of seats with 39.6 percent of the popular vote, while the historically dominant Liberal party was decimated, returning with only 34 seats based on 18.9 percent of the vote. The Bloc was also nearly eliminated, with only four seats and six percent of the national vote. The NDP rose from fourth to second place with 103 seats and 30.6 percent of the vote. Over half of the NDP seats were won in Quebec, which supported a federalist party for the first time since 1993. The Conservative majority was essentially based in English Canada. As a result, even if the BQ had not collapsed and even if the NDP had not swept Quebec, previous predictions of the impossibility of a majority government in modern Canada were rendered false.

PARTY SUPPORT IN CANADA

The role played by the Bloc Québécois between 1993 and 2011 and the recent surge of NDP support in Quebec suggest that, despite the diminishing strength of social cleavages in terms of distinguishing party supporters from one another, and despite the role these cleavages play in the decline-of-party thesis discussed above, social cleavages remain significant in Canadian party politics. While such divisions do not decide elections, they do provide the bases from which parties must build. As Elisabeth Gidengil and her colleagues explain, "regional, religious and ethno-racial cleavages continue to shape Canadians' voting behaviour and it would be difficult to understand recent election outcomes without taking voters' social background characteristics into account."[108]

The obvious starting point is region. The major parties in Canada do not draw their support evenly from across the country. Between 1993 and 2011 the Bloc Québécois contested elections only in the province of Quebec but it generally took around 40 percent of the vote there and won about half of the seats.[109] Conservative strength is also somewhat regional, being primarily in the West and specifically in the Prairies, but that party attracted increased support in Ontario in 2011, especially in the Toronto region.

Between 1993 and 2011 the Liberal party drew large proportions of its seats from Ontario; in the 2008 election, half of its members were from that province.

In 2011, however, the Liberal vote fell both in Ontario and across the country. The New Democrats were able to out-poll the Liberals in all four Western provinces in recent elections, but in each they trailed the Conservatives by a considerable margin. Until its dramatic breakthrough in Quebec in 2011, the NDP was always stronger in Ontario; now, the party is able to regularly win seats in Nova Scotia, New Brunswick, and Newfoundland.

The results in Quebec indicate a linguistic as well as a regional division. One cannot adequately capture the Bloc phenomenon with the region variable, as it is relates to language and Quebec nationalism in a way that is unique. As Blais et al. state, "the impact of language is huge."[110] The Bloc's support base was heavily francophone, while the seats the Liberals won in Quebec often contained large Anglophone populations. The uniqueness of Quebec, including the recent NDP success, has resulted in most interpretations of voting in Canada requiring a separate model for that province.

In the rest of the country religion and ethnicity help us understand partisan support. In writing about the Liberal victory in 2000, Blais et al. make clear the ongoing importance of religion and ethnicity in Canadian politics, claiming, "it would be impossible to understand the Liberals' victory . . . without recognizing the extent to which their strength outside Quebec hinges on the support of Catholics and Canadians of non-European origin. These two groups constitute the core of Liberal support outside Quebec."[111] In analyzing the 2008 election, Gidengil et al. noted a continuing role for religion, but suggested that "we may well be witnessing the emergence of a new religious cleavage based on Christian fundamentalism. Christians who believe that the Bible is the literal word of God preferred the Alliance to the Liberals by a margin of 15 points in 2000. By 2008, they preferred the Conservatives by a margin of almost 50 points. Even controlling for a variety of other social background characteristics, fundamentalist Christians have clearly become less and less likely to vote Liberal. . . . At the same time, voters who profess no religion have become more important to the shrinking Liberal vote."[112]

These are not the only bases of electoral support, as recent work has also pointed out the importance of the urban–rural dimension as well as differences based on gender. The Liberals and NDP do worse in rural areas while the Conservative support is stronger. Furthermore, parties on the left tend to draw more support from women.[113]

CONCLUSION

The world of political parties is complex and evolving and the roles and functions performed by contemporary parties differ from those ideally attributed to them. Critiques of parties focus on the decline in their ability to fulfill the functions identified decades ago as well as their inability to arrest declines in voter turnout and political participation more broadly. Criticism also follows the alleged increase in the power of leaders and the increasing absence of programmatic purity in electoral competition.

It is indisputable that societies have grown in complexity and citizens have seen an increase in their levels of education and a decrease in their long-term commitments to parties. It is equally obvious that technology has dramatically changed the ways in which parties interact with citizens. It would be ludicrous to expect that these changes would not affect the ways parties operate and the functions they perform. Concerns are also expressed about the growing role and authority of leaders. Yet this trend was recognized more than a half century ago by Duverger and in Canada in the 19th century. While the ability of parties to control their leaders may be limited, it is still the parties' prerogative to designate and remove them. Through their authorization of leaders and their role in structuring votes and organizing governments, parties remain critical players in liberal democracies.

Parties provide citizens with choices in elections and offer opportunities for citizens to engage politically. Those who do so can gain the privilege of playing important roles in choosing party leaders and candidates. When they vote, citizens almost always support party-authorized candidates and these candidates go on to occupy the institutional positions of authority within governments. These simple facts make the study of political parties a crucial part of political science and a key foundation for informed citizenship. Despite criticism and concern, the party is far from over.

DISCUSSION QUESTIONS

1. Why are political parties unpopular?

2. How do political parties choose their candidates?

3. What is the best method for choosing party leaders?

4. What types of parties are represented in the Canadian House of Commons?

5. How would you classify the Canadian party system?

FURTHER READING

Cross, William. *Political Parties*. Vancouver: UBC Press, 2004.

Dalton, Russell J. *Citizen Politics*, 4th edition. Washington: CQ Press, 2006.

Diamond, Larry, and Richard Gunther, eds. *Political Parties and Democracy*. Baltimore: The Johns Hopkins University Press, 2001.

Duverger, Maurice. *Political Parties*. London: Methuen, 1964.

LeDuc, Lawrence, Richard G. Niemi, and Pipp Norris, eds. *Comparing Democracies 2: New Challenges in the Study of Elections and Voting*. London: Sage, 2002.

Makarenko, Jay. "Political Parties and the Party System in Canada: History, Operation and Issues," available at http://www.mapleleafweb.com/features/political-parties-and-party-system-canada-history-operation-and-issues.

Michels, Robert. *Political Parties*. Basle, 1915.

Sartori, Giovanni. *Parties and Party Systems*. London: Cambridge University Press, 1976.

ENDNOTES

1. E.E. Schattschneider, *Party Government* (New York: Holt Rinehart and Winston, 1942), p. 1.

2. Giovanni Sartori, *Parties and Party Systems* (London: Cambridge University Press, 1976), p. ix.

3. Russell J. Dalton and Martin P. Wattenberg, "Partisan Change and the Democratic Process," in Russell J. Dalton and Martin P. Wattenberg,

eds., *Parties without Partisans* (Oxford: Oxford University Press, 2002), p. 261.

4. Kay Lawson and Peter H. Merkl, "Political Parties in the 21st Century," in Kay Lawson and Peter H. Merkl, eds., *When Political Parties Prosper* (Boulder: Lynne Reimer, 2007), pp. 1–2.

5. Russell J. Dalton, *Citizen Politics*, 4th edition (Washington: CQ Press, 2006), p. 245.

6. *Ibid.*, p. 255.

7. Larry Diamond and Richard Gunther, "Introduction," in Larry Diamond and Richard Gunther, eds., *Political Parties and Democracy* (Baltimore: The Johns Hopkins University Press, 2001), p. xiv.

8. Sartori, *Parties and Party Systems*, p. 9

9. *Ibid.*, p. 64.

10. Ace Electoral Network, "Guiding Principles of Parties and Candidates," available at http://aceproject.org.

11. John Meisel and Matthew Mendelsohn, "Meteor? Phoenix? Chameleon? The Decline and Transformation of Party in Canada," in Hugh G. Thorburn and Alan Whitehorn eds., *Party Politics in Canada*, 8th edition (Toronto: Pearson Education, 2001). Reprinted with permission by Pearson Canada Inc.

12. *Ibid.*, p. 164. Reprinted with permission by Pearson Canada Inc.

13. Dalton, *Citizen Politics*, p. 191.

14. *Ibid.*

15. S.M. Lipset and Stein Rokkan, *Party Systems and Voter Alignments* (New York: The Free Press, 1967).

16. See for example, Grant Amyot, "The Waning of Political Parties," in Brian Tanguay and Alain G. Gagnon, eds., *Canadian Parties in Transition*, 3rd edition (Scarborough: Nelson, 2007), p. 504.

17. Roland K. Carty, "The Politics of Tecumseh Corners: Canadian Political Parties as Franchise

Organizations," *Canadian Journal of Political Science* 35 (4) (2002): 734.

18. Russell Dalton, "Political Cleavages, Issues, Electoral Change," in Lawrence LeDuc, Richard G. Niemi, and Pipp Norris eds., *Comparing Democracies 2: New Challenges in the Study of Elections and Voting* (London: Sage, 2002), p. 207.

19. See, for example, William Cross, "Candidate Nomination in Canada's Political Parties," in Jon H. Pammett and Christopher Dornan, eds., *The Canadian Federal Election of 2006* (Toronto: Dundurn, 2006), p. 173; and William Cross, "Democratic Norms and Candidate Selection," *Party Politics* 14 (5) (2008): 605.

20. Barbara Norrander, "Democratic Marathon, Republican Sprint: The 2008 Presidential Nominations," in Janet M. Box-Steffensmeier and Steven E. Schier, eds., *The American Elections of 2008* (Lanham: Roman and Littlefield, 2009).

21. Michael Gallagher, "Conclusion," in Michael Gallagher ed., *Candidate Selection in Comparative Perspective: The Secret Garden of Politics* (London: Sage, 1988), p. 273.

22. Cross, "Democratic Norms and Candidate Selection," p. 607.

23. *Ibid.*, p. 609.

24. Kay Lawson, "When Parties Dedemocratize," in *When Political Parties Prosper*, p. 355.

25. *Ibid.*, p. 360.

26. Dalton, *Citizen Politics*, p. 264.

27. *Ibid.*, p. 266.

28. William Cross and Lisa Young, "Are Canadian Political Parties Empty Vessels? Membership, Engagement and Policy Capacity," *Choices* 12 (4) (June 2006): 17.

29. Maurice Duverger, *Political Parties* (London: Methuen, 1964), p. 168.

30. Carty "The Politics of Tecumseh Corners," p. 741.

31. André Siegfried, *The Race Question in Canada*, 1907. (Reprint, Toronto: McClelland and Stewart, 1966), p. 136.

32. Reginald Whitaker, "Virtual Political Parties and the Decline of Democracy," *Policy Options* (July 2001): 17.

33. William Cross, *Political Parties* (Vancouver: UBC Press, 2004), p. 108.

34. Cross and Young "Are Canadian Political Parties Empty Vessels?," p. 20.

35. *Ibid.*, p. 23. See also Lisa Young and William Cross, "Incentives to Membership in Canadian Political Parties," *Political Research Quarterly* 55 (3) (2002): 547–69.

36. Cross, *Political Parties*, p. 157.

37. Robert G. Boatright "Campaign Finance in the 2008 Election," in Janet M. Box-Steffensmeier and Steven E. Schier eds., *The American Elections of 2008* (Lanham: Roman and Littlefield, 2009), p. 138.

38. See Lisa Young, Anthony Sayers, and Harold Jansen, "Altering the Political Landscape: State Funding and Party Finance," in Tanguay and Gagnon, *Canadian Parties in Transition*, 3rd edition, pp. 338–41. See also Tom Flanagan and Harold J. Jansen, "Election Campaigns under Canada's Party Finance Laws," in Jon H. Pammett and Christopher Dornan eds., *The Canadian Federal Election of 2008* (Toronto: Dundurn, 2009), pp. 194–96.

39. Flanagan and Jansen, "Election Campaigns," p. 196.

40. Young, Sayers, and Jansen, "Altering the Political Landscape."

41. Brooke Jeffrey. "Missed Opportunity: The Invisible Liberals," in Pammett and Dornan, *The Canadian Federal Election of 2008*, p. 81.

42. Flanagan and Jansen, "Election Campaigns," p. 207.

43. Elections Canada, Registered Parties Financial Returns, 2008 and 2009. In 2009 the Conservatives raised over $17 million from

101,385 donors while the Liberals gathered $9 million from 37,876 contributors.

44. Young, Sayers, and Jansen, "Altering the Political Landscape," p. 337.

45. Gideon Rahat, "Which Candidate Selection Method is the Most Democratic?," *Government and Opposition* 44 (1) (2009): 68.

46. Duverger, *Political Parties*, p. 361.

47. Hazan, "Candidate Selection," p. 119.

48. *Ibid.*, p. 120.

49. Gideon Rahat, Reuven Y. Hazan and Richard S. Katz, "Democracy and Political Parties" *Party Politics* 14 (6) (2008), p. 663.

50. Rahat, "Which Candidate Selection Method is the Most Democratic?," pp. 73–74.

51. Carty, "The Politics of Tecumseh Corners," p. 735.

52. William Cross, "Candidate Nomination in Canada's Political Parties," in Jon H. Pammett and Christopher Dornan, eds., *The Canadian Federal Election of 2006* (Toronto: Dundurn, 2006), pp. 176–80.

53. Gideon Rahat and Reuven J. Hazan, "Candidate Selection Methods" *Party Politics* 7 (3) (2001): 297–332.

54. Dalton, *Citizen Politics*, p. 235.

55. "Mainstream Republicans in Tea Party primaries setback," BBC Website, available at http://www.bbc.co.uk/news/world-us-canada-11301034.

56. Lawrence LeDuc, "Democratizing Party Leadership Selection," *Party Politics* 7 (3) (2001).

57. Duverger, *Political Parties*, p. 140.

58. LeDuc, "Democratizing Party Leadership Selection," pp. 325–26.

59. *Ibid.*, p. 325.

60. See LeDuc for a discussion of early Labour elections using this model.

61. See Labour Party, "Summary of voting round by round," http://www2.labour.org.uk/votes-by-round; accessed September 28, 2010.

62. Duverger, *Political Parties*, p. 182.

63. *Ibid.*

64. *Ibid.*, p. 134.

65. See, for instance, André Blais, "Accounting for the Electoral Success of the Liberal Party of Canada," *Canadian Journal of Political Science* 38 (4) (2005): 821–40.

66. Other delegates attended as well. They included what can be termed 'super delegates,' those entitled to attend to because of the party or legislative office they held, as well as delegates from youth, women's and aboriginal clubs affiliated with the party.

67. Carty, "The Politics of Tecumseh Corners," p. 737.

68. As Carty explains, political entrepreneurs "mobilize members already in groups—co-religionists, members of one's ethnic community, fellow workers and so forth." "Tecumseh Corners," p. 739.

69. Stephen Clarkson, "Disaster and Recovery: Paul Martin as Political Lazarus," in Jon H. Pammett and Christopher Dornan, eds., *The Canadian Federal Election of 2004* (Toronto: Dundurn, 2004), p. 32.

70. Jeffrey, "Missed Opportunity," p. 65, 81.

71. *Ibid.*, pp. 71–73.

72. *Ibid.*, pp. 72–73.

73. Charles Dornan, "The Outcome in Retrospect," in *The Canadian Federal Election of 2008*, pp. 8–12.

74. Tom Flanagan, *Harper's Team*, 2nd edition (Montreal: McGill-Queen's University Press, 2009), p. 99.

75. See David K. Stewart and R.K. Carty, "Leadership Politics as Party Building: The Conservatives in 1998," in William Cross, ed., *Political Parties, Representation, and Electoral*

Democracy in Canada (Don Mills: Oxford University Press, 2002) for a discussion and analysis of that election.

76. Flanagan, *Harper's Team*, pp. 131–32.

77. See John C. Courtney, *Do Conventions Matter?* (Montreal: McGill-Queen's University Press, 1995) for a discussion of the shortcomings of all-member votes.

78. Duverger, *Political Parties*, pp. 63–71.

79. Otto Kircheimer, "The Transformation of the Western European Party Systems," in Joseph LaPalombara and Myron Weiner, eds., *Political Parties and Political Development* (Princeton: Princeton University Press, 1966).

80. *Ibid.*, p. 188.

81. Angelo Pannebianco, *Political Parties: Organization and Power* (Cambridge: Cambridge University Press, 1988).

82. Richard Katz and Peter Mair, "Changing Models of Party Organization and Party Democracy: The Emergence of the Cartel Party," *Party Politics* 1 (1) (1995): 5–28.

83. Larry Diamond and Richard Gunther, "Species of Political Parties: A New Typology," *Party Politics* 9 (2) (2003) provide a lengthy description of 15 different party types. This is an incredibly rich analysis which provides convincing accounts of the significant differences among political parties.

84. Kircheimer, "The Transformation of the Western European Party Systems."

85. Pannebianco, *Political Parties: Organization and Power*.

86. Cross, *Political Parties*, p. 9. Cross notes, however, that they "have been challenged for voter loyalty in recent elections by more ideological parties and interest groups."

87. Janine Brodie and Jane Jenson, "Piercing the Smokescreen: Stability and Change in Brokerage Politics," in Alain G. Gagnon and Brian Tanguay eds., *Canadian Parties in Transition*, 3rd edition (Toronto: Broadview, 2007), p. 43.

88. Carty, "The Politics of Tecumseh Corners," p. 726.

89. *Ibid.*, p. 729.

90. *Ibid.*, p. 733.

91. Sartori, *Parties and Party Systems*, p. 119.

92. "Final Election Expenses Limits for Registered Political Parties—40th General Election," Elections Canada Website, available at http://www.elections.ca/content.aspx?section=fin&document=index&dir=pol/finalexp/40ge&lang=e.

93. Sartori, *Parties and Party Systems*, p. 64.

94. *Ibid.*, p. 123.

95. Electoral systems permitting members to be elected by receiving more votes than any other candidate are associated with single party governments and a smaller number of parties in the legislature.

96. Cross, "Democratic Norms and Candidate Selection," provides an excellent discussion on the relationship between electoral systems and nominations.

97. Even in the United States, other parties can affect outcomes. For example in the 2000 Presidential election the votes secured by the Green party candidate Ralph Nader may have been sufficient to allow Republican George W. Bush to become President rather than Democrat Al Gore.

98. Jean Blondel, "Party Systems and Patterns of Government in Western Democracies," *Canadian Journal of Political Science* 1 (2) (1968): 180–203.

99. Sartori, *Parties and Party Systems*, p. 179.

100. Stephen B. Wolinetz, "Classifying Party Systems," paper prepared for the Annual Meeting of the Canadian Political Science Association, University of Manitoba, June 2004, p. 6.

101. Alan, Siaroff, *Comparative European Party Systems* (New York: Garland Publishing, 2000).

102. Sartori, *Parties and Party Systems*, pp. 193–200.

103. See Flanagan, *Harper's Team* for an account of this process.

104. Young, Sayers, and Jansen, "Altering the Political Landscape," pp. 344–45.

105. Flanagan and Jansen, "Election Campaigns," pp. 200–01.

106. Dornan, "The Outcome in Retrospect," pp. 8–12.

107. Jeffrey, "Missed Opportunity," pp. 78–79.

108. Elisabeth Gidengil, et al., "The Anatomy of a Liberal Defeat," paper prepared for the Annual Meeting of the Canadian Political Science Association, Carleton University (June 2009), p. 9.

109. Regional voting figures are from Elections Canada.

110. André Blais et al., *Anatomy of a Liberal Victory* (Peterborough: Broadview, 2002), p. 95.

111. *Ibid.*, p. 96; André Blais, "Accounting for the Electoral Success of the Liberal Party of Canada," *Canadian Journal of Political Science* 38 (4) (2005): p. 830.

112. Gidengil, et al., "The Anatomy of a Liberal Defeat."

113. *Ibid.*, Table 1; Blais et al., "Missed Opportunity," *Anatomy of a Liberal Victory*, pp. 91–93; and Elisabeth Gidengil et al., "Gender and Vote Choice in the 2006 Canadian Election," paper presented to the Annual Meeting of the American Political Science Association, Philadelphia, August 30–September 3, 2006.

WWW For various weblinks discussed in this chapter, please go to the book's website at **www.studyingpolitics4e.nelson.com**

Civil Society: Interest Groups and Social Movements in Politics

Miriam Smith

CHAPTER OBJECTIVES

After you have completed this chapter, you should be able to:

- understand what interest groups and social movements are
- enumerate the differences among the major subtypes of interest groups and social movements
- discuss the most common ways in which such groups influence the political system
- engage in the debate over whether such groups are too powerful

INTRODUCTION

Protestors take to the streets of Toronto to protest the G20 meeting. Amnesty International coordinates urgent action campaigns in defence of political prisoners. Greenpeace activists organize to protest BP's actions in the Gulf Oil Spill. Pro-life groups appear before the Supreme Court in the United States to claim that life begins at conception. Anti-government activist and Fox media personality Glenn Beck organizes a mass rally of thousands in Washington. Laid-off workers stage factory occupations and sit-ins in China. What these incidents have in common is that they are expressions of protest based on non-territorial interests, identities, and values: social justice campaigners, environmentalists, libertarians, and pro-life groups.

Much of our everyday discussion of politics is defined by territory. The ideas of government and the state are based on the assumption of a certain geographical region. When we think of Canada or China, we are thinking of a defined geographical territory around which politics is organized. In democratic political systems, voting is often organized around constituencies or districts in which voters elect a representative.

While the electoral system provides for the territorial representation of citizens, groups and movements organize citizens according to non-territorial interests and identities. In the electoral system, voters choose a representative of the geographical area in which they live. In group and movement politics, citizens get together with like-minded citizens to form a group or movement that reflects political cleavages such as economic interests, gender, language, or simply political opinions.[1]

Democratic freedoms are very important for the organization of movements and groups. Without freedom to assemble, freedom of the press, and freedom of expression, it is very difficult for citizens to form groups and movements. Yet even in nondemocratic systems group politics may operate. Authoritarian states may permit certain types of political groups to exist, or may not be able to expend the resources necessary to stop such groups from forming. And movements of political protest may bring people into the streets, leading to the downfall of an authoritarian regime and the transition to democracy.

WHAT ARE INTEREST GROUPS AND SOCIAL MOVEMENTS?

Interest groups and **social movements** bring together people with common interests and/or a common sense of identity for the purpose of influencing the political process. Groups and movements are not part of the state, although in some cases they may have very close relationships with the state. Groups and movements are different from political parties because they do not seek public office. They may seek to influence **public policy** or they may primarily aim to influence the beliefs and values of their fellow citizens.

> **Interest group:** A group that brings together people with common interests and/or a common sense of identity for the purpose of influencing the political process.

> **Social movement:** An informal network of activists who seek to transform the values of society.

Groups and movements form part of **civil society**—that is, social institutions and organizations that are independent of the state and in which citizens pursue their interests, express their beliefs, and live in communities. Examples of institutions of civil society are churches, schools, professional associations, trade unions, companies, and families.

> **Civil society:** Social institutions and organizations that are independent of the state and in which citizens pursue their interests, express their beliefs, and live in communities.

This chapter discusses both interest groups and social movements. Interest groups are formally organized, while social movements function as informal networks of activists. Further, social movements often engage in **contentious politics**—strikes and demonstrations—as a means of achieving their goals, while interest groups usually pursue their goals through conventional means such as lobbying.[2]

> **Contentious politics:** Protests that take the form of disruption of the normal activities of society, such as demonstrations and civil disobedience.

An example of social movement politics is provided by Greenpeace, mentioned at the beginning of this chapter. The organization began in the 1970s as a small group of environmentalists in Vancouver brought together by a sense of common values and identities. In order to stop U.S. and French nuclear testing in the South Pacific, they sailed their ship, the *Rainbow Warrior*, directly into the testing area both to stop the tests and to provide witnesses for the testing. Greenpeace is premised on the effectiveness of direct action and witnessing to achieve their goals. These strategies are typical of social movement organizations, which often use direct action and demonstrations to draw attention to public issues and as a means of effecting change.

The social movement politics of Greenpeace can be contrasted with the interest group politics of, for example, the National Rifle Association (NRA) in the United States. The NRA is well organized with thousands of members and a large budget; it also has spinoff organizations that fund litigation in gun control cases, defend shooting sports, and alert members to upcoming legislation in Congress. The NRA has been heavily involved in lobbying members of Congress on gun control legislation. Moreover, the organization is well known to the public and has a high media profile. It is said that it is almost impossible to change gun control legislation in the United States because of the influence of the NRA on Congress.[3]

The politics of interest groups and social movements can also be distinguished from the activities of lobbying or consulting, in which groups or companies hire professionals to contact and influence government on their behalf. For example, tobacco companies might hire professional lobbyists to influence legislators' and public servants' views on their products and advertising. Typically, lobbyists and consultants are paid well to protect the interests of their clients in government policy. This type of activity is common in most democratic countries; it is a very sizable industry in the United States and increasingly in Canada as well.

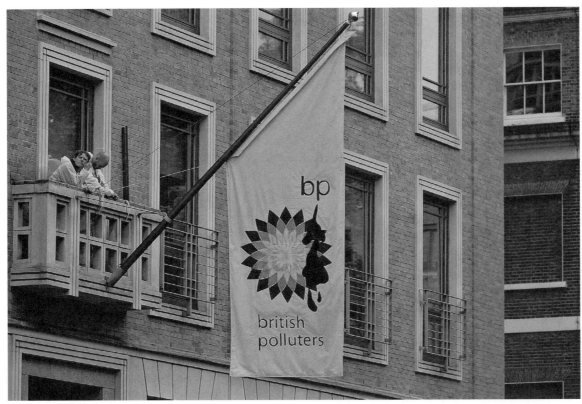

In May 2010, Greenpeace climbers raise flag reading "British Polluters" at BP Head Office, St. James Square, London. Greenpeace was protesting BP's environmental record at the Gulf of Mexico oil spill as well as a controversial tar sands project in Canada.

BEN STANSALL/AFP/Getty Images

Interest groups and social movements are sometimes called **nongovernmental organizations (NGOs)**. This term is particularly common in the fields of international relations and development, but NGOs are also active in domestic politics. Such organizations are part of neither the state nor international organizations such as the United Nations (UN). In addition to targeting states and trying to change domestic policies, they aim to influence international organizations such as the UN and the World Trade Organization (WTO).

> **Nongovernmental organization (NGO):** A non-profit organization that is not part of the state and is not a private corporation. Usually, the term is used to describe organizations that operate across borders in areas such as peace, development, human rights, and international affairs.

FUNCTIONS OF INTEREST GROUPS AND SOCIAL MOVEMENTS

Interest groups and social movements serve a number of functions in the political system, which are:

- to provide a means for citizens to express their views to government and to participate in the political system
- to influence the policies followed by governments, international organizations, and corporations
- to influence views held in society
- to provide information and legitimacy to governments and to international organizations

First of all, group and movement politics provide a link between citizens and government and allow citizens an alternative means of expressing their views. Group and movement organizations allow for the articulation of political opinions that are much more specific than those that can be expressed through voting periodically in an election or even by actively participating in party politics. Some voters may feel none of the political parties represents their views on issues important to them.

Environmentalists, for example, might feel that party politics is a waste of time and that their activism might be more effectively channelled through participation in the environmental movement. People who support the pro-life side of the abortion debate might join a pro-life organization that reflects their specific viewpoint. People might belong to religious and cultural organizations; while these organizations do not exist primarily to influence government, they might from time to time involve themselves in politics and aim to influence policy. Some citizens might feel government is not serving their interests and might organize in their own communities to provide needed services. Many women's organizations such as rape crisis lines and battered women's shelters started out as community-based organizations intended to fill gaps in public services. In this sense, then, group and movement politics provide a means for citizens to express their views to government and to participate in the political system.

Even in authoritarian systems, some forms of group political activity might be permitted and might provide a vehicle for some citizens to express their views to government in a limited fashion. In Box 13.1, you can see an example of the range of interest groups that currently exists in China, which has an authoritarian regime.

BOX 13.1

INTEREST GROUPS IN NONDEMOCRATIC SYSTEMS: THE EXAMPLE OF CHINA

According to Chinese politics experts George Gilboy and Eric Heginbotham, the following important interest groups exist in China, despite the fact that it is not a democratic country:

- *Farmers*. With increasing frequency, Chinese farmers are organizing to protest corrupt local officials, onerous and arbitrary taxes, and extreme poverty. In recent months, farmers have attacked tax collectors, blocked roads, and fought with officials and police.
- *The unemployed*. As economic reform continues, millions of Chinese workers are being laid off each year with little hope of reemployment or adequate social welfare support. In some cities, unemployed workers are now coming together in large-scale protests involving as many as 20,000 people at a time.
- *Consumers*. Today's Chinese consumers frequently speak out and organize against defective products, financial scams, and official corruption.
- *Industry associations*. Because China's official industry associations are weak and dominated by the Communist Party, they are unable to mediate effectively between industry and government. Yet some industry leaders have coalesced to force the central government to change policies on taxes, international trade, and price reforms.
- *Religious and spiritual movements*. The rise of Falun Gong is only the most visible indication of resurgent spiritualism in China. Traditional religions, mystical movements, and cults have attracted millions of followers in recent years.
- *Special-interest groups*. A variety of nascent special-interest groups, ranging from environmental and animal-rights organizations to regional soccer clubs, now place new demands on the state for resources and attention. For example, environmental groups—some with nationwide reach—have sponsored direct actions such as tree-planting programs and petitions calling for better municipal waste management.

Source: Excerpted from George Gilboy and Eric Heginbotham, "China's Coming Transformation." Reprinted by permission of *Foreign Affairs,* 80(4) (July/August 2001). Copyright 2011 by the Council on Foreign Relations, Inc. www.ForeignAffairs.com

Yet interest group and social movement politics raise the problem of collective action and the question of why people join such groups. According to rational choice theorists such as Mancur Olson, people will not join groups that are devoted to goals that will benefit everyone in society. Olson assumes that citizens are rational self-maximizing individuals; that is, they are interested in pursuing their own interests. Given that the individual is primarily concerned with the satisfaction of personal interests and needs, why should he or she join a group or social movement organization? After all, if the group is devoted to goals that benefit everyone, such as clean air, why join? If the goal is achieved, one will benefit regardless of the extent of one's participation.

Because of this, Olson argues that the individual is more likely to *free-ride*—that is, to avoid participating. This creates the problem of collective action: if everyone free-rides, how will groups form? Olson argues that groups will form through the provision of incentives to members.[4]

While many groups do use incentives to encourage membership and participation, other forms of collective action are difficult to explain in terms of incentives for participation. Interest groups and social movements tap into collective identities. For example, nationalist, ethnic, and linguistic groups may form on the basis of a sense of common interests and identity. Historically, business, labour, and farmer groups in Canada have created unity by appealing to a shared sense of political identity and interests.

Second, group and movement politics influence the policies followed by governments, international organizations, and in some cases corporations. Citizens banding together may convince government to follow one course of action rather than another. For example, in recent years, international human rights campaigns have shed light on abuses in many countries around the world and have led to the creation of new international institutions such as the International Criminal Court, which has the potential to bring political leaders to justice for having engaged in atrocities and war crimes. While international action is not new, the ease of transportation and communication in the age of the Internet has made such action more effective.

Third, groups may aim to influence society as much as or more than they may aim to influence the state. For certain types of groups, it may be more important to change what citizens believe about an issue or to change the core political values of citizens than to change public policy. For example, business groups may attempt to use the media to put forth the point of view that free-market policies are superior to state intervention as a means of ensuring economic development and growth. For business groups, it may be just as important to convince citizens to believe in a free-market perspective as to convince governments to undertake a certain policy decision. This is increasingly the case as certain types of decisions by corporations become subject to democratic scrutiny. Whether in the economic or environmental areas, corporations may be scrutinized by groups of citizens and may find it more productive and useful to expend their "political" resources in media and public relations strategies. For example, the Canadian Petroleum Producers Association engaged in a massive media campaign in 2010 designed to convince the public that it was seriously engaged in environmental protection in the Alberta oil sands.

Similarly, social movements may find it more important to influence society than to influence the state per se. The women's movement in many countries has fought for equality with men, a battle very far from over, especially in certain areas of the world. While the state's actions are important in this respect, the movement has also aimed to change public opinion on this issue. Governments may mandate gender equality, but legal rules and regulations are unlikely to make a difference unless citizens believe in them. Similarly, pro-life and pro-marriage groups have defended the traditional family and mounted extensive campaigns to roll back abortion rights, limit the availability of birth control, and defend the importance of heterosexual marriage.

Finally, group and movement organizations may provide information and legitimacy to governments and to international organizations. For this reason, government may support the formation and establishment of groups and movements. Even where governments and organizations have not actually encouraged the establishment of groups or movements, they may promote their involvement in the policy process.

Why? There are two main reasons governments and international organizations might actually welcome input, even pressure, from group and movement organizations. First, in both democratic and nondemocratic states, governments need to know what their citizens think. Groups may provide a barometer of public opinion. Further, precisely because interest groups and social movements bring together citizens with a sense of common interests or a common identity, they are in a position to provide targeted information to governments or international organizations regarding the views of their constituencies on given policies or issues. Governments may wish to know what a given group thinks about a specific issue. If a government wished to know farmers' views on an international trade agreement that was under negotiation, the fastest way would be to ask farmers' groups.

Group and movement organizations may also provide technical information to government and international organizations. In some cases, it may be cheaper for governments and organizations to obtain information from groups and movement organizations than to collect the data themselves. While such data might be tainted by the groups' putting their own claims in the best possible light, governments and international organizations could still find such information useful.

For example, if the government of Botswana wanted to update its information about water availability and quality in villages, it could send out its own inspectors to obtain this data. One could imagine that the task of sending such inspectors to villages would be very expensive and labour-intensive. So instead, the government might seek this information from farmers' organizations and from traditional village leaders. Such civil society organizations and networks would have access to excellent information on water availability and quality, as might NGOs working in the field of development. An NGO that had worked in many parts of the country at the village level might be able to give the government updated information on water. Although NGOs, farmers' groups, or village leaders could provide information that reflects their interests and experience, it might be cheaper and more efficient for government to use the information provided by these groups rather than to collect the information from scratch.

A second reason governments and international organizations might encourage the formation and participation of group and movement organizations in the policy process is that such participation may enhance the **legitimacy** of governments or international organizations. When group or movement organizations participate in the process of policy formation, they send the message that the governments or international organizations with whom they are collaborating are legitimate political actors. If governments can secure the agreement of group or movement organizations to specific policies, those policies will more likely be viewed positively by the public. For example, in almost any democratic system a government that brings down a budget or economic plan will provoke reactions from economic groups such as business, labour, and farmer groups, as well as from others. If every economic group in the country from farmers to business condemns the budget or plan, it is unlikely the public will support it. The same phenomenon exists in other policy areas. Both Presidents George W. Bush and Barack Obama floated plans to change U.S. immigration policy but, in each case, their initiatives were condemned by various stakeholders in the U.S. immigration debate.

> **Legitimacy:** The degree to which citizens accept and tolerate the actions and decisions of social and political actors such as governments, states, international organizations, and civil society groups themselves, usually based on the notion that the decision-makers have a right to such power.

These dynamics are reinforced by the media, which tend to seek out groups and movement organizations that can provide reactions to government initiatives. In this process, some groups—those with economic and media expertise and resources—are better able to exert such influence. Also, the media tend to reinforce existing definitions and concepts of the interests and identities at stake in any given area. For example, economic policy is defined as being of interest to groups that are clearly economic, such as business, labour, and farmers. However, development NGOs, antipoverty groups, and women's groups might all argue that they have a stake as well.

Furthermore, how well a particular group or movement organization can lend legitimacy to government depends in turn on its own legitimacy and visibility in the public eye. Legitimacy and visibility depend on the characteristics of the group or movement organization and the political, social, and economic context in which it operates. In any given context, opponents may attempt to de-legitimate or undermine the group or movement through a wide variety of tactics, from questioning how well it represents the constituency it champions to accusing its leaders of political corruption.

TYPES OF INTEREST GROUPS AND SOCIAL MOVEMENTS

Interest groups and social movements may be classified into various types. When considering these, it is important to remember that such typologies are just approximations of the complex and rich reality of group politics in diverse contexts.

At the beginning of this chapter, we saw that interest groups are more organized than social movements and tend to use more conventional means to achieve their goals; social movements are looser networks of activists who may use unconventional methods such as demonstrations (see Table 13.1).

One way to imagine the variety of possible groups and movements is to use a continuum, with social movements on one end and interest groups on the other.

Interest Groups

The continuum is based on degree of organization. At one end, we have groups, known as *latent groups*, which have no formal organization whatsoever. For example, no organization represents "all taxpayers" collectively. Some organizations might claim to represent their interests and put forth goals and values that purportedly serve them; but "all taxpayers" are not, as such, organized into a formal group in any country. Hence, the category "all taxpayers" is a latent group. Other important latent groups are consumers and the unemployed. Although members of both groups have significant interests in common, neither is organized.

In contrast, some groups are highly organized. In most countries, people that have a stake in business, farming, or labour are organized into **institutionalized groups**, which represent the interests of their members and attempt to influence government policy. In democratic countries, such groups may have very long histories; in many European countries, for example, the employers' federations (or business groups) date back to the late 19th century.

Institutionalized groups are characterized by a permanent organization. This means they have the

---

Table 13.1 **Types of Groups and Movements**	
Institutionalized Groups	Social Movement Organizations
General Features	
Division of labour	Networked
Narrow goals	Broad goals
Well organized	Loosely organized
Formal structure	Informal structure
Many resources	Few resources
State-oriented	Society-oriented
Examples	
Canadian Federation of Agriculture	Egale (gay and lesbian rights)
Canadian Council of Chief Executives	No One is Illegal (immigration and refugee rights)

economic and other resources necessary to sustain ongoing organization. In many cases, institutionalized groups employ professionals to carry out some of the work of the group. In some institutionalized groups, political goals may be secondary to their primary function. For example, religious organizations might have as their first purpose spiritual or religious goals. Yet they may also have political goals, such as to protect the status of their religion within the state, to pursue particular tax or legal advantages in the education system, or to promote strong views on family and gender-related policies such as abortion and birth control or strong preferences in foreign policy. Institutionalized groups also tend to use conventional means to achieve their goals—for example, lobbying politicians or entering into consultations with governments. At times groups may press their case through legal action or by joining forces with political parties.

The more institutionalized interest groups are also characterized by the nature of their goals. Because these groups use conventional strategies, their goals also tend to follow a pattern. In general, they pursue goals that are easily negotiable: they seek more or less of something rather than profound change. For example, regulation and tax policies are divisible—they can be increased or decreased marginally—and hence negotiable; an institutionalized group might advocate a specific regulatory or tax policy that will benefit its constituency. If the group is demanding that certain types of taxes be lowered, taxes can be reduced by a greater or lesser amount. Governments can at least go part way toward meeting the group's aspirations. In this sense, the goals of the group fit with the language and assumptions of government and can be dealt with by politicians and civil servants.

In order to support this high degree of organization, institutionalized groups tend to have access to a stable base of economic resources. Business and professional groups charge their members a substantial fee to join and are able to sustain themselves in this manner. Groups that represent less affluent constituencies may create a stable base of funding by charging a large number of members a smaller fee. Farmers' groups and trade unions are good examples of such groups.

In some cases, groups may receive funding from governments that are interested in the creation and maintenance of organizations representing certain societal interests. In many European countries, for example, governments fund community groups at the local level in hopes that they will help spark urban renewal in areas with social problems and high crime rates. These community organizations become part of consultative processes with governments over urban policy and problems. In other cases, funding may be withdrawn from groups that disagree with the governments. For interest groups and social movement organizations, government funding may be a double-edged sword. While providing a stable base for the organizations' work, it may also hinder their ability to speak freely and influence policy in the best interests of their members.

In Canada, there has been a lively debate over whether the federal government should fund groups that disagree with it.[5] The Conservative Party has argued that government should not fund interest groups that are critics of the government. In this view, such funding only gives the governments' critics more ammunition to disagree with and undermine policy. When the Conservatives were elected in January 2006, one of their first acts was to cut funding to the Court Challenges Program, which funds litigation on *Charter* issues, and to review funding to other social groups. On the other hand, the Canadian government under the leadership of the Liberal Party had become interested in the idea of institutionalizing links with certain civil society groups with the aim of strengthening their place in society. During a period in which government had been expected to do less, not more, and in which large-scale state intervention was out of favour, it was thought government might benefit from downloading tasks to interest groups and from developing a consultative partnership with such groups. In Canada, Australia, and most of the European democracies, state funding of group life is practised to some extent. In the United States, in contrast, groups do not benefit from such systematic state funding.

Social Movements

Moving to the other end of our continuum, social movements tend to be less organized, to use less conventional means, and to have less easily negotiable goals than institutionalized groups. In place of the permanent and professional organization of the institutionalized group, social movements are often composed of networks of activists. These networks may be linked in part by informal ties rather than by large professional organizations.

Social movements often begin life with very broad goals, which may be based on assumptions that are very different from the assumptions of policymakers and power holders. Movements may demand democracy from authoritarian regimes (e.g., democracy movements in the former Eastern bloc and across many developing countries during the 1980s and 1990s), an end to foreign occupation and domination (e.g., anticolonial movements and the Palestinian *intifada*), an end to race-based laws (e.g., the South African anti-apartheid movement), an end to rampant economic growth (e.g., the deep ecology and radical environmental movements in industrialized countries), or peace in a time of war (e.g., the movement against the wars in Iraq and Afghanistan). In these cases, the goals are often not easily negotiable with governments or elites. Even in stable democracies, demands for human rights (e.g., made by the women's movement) or environmental protection may be difficult to negotiate with governments and power holders. In many cases, the goals sought are not easily divisible.

Social movements may have goals that differ profoundly from those of governments. In particular, such movements commonly aim to influence society as well as the state. As mentioned, the women's movement has been concerned with influencing social attitudes as much as changing policy. Further, as politics increasingly moves out to the global level, some organizations have goals that reach beyond the borders of the nation-state—they may aim to influence the policies of other states. Yet, over time, social movements may be tempted to moderate their goals to gain influence with states and international organizations. Some environmental groups may even try to make common cause with government to influence policy. Of course, in addition to influencing states or international organizations, social movements may also aim to influence civil society. For example, some environmental groups might choose to try to change consumer or corporate behaviour directly.

Waterfowl protests against offshore drilling.

Harley Schwadron/Artizans

Social movement organizations often use unconventional means to achieve their goals. These means may include demonstrations and protests, such as those that have occurred in recent years in the anti-globalization movement. The civil rights movement in the United States, drawing its inspiration in part from the anticolonial struggles in India and elsewhere, used the strategies of nonviolence to achieve its goals. Civil disobedience, sit-ins, and marches were used to dramatize and challenge the segregationist laws of the southern U.S. states during the 1950s and 1960s. The pro-life movement in many countries has also used direct action and sit-ins to protest outside abortion clinics and to limit access to abortion.

Another means of influence that may be employed by social movements is direct action, as we saw in the example of Greenpeace. The technique is based on the assumption that changing government policies may not be the most efficient way to achieve a political goal. Direct action has been common in the environmental movement over the past 30 years and, as a strategy, has been publicized best by Greenpeace. The organization has intervened directly to stop environmental damage across the globe as in the case of logging. Other environmental organizations, such as Earth First!, have engaged in tree spiking, that is, hammering a spike into, and then marking, a tree to prevent it from being cut down. At times, such tactics can veer into the realm of violence. Most commentators view organizations that systematically engage in violence as not really social movements but ones engaged in armed struggle.

Social movements are also organized differently from institutionalized interest groups. They tend to function as networks of activists, who may be brought together by shared interests, identities, and values but may not actually belong to formal organizations. Where organizations form, their members may overlap with those of informal networks. Social movement organizations are typically smaller than those of institutionalized interest groups and have fewer economic resources.

Social movements may also overlap with political parties and engage in electoral activity. The environmental movement in many countries has founded Green parties that run in election campaigns. The Tea Party movement in the U.S., a right-wing, anti-tax movement, sprang up informally following President Obama's election victory and, in particular, after the passage of health care reform. The Tea Party is composed of many small informal groups in communities across the U.S., as well as some larger and better financed groups. In the mid-term elections of 2010, some Tea Party candidates were elected for the Republican Party. The diversity of Tea Party organization—from small grass roots groups to larger and better-funded groups—and its role in U.S. elections is another example of the ways in which social movements may cross the line into electoral politics.[6]

The two ends of our continuum of group and movement organizations represent different **organizational cultures**. Social movements and their attendant social movement organizations spring from a political culture that is populist, emphasizing democratic participation in the decisions and actions of the group or network. An important and sizable sector of social movement organizations arise from progressive or left-wing politics; as a result, they share the political cultural heritage of such politics. For example, social movement organizations may make decisions by consensus, allowing each member of the group or each member of the decision-making cadre to approve or veto group decisions.

> **Organizational culture:** Clusters of beliefs about the way groups should be organized. Examples are a belief in hierarchy or in internal democracy.

In contrast, some institutionalized groups share an organizational culture that is markedly different in many ways from the social movement culture. This culture emphasizes majoritarian decision-making rather than consensus decision-making; that is, decisions are made by majority rule rather than by consensus. Further, institutionalized groups, by their very nature, embrace the division of labour. Members may play a passive rather than a participatory role, and professionals often dominate the organization.

The differences between institutionalized interest groups and the social movements that have been highlighted on our continuum represent generalizations about the real-world shape and behaviour of civil society actors. The reality of associational life is much more complex. For example, over time, social movement organizations may take on some of the characteristics of the institutionalized interest group. Some environmental groups have been involved in extensive consultation with government and have developed many of the professional attributes of the institutionalized group, despite their origins in social movement organizing. At times, institutionalized groups may even deploy the tactics of the social movement. Farmers' organizations, for example, have been known to engage in direct action, demonstrations, and occupations in pursuit of their goals. This last example shows the importance of viewing civil society actors in historical context. In most countries, farmers' organizations began as social movements. Similarly, trade unions, usually defined as part of the universe of the stable, institutionalized groups, began as social movements and often deploy the ultimate weapon of direct action—the strike—in pursuit of their goals. Protests against the Iraq and Afghanistan wars in the early 2000s as well as protests against WTO and G20 meetings have also featured massive demonstrations as means of bringing public attention to their point of view. In the 2008–2009 financial crisis, protestors stormed banks in many countries and sometimes directed violence at private property.

Demonstrators clash with police at G20 protest in London, 2009.

Rex Features/The Canadian Press(Justin Williams)

GROUPS AND MOVEMENTS IN PUBLIC POLICY

It is now time to discuss more systematically the means that groups and movements have at their disposal to influence government and society.

Influencing Politicians

Perhaps the most obvious and visible way groups may influence the shaping of public policy in democratic systems is through bringing pressure to bear on politicians. In most democratic countries, the legislature is by definition the key forum for lawmaking; hence, it might seem natural for groups to seek out politicians to champion their views.

However, the influence groups are able to exercise through the legislature depends on the legislature's role within the political institutions of the country. As noted in preceding chapters, legislatures are more important in

some democratic systems than in others. In parliamentary systems, which are common in much of the democratic political world, legislative and executive powers are fused, in the sense that the executive (prime minister and cabinet) is responsible to the legislature and must have the support of the legislature in order to govern. In practice, however, the members of the legislature are loyal to their political parties. The political party that wins the general election forms the government, and for most of the duration of the government's term in office, the prime minister and the cabinet are able to dominate the business of the legislature.

The extent to which prime ministers and their cabinets dominate legislatures in parliamentary systems does vary. In some cases, such as Britain, MPs tend to serve long terms in office and to develop policy expertise; parties allow their MPs some latitude so that the MP can actually play an independent role in lawmaking. In other systems, such as Canada's, there is a higher turnover of MPs and a great concentration of power in the hands of the prime minister and the cabinet; MPs do not have much influence in lawmaking, at least in a majority government situation.

Yet another important difference among parliamentary systems is the type of electoral system used. In the first-past-the-post system, used in Canada and Britain, the candidate with the most votes wins the election; this tends to favour one-party majority governments. In Germany, Italy, and many of the northern European democracies, the system of proportional representation allocates seats in the legislature in part according to the proportion of votes received by each party. In this system, it is rare for one party to have a majority on its own; most of the time, these countries are governed by coalitions.

In presidential systems, such as that of the United States, there is a separation of powers between the legislature and the executive. In contrast to the parliamentary model, the president and the Congress are elected independently, and the tenure of the president does not rest on his or her party's dominance of the congress. President Bill Clinton, a Democrat, ruled with a Republican-dominated Congress, while President George W. Bush governed with a Republican House of Representatives and a Senate that changed hands between the two parties. President Obama began with a Congress that was barely controlled by his own party and had to work to build coalitions to support his policies from among his own fellow Democrats who sometimes disagreed with him; after two years, the Republicans gained a majority in the House of Representatives. This system of divided government means that **party discipline** is not as strong as in parliamentary systems. Cross-party coalitions between Democrats and Republicans sometimes form, and individual members of Congress have much more latitude to make their own decisions about lawmaking.

These political institutional differences play a very important role in determining how interest groups and social movement organizations lobby members of the legislature or the executive. In first-past-the-post parliamentary systems, such as those of Britain and Canada, attempting to influence the legislature is not a very effective strategy for interest group and social movement organizations because MPs do not have much independence in the development of public policy. In the proportional representation system, similarly, lobbying individual MPs is not likely to

have a direct influence on policy formation. In such a system, the parties reach agreement by negotiating among themselves behind closed doors, which tends to decrease the possibility of direct group influence on individual members of the legislature.

In the presidential system, such as the United States with its separation of powers, the situation is quite different. Because of the freedom from party discipline of the individual members of Congress, that body is ripe for group influence. Indeed, the United States is the primary home of pressure group politics, as groups and organizations vie with each other to exercise influence in the Congress.

Another means by which interest groups and social movement organizations may influence politicians is through exerting pressure in electoral politics. In the U.S. system, there is a lack of regulation of campaign finances, which means that groups and social movement organizations can influence the political process by giving money to politicians for their reelection campaigns. Groups often do this through the formation of **political action committees (PACs)**, whose express purpose is to donate to political campaigns and to influence the views of parties and politicians on issues of import to the group (see Figure 13.1, p. 348). Such a system obviously favours groups with plenty of resources.

In parliamentary systems, influence through the electoral system takes different forms. In some cases, groups have formed parties to put forth their views. Trade unions in many countries played an important role in the creation of socialist and social democratic parties such as the British Labour Party. Business groups often have close but informal ties with right-of-centre political parties. Green parties have been established in many democracies to put forth the environmental point of view, and in some countries (e.g., Germany), these parties have been quite successful. In Iceland, the Women's Party was formed to advocate **feminist** views. Groups may also attempt to gain influence within an existing political party. Pro-life and evangelical Christians play an important role in the Republican party in the United States and to some extent played one in the Canadian Alliance.

Influencing the Bureaucracy

In most societies, the **bureaucracy** plays a very important role in the formation and implementation of

Figure 13.1   Top 20 PAC Contributors to Federal Candidates, 2005–2006*

PAC Name	Total Amount	Democrat Percentage	Republican Percentage
National Association of Realtors	$3,752,005	49	51
National Beer Wholesalers Association	$2,946,500	31	69
National Association of Home Builders	$2,900,000	26	73
National Auto Dealers Association	$2,821,600	30	70
International Brotherhood of Electrical Workers	$2,796,875	97	3
Operating Engineers Union	$2,784,435	78	21
American Bankers Association	$2,748,299	36	64
Laborers Union	$2,687,150	85	15
American Association for Justice	$2,558,000	96	3
Credit Union National Association	$2,412,853	45	54
AT&T Inc.	$2,341,683	34	66
Carpenters & Joiners Union	$2,293,923	74	25
United Parcel Service	$2,239,128	32	67
United Auto Workers	$2,220,350	99	1
American Federation of Teachers	$2,113,448	99	1
Teamsters Union	$2,085,100	91	8
American Federation of State/County/ Municipal Employees	$2,048,683	98	1
American Medical Association	$2,011,634	31	69
Plumbers/Pipefitters Union	$1,946,100	91	9
International Association of Fire Fighters	$1,872,105	72	27

* For ease of identification, the names used in this section are those of the organization connected with the PAC, rather than the official PAC name. For example, the "Coca-Cola Company Nonpartisan Committee for Good Government" is simply listed as "Coca-Cola Co." Totals include subsidiaries and affiliated PACs, if any. Based on data released by the FEC on Monday, June 4, 2007.

Source: United States Federal Election Commission, "PAC activity continues climb in 2006", available at: http://www.fec.gov/press/press2007/20071009pac/20071009pac.shtml

public policy. Civil servants often wield a decisive influence over government action, partly because civil servants in many states are experts in their fields. Even in democracies in which civil servants are expected to be accountable to democratically elected politicians, they may still have much influence because of their expertise, stability, and longevity in government positions. This is particularly true of the merit-based bureaucracy, in which civil servants are selected for their positions on their merits rather than on their political affiliations. In authoritarian systems, civil servants may be chosen in part for their political connections, particularly to the party in power.

In any case, in most contexts, influencing the bureaucracy is one of the most effective means for groups to influence public policy. It is important to note that this strategy works best for institutionalized groups because they have the resources, the money, and the expertise to develop stable relationships over time with government bureaucrats. In both democratic and authoritarian systems, governments may cultivate these relationships for the reasons outlined earlier, namely in order to obtain valuable political or technical information from these groups and to use the groups to legitimate the policies of government.

In many democratic systems such as Canada, the United States, and Britain, relationships between interest groups and bureaucrats are so close that these groups and the bureaucracy are involved in institutionalized patterns of relationships and form what scholars call a **policy community**. Groups and the bureaucracy mutually influence each other and collaborate in the formation of public policy. This does not necessarily mean that groups dictate public policy; in some cases, groups may be dominated by government priorities, while in others, groups may indeed play an influential part in policy formation.

Policy community: A collection of groups and individuals (including both state bureaucrats and interest groups or social movement organizations) who influence each other in an effort to shape policy outcomes in their area of interest.

The pattern of relationships between groups and the civil service varies depending on the type of regime and the type of political institutions in place. In authoritarian political systems and in new and fragile democracies, such as Russia, the civil service may be weakened or even corrupted by links to organized crime, making institutionalized group relationships of the type described here impossible. Access may depend solely upon elite connections. In other cases, the civil service may be dominated by appointees of a particular political party, as was the case in Mexico with the dominant party prior to the election of Vicente Fox in 2000. In this case, social groups were institutionalized within the party and dominated by party elites.

Influence Through Lobbying

Those who wish to influence government may choose to do so by hiring professional **lobbyists** to do the job on their behalf. Interest groups may choose this approach if they feel they are unlikely on their own to secure access to the relevant department of government or to the policies that will shape legislation. Corporations or groups of corporations with similar interests may choose this approach because they can afford to pay for lobbying by professionals. Ottawa-based Hillwatch Inc., for example, provides a list of its current and past clients, as well as samples of its work, on its website at http://www.hillwatch.com/About_Us/Clients.aspx. The list shows the type of work lobbyists undertake;

it includes different levels of government (e.g., the City of Ottawa), utilities from outside of Canada (e.g., the New York Power Authority), embassies of foreign governments (e.g., the Embassy of Japan), interest groups that represent particular economic sectors (e.g., the Ontario Lumber Manufacturers' Association), and large corporations (e.g., Nestlé Canada, Paramount Communications, and Honeywell Canada).

Lobbying is effective for those who have relatively narrow, well-defined goals with respect to issues that affect a specific industry, such as levels of taxation or regulations. Tobacco companies, for example, have hired professional lobbyists to influence the Canadian government on advertising. As noted below, they have also hired lawyers to pursue their interests through the courts, arguing that restrictions on tobacco advertising constituted an unconstitutional limit on free expression under the *Charter of Rights and Freedoms*. Lobbying and the use of courts to advance policy goals are similar in that professionals (lobbyists, lawyers, or both) are hired for the express purpose of securing political influence.

Many observers have recognized that lobbyists pose a threat to the democratic process. Because lobbyists are hired by those with money, they may give corporations and well-funded interest groups an advantage in the political process. In recognition of this, some countries have regulated paid lobbying. In Canada, lobbying is regulated by the 1989 *Lobbyists Registration Act*. Lobbyists must register and provide information about each of their efforts undertaken to influence government. Unfortunately, the act does not have much in the way of enforcement mechanisms. When the Conservatives were elected in 2006, they put into place the *Federal Accountability Act*, which created a new Commissioner of Lobbying as an independent officer of Parliament and renamed the law the *Lobbying Act*. Nonetheless, many critics argue that the act does not go far enough.

Influencing the Courts

In democratic societies, the courts also provide a venue for interest groups to exert influence. As in the case of politicians and the bureaucracy, the opportunities for influencing the courts depend on the specific shape of political institutions and the role courts play in the political system. In Britain, for example, groups traditionally have not had much influence on public policy through the courts. Without a written constitution and judicial review, groups did not have strong legal tools to force changes in government policies. Britain's membership in the European Union is changing the role of courts in the British political system, however. Increasingly, groups are turning to European courts, such as the European Court of Human Rights and the European Court of Justice, to influence the British political system. Recent issues in which British laws have been influenced by European court decisions include assisted suicide for the terminally ill and equality of the sexes in entitlement for government benefits.[7]

In the United States, judicial review has formed part of the constitution from an early period. Groups and social movement organizations in the United States often turn to the courts to influence public policies. There are many examples of such influence. In June 2010, the National Rifle Association and other pro-gun rights' groups in the U.S. secured an important victory in the case of *McDonald v. Chicago*, in which the Supreme Court ruled that state and local governments do not have the constitutional right to ban guns. On the issue

of affirmative action for minorities in university admissions, the U.S. Supreme Court struck down a University of Michigan policy that awarded points in admissions to minority candidates in *Gratz v. Bollinger* (2003). These are examples of the role of the courts in influencing public policy and both cases were the object of extensive group mobilization by various stakeholders who sought to influence the court's rulings and reasoning.[8]

In Canada, venues for group influence through the courts were weak before the entrenchment of the *Charter of Rights and Freedoms* in the Canadian constitution in 1982. Since then, many groups have turned to the courts, using the *Charter's* rights guarantees and other provisions of the 1982 Constitution (such as Aboriginal rights' guarantees in Section 35) to achieve important policy objectives. Political scientist Gregory Hein has studied these group efforts to influence public policy through the courts, and his tabulation of frequency of recourse to the courts by different groups in society appears in Figure 13.2. The data show that recourse to the courts has increased across

Figure 13.2 Organized Interests in Court, 1988–1998

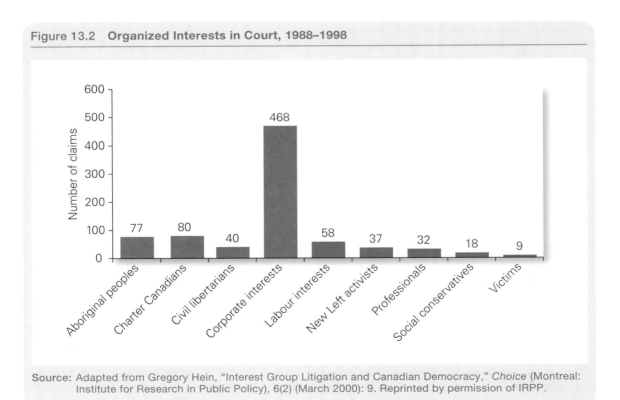

Source: Adapted from Gregory Hein, "Interest Group Litigation and Canadian Democracy," *Choice* (Montreal: Institute for Research in Public Policy), 6(2) (March 2000): 9. Reprinted by permission of IRPP.

different groups in society, although corporations use the courts far more frequently than other groups. In fact, as noted above, corporations have persuaded the Supreme Court that such *Charter* rights as freedom of expression should be extended to themselves! Hein concludes that "interest group litigation is ... an established form of collective action"[9] in Canada.

Influencing the Media

The success of collective actors in challenging government policy or seeking to influence social norms and values may be greatly enhanced through the skilful use of the **mass media**. In particular, when groups seek to influence politicians and elections, the media provide a vehicle for drawing public attention to the groups' point of view. In the cases of gun control, abortion, and lesbian and gay rights, supporters and opponents on each issue attempted to capture the media's attention as a way of bringing pressure to bear on MPs. Because media such as television tend to focus on dramatic conflicts within a limited time frame, groups that can successfully produce quick sound bites tend to receive more attention than collective actors attempting to call attention to the structural forces that shape government policy or societal norms. In the case of environmentalism, for example, a wide variety of deep ecology perspectives emphasize that economic development in many parts of the world threatens humanity's survival. However, complex scientific and philosophical arguments about deep ecology are unlikely to produce the quick media sound bites that television demands. Hence, successful environmental groups have often sought to dramatize environmental issues in ways that can be captured easily for global media consumption. As Stephen Dale has pointed out, Greenpeace is a master of media tactics. By sailing into the U.S. nuclear test site in the Aleutian Islands in 1971, a tiny band of protesters was able to draw worldwide media attention to the test. This was Greenpeace's start; from a few protesters in an old fishing boat, it grew to an international organization with a budget of US$28.3 million by 1994.[10]

Influence at the Transnational Level

Globalization has had important effects on the mobilization of groups and movements. More than ever, public policy is subject to pressures from beyond the borders of one country. Enhanced communications technology facilitates links between groups across borders, while international organizations ranging from the WTO to the UN play an increased role in the making of policy decisions. Regional economic and political integration, as in the European Union, create new transborder policies, and trade agreements, such as the North American Free Trade Agreement (NAFTA), limit the range of policy choices open to governments. This process of "decentring" the state, as Warren Magnusson has termed it, has been characterized by a marked increase in **transnational group** activity in recent years, as is shown in Table 13.2 (p. 352).[11] The table shows the extent to which various types of transnational advocacy groups have grown over the past few decades.

Transnational group: A group that organizes across the borders of nation-states with the aim of influencing national governments, international organizations, or public opinion.

Interest groups and social movement organizations may appeal to international organizations to pressure their own state, or they may form alliances with other groups outside their own state. This may occur when groups have failed in their efforts to achieve positive results through domestic strategies alone. For example, pro-democracy and human rights activists in South Africa were successful in mobilizing international organizations and public opinion to overthrow the apartheid regime. In the last 20 years, First Nations in Canada have developed links with Indigenous peoples around the world, especially through the World Council of Indigenous Peoples. Another example of transnational linkages was the campaign to stop the OECD's Multilateral Agreement on Investment (MAI), a proposed investment treaty. Over 500 NGOs from 67 countries signed a joint statement condemning the MAI; this concentrated effort was widely credited with delaying the ratification of the accord in 1997.[12] Christina Gabriel and Laura Macdonald have demonstrated that, in the wake of NAFTA, incipient linkages are developing between

---

Table 13.2 International Nongovernmental Social Change Organizations

Issue Area	1953		1963		1973		1983		1993	
	#	%	#	%	#	%	#	%	#	%
Human rights	33	30.0	38	27.0	41	22.4	79	22.7	168	26.6
World order	8	7.3	4	2.8	12	6.6	31	8.9	48	7.6
International law	14	12.7	19	13.4	25	13.7	26	7.4	26	4.1
Peace	11	10.0	20	14.2	14	7.7	22	6.3	59	9.4
Women's rights	10	9.1	14	9.9	16	8.7	25	7.2	61	9.7
Environment	2	1.8	5	3.5	10	5.5	26	7.5	90	14.3
Development	3	2.7	3	2.1	7	3.8	13	3.7	34	5.4
Ethnic unity/ Group rights	10	9.1	122	8.5	18	9.8	37	10.6	29	4.6
Esperanto	11	10.0	18	12.8	28	15.3	41	11.8	54	8.6

* The percentages in any one decade do not add up to 100 because groups that champion other causes have not been included.

Source: Material reprinted from *Activists Beyond Borders: Advocacy Networks in International Politics,* by Margaret E. Keck and Kathryn Sikkink. Copyright © 1998 by Cornell University. Used by permission of the publisher, Cornell University Press.

---

feminist activists in Canada and Mexico, as women attempt to deal with the economic, social, and political consequences of North American economic restructuring.[13]

Interest groups and social movement organizations within one country may mobilize to influence politics elsewhere in the world, targeting foreign states or international organizations in an effort to influence the behaviour, policies, and practices of foreign states and international actors. One of the best examples of this was mentioned above: the campaign against South Africa's apartheid regime, in which many solidarity groups from other states, international organizations, private companies, and other institutions in developed democracies sprang up to put pressure on South Africa. For example, the divestment campaign in North America and Europe pressured social institutions such as universities to cancel their investments in companies doing business with the country. International pressure played a key role in instituting change.[14]

The antiglobalization protests of the past few years have had important effects on how multilateral economic institutions function. According to Robert O'Brien and his colleagues, the labour,

women's, and environmental movements have all had a very important impact. Organizations such as the **IMF**, the **WTO**, and the **World Bank** have responded to such pressure. Scholars argue that transnational social movement advocacy is creating a new and complex form of global governance as political issues move from the domestic to the international and global levels.[15] In this sense, the contestation and social movement tactics we have seen on television at antiglobalization protests such as those in London in 2009 and Toronto in 2010 are counterbalanced by the actions of more institutionalized groups, which serve some of the same functions for international institutions and for multilateral economic organizations as we have identified at the domestic level. While the social movements protest in the streets and put pressure on such organizations through the media, the more established groups are developing institutionalized relationships with these organizations. As on the domestic level, interest groups at the international level provide international organizations and institutions with information about complex areas of public policy. Also at the domestic level, transnational advocacy groups lend legitimacy to the actions of international organizations such as the World Bank and the IMF. In an era of heightened and increasingly competitive and globalized media scrutiny, special-interest social movement groups are valuable potential allies for such international organizations.

ARE INTEREST GROUPS TOO POWERFUL?

Are interest groups and social movement organizations too powerful? In the media, one often hears the view, at both the domestic and the international level, that special-interest groups should not be able to dominate policymaking. This debate revolves around the question of democratic legitimacy. Are groups and social movements legitimate representatives of citizens, thus advancing the process of democratization? Or do they pervert and distort the process by using money and other illegitimate means to pursue their interests? Do such groups and movements reflect or impede the spirit and practice of democracy?

Which side we take on this question may well depend upon the context. In an undemocratic system such as Mexico's before the Fox election, we might favour the mobilization of societal interests to facilitate the transition to democracy. In recent years many mobilizations have pushed forward democratic transitions, as noted in Chapter 15. In Eastern Europe's struggle against communism, in the (failed) Iranian Green movement, and in South Africa's anti-apartheid movement, we see street power, demonstrations, and other tactics of social movement protest bringing about democracy. Even in existing authoritarian regimes, groups may play an important role in permitting channels for the expression of public opinion between citizens and the state. Such channels, though likely narrow and circumscribed, are even more important in the absence of free elections.

Furthermore, many scholars believe interest groups and social movement organizations are essential to the healthy functioning of democratic political institutions, and a prerequisite to the establishment of democracy. In the 19th century, observers such as Alexis de Tocqueville (in his famous book, *Democracy in America*) and French sociologist

Émile Durkheim argued that democratic political institutions required the healthy soil of associational and group life in order to flourish. Some scholars have argued that societies in which interest groups and social movements do not exist or in which they have been weakened by a strong and repressive state (e.g., Russia) may find it difficult to make democracy work.[16]

On the other hand, in capitalist democracies the power of groups and movements may in part depend upon their access to money. Left-wing and populist critiques of group involvement in democratic politics emphasize how business groups may use their financial resources to access and influence political elites. By this view, in a market society the playing field is not level for interest group and social movement activity; certain groups have more power than others because of their ability to mobilize economic resources. Many argue that interest group activity during election campaigns should be limited because of the fact that monied groups (such as the PACs in the United States) can circumvent election spending laws and influence election outcomes. From a right-wing perspective, it is sometimes argued that certain minority groups have too much power and have been able to influence public policy against the interests of the democratic majority. Right-wing critics of interest group and social movement activism often point to feminism as an example of a negative identity politics that has produced public policy outcomes that ignore the wishes of the majority.

CONCLUSION

Debates over the power of groups and movements as political actors go to the heart of the question of the nature of political power itself. How is such power exercised? Who has it and who doesn't? Who should have it? Should politics be restricted to politicians? How can citizens engage in democratic deliberation, and how can group politics and associational life facilitate citizen engagement? There are no easy answers. These questions extend from the realm of political debates in any one country into the international arena as groups increasingly overlap across borders in the new political spaces of our globalized world.

DISCUSSION QUESTIONS

1. Choose one social movement organization or interest group and trace its attempts to influence public policy.

2. Are demonstrations and civil disobedience a legitimate means of influencing public opinion and public policy?

3. Should interest groups and social movement organizations have the right to spend money during election campaigns?

4. What are the main similarities and differences between institutionalized interest groups and social movement networks?

FURTHER READING

Broder, David S. *Democracy Derailed: Initiative Campaigns and the Power of Money.* New York: Harcourt Brace, 2000.

Graziano, Luigi. *Lobbying, Pluralism and Democracy.* London: St. Martin's Press, 2001.

Keck, Margaret E., and Kathryn Sikkink. *Activists Beyond Boarders: Advocacy Networks in International Politics.* New York: Cornell University Press, 1998.

Roberts, Alexander, ed. *The Classics of Interest Group Behavior.* New York: Wadsworth, 2004.

Smith, Miriam. *A Civil Society? Collective Actors in Canadian Political Life.* Peterborough: Broadview Press, 2005.

Smith, Miriam, ed. *Groups and Movements in Canadian Politics.* Peterborough: Broadview Press, 2008.

Staggenborg, Suzanne. *Social Movements.* Toronto: Oxford University Press, 2008.

Tarrow, Sidney. *The New Transnational Activism.* Cambridge: Cambridge University Press, 2005.

ENDNOTES

1. John Agnew, *Geopolitics: Re-visioning World Politics* (London and New York: Routledge, 1998).

2. Sydney Tarrow, *Power in Movement: Social Movements, Collective Action and Politics* (Cambridge: Cambridge University Press, 1994).

3. Osha Gray Davidson, *Under Fire: The NRA and the Battle for Gun Control* (Iowa City: University of Iowa Press, 1998).

4. Mancur Olson, *The Logic of Collective Action: Public Goods and the Theory of Groups.* Cambridge, Mass.: Harvard University Press, 1965.

5. Leslie A. Pal, *Interests of State: The Politics of Language, Multiculturalism and Feminism in Canada* (Montreal and Kingston, ON: McGill-Queen's University Press, 1993).

6. David Barstow, "Tea Party Lights Fuse for Rebellion on Right," *New York Times*, February 16, 2010, available at http://www.nytimes.com/2010/02/16/us/politics/16teaparty.html?pagewa; and Kate Zernike, "Tea Party Comes to Power on an Unclear Mandate," *New York Times*, November 2, 2010, available at http://www.nytimes.com/2010/11/03/us/politics/03repubs.html?_r=1&ref=politics.

7. *Pretty v. the United Kingdom*, European Court of Human Rights, January 18, 2002; *Fielding v. the United Kingdom*, European Court of Human Rights, January 29, 2002.

8. Charles Epp, *The Rights Revolution* (Chicago: University of Chicago Press, 1998).

9. Gregory Hein, "Interest Group Litigation and Canadian Democracy," *Choices* (Montreal: Institute for Research in Public Policy) 6 (2) (March 2000): 9.

10. Stephen Dale, McLuhan's Children: The Greenpeace Message and the Media (Toronto: Between the Lines, 1996), pp. 4, 15ff.

11. Warren Magnusson, "Decentring the State," in James Bickerton and Alain G. Gagnon, eds., *Canadian Politics* (Peterborough, ON: Broadview Press, 1994).

12. Council of Canadians, "Joint NGO Statement on the Multilateral Agreement on Investment (MAI)

to the Organization for Economic Cooperation and Development," available at http://www.canadians.org/ngostatement.html; accessed June 13, 2008.

13. Christina Gabriel and Laura Macdonald, "NAFTA, Women and Organizing in Canada and Mexico: Forging a Feminist Internationality?," *Millennium* 23 (3) (Winter 1994): 535–62.

14. Audie J. Klotz, *Norms in International Relations: The Struggle Against Apartheid* (New York: Cornell University Press, 1996).

15. Robert O'Brien, Anne Marie Goetz, Jan Aart Scholte, and Marc Williams, *Contesting Global Governance: Multilateral Economic Institutions and Global Social Movements* (Cambridge: Cambridge University Press, 2000).

16. Robert Putnam, *Making Democracy Work* (Princeton: Princeton University Press, 1994), pp. 163–86.

W W W For various weblinks discussed in this chapter, please go to the book's website at **www.studyingpolitics4e.nelson.com**

PART 6

Political Development and Change

Courtesy of Grant Budding

GRANT BUDDING

Grant Budding chose to study Political Science at Brock University in St. Catharines, Ontario because he hoped to find a career in an international development organization—a job that would allow him to travel as well as to make a positive contribution in people's lives. The subject of his honours thesis was ethnic conflict. After graduation, he did not quite know what he wanted to do with this degree but realized that he would not find this out simply by remaining in Canada and looking for work. He therefore made what he credits as the best decision in his life and moved to the city of Van in Eastern Turkey, where he saw first-hand the effects of ethnic conflict, forced migration, and terrorism that resulted from the war in the 1990s.

Grant began to teach English at a private school in Van and was able to learn Turkish and some Farsi. This allowed him to establish himself in the city and to meet a large number of people who worked in both the government and civil society. Eventually he was put into contact with the local office of the United Nations High Commission for Refugees where, after a short internship, he acquired a contract to do refugee status determination for the Iranian and Afghan asylum seekers fleeing to Turkey. He was able to glean insights into the operations of the UNHCR, as well as meet many people engaged in human rights and refugee-related issues through the world.

Grant's interest in Afghanistan and Iran has continued, and he is currently enrolled at Oxford University in England in a Master of Science program for Migration Studies. He is writing his dissertation thesis on Development and Migration in Afghanistan. He spent last summer travelling around Iran where he experienced Persian hospitality and culture and was able to glimpse into the politics of the country. After graduating, he will be going to Morocco through a cultural tourism program, and following that, he plans to stay and learn French (it's essential!) and Arabic. He eventually hopes to achieve his goal of a career in working with development and refugees in the broader Middle East and Central Asia. He believes that he has made the right choices, precisely because when he didn't see opportunities at home he moved to places where he knew his skills and personal interests would naturally lead to opportunities, and he encourages others to do the same.

The Politics of Development and Underdevelopment

James Busumtwi-Sam

CHAPTER OBJECTIVES

After you have completed this chapter, you should be able to:

- identify some of the dimensions of global inequality, including inequality between men and women
- discuss the history and sources of development as a global issue and the evolution of the dialogue between rich countries and poor countries over how best to achieve development
- identify some of the main explanations offered for patterns of development and underdevelopment
- outline the contemporary issues and debates that arise from processes of development and change.

INTRODUCTION

Economic growth and industrialization, as well as advancements in science and technology, have resulted in a level of prosperity and material well-being unparalleled in human history. But these very same forces of development and change have generated deepening imbalances among countries, individuals, and groups; between men and women; and between human civilization and the natural environment. These imbalances have been a source of past and continuing political conflict and disagreement. In this chapter, we examine "development" as an international issue and discuss some key questions arising from processes of development and change. What does development entail? Why do some countries and peoples enjoy very high standards of living while others live in poverty? What are the consequences of underdevelopment, and what prescriptions are available for addressing these consequences? The phrase "politics of development and underdevelopment" in the title of this chapter draws attention to the fact that the answers to these questions are not straightforward, but have been and continue to be highly contentious.

We begin with an overview of some key challenges to development globally, highlighting the dimensions of the gap between the "haves" and "have-nots" of the world, and then proceed to examine the question of what "development" entails by investigating the different circumstances of countries classified as "developing." Having a good sense of the relevant history helps our understanding of the present, and thus this chapter discusses the history and legacy of colonialism in the Americas, Asia, and Africa. The countries in these regions were subject to European colonial expansion between the 17th and early 20th centuries. In the contemporary period, as a group, they generally fall into the "have-nots" category. The efforts by these countries to effect change in international economic and political relations is also examined. The chapter will then consider the difficulties in, and controversies surrounding, the measurement and explanation of patterns of development and underdevelopment. Here we examine different ways of looking at development—political, economic, and social—as well as some of the theories and explanations offered for development and the lack thereof. Worldwide, women fare comparatively less well than men on various indicators of development, and we will examine aspects of the debate over women in development including the gender dimensions of global inequality.

To conclude, the chapter will explore some contemporary issues and debates arising from processes of development and change, including the debate over the role of foreign aid in development and that over the environment and development captured by the term "sustainable development." Also examined is the role of democracy and "civil society" in development, as well as problems of political violence and civil strife in many poorer countries.

CHALLENGES OF GLOBAL DEVELOPMENT

Development entails the transformation of human, natural, and material resources at various levels of social interaction (local, national, regional and international/global) in order to enhance the quality of life of individuals and groups.[1] Challenges to development globally are manifest in a number of ways. These can usefully be grouped into three broad categories: challenges arising from global poverty and inequality, challenges in the area of human security, and challenges arising from environmental stress and degradation.

Global Poverty and Inequality

Since the early 1960s considerable advances have been made in improving living standards for people around the world. Overall production of wealth has increased sevenfold globally since the early 1960s; however, this wealth is not evenly distributed. The World Bank, the world's leading development institution, recently changed the way it calculates global poverty, revising the figure for gauging *extreme* income poverty from US$1.00 per day to US$1.25 per day. The figures were revised to include new cost-of-living data and show that extreme poverty has been more widespread across the developing world over the past 25 years than previously estimated using the $1 per day standard. The new figures reveal that out of an estimated world population of about 6.5 billion in 2005, approximately 1.37 billion people lived below the income poverty line of US$1.25 per day, 400 million more people than previous estimated, and almost half the world's population lived on less than US$2.50 per day.[2] The proportion of the world's population living in poverty decreased (from about 41 percent in 1990 to about 25 percent in 2005), but the total number of poor people actually increased in many regions of the world, particularly in sub-Saharan Africa and parts of Latin America, Eastern Europe, the Middle East and South Asia (see Table 14.1, p. 360). The majority are women and children. Income disparities between the richest 20 percent and the poorest 20 percent have also more than doubled since the early 1960s. The richest 50 individuals in the world have a combined income greater than that of the poorest 416 million. The assets of the 200 richest people exceed the combined income of 41 percent of the world's total population. Almost half the world's population receives only five percent of global income, while 54 percent of global income goes to the richest 10 percent of the world's population.

While income measures provide useful shorthand for gauging standards of living, it is now widely accepted that income and money alone cannot provide a comprehensive picture of the deprivations associated with poverty. The United Nations Development Program's (UNDP) *Human Development Report for 2010* uses a Multidimensional Poverty Index that measures not only incomes but also deprivations at the individual level in health and education. This new measure estimates that globally 1.75 billion people lived in poverty in 2010.

Table 14.1   Population Living on Less Than US$1.25 Per Day

Region	No. (millions) living on less than $1.25/day		% living below $1.25 a day	
	1990	2005	1990	2005
East Asia and Pacific	873.3	316.2	36.0	16.8
Eastern Europe and Central Asia	9.1	17.3	2.0	3.7
Latin America and Caribbean	42.9	46.1	9.8	8.2
Middle East and North Africa	9.7	11.0	4.3	3.6
South Asia	579.2	595.6	51.7	40.3
Sub-Saharan Africa	299.1	390.6	57.9	50.9
Total	1813.4	1376.7	41.6	25.2

Source: International Bank for Reconstruction and Development/The World Bank: S. Chen & M. Ravallion, "The Developing World Is Poorer Than We Thought, But No Less Successful in the Fight against Poverty," World Bank Policy Research Paper WPS 4703, (Washington, DC: World Bank, August 2009), Table 6(b) p, 42 and Table 7(b) p. 44.

Human Security

Another major challenge to global development lies in the insecurities faced by large numbers of individuals and groups around the world. The word security means different things to different people but, in general, achieving security entails protecting certain core values (human life, livelihoods, property, etc.) from sudden disruption or harm. The notion of **human security**, which was first introduced by the 1994 *Human Development Report* published by the UNDP, articulates an approach that places individuals and communities at the centre of efforts to enhance security globally. This is in contrast to the traditional approach to security in international affairs that emphasized the security of states and governments (i.e., national security). Since 1994, the human security concept has been widely embraced by international development agencies, **nongovernmental organizations**, and national governments, and Canada has played a leading role. This widespread acceptance is in recognition of how disparities in patterns of inequality globally and nationally affect security.

Human security: A broadened concept of security focusing not only on national security and interstate war but also on threats to the safety of individuals and groups.

Human security is said to include freedom from fear and freedom from want. The former focuses on violence associated with repressive government, armed conflicts, genocides, and other forms of political violence. Those who emphasize this dimension of human security note that the majority of armed conflicts since World War II have occurred in the developing world. Most of these conflicts, with a few notable exceptions in the Middle East and South Asia, have not been traditional inter-state wars between two or more states but intra-state wars (civil wars, communal violence, insurgencies, genocides, etc). More than one-half of the world's 35 poorest countries experienced a major armed conflict in the past 20 years. These armed conflicts have been accompanied by some of the most gruesome violations of human rights and humanitarian law, including the use of child soldiers and the direct targeting of civilian populations. The proportion of civilian casualties soared from five percent of total casualties in World War I to 80 percent in armed conflicts that occurred during the 1990s. The Human Security Report notes a decline in violent intra-state conflict worldwide since the late 1990s, possibly indicating some success in the "freedom from fear" dimension of human security.[3] However, the incidence of violent crime within nations, as well as internationally, is on the increase. This has led to recognition of the phenomena of transnational organized crime and **terrorism** as global issues. The issue of political violence and warfare is discussed in a later section of this chapter and in more detail in Chapters 15 and 16.

With freedom from want the focus is on insecurities arising from a broader set of deprivations, including chronic hunger and malnutrition, endemic disease and ill-health, lack of access to safe drinking water and sanitation, and environmental pollution. Those who emphasize this aspect of human security paint a much bleaker picture of insecurity in the developing world by noting that poverty-related disease and ill health combined with other deprivations such as malnutrition, lack of basic sanitation and access to clean drinking water, and environmental pollution and degradation kill more people annually than armed conflicts and that many of these deaths are preventable.[4] While poverty does not directly cause insecurity, the deprivations associated with extreme and/or endemic poverty and inequality contribute to insecurity by amplifying vulnerabilities to harm. In the poorer areas of the developing world, food insecurity is pervasive and the urban and rural poor, many of them women and children, have been more vulnerable to preventable diseases and deaths, to the harmful effects of environmental pollution and degradation, and to violence. The issue of vulnerability and insecurity is discussed in a later section on the environment and development in this chapter.

Environmental Stress and Degradation

Challenges to development are also evident in the area of increased pressure on the earth's natural environment. According to the United Nations Environment Program (UNEP), one of the most authoritative scientific reports on the global environment, climate change, the collapse of fish stocks, biodiversity losses, and the extinction of species have reached a point where they threaten the survival of humanity.[5] Only 1.7 million out of an estimated 30 million species living on the planet have been identified. However, natural habitats including forests and wetlands, where many of the unidentified species live, are disappearing at a rate of 0.5 to 1.0 percent per year. According to the United Nations Population Division, the world population reached an estimated 6.8 billion in 2009, is expected to reach seven billion by 2012, and increase to over nine billion by 2050. Most of this growth will occur in regions of world classified as "developing."[6] To keep pace with this growth, world food production will need to double in the next

30 years. Mass migrations of people within nations and across borders fleeing persecution or seeking better economic conditions and livelihood security can also be a source of insecurity and conflict. Internally displaced persons (internal refugees) and international refugees are among the most vulnerable populations in the world.

Environmental stress and degradation can also induce mass migrations of people (so-called "environmental refugees"), which can also be a source of insecurity and conflict. Approximately 1.3 billion people world-wide have no access to safe drinking water or basic sanitation, while 800 million people—200 million of them children—are at risk of disease and malnourishment. More than two million people are possibly dying prematurely from air pollution and close to two billion, most of them in the developing world, are likely to suffer absolute water scarcity by 2025. Resource scarcity, including a decline in arable land, compounds the insecurities faced by individuals and groups around the world and can contribute to the incidence of violent conflict, both within and between nations.

DEVELOPMENT AND UNDERDEVELOPMENT: PROBLEMS OF CLASSIFICATION

Considerable differences exist among the 193 sovereign states in the world today in terms of their levels of development. Generally, discussions of development internationally have focused on how to improve the conditions or circumstances of people living in a group of countries variously described as *developing countries, less developed countries, underdeveloped countries*, the *Third World*, or the *South*. This group is said to include all countries in Central and South America and the Caribbean, Africa, Asia and the Middle East (excluding Japan), and the Pacific islands excluding Australia and New Zealand. In all, about 140 countries are represented here (see Figure 14.1, p. 362). These various terms are used to differentiate this group from the *developed* countries (also called the *North*) which includes Canada and the United States, Europe, Australia, New Zealand, and Japan.

Figure 14.1 **The North and the South**

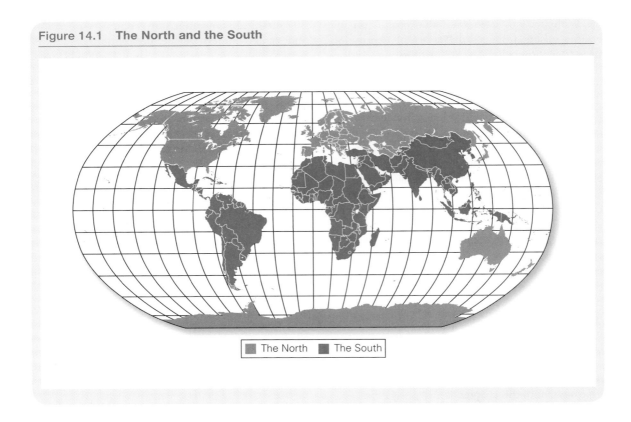

The North ■ The South

Some analysts question whether such classifications and generalizations are still relevant today.[7] They point to the fact that the term *Third World* was originally a political classification to describe one of the "three worlds" that existed during the Cold War—a "first world" of western industrialized states, a "second world" comprising the Soviet Union and its allies in eastern Europe, and a "third world" that included all other countries that were not aligned with either of these groups. Now that the Cold War is over, the argument states that this classification is no longer relevant.

Some postmodernist critics, noting the Cold War context within which "development" first came to be used, reject the very notion of development as a discourse of power, imposing on the world a modernity that many in it do not necessarily want or need.[8] Others point to the increased diversity within the group of developing nations. For example, the group includes countries such as Singapore and South Korea that have been among the fastest-growing economies in the world over the past three decades. On some

economic indicators of development, these countries are comparable to many developed western states. Singapore, for example, had a higher average national income (US$32,470) than Spain (US$29,450) in 2007.[9] While these criticisms have merit, the fact remains that diversity within the group of developing countries tends to be exaggerated when the focus is mainly on economic indicators of development. When the concept of development is disaggregated into its economic, social, and political dimensions, it becomes evident that the developing countries as a whole tend to score lower on all three dimensions than developed countries. These dimensions are explored in greater detail below. Other critics object to the terms *underdeveloped* and *less developed* on normative grounds. They are essentially negative concepts that describe and classify a group of countries and people by what they do not have in comparison to what another group of countries has (i.e., they are not developed).[10]

In deference to some of these negative connotations, the subsequent discussion in this chapter will use the terms "South" or "developing" countries interchangeably. As Figure 14.1 indicates, most of the countries that make up the "developing world" are located in the southern hemisphere or to the south of the developed countries. Most developed states, with the notable exceptions of Australia and New Zealand, are located in the northern hemisphere.

Another important factor that unites the developing countries of the South vis-à-vis the developed North is a technological gap or dependence. "Technology" as used here does not simply mean machines and physical tools, but rather applied knowledge—the instruments and processes used to solve social, economic, and political problems. For much of the post-World War II period, "development" in practice has been virtually synonymous with modernization and Westernization—the adoption of Western forms of social, political, and economic organization. Even non-Western developed countries such as Japan owe their success in part to their ability to adapt their indigenous practices to Western forms of technology and organization.

For example, although bureaucracy may have originated in China, the modern bureaucracy—based on rational-legal authority and an efficient technocracy—is very much a Western invention. As the discussion later in this chapter shows, the emergence of such rational-legal authority is seen by some as a key to successful political development. Furthermore, the most dominant form of political organization in the world today, the sovereign territorial state, is also a Western invention. Almost all present-day developing countries in Africa, Asia, and the Americas were once colonies of European states, and all are the product of a process that began in the late 15th century in Europe by which scattered peoples throughout the world were brought together into a single society of sovereign states and a single global economy.[11] The history and legacy of colonialism is examined below.

COLONIALISM IN THE AMERICAS, ASIA, AND AFRICA

By far the greater part of what is currently the South was at one time or another subjected to formal colonial rule by European states.[12] Even those non-Western societies that retained their independence, such as Japan and China, were forced both to come to terms with a world in which European technology and influence were dominant and to adapt their own domestic political structures to meet the European prerequisites of statehood. European **colonialism** took different forms depending on the colonizing state itself, the reasons for which it undertook colonialism, and especially, the sociopolitical organization and response of the colonized peoples. In many cases, colonialism was part of a broader process of European **imperialism** that resulted in the establishment of large European empires.

> **Colonialism:** The ownership and administration of one territory and people by another, as if the former were part of the latter.

> **Imperialism:** A broader term than colonialism that literally means "empire building." Imperialism occurs when one country dominates another with the aim of controlling and/or exploiting the latter. The domination can be economic, political, social, or cultural.

Colonialism in the Americas

European colonialism in the Americas was distinguished from Africa and Asia by the thoroughness with which it displaced indigenous societies. In the islands of the Caribbean, the first point of contact in the Americas, indigenous populations almost entirely disappeared within a few generations. In Central and South America, strong indigenous empires, such as the Aztec and Inca, could not resist European expansion. However, the extent to which indigenous populations were displaced varied in the Americas. In the northwest portion of the South American continent and in Central America, indigenous populations still account for a significant proportion of the population—Bolivia (70 percent), Peru (46 percent), Ecuador (39 percent), and Mexico (30 percent). In the southern part of South America and the Caribbean islands, however, they have all but disappeared. Although substantial indigenous populations still exist in Canada and the United States, they remain socially, politically, and economically peripheral.

The displacement of local populations in the Americas was due to a variety of factors. Many of these territories, which had a more temperate climate similar to that in Europe, were designated "white settler" lands—especially in Canada, the United States, Argentina, and Chile. The more tropical areas of the Americas (the Caribbean, Brazil, southern U.S., etc.) were designated for the production of "cash crops" for the European market—sugar, cotton, tobacco, and coffee. For various reasons, the indigenous populations were deemed "unsuitable" for the production of cash crops, and the solution was to import people from the African continent to work as slaves. This led to the trans-Atlantic slave trade, which began in the mid-16th century, continued for 300 years, and poured millions of Africans into the Americas, some estimates putting the figure as high as 100 million people. A renewed demand for plantation labour in the 19th century after the demise of the slave trade led to the importation of indentured labourers from India and China.

Colonialism in Asia

What distinguished colonialism in Asia from the Americas was the comparative strength and resistance of its indigenous cultures and societies. In no case (except for small islands in the Indian Ocean such as Mauritius) could these be destroyed or completely subordinated to a predominantly European settler society. Even though Asia had been the prime target for European mercantilist expansion even prior to the "discovery" of the Americas (in the late 15th century), the cohesiveness of Asian societies restricted European incursions to coastal trading posts. The formal imposition of colonial rule in Asia occurred mainly in the 19th century, and was made possible by European technological advances; however, a number of political entities such as Iran, Afghanistan, and Thailand were never subject to formal colonial rule.

European colonialism in Asia proceeded by taking over existing political systems, including preserving their political leaders (e.g., in India). Societies were taken over in their entirety and the new, fixed colonial territorial frontiers roughly coincided with the undemarcated boundaries within which the pre-colonial rulers had ruled. The Middle East also experienced a unique brand of colonialism. This region had been subject to European expansion since the time of the crusades (5th–10th centuries), and by the mid-17th century had come under the control of the Ottoman Empire. At the end of World War I, European powers such as France

and the United Kingdom ruled most of the territories formerly controlled by the Ottoman Empire under the League of Nations Mandate system in conjunction with local dynasties. The impact of European incursions here was limited by the strength of the local dynasties and by the force of "pan-Arabism" that produced a very strong sense of regional identity.

Colonialism in Africa

Unlike Asia, Africa was initially perceived to have little economic worth (except for its people to be exported as slaves); it had an interior that was difficult to penetrate, and was perceived to have a climate inhospitable for European settlement. Thus, except for a few coastal trading forts and settlements that were used primarily for slave raids and storage of slaves for export, formal imposition of colonial rule did not occur until the end of the 19th century (except Algeria, colonized by France in 1830). By the time Africa began to be formally colonized in the late 1800s most colonies in the Americas (except the Caribbean) had already become independent states.

Colonialism in Africa, like Asia but unlike the Americas, did not involve the displacement of indigenous peoples. But unlike Asia, no attempt was made to create colonial boundaries that broadly coincided with existing cultures and political systems. Instead, colonial boundaries in Africa were demarcated by European powers at the Berlin Conference of 1884–1885. Only one existing African state (Ethiopia) retained its independence for much of the colonial period (save for a brief period in the 1930s when Mussolini of Italy attempted to colonize it). By 1914, all of Africa (except Liberia— created as an independent state in 1822 for freed slaves from the USA, Lesotho, Ethiopia, and South Africa) was made up of colonies of the European powers.

DECOLONIZATION AND THE POLITICS OF NORTH–SOUTH RELATIONS SINCE 1950

The collapse of European colonialism was rapid and, with very few exceptions, is virtually complete today. **Decolonization** began in Central and South America

Decolonization: The process in which a population and territory formerly under colonial domination achieve formal political independence and become a sovereign state.

in the 1820s with the independence of Brazil and Mexico. The relative decline of Spain and Portugal—the main colonizers of the region—as major European powers contributed to this early start in the process. In most of Africa and Asia, however, decolonization did not begin until after World War II, with the independence of India and Pakistan in 1947. As a result, the term *post-colonial era* usually refers to the period after 1945. A number of factors contributed to decolonization on these continents, including the weakening of European colonial powers as a result of the war, the rise of nationalist movements in the colonies demanding political independence, and the emergence and institutionalization of new norms in international relations that de-legitimized colonialism.[13] These norms centred on a new interpretation of the principle of **self-determination**.

Self-determination: A principle of international law that grants all peoples/nations the right to determine their political status, and pursue their economic, social, and cultural development free from external domination or interference.

The resolution adopted by the United Nations General Assembly in 1960, called the Declaration on the Granting of Independence to Colonial Countries and Peoples, sums up the new views on self-determination: "All peoples have the right to self-determination; by virtue of that right they freely determine their political status and freely pursue their economic, social and cultural development…. Any attempt aimed at the partial or total disruption of the national unity and the territorial integrity of a country is incompatible with the purposes and principles of the Charter of the United Nations" (UN General Assembly Resolution 1514—XV, December 14, 1960).

Prior to 1945, the international system was very much a European state system (with countries such as the United States and Japan emerging in the early 20th century). The founding of the **United Nations**

in 1945 involved only 51 states as members. By 2011, the UN had a total of 193 member states. This phenomenal growth is largely due to decolonization. Once political independence was attained, the countries of the South, through a series of international conferences and negotiations beginning in the mid-1950s, sought to achieve changes in the international political and economic order. These demands often brought the interests of the South into conflict with the interests of the North. Five stages or phases can be discerned in the evolution of the dialogue between North and South.

Phase One: The 1950s and 1960s

The first phase of decolonization, which occurred in the 1950s and 1960s, was characterized by the South's attempt to carve out a separate identity in world politics. Two international conferences highlighted these efforts: the Afro-Asian Conference held in Bandung (Indonesia) in 1955, and the first meeting of the Non-Aligned Movement (NAM) held in Belgrade (Yugoslavia) in 1961. By the early 1960s a more focused strategy to influence international events began to emerge on the part of the South. This involved an attempt to extend the international normative consensus that had emerged in favour of decolonization and political independence into international support for development. Through the UN system and the creation of new institutional frameworks, such as the UN Conference on Trade and Development (UNCTAD), the countries of the South were successful in making the issue of "development" a priority on the international agenda. Their objectives during this period were defined mainly in terms of "closing the gap" with the North.

Phase Two: The 1970s

At the beginning of the 1970s, a series of events occurred that changed the strategy of the South, including the quadrupling of oil prices by the Organization of Petroleum Exporting Countries (OPEC) after the 1973 Middle East war. This new strategy was more explicitly redistributive and combined the threat of negative sanctions (on the North) with the promise of mutual gains for both North and

South. This strategy, known as the **New International Economic Order (NIEO)**, represented an attempt by the South to affirm a "right to development," and to convince the North that reform of existing institutions and practices in the global political economy was needed (see Box 14.1).[14] The call for the NIEO, however, failed to produce the results that developing countries expected.

New international economic order (NIEO): A set of proposals launched in 1974 for reform of the international economic order, with the goal of enhancing the self-reliance of the South and its influence over international institutions and events and achieving an increase in resource flows from the North to the South.

BOX 14.1

THE NEW INTERNATIONAL ECONOMIC ORDER (NIEO)

The New International Economic Order refers to a set of proposals made by the South for reform of the international economic order. The idea for the NIEO took shape first within the Non-Aligned Movement and subsequently in the United Nations. Two resolutions adopted by the UN General Assembly (UNGA) in 1974 launched a series of global negotiations between North and South. These were UNGA Resolution 3202, "The Program of Action on the Establishment of the New International Economic Order," and Resolution 3281, "The Charter of Economic Rights and Duties of States." Three sets of reforms were proposed:

1. the self-reliance reforms, designed to increase the control of developing countries over their natural resources
2. the resource-transfer reforms, designed to achieve greater and more regular flows of financial resources from North to South (e.g., an increase in grants and concessional foreign aid)
3. the international influence reforms, designed to increase the participation of developing countries in the central institutions that regulated international economic and political interactions

Some modest changes occurred as a result of these negotiations but the fundamental reforms sought by the South did not occur. By the early 1980s, negotiations for the NIEO were effectively over.

Phase Three: The 1980s

During the 1980s, several events displaced the NIEO from the top of the international agenda including the worldwide recession of the early 1980s precipitated by a second round of oil price increases in 1979, and the emergence of the first developing country debt crisis in 1982 (see Box 14.2). These events undermined the unity of the South, weakened its bargaining position vis-à-vis the North, and led to a new strategy that deemphasized redistribution and focused on common problems and the interdependence between North and South. The premise was that the development problems of the South and their political, social, and environmental consequences were very much a concern for the North. Hence, the efficient working of the international system as a whole required cooperation between North and South. This new emphasis on interdependence and multilateralism was articulated through a series of reports commissioned by the UN.[15]

Phase Four: The 1990s

For most of the 1980s, issues arising from the (1982) debt crisis dominated North–South relations. Debt problems of developing countries continued into the 1990s, with a number of currency and financial crises including the Mexico Peso crisis in 1994 and the Asian financial crisis that began in 1997. Thus a key issue in the 1990s was how to manage the mountain of debt accumulated by countries in the South. One initiative was the Highly Indebted Poor Countries Initiative (HIPC), launched in 1996, which offered some debt-relief to low-income developing countries. An enhanced version of the HIPC (the EHIPC) was introduced in September 1999 to strengthen the link between debt relief and poverty reduction. Although managing debt problems was dominant, a number of other significant issues were added to the agenda of

BOX 14.2

THE FIRST DEVELOPING COUNTRY DEBT CRISIS

The causes of the first debt crisis can be traced to the impact of the 1973 quadrupling of oil prices that resulted in severe deficits in oil-importing developing countries.[16] Many of these countries, faced with a choice between a swift but painful adjustment that would have entailed a reduction in imports and strict austerity measures, chose instead to finance their deficits by borrowing money from the "offshore" private capital markets (branches of commercial banks in the North located offshore). The second round of oil price increases in 1979 led governments of industrialized countries, particularly the United States, to make controlling domestic inflation a key priority. These policies were deflationary and resulted in a reduction in the demand for and prices of exports from developing countries, increased protectionism, and a steep rise in interest rates to unprecedented levels.[17] The export earnings of countries in the South declined relative to the prices of their imports. Debt-service obligations rose while the income to meet them declined. At the same time, commercial bank lending dried up. By late 1982 there were widespread difficulties in servicing the mountain of accumulated debt. The actual onset of the crisis is dated from August 1982, when Mexico announced a moratorium on repayments. By the end of 1983, over 30 countries had suspended repayments of their debts. Total external debt of low- and middle-income developing countries increased from US$480 billion in 1980 to over US$1.3 trillion in 1990. By 2005 it had reached over US$2.8 trillion.[18]

In the mid-1980s the **International Monetary Fund (IMF)** and the **World Bank** became major players in the management of the international debt problem, because of the leverage they had over countries seeking to refinance and reschedule their debts. The source of this leverage lay in the conditionality attached to their lending facilities. The linchpin of the debt management system was a package of policies known as "structural adjustment," in which debtor countries had to agree to restructure their economies according to market-oriented principles (more on this in the section on the "Washington Consensus" later in this chapter). In addition, through the Consultative Groups, chaired by the World Bank, which brought together the major foreign aid donors in the international community, and the Paris Club of debt rescheduling chaired by the IMF, all other forms of assistance and aid were linked to IMF and World Bank programs. As a result, developing countries today as a whole face a much tighter system of conditionality than ever before.

North–South relations, aided by the end of the Cold War in 1990, which created the space for these newer issues to emerge.

One of the most prominent of these was the increased concern over the relationship between development and the natural environment, encapsulated in the concept of "sustainable development," which was given institutional expression at the 1992 United Nations Conference on the Environment and Development (UNCED). A number of important agreements were signed, including treaties on Climate Change and Biodiversity. The conference also exposed some strong differences between North and South on how to achieve sustainable development, which is discussed later in this chapter. Other significant issues that emerged in the 1990s included debates on the role of foreign aid and trade in development, and debates over democracy, human rights, and development. Also in the 1990s, increased attention was paid to the issue of gender and development. In addition, the end of the Cold War focused attention on problems of human security in the context of civil war, state failure, and ethnic conflict in various regions of the world. Each of these contemporary issues is explored in more detail later in this chapter.

Phase Five: The Millennium Development Goals (MDGs)

The new century appeared to usher in a new era of cooperation between North and South marked by a determination to meet some of the challenges of global development outlined at the beginning of this chapter. In September 2000, 189 countries at the largest-ever gathering of heads of state signed the United Nations Millennium Declaration, which led to the adoption of the Millennium Development Goals (MDGs). This declaration committed all countries, rich and poor, to eradicate poverty, promote human dignity, achieve greater gender equality, and achieve peace, "good governance," and environmental sustainability (see Box 14.3). They also include actions to reduce debt and increase aid, trade, and technology transfers to poor countries. The MDGs provide important benchmarks for measuring global progress on key development outcomes, and focus attention on the enormous challenges in the poorest countries. Since the adoption of the MDGs in 2000, a number of other international conferences have sought to provide a framework for a partnership between North and South to help achieve the MDGs, including the November 2001 Doha Declaration, the March 2002 Monterrey Declaration, the September 2002 Johannesburg Declaration on Sustainable Development, and the 2005 Paris Declaration on Aid Effectiveness.

Assessing Outcomes of the North–South Dialogue

At the beginning of the new millennium, assessing the outcomes of the over 50-year dialogue between North and South is difficult. On the whole, the fundamental changes in international political and economic relations that the South wanted have not been achieved. Nevertheless, some changes have occurred. Perhaps the most visible impact of the South has been normative and institutional. In normative terms, countries of the South have been successful to a degree in placing issues on the international agenda that, arguably, would not be there otherwise, such as the very notion of "development" as an international issue. Even more important has been the impact of the South on international institutionalization, especially within the United Nations system. The Millennium Declaration was supposed to signify a new era of cooperation between North and South, but it remains to be seen whether the specified MDG targets are indeed achieved by 2015. The global financial and economic crisis that began in 2008 had

---

BOX 14.3

THE MILLENNIUM DEVELOPMENT GOALS (MDGs)

The MDGs are set of eight goals for which a number of numerical targets have been identified.[19] These goals and targets are to be achieved by the date of 2015 or earlier.

Goal 1: Eradicate Extreme Poverty and Hunger
Halve by 2015 the proportion of people whose income is less than $1 a day and the proportion of people who suffer from hunger.

Goal 2: Achieve Universal Primary Education
Ensure that by 2015 children everywhere, boys and girls alike, will be able to complete a full course of primary schooling.

Goal 3: Promote Gender Equality and Empower Women
Eliminate gender disparity in primary and secondary education, preferably by 2005 and in all levels of education no later than 2015.

Goal 4: Reduce Child Mortality
Reduce by two-thirds the under-five mortality rate.

Goal 5: Improve Maternal Health
Reduce by three-quarters the maternal mortality ratio.

Goal 6: Combat HIV/AIDS, Malaria, and Other Diseases
Reverse the spread of HIV/AIDS.

Goal 7: Ensure Environmental Sustainability
Integrate sustainable development into country policies and reverse loss of environmental resources. Halve the proportion of people without access to potable water. Significantly improve the lives of at least 100 million slum dwellers.

Goal 8: Develop a Global Partnership for Development
Raise official development assistance. Expand market access in international trade.

a negative impact on progress towards achieving the MDGs, and the ability to recover will vary across countries and regions. While the longer-term effects of the global economic crisis are unknown, by the end of 2010—just five years to the target year of 2015—an important World Bank publication noted the lack of progress in several key MDG indicators in poorer countries including education, health, nutrition, and poverty indicators.[20]

MEASURING DEVELOPMENT: ECONOMIC AND POLITICAL DIMENSIONS

The study of development is the study of social transformation or change, particularly those changes that affect the *quality of life* of individuals and groups. The synopsis of North–South relations above shows that the question of "development" is a highly contentious one. Defining exactly what "development" entails is, like many other concepts in the study of politics, subject to much debate. While analysts agree that development involves processes of change, considerable debate has revolved around specifying who or what the target or object of "development" is, exactly what these processes of change involve, and what the desirable goals of such development processes are. Despite these disagreements, the practice of development internationally as it has evolved over the past 50 years has generally included economic, social, and political dimensions. These three aspects of development are analyzed below.

Economic Development

The economic dimension of development refers to the *production* and *distribution* of wealth and income in a country.[21] Perhaps the most widely used measure of the production of wealth in a country is the *gross domestic product (GDP)* or *gross national product/gross national income (GNP/GNI)*.[22] The GDP or GNP/GNI can also be expressed as a ratio of a country's population to provide a representation of that country's average national income (the GDP or GNI per capita). Less economically developed countries tend to produce less wealth and income than more economically developed countries. For example, in 2007, the per capita GNI for the United States, one of the wealthiest countries in the world, was over US$46,040. In comparison, Ethiopia, one of the poorest countries, had a GNI per capita of only US$220. The 18 richest countries in the world—the United States, Japan, and Canada, plus the 15 countries of the European Union (EU) prior to its May 2004 enlargement—accounted for about 47 percent of total global GDP in 2003.

The World Bank, the leading institution charged with promoting development internationally, has developed a fourfold classification of countries to distinguish their level of economic growth (see Table 14.2).

In addition to GDP/GNI per capita and GDP/GNI growth, levels of economic development are measured by how that wealth and income are distributed. Not only do developing countries tend to produce less wealth and income, but whatever they do produce is often poorly distributed. One way of measuring inequality is the *Gini Index*, which measures the extent to which the distribution of income (or consumption) among individuals or households within a

Table 14.2 The World Bank's Classification of Levels of Economic Growth		
Classification	GNI per Capita (US$)	Example (US$ 2007)
Low income	$935 or less	Bangladesh ($470)
Lower middle income	$936–3,705	Egypt ($1,580)
Upper middle income	$3,706–11,455	South Africa ($5,760)
High income	$11,456 or more	United Kingdom ($42,740)

Source: International Bank for Reconstruction and Development/The World Bank: *World Development Report 2009*, p. 350, and Annex Table 1, pp. 352–253. Annex Table 1.

Table 14.3 Gini Index of Income Inequality Within Countries				
Lower Inequality			**Higher Inequality**	
Country	Gini		Country	Gini
Finland	0.25		Haiti	0.68
Denmark	0.27		Botswana	0.63
Norway	0.27		Brazil	0.59
Canada	0.33		Bolivia	0.58
United States	0.38		Columbia	0.54

Source: International Bank for Reconstruction and Development/The World Bank: *World Development Report 2006*, Table A2, p. 280.

country deviates from a perfectly equal distribution. The Gini is expressed on a scale between 0 and 1, zero representing perfect equality and one perfect inequality. No country ever scores a perfect 0 or 1, and generally countries with Ginis closer to 0 are considered to have lower income inequality (see Table 14.3). Most developed countries have Ginis below 0.4.

Social Development

The social dimension refers to the development of a country's human resources.[23] Indicators such as levels of education, school enrolments, literacy rates, life expectancy, and levels of nutrition are often used as measures of a country's social development. The United Nations Development Program (UNDP), an agency of the UN, has developed a **Human Development Index (HDI)**, a composite index that contains three variables: longevity (measured by average life expectancy); knowledge (measured by adult literacy and combined primary, secondary and tertiary enrolment); and standard of living (measured by the real GNI per capita).

> **Human development index (HDI):** A composite index measuring longevity, knowledge, and standard of living, designed to give an indication of and a basis for comparing the quality of life in various countries.

The HDI is calculated for each country and expressed on a scale between 0 and 1 to allow for comparisons. A score of one indicates that a country has attained the highest possible quality of life for its citizens. HDI scores of less than one indicate how far a country

must go to reach this ideal. All countries are ranked from "high" (scores of 0.81 and above) to "medium" (0.51 to 0.80) and "low" HDI (less than 0.50). Since the HDI was introduced in 1990, no state has ever scored a perfect 1. Generally, developed countries of the North tend to score higher than developing countries of the South. For example, in 1998 Canada achieved the highest HDI score of 0.960. The lowest was Sierra Leone with a HDI of 0.185. In effect, Canada was rated the "best country in the world to live," while Sierra Leone—a country afflicted with civil war and extreme poverty—was the "worst country in the world to live." In 2010, however, Canada was eighth in the HDI rankings (see Table 14.4). Singapore at 27th was the highest-ranked country in the South in 2010, and Zimbabwe at 169th was the lowest.

Political Development

Measuring **political development** is far more difficult than measuring economic and social development.[24] Because no widespread agreement on the suitable indicators of political development exists, political variables—dealing with values and beliefs, institutions,

> **Political development:** A concept that describes how well a society has developed politically, usually measured by the degree of state capacity to effectively carry out the legislative, executive, and judicial functions of government; the degree of political stability, or ability to resolve political conflicts in a peaceful manner; and the degree of governmental responsiveness to public demands and respect for fundamental rights.

Table 14.4   Human Development Index Rankings (2010)

High Human Development (Top 10)		Low Human Development (Bottom 10)	
Country Rank	HDI	Country Rank	HDI
1. Norway	0.938	160. Mali	0.309
2. Australia	0.937	161. Burkina Faso	0.305
3. New Zealand	0.907	162. Liberia	0.300
4. United States	0.902	163. Chad	0.295
5. Ireland	0.895	164. Guinea-Bissau	0.289
6. Liechtenstein	0.891	165. Mozambique	0.284
7. Netherlands	0.890	166. Burundi	0.282
8. Canada	0.888	167. Niger	0.261
9. Sweden	0.885	168. Congo, DR	0.239
10. Germany	0.885	169. Zimbabwe	0.140

Source: UNDP, *Human Development Report*, 2010, Table I pp. 143–146.

and power—cannot be quantified as readily as economic and social variables. Ideological and cultural differences also further complicate the debate. Despite these disagreements within the literature, several influential views on measures of political development may be discerned. These include the degree of state capacity and the degree of political stability. More recently, issues of governmental responsiveness and representation have been added as criteria.

Degree of State Capacity Political development involves the creation of specialized and differentiated government institutions that have the capacity to effectively carry out the functions of government—making (legislative functions), implementing (executive functions), and adjudicating (judicial functions) public policy and laws. The idea here is that political development entails the institutionalization of rational-legal authority and the establishment of an effective state **bureaucracy**. Although they possess all the attributes of statehood such as population, demarcated territories, and so on, many states in the South do not have governments that can discharge these functions effectively. In some extreme cases—what are known as *failed states*—government capacity is virtually nonexistent. Examples include Somalia and Afghanistan.

Degree of Political Stability Countries that are politically developed enjoy a degree of political stability.

The notion of political stability addresses the issue of how political conflicts and disputes are resolved. Stable polities are those in which political conflicts can be resolved in a peaceful manner without recourse to widespread violence. In contrast, less developed polities are plagued by instability—civil strife, communal violence, military coups, and sometimes outright civil war. Generally, developed countries of the North tend to be more stable than those in the South. Indeed, as shown later in this chapter, since 1945 almost all major armed conflicts in world have been located in the South.

Degree of Governmental Responsiveness and Representation In addition to state capacity and political stability, some observers include the degree of governmental responsiveness and representation as indicators of political development. The idea here is that politically developed countries have governments that are responsive to broad segments of society, and show respect for that population's fundamental rights and freedoms. Representative governments reflect the wishes of their populations, and govern with the consent, or at least the acquiescence, of that population. Responsive and representative governments would enjoy a high degree of **legitimacy**, they would allow their citizens to pursue their values, interests, and goals peacefully, have mechanisms and procedures in place to prevent the abuse of power, and allow for a peaceful change in government.

The criteria of responsive and representative government sound very similar to those associated with the form of government known as *democracy*. Does this mean political development is synonymous with democratization? Early works on political development gave ambiguous answers to this question to avoid the accusation that they were attempting to impose Western values. However, today the widespread view is that political development does entail the emergence and consolidation of some type of democratic political institutions and procedures, for democratic governments tend to have greater political capacity, are more responsive and representative, and

tend to be more stable than authoritarian governments. This issue of democracy and development is examined in greater detail later in this chapter and in Chapter 15.

Using the three broad measures of economic, social, and political development we can generally say that more developed societies have achieved higher levels of economic growth with a degree of equity in their income distribution, have a relatively high level of social development, and have a higher degree of state capacity and political stability with governments that are responsive to and representative of their populations. In Box 14.4, we look at the interesting case of Ghana.

BOX 14.4

GHANA: DEVELOPMENT, DECAY, AND RECOVERY

Ghana is a relatively small country located on the west coast of Africa with a population of about 18 million. It was one of the first sub-Saharan African countries to achieve political independence (from Britain) in 1957. In the immediate post-independence period, Ghana's future development prospects looked bright. It was relatively well endowed with natural resources (gold, manganese, timber, bauxite) and by the standards of colonial Africa at the time (generally very low) it had a relatively well-educated population. In 1960, Ghana's per capita income was similar to that of South Korea. But by 1998 South Korea's per capita income (US$10,550) was more than 20 times greater than that of Ghana (US$400), and by 2007 the gap was even wider with South Korea at US$19,690 and Ghana at US$590. South Korea is generally seen as a "success story" of development (see Box 14.5 for more on South Korea and other Asian countries), having achieved marked improvements in the economic, social, and political dimensions of development. The experience of Ghana between 1960 and the early 1980s, on the other hand, appeared to demonstrate everything that might go wrong in the development of a country.

For example, between 1970 and 1982, income per capita in Ghana fell by 20 percent, and almost every social indicator of development, including school enrolments, declined. Politically, Ghana's post-independence history has been unstable, having experienced five successful military coups d'état, in which incumbent governments were violently overthrown. The country has also experimented with a wide range of governments, civilian and military-authoritarian. By the early 1980s, the central institutions of the state were near collapse. However, at the end of 1981, an authoritarian military leader took power who was determined to break the cycle of economic, social, and political decay, and set the country on a path to development. He rigorously implemented policy reforms. These reforms appear to have reversed the cycle of decline, and resulted in improvements in economic, social, and political development.

From the mid-1980s and throughout the 1990s, for example, Ghana's economic growth rate exceeded the average for sub-Saharan Africa (about five percent per annum as against the continental average of about two percent). Ghana has also shown signs of political development. In 1992, Ghana made a transition from authoritarian to democratic government, and since then a degree of political stability has been achieved, and the capacity of state institutions has been strengthened. Five successful rounds of democratic elections have been held (1992, 1996, 2000, 2004 and 2008). The 2000 and 2008 elections resulted in peaceful transfers of power, which are significant in Africa where incumbent governments rarely accept defeat in elections. As a result of the dramatic turnaround in the country's political, economic, and social development, Ghana today is considered to be one of the countries in sub-Saharan Africa that is on a road to recovery and development.

POLITICAL, ECONOMIC, AND SOCIAL DEVELOPMENT: ISSUES OF DEBATE

The relationship among the three dimensions of development has generated considerable debate on whether they might be achieved simultaneously. Influential works have identified important tradeoffs and tensions within each dimension as well as between the economic, political, and social dimensions of development. In terms of political development, for example, some analysts have argued that to achieve the goal of political stability, a country in the early stages of development has to forgo a degree of political participation and representation. The argument was that for many of the new countries in the South, democracy was incompatible with order and stability—indeed, that premature democratization created political instability. Thus, from this perspective, priority was to be given to stability at the expense of democracy.[25]

Some versions of this argument went further, positing a tension between political and economic development, such that premature creation of democratic governments in developing societies would impede economic growth. Or, to put it another way, strong authoritarian government was necessary for economic growth. Only a strong authoritarian government free from particular interests in society could take the necessary measures. This was the so-called "liberty–growth" trade-off. To support this argument, they pointed to the successes of the Asian newly industrialized countries (NICs)—Singapore, South Korea, and Taiwan—each of which achieved impressive rates of economic growth in the 1970s and 1980s under authoritarian governments. More recently China has adopted elements of this approach and is also recording impressive rates of economic growth (see Box 14.5). However, the empirical record supporting a direct correlation between type of government and economic growth is mixed. While the Asian NICs did achieve impressive rates of economic growth under authoritarian governments, they were the exception, not the rule. The majority of such governments elsewhere in the South—in most Latin American and African countries—failed to achieve sustained growth. With respect to democratic government, the historical record is also mixed. While some democratic governments (such as Botswana) have been able

---

BOX 14.5

THE EAST ASIAN EXPORT-ORIENTED "DEVELOPMENT-STATE" APPROACH

For much of the early post-colonial period in the 1950s and 1960s there was little variation in the domestic economic structures throughout the South—in Asia, Latin America, and Africa. The period from the 1970s onwards, however, began to see significant variations in domestic economic performance, especially between those in Southeast Asia (and a few Latin American states on one hand) and the rest of the South. Observers have argued that the explanation of these differences lies in a particular model of development adopted by the south East Asian countries—the "development state" model.

The success of the East Asian newly industrialized countries (NICs), including Singapore, South Korea, and Taiwan, is attributed to an outward-oriented growth strategy based on export growth and a strong private sector. Centralized and authoritarian economic management was a major ingredient in this model. In each of these NICs, state agents and administrators, backed by government-financed "think-tanks," played a key role in the direction of economic policy, with little public debate and input. Government intervention was directed at ensuring an efficiently working market economy, including policies of trade liberalization, currency devaluations, reductions in wasteful government spending, and the reduction of barriers to foreign investment. In contrast to this outward-oriented set of policies, the majority of countries in Latin America, Africa, and the rest of Asia pursued inward-oriented growth strategies involving extensive state interventions, economic nationalism, and import-substitution, which distorted markets and discouraged production.

(continued)

BOX 14.5

THE EAST ASIAN EXPORT-ORIENTED "DEVELOPMENT-STATE" APPROACH *(Continued)*

In summary, the three key ingredients of the Development State model, first developed by Japan and subsequently adopted by East Asian NICs, include:

1. *Strong centralized economic management.* This is essentially a market economy; however, the government intervenes into and controls the operation of the economy in the areas of finance, foreign investment, and industrial and export development.
2. *Emphasis on the promotion of exports*, with preferential access to credit for exporters, investment incentives, and other trade interventions (e.g., the use of trade tariffs).
3. *Emphasis on industrialization,* but also support for more efficient agricultural production.

Much debate continues on whether the success of the East Asian countries can be replicated elsewhere in the South. Those who question the transferability of this model point to the changed international environment of today compared to that of the late 1960s and 1970s when these NICs began their phenomenal growth. They note, for example, that the NICs received large amounts of foreign aid, particularly from the United States and Japan, which assisted in their economic growth. However, foreign aid to many other countries in the South has declined considerably since the early 1990s. Also, the financial crises that hit several East Asian countries in 1997 have led to questions about the durability of this model.

to manage impressive rates of economic growth, others such as Bolivia have not.

Another important tension that has been identified is between economic growth and equity. This view argued that economic growth should be accorded priority over income distribution and equity. One influential theory that became known as the "trickle-down" doctrine posited that income inequality was indeed necessary to provide incentives for investment. If investors were allowed to reap differential rewards for their entrepreneurial efforts, total societal income would be maximized and the benefits would eventually trickle down to those less well off in that society. However, here again the empirical record to support the trickle-down theory is mixed. For example, rapid economic growth in South Korea and Singapore was achieved together with a marked reduction in levels of poverty and income inequality. In contrast, other countries that pursued growth-first strategies, such as Mexico and Brazil, did so at the cost of widening income disparities and increased inequality. Furthermore, countries such as Cuba and Costa Rica, which recorded comparatively slow rates of economic growth nevertheless recorded impressive gains in the area of social development, including marked improvements in literacy, school enrolments, and the reduction of infant mortality rates.

Thus, the relationship among the three dimensions of development (especially between political and economic

development) is very complex and continues to be the subject of much debate. These debates, in turn, have been influenced by strong disagreements among analysts on the causes of development and underdevelopment.

THE CAUSES OF DEVELOPMENT AND UNDERDEVELOPMENT

Debates over development have revolved not only around how best to measure levels of development, but also around how to understand and explain the present condition of poorer countries and societies, and possibly shape and predict the future direction of change. The kinds of answers to these questions have depended on the type of theoretical framework or *paradigm* employed. A paradigm can be defined as a model or a worldview from which springs a coherent tradition of research. Paradigms include collections of theories that rely on a common set of assumptions, and a common set of questions and methodological tools that shape the way they diagnose the problem to be investigated and the solutions or prescriptions they offer.

We will examine early views on development provided by modernization theories, and then explore the dependency and world system theories that put forth an alternative explanation of development. That will bring us to the view called the "Washington Consensus" that became dominant in the 1990s (subsequently modified to become a "post-Washington Consensus"), as well as to some of the critical perspectives on gender and development.

The Modernization Paradigm

As the name implies, theories within the modernization paradigm which emerged in the 1950s and 1960s saw development as a process of progressive transformation in which societies moved from "traditional" through a series of stages to "modern" (see Box 14.6).[26] In effect, this meant that present-day developing countries were at an earlier stage in the historical trajectory of development through which all states had to pass. The obstacles to development thus lay within the countries of the South—in the nature and operation of their political institutions and processes, and in their economic and social systems. These political institutions were still steeped in ancient traditions and cultures and had not yet acquired the rational institutions and processes found in the North.[27]

In their prescriptions for change, modernization theories emphasized the creation of institutions and processes within poorer countries that would allow for more rational and efficient public-policy making and administration by doing away with practices such as nepotism and corruption. A more efficient system for allocating and distributing economic resources (the operation of competitive market forces) was also needed to allow economic growth to occur. The diffusion of technology, skills, capital, and other values from North to South, through trade and other international transactions, was also seen as a key instrument of change. In this respect, modernization theories drew on the works of Max Weber on political organization, authority, and bureaucratic rationalization, as well as the ideas of classical economists such as Adam Smith who championed **laissez-faire** economics, in which the "invisible hand" of the market was the best mechanism to allocate economic resources for development.

Modernization theories were criticized on a number of fronts including their view of what development entailed, their diagnosis of development problems, and their prescriptions for change. With respect to the first, modernization theories were accused of being ethnocentric because of the notion that development was synonymous with Westernization. Their view of history was also criticized for being

---

BOX 14.6

WALT W. ROSTOW'S FIVE STAGES OF ECONOMIC GROWTH

The work of Walt W. Rostow is considered to be a classic in the modernization paradigm. In 1960 he identified five stages through which all countries had to pass on the path to modernization and development.

1. *Traditional society.* Characterized by an agrarian economy, the existence of traditional authority structures, a high level of subsistence, and low levels of technological and scientific knowledge.
2. *The preconditions for takeoff.* This is a period of transition from tradition to modernity, and is characterized by the development of new ideas and processes, and advances in education. A change occurs in the balance of social forces, away from traditional authority structures toward new elites. This period also sees the creation of a centralized state.
3. *The takeoff.* This is the stage where the old traditional pre-modern ways of doing things are finally overcome. Technology plays a key role. Rapid increases in agricultural productivity and industrialization occur, together with the emergence of elites who champion modernization of the economy.
4. *The drive to maturity.* This is a period of fluctuating but sustained progress. Here a society and economy demonstrate the ability to move beyond the original industries that fuelled takeoff. Rostow argued it took roughly 60 years from the stage of takeoff for an economy to reach maturity.
5. *The high mass-consumption society.* At this stage an economy and society move toward the production of consumer goods and provision of services, and away from a reliance on heavy industry. It is characterized by a rapid rise in per capita incomes and overall living standards. Also at this stage we see the development of social welfare programs.

"linear"—they assumed there was only one path to development and that path was the one followed by the present-day developed states. Modernization theories also came under criticism for, in effect, blaming the poor for their poverty. They implied that the poor were poor because they were inefficient. They were also criticized for placing too much emphasis on domestic changes within developing countries and ignoring the international aspects of the problem such as the protectionist practices of developed countries in international trade relations that discriminated against exports from the South. In response to these criticisms, various attempts were made to modify modernization theories, by rejecting the linear view of history, identifying important tradeoffs in the development process, and attempting to acknowledge the special political and historical circumstances of developing countries.[28]

Dependency and the World Systems Paradigm

By the beginning of the 1970s, the influence of modernization theories began to wane. The initial optimism that countries in the South recently emerged from colonialism would rapidly modernize was soon replaced by pessimism. This pessimism in part reflected events in the real world such as the fact that a majority of states in Africa, Asia, and Latin America had adopted various types of military and authoritarian governments; and the fact that although some economic growth had been achieved throughout the developing world, less progress had been made in reducing poverty.

The most serious challenge to the modernization paradigm came from theories in an alternative paradigm of development—theories of **dependency** and the world system—that provided a very different explanation of problems of poverty and underdevelopment in the south. World system theories were broader in scope. They provided an explanation of the evolution and impact of imperialism and capitalism on political and economic organization throughout the globe since the 16th century. Dependency theories had

> **Dependency:** A condition in which countries in the South lack any degree of autonomy in their political, economic, and social development by virtue of their reliance on countries in the North for access to capital, technology, and markets.

a narrower focus. They examined the consequences of imperialism, colonialism, and global capitalism for the development of countries in the South.[29] As a result, dependency theories may be seen as a subset of world system theories.

Theories of dependency and the world system, despite considerable differences among them, saw a causal relationship between the historical expansion of western European political and economic influence, beginning with the industrial revolution and the expansion of European colonial empires on the one hand, and the progressive impoverishment of countries in Africa, Asia, and the Americas on the other. Unlike modernization theories, which saw underdevelopment as a natural stage or condition on a linear process of development, for theorists of dependency there was nothing natural about underdevelopment. It was a specific historical creation, a product of unequal political and economic relations between developed countries located at the "core" of the world system and underdeveloped countries located at its "periphery." In the words of one prominent dependency theorist, "underdevelopment was developed."[30]

The central concern for dependency theories in their diagnoses of the problems of underdevelopment was an analysis of how power was used to allocate and distribute resources, especially economic resources. Two broad positions emerged, the neo-Marxists and the structuralists. The neo-Marxists, who drew on the earlier works of Karl Marx focused on the internal class structure within countries on the periphery, while the structuralists focused on the international linkages between core and periphery. For the structuralists, in the contemporary period, the unequal relationships between core and periphery were described in terms of an "international division of labour" created by core states. This international division of labour was the prime determinant of economic and political outcomes in the developing countries. In effect, the poor were poor not because they were inefficient, but because of their exploitation by the rich and powerful.

Such dependency relationships were maintained by the cooperation of classes and elites in the periphery who profited from their economic links with the core, and whose common identity and survival as a class derived from subordination to the international economy. In effect, although formal political independence had been achieved, exploitative economic relationships were maintained by former colonial and imperial powers—a situation described by some analysts as "neocolonialism." The neo-Marxists, on the other hand, while acknowledging the exploitative international linkages between rich and poor countries, diagnosed the problem of underdevelopment primarily in terms of the weaknesses of domestic classes within poor states and their failure to play their "historic role" of overturning traditional elites and practices and spearheading economic and political development.

Theories of dependency and the world system were criticized for being too deterministic by overemphasizing the role of international and global forces on countries in the South. Other critics rejected them as little more than "conspiracy" theories for implying that rich countries deliberately kept the poor impoverished. One of the most serious criticisms was that dependency theories were better at explaining why countries did not develop than they were at explaining how countries actually did develop. In other words, unlike modernization theories, dependency theories had no explanation of how development occurred, and thus no vision of the future. In response to these criticisms, a "soft" variant of dependency emerged. It argued "dependent capitalist development"—a form of development that did not fundamentally alter the unequal relationship between core and periphery—was possible, but only when it was in the interests of the developed core states.[31]

The ideas developed by dependency and world system theories were embraced by many developing countries. Here was a paradigm that had been developed in large part by scholars from developing countries themselves, and that reflected their sense of exploitation going back to the era of European colonialism. Indeed, the demands by the South for the NIEO outlined above were strongly influenced by theories of dependency and the world system.

The Washington Consensus on International Development

The influence of dependency theories was relatively short-lived. By the mid-1980s a newer perspective on development called the "Washington Consensus" began to take hold.[32] In part, the shift occurred in response to the series of international crises that occurred during the 1970s and 1980s that produced important changes within the South and in their relations with the North. They included the oil crises of 1973 and 1979, the international recession of the early 1980s, and the debt crisis that emerged in 1982.

The *Washington Consensus* is so named because it was strongly endorsed by agencies within the United States government and by the two central institutions of the global economy—the International Monetary Fund (IMF) and the World Bank—both having their headquarters in Washington, DC. This view is based on the classical economic principles developed by Adam Smith, which put emphasis on a free, competitive market in which rational economic agents could make choices to overcome scarcity and efficiently use productive resources. Government intervention in the economy is to be minimal ("*laissez-faire*") and is to focus on stimulating savings, investment, and production by the private sector. This would ensure that the economy produced the desired goods in the most efficient manner. Market instruments are supposed to encourage greater allocative efficiency, increased investment, faster economic growth, and increased standard of living. From this perspective, the obstacles to development in the South lie in government interventions into the market, which result in an inefficient allocation of resources.

Some analysts talk of a post-Washington Consensus emerging at the end of the 1990s and into the new millennium, entailing increased attention to reducing poverty and improving other social variables (education, health, etc). This new version sought to soften (but not eliminate) the emphasis on market-driven economic growth in the original Washington Consensus. Both the IMF and World Bank, for example, made poverty reduction a cornerstone of their lending programs, and initiated a special Poverty Reduction Growth Facility (PRGF) in 1999, designed to accommodate higher pro-poor public expenditure by governments in the South.[33] In addition, greater emphasis was placed on debt-relief and making foreign aid more effective within the overall context of achieving the Millennium Development Goals.[34]

In some respects, then, the Washington Consensus can be seen as a contemporary restatement of some of the ideas that informed earlier works in modernization theory. The influence of the Consensus has been extended in part through the lending conditions of the IMF and World Bank to countries in the South that required assistance in managing their debts. These loans come with a package of conditions linked to specific economic and institutional reforms known as

BOX 14.7

**SOME TYPICAL REFORMS UNDER
STRUCTURAL ADJUSTMENT**

- Currency devaluation and market-determined exchange rate adjustments
- Anti-inflationary demand management measures, reduction in rate of growth of money supply, and wage restraints
- Reduction in the state's role in the economy through retrenchment and divestment of state-owned enterprises and elimination of subsidies
- Restoration or construction of market mechanisms through price liberalization and deregulation
- Privatization
- Trade and financial sector liberalization
- Redirection of public expenditure toward infrastructure (schools, hospitals, etc.) and, more recently, to poverty reduction

structural adjustment (see Box 14.7). The neoclassical economic principles on which the Consensus is based have also become an integral part of the contemporary phenomenon known as **globalization**, which is explored in greater detail in Chapter 17.

Perspectives on Women and Gender in Development

For most of the post–World War II period, scholars and policymakers were largely oblivious to the role of women in development. In the past two decades, however, the rise of gender-related social science research led to the emergence, in chronological order, of *women in development (WID)*, *women and development (WAD)*, and most recently, *gender and development (GAD)* perspectives. The inclusion of gender-related issues in the study of development draws attention to the sources and dimensions of gender inequality and the victimization of women, the analysis of structures of power and patriarchy, and the ways to empower women and increase their participation in development processes.[35]

For example, with respect to the dimensions of gender inequality and victimization, women tend to be relegated to particular occupations. In Africa and South Asia, women dominate in the informal sector and in agricultural labour. In Southeast Asia and parts of Central and South America, women (and children) are largely found in low-wage, labour-intensive industry. Even in developed countries, a "gendered division of labour" is evident in the overrepresentation of women in the so-called "nurturing professions" such as teaching, nursing, social work, and so on. Furthermore, women tend to be underrepresented in the public sphere of politics and business. With a few notable exceptions throughout the developing world, women hold fewer government positions and their representation decreases as one moves up the ladder of political power. In addition, women worldwide are subject to a litany of abuses, injustices, and acts of violence.

Most official statistics on economic activity have tended to overlook women's participation and contribution. Informal sector activities and production for household consumption, where women tend to dominate, for example, are not normally included in official GNP/GNI accounts. The UNDP has created a *Gender Development Index (GDI)* and *Gender Inequality Index (GII)* to complement the HDI. The GDI measures the gap between scores obtained by women and men on the HDI. In 2007, the country with the highest GDI (i.e., the lowest human development gap between men and women) was Australia followed closely by Norway and Iceland (see Table 14.5). In general, countries of the North score higher on the GDI than countries in the South. The highest-rated country in the South in 2007 was South Korea (rated 25). However, in every country in the world—developed and developing—women generally fare less well than men in virtually all indicators of development.

Sources of gender inequality in the South include traditional beliefs and cultural practices such as the preference in many parts of Africa and Asia for male children over females. Colonialism also compounded women's inequality by changing some traditional patterns of authority and economic activity. In some west African societies, for example, matrilineal patterns of lineage enabled women to play important political roles as clan elders, in the selection of traditional chiefs and kings, and even as chiefs. This system was eroded under British colonialism. Other factors affecting women's inequality include social class, ethnicity, religion, urbanization, and levels of education.

Table 14.5   Gender Development Index Rankings, 2007

Top Ten		Bottom Ten	
Country Rank	**GDI**	**Country Rank**	**GDI**
1. Australia	0.966	146. Burundi	0.390
2. Norway	0.961	147. Burkina Faso	0.383
3. Iceland	0.959	148. Guinea-Bissau	0.381
4. Canada	0.959	149. Chad	0.380
5. Sweden	0.956	150. Congo (DR)	0.370
6. France	0.956	151. Central African Republic	0.354
7. Netherlands	0.954	152. Sierra Leone	0.354
8. Finland	0.954	153. Mali	0.353
9. Spain	0.949	154. Afghanistan	0.310
10. Ireland	0.948	155. Niger	0.308

Source: UNDP, *Human Development Report*, 2009, Table J, pp. 181–184.

Studies on gender and development also identify ways to enhance women's participation in development processes. This has led to a focus on the issue of women's empowerment designed to meet "strategic gender needs" of women in addition to their "practical gender needs." Practical gender needs include the basic necessities of survival such as health care, water, housing, food, and employment. Strategic gender needs are designed to address the structural inequalities between men and women, and the processes that have served to keep women in an inferior position. The premise underlying empowerment is that rights are not given but are instead won through political action. Greater equality for women will only come about through mobilization, activism, and participation.[36]

CONTEMPORARY ISSUES AND DEBATES

A number of issues and debates arising from processes of development and change have become prominent in our period: the role of foreign aid and the impact of globalization on national development, sustainable development, democratization and development, and the management of political violence and war.

Foreign Aid, Globalization, and Development

Foreign aid might be defined as the administered transfer of resources from rich to poor countries ostensibly to promote the latter's welfare and development. The term *foreign aid* is usually reserved for official (i.e., government-to-government) transfers and resource flows as distinct from private resource flows. Foreign aid is also known as *official development assistance (ODA)*. ODA can be provided as *bilateral aid*, in which the assistance flows directly from a donor to a recipient government, and as *multilateral aid*, in which the assistance flows from donor governments through international organizations (such as the World Bank) to recipients. The largest source of Bilateral ODA comes from the 22 member states of the Development Assistance Committee (DAC) of the Organization for Economic Cooperation and Development (OECD).

The practice of giving aid emerged mainly in the post-World War II era, and was driven by a mixture of self-interest and altruism on the part of donors. Aid was used to promote the strategic and political interests of donors (e.g., to counter the threat of communism) as well as to promote long-term development of countries in the South. The amount of foreign aid increased steadily from the 1960s but declined during the 1990s. For example, in 1974 aid totalled $41.3 billion, reached $69 billion in 1991, but in 2001 the figure was down to $63.8 billion.

Table 14.6 provides a summary of foreign aid as a percentage of the GNIs of DAC members in 2008. In 1974 the UN recommended that donor countries devote a minimum of 0.7 percent of their GNP/GNI to development assistance. However, as the table shows, most of the major aid donors including Canada did not meet the target. Table 14.7, which shows long-term trends in ODA, reveals that some of the richest countries in the world, including the United States and Japan, devoted a smaller proportion of their national income to development assistance in 2008 than in 1960.

The reasons for the decline in foreign aid from the early 1990s into the early 2000s include the end of the Cold War, which reduced the strategic importance of the South to aid donors, and the emergence of unfavourable public attitudes within donor countries to foreign aid reinforced by the perception that aid was wasted and supported corrupt regimes in the South. Other important factors that contributed to the decline in ODA included the emergence of the Washington Consensus described above and the expansion and integration of global financial markets and expansion in private capital flows. Worldwide, private capital invests about $4 trillion annually, of which about $1.5 trillion is invested in developing countries. This figure is six times greater than the amount invested by governments. These factors led to serious questions about the relevance of foreign aid in a globalized world. The new slogan became "trade not aid."

Indeed, some have characterized the contemporary period as a "post-aid" world—that globalization has rendered redundant the kinds of official financial transfers between governments that we call foreign aid. Supporters of this view argue that instead of receiving aid from donor governments in the North, countries in the South should adopt the policy prescriptions of the Washington Consensus, "get their houses in order," and thereby attract foreign private capital investment. Such private investment plus increased trade opportunities, they argue, are more effective avenues for achieving development than official government-to-government

Table 14.6   ODA/GNI Rankings of the Major Aid Donors, 2008

Country Rank	Net ODA/GNI (%)
1. Sweden	0.98
2. Luxembourg	0.97
3. Norway	0.88
4. Denmark	0.82
5. Netherlands	0.80
0.7% GNI Target	
6. Ireland	0.59
7. Belgium	0.48
8. Spain	0.45
9. Finland	0.44
10. Austria	0.43
11. United Kingdom	0.43
12. Switzerland	0.42
13. France	0.39
14. Germany	0.38
15. Australia	0.32
16. Canada	0.32
17. New Zealand	0.30
18. Portugal	0.27
19. Italy	0.22
20. Greece	0.21
21. Japan	0.19
22. United States	0.19

Source: Based on data from OECD, *Development Co-operation Report 2010,* Statistical Annex Table 1, p. 172, OECD Publishing, http://dx.doi.org/10.1787/dcr-2010-en

Table 14.7   Long-Term Trends in ODA, 1960–2008 (selected countries)

Country	ODA as Percentage of GNP/GNI*						
	1960	1970	1980	1990	1997	2004	2008
Canada	0.19	0.43	0.43	0.44	0.31	0.26	0.32
Denmark	0.09	0.38	0.74	0.94	0.97	0.84	0.82
Germany	0.31	0.32	0.44	0.42	0.28	0.28	0.38
Japan	0.24	0.23	0.32	0.31	0.22	0.19	0.19
Netherlands	0.31	0.63	0.97	0.92	0.81	0.74	0.80
Sweden	0.05	0.37	0.78	0.91	0.76	0.77	0.98
United Kingdom	0.56	0.37	0.35	0.27	0.26	0.36	0.43
United States	0.53	0.31	0.27	0.21	0.08	0.16	0.19

* After 2000, figures are expressed as a percentage of GNI.

Source: Based on data from OECD, *Development Cooperation Reports,* various years, doi 10.1787/20747721 (http://www.oecd-ilibrary.org/development/development-co-operation-report_20747721)

aid transfers. Critics also point to a "moral hazard" of aid—that recipient governments become dependent on aid and have little incentive to undertake the actions necessary to break that dependency and develop their countries.

Supporters of increased foreign aid, however, take a very different view. They point to the paradox of "globalizing poverty amidst global prosperity" evident in the increased levels of poverty and inequality worldwide noted at the start of this chapter.[37] Other critics question the ability of private capital to foster stable development. For example, they note the volatility and instability of such investment, evident in the major financial and debt crises that occurred in the South in the 1980s and 1990s.

Supporters of foreign aid also observe that aid played a large role in the successful development of many countries in the postwar era. For example, they point to the Marshall Plan, named after U.S. Secretary of State George C. Marshall, in which the U.S. government provided aid to Western Europe that played a significant role in reconstruction and development after 1945. At its peak, the Plan represented about 2.0 percent of U.S. GNP. However, U.S. aid in 2008 was 0.19 percent of its national income. Furthermore, foreign aid, as noted in Box 14.5, was a key ingredient in the development of some of the East Asian NICs.

In the contemporary period, debates about the role of foreign aid in development continue as processes of globalization intensify and global inequities widen. The adoption of the MDGs in 2000 provided a new context for ODA. The major donors pledged to increase aid to help achieve the MDG poverty reduction and other targets, and in 2005 at Paris they pledged to make aid more effective. A key aspect of the debate over aid effectiveness involves questions about what counts as foreign aid.

Aid flows to the South increased from US$63 billion 2001 to a record high US$122 billion in 2008. The amount decreased slightly to US$119.6 billion in 2009 partly in response to the global economic and financial crisis that began in 2008.[38] On the surface, the numbers show a remarkable increase in ODA but the reality is less encouraging because donor foreign aid practices involve a whole lot more than giving money.

For example, many donors include "debt forgiveness" (where the donor reduces or cancels loan repayments of a recipient) as "aid." Donors also include "technical assistance" as aid. Here, instead of sending money the donor sends "experts" (usually the donor's nationals) to offer *advice* and other services to the recipient. Many donors also include "emergency relief/assistance" as foreign aid. Funds for emergency assistance, however, are designed to address short-term suffering (e.g., after a natural disaster) rather than longer-term development needs. Another problem arises from the practice of "tied aid" where donors require that recipients use aid funds to purchase equipment and services from the donor. Furthermore, many donor aid agencies are heavily bureaucratized with high administrative overhead costs (e.g., salaries, wages, etc). These administrative costs are sometimes counted as "aid."

When considering the total aid given by donors, therefore, amounts for debt forgiveness, technical assistance, administrative overheads, and emergency assistance must be subtracted before an accurate picture of what is actually available to finance development projects and programs is obtained. According to one estimate, for example, of the $100 billion in aid for 2005, only $38 billion (37 percent) was actually available for development "on the ground" in recipient countries.[39] This raises questions about donor generosity and commitment to the MDGs.

Sustainable Development

The concept of **sustainable development** emerged in the 1980s and was popularized through the publication of a report *Our Common Future* by the World Commission on Environment and Development (WCED) in 1987.[40] According to the WCED report, sustainable development is "development that meets the needs of the present without compromising the ability of future generations to meet their needs." It is "a process of change in which the exploitation of natural resources, the direction of investments, the orientation of technical development, and institutional change are all in harmony and enhance both current and future potential to meet human needs and

> **Sustainable development:** An approach to development that makes environmental conservation and protection an integral part of development processes, in order to enhance the ability of current and future generations to meet their needs.

aspirations." Since the report's publication, the concept of sustainable development has become a vital feature in discussions of development, and debates have centred on how to solve the "environmental paradox"— the mismatch between the demands placed on Earth's resources and what Earth is capable of supplying. A healthy natural environment is the lifeblood of successful development. However, many contemporary development practices are unsustainable, because they create numerous environmental problems including the depletion of natural resources, destruction of ecosystems, and air and water pollution. In the quest for economic growth, the environment had traditionally been seen as little more than a resource to be used and exploited. When environmental problems arose, they were considered as discrete technical problems requiring technical solutions, rather than as interconnected problems producing wide-ranging and often unforeseen consequences that required broader political and socioeconomic as well as technical solutions.

Two broad views on how to solve the environmental paradox and achieve sustainable development have emerged in the literature. The first, "weaker sustainability" (or "shallow environmentalism") sees the solution in the expansion of the stock of resources by, for example, developing renewable resources, creating substitutes for non-renewable resources, and applying new technologies to solve problems such as resource depletion and pollution. The second view, "stronger sustainability" (or "deep ecology"), argues that nature is finite and thus rather than attempting to adapt the natural environment to meet the increased demands of the world's population, the demands made on the world's resources need to be changed and reduced.[41]

The first major global conference on the environment was the 1972 United Nations Conference on the Human Environment (UNCHE) held in Stockholm in Sweden. Since the early 1990s, a number of international conferences have been convened (and agreements signed) with the objective of implementing sustainable development programs worldwide. The most prominent of these have been the series of Earth Summits that began with the 1992 United Nations Conference on the Environment and Development (UNCED) held in Rio de Janeiro in Brazil. The second conference was held at UN headquarters in 1997 and the third in Johannesburg in 2002. While a measure of international agreement exists on the desirability of environmentally sound development, considerable challenges exist in implementing sustainable development programs. Many of these challenges have assumed a distinct North–South dimension, and revolve around questions of who should bear the costs of cleaner and more environmentally friendly products and development processes,

Many countries in the South, for instance, take the position that the North has contributed disproportionately to global environmental degradation. Relative to its population, the North produces a greater amount of pollutants and consumes a larger amount of global resources. At the Rio Conference in 1992, concerns were expressed that the emphasis on sustainable development may place too strong an emphasis on the environment at the expense of development in the South. Furthermore, some of the issues at the core of the environment–development debate, such as population growth, access to fresh water supplies, conserving biological diversity, and combating climate change are among the most divisive political issues. For example, with respect to population growth, debates have reflected differences between North and South and between the "neomalthusians" who see dire negative consequences arising from unchecked population growth, and "cornucopians" who look to technology, increased production, and economic growth to meet demands of increased populations. Issues arising from women's rights and reproductive health are also at the centre of the debate. In addition, matters of national power and prestige, culture, race, and religion further complicate the debate over population growth.

Global efforts to address climate change have occurred within the framework of the 1992 United Nations Framework Convention on Climate Change (UNFCCC) and the 1997 Kyoto Protocol. Together these agreements established broad principles and concrete measures to combat climate change. These measures can generally be grouped into climate change "mitigation" and "adaptation."

Mitigation entails measures to reduce the *sources* of greenhouse gas (GHG) emissions (mainly carbon dioxide, methane, and nitrous oxide) from industry, agriculture, commerce, energy production, household use, etc.). Under the Kyoto Protocol, the major GHG producing-states (mainly in the global North) pledged to reduce their emissions to 95 percent of 1990 levels by 2012. Climate change adaptation entails measures to address the *impacts* of climate change. According to the

Intergovernmental Panel on Climate Change (IPCC) the world's most authoritative source on Climate Change, these impacts will result from changes in the earth's geophysical, biological, and social systems.[42] The UNFCCC and Kyoto Protocol created special funding mechanisms (financed mainly by the North) including an Adaptation Fund to help address these impacts.

Adaptation is particularly important to the South because of the "triple inequality" of climate change— inequality in historical responsibility for climate change, where the North has been responsible for a far greater proportion of GHG emissions than the South; inequality in vulnerability to climate change impacts; and inequality in the ability to cope with and manage those impacts.[43] And although climate change impacts will be world-wide and affect all nations and peoples in different ways and to varying degrees, as the IPCC's 4th Assessment Report notes, people in poorer developing nations are more vulnerable to and less able to cope with key harmful impacts. These include intense droughts and scarcity of freshwater water supplies, sea level rise, and extreme weather events (cyclones, changes in precipitation, heatwaves, etc.). The most vulnerable regions include Africa and the Middle East where droughts and acute water shortages are expected to worsen; South Asia where extreme weather events are expected to intensify; and the so-called Small Island Developing States, some of which are already experiencing land loss due to rising sea levels.

Despite the mitigation and adaptation measures outlined above, troubling questions are raised about the effectiveness of the UNFCCC and Kyoto Protocol. None of the major GHG producing countries in the North including Canada is on track to meet established emissions reduction targets (ERTs) by 2012 when the Kyoto Protocol expires. Efforts at a 2009 meeting in Copenhagen to sign a new binding agreement beyond 2012 failed, producing instead a non-binding agreement.

Democracy, Civil Society, and Development

The term **democratization** describes the processes involved in the creation of democratic governments. This process entails the relaxation of authoritarian political control by political leaders, the expansion of political and civil liberties, and the creation of institutional mechanisms that open up a political system to greater representation and participation. On the basis of this definition, analysts have identified three "waves" of democratization, as discussed in more detail in the following chapter.[44] The "first wave" occurred between the 1820s and the 1920s with the expansion of the franchise and the creation of universal adult suffrage. The "second wave" occurred between 1945 and the early 1960s. This was largely due to decolonization in Asia and Africa. By the end of the 1960s, however, the trend toward democratization was reversed. Many of the newly emergent democratically elected governments in these countries were replaced by military dictatorships and single-party authoritarian systems. The current or "third wave" of democratization began in the mid-1970s, continued in the 1980s with democratic transitions in South and Central America, and intensified in the 1990s with the collapse of authoritarian communist governments in the Soviet Union and Eastern Europe, and the emergence of democratic forms of government in Africa and Asia.

Democracy and democratization have become important issues in discussions of development, and have generated a number of interesting debates. One of these debates centres on identifying the conditions that promote "democratic transitions" and the consolidation or deepening of democratic systems of government. One of the factors identified as playing a central role in processes of democratization is the role of **civil society**. Civil society is seen as the realm of organized private social life represented by nongovernmental actors and associations, which emerges through the organization of individuals and groups in society in pursuit of their interests.

Another aspect of the debate centres on the role of democracy in development. Some of the key issues informing this debate were outlined above when we discussed the relationship between political and economic development. While the empirical record does present inconclusive results, the widely held view today, influenced in part by the Washington Consensus, is that some form of democratic government is conducive to economic growth, if not an essential prerequisite for such growth. This is because the procedural aspects of democratic government are more likely to produce "good governance"— upholding the rule of law, ensuring transparency in the administration of justice, and allowing for citizen participation in decision making. These are seen as essential for private capital investment and market-driven economic growth.

The issue of democracy is important in discussions of development for yet another reason—the apparent relationship between democracy and peace and stability. This idea is captured in the notion of "democratic peace," which suggests that democratic governments tend to be more peaceful because they have institutional and procedural safeguards that make it difficult to go to war and because democratic norms encourage negotiation, compromise, and the peaceful settlement of disputes. This issue is of particular importance in view of the problems of civil war and state failure in many regions of the developing world, examined briefly below and in more detail in the following chapter.

Political Violence and Civil Strife

While the incidence of interstate war declined since the end of World War II in 1945, the incidence of various types of such war and other forms of organized group political violence within states increased. Almost all the major wars since 1945 have been in the developing world, with the exception of those that erupted in central and eastern Europe following the breakup of Yugoslavia and the USSR in the early 1990s. That decade saw an average of 30 ongoing civil wars per annum, most of which were in developing countries especially in Africa, South and Central America, and South Asia. Although the incidence of wars in these regions has declined in the new millennium, major peacebuilding and development challenges remain because of the devastating consequences the wars had on the political, economic, and social development of the affected countries. Table 14.8 provides a list of countries that experienced major armed conflicts between 1970 and 2000.

Table 14.8   Countries Experiencing Major Armed Conflicts, 1970–2000

Africa	The Americas	Asia/Middle East	Europe
Algeria	Colombia	Afghanistan	Armenia
Angola	El Salvador	Burma (Myanmar)	Azerbaijan
Burundi	Guatemala	Cambodia	Bosnia/Herzegovina
CAR	Haiti	Indonesia	Croatia
Chad	Nicaragua	Iraq	Georgia
Congo	Peru	India/Pakistan	Russia (Chechnya)
DR Congo		Israel/Occupied	Yugoslavia (Kosovo)
Djibouti		Territories	
Eritrea		Lebanon	
Ethiopia		Sri Lanka	
Guinea Bissau		Tajikistan	
Liberia		Vietnam	
Mali		Yemen	
Mozambique			
Namibia			
Niger			
Rwanda			
Sierra Leone			
Somalia			
South Africa			
Sudan			
Uganda			

Source: Carter Center, State of World Conflict Report, 2000. Reproduced with permission

Thus, one key debate has focused on identifying the factors that lead to civil war and other forms of political violence. Some have sought the sources of war in economic factors; others have looked to the legacy of colonialism, and to the role of external powers which have intervened openly or covertly in many countries in the South. Some analysts examine social factors such as ethnic, cultural, and religious differences, and yet others examine the political sources of war. Here, the concept of **state failure**—a situation that arises when central governmental authority breaks down—has emerged as a key variable in the study of war.[45] Other aspects of the debate have centred on how best to manage, resolve, and prevent various types of armed conflicts, and on the conditions for successful post-conflict reconstruction and peacebuilding. As noted early in this chapter, the concept of human security attempts to locate the sources of and possible solutions to insecurity, state failure, and political violence in processes of development and change.

CONCLUSION

The comparative study of development is a broad sub-field within the discipline of political science, and a single chapter cannot hope to cover all of the topics, issues, themes, approaches, and methods that make it up. Nevertheless, we have provided an introduction to some of the main issues that arise from the politics of development and underdevelopment. We have outlined some of the dimensions of global inequality, introduced some key concepts, provided a brief history of the evolution of the dialogue between rich countries of the North and the poorer countries of the South, offered some of the major explanations for patterns of development and underdevelopment, and discussed some of the contemporary issues and debates that arise from ongoing processes of development and change.

DISCUSSION QUESTIONS

1. Why has democracy become important in the study of development?

2. Are the explanations offered for development and underdevelopment by modernization and dependency theories still relevant today? Why or why not?

3. Should rich countries provide more aid to poorer countries? How can aid be more effective?

4. In what ways does the inclusion of gender-related issues alter the way we think about development?

5. Why have issues of development generated conflict between rich countries of the North and poorer countries of the South?

FURTHER READING

Chilcote, Ronald H. *Theories of Development and Underdevelopment*. Boulder, CO: Westview Press, 1984.

Escobar, Arturo. *Encountering Development: The Making and Unmaking of the Third World*, Cambridge, MA: Princeton University Press, 1996.

Handelman, Howard. *The Challenge of Third World Development*, 4th ed. New York: Pearson-Prentice Hall, 2006.

Huntington, Samuel P. *The Third Wave: Democratization in the Late Twentieth Century*. Norman, OK: University of Oklahoma Press, 1992.

Kiely, Ray, and Phil Marfleet, eds. *Globalization and the Third World*. London: Routledge, 1998.

Moser, Caroline. *Gender Planning and Development: Theory, Practice and Training*. New York: Routledge, 1993.

Roberts, J. T., and Bradley C. Parks. *A Climate of Injustice: Global Inequality, North–South Politics, and Climate Policy*. Cambridge, MA: MIT Press, 2007.

Rostow, Walt W. *The Stages of Growth: A Non-Communist Manifesto*. Cambridge: Cambridge University Press, 1960.

Schurman, Frans J. "Paradigms Lost, Paradigms Regained? Development Studies in the Twenty-First Century," *Third World Quarterly* 21 (1) (2000): 7–20.

Sen, Armatya. *Development as Freedom*. New York: Alfred Knopf, 1999.

Weatherby, Joseph N., et al., eds. *The Other World: Issues and Politics of the Developing World*, 2nd ed. New York: Addison Wesley Longman, 2005.

Weiner, Myron, and S.P. Huntington, eds. *Understanding Political Development*. Boston: Little, Brown & Co, 1987.

World Commission on the Environment and Development. *Our Common Future*. New York: Oxford University Press, 1987.

ENDNOTES

1. Statistical figures in this section are drawn from the following sources: World Bank, *World Development Report* (New York: Oxford University Press, various years); United Nations Development Program (UNDP), *Human Development Report*, New York: Oxford University Press, various years; and United Nations Environment Program, *Global Environmental Outlook*, various years.

2. See "World Bank Updates Poverty Estimates for Developing World," http://econ.worldbank.org/WBSITE/EXTERNAL/EXTDEC/EXTRESEARCH/0,contentMDK:21882162~pagePK:64165401~piPK:64165026~theSitePK:469382,00.html; accessed October 28, 2010.

3. Human Security Centre, *Human Security Report, 2005* (New York: Oxford University Press, 2005).

4. See for example, C. Thomas, "Global Governance, Development, and Human Security: Exploring the Links," *Third World Quarterly* 22 (2) (2001): 159–175; A. Surhke, "Human Security and the Interests of States," *Security Dialogue* 30 (3) (1999): 265–276.

5. United Nations Environment Program, *Global Environment Outlook 4* (UNEP, 2007).

6. UN Population Division, "World Population to Exceed 9 billion by 2050", Press release, March 2009.

7. See, for example, Allen H. Meriam, "What Does 'Third World' Mean?," in J. Norwine and A. Gonzalez, *The Third World: States of Mind and Being* (Boston: Unwin Hyman, 1988); and Richard E. Bissell, "Who Killed the Third World?," *The Washington Quarterly*, 13 (4) (Autumn 1990): 23–32.

8. See, for example, Arturo Escobar, *Encountering Development: The Making and Unmaking of the Third World* (Princeton: Princeton University Press, 1996) and Wolfgang Sachs, ed., *The Development Dictionary* (London: Zed, 1992).

9. World Bank, *World Development Report, 2009*, Annex Table 1, pp. 352–53.

10. See, for example, Meriam, "What Does 'Third World' Mean?"

11. See Christopher Clapham, *Third World Politics* (London: Croom Helm, 1985).

12. For more on colonialism in the Americas, Africa, and Asia, see Clapham, *Third World Politics*; Joseph N. Weatherby et al., eds., *The Other World: Issues and Politics of the Developing World* (New York: Addison Wesley Longman, 2000), pp. 113–25.

13. See Robert H. Jackson, *Quasi-States: Sovereignty, International Relations and the Third World* (Cambridge: Cambridge University Press, 1990).

14. For more on the NIEO, see Jagdish Baghwati and John Ruggie, *Power, Passions and Purpose: Prospects for the North-South Negotiations* (Cambridge: Cambridge University Press, 1984).

15. These included the Independent Commission on International Development Issues (Brandt Commission, 1980); the Independent Commission on Disarmament and Security Issues (Palme Commission, 1982); the World Commission on Environment and Development (Brundtland Commission, 1987); the South Commission (1990); and the Commission on Global Governance (1995).

16. For more on the debt crisis, see James Busumtwi-Sam, "International Financial Institutions, International Capital Flows, and Financial Liberalization in Developing Countries," in Stephen McBride and John Wiseman, eds., *Globalization and Its Discontents* (London: Macmillan & NY: St. Martin's Press, 2001), pp. 84–96.

17. *Report of the South Commission*, 1990, pp. 50–55.

18. World Bank, *World Development Indicators*, external debt tables, various years; *Recent Developments in External Debt*, Report of the United Nations Secretary-General, A/61/152, July 2006, p. 3.

19. For more on the MDGs, see World Bank, *World Development Report*, 2004, p. 2.

20. See World Bank, *Global Monitoring Report 2010: The MDGs After the Crisis,* Washington DC: World Bank, 2010) pp. 1–9

21. Figures in this section are from the World Bank, *World Development Report,* 2006 and 2009.

22. GDP measures the total economic output of a country for a given period, usually a year. This figure is then divided by the total population to obtain the GDP per capita. Production of wealth is also sometimes expressed as the gross national product (GNP) or the gross national income (GNI) which replaced the GNP in World Bank Classifications in 2000. The GDP excludes net income earned from abroad, while the GNP/GNI includes this income. Of the two, the GDP is more commonly used to compare economic production across countries.

23. Figures in this section are from the UNDP, *Human Development Report,* 2009 and 2010 (New York: United Nations).

24. For more on political development, see Myron Weiner and S. P. Huntington, eds., *Understanding Political Development* (Boston: Little, Brown & Co, 1987); and Howard Handelman, *The Challenge of Third World Development,* 2nd ed. (Prentice Hall, 2000).

25. See, for example, Samuel P. Huntington, *Political Order in Changing Societies* (New Haven: Yale University Press, 1968).

26. See Walt W. Rostow, *The Stages of Growth: A Non-Communist Manifesto* (Cambridge: Cambridge University Press, 1960).

27. Notable works on modernization include Clifford Geertz, *Old Societies, New States: The Quest for Modernity in Asia and Africa* (New York: Free Press, 1963); Gabriel A. Almond and James S. Coleman, *The Politics of Developing Areas* (Princeton: Princeton University Press, 1960); Edward Shills, *Political Development in the New States* (The Hague: Mouton, 1966); David Apter, *The Politics of Modernization* (Chicago: University of Chicago Press, 1965); A.F.K. Organski, *Stages of Political Development* (New York: Knopf, 1965). For a recent discussion of modernization

theory, see Samuel P. Huntington and Myron Weiner, eds., *Understanding Political Development* (Boston: Little, Brown, 1987).

28. See, for example, Samuel P. Huntington, *Political Order in Changing Societies* (New Haven: Yale University Press, 1968).

29. Prominent works in the dependency tradition include A.G. Frank, *Capitalism and Underdevelopment in Latin America* (New York: Monthly Review Press, 1966); Samir Amin, *Accumulation on a World Scale* (New York: Monthly Review Press, 1975); Ronald H. Chilcote, *Theories of Development and Underdevelopment* (Boulder, CO: Westview Press, 1984); F. Cardoso and E. Falletto, *Dependency and Development in Latin America* (Berkeley: University of California Press, 1979); Walter Rodney, *How Europe Underdeveloped Africa* (London and Dar-es-Salaam: Bogle L'Ouverture and Tanzania Publishing House, 1972); and Immanuel Wallerstein, *The Modern World System* (New York: Academic Press, 1974).

30. André Gunder Frank, *Capitalism and Underdevelopment in Latin America* (New York: Monthly Review Press, 1966).

31. See, for example, F. Cardoso, "Dependent Capitalist Development in Latin America," *New Left Review* 74 (1972); and Peter Evans, *Dependent Development: The Alliance of Multinational, State and Local Capital in Brazil* (Princeton: Princeton University Press, 1979).

32. For more on the Washington Consensus, see John Williamson, "What Washington Means by Policy Reform," in John Williamson, ed., *Latin American Adjustment: How Much Has Happened?* (Washington, DC: Institute for International Economics, 1990); and Charles Gore, "The Rise and Fall of the Washington Consensus as a Paradigm for Developing Countries," *World Development* 28 (5) (2000): 789–804.

33. International Monetary Fund, "Poverty Reduction Strategy Papers: A Fact Sheet," 2005, available at http://www.imf.org/external/np/exr/facts/prsp.htm; accessed February 9, 2006.

34. See D. Porter and D. Craig, "The Third Way and the Third World: Poverty Reduction and Social Inclusion in the Rise of 'Inclusive' Liberalism," *Review of International Political Economy* 11 (2) (2004): 387–423.

35. See Caroline Moser, *Gender Planning and Development: Theory, Practice and Training* (New York: Routledge, 1993); Eva Rathgeber, "WID, WAD, GAD: Trends in Research and Practice," *Journal of Developing Areas* 24 (1990): 489–502.

36. Jane L. Parpart, "Rethinking Participation, Empowerment and Development from a Gender Perspective," in Jim Freedman, ed., *Transforming Development* (University of Toronto Press, 2000), pp. 222–34.

37. See Ray Kiely and Phil Marfleet, eds., *Globalization and the Third World* (London: Routledge, 1998).

38. OECD, *Development Cooperation Report 2010*, and World Bank, *Global Monitoring Report, 2010*, pp. 5–6.

39. See Homi Kharas, *The New Reality of Aid.* Washington, DC: Brookings, 2008.

40. World Commission on the Environment and Development, *Our Common Future* (Oxford: Oxford University Press, 1987).

41. Colin C. Williams and Andrew C. Millington, "The Diverse and Contested Meanings of Sustainable Development," *The Geographical Journal* 170 (2) (June 2004): 99–104.

42. IPCC, *Fourth Assessment Report: Climate Change 2007: Impacts Adaptation and Vulnerability* (New York: Cambridge University Press, 2007).

43. See J. Timmons Roberts and Bradley C. Parks, *A Climate of Injustice: Global Inequality, North–South Politics, and Climate Policy* (Cambridge, MA: MIT Press, 2007).

44. See Samuel P. Huntington, *The Third Wave: Democratization in the Late Twentieth Century* (Norman, OK: University of Oklahoma Press, 1992).

45. Michael Brown, ed., *Ethnic Conflict and International Security* (Princeton: Princeton University Press, 1993), and I. William Zartman, ed., *Collapsed States: The Disintegration and Restoration of Legitimate Authority* (Boulder, CO: Lynne Rienner, 1995).

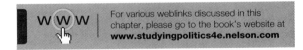

W W W For various weblinks discussed in this chapter, please go to the book's website at **www.studyingpolitics4e.nelson.com**

Regime Change in An Era of Globalization

Peter A. Ferguson

CHAPTER OBJECTIVES

After you have completed this chapter, you should be able to:

- describe how the state of global democracy has changed over the past 40 years
- explain the causes and consequences of the regime breakdown process
- discuss the implications of a democratic transition
- discuss the impediments to and the consequences of democratic consolidation.

WHY STUDY REGIME CHANGE?

During your lifetime, the world has experienced a dramatic transformation in the way most people are governed. The number of democratic governments worldwide has surged over the past 30 years to the point that there are many more countries with democratic governments than with nondemocratic ones. This wave of democracy has extended across the globe from southern Europe to Latin America, Southeast Asia, Eastern Europe, and Africa. The implications of this change can be seen from things as simple as where you are now able to travel to where you may end up working or doing business when you graduate from school. On a national level, the countries with which Canada interacts have radically changed.

Recent negotiations dealing with expanding the North American Free Trade Agreement (NAFTA) to include all the Americas, for example, included discussions about the importance of maintaining democracy throughout the Americas. On an international level, as the forces of globalization and interdependence "shrink" the size of the world we live in, the scope of incentives (and disincentives) for these new democracies to avoid nondemocratic change has greatly increased. As demonstrated in Figure 15.1, while 45 percent of the countries in the world operate under democratic regimes and 31 percent have some of the characteristics of democracy, almost a quarter (24 percent) of the countries in the world are fully nondemocratic. Figure 15.2 shows that 35 percent of the world's population lives under a nondemocratic regime.

Why, then, should you be interested in the global democratic transformation? The answers are the same as the ones found in Chapter 1 when we discussed the reasons to study politics. Global democratization is fascinating—there are colourful characters and interesting stories about faraway places. Beyond that, democratization is very important. It has serious implications not only for the people who live in countries that experience such transitions, but also for people who come

Figure 15.1   Country Breakdown by Freedom Status, 2011

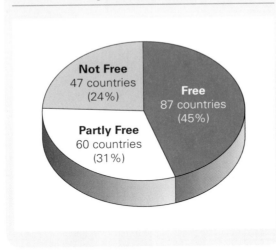

Not Free
47 countries
(24%)

Free
87 countries
(45%)

Partly Free
60 countries
(31%)

Figure 15.2   Population Breakdown by Freedom Status, 2011

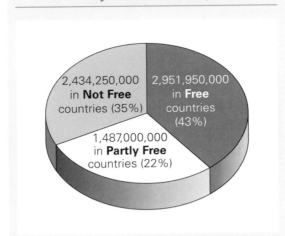

2,434,250,000
in **Not Free**
countries (35%)

2,951,950,000
in **Free**
countries
(43%)

1,487,000,000
in **Partly Free**
countries (22%)

Source: Adapted from Freedom House, *Freedom In The World 2011: The Authoritarian Challenge To Democracy* (New York: Freedom House, 2011). Reprinted by permission of Freedom House.

into contact with those countries, whether through family, business, or travel. The issues surrounding the questions of citizenship are galvanized around democratization. At a time when many Canadians no longer seem to care about politics, reading a story about people waiting in line for eight or nine hours while facing military forces bent on intimidation—simply to be able to exercise their right to vote—should help us all appreciate the importance of democratic citizenship. Finally, the wave of democracy that has transformed the world we live in holds great opportunities for political science graduates. In this era of globalization, companies, governments, and all sorts of organizations need to hire people knowledgeable about this expanding list of democratic countries—about which they lack a real understanding but are now forced to interact with on a variety of levels. Understanding the material in this chapter could lay the foundation for you to take one of these exciting jobs.

REGIME BREAKDOWN

Change is the one constant in politics, and this is especially evident in the examination of political **regimes**. This section examines issues surrounding regime breakdown. Why should we be interested in such breakdowns? The most important reason is that democracy has not won the day. Throughout history, one sees the rise and fall of regimes. Despite the rhetoric surrounding the advancement of global democracy across the last four decades, it is important to remember that democracy is at risk in large portions of the world. As demonstrated in Figure 15.3 (p. 392), between 2005 and 2010, and for the first time since the fall of the Berlin Wall, the number of countries experiencing declines in freedom exceeds those experiencing increases. Democratic gains are under threat across the globe, from Latin American to Africa to Eastern Europe to Central Asia to South Asia and to Southeast Asia. If we are to understand why some countries become democracies and others do not, and why democracy

Regime: The whole decision-making apparatus of the state; the constitutional principles and arrangements according to which government decisions are made; the fundamental rules of the game.

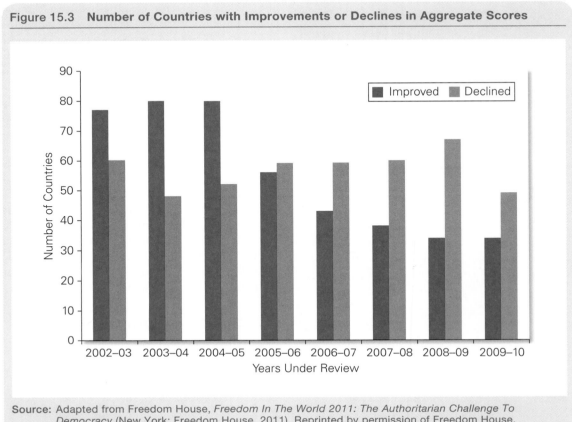

Figure 15.3   **Number of Countries with Improvements or Declines in Aggregate Scores**

Source: Adapted from Freedom House, *Freedom In The World 2011: The Authoritarian Challenge To Democracy* (New York: Freedom House, 2011). Reprinted by permission of Freedom House.

persists in some countries and not in others, we must first understand the roots of such change. These are found in an examination of the breakdown of the prior nondemocratic regimes. One thing that is important to understand from the beginning is that the collapse of a nondemocratic regime does not necessarily result in a democratic regime coming to power. Historically, the most likely result of a nondemocratic regime breakdown has been the institution of another nondemocratic regime—not the establishment of a democracy. To understand why, we must first look at the various trigger events or causes of breakdown and then examine the various actors that play a part in such an occurrence. On that basis, we can turn our attention to the various consequences of these breakdowns.

Breakdown Causes

What are the events or situations that raise the possibility of regime breakdown? This chapter argues that the causes of breakdowns interact with the actors in a particular country to lay the foundation for breakdown. These causes set the table for change. Once the table has been set, we need to examine the various actors to determine not only if the regime will break down but also what outcome will be produced. For ease of understanding, the trigger events are divided into economic, social, and political explanations.

Economic Causes One of the most widely studied concepts in political science is the idea of modernization. Seymour Martin Lipset advanced the argument that socioeconomic development is a prerequisite for democracy. In order for nondemocratic countries to become democratic, they must achieve a certain level of development. The idea is that as a country modernizes, its social structures become increasingly complex and a variety of new groups emerge; this produces a system that can no longer be effectively governed by command, and democracy emerges.[1] This theory makes sense in that poor countries tend to be nondemocratic, whereas rich countries tend to be democratic. The fate of middle-income countries, however, varies widely. The search for an economic threshold for democracy continues to be a highly contested idea in political science.

A second potential economic explanation examines the economic performance of regimes. Unlike the modernization theory, this approach argues that enduring levels of poor economic performance trigger regime changes. As the economy in a country deteriorates, the resources available are reduced, making it harder to maintain the regime's bases of support. One way of thinking about this is that political regimes usually have a group of allies. The regime receives support from its allies, which allows it to continue to run the country. In exchange for this support, the regime's allies receive benefits, many of which cost the regime money (tax breaks, subsidies, and so on). As the economy deteriorates, the amount of money available to the regime is reduced, resulting in a reduction of the regime's ability to deliver benefits to its supporters. At some point, benefits are reduced to such an extent that support is withdrawn and the regime collapses.[2]

Social Causes A variety of explanations for regime breakdown revolve around social (and psychological) issues in a country. The theory of rising expectations recognizes that people have a set of expectations about their future and significant events, such as a regime change, cause people to raise their expectations. These expectations are commonly economic in nature but can also include things such as human rights. The difficulty with such expectations arises when they go unmet, causing people to agitate for change. When a new regime comes to power, such as when Nelson Mandela was elected in South Africa, people expect that their economic situation will improve. In this case, as in others, they expected that jobs would be more plentiful, that they would earn more money,

and that they would be able to buy more goods. As the euphoria surrounding the demise of apartheid and Mandela's election began to fade from memory, the people of South Africa started asking themselves if they were, in fact, better off than they had been before these changes. Many observers of South Africa believe these unmet expectations hold the seeds for significant tensions in the future.

A second theory, the theory of relative deprivation, looks at situations in which the conditions people have come to understand as normal change for the worse. Unlike the rising expectations theory, this theory examines the circumstance where people have a relatively stable set of expectations that have been met over time. When these expectations are no longer met, people begin to support systemic change. A number of Eastern European countries saw communist parties return to power in the second round of elections following the demise of the Soviet Union. Many observers have argued that some of this shifting support can be explained by the idea that the initial post-Soviet regimes were forced to cut back on commodity price supports and to slash the size of the public sector. As a result, concerns and expectations that people had regarding issues ranging from the price of food to job security significantly worsened and caused them to throw their support behind parties that had maintained acceptable levels of these values in the past. Such a shifting of support back to past nondemocratic actors increases the chances of regime change.

A third set of theories relevant to regime breakdown surrounds the issue of ethnic conflict. Many countries throughout the world are now home to numerous ethnic groups. In some places, two main groups vie for power. In India, for example, the Hindu majority makes up more than 80 percent of the population, while the Muslim minority makes up a little more than 10 percent. Other countries face more severe **cleavages**. Nigeria contains people of more than 250 languages and tribes, of which the three main groups make up two-thirds of the population. Such cleavages do not always trigger serious problems, however, as the experiences of Canada and the United States attest. Donald Horowitz argues that ethnic divisions threaten regimes due to problems with inclusion and exclusion. Those included in power structures receive certain privileges while those excluded from power receive penalties. The difficulty arises when groups begin to feel that the exclusions from power are permanent. If groups foresee that there is no possibility for them to receive the privileges of power, they may begin to cause problems for the regimes, especially through violent actions. The groups in power, likewise, feel the need to protect their power and often resort to violence in order to do so.[3] The postcolonial histories of the Central African countries of Burundi and Rwanda demonstrate that when ethnic divisions explode, in this case between the Hutu and the Tutsi, hundreds of thousands can die in the subsequent fighting.

Political Causes One of the most common explanations of regime breakdown is corruption. While a certain amount of political corruption is found everywhere, the level in some states is extremely high, and it is generally highest in developing countries. Almost without fail when a regime is overthrown the victors point to the endemic levels of corruption found in the old regime as a justification for taking power. Their argument is that such corruption creates economic inefficiencies that make it impossible for the country to develop. They also point out that it becomes increasingly difficult for the mass public to trust political leaders who are seen as personally benefiting from the fruits of corruption. Transparency International is an international nongovernmental organization devoted to studying the causes and consequences of and cures for corruption. Their website, http://www.transparency.org, contains a wealth of information on this issue.

A second set of political explanations can be found in the idea of institutional failure. When the institutions of government cease to function, it becomes increasingly difficult for a regime to sustain itself. Legislative assemblies that can no longer pass legislation because of fractionalized party systems make it virtually impossible for a regime to solve the problems it faces. Bureaucracies that have extensively relied on patronage appointments may no longer be capable of administering the country. This is especially problematic when the effectiveness of the tax (revenue) agency is compromised. The problems a regime faces when institutional failure begins to occur are manifold. In Turkey, for example, the military has intervened at least three times since independence because of institutional failure. In 1980, the situation reached such an extreme that the military argued the government could no longer control the spread of violence

across the country, so they took over. Every time the Turkish military stepped into power, they vowed to return power to civilian governments as soon as they got the situation under control. And, every time, they did so—something that cannot be said of many other military regimes.

A final political explanation can be found in war. History is replete with examples of defeated regimes breaking down and being replaced by new ones. If a regime cannot maintain the integrity of its borders, it has little hope of surviving. Following World War II, political regimes in defeated Germany and Japan had new, democratic regimes imposed on them. Shortly after losing the Falklands War to Britain, the military regime governing Argentina collapsed. It is not always the case, however, that military defeat signals the demise of a regime. Most would argue that the first Gulf War coalition led by the United States defeated Iraq; however, the regime led by Saddam Hussein emerged more fully entrenched. Of course, the other side of the coin was demonstrated following the second Gulf War with the capture and execution of Mr. Hussein. In general, though, military defeat signals to regime opponents that there is a vulnerability that can be exploited, raising the risk of regime breakdown.

Breakdown Actors

A variety of actors and groups are involved in and affected by any type of political regime. We will discuss here five sets of actors: political elites, business elites, the military, the mass public, and the international community. These rather large groupings are not necessarily mutually exclusive—a member of the military might also belong to the political elite, for example. Nor do these groups function as a unified whole; there is certainly no agreement within any one group across all issues and concerns. Such a basic division of actors, however, will provide us with an understanding of the set of players within a regime and help explain why one or more of these groups might seek to change it.

Political Elite The political **elite** is a group that is interested in the functioning and overall success of any regime. This group consists of more than just the political leader and his or her immediate advisors. Also included is the upper echelon of the various

departments of the bureaucracy, members of the legislature, the leadership of any recognized "loyal" opposition, important regional and local leaders, and a variety
of civilian leaders who play a vital role in the support
and operation of the government. These people are
powerful players in the country because of their ability
both to influence government policy and to distribute
the benefits of such policy. These benefits may include
such disparate things as providing family and friends
with jobs, securing public works projects for one's
home region, and getting a tax policy approved to
benefit an important domestic industry.

If these people are most directly responsible for the
functioning of politics in a country, why would they
ever take part in its demise? As in most sporting events,
politics creates winners and losers. The winners seek
to maintain or augment their power. If, for example, a
finance minister in a country feels he has reached the
apex of power under the current regime but has aspirations to be leader himself, he might conceivably support change, anticipating that he will become the leader
of the new regime. If someone at such a high level in
government could defect (withdraw support from the
existing regime), it should be fairly easy to understand
why those within the political elite who have not
attained such powerful positions might also withdraw
their support. Beyond the desire to improve personal
or group position and power, there might also be concern about the direction in which important policy is
heading or for the overall welfare of the country. Likely
some combination of all of these factors is at play.

Business Elite The second important group
of actors is the business elite. This group consists of
the people outside of government involved in the
functioning of the country's economy, including
the leaders of the country's largest corporations, key
associational groups (such as lawyers or engineers),
and trade groups (such as major unions). These people
and groups are important players because they are
responsible in large part for the health and direction
of the country's economy: they provide the people
with jobs, the government with tax revenues, and the
country with regional or global prestige. Most obviously, the business elite may withdraw their support
from a regime if the economy is performing poorly
or if it is in the midst of a severe crisis. However,
it may happen that regimes also break down during

relatively stable or prosperous economic times. Why?
It could be that certain groups, such as labour unions,
feel left out of the political process. Others may feel
that while the economy is in good shape, in order
for the country to experience real success government
policies must be changed; for example, opening the
country to more global trade or restricting the flow
of goods entering the country. The point is not the
particular policy or problem; it is that sometimes the
economic losers are willing to gamble to improve
their position, while the winners feel they might do
even better under a new regime.

The Military The group most often considered when
examining regime change is the military. It is the military that executes coups and crushes rebellions. If,
as Mao said, power grows out of the barrel of a gun,
then surely the military will always be a key actor in
regime breakdown. Unlike in Western democracies,
the military in most nondemocratic regimes plays an
important role in both external and internal security.
Political leaders rely on the support of the military for
their survival. There are numerous explanations as to
why the military might withdraw its support from a
regime. It is useful to divide such explanations into
internal and external rationales. Internally, the military
is usually concerned, first and foremost, with its institutional survival. Actions, events, and circumstances
that the military perceives as threats to its survival can
include things such as the dismissal of popular or powerful military figures, the undermining of military discipline, and severe budget cuts. Additionally, internal
conflicts can arise when junior officers see no room
for promotion, or when traditional elements perceive
the institution as becoming too politicized. External
rationales might include a perception that the civilian
government is corrupt or unable to deal with economic or political crises, and the desire on the part
of the military to seek a stronger role in influencing
the direction the country is taking. Most often several
reasons interact with one another and serve as justification for military intervention. The role of the military
in Pakistan is discussed in Box 15.1 (p. 396).

Mass Public The mass public also has a role to
play in the breakdown of nondemocratic regimes.
Too often people think of such regime change as an
elite-driven process, but as events ranging from the

BOX 15.1

CASE STUDY: PAKISTAN

To understand the role of the military as an obstacle to democratization in developing countries, we need look no further than the Pakistani model. In 1997, Nawaz Sharif, leading a 14-party coalition, was elected to the post of prime minister. Following his election Sharif sought to "undermine every institution capable of challenging him, including the judiciary and the press" (Freedom House, 2007). It was only after Sharif sought to undermine the primacy of the military, however, that his leadership was compromised. In October 1999, after Nawaz attempted to remove General Pervez Musharraf, the Chief of Army Staff, Musharraf returned to Pakistan and seized control in a bloodless coup, becoming the fourth Army chief to take control of the country. Musharraf ruled in a similarly authoritarian manner by suspending the constitution, dismissing or jailing several judges, and arresting political dissidents. Later elected President, he was forced to resign for his misdeeds in 2008. During his recent global book tour he has repeatedly vowed to return to Pakistan to contest the next presidential election.

Source: Based on "Freedom in the World: Pakistan, 2007," *Freedom in the World* (New York: Freedom House, 2007). Reprinted by permission of Freedom House.

fall of the Berlin Wall to the "people power" movement in the Philippines demonstrate, the power of the mass public should not be ignored. The mass public consists of all the people in a country not included in the first three groups—the "regular" citizens. The raw numbers of people involved is what makes this group powerful. Nothing makes elite groups sit up and pay attention as 100,000 people, normally only marginally involved in politics, marching in the streets. As a result, the public can wield a lot of power. It also represents a significant source of potential power for other groups to use or threaten to use. Groups perceived to have the support of the masses can often increase their power simply by threatening to mobilize mass demonstrations. Likewise, groups occasionally may set out to mobilize the masses to push for reforms, but end up frightening other actors (such as the military) into much more extensive responses because of these actors' fear of such mobilization.

The public may withdraw its support for the old regime for a variety of reasons. Economic reasons span a wide spectrum, which includes factors such as poor economic performance, the onset of economic crisis, the failure to meet expectations raised by initial successes, and a lack of hope for the future among the rising middle classes. Political reasons can range from scandals involving key leaders to extensive levels of corruption to assassinations of sympathetic or popular figures. In November 2004,

despite subzero temperatures, tens of thousands of citizens camped out in central Kiev, the Ukrainian

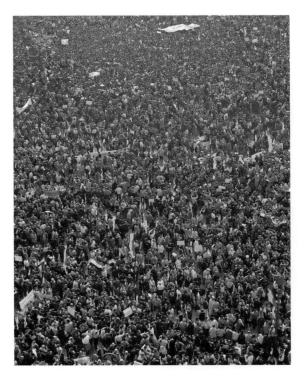

Protesters gather in Tahrir Square in Cairo, Egypt, January 2011, calling for President Hosni Mubarak to resign.

Lewis Whyld/The Canadian Press

capital, for several weeks in support of efforts to overturn the results of an obviously fraudulent presidential election. Bowing to this pressure, as well as that of opposition politicians and the international community, the government arranged for new elections to be held the day after Christmas. The vote reversed the previous result and elected opposition leader Viktor Yushchenko. This example aside, it is important to remember that there is a normal level of public activity in most countries that is usually not exceeded. It is rare for the public to be mobilized to an extent necessary to trigger regime change. While it does happen, the role the public more often plays is in the credible threat that another actor may gain its support and mobilize it.

International Community The final player in regime change is the international community. This group includes any actors not resident in the country in question. It may include actors in neighbouring countries, in countries with economic or political involvement in the country, and in regional and international organizations. During the Cold War, the role of the international community was defined more by strategic interests than by other considerations. The international influence on regime breakdown was more a function of whom the regime (or its opponents) supported at the global level and how important its strategic position was to the superpowers. Immediately following the end of the Cold War, the international community became much more involved in expressing its support for democracy as the preferred regime type. The international community, owing in significant part to the influence of the United States and its closest allies, became decidedly more active and aggressive in the promotion of global democracy. Following the events of 9/11, the U.S. became more tolerant of nondemocratic regimes, such as Pakistan, in exchange for their support for the "war on terror." Former President Bush made a concerted effort to tie support for democracy and opposition to terrorism together into one overarching test of whether a country deserved the support of the United States and its allies (Box 15.2, p. 398, outlines the Bush Doctrine in more detail).

When attempting to influence regimes, a variety of tools are available, including, most importantly, aid and trade. Countries desiring aid from the West and from international organizations such as the **World Bank** and the **International Monetary Fund (IMF)** are much more likely to receive that aid if they are democratic or if they undertake democratic reforms (and/or support U.S. efforts against terrorism) than if they operate in a nondemocratic fashion (and/or oppose U.S. efforts against terrorism). Increasingly, democratic reforms are one of the main preconditions for such countries to receive economic assistance. Countries experiencing democratic reversals are much more likely to come under pressure to return to democracy or face the prospect of losing access to such assistance. Likewise, trade relations are increasingly becoming tied to democracy and democratic reform. Western countries have become more reluctant to trade with countries that are not democracies; when they do trade with such countries, they often attempt to use the expansion (or restriction) of trade as a tool to encourage democracy. As mentioned, the proposed FTAA treaty text includes provisions for the exclusion of countries that experience democratic reversals. It is important to remember that international economic levers are not all employed in support of democracy. Recently, China's policies vis-à-vis Africa have come under increasing scrutiny. A number of scholars and NGO officials have pointed out that it is increasingly difficult to employ economic levers in support of African democracy if China will provide aid and conduct trade with African countries regardless of their regime type or human rights policy. Despite this example, economic assistance and trade relations remain a powerful tool used to push for democratic reform in nondemocratic countries and to prevent democratic breakdown in existing democracies.

Breakdown Consequences

Having outlined the major actors in the regime breakdown process, we can now turn our attention to the consequences of such breakdowns. This section will address three basic consequences: nondemocratic change, liberalization, and democratization. As previously stated, the most common result of the breakdown of a nondemocratic regime is its replacement with another: one military government replaces another or one dictator replaces another. If one is able to identify

BOX 15.2

THE BUSH DOCTRINE

Addressing the graduating class of 2002 of the U.S. Military Academy at West Point, President Bush introduced what became known as the "Bush Doctrine" when he announced the end of foreign policy based on containment and deterrence. In an era defined by the threat of terrorism, he argued, if you wait for threats to fully materialize, you have waited too long. Instead, the security of the United States required all Americans to "be ready for pre-emptive action when necessary to defend our liberty and our lives." The policy of pre-emption was described more formally in the *National Security Strategy of the U.S.A.* released on September 17, 2002 (http://www.whitehouse.gov/nsc/nss.html).

This document points to a new vision of American interaction with the world: rogue states and terrorists will be confronted pre-emptively, the United States will not allow its military superiority to be challenged, and the U.S. will use its economic and military power to encourage the spread of freedom and democracy. Recognizing the potential for international resistance, the policy further states that when American vital interests are at stake, the United States will seek international approval for its actions but will go it alone if necessary.

In 1992, following the failure to oust Saddam Hussein from power during the first Gulf War, Paul Wolfowitz (the Pentagon's third-highest-ranking civilian at the time) drafted a set of guidelines titled "Defence Planning Guidance" calling for America to "talk loudly, carry a big stick, and use its military power to pre-empt the proliferation of weapons of mass destruction" (http://www.pbs.org/wgbh/pages/ frontline/shows/iraq). Further, he argued that coalitions of the future would be ad hoc collections of states and that the United States should be prepared to act independently when collective action cannot be orchestrated. The document was leaked to the press, triggering controversy, and Secretary of Defence Dick Cheney was forced to rewrite it, removing all reference to pre-emptive action.

Nevertheless, the Bush Administration put the policy of pre-emption to the test in Iraq during the second Gulf War. While evaluations of events surrounding this war widely vary, supporters of the Bush Doctrine not only viewed it as a success in Iraq but also as a template for further action. In his 2005 State of the Union address and in a number of subsequent speeches, President Bush indicated that the United States continued to view pre-emptive military action as a viable strategy, specifically pointing to Iran and Syria as potential future targets. In meeting the objective of spreading democracy throughout the Middle East and the rest of the world, the president argued that no tools should be taken off the table. There was a widespread expectation that the election of President Obama would consign the Bush Doctrine to the history books, but the reality has been quite the opposite. The foreign policy of the Obama White House, particularly with regards to Afghanistan and Pakistan, has closely resembled the policies of his predecessor.

When discussing the potential application of pre-emptive military strikes we should, at minimum, evaluate questions of imminence and globalism. In most societies, self-defence is justified if someone points a gun at you and threatens your life; there is no requirement to wait until after you are shot to act. The key to resolving the situation, legally and morally, is evaluating the credibility of the threat. Similarly, on the international level, the key is to understand both whether there is a threat and, if so, whether it is imminent. If the threat is not judged imminent, "just war" theory would counsel consideration of nonmilitary solutions. In this regard the globalization of international relations seems to point up the importance of allowing the international community to make judgments about and participate in solutions to such threats. Indeed, following President Bush's address to the UN General Assembly on September 12, 2002, Secretary-General Kofi Annan explained this position when he told the Assembly that while the UN Charter recognizes the inherent right of self-defence, solutions to terrorism and the spread of weapons of mass destruction can only be found in multilateral action.

the key actors and their interests, it is not difficult to see why they may not favour a democratic outcome. If the goal is to get rid of the old regime in order to take power, there is no real desire for open competition. In certain cases, however, regime breakdown holds the potential to start the democratization process.

A second potential outcome is liberalization. Liberalization occurs when a regime significantly expands civil and political liberties in the country or opens itself up, at some level, to more meaningful competition from opposition forces. This does not mean that it becomes a democracy, but rather that it takes on some of the trappings of democracy. Why would a regime do such a thing? First, a regime that finds itself in trouble may seek to avoid radical change and total loss of power by agreeing to ease some of the restrictions it has in place. It may attempt to address problems of human rights violations; allow increased group formation (e.g., labour organizations); ease restrictions on freedom of the press, religion, association, or speech; or allow opposition parties to compete in a more meaningful fashion at the local, regional, or national level. It undertakes these actions not to begin the process of democratic change but rather to stave it off. The idea is to change certain policies to address the concerns of powerful opposition forces in order to guarantee the survival of the regime.

Second, regimes may pursue liberalization because they seek to expand their power and influence. Occasionally, very stable nondemocratic regimes pursue liberalization exactly because they feel secure and powerful. As the above discussion about the international community points up, a number of advantages (such as access to aid and trade) are available to regimes that undertake some type of democratic reform that are not available to nondemocratic regimes. Therefore, regimes that feel they can undertake some democratic reforms while continuing to maintain their control and power liberalize in an attempt to receive these extra benefits.

In both cases, the difficulty is that, once started, liberalization is difficult to control. As the different actors begin to get a taste of the advantages of change, they are often tempted to push for even more change. Such reforms also send unintended signals to opponents of the regime. Rather than seeing such reforms as a decision made from a position of strength, opponents often interpret them as a sign of weakness and redouble their efforts to overthrow the regime. This is especially true in regimes attempting to save themselves from mounting problems. Finally, almost all nondemocratic regimes overestimate their power and popularity. When the means to express dissatisfaction with the system are restricted long enough, leaders often (incorrectly) take silent acquiescence as a positive sign of support for the regime. This combination produces a situation in which the regime overestimates its power, while signalling to the opposition that it is vulnerable and providing an opportunity for all the actors—both its supporters and its opponents—to experience the benefits of reform. The bottom line is that while liberalization often seems to be a sound strategy for a regime to maintain its control over a country, it proves difficult to control in the end.

The final potential outcome of regime breakdown is some form of transition to democracy. Most often, this involves the announcement that democratic elections will be held at some future date. Depending on the circumstances and the degree of power the old regime still holds, several events follow from such an announcement. One has to do with the country's constitution. In order to accommodate democracy, countries often have to write an entirely new constitution or radically overhaul the old one. The terms of such constitutional reforms are a function of the power and desires of the old regime and the opposition. A second issue arises from the fact that the old regime has to make political room for the opposition, usually in the form of political parties. Again, the strength of the old regime dictates its ability to control this process. Outgoing regimes that maintain a significant power base often attempt to exclude popular leaders or parties that might threaten the success of their preferred candidate or party. Regimes with little power may attempt to exclude only anti-system parties, such as rebel groups or communists. A last issue surrounds the election itself. Regimes attempt to control such things as the timing of the election, voter eligibility and registration, access to the media, the runoff process, and the transparency of tabulating the results. As with the other issues, the ability to control the election is a function of the distribution of power of the players and their various objectives.

NONDEMOCRATIC REGIME CHANGE

The most common historical outcome of regime breakdown is nondemocratic change, of which there are three main forms. The first is *political dissent*, which can range from protest to domestic violence to international terror. The second is *rebellion*, which for purposes of this section refers to military coups and *autogolpes* (leaders' coups against their own democratic regime). The third is *state failure*, which can be understood by examining civil war and social breakdown.

Political Dissent

Political dissent involves some form of action taken to indicate a rejection of the existing order. Protest is one aspect of dissent that is both widespread and accepted throughout the world. People who feel they are unable to effect change through the mechanisms of government turn instead to protest. When groups feel that government is no longer paying attention, one option they have is to expand the scope of the conflict. By organizing rallies and demonstrations, they hope to inform a greater portion of the population about their cause and thus force the government to act. It is important to remember that protest can produce results ranging from no change to a crackdown on protesters to wider recognition of the issues to the initiation of regime change. The world has recently seen many protests surrounding the issues of globalization. The first major action in this regard took place in November 1999 when protesters attempted to disrupt the World Trade Organization's meetings in Seattle, Washington. One of the major difficulties with protest is that it may turn violent. While many protesters look to the likes of Gandhi and Martin Luther King for examples of nonviolent protest, others believe the only way to galvanize opinion (and media coverage) is through violent protest. Students protesting economic and human rights conditions in South Korea during the late 1980s routinely hurled rocks, bottles, and Molotov cocktails at the police. Anyone following the protests of Palestinian youths against Israel has probably seen similar pictures. The point here is that protest is undertaken for many different reasons, can take many forms, and can have a variety of effects. The importance of protest for our purposes is that it can signal that there is a potential for regime change.

A second form of political dissent can be found in domestic violence and terror. Groups seeking systemic change in a country sometimes turn to organized violence in an attempt to force change. The battle between the Irish Republican Army (IRA) and the British government is a prime example. Feeling that the British had no legitimate claim to rule Northern Ireland, the IRA, which was formed following the Easter Rebellion in 1916, undertook a sustained campaign of terrorism in both Ireland and England. The aim was to force change by constantly reminding the people of the IRA's cause and making them doubt their personal security. In December 1999, the political arm of the IRA (Sinn Fein) formally entered into the governing process in Northern Ireland in exchange for the disarmament of the IRA. Following a series of negotiations in 2006, both Britain and Ireland declared that the IRA no longer represented a terrorist threat. Another example of domestic terror involves the Shining Path (Sendero Luminoso) in Peru. This group was a communist guerrilla force that turned

The Grim Reaper takes on the United States and Afghanistan.

Carlucho, Cartoonists & Writers Syndicate/cartoonweb.com

to domestic violence in the 1980s. By the late 1980s, the Shining Path found a great deal of success in targeting urban infrastructure so as to disrupt the lives of Peruvian citizens. The country's democratic regime broke down in 1992 when President Alberto Fujimori suspended the constitution, one of his justifications being the need to defeat the Shining Path and capture its leader, Abimael Guzmán Reynoso. Guzmán was captured within six months, which greatly diminished the activities of the organization. Once Fujimori fled the country in 2000 a fragile democracy was restored, but during the 15 years of terror in Peru more than 25,000 people (mostly civilians) died. The examples of both the IRA and the Shining Path should point to the potential importance of domestic terror in the regime change process.

A third form of political dissent can be found in international **terrorism** (see Box 15.3, p. 402). The events of September 11, 2001 drove home the relevance of this phenomenon. The actions of the United States and its coalition partners in response to what came to be known as "9/11" aptly demonstrate the linkage between international terrorism and regime change. The ramifications of this act of terror went far beyond the deaths and injuries of a single day. For example, the global economy was seriously damaged. Illustrating the effects of interdependence, economies from Europe to Asia to North America declined. Contrary to the intentions of the initiators of this act, at least two countries— Afghanistan and Iraq—experienced a regime change in the subsequent U.S.-led war on terrorism. While 9/11 certainly was not the first example of international terrorism, it demonstrated the vulnerability of even the United States, and it serves as a prime example of how such events can play a role in regime change.

> **Terrorism:** The threat or use of violence, usually directed at civilian populations, in order to create some form of political change.

Rebellion

The most common form of regime failure involves some form of rebellion. The two most salient examples of rebellion are military coups and *autogolpes*. A **coup d'état** is the mechanism most people understand as the cause of nondemocratic regime change; it is defined as the overthrow of a political regime or leader by military force.

A quick reference to the motivations of the military as an actor in the regime change process should indicate why it may step in and overthrow a regime. While many motivations may appear reasonable, there are two basic sets of theories explaining why militaries seize power. The first revolves around the national interest of the country. This view sees the military as the nonpartisan adjudicator of politics in the country. As such, it will seek power when the existing government has lost legitimacy and can no longer govern effectively. Exactly when this point is reached is the subject of much debate. Typically, the military will point to economic crisis, a deadlocked or ineffective legislature, or widespread governmental corruption to indicate that the current regime has put the national interest at risk. The Turkish military is a prime example of this approach, having executed three military coups. Whenever it has stepped into politics in the form of bloodless coups, it has cited legislative deadlock that left the country unable to confront crises. It established control over the country, made constitutional changes, and then withdrew from power in favour of an elected civilian government. The counter-example to Turkey is Thailand, a country that has experienced at least 15 successful coups including the one in September of 2006 that removed Thaksin Shinawatra from office ending 15 years of civilian rule. Upon taking power, the Thai military announced that elections would be held and civilians returned to power, a promise that may have been fulfilled in 2011.

The second theory explaining military motivation involves the corporate interest of the military. From this perspective, if it feels its very existence is at risk under the current regime, it fights to defend itself. What types of actions or events trigger such a feeling? For one, they may concern money. From this perspective, the chief corporate concern of the military is its budgetary support. If the institution's funding is endangered (or significantly reduced), it may feel it can no longer meet obligations to its members or to the nation. Another triggering factor has to do with autonomy. Threats to the military's autonomy can be found when the existing regime attempts to interfere in that body's internal affairs: for example, the education and training curriculum, the assignment of posts, the promotion of all but the most senior officers, and the crafting of national

> **Coup d'état:** The overthrow of a political regime or leader by military force.

BOX 15.3

INTERNATIONAL TERRORISM

The question of what constitutes terrorism has been debated for decades without being definitively answered. The oft-heard comment that one person's terrorist is another's freedom fighter underlies the difficulty of achieving a consensus definition. Unable to unravel this problem, the United Nations continues to identify terrorism via 12 piecemeal conventions and protocols (http://www.unodc.org/unodc/ en/terrorism/conventions.html). Rather than defining the term, they identify events that most agree constitute terrorist activities, such as taking hostages, harming diplomatic agents, and hijacking planes. The government of Canada is no clearer. The Supreme Court of Canada, in *Suresh v. Canada*, argued that there is no authoritative definition of terrorism, in large part because the term is open to "politicized manipulation, conjecture and polemical interpretation." Instead of undertaking such an effort, the *Anti-Terrorism Act* defines terrorism by recognizing 10 of the UN antiterrorism conventions and protocols. Some in the UN have proposed relying on A.P. Achmid's "short legal definition," which states an act of terrorism is "peacetime equivalents of war crimes." When evaluating any proposed definition, keep in mind the three elements of motive, identity, and method.

Terrorism has historic roots stretching back more than 2,000 years; however, the first example within the last 100 years was the assassination of the Archduke Franz Ferdinand on June 28, 1914 in Sarajevo—an act carried out by an activist from a group known as the Young Bosnians. Following World War II, terrorism was mainly employed by non-state groups including nationalist and anticolonial groups in Asia, Africa, and the Middle East. The 1960s and 1970s witnessed the prominence of nationalist groups such as the Provisional IRA, the PLO, and the Basque ETA and of groups motivated by ethnic and ideological considerations, such as the Red Army Faction and the Italian Red Brigade. During the 1980s, state-sponsored terrorism, backed by countries such as Iran, Iraq, Libya, and Syria, reemerged in the form of attacks against American and other Western targets in the Middle East. More recently, the world has witnessed the reemergence of religiously motivated terror culminating in the Al-Qaeda attacks of September 11, 2001.

While the United States has attempted to focus global attention on Al-Qaeda, it is important to remember that people in other parts of the world may be more concerned with other groups—FARC in Columbia, the Liberation Tigers of Tamil Eelam (LTTE) in Sri Lanka, Chechens in Russia, etc. That said, Al-Qaeda remains the focus on the U.S.-led "war on terrorism." *Al-Qaeda*, an Arabic word meaning "the base," was built on the foundation of the mujahideen resistance movement against the Soviet invasion of Afghanistan sometime around 1989 by Osama bin Laden and Muhammad Atef and was dedicated to opposing non-Islamic governments with force and violence. Prior to 9/11, Al-Qaeda was behind numerous terror attacks: 1992 bombings in Yemen targeting U.S. troops; training those responsible for attacks in 1993 on U.S. military personnel in Mogadishu, Somalia; the 1998 bombing of the U.S. embassies in Nairobi, Kenya, and Dar es Salaam, Tanzania; and the 2000 bombing of the USS *Cole* in Yemen.

Following the 9/11 attacks, the United States led a military campaign in Afghanistan that ousted the Taliban from power, forcing the leadership of Al-Qaeda to flee its bases in that country. Subsequently, President Bush advanced a foreign policy agenda based on the "war on terrorism." This policy was used, in part, to justify the U.S. invasion of Iraq. As well, most Western countries have passed legislation aimed at bolstering the domestic tools to fight terrorism including the *Patriot Act* in the United States, the *Anti-Terrorism Act* in Canada, and the *Anti-Terrorism, Crime and Security Act* in Britain. Such legislation usually aims to provide new investigation tools to law enforcement and intelligence agencies in areas such as tracking and intercepting communications, thwarting money-laundering efforts, and increasing control over border entries. Opponents of such legislation point out that these efforts to fight terrorism directly trade off with the civil and political liberties of citizens. They argue that while suspending constitutional rights of citizens certainly makes it easier to combat the threat of terrorism, it exacts a high democratic price. The tradeoffs between protecting individual rights and preventing terrorism are sure to remain at the core of future debates surrounding this issue.

defence strategy. Militaries express concerns that such interference puts the chain of command at risk and thus threatens the entire institution.[4] When the Goulart regime in Brazil changed promotion patterns and then proclaimed amnesty for all involved in a sailors' revolt, the military took control of the country by coup.

A second example of rebellion is the *autogolpe*, a kind of self-coup in which a country's leader (usually elected) decides to rule by decree. This normally takes place when a country faces an economic crisis at the same time as an ambitious leader experiences institutional gridlock. A classic example was President Alberto Fujimori of Peru's forcible closure of the congress and suspension of the country's constitution in April 1992. This action was greeted with massive public support because of Peruvians' weariness with the corrupt and incompetent congress. The international community, on the other hand, overwhelmingly opposed the "coup," and moved to isolate Peru and force it back to democracy. Fujimori's success in dealing with the economic problems and defeating the Shining Path earned him reelection in 1995.[5] It was only when his right-hand man was caught on video bribing a member of congress that he was forced to flee to Japan, ending his rule.

State Failure

The third form of nondemocratic regime change involves **state failure**. State failure involves more than simply rebellion, coups, or riots; it refers to "a situation where the structure, authority (legitimate power), law, and political order have fallen apart and must be reconstituted in some form, old or new."[6]

> **State failure:** A situation in which the structure, authority, law, and political order have fallen apart and must be reconstituted in some form.

The clearest example of such failure is civil war. When two or more factions within a country take up armed struggle against one another, it puts the state at risk. History is replete with examples of civil war and the threats they posed to regimes. The civil war in the United States threatened to tear the country apart and throw it into chaos; John A. Macdonald drew on the lessons of that conflict in arguing that Canada should not provide too much power to the provinces. The

bloody civil war in El Salvador in the 1980s can be understood in light of the Cold War politics of the times. The civil war fought in Ethiopia really began after World War II as a result of the unification of two historically distinct groups by European powers. The effects of civil war extend well beyond body counts. The death and destruction are truly awful, of course, but such wars also serve to divide the loyalties of citizens and put the very survival of the state in jeopardy.

A second example of state failure is total social breakdown. Occasionally, events in a state reach such a point that the state basically ceases to exist. It is under these circumstances that humans find themselves closest to a Hobbesian "state of nature," in which life is "solitary, poor, nasty, brutish and short." In 1991, the leader of Somalia was ousted from power, which plunged the country into civil war. A significant portion of northern Somalia announced it had seceded. A devastating famine the following year killed an estimated 300,000 people, triggering an attempt by the United Nations to broker a truce that would allow peacekeepers and famine relief workers and supplies into the country. For all practical purposes, the truce was ignored. Attempts by the international community to prevent looting only served to draw it in to the burgeoning tribal conflict. The escalating fighting resulted in deaths and casualties among the international peacekeeping forces and led to the departure of the UN by 1995. In the period that followed, the country was ruled by tribal warlords. There was no central government and all services usually carried out by a state ceased to function. At that point, Somalia was close to anarchy, a situation that has not yet greatly improved. The country faced another famine crisis in 2011.

THE TRANSITION TO DEMOCRACY

The world has seen a remarkable wave of **democratic transitions** over the past three decades. Thus, it is important to have a more complete understanding of

> **Democratic transition:** The change from nondemocratic to democratic government, usually indicated by the existence of at least one free and fair election.

the issues surrounding the transition itself. To more fully understand democratic transition, we must first define "democracy." While it is possible to define it in terms of the roots of authority and the ideal outputs of democratic regimes, this chapter defines it in terms of the procedures for constituting government, and therefore focuses on free and fair **elections**. We then explore the historic evolution and the current state of global democracy. Finally, we turn our attention to the defining event of the transition—the election. For an election to be considered the end of a transition to democracy, it must be seen as "free and fair," so we examine what is meant by this phrase, and explore the limitations of the groups that arrive at such judgments—election observers.

Defining Democracy

The idea of democracy has meant different things to different people over the ages, as noted in other chapters in this book. One approach is to focus on the source of authority. From this point of view democracy means government by the people. We might debate the question of whether history has ever witnessed a regime that operated as a true direct democracy, in which the people really govern. Certainly women and other people not offered the advantages of citizenship would disagree with even the "best" cases of ancient democracy. In the modern age there are no examples of the people directly governing. Such a solution is simply not practical. So while this approach offers interesting food for thought, it does not provide guidance for discriminating between democratic and nondemocratic cases in today's world.

Another approach is to focus on the outputs of government. We all know that democracies are supposed to protect the common good: safeguard individual rights, provide equality, and guard against tyranny (see Figure 15.4). The question that must be asked is whether these are defining features of democracy as a form of government or objectives democracies are supposed to strive toward. Put another way, if a regime must accomplish the objectives set out in our list before being considered a democracy, how many democracies actually exist in the world? Surely we could come up with examples in which Canada and the United States themselves

violate some of these requirements, such as their early treatment of women and their dealings with Aboriginal peoples. If we can use the terms of the definition to question even the most well-established democracies in the world, how useful is the definition in examining newly formed democracies? This approach does not allow us to distinguish between democracies and nondemocracies in the countries we are interested in during the post-World War II period.

The third approach is much more limited. It focuses on the procedures for constituting the government, arguing that we must examine the method of leadership selection. This definition, first advanced by Joseph Schumpeter, argues that democracy is "that institutional arrangement for arriving at political decisions in which individuals acquire the power to decide by means of a competitive struggle for the people's vote."[7] Several scholars have pointed out additional elements necessary to improve on this definition. Robert Dahl argued that democracy requires contestation, participation, and civil and political liberties. There must be meaningful competition (also called *contestation*) for the effective positions of power in government. This is accomplished through regular elections. These elections must allow for a highly inclusive level of political participation that excludes no major social group. In order to carry out such elections, a minimum level of civil and political liberties such as those of speech, press, and association is necessary.[8] This is a very *limited* definition of democracy but it is employed here because it allows for the inclusion of newly formed democracies and provides us with a reasonable list of factors to examine when determining whether a country is a democracy.

The State of Global Democracy

Samuel P. Huntington has advanced a widely cited theory that there is an observable historical pattern of global political change. He refers to the patterns of change as waves, and notes that history is not unidirectional: countries can experience transitions to democracy but they can also experience transitions away from democracy. Transitions away from democracy are referred to as reverse waves. While recognizing that the events of history are messy and therefore difficult to sort

Figure 15.4 **The Map of Freedom, 2011**

■ Free ■ Partly Free ■ Not Free

Source: Reprinted by permission of Freedom House.

into nice, neat boxes, Huntington argues that there have been three waves of **democratization** and two reverse waves in modern history[9].

> **Democratization:** A group of transitions from nondemocratic to democratic regimes, involving the relaxation of authoritarian political control by political leaders, the expansion of political and civil liberties, and the creation of institutional mechanisms that open up a political system to greater representation and participation. Democratization can be seen to occur in waves. A reverse wave occurs when some of the countries that had previously made the transition to democracy revert to nondemocratic forms of government.

According to Huntington, the first wave of democratization occurred between 1828 and 1926. This was followed by the first reverse wave during the 20-year period following 1922. The second wave of democratization began in 1943 and lasted until 1962, but before it was over, the second reverse wave started in 1958 and lasted until 1975. Finally, Huntington designates the period since 1974 as the third wave of democratization. Although he was writing in 1990, and although there have been a few bumps in the road along the way, it seems fair to say that we are still living in that phase of history.

Even a cursory examination of these dates reveals that the waves overlap; for example, the first wave did not end until 1926, but the first reverse wave began in 1922. This should reinforce the *inexact nature* of attempting to divide history into neat groupings. Nevertheless, Huntington's classification provides an easy way to conceptualize the ebb and flow of democracy over time.

The first wave is rooted in the American and French **revolutions**. Exactly when these countries became democratic is a subject of ongoing debate. Nevertheless, when we employ even a basic democratic qualification of 50 percent adult male suffrage and some type of responsible executive (either through parliamentary support or periodic election), we can see that the United States began this wave with the 1828 presidential election. By the end of the first wave, 33 countries—including Canada and most of Europe—experienced some form of democratic

transition. The first reverse wave began in 1922 with Mussolini's rise to power in Italy, and continued with Hitler's rise to power in Germany. During this period, military coups resulted in the overthrow of democracy in numerous places across the globe, ranging from the Baltic states to a number of South American countries.

The second, short wave of democratization began during World War II but lasted only through the early 1960s. Countries such as West Germany and Japan adopted democratic forms of government following occupation by Allied forces. Others, such as a number of Latin American states, seemed to follow the lead of the Allied democracies, which facilitated improved aid and trade relations. In addition, a number of countries "created" during this period due to the decline of Western colonial rule began as democracies. Most of these postcolonial democratic experiments, however, were short-lived. The second reverse wave saw a return to nondemocratic regimes across the globe. From Latin America to Asia to southern Europe, democratic governments were swept from power through military force.

The third wave of democratization began in southern Europe with the end of dictatorial rule in Portugal, followed quickly by a return to democracy in Greece and Spain. This wave picked up steam during the late 1970s in Latin America. Ecuador, Peru, and Bolivia all saw military governments attempting to withdraw from power. The movement to democracy subsequently spread throughout Latin America. At the same time, beginning with India and continuing from the Philippines to South Korea, Taiwan, and Pakistan, the democratic wave spread throughout Asia. The collapse of the Soviet Union triggered a surge of democracy across Eastern Europe. Beginning with Hungary in 1988, the world witnessed a rapid and dramatic spread of democracy across the countries formerly behind the Iron Curtain. The 1990s saw the third wave spread into Africa.

Most recently, the debate on democratic reform has spread to the Middle East. Putting aside the issues around weapons of mass destruction, one of the objectives of the most recent war in Iraq was to attempt to put a democratic government in control of the country. Despite an ongoing insurgency conflict the Iraqi people went to the polls on January 30, 2005 in the country's first free election in at least half a century. The Iraqi people returned to the polls on March 7, 2010 in what has been widely recognized as the most open and competitive election in the country's history. Iraq was not the only Middle Eastern country to experience a democratic push. Following the February 14, 2005 murder of popular former prime minister Rafik Hariri, at least one million Lebanese citizens demonstrated in Beirut calling for the withdrawal of Syrian troops and democratic elections. Since then, the pro-Syrian Lebanese government was forced to resign and Syria has begun a military withdrawal. In 2011 the world witnessed uprisings across the Arab world including Tunisia and Egypt, referred to as the "Arab Spring." While it is too early to assess the democratic possibilities for any of the countries involved, these events seem to indicate that the third wave has the potential to finally reach the Middle East.

Free and Fair Elections

The defining moment of the democratic transition is the initial election. Whether the regime is ultimately viewed by the international community as a democracy comes down to a judgment on whether the transition election is free and fair. In this context, the word *free* gets at the element of participation, whereas the word *fair* refers to contestation. The idea of civil and political liberties underpins both the "free" and the "fair." Therefore, the first question we must ask is: How are these two things determined? When evaluating this question, keep in mind the discussion in Chapter 11, particularly the information in Box 11.1.

Whether an election is free usually comes down to the issues of suffrage and coercion. Is there universal suffrage? To determine this, we examine whether virtually all of the adult citizens in the country are eligible to vote. Are women excluded? Are significant minority groups—especially ethnic and religious—excluded? If there is universal suffrage, then the question of whether the election was also generally free from coercion must be examined. To determine this, we usually ask whether voters were intimidated, either when registering or when actually voting. A certain degree of intimidation is allowed for; however, turning large numbers of voters away from polling stations or widespread, especially targeted, violence during the election

period is usually grounds for declaring an election to have been not free.

Whether an election is fair usually comes down to restrictions placed on candidates and parties, as well as to the level of corruption throughout the process, especially in the tabulation of votes. While some restrictions on contestation are accepted—for example, excluding anti-system and communist parties—we have to examine whether the major opposition leaders and parties were, in general, allowed to have candidates run in the election in an open fashion. If they were, then we turn to the issue of corruption. It is widely recognized that no election is totally free from corruption. The questions become how pervasive the corruption was and whether it affected the outcome. While minor indiscretions during the campaign may be tolerable, stuffing the ballot box or not counting ballots from opposition strongholds is usually not. Of course, out-and-out fraud in the reporting of election results, assuming such fraud can be identified, results in a declaration that the election was not fair.

The issue of civil and political liberties, while recognized as important to the definition of democracy, does not extensively come into play when examining the issue of free and fair elections. It is generally accepted that significant restrictions on such liberties will exist. As long as the outgoing regime loosens them to some extent, such restrictions rarely result in a declaration that the election was not free or fair. Aside from the elements of the free-and-fair determination that overlap with such liberties, the question usually comes down to media access. In most countries experiencing transition elections, the major media in the country are state-owned and thus dominated by those loyal to the old regime. If the opposition forces are excluded from all media access the election risks losing the free-and-fair determination. But as long as they have some degree of access issues such as the state media's bias against the opposition are generally ignored.

There is one outcome that always results in a declaration that the election was free and fair: if the opposition wins the election. Regardless of any violations mentioned above, such a victory is seen as prima facie evidence that it was a democratic election. If the opposition does not win, analysts examine whether the opposition forces were provided with a chance to win. They may not take advantage of such opportunities, of course, and even if they do they may still not win.

In the end, the real question is simply the existence of such opportunities.

An important question to keep in mind when considering the issue of free and fair elections is: Who decides? The problem with making such a determination is that it is almost entirely subjective. Elections are inherently imperfect, even in developed democracies. Answering questions dealing with the allowable degree of exclusions, intimidation, and corruption is ultimately a judgment call. Who then is making this call? The answer varies over time and across countries. As the third wave of democratization has matured, a system of international election observers has developed. Observer missions operate under the umbrella of international organizations such as the United Nations or the Organization of American States; think tanks such as the Carter Center at Emory University and the National Endowment for Democracy; and individual countries such as Canada and the United States.

While generally well intentioned, election observation missions face numerous difficulties. The first is the issue of *access*: Will the government allow observers access to the entire country during both the campaign and the election itself? If so, can these observers be offered a reasonable guarantee of safety? Will the government allow access to party officials, candidates, party headquarters, and domestic media? What about outside observation of the vote count? The second is the issue of *money*. Assuming reasonable access is granted, can observer missions afford to take advantage of it? This is usually a function of the size of the country, its location, the infrastructure (travel and telecommunications), and the importance the international community attaches to the election. The bigger, the farther away from the West, the poorer, and the less important a country is, the harder it is to gather even minimally sufficient funds to observe the election. Finally, there is the question of *timing*. As the world has moved to real-time communications, people have become much less patient about receiving judgments on international events. If missions wait several weeks to gather all the data they believe to be necessary to judge the election, the media have either already passed judgment without their input or are no longer interested in the story. On the other hand, if observer missions attempt to make judgments according to the news cycle of the Western media, how informed can such decisions actually be? The best most missions can usually hope for is to have people covering a small sample of the important or controversial polling stations, some form of limited access to the vote count, and enough clear information to make their best guess in time to receive international media attention. These are important yet difficult tasks indeed.

DEMOCRATIC CONSOLIDATION

Once an election that is certified as free and fair occurs, does the world have another democracy? Is that the end of the story? No. At this point, all that has happened is this: the nondemocratic regime experienced a breakdown, and subsequently there was a democratic election. If you compare a country that has just gone through this process to Canada, it is difficult to make the case that they should be considered equal in terms of democracy. Canada has well-developed democratic political institutions, a vibrant democratic political culture, and minimal prospects of reverting to a nondemocratic form of government in the foreseeable future. In comparison, we should remember that countries such as Iraq have only succeeded in concluding one or two free and fair elections. Rather than indicating an attainment of the democratic condition, such events are really indicative of the beginning of a long challenge. In political science, the issues

People line up to vote in the black township of Soweto, South Africa, in April 1994.

AP Photo/Denis Farrell

surrounding this challenge are known as **democratic consolidation**.

> **Democratic consolidation:** The achievement of a situation in which none of the major political actors, parties, organized interests, forces, or institutions consider that there is any alternative to democratic processes to gain power, and in which no political institution or group has a claim to veto the action of democratically elected decision-makers.

Consolidation Definition

Now that a fledgling democracy has been put in place, what needs to happen for that country to remove the "fledgling" tag? Democratic consolidation exists when none of the major political actors, parties, organized interests, forces, or institutions consider that there is any alternative to democratic processes to gain power, and when no political institution or group has a claim to veto the action of democratically elected decision-makers.[10]

A consolidated democracy may have small anti-democratic actors and groups. The important idea here is that the major actors in the regime, especially in times of crisis, do not turn to such groups for assistance. Rather than seeking such support, groups embrace the uncertainty of democracy—the idea that winners and losers are temporary and prone to change from election to election. It is this uncertainty that tempers the interactions and competition of groups both in and out of power. Out-of-power groups recognize that the uncertainty of democracy guarantees them a chance to regain power during the next election. Rather than attempting to take power by force, they put their energies into attempting to turn this uncertainty to their advantage. Likewise, groups in power recognize that the uncertainty of democracy means they may lose the next election and so rather than planning to stay in power by force, they plan for how to maintain their power through elections—and, if they lose, how to regain it next time. Because of this ebb and flow of groups in power and the likelihood that even though a party is a winner today, it may not be a winner after the next election, it behooves each group to treat its opposition with some level of respect at all times. The objective of the post-transition period is to get actors to embrace the advantages of uncertainty. Thus, as Juan J. Linz put it, a democracy is consolidated when democracy becomes "the only game in town."[11]

Consolidation Challenges

How do democracies become consolidated? New democratic regimes face at least four common challenges: asserting civilian control over the military, reforming the institutions of government, fostering the growth of civil society, and improving relations with the international community.

Asserting civilian control over the military is likely the most important challenge confronting a new democratic regime. Given that new regimes often face numerous threats and contenders for power, they may require more from the military than simply a "return to the barracks." Newly formed democracies often find themselves turning to the military to actively assist them in defeating challengers. For this to take place, the civilian government has to achieve some level of control over the military. A number of problems stand in the way of such control. The first is the issue of what to do about past human rights violations. The government is often left in a no-win situation: if it prosecutes the military it greatly increases the risk of a coup but if it ignores past violations it may anger the mass public. Countries such as South Africa have tried to deal with this problem via "truth and reconciliation commissions." Such commissions attempt to uncover information about past injustices, but they do not aim to prosecute the people behind the acts.

Another issue confronting civil–military relations in new democracies revolves around the military's budget. Most third-wave democracies have sprung up in relatively poor countries facing severe economic problems and pressure from international lenders (such as the IMF and World Bank) to drastically reduce government spending. Generally speaking, governments can cut military budgets in countries where the military has lost a significant amount of prestige and influence but they try to insulate the military from cuts where it still retains significant power. However, it may be that just the opposite should occur: powerful militaries should be confronted if the civilian government ever hopes to gain dominance, while defeated militaries should not be pushed into a corner where they feel they have nothing else to lose.

Given these and other challenges, how should the new regime respond to the military? The overarching object must be democracy's survival. In the short term, this may require the regime to appease the military. In the long run, however, the civilian regime must assert its control over the military. Democracies must figure out how to send the military back to the barracks and how to keep them there. What this means is that military professionalism must be increased. The military must come to understand that its job exists in the military realm, not in the political or economic realms.

A second major challenge that transitional democracies face is how to build and reform the democratic institutions of government. The most obvious targets are the legislature, the courts, and the bureaucracy. Outside of the executive, these three institutions are most responsible for the functioning of government—for making, enforcing, and carrying out the law—and are crucial to the government's ability to operate as a democracy. The root of the problem is that these same institutions were also responsible, in some manner, for the operation of the previous, nondemocratic regime. As such, we should expect them to experience difficulties making the transition to a completely new set of rules. Specifically, these institutions must somehow confront issues surrounding responsiveness and corruption.

The legislature must learn how to function in a democracy. New rules must be established to allow the legislature to actually legislate. This demands attention to everything from how to form committees to how question period will work. A variety of challenges also surround the funding necessary to undertake new responsibilities ranging from constituency service to legislative research to public communication. In addition, the legacy of corruption must be confronted. The list of necessary reforms is almost endless but the legislature has to undergo a radical makeover before the people come to see it as a democratic institution.

Similar challenges are found when examining the courts. For a consolidated democracy to function properly the courts must be able, at minimum, to check abuses that occur in the rest of the government. Instead of relying on the desires of the executive the courts have to be put in a position to rely on the law. Here, too, the legacy of corruption must be overcome. To accomplish this the courts will require additional funding for the recruitment of new judges and staff

members. The corrupt judges of the old regime must be retrained or retired.

Finally, the bureaucracy also faces challenges. Citizens are much more likely to have direct interactions with the bureaucracy than with the legislature or the courts. One of the toughest tasks in reforming the bureaucracy is the implementation of merit-based hiring practices. In most nondemocratic (and even many democratic) regimes staffing in the bureaucracy is used as a way to reward followers. An important job allows one to employ family and friends, regardless of qualifications. Such jobs are powerful, not because of the missions or objectives of the position but rather as a function of their ability to deliver goods. The most straightforward solution to the problem is to hire civil servants on merit, although such reforms are likely to receive resistance from within the institution.

The proper functioning of government is not enough to push a democracy toward consolidation; democracy also requires a functioning **civil society** (see Box 15.4). Civil society refers to nongovernmental groups in society, but in nondemocratic political

---

BOX 15.4

CIVIL SOCIETY IN TRANSITIONAL DEMOCRACIES

Civil society is a set or system of self-organized intermediary groups that: 1) are relatively independent of both public authorities and private units of production and reproduction, that is, of firms and families; 2) are capable of deliberating about and taking collective actions in defence or promotion of their interests or passions; 3) do not seek to replace either state agents or private (re)producers or to accept responsibility for governing the polity as a whole; and 4) agree to act within pre-established rules of a "civil" nature, that is, conveying mutual respect.

Source: Philippe C. Schmitter, "Civil Society East and West," in Larry Diamond, Marc F. Plattner, Yun-han Chu, and Hung-mao Tien, eds., *Consolidating the Third Wave Democracies: Themes and Perspectives* (Baltimore: Johns Hopkins University Press, 1997), p. 240.

systems the term goes beyond the definition provided in Chapter 13.

The idea is that as more groups are created and as more people join them, the chances of democratic consolidation increase. At an individual level, membership in such groups helps develop people's understanding of the way democracy functions and therefore serves as an incubator for democratic political culture in the country. At a group level, such organizations offer a check against the abuse of power and a backstop support for democracy. These two points make it clear that democratic consolidation is dependent, not only on the groups that make up civil society, but also on how these groups interact with their members, each other, the business sector, and the government. While such groups are more likely to form spontaneously in a democracy, anything transitional governments can do to foster their formation and survival will assist in the consolidation process.

A final element to consider is the role of the international community. As the forces of the Cold War have faded and the forces of **globalization** have spread around the world, the role the international community plays in democratic consolidation has greatly increased. During the 1990s, it became clear that the international community, especially the Western world, favours democracy and actively works to foster and maintain it. The West relies on economic tools to accomplish its objectives. Western-backed international organizations, such as the World Bank and the International Monetary Fund, condition aid packages to new democracies on a set of economic reforms theoretically aimed at making these fledgling democracies more competitive. Individual donor countries often tie aid not only to meeting conditions set out by the World Bank and the IMF but also to consistent progress toward democratic consolidation. The effectiveness of conditioning aid on the achievement of democracy (or democratic progress) is still much disputed.

The other tool employed in this respect is international trade. Given that the world is becoming more interdependent, countries that desire economic success must become more open and active in the realm of international trade. Aid and trade are also used to foster consolidation by delivering needed short-term assistance, which helps countries get their economic houses in order, and then to offer these new democracies prospects for long-term success by putting them in a position where they can take advantage of globalization and world markets.

Unconsolidated Democracy

An understanding of the challenges facing countries during the consolidation period should lead one to understand that consolidation is not easily achieved. In fact, depending on how one defines and measures democratic consolidation, it is more typical for a country that experiences a democratic transition *not* to achieve consolidation. Throughout Latin America and Asia, countries that have experienced democratic transitions have more often than not found a sort of semi-democracy persisting in their country, rather than a move to eventual consolidation. One way of looking at this is to label such states as "electoral democracies." These states have experienced one or more free and fair elections but have failed to consolidate. There are still serious nondemocratic actors in the country, and the levels of civil and political freedoms common in Western democracies have not materialized. This is not to say that electoral democracies can never consolidate. Rather, their condition should serve as a reminder that there is no natural pattern of regime evolution. Not only is it possible for countries to experience a democratic transition that never results in democratic consolidation; it is also important to remember that democracies can and do break down.

Consolidation Consequences

Having laid out the issues surrounding the challenge of democratic consolidation, we will now consider its consequences. What are the practical effects of consolidation? Life in a country that has experienced a nondemocratic regime breakdown, an initial democratic transition, and the successful completion of the democratic consolidation will be much different at the end of the process. The domestic and international implications vary across individual countries and across time but it is possible to isolate some common consequences of a successful democratic consolidation. Political rights, including things such as the right to vote, the fairness of electoral rules, the principle that votes endow actual power, the ability to organize political parties, and the existence of meaningful opposition are the norm and are almost taken for granted.

Civil liberties, encompassing the freedoms to hold views, maintain institutions, and possess personal autonomy apart from the state, are widespread.[12] While they may come under attack from time to time, society recognizes their importance and strives to protect the core set of liberties. The political elite sees democracy as the only possible regime and spends its time trying to take advantage of the rules in order to gain power. The military takes its orders from the civilian government and is now considered professional and divorced from politics. Civil society has blossomed as people are more engaged in group activities and government is more responsive to and inclusive of outside groups' views. The socioeconomic situation of the country has gradually improved and gross distributional problems such as famine have become much less frequent. On the international level, the country is much more fully involved in the globalized world. Aid donors and trade partners no longer question whether they should be engaged with the country. While there may be disagreements as to the degree or type of engagement, the regime is no longer questioned over democratic legitimacy. While this is obviously an idealized picture, and even consolidated democracies will have trouble achieving all of the benefits just described, it does provide the rationale for attempting the consolidation process.

CONCLUSION

During the past four decades, the world has undergone a radical transformation toward democracy. The third wave of democratization began in the early 1970s and continues today. For this reason, the study of democratization has never been more important. In order to understand this process, it is essential to begin with an examination of the key actors: political elites, business elites, the military, the mass public, and the international community. With an understanding of their interests and strengths, the reasons why some of these groups may withdraw their support from nondemocratic regimes and thus break those regimes down become more apparent.

It is important to remember that the consequence of such breakdowns is, more often than not, the installation of another nondemocratic regime. Sometimes, however, the result is a transition to democracy. The defining moment of any transition is the election itself.

In the end, whether a country is considered by the international community to be democratic depends on the judgment of election-monitoring teams on whether the election was free and fair. Having completed a free and fair election, the democratic regime enters into the consolidation phase of democratization, in which the objective is to make democracy the only game in town. Once this is accomplished a country can expect the benefits of democracy to take on a more permanent status.

DISCUSSION QUESTIONS

1. Identify and discuss the importance of the different actors in the democratization process.

2. Identify and discuss the importance of the different consequences of the breakdown of nondemocratic regimes.

3. Compare and contrast the different approaches to defining democracy.

4. What is meant by "free and fair" elections?

5. Discuss the challenges that regimes face during the democratic consolidation process.

FURTHER READING

Diamond, Larry. *Developing Democracy: Toward Consolidation.* Baltimore: Johns Hopkins University Press, 1999.

Haggard, Stephan, and Robert R. Kaufman. *The Political Economy of Democratic Transitions.* Princeton: Princeton University Press, 1995.

Huntington, Samuel P. *The Third Wave.* Norman, OK: University of Oklahoma Press, 1990.

Mainwaring, Scott, Guillermo O'Donnell, and J. Samuel Valenzuela, eds. *Issues in Democratic Consolidation: The New South American Democracies in Comparative Perspective.* Notre Dame, IN: Notre Dame University Press, 1992.

Przeworski, Adam, et al. *Democracy and Development: Political Institutions and Material Well-Being in the World, 1950–1990.* Cambridge: Cambridge University Press, 2000.

ENDNOTES

1. Seymour Martin Lipset, "Some Social Requisites of Democracy," *American Political Science Review* 53 (1959): 69–105; Adam Przeworski, et al., *Democracy and Development: Political Institutions and Material Well-Being in the World, 1950–1990* (Cambridge: Cambridge University Press, 2000), pp. 78–80.

2. Stephan Haggard and Robert R. Kaufman, *The Political Economy of Democratic Transitions* (Princeton: Princeton University Press, 1995), pp. 25–32.

3. Donald Horowitz, *Ethnic Groups in Conflict* (Berkeley: University of California Press, 1985).

4. Eric A. Nordlinger, *Soldiers in Politics: Military Coups and Governments* (Englewood Cliffs, NJ: Prentice-Hall, 1977).

5. Maxwell A. Cameron and Philip Mauceri, eds., *The Peruvian Labyrinth: Polity, Society, Economy* (University Park, PA: Pennsylvania State University Press, 1997).

6. I. William Zartman, "Introduction: Posing the Problem of State Collapse," in I. William Zartman, ed., *Collapsed States: The Disintegration and Restoration of Legitimate Authority* (Boulder, CO: Lynne Rienner Publishers, 1995), pp. 1–11.

7. Joseph Schumpeter, *Capitalism, Socialism, and Democracy*, 2nd ed. (NewYork: Harper, 1947), p. 269.

8. Adapted from Samuel P. Huntington, *The Third Wave* (Norman, OK: University of Oklahoma Press, 1990), p. 6; and Georg Sorensen, *Democracy and Democratization* (Boulder, CO: Westview Press, 1993), pp. 12–13.

9. Huntington, pp. 15–26.

10. Juan J. Linz, "Transitions to Democracy," *Washington Quarterly* 13 (3) (1990): 158.

11. *Ibid.*

12. See the checklist of political rights and civil liberties employed by Freedom House for their Freedom in the World reports, available at http://www.freedomhouse.org.

W W W For various weblinks discussed in this chapter, please go to the book's website at **www.studyingpolitics4e.nelson.com**

International Politics

Courtesy of Katrina Burgess

KATRINA BURGESS

Katrina Burgess graduated with an honours Bachelor of Arts degree in politics from Queen's University. While completing her degree, she spent one year as an exchange student at L'Institut d'Études Politiques in Lyon, France. While at Queen's, Katrina participated in the Model Parliament and Model United Nations, volunteered in a number of extracurricular causes, and became involved in many athletic activities.

Immediately after graduating from Queen's, Katrina accepted a position as an English teacher in Japan for a year, and after that she studied for a master's degree in international relations at the London School of Economics. In London, she learned about both international security threats and the dangers that arise from drinking with the Brits!

Katrina joined Foreign Affairs Canada in September 2004. She began her work there as a policy advisor in the federal–provincial–territorial relations division, dealing with the provinces' role in Canada's international affairs. She followed that with a position in the Human Security Policy Division, working on war-affected children and representing Canada at ministerial meetings in Bangkok, Ljubljana, and New York.

Katrina took a six-month leave from the Human Security work to undertake a special assignment in Rome, where she liaised between the Ambassador and Ottawa on Canada's response to Darfur, and participated in the Canadian delegation to the annual G8 Africa Partnership meeting in Maputo, Mozambique. The highlight was a project site visit trip to Malawi to evaluate Canada's development aid and ascertain how to better respond to what is referred to as Malawi's triple threat: famine, HIV/AIDS, and poor governance.

Katrina then spent two years on a posting in Venezuela where she was the Second Secretary responsible for political reporting on domestic issues and human rights, as well as managing the education and academic affairs program at the embassy. She observed and reported on three elections while there, worked closely with civil society to build capacity and get youth involved, survived milk and sugar shortages, and, perhaps more seriously, reggaeton.

Katrina has spent the last two years working in the Humanitarian Affairs and Disaster Response Division where she deals with international humanitarian law and humanitarian policy challenges in the Middle East and the Americas. She was part of the initial Government of Canada team deployed to Haiti immediately after the earthquake and spent a month there as a humanitarian advisor to the DART Commander in Jacmel.

Katrina will be heading to New York this summer to take up a posting at Canada's Permanent Mission to the United Nations to continue working on human rights and humanitarian issues.

Katrina excels at both languages and athletics. She is fluently bilingual in English and French and almost there in Spanish. As an athlete, she participates in skiing, soccer, running, and diving, and has a surfboard that currently decorates her Ottawa townhouse.

International Relations: Global Anarchy, Conflict, and Cooperation

Claire Turenne Sjolander

CHAPTER OBJECTIVES

After you have read this chapter, you should be able to:

- discuss the role of theory in International Relations, including factual, normative, problem-solving, and critical theories
- define the Realist approach to international relations, including the role of states, power, and anarchy
- assess Liberal theory and the significance of international organizations and other forms of international cooperation
- discuss the Marxist and Marxist-inspired contributions to the explanation of international relations
- evaluate the contribution of feminist theory to the explanation of international relations.

INTRODUCTION

International Relations courses often attract the largest enrolments in university Political Science Departments. Students signing up for these courses imagine that they will learn everything there is to know about wars, revolutions, terrorism, and any other manner of threat to world peace and stability. Who can blame students for being drawn to a subject matter that is glorified in countless Hollywood blockbusters? It often comes as a surprise to students, therefore, to discover that the study of International Relations seems to have less to do with identifying Hollywood's global "good guys" and "bad guys," that is, those with the potential to take the world to the brink, than it does with learning about different theoretical models

or approaches that provide contrasting and sometimes contradictory interpretations of the reasons for, and possible solutions to, global problems.

What is the field of International Relations? Despite the fact that it is usually taught as part of Political Science programs, most scholars of International Relations argue that it is a distinct academic discipline—related to Political Science, of course, but also connected to Economics, History, Sociology, Anthropology, and Geography. Well before it was ever considered as a self-contained area of study, however, the major themes that have continued to preoccupy the discipline since its inception had long been identified. Leon Tolstoy published *War and Peace* in 1869. Questions of global order and anarchy had consumed generations of philosophers, historians, and economists. Concerns over injustice and equality had motivated social revolutions and brought about regime change throughout the world. In other words, the major questions of International Relations—and the range of options or choices confronting the international system—are, and have always been, widely understood. We know *what* the choices are. What has been less clear is the question of how we, as analysts and scholars, should interpret the meaning of the circumstances that condition these choices. What are the best ways to achieve peace, justice, equality, and order? Is it even possible to achieve all these ends? Is it desirable to try to do so? How do we interpret the reasons the world is able, or unable, to achieve that for which humanity strives?

Theories, Approaches, and Facts

What should be immediately clear is that if the problems posed by International Relations seem obvious, the answers are far less so. These are big questions that are global in scope. The world is a very complicated place and it is hard to judge which information is relevant in affecting both the choices that need to be made and the reasons that particular outcomes have been reached. It is simply hard to know where to start in the search for explanation and understanding. Facts can be confusing, partial, and contradictory. They do not "speak for themselves"—too often, when facts "speak," we cannot figure out what they are saying because there are too many facts claiming our attention at once. That is why theoretical models and approaches are so important in Political Science in general and in International Relations more specifically; it is theory that helps us to make sense of the complexity of the world. Theory is what helps us to know what is relevant and what does not need to be taken into account, at least not as a primary explanatory factor. This chapter will present some of the different theories in International Relations and explain some of the reasons for their emergence in the field. Before we do this, however, two cautionary notes are needed.

First, if we know what the choices in international relations are, but we have many different theories guiding us in our interpretation of the conditions that give rise to them or the factors that we need to take into consideration, it should seem obvious that theory is not necessarily a perfect reflection of reality. Theories are possible *interpretations* of reality. Because there are many possible interpretations, there are many theoretical approaches and perspectives. This can make the study of International Relations seem terribly confusing—the answer to the question of "what is the truth?" inevitably has to be "well, it depends." Theories are prisms that allow us

to make sense of the world, but as with any prism they almost invariably distort the world, at least to some extent. Theories tell us what to look for and what is important. Different theories point to different things as being the most important in understanding a particular aspect of international reality. Theories are more than our opinions, of course. They have an important relationship to reality in the sense that we need to find evidence to support our theories. But theories are not, in themselves, unvarnished reality. They are not facts speaking for themselves, but instead they are a simplification of the world. The problem for us as scholars is that the world is too complex for us to understand without theory. We have to accept that different perspectives tell us different (sometimes contradictory) things about the world, but that no one theory is able to tell us everything about the world.

The second cautionary note follows from the first. Theories are distinct from facts; they are systems of interpretation that allow us to make sense of facts. Because of this, one of the most important Canadian scholars of International Relations, Robert W. Cox, argued that: "theory is always *for* someone and *for* some purpose."[1] In saying this, Cox was reminding us that theories are anchored in normative positions. Many theories in International Relations claim to advance arguments about the way the world *is*—scholars refer to theory that does this as "positive theory." The arguments might be correct or they might be wrong (because they do not correspond to the evidence we uncover), but in telling us how the world *is*, a theorist does not appear to be advancing a judgment about the world (either approval or disapproval). A theorist can say: "states are prone to conflict, and the only way to reduce the chance of conflict is to make sure that one state is more powerful than all the others." This appears to be a positive statement, or a statement of fact; even the theorist authoring the statement could say that he or she does not agree with what has been observed, but that it is nonetheless the way the world is.

Cox argues, however, that even positive theories are normative; that is, that they are theories that advance a judgment or a position: they are for someone or for something. A theory that tells us that the only way to reduce the possibility of international conflict is to ensure that there is a global superpower, for example, is implicitly arguing a number of normative positions: that conflict is always bad and that reducing of the possibility of conflict is always good, and therefore having a global superpower is a beneficial thing because it is the only way to reduce the chance of conflict. Even though they do not appear to be, Cox would say that these are also statements about the way the world *should* be—it *should* be defined by an unequal distribution of power and resources (this, after all, is what defines a superpower), and this unequal distribution is the best way to ensure that the world remains as stable and conflict-avoiding as possible. While stability seems to be a good thing, stability also means that the distribution of power and resources in the world will not change, and that the superpower will always be the superpower, even if other states have to remain poor and marginal as a result. In this positive theoretical statement about the necessity of a global superpower (or a global hegemon), there are clear normative choices that define stability as more important than equality or justice. Debates in International Relations theory are less about the truth of specific facts (although these debates do take place) than they are about the merits of particular

normative positions and whether or not these positions are actually made explicit by the theorist.

Expansion of the Field

What does this mean for the student of International Relations? To begin, the field must be thought of as very fragmented; there are many different approaches and many different theories. There is no one "truth" about the way the world works. This is not only because scholars hold different normative positions; it is also, as we will see, because the object of study that is International Relations has become much more complicated over the past seven or so decades. International Relations might be about contending theoretical approaches, but theoretical approaches evolve and change as a result of the changing world, however partially we can observe these changes. As a result of globalization, the end of the Cold War, the growth of new information technologies, the rapidity with

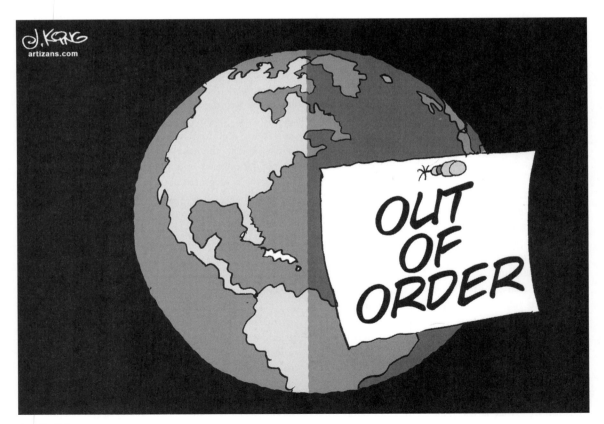

Jerry King/Artizans

which information is shared across borders, and the realization that many of the most pressing issues in the world today (such as the environment or health) have causes and consequences beyond the capacity of any one state to manage, our object of study has grown exponentially. It is increasingly difficult to know where the boundaries between national and international politics, economics, and society, are drawn. Because the object of the study is so vast, International Relations, bluntly put, can be confusing and the analyses can be ambiguous. There are no readily apparent "right" or "wrong" answers—at least, if what we are trying to identify are answers that are *always* right or *always* wrong, no matter where or when they are applied. In the midst of the confusion and ambiguity, however, International Relations is a field of study characterized by vigorous debate, touching on some of the questions that are most important to the survival of our planet and the quality of life of its people. In that respect, there might be no more important field of study, despite—and perhaps because of—its messiness.

WAR AND PEACE

What we have discussed elaborates some of the reasons for the importance of theory and the seemingly never-ending debates that characterize the development of International Relations. Beyond this, however, what is the field of International Relations about? Unlike some disciplines related to Political Science (and unlike Political Science itself), International Relations (IR) is largely a post-World War II phenomenon. This does not mean, of course, that no scholars were interested in International Relations before the end of the Second World War in 1945, but rather that those who were interested defined themselves as scholars of something else—history, international law, economics, or philosophy, for example. Yet, if something was very clear in the period between the start of the First World War and the end of the Second it was that international developments were critically important and profoundly reshaped societies throughout and beyond Europe. Understanding the causes of the international conflict which had so significantly engulfed substantial parts of the world twice in 25 years quickly seemed one of the most pressing scholarly concerns.

This is not to say that there had not been attempts after World War I to avoid the conflagration brought about by World War II. The League of Nations had been proposed by U.S. President Woodrow Wilson as a solution to the instability that had brought about the first war. According to Wilson, "a general association of nations… [needed to] be formed under specific covenants for the purpose of affording mutual guarantees of political **independence** and territorial integrity to great and small states alike."[2] The League was hampered from the start—not least by the refusal of the United States Senate to permit the U.S. to join. In the absence of the United States, the authority of the League was weakened and major powers (Germany, Japan, and Italy) began to withdraw from the League rather than to respect its decisions. The collapse of the promise of the League of Nations as a dispute-resolution mechanism was epitomized by the start of World War II—the League had been unable to forestall the very event it was created to prevent.

The Realist Approach

The failure of the League of Nations to prevent World War II raised two issues upon which the discipline of International Relations was founded: first, the problem of **security** (can we avoid interstate conflict?) and second, the problem of **global governance** (can any international organization ever be successful in enabling states to resolve their differences, thereby preventing these major international conflicts?). The approach to the study of International Relations that gained the ascendancy was the approach identified as "Realist"—that is, the approach that argued that it was naïve to think that international organizations might be able to assist states in finding a peaceful resolution to their differences. The perspective of Realists made a great deal of sense given the cumulative experiences of the failure of the League of Nations and the disasters of the two world wars. These experiences are critical in understanding the focus of **Realist theory**—if the

> **Global governance:** Collective policy-making aimed at addressing global problems in the absence of a formal governing structure for the whole world.

> **Realist theory:** A foundational theory in international relations, usually identified with Hans J. Morgenthau, that emphasizes the anarchy of the international system and the interaction of states based on their respective power.

failures of great power politics had led to two devastating world wars, then surely a sustained focus on great power politics and the instability of the international system was needed. It is within the context of these experiences that Realists began to define the basis of their positive theory of International Relations. For Realists, the problem with the League of Nations and other similar efforts to find collaborative solutions to international differences was simple: the League could not work because it was designed on the basis of ideals—on the promise that the world could change and become a better place—rather than on a hard-nosed "realistic" assessment of the way the world *really* is.

As Realists, these theorists argued, we needed to understand that states were conflict-prone by nature, just as individual human beings can be seen to be conflict-prone. Further, even if states tried to avoid conflict, defending oneself (and preparing for that defence by having available the needed weapons) can sometimes be the only choice—particularly if the state's very survival was at stake. The absence of a world **government** to resolve disputes between states made it more likely that states would have to resort to behaving in their nature if they felt threatened. The "true" nature of states, early Realist theory told us, made international conflict inevitable. International organizations could not stop states from pursuing their own national interests and taking steps to ensure their national survival. As a result, it was simply wrongheaded to think that such organizations could be guarantors of world peace. Rather, a "realistic" assessment of the world dictated that we try to determine the best ways to bring about international stability, even if that stability could not be a permanent feature of the international system given the true nature of states.

Anarchy and Power

While not the first "Realist," Hans Morgenthau quickly became the best-known Realist scholar and his principles became the bedrock of the new discipline of International Relations. His book, *Politics Among Nations*, first published in 1948 (but reissued many times in revised editions),[3] became the most widely used textbook in International Relations courses in the United States as well as in many other countries. Born in Germany to a Jewish

> **State:** A modern form of organizing political life that is characterized by a population, territory, governing institutions, and a government that claims a monopoly of legitimate force; recognition by the international community of states (most often by the United Nations) may also be key.

family and educated in Germany and Switzerland, Morgenthau had immigrated to the United States in 1937 and accepted a teaching position at the University of Chicago. Morgenthau's contribution to Realist theory, and thus to the entire discipline of International Relations, was powerful in its simplicity. **States** were the central and most important international actors, and the concern of states (and indeed, of the entire field as a scholarly enterprise) was **power**. Morgenthau emphasized the importance of national interest as the determinant of state behaviour (with the ultimate national interest being national survival), and defined that interest in terms of power. For Morgenthau, the field of International Relations was really about International Politics. The field at its inception, therefore, was narrowly defined; it was concerned with the ultimate political actors— **nation-states**—and their interactions in a sphere characterized by the absence of any central authority. In other words, International Politics as a field of study would look at states and their interactions in the international arena under conditions of **anarchy**.

> **Power:** The ability of one actor to impose its will on another, to get its own way, to do or get what it wants.

> **Nation-state:** A term sometimes used synonymously with state, but implies that the citizens share a common ethnic or cultural background. In the modern world, few such homogeneous states remain, most either being multicultural, multiethnic, or multination states.

> **Anarchy:** A system of social, political, and economic relations without formal institutions of governance to define enforceable rules or exact obedience from the governed; as such, it is more characteristic of world politics than of politics within communities.

States, power, and anarchy became the Realist trinity of the study of International Relations.

For these early Realists, domestic politics did not play a role in the analysis of a state's international interactions because domestic politics are not played out under the same circumstances as international politics. Domestic politics do not take place under conditions of anarchy; in the domestic arena, the state holds the legitimate monopoly over the use of force in a defined national territory. There is no analogous situation in the international realm—whatever the different domestic circumstances of individual states, their behaviour internationally would adhere to the same logics: those dictated by anarchy. Without a **supranational** authority, states could only rely on themselves to ensure their ultimate national interest (survival) in what became known as a system of self-help. Self-help requires states to acquire and maintain the power resources that might conceivably be necessary to protect their national interests from potential threats emanating from other states. For a number of Realists, writing three decades after Morgenthau, the anarchic structure of the international system was seen to be a more important determinant of state behaviour than their "true" nature as conflict-prone. For these Realists, led by Kenneth Waltz,[4] the structure of anarchy compelled states to behave under the self-help logic, no matter how "nice" a state might be or how altruistic its foreign policy intentions. Anarchy determined state behaviour.

> **Supranational:** A sphere of politics and political institutions that exists "above" the nation-state but usually "below" the global level. The only supranational polity in the world is the European Union.

Given that under conditions of anarchy a threat can come from any direction, the prospects for peace are fragile at best. International stability, however, could emerge from coalitions of states with similar interests that could balance coalitions of states with opposing interests. This effort to achieve a "balance of power" contributes to stability, in Realist thought, because it diminishes the risk—a state in one coalition knows who its enemies might be (those in opposing coalitions), so it does not need to protect itself from all states. Threat does not come from anywhere or from everywhere; instead, it comes from a very specific group, or groups, of opposing states.

The Cold War

Despite the fact that Realist theory was first elaborated using European politics of the 19th and 20th centuries as examples, the period of the **Cold War** seemed to confirm what Realists were saying about the nature of states and their power-balancing behaviour under conditions of anarchy. The decades-long "cold" confrontation between the United States and the Soviet Union appeared to illustrate the importance of states and power in the international system, as well as the precariousness of the international stability that could emerge as a result. For Realist theory, it did not really matter that the United States was a **capitalist** democracy or that the Soviet Union was a **socialist** dictatorship. What was important was that both countries, as leaders

> **Cold War:** The period in international relations between 1945 and 1990 which was dominated by global political conflict and economic competition between the United States and the Soviet Union, each with its ideology and allies, in which major wars were precluded by a military balance between the two superpowers, but which was marked by many regional proxy conflicts.

> **Capitalism:** An economic system in which the means of production (land, factories, technology, etc.) are privately owned and operated according to the profit motive. Decisions about production, investment, and distribution are determined according to market forces (i.e. whether a profit can be made producing and marketing a product), rather than collective or community priorities.

> **Socialism:** The doctrine advocating economic equality of the classes and the use of government to serve the collective good of the whole society. Socialists value the collective good over the private interests of individuals and emphasize cooperation over competition. Socialists support a positive role for government in the economy. They advocate public ownership of key industries, regulation of the market, redistribution of resources, and protection of fundamental social rights and freedoms.

of their respective coalitions—the North Atlantic Treaty Organization, or NATO, in the case of the United States, and the Warsaw Pact, in the case of the Soviet Union—behaved following the logic of self-help under conditions of anarchy. Waltz went so far as to argue that because the international rivalry was bipolar (between two superpowers), this distribution of power and resources made the international system more stable than could be achieved under any other distribution of power and resources: both the United States and the Soviet Union were clear on who the enemy was, so both could focus their attention on protecting themselves from the threat presented by the other (see Box 16.1).

The focus on the centrality of the state and the importance of anarchy became defining characteristics of the study of International Relations. Because Realism seemed to be able to account for the persistence of the Cold War, it was lent theoretical credibility in the field. This does not mean, however, that there were no critiques of Realism, or that serious problems with this theoretical approach were not identified. One of the most powerful critiques raised argued that Realism best corresponded to an analysis of how a superpower might conduct its foreign policy. At one level, this is hardly surprising. Morgenthau's work was quite explicit in that respect; he saw his book as a manual for U.S. foreign policy

---

BOX 16.1

THE COLD WAR AND THE BALANCE OF POWER SYSTEM

For many Realists, the period of the Cold War (1945–1991) between the United States and the Soviet Union represented the classic example of the workings of the balance of power system fundamental, at least from their perspective, to international stability. The Cold War rivals differed in their systems of government: liberal democracy versus one-party rule, in their opposite understandings of the hierarchy of rights (individual rights, especially rights to property versus collective rights), and in their very different economic systems (a capitalist free market versus a centrally-planned economy, otherwise known as communism). These fundamental differences in world view or ideology set the stage for a global rivalry which largely defined international politics in the second half of the 20th century.

During the period of the Cold War, both the United States and the Soviet Union developed formal military alliances—NATO in the case of the United States, comprising most of the Western half of Europe and North America, and the Warsaw Pact in the case of the Soviet Union, comprising the eastern half of Europe. Each of these alliances represented a formidable military bloc targeting the other. Both the United States and the Soviet Union amassed huge stockpiles of nuclear weapons that targeted the military installations and major population centres of the opposite alliance. Estimates suggested that each side had enough nuclear fire power to destroy not only each other, but the world, many times over if the Cold War ever became a "hot" confrontation.

Despite the fact that the two superpowers conducted "proxy" wars through their client states in various areas of the world (especially Southeast Asia and Africa), the two superpowers and their alliances never engaged in a direct confrontation—although they did come close during the Cuban missile crisis of 1962. For a number of Realist scholars, the military power at the hands of each alliance and the threat that this power posed to the other contributed directly to stability between the two superpowers during the Cold War. The threat of "mutually assured destruction" (MAD) should one side launch a nuclear strike against the other was one the most significant reasons for this bipolar stability, as the Realist balance of power was equally a balance of terror. For such scholars, the fact that the Cold War was a bipolar rivalry also simplified things, because each of the superpowers always knew who the enemy was. When the Cold War ended with the collapse of the Soviet Union, John Mearsheimer lamented that "we will soon miss the Cold War" as the world moved toward what would be, in Realist eyes, a less stable multipolar system.

makers. *Power Among Nations* was radical for its day: Morgenthau was telling the United States that it needed to understand that all nation-states behave in the same way in the international system, and have the same basic national interest—survival. The political rhetoric that often accompanies international conflict (the demonization of the enemy, whether Adolph Hitler's Germany or Saddam Hussein's Iraq) was not helpful from Morgenthau's perspective. Such rhetoric tended to cloud the fact that all states want to protect themselves and ensure their survival, and that they will all take the steps they deem necessary to do so. Morgenthau wanted to teach American foreign policy makers to be prudent and to engage in wars only if national survival was truly at stake. (As such, Morgenthau was a passionate opponent of the U.S. intervention in Vietnam, which he did not believe could be justified on the grounds of national interest).

Over the decades, however, Realism had insisted upon its nature as positive theory, particularly when it evolved towards a structural understanding of state behaviour (whereby anarchy defined the parameters of state action). Positive theory tries to be general theory; Realism identified the "reality" of the international system (anarchy) and the necessary impact of anarchy on state behaviour. Realist theory claimed applicability to all states or, at the very least, to all great powers. This of course was a source of frustration for scholars who were *not* primarily interested in the foreign policy of the United States (or other larger powers). The stability of the bipolar period really depended on where you lived; it might have seemed to be a stable period if you lived in the United States or Canada or even Western Europe, but it looked a lot less stable to those living in any number of other countries where wars killed hundreds of thousands, if not millions, of people (Korea, Vietnam, Cambodia, Laos, Rwanda, Burundi, Nigeria, Bangladesh, Ethiopia, Afghanistan, Sudan . . . the list goes on). Realism, however, was interested in telling us that the *world* was stable in the bipolar era.[5]

Actors Other Than States

Other scholars reproached the Realists for their excessive focus on states as the primary actors in the international system. They pointed to a number of problems

with this premise, such as its inability to recognize the importance of **social movements** because of its unwillingness to treat domestic politics seriously. As a result, these critics argued, Realism was unable to predict the end of the Cold War—which seemed ironic given the importance of the Cold War in Realist thought. The lack of attention paid to social movements blinded many Realists to the social **revolutions** taking place in many Eastern European countries as well as in the Soviet Union at the end of the 1980s, just as some Realists have been surprised by the social revolutions taking place in a number of Middle Eastern and North African countries in 2011. These social movements, however, were critical to the evolution of the world's political and economic structures because their ability to push for fundamental political change effectively ended the Cold War.

> **Social movement:** An informal network of activists who seek to transform the values of society.

The lack of attention paid to social movements was not the only criticism levelled against the state-centricity of Realism. Its early unwillingness to take the global economy seriously limited its capacity to understand the power and influence of **transnational corporations** (many with annual budgets and revenues greater than those of a significant number of states, as noted in Chapter 1). Further, the lack of attention paid to the global economy, critics argued, led Realists to overstate the importance of the anarchic features of the international system; because trade and investment relations created powerful webs of interdependence between countries, the potential to constrain state behaviour (limiting the prospect of armed conflict between countries with largely interdependent economies, for example) existed. Focusing on the state, they argued, created an artificial "billiard-ball" model of International Relations and made it appear that states were hermetically sealed units, bumping into each other along their own independent trajectories. This

> **Transnational corporation:** Business firms that are headquartered in one country but have plants or places of operation around the world permitting them to integrate their business activities on a global scale.

model appeared to be increasingly and fundamentally incompatible with the growing interdependence of a **globalizing** world economy.

Social movements and patterns of economic exchange were not the only things marginalized by Realist theory, according to its critics. The events of

> **Globalization:** The movement of goods, capital, ideas, and people across geopolitical boundaries today and in the past. Contemporary patterns of globalization involve a deepening constellation of economic, technological, and cultural changes that are worldwide in scope and that challenge the sovereignty of the state; a process that is leading to ever closer economic relations among the countries of the world, based on increased trade, foreign direct investment, activity by multinational corporations, and financial flows.

Terrorism in New York City, September 11, 2001.

The Canadian Press(Todd Hollis)

September 11, 2001 underscored the extent to which states were not the only international actors capable of deploying deadly force. The international webs of the **terrorist** network Al-Qaeda could not be easily understood in statist terms, although the international community reacted militarily against one state (Afghanistan) in seeking to avenge the attacks on the United States. Both Realist theory and the foreign policy actions of states seemed to have difficulty moving beyond the state centricity of their understanding of the relationship between states and the global distribution of power. For many scholars, Realism's difficulty in responding to an evolving global reality was due to the fact that, in its essence, it was a theory of great power politics that responded to the interests of those powers when it argued that great powers were necessary to the stability of the international system. In response to Cox's observation that theory is always for someone and something, Realism appeared to be a theory for the status quo defined in terms of the unequal distribution of resources and power between states. While Realism has been able to integrate some of these criticisms in order to broaden its focus, other issues still remain.

> **Terrorism:** The threat or use of violence, usually directed at civilian populations, in order to create some form of political change.

ORDER AND ANARCHY

As we noted, the original Realist premise was based on the idea that the true nature of states existing in an anarchic international system precluded their ability to cooperate over any significant period of time. States, Realists argued, would cooperate but only so long as this cooperation was seen to be in their national interest. As soon as cooperation no longer responded to the national interest, states would defect and leave the international organizations to which they belonged. The prospects for **international organizations**, therefore, seemed quite slim—at least, from a Realist perspective. Despite this, however, international organizations multiplied

> **International organization:** An organization, such as the United Nations, the WTO, or NATO, whose members are typically sovereign states.

in the period after World War II. The **United Nations** was created (although through the attribution of a veto in the Security Council to the post-World War II great powers, the United Nations exempted certain states from the obligation of respecting the will of the broader international community) and a host of specialized agencies were brought under the UN's umbrella, each endeavouring in a specific sphere of international activity (global health, children's welfare, the rights of women, aviation, the global environment, the AIDS pandemic, among many others), (see Figure 16.1, p. 426). While the Security Council of the United Nations has not always been able to act (or to prevent the action of one of its members), the UN specialized agencies have demonstrated the extent to which states are able to cooperate along a vast range of issues in order to favour the achievement of transnational solutions. Further, the network of international financial organizations created in the post-war period known collectively as the Bretton Woods organizations (the **World Bank** and the network of regional development banks; the **International Monetary Fund**; the General Agreement on Tariffs and Trade, later supplanted by the **World Trade Organization**) were *not* predicated on a vision of the international system defined by anarchy but rather on an understanding of international relations as a system of rules, patterns of behaviour, expectations, and norms that could and should be enshrined in international organizations.

> **United Nations:** An international organization formed in 1945 as a successor to the League of Nations; it has become the largest and most ambitious international governmental organization in world history, consisting of a vast array of organs and agencies. Its membership now includes almost every country in the world. Less than a world government, it attempts to promote peaceful relations among states and economic and human rights for all people.

Liberal Theories: International Cooperation

More than this, however, the post-war period also witnessed the growth of regional economic organizations which not only sought to define and codify the rules of exchange in a specific geographical region, but which also attempted to facilitate greater exchange and integration within that region. The progression of integration in Europe, beginning with the establishment of the European Coal and Steel Community, through to the creation of the European Economic Community, and, finally, to the ongoing expansion and deepening of integration in the **European Union**, appeared to demonstrate that the international system might be structured by something more than anarchy. Inspired by the pioneering work of theorists David Mitrany[6] and Ernst Haas[7] (who developed the theory of functionalism in International Relations), Liberal theorists argued that international organizations could not only codify or embed cooperative norms; they could also seek to advance or extend greater cooperation between states.

For these theorists, states were not the only significant actors on the international stage; international organizations could be just as, and perhaps more, important than states. Mitrany, writing in *A Working Peace System* (first published as a pamphlet in 1943), saw states as an obstacle to cooperation or peace in the international system. In this respect, Mitrany's understanding of the consequences of the "true nature" of states was not widely different from that proposed by Morgenthau. Where Mitrany differed, however, was in his belief that citizens and bureaucrats could understand the merits of transnational cooperation better than the political leadership of states could. A certain number of problems require international solutions, Mitrany argued, and people know this. But it is not important that they be carried out by any one specific actor. As a result, people will pressure states to collaborate, and those bureaucrats charged with moving such collaboration forward will begin to realize the virtues of international cooperation in carrying out necessary functions. For Mitrany, the issues most apt to be resolved through international cooperation, at least at the outset, were those that were not deemed to be "political"—issues of health and welfare, for example. Mitrany appeared to be arguing that while there was little to be done with the state's obsession over the "high politics" of conflict, much cooperation could and did take place under the surface in those areas of everyday life of most interest to ordinary citizens. Over time, the habits and benefits of cooperation would become ever more apparent and state power

Figure 16.1   The United Nations System

Main Committees
Standing Committees
Other Ad Hoc Subsidiary Organs

Trusteeship Council

Security Council

MINURSO
MONUC
UNAMSIL
UNDOF
UNFICYP
UNIFIL
UNIKOM
UNMEE
UNMIBH
UNMIK
UNMOGIP
UNMOP
UNOMIG
UNTAET
UNTSO

Military Staff Committee
Standing Committees
Ad Hoc Committees

International Court of Justice

General Assembly

Secretariat

MICAH
MINUGUA
UNRWA

IAEA

INSTRAW
UNCHS/HABITAT
UNCTAD
UNDP
UNEP
UNFPA
UNHCR
UNICEF
UNITAR
UNU
UNV

Economic and Social Council

Regional Commissions
Functional Commissions
Other Committees

FAO
ICAO
IFAO
ILO
IMF
IMO
ITU
UNESCO
UNIDO
UPU
WHO
WIPO
WMO
World Bank
WTO

IDA
IBRD
IFC

WFP

N.B. The establishment of an International Criminal Court was approved in July 1998 at a UN conference, but is not included on this chart.

- ● Principal organs of the United Nations
- ○ United Nations programs and organs
- ● Specialized agencies and other autonomous organizations within the system

Source: United Nations, "The United Nations System," available at http://www.un.org/aboutun/chart_en.pdf; accessed June 11, 2008.

would become marginal by comparison to the extensive webs of international cooperation.

For Ernst Haas, writing more specifically about the prospects of European integration, politics could not so easily be separated from economics or other spheres of human activity—*all* spheres were inherently political. For Haas, though, this was not an obstacle to cooperation or integration because states could genuinely choose to collaborate. The European project was not one in which states had stood aside as bystanders, but rather one in which states had been active participants, choosing to "share" power with a regional organization and to cede authority where it made sense to do so according to both national and regional interests. Cooperation rather than conflict was the key to prosperity and growth, and cooperation was a source of predictability and order in the international system, even if, for some, anarchy remained an underlying feature of the system.

As with the Realists, Liberal theorists were and are interested in providing solutions to the problem of how to make the existing international structure function more effectively. This is hardly a bad thing, and is in fact what most positive theory in International Relations attempts to do. Robert Cox named this positive theory "problem-solving theory." Problem-solving theory "takes the world as it finds it, with the prevailing social and power relationships and the institutions into which they are organized, as the given framework for action. The general aim of problem-solving is to make these relationships and institutions work smoothly by dealing effectively with particular sources of trouble."[8] Liberals try to theorize the ways in which states can cooperate more effectively, but they do not question the relationships and institutions in which such cooperation takes place. The fact that cooperation may work to deepen patterns of inequality, exploitation, and injustice, as scholars in some developing countries would argue has been the result of international financial and economic cooperation, goes beyond the scope of problem-solving theory—which in this case is to enhance the prospects for cooperation (see Box 16.2).

BOX 16.2

THE TECHNICAL SIDE OF THE UNITED NATIONS SYSTEM

As Liberal theorists such as David Mitrany suggest, international cooperation has been possible and successful in a number of areas that might be considered to be more "technical" in nature. The United Nations system currently includes 15 of these agencies, known as specialized agencies, which reflect the compartmentalization of international relations into a large number of specialized areas. These agencies are generally less well known than the United Nations General Assembly or the Security Council and yet they arguably have been more significant to the day-to-day functioning of international affairs than either of these two much more explicitly political bodies. Two of these organizations, the ICAO and the WHO are profiled below but a list of all 15 agencies can be found at http://www.un.org/en/aboutun/structure.

The International Civil Aviation Organization (ICAO) is headquartered in Montreal. Formally established in 1947 (although an interim agency existed between 1945 and 1947), the ICAO is responsible for the development of procedures and regulations governing international civil aviation, including "generally applicable rules and regulations concerning training and licensing of aeronautical personnel both in the air and on the ground, communication systems and procedures, rules for the air and air traffic control systems and practices, airworthiness requirements for aircraft engaged in international air navigation as well as their registration and identification, aeronautical meteorology and maps and charts" (http://www.icao.int/cgi/goto_m.pl?icao/en/hist/history02.htm).

The rules and regulations the ICAO developed enabled air navigation to become truly international—not to mention that these rules ensure that commercial aircraft from everywhere in the world do not run into each other in flight! The ICAO establishes procedures permitting the orderly growth of

(continued)

BOX 16.2

BOX 16.2

THE TECHNICAL SIDE OF THE UNITED NATIONS SYSTEM (CONTINUED)

an international air transport system to which all countries with a commercial aviation industry belong.

The World Health Organization (WHO) is another example of a specialized agency that has proven very significant to the functioning of the international system since its creation. Created in 1948, it is the public health arm of the United Nations system. At the first World Health Assembly held in June 1948, leaders agreed that the WHO's priorities would be malaria, women's and children's health, tuberculosis, venereal disease, nutrition, and environmental sanitation. Many of these issues are still relevant today, although the WHO's work has also grown to cover health problems that were not known in 1948, including relatively new diseases such as HIV/AIDS. The WHO also sends response teams to contain the outbreak of disease (such as during the SARS epidemic that affected Toronto in 2002), provides emergency assistance to people affected by disasters, and organizes mass immunization campaigns to protect children from disease.

The WHO also does work which is less visible, including monitoring health trends throughout the world in order to inform the development of public policy and establishing a single international name for drugs so that individuals can be assured that prescriptions filled away from home will be what the doctor ordered (http://www.who.int/about/brochure_en.pdf).

Marxist Theory

It should come as no surprise, given that both theoretical approaches are preoccupied with making the "problem" of conflict and disorder a less threatening one, that certain Realist and Liberal theorists have been able to forge some common ground in a debate over the extent to which national interest permits cooperation even under conditions of anarchy. Other theorists concerned with patterns of economic exchange have rejected entirely the notion that the international system can ever be seen as defined by anarchy. These scholars, inspired by more radical **Marxist** and neo-Marxist writings, have argued that the world is not anarchic—it is capitalist. Further, these authors contend that the capitalist system of exchange has implied clear rules and patterns, supported by states but not defined by them. Rather, capitalist interests (the interests of large firms and banks, for example), have worked together with states to structure an international system that would be most profitable to their economic and political interests.

Immanuel Wallerstein produced a very important three-volume work (*The Modern World-System*)[9] arguing that global capitalism defined the nature of the modern international system. The exchange relationships embedded within the capitalist world-system were unequal, however, and contributed not only to the creation of rich and poorer regions in the world, but equally to their maintenance. Wallerstein argued that countries of the wealthy centre (the developed countries) remained wealthy because they benefited from a pattern of unequal exchange with poorer countries (countries of the periphery, or less developed countries). Countries of the semi-periphery situated themselves somewhere between these two extremes and shared some of the characteristics of wealthier economies (some industrial production, for example) as well as some of the characteristics of the periphery (such as a heavy dependence on resource extraction). For Wallerstein, the primary role of the semi-periphery was political: to mitigate the potential for conflict between the centre and the periphery, since the semi-periphery made it appear that it might be possible to progress from one category (the periphery) to another (the centre). These issues were also addressed in Chapter 4 and 14.

Wallerstein's Marxist theory of the international system was heavily criticized as being static and largely incapable of explaining the emergence of dynamic economies in what has been labelled the "developing world" (economies such as Singapore, South Korea and Thailand, for example). His contribution was influential in International Relations, however, in so far as it reminded scholars that Realists had not developed the first theory of conflict in the international system—Marxists had. Well before Morgenthau, Marxist scholars—from Rosa Luxembourg to Lenin—were arguing that war was the natural consequence of rivalry between capitalist countries seeking to expand in order to find new markets and new wealth in the interests of their national capitalist classes. Here, conflict was not the product of anarchy but was the inevitable result of capitalist expansion.

Marxist-inspired Theory

Marxist-inspired theory has moved far beyond Wallerstein's contributions. Work of scholars such as Robert Cox (his most influential book is *Production, Power and World Order*)[10], moved beyond the static portrait painted by Wallerstein to explore the relationships between forms of capitalist production, forms of state power, and forms of world order. Cox brings international organizations squarely into focus in his analysis, and he identifies them as the crystallization of moments of hegemony. Where Realists will speak of the hegemony of states, however, Cox will speak of the hegemony of dominant classes working with and through dominant states. The international financial institutions created after World War II, therefore, represent particular patterns of hegemonic consensus (the principles of non-discrimination and reciprocity in international trade, for example). This hegemonic consensus permitted not only the systemic hegemon (the United States) to reap the rewards of trade liberalization, but also permitted other states (such as Canada) and their dominant social classes, wholly integrated into the American economic system, to benefit as well. The threat of conflict, always present in Wallerstein's scholarship as well as that of earlier Marxists, is considerably muted here, as Cox reminds us of the power and influence of these institutionalized international norms. As long as they represent a hegemonic consensus, they do not need to be backed up by the threat of force because they are seen as normal and inevitable. While this radical scholarship differs

substantially from that of both the Realists and the Liberals in that it is explicitly normative, asking whose interests are being supported by a particular configuration of world order (rather than assuming that the order of the international system is simply a given), Cox's work reminds us that even when an order is working to the advantage of particular interests, those who are disadvantaged might well simply accept the situation as normal or as one for which there is no alternative. Cox's work, as well as the work of other critical scholars, was reflective of a trend to normative, or "critical theory," rather than problem-solving theory. Critical theory "is critical in the sense that it stands apart from the prevailing order of the world and asks how that order came about. Critical theory, unlike problem-solving theory, does not take institutions and social and power relations for granted but calls them into question by concerning itself with their origins and how and whether they might be in the process of changing."[11] The explicitly normative focus of this critical scholarship underscored the extent to which its objectives were not defined in terms of the maintenance of the status quo.

While Marxist scholarship in International Relations has, in some respects, been transcended by a new generation of scholarship (some of which we will discuss in the next section of this chapter, looking particularly at the contributions of feminist scholarship in International Relations), the insights of Marxist scholarship continue to resonate in some aspects of international practice. Just as Realism continues to capture some elements of great power foreign policy and Liberalism contributes to our understanding of some processes relating to integration and regional cooperation, Marxist-inspired theories provide a lens through which we can assess the evolution of aspects of the relationship between developed and developing economies. The Doha Round of trade negotiations launched in 2001 under the auspices of the World Trade Organization (WTO), for example, became known as the "Doha Development Round" or the "Doha Development Agenda" under pressure from developing countries trying to push for trade rules that would be fairer to their economies. Underlying this pressure was the analysis by a significant bloc of developing countries that the trading system has worked to entrench the

Children drive a donkey cart through the Otash refugee camp in Darfur, Sudan. Having fled there to avoid violence, they were under increasing pressure to leave.

AP Photo/Alfred de Montesquiou

interests of the industrialized world and to ensure that developed economies would continue to prosper disproportionately from international trade when compared to developing countries, notably, but not exclusively, in agricultural trade. For these countries, the problem of the international system is hardly the instability that is the consequence of anarchy; rather, it is the *stability* of international trade rules and practices that have consistently discriminated against developing economies and ensured that the benefits of capitalism returned to the rich.

INJUSTICE AND EQUALITY

Marxist-inspired theories of International Relations are explicitly normative and critical; in identifying the interests that are served by the workings of the international capitalist system they also identify those segments of the global economy that suffer in the bargain. Their insights lead them to point to injustice and inequality as being a fundamental feature of the international system and a consequence of the workings of global capitalism. International policy efforts, for these authors, must be targeted towards reducing the inequalities (in the short, "problem-solving" term) and planning for system transformation in the longer term. The normative component of Marxist-inspired theories is much easier to identify than in Realist or Liberal theories, since Marxist theories are explicit about their normative concerns.

Over the past two decades, International Relations theory has seen an important normative turn with the advent of many different critical approaches to the study of IR. Inspired in part by the Marxist concern for inequality and injustice, various schools of thought new to International Relations have begun to make their mark. What unites these theories is a concern with injustice, as well as the way in which the practice of international relations is represented in speeches, media reports, television images, and popular culture. For these critical scholars, the study of International Relations must be concerned with far more than state-to-state relations, the role of international organizations, or the formal workings of the global economy. The practice of international relations is made possible and is sustained by the ways in which the world and those within it are represented. Where international practices produce injustice or inequalities, these are caused, permitted, and sustained by the representations of what is "normal" practice in International Relations. This common orientation of critical scholarship brings us back to the beginning of the chapter; if facts cannot speak for themselves, how do we understand them through theory. In other words, how do we make them speak? Further, since we are making the facts speak, should we not listen to what the theories are saying when we do so? After all, our theories help to construct the prevalent interpretations of the world. In order to examine some of the ways in which this is done, we will turn our attention to some of the feminist interventions in the field of International Relations, all the while recognizing that this represents but one of the critical turns in International Relations.

Feminist Approaches

Feminist scholars of International Relations began by asking a series of questions about where women are to be found in international politics and economics (why are so few leaders, foreign

Feminism: A belief in the full equality of men and women and the insistence that all barriers to such equality be removed.

ministers, generals, and diplomats women)? Realist International Relations included very few spaces to speak about people but there was never any doubt that the individuals who "counted" in international practice (the above mentioned leaders, foreign ministers, generals, and diplomats) were largely men. More specifically, pioneering scholars such as Cynthia Enloe[12] asked if the places in which women are more often found (from the household to the brothel) sustain International Relations, and if so, how it is that women are also made invisible by the same theories of International Relations? For example, many feminist scholars have argued that the war-making capacity of states could not be sustained if mothers were not prepared to allow their children (mostly their sons) to enlist in the military to be sent off to war. The willingness of mothers to do so makes women an integral part of the foreign policy machinery of states; however, when we speak about the military we tend not to mention the women who bear, nurture, and raise the manpower staffing those very military forces. The wives of diplomats have played and continue to play a substantial role—at no cost to the public purse—in the intricacies of the state's foreign representational

activities.[13] Spouses (read: wives) are seen as part of the "package deal" when a man—the husband—is posted abroad to represent his country. (Despite the increasing number of women in the foreign service, spouses are still understood to be women who are largely occupied with the task of raising children at home—to the profound frustration of the men who are following their diplomatic wives abroad).[14] The (unpaid) labour of the spouse is assumed and is neither compensated nor remarked upon in an analysis of International Relations, despite the fact that international diplomatic practice could not function (at least not at the highest levels) without the spouse.

Gender and Race

In a similar way, international financial negotiations to restructure developing economies in order to enable them to service their debt are not only about arrangements made between national leaders and international financial institutions. The very success of these austerity and restructuring measures depends on the capacity of women—with disproportionate responsibilities for household management—to absorb the additional burdens that will result from cutbacks in social spending.[15] Authors such as Marianne Marchand have pointed to the ways in which globalization is itself premised on a gendered and **racialized** division of labour. The image of the (mainly white male) risk-taking captains and warriors of the global financial industry (even if their risks are sometimes too great, as the 2008–2010 financial crisis revealed) conceals the extent to which this industry depends on an "internationalized service economy in both the public and private spheres." These services are characterized by large numbers of migrant (non-white) women employed in the world's financial centres as domestic help and nannies, and by (non-white) migrant men who clean the offices of financial institutions, mostly overnight or who work in low-paying jobs as data-entry clerks for these institutions' offshore offices.[16] International Relations, however, both as an academic discipline and as political and economic practice in the "real world," makes these racialized women and men invisible, even in discussions of

Mary Robinson, former President of Ireland; Margot Wallstrom, Vice President of the European Commission; Kim Campbell, former Prime Minister of Canada; and Jenny Shipley, former Prime Minister of New Zealand at the International Women Leaders Global Security Summit in New York, November 2007, evaluate meaningful strategies for global security.

AP Photo/The Canadian Press(David Karp)

global financial restructuring and globalization. It does not ask how the financial warriors with all their riches and the financial institutions they lead depend on an invisible racialized and gendered class of people earning very little indeed. While Marxist-inspired International Relations theorists pose questions about which **classes** are exploited in global capitalist exchange, they have had less to say about the extent to which such exploitation and inequality is also a function of gender and race, rather than exclusively or predominantly one of class.

Beyond asking where the women are in the practice of international politics, however, feminist critical scholars have also pointed to the ways in which the representations of International Relations are themselves profoundly gendered. Addressing Realist theory, for example, Ann Tickner has raised the issue of the extent to which Hans Morgenthau's principles of Realism reflect a masculinist understanding of the world. While Tickner takes on all

aspects of Morgenthau's theorizing, we will limit ourselves to the discussion of only part of his theoretical framework, that which looks at power. Morgenthau's conception of power as the control of man over man, Tickner argues, represents a very narrow understanding of power typically associated with masculinity. Yet this is not the only understanding of power possible. She identifies other ways in which power has been understood: as the human ability to act in concert, or as persuasion and coalition-building.[17] These are collaborative behaviours that lead to positive outcomes and those who are able to encourage such collaborative behaviours demonstrate a form of power often associated (because of its non-combative nature) with women. Yet this understanding of power is completely absent from Morgenthau's discussion of International Relations; power is control and domination, not collaboration and persuasion. For an account of the importance of gender on the international agenda, see Box 16.3.

BOX 16.3

THE STATUS OF WOMEN AS AN INTERNATIONAL ISSUE

The United Nations system, pressured by many women's organizations working both with the UN and as critics of it, has worked to address the issues surrounding the status of women internationally. In 1975 the United Nations observed the first International Women's Year and held the first of four UN conferences on women in Mexico City. The Mexico City conference was held to remind the world that discrimination against women continued to be a problem in most areas of the world. In addition to leading to the declaration of the United Nations Decade for Women (1976–1985), the Mexico City conference launched a new global dialogue on gender equality. In particular, the United Nations General Assembly identified three key objectives that would become the basis for the work of the United Nations on behalf of women: (1) full gender equality and the elimination of gender discrimination, (2) the integration and full participation of women in development, and (3) an increased contribution by women in the strengthening of world peace (http://www.5wwc.org/conference_background/1975_WCW.html).

In 1980 the Second World Conference on Women was held in Copenhagen. Halfway through the UN Decade for Women, this conference was spurred by the adoption by the General Assembly in late 1979 of the United Nations Convention on Elimination of All Forms of Discrimination Against Women (CEDAW), a very powerful international instrument for women's equality. Despite this important milestone, however, the Copenhagen conference noted a significant gap between the legal breakthroughs in favour of women's equality internationally and the practical ability of women to exercise these rights. As such, the conference built upon the general areas identified as the basis for work stemming from Mexico City by adding three specific areas where action needed to be taken if the goal of women's equality was to be reached: (1) equal access to education,

(continued)

BOX 16.3

THE STATUS OF WOMEN AS AN INTERNATIONAL ISSUE (CONTINUED)

(2) employment opportunities, and (3) health care services (http://www.5wwc.org/conference_background/1980_WCW.html).

The 1985 Third World Conference on Women, held in Nairobi, Kenya, unleashed a powerful push for women's rights. Observing that NGOs championing women's rights and women's equality were increasing in numbers and scope, the conference hosted 1,400 official delegates and 15,000 NGO delegates. The issue of violence against women was given focused attention as an essential component of the promotion and maintenance of peace internationally. The Nairobi Conference established a set of Forward Looking Strategies to address outstanding obstacles in the path of women's equality—and it was notable for the fact that the 157 governments participating put their many differences aside and unanimously adopted these strategies (http://www.5wwc.org/conference_background/1985_WCW.html).

The impetus provided by the Nairobi Conference laid the groundwork for the Fourth World Conference on Women in 1995, better known as the Beijing Conference. This was the most important, most influential of the world conferences on women, and it was attended by nearly 180 government delegations and 2,500 NGO delegations. The Beijing Platform for Action laid out twelve critical areas for concern:

1. The persistent and increasing burden of poverty on women
2. Unequal access to and inadequate educational opportunities
3. Inequalities in health status, and unequal access to and inadequate health-care services
4. Violence against women
5. Effects of armed or other kinds of conflict on women
6. Inequality in women's access to and participation in the definition of economic structures and policies and the production process itself
7. Inequality between men and women in the sharing of power and decision-making at all levels
8. Insufficient mechanisms at all levels to promote the advancement of women
9. Lack of awareness of and commitment to internationally and nationally recognized women's human rights
10. Insufficient mobilization of mass media to promote women's positive contribution to society
11. Lack of adequate recognition and support for women's contribution to managing natural resources and safeguarding the environment
12. The girl-child (http://www.5wwc.org/conference_background/Beijing_Platform.html)

The Beijing Declaration set out clear objectives and commitments on behalf of international organizations and national governments to address the critical areas for concern. In so doing, the Beijing Declaration provided a global benchmark against which policies for women's equality are measured. Five-year annual reviews of the international community's progress in meeting the Beijing commitments have been held (known as Beijing +5, +10, +15). Since 2006, pressure has been increasing from the global women's NGO community to convene a 5th World Conference on Women (http://5WCW.org/) rather than holding a Beijing +20 conference.

Other feminist scholars have looked at the ways in which international politics and economics are represented in the public sphere in very gendered ways. For example, Sandra Whitworth has brought an important feminist contribution to those scholars interested in critical security studies. Emerging after the end of the Cold War, critical security studies began to ask if the state was the only, or even the most important, object of security (as was the clear consensus in Realist analyses of International Relations). Who should be secured? The state? Privileged groups? All people? And from what should they be secured? Finally, who gets to decide what constitutes a security threat, what does not, and who is the object of security?[18] Whitworth's study of **peacekeeping** picks up on these questions in order to raise fundamentally political concerns about the nature of peacekeeping and the contradictions upon which it rests. She contrasts the way in which peacekeeping is represented, not only in Canada but also internationally, as "benign and altruistic," with the reality that peacekeeping is performed by soldiers who have been taught to kill.[19] This contradiction, Whitworth describes, is the result of the incoherence between "the messages a soldier receives about appropriately masculine soldierly behaviour" and peace operations (often with restrictions imposed as to the use of force) which are neither fully nor properly militaristic.[20]

Whitworth's inquiry, therefore, goes beyond the traditional questions of International Relations in that it asks how our understandings of what it is to be masculine (and feminine) inform the military and military operations, and what happens when the representations of gender and the expectations of appropriate militarized gender roles do not coincide with the mission on the ground. Gender here is not so much about women and men as biological subjects, but about the way in which representations of what it is to be "masculine" in the military have practical consequences. These are illustrated in Whitworth's study, whether in the outburst of sexualized or racialized violence by military troops, or in the increase in cases of post-traumatic stress disorder (PTSD) in soldiers who have not been able to respond to violence in the defensive ways in which they have been trained as soldiers because the peace mission cannot and does not permit it. These practical consequences raise real questions about who is being made secure in International Relations. Using gender or race as a prism through which to view International Relations both as a field of study and as an international "reality" leads us to pose questions about the way in which we construct what is legitimate and what is not on the

international stage, as well as the consequences of so doing. What are the injustices and inequalities that are perpetuated by maintaining specific gendered or racialized ideas of what is appropriate and legitimate or not?

CONCLUSION

As we have seen, International Relations as a field of study is characterized by a series of different theoretical interventions in the study of the international arena. These theories put their emphasis on states, anarchy, and power, or on collaboration and order, or on justice and inequality (through examinations of class, gender, or race, for example). In a field of study as complex as International Relations, it is no surprise that the number of theories far surpass those few we have been able to examine here. The point of this chapter has not been to provide a comprehensive listing of the various approaches to International Relations, however, but rather to highlight the way in which the discipline evolves through theoretical debate. These theories structure the way we understand the world and therefore colour our understanding of what is possible in that world.

As Cox reminds us, theory is always for someone and for some purpose, and his observation heightens the distinction between positive (problem-solving) and normative (critical) theory. As the field of International Relations has evolved and broadened its scope, normative or critical theory has begun to play a greater role. This form of theorizing turns the discipline on its head because instead of trying to develop theories that explain the world the way it *is*, critical theory asks us to think of the consequences of the way we theorize or represent the world to ourselves. If our theories blind us to the way in which the international system produces and sustains patterns of class, racial, and gender inequalities (among others), or habits of environmental exploitation and degradation, our theories are complicit in perpetuating the very injustices we as scholars should strive to overcome. As Steve Smith argues, "International Relations theory has concentrated almost exclusively on a particular world of international relations, and that has not been a world that most of the world's population could relate to. Their concerns, the violences that affected them, the inequalities they suffered, were all invisible to the gaze of the discipline, and in that very specific way the discipline, my discipline, my work, was culpable in serving specific social interests and explaining their agenda."[21] While the critical or normative turn in International Relations does not make the discipline more coherent or less messy, it can be hoped that it contributes to a greater ethic of responsibility and theoretical humility. The world as it *is*, is also the world as we make it.

DISCUSSION QUESTIONS

1. Did the Cold War contribute to global stability? What promotes international stability in the world today?

2. Do you agree with the Realist theory of International Relations? Why or why not?

3. How realistic is the Liberal theory that emphasizes international cooperation? Do the functional accomplishments of the United Nations justify its existence?

4. To what extent do Marxist and Marxist-inspired theories explain International Relations?

5. What has the feminist approach added to the study of International Relations?

FURTHER READING

Buzan, Barry, and Lene Hansen. *The Evolution of International Security Studies*. Cambridge: Cambridge University Press, 2009.

Cox, Robert W. *Production, Power and World Order: Social Forces in the Making of History*. New York: Columbia University Press, 1987.

Cox, Robert W. "Social Forces, States and World Orders: Beyond International Relations Theory," *Millennium: Journal of International Studies* 10 (2) (1981): 128.

Donaghy, Greg, and Kim Richard Nossal, eds. *Architects and Innovators: Building the*

Department of Foreign Affairs and International Trade, 1909–2009. Montreal and Kingston: McGill-Queen's University Press, 2009.

Enloe, Cynthia H. *Bananas, Beaches and Bases: Making Feminist Sense of International Politics*. Berkeley: University of California Press, 1990.

Haas, Ernst B. *Beyond the Nation-State: Functionalism and International Organization*. Palo Alto, CA: Stanford University Press, 1968.

Mitrany, David. *A Working Peace System*. Chicago: Quadrangle Books, 1966.

Morgenthau, Hans J. *Politics among Nations: The Struggle for Power and Peace*, 5th ed. New York: Knopf, 1978 (first published in 1948).

Smith, Steve. "Singing Our World into Existence: International Relations Theory and September 11," *International Studies Quarterly* 48 (3) (2004): 514.

Tickner, J. Ann. "Hans Morgenthau's Principles of Political Realism: A Feminist Reformulation," *Millennium: Journal of International Studies* 17 (3) (December 1988): 434.

Turenne Sjolander, Claire. "Adding Women but Forgetting to Stir: Gender and Foreign Policy in the Mulroney Era," in Kim Richard Nossal and Nelson Michaud, eds., *Diplomatic Departures: The Conservative Era in Canadian Foreign Policy*. Vancouver: UBC Press, 2001.

Kenneth N. Waltz, *Theory of International Politics*. New York: Random House, 1979.

ENDNOTES

1. Robert W. Cox, "Social Forces, States and World Orders: Beyond International Relations Theory," *Millennium: Journal of International Studies* 10 (2) (1981): 128.

2. Woodrow Wilson, "Fourteen Points: President Woodrow Wilson's Address before a Joint Session of the United States Congress, January

8, 1918," *Virginia Center for Digital History,* available at http://www.vcdh.virginia.edu/solguide/VUS09/vus09b05.html; accessed March 9, 2011.

3. Hans J. Morgenthau, *Politics among Nations: The Struggle for Power and Peace,* 5th ed. (New York: Knopf, 1978; first published in 1948).

4. Kenneth N. Waltz, *Theory of International Politics* (New York: Random House, 1979).

5. See, for example, John J. Mearsheimer, "Why We Will Soon Miss the Cold War," *The Atlantic Monthly* 266 (2) (August 1990).

6. David Mitrany, *A Working Peace System* (Chicago: Quadrangle Books, 1966).

7. Ernst B. Haas, *Beyond the Nation-State: Functionalism and International Organization* (Palo Alto, CA: Stanford University Press, 1968).

8. Cox, "Social Forces, States and World Orders: Beyond International Relations Theory," pp. 128–29.

9. Immanuel Wallerstein, *The Modern World-System, Vol. I: Capitalist Agriculture and the Origins of the European World-Economy in the Sixteenth Century* (New York/London: Academic Press, 1974); *The Modern World-System, Vol. II: Mercantilism and the Consolidation of the European World-Economy, 1600–1750* (New York: Academic Press, 1980); *The Modern World-System, Vol. III: The Second Great Expansion of the Capitalist World-Economy, 1730–1840s* (San Diego: Academic Press, 1989).

10. Robert W. Cox, *Production, Power and World Order: Social Forces in the Making of History* (New York: Columbia University Press, 1987).

11. Cox, "Social Forces, States and World Orders: Beyond International Relations Theory," p. 129.

12. See, in particular, Cynthia H. Enloe, *Bananas, Beaches and Bases: Making Feminist Sense of International Politics* (Berkeley: University of California Press, 1990).

13. See, for example, Cynthia H. Enloe, "Diplomatic Wives," *Bananas, Beaches and Bases: Making Feminist Sense of International Politics*; for a Canadian take on the question, see Claire Turenne Sjolander, "Adding Women but Forgetting to Stir: Gender and Foreign Policy in the Mulroney Era," in Kim Richard Nossal and Nelson Michaud, eds., *Diplomatic Departures: The Conservative Era in Canadian Foreign Policy* (Vancouver: UBC Press, 2001).

14. See Claire Turenne Sjolander, "Margaret Meagher and the Role of Women in the Foreign Service: Groundbreaking or Housekeeping?" in Greg Donaghy and Kim Richard Nossal, eds., *Architects and Innovators: Building the Department of Foreign Affairs and International Trade, 1909–2009* (Montreal and Kingston: McGill-Queen's University Press, 2009).

15. Cynthia H. Enloe, "Just Like of the Family: Domestic Workers in World Politics," *Bananas, Beaches and Bases: Making Feminist Sense of International Politics*, pp. 184–85.

16. Marianne Marchand, "Gendered Representations of the 'Global': Reading/Writing Globalization," in Richard Stubbs and Geoffrey Underhill, eds., *Political Economy and the Changing Global Order* (Toronto: Oxford University Press, 2000), p. 223.

17. J. Ann Tickner, "Hans Morgenthau's Principles of Political Realism: A Feminist Reformulation," *Millennium: Journal of International Studies* 17 (3) (December 1988): 434.

18. For a summary of the changes in the field of security studies, see, for example, Barry Buzan and Lene Hansen, *The Evolution of International Security Studies* (Cambridge: Cambridge University Press, 2009).

19. Sandra Whitworth, *Men, Militarism and UN Peacekeeping: A Gendered Analysis* (Boulder, CO: Lynne Rienner Publishers, 2004), pp. 183–87.

20. *Ibid.*, p. 16.

21. Steve Smith, "Singing Our World into Existence: International Relations Theory and September 11," *International Studies Quarterly* 48 (3) (2004): 514.

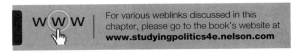

The Politics of Globalization

William D. Coleman

CHAPTER OBJECTIVES

After you have completed this chapter, you should be able to:

- define globalization and assess the degree to which globalization is taking place in a domain of the economy, culture, or politics

- assess how politics at the global and local levels are increasingly intertwined

- evaluate how the role of the nation-state might be changing as a result of globalization

- identify four challenges to accountability and legitimacy posed by globalization.

INTRODUCTION

Over the past several decades, processes now termed *globalization* have been steadily reshaping how many of us live and relate to others across the world. They are reducing many limits on the interactions between individuals and communities once imposed by physical location. They are destabilizing existing centres of authority and security such as nation-states, with new centres emerging at various scales of social life, from global down to local levels. The organization and scope of markets and the production and diffusion of cultural forms, like movies and literature, and practices, like the choices of foods, have taken on even more global dimensions. Many concerned citizens the world over have mobilized politically in order to oppose or reshape some of the changes involved. The changes are potentially so profound that they may be altering some of the basic elements of the human condition.

One of the most basic of these elements is autonomy. The term *autonomy* is used in two ways. First, it refers to the situations of individual persons and usually to their capacity to shape the conditions under which they live.[1] It is also used in connection with collective bodies, such as **nation-states**, minority groups within states, indigenous peoples, and religious movements. In this collective sense, autonomy usually means something closer to the Greek roots of the term: the capacity to give oneself laws. Individual and collective autonomy are linked and globalization shapes these linkages in important ways. Protesters have gathered in the streets at meetings of major global institutions over the past few years to register their worries about a loss of control over their lives. These worries extend, however, well beyond these street protests. Concerned about collective autonomy, African political leaders note the increased marginalization of their economies and societies in the world system. Peasants throughout the Global South countries and many workers in manufacturing sectors such as auto-making in wealthy countries see international trade rules as inevitably bringing an end to what individual autonomy they might have had. Ministers responsible for culture in countries outside the United States have formed a worldwide alliance in pursuit of the preservation of collective autonomy in the cultural realm in the face of such U.S. corporations as Disney and McDonald's. Fears have become more widespread about climate change and about the growing inability of communities to have any control or say in how such change might affect their futures. Ethnic nationalist movements and religious fundamentalist communities have sought new forms of collective autonomy as they have become more anxious and even violent. As "modernity" is globalized, they see their "traditional" practices threatened.

Others speak of new possibilities. Changes in communications and information technologies have created surprising openings in high-technology industries in developing countries, as the software sector in India illustrates, and with them new avenues for individual autonomy. Aspects of culture such as music, literature, and films produced in one part of the world are increasingly accessible to large numbers of people in other parts, thanks to some of these same technologies. Attempts to establish an international human rights regime have helped some individuals and communities to imagine autonomy in different ways, breathed new life into cosmopolitan thinking, led to new global institutions like the International Criminal Court, and encouraged the growth of such notions as global justice and global citizenship.

This chapter examines the politics of globalization. It is divided into two sections. The first focuses on the meaning of globalization and explores the several dimensions of the concept. It shows how globalizing processes bring about new linkages between what happens globally and what occurs locally in our communities and in our daily lives. The second section builds on this definition by examining the kinds of changes to politics that have come about with globalization and **global governance**. In this section, we address four inter-related dimensions of these politics: the acceleration in the number of problems on a global scale and

the accompanying growth in global consciousness, the disorderly politics of global governance, changes in the roles played by nation-states, and what accountability and legitimacy might mean for global governance.

WHAT IS GLOBALIZATION?

In political science, we often work with concepts that are highly charged with political meaning. On the one side, they are used in everyday political practices and discourse, while on the other, scholars debate them and adapt them for the analysis of politics. Globalization has become one of these kinds of concepts. Social movements, corporate executives, politicians, and public intellectuals writing in popular magazines or appearing on television refer to it often. In these public usages, globalization takes on a number of different meanings. When many social movements say that they are "anti-globalization" (see Chapters 3 and 13) or seek an alternative globalization ("alter-globalization"), they usually mean they are opposed to unchecked power of **transnational corporations**. Sometimes, they mean simply that they are opposed to capitalism becoming entrenched as the sole system for organizing economic activity. Others use

> **Transnational corporations:** Business firms that are headquartered in one country but have plants or places of operation around the world permitting them to integrate their business activities on a global scale.

> **Global governance:** Collective policy-making aimed at addressing global problems in the absence of a formal governing structure for the whole world.

KFC in Beijing.

Yanqiu Rachel Zhou

"globalization" synonymously with Americanization. They see the growing economic and military dominance of the United States, whether through the spread of American movies and fast food outlets; through the global role taken on by U.S. multinational corporations such as Monsanto, KFC, and Disney; or through the extensive reach of U.S. military power. Still others see globalization as another way of saying that capitalism is extending itself on a global scale.

Like other social scientists, political scientists examine carefully the way terms are used by various persons and organizations in society. They reflect upon these usages and seek to distil the core ideas and concerns implicit to them. Building on these core ideas and concerns, they begin to develop an analytic definition of the phenomenon. This analytic definition then takes on a life apart from how the concept might be used by political actors in broader society. It becomes a tool for analyzing politics. Eventually, such a definition might, in turn, become adopted by people more generally, changing their behaviour and attitudes toward globalization. Social scientists refer to this process as *reflexivity*.

Many social scientists have engaged in this careful process of reflection when it comes to **globalization**. After examining the competing definitions of globalization, political scientist Jan Aart Scholte suggested that globalization involves "the spread of transplanetary—and in recent times also more particularly supraterritorial—connections between people."[2] *Supraterritorial* refers to relations that are "above" territory or relatively unconstrained by one's physical location. John Tomlinson characterizes this "empirical condition" of "supraterritoriality" as one of "complex connectivity," a set of "connections that now bind our practices, our experiences and our political, economic and environmental fates together across the

> **Globalization:** Globalization is the transformative growth of connections among people across the planet. In the contemporary era, many of these connections take a supraterritorial form. In ever more profound ways, globalization ties together what people do, what they experience, how they perceive that experience, and how they reshape their lives. In short, individuals and communities begin to see the world as one place and to imagine new roles for themselves within it.

modern world."[3] Associated with this change in the character of social relationships for both authors is "deterritorialization." The relative importance of physical location as a basis for building social relationships is declining as supraterritorial ties grow in significance. In this respect, globalization is bringing far-reaching changes to the nature of social space: it is less and less defined by the physical place in which we live.[4]

Following David Held and his colleagues, we can begin to assess the scope of these changes by looking at three properties of supraterritorial relations.[5] First, we can observe shifts in *extensity*, the degree to which cultural, political, and economic activities are stretching across the whole world, thus taking place in a global space. For example, suppose we are interested in global environmental problems such as the climate change triggered by increased human creation of greenhouse gases like carbon dioxide (CO_2). We can ask whether the human production of excessive greenhouse gases has extended to include more parts of the world than it did 20 years ago. If the answer is yes, we can argue that the propagation of greenhouse gases is becoming more extensive over time. Second, we can assess *intensity*—changes in the magnitude and regularity of interconnectedness. To continue with our climate change example, if we observe that more and more presumed effects of climate change such as intense, destructive storms and higher temperatures are affecting the everyday lives of more persons in the world, we can argue that the effects of climate change are becoming more intensive. Third, Held et al. draw our attention to the property of *velocity*—changes in the speed of global interactions and processes. If the increasing levels of greenhouse gases are leading to a faster rise in temperatures and a greater increase in the number of destructive storms than historical averages, we can say that the velocity of global climate change is increasing. Some of these processes are captured in the graph of CO_2 emissions shown in Figures 17.1a and 17.1b (p. 442). Formerly poorer countries like China and India are generating more emissions every year, while rich countries like Canada still produce many more emissions *per person* than in poorer countries.

Together these three properties contribute to a fourth: *enmeshment*—changes in the interdependence of the global and the local (see Box 17.1). Suppose we

Figure 17.1a **Amount of CO$_2$ Emissions: Total and Per Capita, Selected Countries**

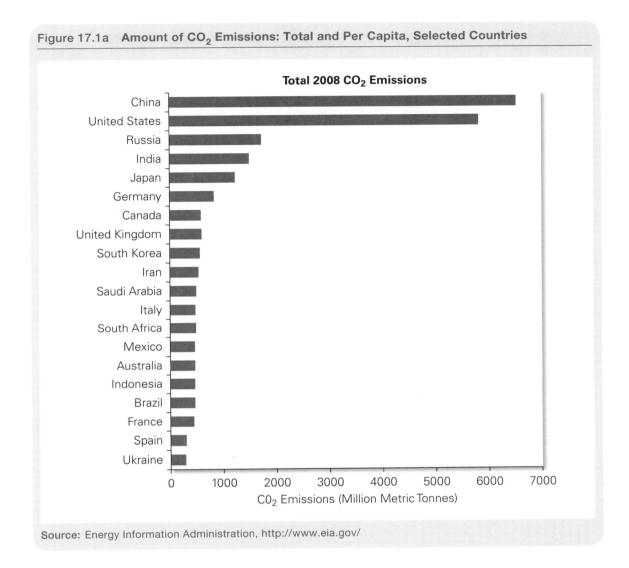

Total 2008 CO$_2$ Emissions

Source: Energy Information Administration, http://www.eia.gov/

BOX 17.1

PROPERTIES OF SUPRATERRITORIAL RELATIONS

- *Extensity*. The extent to which cultural, political, and economic activities are stretching across a global space.
- *Intensity*. The magnitude and regularity of the global connections that occur.
- *Velocity*. The speed at which global connections occur.
- *Enmeshment*. The degree to which what happens locally is tied to global events and the degree to which what happens globally is tied to local events.

Figure 17.1b   Amount of CO$_2$ Emissions: Total and Per Capita, Selected Countries

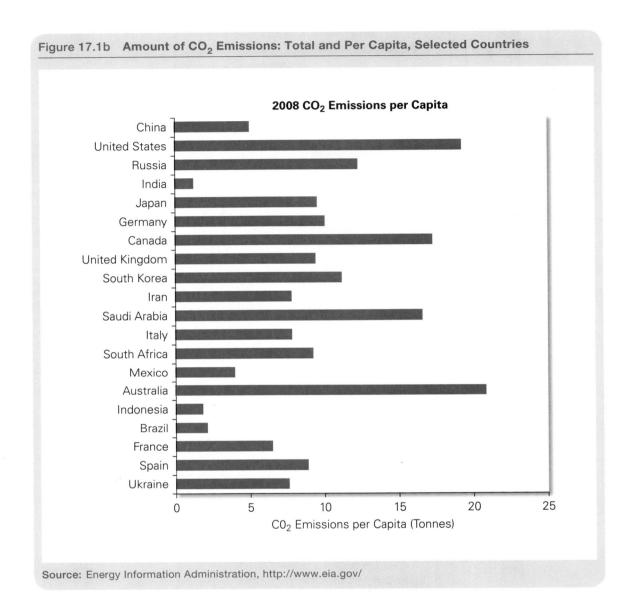

2008 CO$_2$ Emissions per Capita

CO$_2$ Emissions per Capita (Tonnes)

Source: Energy Information Administration, http://www.eia.gov/

look at small villages in the Canadian Arctic. If temperatures have risen significantly over the past 20 years, and if these changes have consistently led to a melting of polar ice, making it more difficult to do traditional subsistence activities like hunting and fishing, we can say that the people living in this rather remote region of the world are more enmeshed in global economic and environmental processes today than they were two decades ago. What happens in the small settlements in the Canadian north is more closely linked to what is happening globally in the creation of greenhouse gases—the so-called **greenhouse effect**.

Contrary then to what might have happened in the past, globalization is not just a matter of the rich and the famous travelling the globe. Rather, it involves changes to the lives of more people in all walks of life, living in an even more diverse range of local communities. Robertson offers the concept of

Greenhouse effect: A warming of the surface and lower atmosphere of the earth caused by the increased presence of various pollutants that break down the ozone layer of gases that protects life from harmful rays from the sun. The process leads to rising temperatures and climate change; it is also known as global warming.

"global unicity" for understanding how these changes are linked to one another.[6] Unicity comes first from a global context of trading rules, of international regimes, including those related to the environment, of cultural transmission, and of corporate activities that has an ever-increasing impact on how individuals and groups relate to one another in their local settings. Second, it arises from the creation of global frames of reference within which social actors increasingly understand who they are and how they should orient their activities. Accordingly, even acts of resistance—whether they are attempts to prevent massive depopulation of agricultural areas or to secure the traditional family in a strong religious community—are done with an eye to what is happening globally. For example, demonstrations by farmers about agricultural policies were targeted to what is happening at negotiations on an Agreement of Agriculture at the **World Trade Organization (WTO)**. Religious fundamentalists make effective use of current communications technologies to send out their message about resisting secularization, thereby seeking to build alliances with other religious communities with similar concerns around the globe.

When we speak of globalization, therefore, we are referring to a complex phenomenon. It occurs in many aspects of our lives. We have spoken earlier about global climate change and cultural phenomena like religious fundamentalism. There are examples in other domains. In the economy since 2007 the world has experienced a severe financial (banking) and economic crisis. Many have observed that the depth and severity of the crisis have been a result, in part, of globalization. The effects of the crisis have certainly been extensive, touching virtually every financial market in the world as well as lowering employment in most countries. The depth of the crisis has been such that large global banks have either collapsed or had to be bailed out by governments in many countries (more intensive). And

the crisis developed very quickly, impacting the whole world in a matter of hours (high velocity). Across the world, millions of people lost their jobs and their homes. In the social realm, migration to Canada now draws from all parts of the globe and not just Europe (more extensive); we have been admitting between 200,000 and 250,000 immigrants per year since the 1980s (more intensive); people can get here more quickly by airplane than in the past (higher velocity); and many of our cities are becoming much more culturally diverse (more enmeshment of the local and the global). See Figure 17.2, p. 444.

In politics, the rules of the international trade regime at the WTO now bind the activities of 153 states including China (more extensive), these rules affect a large range of policies (more intensive), meetings on the interpretation and implementation of these rules go on almost constantly (higher velocity), and the economic fates of a larger number of workers and firms are affected by these rules (greater enmeshment of local production with global rules). The international agreement on trade is just one of an increasing number of international treaties in the economic arena.

Across the world, however, people do not participate equally in these processes. Scholars emphasize the importance of communication and information technologies for supporting growing extensity, intensity, and velocity. These technologies facilitate the development of the supraterritorial relations particularly characteristic of contemporary globalization. The International Telecommunications Union has devised an index that permits it to calculate the extent to which countries have integrated these technologies into daily living. The story of a "digital divide" between wealthier and poorer countries told by information in Table 17.1, p. 444, is a familiar one. It shows that the persons living in the wealthier countries of the world have far higher access to these technologies than their counterparts living in the poorer, so-called "developing" countries. Without access to these technologies, individuals and communities will have less power to contest globalization and to shape it in ways they might wish. Thus, this table points to a more general argument made by some scholars: globalization is deepening inequalities between the rich and the poor, rather than reducing them.

Figure 17.2   **Increasing Immigration from Asia and the Middle East**

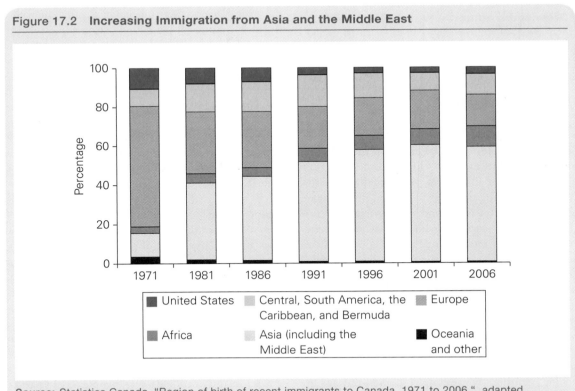

Source: Statistics Canada, "Region of birth of recent immigrants to Canada, 1971 to 2006 ", adapted from Statistics Canada publication Immigration and citizenship, 2006 Census, Catalogue 97-557-XIE2006001, page 9, http://www12.statcan.ca/census-recensement/2006/as-sa/97-557/pdf/97-557-XIE2006001.pdf

Table 17.1   **Countries Grouped by Access to Technologies**

High	Upper	Medium	Low
Australia	Argentina	Albania	Angola
Austria	Belarus	Algeria	Bangladesh
Bahrain	Bosnia and Herzegovina	Armenia	Benin
Belgium	Brazil	Azerbaijan	Bhutan
Canada	Brunei Darussalam	Bolivia	Burkina Faso
Denmark	Bulgaria	Botswana	Cambodia
Estonia	Chile	Cape Verde	Cameroon
Finland	Colombia	China	Chad
France	Croatia	Costa Rica	Comoros
Germany	Cyprus	Cuba	Congo
Greece	Czech Republic	Dominican Rep.	Congo (Dem. Rep.)
Hong Kong, China	Hungary	Ecuador	Côte d'Ivoire
Iceland	Kuwait	Egypt	Djibouti
Ireland	Latvia	El Salvador	Eritrea
Israel	Lithuania	Fiji	Ethiopia

Table 17.1 *(Continued)*

High	Upper	Medium	Low
Italy	Malaysia	Gabon	Gambia
Japan	Montenegro	Georgia	Ghana
Korea (Rep.)	Panama	Guatemala	Guinea
Luxembourg	Poland	Honduras	Guinea-Bissau
Macao, China	Qatar	Indonesia	Haiti
Malta	Romania	Iran (I.R.)	India
Netherlands	Russia	Jamaica	Kenya
New Zealand	Saudi Arabia	Jordan	Lao P.D.R
Norway	Serbia	Kazakhstan	Lesotho
Portugal	Seychelles	Kyrgyzstan	Madagascar
Singapore	Slovak Republic	Lebanon	Malawi
Slovenia	St. Vincent and the	Libya	Mali
Spain	Grenadines	Maldives	Mauritania
Sweden	TFYR Macedonia	Mauritius	Mozambique
Switzerland	Trinidad & Tobago	Mexico	Myanmar
United Arab Emirates	Turkey	Moldova	Namibia
United Kingdom	Ukraine	Mongolia	Nepal
United States	Uruguay	Morocco	Niger
	Venezuela	Nicaragua	Nigeria
		Oman	Pakistan
		Paraguay	Papua New Guinea
		Peru	Rwanda
		Philippines	Senegal
		South Africa	Sudan
		Sri Lanka	Swaziland
		Syria	Tanzania
		Tajikistan	Togo
		Thailand	Uganda
		Tunisia	Yemen
		Turkmenistan	Zambia
		Uzbekistan	Zimbabwe
		Viet Nam	

Source: International Telecommunications Union, *Measuring the Information Society: The ICT Development Index.* Geneva: ICT, 2010, p. 45. http://www.itu.int/ITU-D/ict/publications/idi/2010/Material/ MIS_2010_without_annex_4-e.pdf

GLOBALIZATION AND GLOBAL GOVERNANCE: CHANGING POLITICS

In December 2009, under the auspices of the United Nations Framework Convention on Climate Change, the UN convened a conference in Copenhagen, Denmark with the goal to move toward a new global agreement on reducing greenhouse gases, a major cause of climate change. At this meeting, not only were heads of government present, but also transnational corporations, **nongovernmental organizations**, global social movements, and scientists with expertise in the area, among others. Although **states** remained key actors around the table, coming up with an agreement had come to involve many other actors as well. When the formulation of policies and decisions about how to implement these policies take place in global meetings like this one, political scientists tend to speak of "governance" rather than "government." There is no world government in place and maybe there never will be. Political scientists use the word "governance" to indicate that this kind of politics takes a different form than the politics within states where there are governments. Governance refers, then, to a collective way to try to address global problems in the absence of a formal governing structure for the whole world.

In this section of the chapter, we explore more fully how globalization has affected politics by looking at four inter-related changes: the increase in both political challenges that are global in scale and in global consciousness; the disorderly politics that comes with global governance; changes in states themselves, including how they are organized for global governance and how increased cultural diversity in many countries including Canada affects politics; and, finally, the implications of all of these changes for political legitimacy and accountability.

Global Problems, Global Consciousness

With globalization, an increasing number of problems are global in scale; that is, they touch directly the lives of individuals living in most parts of the world. We have already spoken about greenhouse gases as one example. As different parts of the world come to rely on fossil fuels to power factories, homes, transportation, heating, cooling, and the cultivation of plants and animals for food, they increase the release of carbon dioxide into the atmosphere. With these increases, the world is becoming warmer, which is upsetting ways of living in all parts of the world. For example, ice long frozen permanently in the Arctic and Antarctic and on the peaks of high mountains in ranges like the Himalayas, is melting. As this melting continues and more water flows through rivers to the sea, many towns and cities on the shores of oceans or on islands in the middle of oceans may gradually become submerged. Reducing greenhouse gases requires all parts of the world to collaborate and to agree upon a strategy.

No one state or even a group of states can solve the problem alone.

There are other examples. Beginning in late 2007, we learned that financial markets had become so integrated on a global scale, with transactions taking place virtually instantly, that a problem like the collapse of U.S. banks resulting from wrong-headed mortgage loan policies (among other problems) had a global domino effect. Within days, every economy in the world was touched and no national government had the power to isolate itself from the contagion. In 2003, an outbreak of an uncommon illness in farmers' markets in eastern China quickly created a global panic as the disease—now known as SARS—quickly spread to other parts of the world, including a major outbreak in Toronto. The attack on the World Trade Center in 2001 showed that networks of highly alienated men and women could communicate on a global scale and threaten people not only in North America, but also in Europe, the Middle East, South Asia, South-East Asia, and Australia. The combination of rapid air transportation and new communications technologies made possible global forms of terrorism. The sociologist Ulrich Beck characterizes the contemporary situation as one of living in a "world risk society."[7]

Globalization also has the effect over time of making people more conscious of the world as one place; they come to face the reality that despite cultural, religious, economic, and social differences, they share one planet and some things that they do affect the lives of others, even those far away. Accordingly, in 2001 when the Taliban government blew up the two huge statues of the Buddha carved into the mountainside in the Bamiyan province in Afghanistan in the 6th century, people from many faiths from across the world expressed their sense of loss. When Siberian tigers in northern Asia or pandas in China diminish to such a degree that extinction is on the horizon, the threat is felt everywhere in the world. When an iconic figure like Princess Diana dies in an automobile accident, millions and millions of people across the world watch her funeral, often in tears. When a tsunami swept across the Indian Ocean in 2004 hitting South and South-East Asia or when much of Haiti was flattened by an earthquake in 2010, not only Canadians but persons from all parts of the world reacted in varying ways to help out. In short, the global consciousness that comes with globalization makes seemingly local events or changes felt in many different parts of the world.

> **Declaration on the Rights of Indigenous Peoples:** An agreement reached at the United Nations to outline clearly and in some detail the rights of Indigenous Peoples that should be respected everywhere in the world.

Disorderly Politics of Global Governance

From the middle of the 19th century until the beginning of the 1980s, the principal form of politics addressing collective problems facing states was *international*: states concerned by a problem met together and set up rules for addressing the problem whether it be the international sanitary regulations of late 19th and early 20th centuries, a system for sharing radio signals in the 1920s, or rules for regulating trade between countries. No other actors besides states had a significant role and usually states from the wealthy countries of North America and Europe dominated these negotiations.

As the world faces more and more complex global challenges and the need for global governance, states have found it necessary to work with other organizations: transnational corporations, globally organized interest groups (e.g. the International Institute of Finance, which represents global banks; World Medical Association), transnational social movements (Greenpeace International, Via Campesina), other international organizations, and so on. In addition, the representation of countries outside the long dominant wealthy ones has improved steadily as countries like Brazil, China, and India become more present in global policy discussions. No longer is policy-making controlled and exclusive to a small group of wealthy states from one part of the world. In this situation of global governance, politics becomes more disorderly and less predictable. Despite these characteristics, however, global governance can be effective.

An example of global governance that illustrates some of these changes is the process that led to the drafting and ultimate adoption of the **Declaration on the Rights of Indigenous Peoples** at the United Nations in 2007. The Declaration has since been ratified by most countries in the world, with the United States being notable in refusing to do so. The governance process began in the 1970s, when, following a

UN conference, indigenous peoples' groups became more aware of each other and began to understand that the problems they faced in North America, South America, Australia, New Zealand, Scandinavia, and parts of Africa and Asia were relatively similar. Despite being victims of colonization, they were not being recognized as having the right to self-determination and other human rights outlined by the UN and applied to many formerly colonized peoples, which had gained their "independence" in the 1950s and 1960s. Beginning with the International NGO Conference on Discrimination Against Indigenous Peoples in the Americas in 1977 under the auspices of the UN Decade to Combat Racism and Racial Discrimination begun in 1973, collaboration among Indigenous peoples gradually expanded on a global scale as they earned increasing institutionalization within the UN System. Accompanying this institutionalization was the adoption of a global indigenous identity, an understanding of a meaning of "indigenous" that was shared by indigenous peoples wherever they lived on the planet.[8]

In 1982, the UN responded to increasing pressure from the growing cognitive and social justice global networks of indigenous persons sharing this new global identity by setting up a "Working Group on Indigenous Populations" as a subgroup of the UN Commission on Human Rights Sub-Commission on Prevention of Discrimination and Protection of Minorities. The network's continuing work in this forum led successively to new standards in UN law, the most comprehensive being the 1989 International Labour Organization (ILO) Convention on Indigenous and Tribal Peoples. They lobbied successfully for a special chapter for Indigenous peoples' programs in Agenda 21, a comprehensive plan of action to be taken globally, nationally, and locally by organizations of the **United Nations** system, governments, and major groups in every area in which human impacts on the environment exist. Agenda 21 was adopted by the UN Conference on the Environment in 1992. Indigenous peoples then pressed successfully for the inclusion of their traditional ecological knowledge in the UN Convention on Biological Diversity in 1993. The same year, the UN proclaimed 1993 to be the International Year of the World's Indigenous Peoples. Two years later, an International Decade for Indigenous Peoples was declared by the UN. These events culminated in the establishment of a Permanent Forum for Indigenous Peoples at the UN in 2000.

This forum, in turn, became the Indigenous peoples' launching pad for the eventual design and subsequent adoption of the Declaration on the Rights of Indigenous Peoples. The various Indigenous organizations and their networks engaged with nation-states, UN agencies, and other interested or affected parties to draft, debate, revise, and eventually conclude the final text of the Declaration. The resulting Declaration affirms the rights of Indigenous peoples to self-determination and self-government as well as the right:

- not to be subjected to forced assimilation or destruction of their culture
- to practise and revitalize their cultural traditions and customs
- to manifest, practise, develop, and teach their spiritual and religious traditions, customs, and ceremonies
- to revitalize, use, develop, and transmit to future generations their histories, languages, oral traditions, philosophies, writing systems, and literatures, and to designate and retain their own names for communities, places and persons
- to establish and control their educational systems and institutions providing education in their own languages, in a manner appropriate to their cultural methods of teaching and learning.

In summary, this example illustrates how globalization can lead to global governance initiatives. Coming together were a growing global consciousness of being indigenous, world-wide networks of indigenous groups, a global debating forum at the UN, and the eventual involvement of states and other actors including transnational corporations and various non-governmental organizations. The debates and negotiations were "messy" in the absence of any world government and were prolonged. The Declaration eventually emerged when all of these actors collaborated in a planet-wide process culminating with 144 countries voting for it in the UN General Assembly (http://www.un.org/esa/socdev/unpfii/en/declaration.html).

Global Governance and Nation-States

Our discussion thus far already hints that there will be changes experienced by nation-states like Canada with the growing importance of global policy-making. First, within countries, these changes are leading to a gradual end to the traditional distinction between "domestic" and "foreign" policy. In this older arrangement, one part of the government—the Department of Foreign Affairs—would be responsible for all of the "foreign" activities of the government. Other departments like Industry, Agriculture, Environment, or Finance would be devoted to policy-making within the country only. With increasing globalization, however, it becomes more and more necessary for those responsible for industry, environment, natural resources, agriculture, and finance, among other areas of government, to engage with their counterparts in other countries. Hence, finance ministers meet twice a year with each other at the semi-annual meetings of the International Monetary Fund to discuss the global economic situation. They have become part of new transnational policy forums like the Group of 20 and the **Group of 8 (G8)**. In fact, these developments have become sufficiently important that the political scientist Anne-Marie Slaughter describes the changes as part of a "new world order." She documents how these networks of government officials have become more and more active, dealing with sharing information, harmonizing policies, and developing common regulatory procedures in more and more areas.[9] As these changes become more common, the long-standing line drawn between "international affairs" or "foreign policy" and "domestic policy" becomes more and more blurred. What is global becomes national, and what is national becomes global.

The blurring of the distinction for nation-states between what is "national" or "domestic" and what is "foreign" extends beyond policy-making to the very identities of the citizens of those states. Even while nation-states are being drawn into multilevel governance arrangements to accomplish their domestic policy goals, the "national" identities of their

Anti-globalization protesters use global products.

Malcolm Mayes/Artizans

citizens are becoming more fluid (see Chapter 3). In the 18th and 19th centuries, when the nation-state was rising to become the dominant organizational form in the world, states invested considerable energies in constructing a national identity. In the United Kingdom, a "British" identity was forged out of the separate distinct identities of peoples living in England and in the Celtic regions of Scotland and Wales. France melded the Celtic Bretons, the Provençal in the south, and the German-speaking Alsatians in the east into a single, universalistic French identity. Canada adopted a slightly different approach by building a political nationality composed of two supposedly complementary identities: those of English and French Canadians. All persons

were pushed to adopt one of these identities, whether these be the original settlers in the area (Indigenous peoples), or new arrivals (immigrants).

These same national identities are now weakening and becoming part of more complex forms of citizenship. In the United Kingdom, a Scottish identity has strengthened over the past 20 years, as has a sense of being European. This idea is captured in the slogan of the Scottish nationalists, "An independent Scotland in a united Europe." Similar developments may be seen in France as the Breton language (Breizh) has resurfaced at the same time as discussions of European citizenship are increasingly important. In Canada, the former French-Canadian identity has evolved into a Québécois one, which is much less complementary to the traditional English Canadian identity. At the same time, the Québécois have been enthusiastic about the arrival of the North American Free Trade Agreement (NAFTA). Mimicking the Scots, we could say that they embrace the idea of "an independent Québec in a united North America." In all parts of Canada, Indigenous peoples have asserted an identity based on their being the "first peoples" in North America and on their recognition as "peoples" by the United Nations. All these developments mean that the traditional national identity constructed in the past 300 years in many nation-states has declined in importance. Simultaneously, it has become coupled to new identities that transcend national borders or that are unique to ethnic minorities within those borders.

For countries like Canada which receive relatively large numbers of immigrants, these changes become even more pronounced because of the growing **diaspora** or transnational communities in their midst. In Chapter 3, these were described as ethnic groups who experience dislocation in multiple states yet typically nurture narratives about their specific "homeland," held out as a place of possible return. For example, we might speak of part of a Tamil diaspora or transnational community living in Canada. Tamils are a minority ethnic group living in Sri Lanka and they have been fighting the majority Sinhalese group for many years in pursuit of more political autonomy. The fierce fighting in their "homeland" has forced many to leave Sri Lanka for Canada, the United Kingdom, the United States, and other countries. Many of these emigrants remain attached to Sri Lanka and would like to return when political autonomy has become a reality or when the fighting has ended.

With the onset of contemporary transportation and communication technologies, these local, often marginalized, communities can become global political actors. Members can travel back and forth to the "homeland" or to other states hosting their ethnic group more easily than before. Using the Internet they can communicate with their relatives, friends, and political allies on a daily basis. They can import clothing and food more easily, thereby reproducing more aspects of the lives they were familiar with in their homeland. The international right of freedom of conscience gives them more room to practise their religion, with perhaps less fear of persecution or discrimination. With all of these changes, they can imagine their local group as part of a global community of Tamils, Jains, Chinese, or Serbians more easily than in the past. Moreover, their local politics often tends to reflect politics in the homeland, which in turn is reproduced in local communities of these groups around the world. When Pakistan and India clash over Kashmir, for example, dimensions of this same struggle may surface simultaneously in the Pakistani and Indian transnational communities living in Toronto, Hamilton, Vancouver, New York, London, Manchester, and Sydney. When Tamils are being slaughtered in Sri Lanka, Tamils in Toronto demonstrate and occupy the Gardiner Expressway which runs through the heart of the city.

Globalization, Accountability, Legitimacy

Based on our analysis thus far, it becomes increasingly clear that changes in governance and the roles of nation-states raise questions about how governance can be *accountable* to those affected by political decisions. And this accountability will affect whether or not these decisions are accepted by affected populations as ones they should respect. In other words, do these decisions have **legitimacy**? These questions arise for both nation-states and global governance decision-making.

***Nation-States*: Accountability and Legitimacy** Within nation-states, these questions are often discussed in terms of the concept of democracy. Crucial to this concept have been two assumptions:

1. Citizens are able to hold *accountable* all the political leaders who make decisions affecting their daily lives. For example, if citizens are concerned about air pollution, they can express these concerns to, and hold to account, all the political leaders governing the territories and firms that are the source of the air pollution.
2. Citizens can bring about changes in the political factors affecting their daily lives by using democratic procedures to pressure or to change their political leaders. We refer to this aspect of democracy as *popular sovereignty*. For example, if citizens

KEY DIMENSIONS OF DEMOCRACY

- *Accountability*. Citizens can make demands on, and hold accountable, the political leaders making decisions that affect them in their everyday lives.
- *Popular sovereignty*. Citizens can bring about changes in the political factors affecting their daily lives by using democratic processes to influence or to change their political leaders.

are unhappy about the quality of the air they breathe, they can choose new leaders who will have the necessary power and authority to respond to their concerns.

These assumptions are important because globalization appears to be placing both of them into doubt. In particular, globalization makes it more difficult to retain the sense of *solidarity* needed for popular sovereignty and blurs our usual understandings of *accountability*.

The Solidarity Challenge Political scientists use the Greek term *demos* to refer to the idea of a people who have a sense of community and of common purpose. The *demos* (or sovereign people) within the nation-state has changed drastically over the past 150 years. Let us think back to 1867, when the Dominion of Canada came into being. Who constituted the *demos* at that time—that is, the people who exercised some measure of democratic rights? First of all, it was men only. Women were not considered to be part of the people for the purpose of political decisions. And this group of men itself was a highly restricted one. It certainly did not include the men in First Nations communities, nor did it include men who had lower incomes and little personal property. At the time of Confederation, only those men who possessed a certain amount of property and wealth actually exercised democratic rights. Historians estimate that about 13 percent of the male population of the Dominion had the vote in 1867.

So the Canadian *demos* has travelled a long way from the small, relatively wealthy group of principally British and French men who exercised power

in 1867. Women began to get the vote beginning in 1916 in Manitoba and ending in 1940 in Quebec. Chinese and Japanese Canadians *lost* their right to vote in the interwar period, and only regained it in the late 1940s. Aboriginal peoples did not obtain the vote until 1960. Moreover, as we have seen, the addition of women and First Nations peoples is not the only complicating factor to the Canadian political community. Since 1960, our political community has become much more heterogeneous in terms of diaspora communities, visible minorities, and religions (see Table 17.2, p. 452). If we add to these categories the **identity politics** associated with the second wave of the women's movement, the gay and lesbian movement, and various **social movements** interested in the environment and world peace, we have a much more complex political community. And as we have argued above, globalization intensifies these complications because it enables the construction of identities that transcend borders more easily.

Should we be worried about such developments? The problem is that our whole conception of democracy within the nation-state involved the development of a common political identity as Canadians, or Americans, or French. Nation-states have worked to develop a common understanding of a shared history, a common political culture. They have sought to cultivate identification with common symbols such as the Maple Leaf flag or "O Canada" or common practices such as universal health care. They have stressed the institutions we have in common—parliament, a public education system, modern hospitals, and so on. Behind these efforts to develop this sense of national community and identity are two qualities assumed to be important to democratic governance: trust and solidarity.

It is important, many will argue, that citizens trust one another. If I have faith in my co-citizens that they will fulfil their duties, then I will fulfil mine. I will obey the laws and follow the general rules of my political community because I trust that others will do the same. Solidarity is also important. Citizens must believe that their compliance with laws, including the paying of taxes, is important even if it does not bring them direct personal benefit. They must feel sufficient sense of solidarity with their co-citizens that they are willing to help improve the

Table 17.2	Religious Affiliation of Immigrant Population, Non-immigrant Population, Over Time								
Religion	Non-immigrant Population	Immigrant Population	Before 1961	1961– 1970	1971– 1980	1981– 1990	1991– 2001	1991– 1995	1996– 2001
Catholic	46.2	32.8	40.6	43.8	34.1	33.4	23.6	27.4	20.1
Protestant	31.4	20.1	39.2	26.9	21.1	14.5	10.7	11.4	10.2
Christian Orthodox	0.9	4.8	3.8	6.3	3.8	3.0	6.3	5.4	7.1
Muslim	0.6	7.6	0.2	1.3	5.4	7.5	15.1	11.5	18.3
Jewish	0.9	1.9	2.7	2.0	2.2	1.9	1.2	1.2	1.3
Buddhist	0.3	4.0	0.4	0.9	4.8	7.5	4.6	5.7	3.7
Hindu	0.3	3.9	0.1	1.4	3.6	4.9	6.5	6.7	6.3
Sikh	0.4	3.2	0.1	1.1	3.9	4.3	4.7	4.8	4.5
Aboriginal spirituality	0.1	0.0	0.0	0.0	0.0	0.0	0.0	0.0	0.0
No religious affiliation	16.3	17.2	11.3	13.8	16.9	17.5	21.5	20.2	22.7
Other	2.5	4.3	1.5	2.5	4.2	5.6	5.8	5.8	5.8
	100.0	100.0	100.0	100.0	100.0	100.0	100.0	100.0	100.0

Source: Statistics drawn by author from Statistics Canada, "Religion (95) and Immigrant Status and Period of Immigration (11) for Population, for Canada, Provinces, Territories, Census Metropolitan Areas and Census Agglomerations, 2001 Census—20% Sample Data," available at http://www.statcan.ca/bsolc/english/bsolc?catno=97F0022XCB2001004; accessed June 8, 2008.

situations of others who are elderly, ill, or disabled, or temporarily out of work.

The problem then is that the cultivation of trust and solidarity becomes ever more difficult the more different we citizens become from one another. Differences based on gender, religion, or ethnicity can be thought so deep that women may not trust men, or that Muslims and Christians do not trust one another, or that immigrants from Sri Lanka may find it difficult to feel solidarity with immigrants from Jamaica. What steps can we take to improve solidarity and trust? We have adopted a *Charter of Rights and Freedoms*, other countries have similar charters, and the UN also has covenants on political, civic, and human rights. Are these steps enough? Do we need to do more? If so, what should we be doing? If we want to preserve the principles of democracy within the nation-state, we are going to have to work much harder at trust and solidarity in this globalizing era.

The Accountability Challenge Working hard at trust and solidarity may become more difficult, however, because globalization is shrinking somewhat the areas of public policy to which citizens can hold their political leaders to account. Democracy requires that citizens are able to hold accountable all the political leaders who make decisions affecting their daily lives. Such accountability is diminishing in certain key areas as our discussion of global governance above has indicated. Our politicians cannot address by themselves an increasing number of problems that we face without help from others. For example:

1. Important changes in the value of our money are taking place very far away and there is little that our political leaders can do about it. For instance, as the Canadian dollar appreciated in value by close to 20 percent against the U.S. dollar in 2007, our politicians did not take action, and there was virtually nothing they could do. Nevertheless, this

change had a significant impact on the economic situation of thousands of Canadians. In particular, thousands of automobile and forestry workers lost their jobs.

2. It is very difficult for a country like Canada to have its own autonomous policy favouring economic growth and full employment. With the liberalization of capital movements, we lose important degrees of freedom in this realm. This change is important, because the postwar economic order postulated that countries would have control over their own macroeconomic policies so they could promote full employment and provide a social safety net for those in need: the ill, the elderly, the disabled, and the unemployed. Have Canadians and citizens in other countries asked that their healthcare budgets, their education budgets, and other, related social policies be cut or held constant while needs for such services increase? Probably not. None the less, their politicians have gone ahead and done these kinds of things in response, in part, to external financial pressures. Such political outcomes indicate, in turn, a decline in accountability.

3. Developments in the area of the environment illustrate the problem as well. Virtually everyone is familiar now with the fact that the size of the ozone layer that protects us from some of the harmful consequences of the sun's radiation is gradually retracting. Over the past 20 years there has been a steady decline in levels of ozone. Again, we have here a global problem that requires a set of global political decisions. It is also an area where accountability is low. Decisions about ozone depletion that are affecting us as Canadians are being made by governments and others who are well beyond our capacity to hold accountable. The possibility of a nuclear accident is in the same category. Think of the accident in Chernobyl in the Ukraine in 1975 as the radioactive fallout drifted over Western Europe and other parts of the globe with the winds. How could the citizens of Sweden, for example, hold any politicians to account for the radiation found in the vegetables growing in their backyard gardens?

4. Let us think of still another area of public policy: security. Since the end of World War II, there has been a steady growth in the number of countries

with research into, potential for, and possession of nuclear weapons. Not only are these weapons terrifying technologies, but they are also ones whose use has global ramifications. If even a small nuclear war were to break out virtually anywhere on the globe, the radioactive fallout and other disastrous consequences would have very significant effects well beyond the territorial borders of the states involved. In February 1945, when the German city of Dresden was firebombed, the effects were felt principally in that city alone. If Pakistan and India were to begin dropping nuclear bombs on one another tomorrow, the radiation produced would have direct, immediate impacts well beyond the territorial borders of those states. Citizens of Sri Lanka or Iceland or Canada, however, have little capacity to affect such matters.

In short, the accountability challenge is whether we as citizens can bring about changes to our life circumstances through political action directed at the relevant decision-makers. The previous discussion will already have raised questions about this possibility. Many of the key decisions, it would appear, are being made either by other states or in global governance decision-making. So it is difficult for citizens to have any impact on the kinds of political outputs that they might want in their lives.

Leaders of nation-states are discussing policy options and reaching decisions in international and global settings much more than in the past. As the importance of these discussions has increased, it has brought about changes in the organization of government. Certain officials (prime ministers and ministers of finance and trade) have grown in importance, as have the bureaucracies underneath them. What is more, because they are making policy beyond the framework of the nation-state and they have to make decisions relatively quickly, the usual institutions for holding political leaders to account do not work well. This kind of decision-making does not fit easily into cabinet government in a parliamentary system, nor does it provide much of a role for the parliament or legislature. In fact, in the United States the president usually seeks "fast track" authority from Congress so that he does not need to consult the elected representatives until the very end, when an international deal has already been struck. In short, as political decisions become globalized, citizens seem to be losing control over the persons making those decisions, even though the decisions might have an impact on their lives in crucial ways. Such a development is inconsistent with popular sovereignty—the idea that the "people" have the ultimate power and authority over their lives.

Global Governance Decision-making: Accountability and Legitimacy

In the face of these kinds of changes to accountability and legitimacy for nation-states, the question arises as to what it might mean to speak of these principles for international and global decision-making. International agreements affecting such policy areas as the environment and trade have increased significantly during the most recent period. Associated with many of these agreements is the development of international secretariats or committees that oversee the agreements and provide a site for ongoing decision-making. Other international organizations have developed without the signing of formal agreements. And a global civil society has evolved in response to the growth of these organizations.

It is important to recognize that these global institutions are increasingly parts of systems of multilevel governance that in many instances include decision-making, not only by regional organizations or national governments, but also by subnational governments. Accountable, legitimate governance requires, therefore, that certain principles be followed and inform policy processes at *all levels of decision-making*. Accountability at the **supranational** level becomes a hollow concept if it is lacking at the regional, national, or subnational level. Legitimacy will only result if accountability is entrenched throughout the system. For example, in a country with a federal system, such as Canada, the United States, or Germany, it would not make sense to have an accountable federal government and autocratic provinces or states. Similarly, it is no use reforming global governance institutions if some of the problems in domestic governance we have noted above are not also addressed.

At this point, we are some distance away from institutions at the global level that might conform fully to democratic principles. What we can do at this stage is to identify some criteria that might be used to assess accountability in existing institutions. The criteria proposed below extract key underlying principles of democratic accountability that have emerged within nation-states. They are applied, however, in a way that does not tie them to political institutions, such as legislatures, that do not (yet) exist globally.

Assessing Levels of Democracy in Global Governance Institutions

There are six main criteria by which we can assess the levels of accountability in international institutions.[10] They are listed in Box 17.3.

Transparency Can all interested observers inform themselves fully on the core questions and tradeoffs under consideration? Policies are often developed in locations or technical languages that remove them from the scrutiny of citizens. Transparency can be enhanced by such techniques as the posting of policy documents and other reports in technical and lay language on websites. The World Trade Organization has adopted these kinds of practices more and more.

Openness to Direct Participation Global governance only becomes accountable when political

---

BOX 17.3

CRITERIA FOR ASSESSING LEVELS OF ACCOUNTABILITY IN GLOBAL GOVERNANCE INSTITUTIONS

1. Transparency
2. Openness to direct participation
3. Quality of discourse and its accessibility to all interested citizens
4. Degree of representativeness
5. Capacity to make decisions (effectiveness)
6. Fairness (procedural and substantive)

influence within processes of deliberation and decision-making is equally accessible or available to affected or concerned parties. Similarly, because the interests at stake in an issue area may change as the issue develops it is problematic to restrict access permanently to a specified set of actors. Evidence that international institutions are satisfying this criterion, therefore, will be found primarily when they let citizens' organizations have some access to the policy process. Many of the global civil society movements argue that the WTO and the IMF are closed off to such citizens' organizations.

Quality of Discourse Accountability requires the existence of public arenas or spaces where open, informed debates can take place about possible policy options. Such public spaces are often absent at supranational levels. Accordingly, public spaces where debates can take place must be created for supranational governance arrangements. These debates must permit the "translation" of technical issues into language for a lay public, so that as many citizens as possible can inform themselves about the stakes involved and about the advantages and disadvantages of choosing one policy option over another. For example, if intellectual property rules at the WTO are to govern the duration of the patents that transnational pharmaceutical companies can hold on their medicines, all countries and the WTO itself should have a "place" where citizens can debate the pros and cons of different proposals.

Representation Representation is a formal means of aligning the interests of citizens at large with the smaller number of actors required if bargaining, deliberation, or decisions are to be effective. Practices well established at the domestic level, such as electing representatives on the basis of majority voting in territorial constituencies, are often inapplicable or not yet available at supranational levels. Although its application may be complex, the idea is simple: all those potentially affected by policymaking in a given supranational institution should be represented in some way in the policy process. In the area of global finance, representation is often a problem. For example, even though the actions of the IMF and the World Bank are directed primarily toward developing countries, these institutions are led by persons from the wealthy countries. The managing director of the IMF is always nominated by the member states of the European Union, and the president of the World Bank has always been an American recommended by the U.S. president. Rules that have global effects are too often devised by leaders from a limited number of highly wealthy states. Citizens in less wealthy countries have no voice or representation in these organizations.

Effectiveness There is little value in having open, transparent, representative institutions if they cannot make decisions and implement them. Effectiveness refers to the ability of institutions to do these things, and it normally involves the creation of an executive-like grouping for taking decisions and a bureaucracy for implementing them. This bureaucracy may, in fact, be located at the nation-state level, provided that participating governments have agreed upon rules for implementing decisions taken at a higher level. In the absence of effectiveness, the legitimacy of institutions may come into question, thereby undermining accountability. For example, if political leaders operating in open, transparent, and representative institutions cannot reach agreement on rules to reduce the pollution responsible for climate change, they are not effective and the democratic institutions within which they are working may be questioned. Or if they can agree on the rules but have no bureaucracies with the needed expertise to implement them, decision-making is again not effective, leading to doubts about the legitimacy and value of the given institutions.

Fairness Political theorists talk about fairness in two ways. *Procedural* fairness refers to the types of considerations that have been discussed in the first four criteria listed earlier. *Substantive* fairness refers to the distribution of benefits from policy outcomes. Are some nation-states and some citizens systematically excluded from the distribution of benefits by given institutions? For example, if the WTO becomes more open, more transparent, and more representative and still the citizens of less wealthy countries receive little benefit from stronger international trade rules, then the criterion of substantive fairness is being compromised.

CONCLUSION

If individual citizens wish to continue to preserve accountability and build legitimacy in this globalizing era, they will need to be more demanding of their political leaders at the nation-state level. They must work to ensure that accountability principles are not marginalized by the growth of supranational decision-making. Further, they must resist closed-door decision-making at transnational levels. Individual citizens may need to join organizations that are active on transnational levels and that are seeking more accountability along the lines described in this chapter. Whatever the nation-state in which they find themselves governed, citizens may no longer have the luxury of keeping their political activity within their own national borders. Too much crucial to their lives is now being decided elsewhere.

It took at least two centuries of struggle to realize some of the potential of democracy within the nation-state. Now that globalization has given rise to centres of power and authority outside the control of the nation-state system, those believing democracy is important will have to target some of their energies on these centres if they are to have any hope of controlling the conditions under which they will live.

DISCUSSION QUESTIONS

1. Can you identify areas of the economy or culture where there is increasing extensiveness, intensity, and velocity in human social relationships?

2. Is globalization a welcome process or an unfortunate development?

3. Some scholars argue that globalization has been going on for 500 years or more. What factors might differentiate contemporary globalization from globalizing periods in the past?

4. What is the significance of the large "global civil society" protests taking place at meetings of world political leaders and at meetings of such organizations as the WTO or the G20?

5. Give some examples of where nation-state governments have lost power as a result of globalization. Give some examples of where nation-state governments remain very powerful, if not more so.

How do we explain these apparently contradictory changes?

6. Take an international organization such as the United Nations Human Rights Council or the World Trade Organization and use the criteria presented in this chapter to assess where they are accountable and where they are lacking in accountability.

FURTHER READING

Bernstein, Steven, and William Coleman, eds. *Unsettled Legitimacy: Political Community, Power and Authority in a Global Era.* Vancouver: University of British Columbia Press, 2009.

Pauly, Louis, and William Coleman, eds. *Global Ordering: Institutions and Autonomy in a Changing World.* Vancouver: University of British Columbia Press, 2008.

Scholte, Jan Aart. *Globalization: A Critical Introduction,* 2nd ed. Basingstoke, UK: Macmillan/ Palgrave, 2005.

ENDNOTES

1. David Held, *Democracy and the Global Order* (Stanford: Stanford University Press, 1995), p. 145.

2. Jan Aart Scholte, *Globalization: A Critical Introduction,* 2nd ed. (Basingstoke, UK: Macmillan/Palgrave, 2005), p. 59.

3. John Tomlinson, *Globalization and Culture* (Chicago: University of Chicago Press, 1999), p. 2.

4. William D. Coleman, Louis Pauly, and Diana Brydon, "Globalization, Autonomy and Institutional Change," in Pauly and Coleman, eds., *Global Ordering: Institutions and Autonomy in a Changing World* (Vancouver: University of British Columbia Press, 2008).

5. David Held, Anthony McGrew, David Goldblatt, and Jonathan Perraton, *Global Transformations* (Palo Alto, CA: Stanford University Press, 1999).

6. Roland Robertson, *Globalization: Social Theory and Global Culture* (London: Sage, 1992).

7. Ulrich Beck, *World at Risk* (Cambridge, UK: Polity Press, 2009).

8. Ronald Niezen, *The Origins of Indigenism: Human Rights and the Politics of Identity* (Berkeley, CA: University of California Press, 2003).

9. Anne-Marie Slaughter, *A New World Order* (Princeton, NJ: Princeton University Press, 2004).

10. William D. Coleman and Tony Porter, "International Institutions, Globalisation and Democracy: Assessing the Challenges," *Global Society* 14 (3) (2000): 377–98.

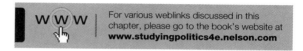

For various weblinks discussed in this chapter, please go to the book's website at **www.studyingpolitics4e.nelson.com**

Glossary

Note: Numbers in parentheses refer to the chapters in which the term in question is discussed.

Aboriginal self-government Diverse arrangements whereby the authority of Aboriginal or Indigenous groups to govern themselves is recognized; such authority (over various aspects of community life) would have to be consistent with the laws operating within existing states. (2, 7)

Absolute monarchy A system of government ruled, at least in name, by one individual whose authority is unchecked, final, and permanent. (2)

Administrative tribunals Boards or commissions established by the government to adjudicate certain disputes by applying laws to the facts; also called quasi-judicial tribunals or regulatory agencies. These tribunals are not proper courts presided over by judges. (8, 10)

Affirmative action The giving of preferential treatment to targeted groups in such areas as employment, promotion, housing, or education to redress the effects of past discrimination. (3, 6)

Agents of political socialization Those groups of people or institutions that convey political attitudes and values to others in society. (5)

Amending formula The procedure by which a constitution may be amended; in most states, it is a more onerous procedure than that which applies to the amendment of ordinary legislation. (7)

Anarchism A political ideology that sees no need to impose government order on a society, because of the essential goodness of human beings; it assumes harmony will naturally prevail when free individuals participate equally in mutually beneficial decisions. (6)

Anarchy A system of social, political, and economic relations without formal institutions of governance to define enforceable rules or exact obedience from the governed; as such, it is more characteristic of world politics than of politics within communities. (2, 16)

Aristocracy Government by an elite or privileged class or by a minority regarded as those best fit to rule. (2, 6)

Authoritarian government A nondemocratic form of government that is not based on free and fair elections, severely curtails public participation in political life, and holds the actions of the state to be above the law; such regimes often commit gross human rights violations in order to maintain their power. (2)

Authority The imposition of one's will on another by reason of legitimacy—because the subject regards the decision-maker as having a right to make such a binding decision. (1)

Backbenchers Members of parliament who, if they are in the governing party, are not cabinet ministers, or, if in an opposition party, are not among the important party critics. (9)

Bicameral legislature A legislature that has two separate houses, or chambers, each with its own set of members. (9)

Bill The formal text of a proposed law before it has been enacted into law. When a bill has completed all stages of the legislative process, it becomes a law and is known as a *statute* or an *act*. (9)

Bourgeoisie In Marxist theory, the ruling class in capitalist society consisting of those who own the means of production, such as factories or mines. This capitalist class rules over the proletariat or working people. (6)

Brokerage party system A definition of Canada's national party system which argues that ideological polarization is less pronounced in Canadian politics than in many other countries; instead, the main parties are said to attempt to aggregate enough diverse interests to win elections. (4, 12)

Bureaucracy The expert, permanent, non-partisan, professional officials employed by the state to advise the political executive and to implement government policies. (1, 2, 8, 13, 14)

Cabinet The group of people chosen by the prime minister or president to provide political direction to government departments; in Canada, cabinet members act collectively to make the key government decisions. (8)

Cabinet government A system of government in which the major political decisions are made by the cabinet as a whole, as opposed to one in which the prime minister or president acts with considerable autonomy. (8)

Cabinet solidarity The constitutional duty of ministers to publicly support the policy of the government. Ministers who openly dissent from government policy must resign from the government. (8)

Capitalism An economic system in which the means of production (land, factories, technology, etc.) are privately owned and operated according to the profit motive. Decisions about production, investment, and distribution of resources are determined according to market forces (i.e. whether a profit can be made producing and marketing a product), rather than collective or community priorities. (4, 6, 16)

Catch-all party A political party that takes a pragmatic approach to elections and focuses its agenda on securing electoral victory. See also *electoral-professional party*. (12)

Caucus A group composed of all members of a legislature that belong to a particular party or legislators who meet to further a specific policy interest. (9, 12)

Central agencies Those agencies of the state that assist the political executive to coordinate and control overall government operations. They provide both policy advice and administrative support. (8, 16)

Checks and balances A constitutional system of power-sharing under which powers are assigned to different branches of government (especially executive, legislative, and judicial) so as to enable each branch to curb the unilateral exercise of power by the others. (6, 8)

Citizenship Legal membership in a political community, especially in a nation-state, entailing rights and responsibilities. (1)

Civil rights and liberties Those legal and constitutional guarantees, such as freedom of speech, the right of *habeas corpus*, and nondiscrimination rights, that govern the conduct of the state, and some private power holders, in relation to citizens and certain minority groups. (7)

Civil society Social institutions and organizations that are independent of the state and in which citizens pursue their interests, express their beliefs, and live in communities. (2, 5, 6, 11, 13, 14, 15)

Class A concept that describes hierarchical groupings within societies based on social and economic factors such as income, occupation, education, and status. (4, 5, 6, 16)

Class consciousness An awareness of the divisions in society based on social and economic differences and a sense of identification with the appropriate division. (5)

Cleavage A persistent division among two groups of voters, based on long-term demographic or economic characteristics. Examples include language, religion, class, and region. Groups on either side of the cleavage may be mobilized into a subculture which shapes the voting patterns and political perceptions of its members. (5, 11, 12, 15)

Closure A term used to describe procedural rules that permit the majority to put an end to debate on a motion and require that a vote on the matter be held; also known as cloture or the guillotine or time allocation in various countries. (9)

Coalition government A government that occurs when two or more parties hold seats in cabinet supported by a combination of parties that forms a majority in the legislature. (9, 12)

Coercion The imposition of one's will on another by the use of penalty, force, or the threat of force. (1)

Cold War The period in international relations between 1945 and 1990 which was dominated by global political conflict and economic competition between the United States and the Soviet Union, each with its ideology and allies, in which major wars were precluded by a military balance between the two superpowers, but which was marked by many regional proxy conflicts.

Collective responsibility In Westminster parliamentary systems, members of the political executive are collectively responsible to parliament for government policy and for the overall administrative performance of the government. (8)

Colonialism The ownership and administration of one territory and people by another, as if the former were part of the latter. (2, 3, 14)

Common law A system of law in which precedents from relevant cases in the past are applied to current cases. Judges are bound by precedent and should decide like cases alike. (10)

Communism A political ideology based on eliminating exploitation through nearly total public ownership, full state control, and central planning of the economy. (2, 6)

Concurrent powers Those fields of shared jurisdiction under a federal constitution in which both the national and the subnational government may act and pass laws. (7)

Confidence (or nonconfidence) vote Alternatively, an explicitly worded motion indicating that the legislature either has or does not have confidence in the government; a vote on a matter that the government has previously declared to be a matter of confidence; or a vote on important measures central to the government's plans, such as the budget. (8, 9)

Conservatism The ideology of defending the status quo against major social, economic, and political change. Today conservatism is often used to label anyone on the political right, especially those who want to conserve the free-market capitalist system against radical demands for progressive reforms. (6)

Constituency A geographical electoral district or the group of people represented by a member of a legislature. (9)

Constitution The body of fundamental laws, rules, and practices that defines the basic structures of government, allocates power among governmental institutions, and regulates the relationship between citizens and the state. (1, 7)

Constitutional convention An unwritten rule of constitutional behaviour that fills in gaps in the written constitution and conditions the exercise of legal powers under the constitution. While considered obligatory, such rules are not legally enforceable. (7)

Constitutionalism The idea that the constitution should limit the state by separating powers among different branches of government and protecting the rights of individuals and minorities through a bill of rights. (7)

Contentious politics Protests that take the form of disruption of the normal activities of society, such as demonstrations and civil disobedience. (13)

Corporatism A political economy in which formal bargaining and compromises among leading societal interests, above all business and labour, are very important for social and economic outcomes. (4)

Coup d'état The overthrow of a political regime or leader by military force. (15)

Crown corporation A corporation owned by the government that assumes a structure similar to that of a private company and that operates semi-independently of the cabinet. (8)

Cultural pluralism The coexistence of many ethnic and cultural groups within a country. Such diversity is the starting point in arguing that all groups in a society can maintain their linguistic, cultural, and religious distinctiveness without being relegated to the economic or cultural margins, and is achieved through the creation of a common set of values and institutions. (3, 5)

Declaration on the Rights of Indigenous Peoples An agreement reached at the United Nations to outline clearly and in some detail the rights of Indigenous Peoples that should be respected everywhere in the world. (17)

Decline of party thesis A theory that many of the traditional functions performed by parties are in decline or have been taken over by other actors. (12)

Decolonization The process through which a population and territory formerly under colonial domination achieve formal political independence and become a sovereign state. (14)

Democracy See *liberal democracy*.

Democratic consolidation The achievement of a situation in which none of the major political actors, parties, organized interests, forces, or institutions consider that there is any alternative to democratic processes to gain power, and in which no political institution or group has a claim to veto the action of democratically elected decision-makers. (15)

Democratic deficit The perceived gap between the theoretical principles of democracy and the actual practice of ostensibly democratic institutions, including national governments and international organizations. (2, 10, 11)

Democratic transition The change from a non-democratic to a democratic government, usually indicated by the existence of at least one free and fair election. (15)

Democratization A group of transitions from nondemocratic to democratic regimes, involving the relaxation of authoritarian political control by political leaders, the expansion of political and civil liberties, and the creation of institutional mechanisms that open up a political system to greater representation and participation. (2, 14, 15)

Department of finance The department referred to as the government's chief economic advisor, responsible for overall economic management, raising revenue, preparing economic forecasts, and determining government expenditure levels. In Britain, it is called the Treasury. (8)

Dependency A condition in which countries in the South lack any degree of autonomy in their political, economic, and social development by virtue of their reliance on countries in the North for access to capital, technology, and markets. (14)

Deputy minister The minister's chief policy advisor, the department's general manager, and a key participant in the collective management of the government; known in Britain as the permanent secretary. (8)

Devolution The delegation of administrative or limited legislative powers by a central government to regional or local governments. (7)

Diaspora An ethnic group that has experienced or currently experiences dislocation across multiple states, yet typically nurtures narratives and political projects about a specific "homeland" as a place of eventual return. (3, 17)

Dictatorship of the proletariat A Marxist concept that refers to the interim period immediately after the proletariat (the working class) has triumphed in revolutionary class war over the bourgeoisie (capitalists). In theory, the rule of the proletariat was expected to give way to the classless society in the final stage of history, when full communism is realized. (6)

Digital democracy A broad term meant to encompass the application of technological innovation to politics and political participation; also called *e-democracy* or *e-politics*. (11)

Direct democracy A political system in which citizens hold power directly rather than through elected or appointed representatives. (2, 11)

Dominant conformity A model of ethnic group integration holding that all groups in a society should conform to the language and values of the dominant group. In the case of Canada, this is the idea behind historical policies emphasizing Anglo conformity, which aimed to have all groups assimilate by speaking English and holding the values of the dominant British-origin group. (3)

Dual executive A form of executive in which the posts of head of state and head of government are divided and each is held by a separate officeholder. In parliamentary systems, the head of state is a constitutional monarch or an elected president and the head of government is the prime minister. (8)

Egalitarianism The doctrine that advocates equal social and political rights for all citizens, regardless of class, sex, religion, ethnicity, etc. Reform-oriented liberals emphasize the need for an equality of opportunity, which guarantees to all the equal chance to compete for the social, economic, and political benefits available in society. Socialists often interpret egalitarianism to require an equality of condition, so that all goods and resources in a society would be distributed equally. (6)

Election A mechanism by which the expressed preferences of citizens in democratic states are aggregated into a decision regarding who will govern. (1, 11, 12, 15)

Electoral-professional party A political party whose primary goal is to form a government rather than to advance a particular ideology. It is characterized by a small membership, a reliance on corporate donors, and capital-intensive campaign techniques. See also *catch-all party*. (12)

Elite A small group of individuals who have significantly more power than other members of their community. They are either in a position to make authoritative decisions or have privileged access to decision-makers. (5, 6, 11, 12, 15)

Enumerated powers Those areas of legislative authority in a federal state that are specifically listed in the constitution and assigned to one level of government or the other, or to both. (7)

Ethnic cleansing The removal of one or more ethnic groups from a society, by means of expulsion, imprisonment, or killing. The term entered the political lexicon in reference to the former Yugoslavia; it was first used to describe the violent measures and policies designed to eliminate or dramatically reduce the Muslim and Croat populations in Serb-held territory. (3, 5)

European Union A unique supranational organization made up of 27 European states characterized by increasing economic and political integration. (2, 3, 7, 16)

Executive That branch of government concerned with the implementation and enforcement of laws and other authoritative decisions of the state. The executive also formulates public policy and provides political leadership. (1, 8)

Executive Office of the President Offices and agencies attached directly to the President of the United States that provide advice on decisions and help develop and implement policies and programs. (8)

Fascism The political system of the extreme right, based on the principles of the strong leader (dictator), a one-party state, nationalism, total control of social and economic activity, and arbitrary power, rather than constitutionalism. In 1922, in Italy, Benito Mussolini created the first fascist regime, emulated by Adolf Hitler in Germany. Fascist regimes also held power in Spain and Argentina. Today there are numerous neofascist movements advocating ultranationalist, racist, and anti-immigrant political positions. (2, 6)

Federalism A form of government in which the sovereign powers of the state are formally divided under the constitution between two levels of government, neither of which is subordinate to the other. (5, 7)

Feminism A belief in the full equality of men and women and the insistence that all barriers to such equality be removed. (6, 11, 13, 16)

Filibuster A device used by a member or group of members who take advantage of the procedural rules of a legislature that allow members to speak for extended periods of time in order to stall proceedings. (9)

First-past-the-post (FPTP) An electoral system that requires the winning candidate to receive more votes than any other in order to win the seat—that is, to receive a plurality of votes. The majority of first-past-the-post systems employ single-member electoral districts. (9, 11, 12)

Fiscal imbalance In federal states the constitutional responsibilities of the provincial or state governments to deliver a wide range of public services often greatly exceed the financial capacity of such governments. This gulf between public expenditures and public finances usually requires the central government to provide cash and other transfers to the provinces. (7)

Flexible amending formula A constitution whose provisions may be amended with relative ease. (7)

FPTP See *first-past-the-post (FPTP)*.

Franchise The right to vote in public elections. (11)

Fusion of powers In parliamentary systems, the joint exercise of legislative and executive powers by the prime minister and members of the cabinet who simultaneously hold office in both the legislative and executive branches of government. (8)

Genocide The deliberate and systematic extermination of a national, ethnic, or religious group. The term was developed in response to the horrors of the Holocaust. (3, 5)

Global governance Collective policy-making aimed at addressing global problems in the absence of a formal governing structure for the whole world. (2, 16, 17)

Globalization (a) The transformative growth of connections among people across the planet. In the contemporary era, many of these connections take a supraterritorial form. In ever more profound ways, globalization ties together what people do, what they experience, how they perceive that experience, and how they reshape their lives. In short, individuals and communities begin to see the world as one place and to imagine new roles for themselves within it. (b) The movement of goods, capital, ideas, and people across geopolitical boundaries today and in the past. Contemporary patterns of globalization involve a deepening constellation of economic, technological, and cultural changes that are worldwide in scope and that challenge the sovereignty of the state. (c) A process that is leading to ever closer economic relations among the countries of the world, based on increased trade, foreign direct investment, activity by multinational corporations, and financial flows. (1, 2, 3, 4, 11, 13, 14, 15, 16, 17)

Government The set of institutions and practices that make and enforce collective public decisions for a society. (1, 2, 4, 16)

Greenhouse effect A warming of the surface and lower atmosphere of the earth caused by the increased presence of various pollutants that break down the ozone layer that protects life from harmful rays from the sun. The process leads to rising temperatures and climate change; it is also known as *global warming*. (17)

Group of 8 (G8) Canada, France, Germany, Italy, Japan, Russia, the United Kingdom, and the United States, whose leaders meet once a year to discuss how they might coordinate their economic activities to ensure that the global economy functions well. (4, 16, 17)

HDI See *Human Development Index (HDI)*.

Head of government The person in effective charge of the executive branch of government, namely the prime minister in a parliamentary system. (8)

Head of state The person who symbolizes and represents the state but does not exercise effective political power, namely the monarch in a parliamentary system. (8)

Human Development Index (HDI) A composite index measuring longevity, knowledge, and standard of living, designed to give an indication of and a basis for comparing the quality of life in various countries. (1, 14)

Human rights Rights enjoyed by individuals simply because they are human beings, primarily including the prevention of discrimination or coercion on grounds of ethnicity, religion, gender, or opinion. (2)

Human security A broadened concept of security focusing not just on national security and interstate war but also on threats to the safety of individuals and groups. (14)

Identity politics Political activity of particular groups for recognition of their status and identity, as well as of the ways their beliefs and value systems differ from those of others. (5, 17)

Ideology A fairly coherent set of beliefs that not only explains what may be wrong with society, but also provides a vision of what society should be like. (1, 4, 5, 6, 12)

IMF See *International Monetary Fund (IMF)*.

Imperialism A broader term than colonialism that literally means "empire building," imperialism occurs

when one country dominates another with the aim of controlling and/or exploiting the latter. This domination can be economic, political, social, or cultural. (3, 14)

Independence The state of being free from the control of others; the ability to make one's own decisions, not having to rely on anyone else. In the context of world politics, it is the ability of a political community to govern itself rather than be governed by others. (16)

Influence The imposition of one's will on another through persuasion and voluntary compliance. (1)

Initiative A mechanism that allows citizens to petition the government to introduce or adopt specific pieces of legislation or force a referendum on an issue. (11)

Institutionalized group A highly organized interest or pressure group that has a permanent, professional staff. (13)

Interest group A group that brings together people with common interests and/or a common sense of identity for the purpose of influencing the political process. (1, 13)

International law A complex body of rules, derived principally from the treaties, covenants, and declarations signed by the governments of various countries. The resolutions of international organizations, the writings of academics, and rulings of domestic and international courts can also be sources of international law when the rules are not otherwise clear. (10)

International Monetary Fund (IMF) A sister of the World Bank and a branch of the United Nations that regulates the international monetary system in order to stabilize national currencies, and that, subject to certain conditions, makes loans to developing countries. (4, 13, 14, 15, 16)

International organization An organization, such as the United Nations, the WTO, or NATO, whose members are typically sovereign states. (16)

JCPC See *Judicial Committee of the Privy Council (JCPC)*.

Judicial activism A style of judges' decision-making that involves an active use of their discretion to create new policies. (10)

Judicial Committee of the Privy Council (JCPC) A British court that was the final court of appeal for Canada until 1949, when the Supreme Court of Canada took over this function. (10)

Judicial impartiality A state of mind in which judges preside over and decide cases with an open mind toward the parties and issues involved. (10)

Judicial independence A relationship between the courts and the other branches of government that allows judges to function without interference from other government officials. (10)

Judicial review A function of the courts in which judges examine actions of the government to determine whether they are authorized by law. This may also include a determination of whether statutes and regulations are contrary to the constitution. (7, 10)

Judiciary The term used to refer to all the judges collectively in a country. It can also mean the whole judicial branch of government, including juries and the courts' administrative staff. (1, 10)

Laissez-faire A French phrase meaning literally "Let do"; this economic theory provides the intellectual foundation for the system of free-market capitalism. Following the principles of Adam Smith, proponents of *laissez-faire* believe that the economy works best when there is no government intervention. Thus, the theory rejects state ownership or control, advocates a free market, values individualism, and promotes free trade. (4, 6, 14)

Law A type of rule that has been formally approved by the legislature or the executive or declared by the courts and that people are obliged to obey. (8, 9, 10)

Left That part of the ideological spectrum that believes in equality in society and the intervention of government via such collectivist measures as taxation, regulation, redistribution, and public ownership to effect such equality. (6)

Legislature An institution with primary responsibility to enact laws. (1, 9)

Legitimacy A measure of the degree to which citizens accept and tolerate the actions and decisions of social and political actors such as governments, states, international organizations, and civil society groups themselves, usually based on the notion that the decision-makers have a right to such power. (1, 2, 7, 11, 13, 14, 17)

Liberal democracy A form of government common to Western political systems in which there is a combination of the "liberal" right to individual freedom and the "democratic" right to representative government. Hence, the ability of the elected representatives to exercise decision-making power is subject to the rule of law as established by a constitutional system that recognizes fundamental rights and freedoms (e.g. free speech, freedom of the press and religion, and the right to free association) along with certain legal rights to property, privacy, equality under the law, etc. Liberal democracies also include protection for minorities against possible encroachment on their rights by the majority and such institutional structures as open and free elections with multiple party systems, civilian rule, separation of powers between the executive and legislative branches, an independent judiciary, and a political culture of tolerance and pluralism. (6)

Liberalism The ideology based on the paramount value of individual liberty. Liberals regard the individual as a rational creature who can use his or her intelligence to decide how best to live life and maximize his or her own well-being. Liberalism assumes that all humans are free and equal by nature, and that society is a vehicle for the protection and enhancement of our natural rights. In its earlier form, often called classical liberalism, this ideology assumed a limited role for the state. In later years, liberals tended to advocate a larger role for the state to guarantee equality and to help foster the full development of the individual. (6)

List system The most commonly adopted form of proportional representation, employing relatively large multimember electoral districts and a ballot that requires voters to choose from among party lists or candidates on party lists. (11)

Lobbyists Those professional, private sector firms and individuals that are paid by companies or groups to influence and access government. (13)

Maastricht treaty A 1993 European treaty that created an economic and monetary union for the countries joined in the European Union, specifying that they have a single currency (the Euro) and one common central bank (the European Central Bank); it also introduced a citizenship of the European Union. (3, 7)

Majoritarian system An electoral system that requires the winning candidate to receive a majority of votes to win the seat. The majority is normally achieved through a second ballot or by an alternative voting system. (11)

Majority government   A government in which one party holds all the seats in the cabinet as well as the majority of seats in the legislature (or lower house in bicameral legislatures). (8, 9, 12)

Marxian political economy   An approach to political economy that stresses the importance of social classes and of class conflict, and that identifies the interests of the dominant class, the capitalist one under capitalism, as the main influence on social institutions, including the state. (4, 16)

Mass party   A political party with a large, involved membership and a central set of principles that it promotes at the same time as it seeks electoral support. (12)

Mass media   The methods of mass communication, such as television, radio, and newspapers, designed to reach large numbers of people. (1, 2, 5, 11, 13)

Merit principle   A system of hiring or promoting public servants on the basis of their merit (education, training, experience, and so on), rather than on the basis of party preference or other considerations. (8)

Ministerial responsibility   The responsibility of individual ministers to answer to parliament for the administration of their departments, including the actions of public officials employed in such departments. (8)

Minority government   A government in which one party holds all the seats in the cabinet but has less than 50 percent of the members in the legislature. (9)

Mixed Member Proportional electoral system (MMP)   An electoral system that seeks to balance geographical representation with proportionality of party support by combining single-member electoral districts with other seats in the legislature distributed on the basis of the proportion of votes each party wins. (11)

Multiculturalism   A policy sometimes adopted in a state characterized by cultural pluralism that supports ethnic and cultural groups in maintaining their customs and traditions, often with public financial assistance. (2, 3)

Multination state   A state that contains more than one nation. (2, 3, 5)

Multinational corporations   See *transnational corporations.*

NAFTA   See *North American Free Trade Agreement (NAFTA).*

Nation   A community of people, normally defined by a combination of ethnicity, language, and culture, with a subjective sense of belonging together. (2, 3)

Nation-state   A term sometimes used synonymously with state, but implies that the citizens share a common ethnic or cultural background. In the modern world, few such homogeneous states remain, most either being multicultural, multiethnic, or multination states. (2, 3, 6, 16, 17)

Nationalism   An ideology that holds that certain populations are nations, that the world is divided into nations, and that a nation should be self-determining (i.e., able to establish its own institutions, laws, and government and to determine its future). (3, 6)

Neoconservatism   A social ideology that advocates a traditional, hierarchical, patriarchal, authoritarian, and inequitable society; it usually overlaps with neoliberalism in economic terms. (6)

Neoliberalism   An economic ideology that advocates an economic arena free of government regulation or restriction and free of government participation in the marketplace via public ownership; usually overlaps with neoconservatism in economic terms. (6, 8)

New International Economic Order (NIEO)   A set of proposals launched in 1974 for reform of the international economic order, with the goal of enhancing the self-reliance of the South and its influence over international institutions and events and achieving an increase in resource flows from the North to the South. (14)

New Public Management   A bureaucratic transformation occurring in many states over the past 15 years involving downsizing government, technological change, providing public services in new (alternate) ways, and forming partnerships with private sector agencies. (8)

NGO   See *Nongovernmental Organization (NGO).*

NIEO   See *New International Economic Order (NIEO).*

Nonconfidence vote   See *confidence (or non-confidence) vote.*

Nongovernmental Organization (NGO) A non-profit organization that is not part of the state and is not a private corporation. Usually, the term is used to describe organizations that operate across borders in areas such as peace, development, human rights, and international affairs. (1, 13, 14, 17)

North American Free Trade Agreement (NAFTA) An agreement ratified by the United States, Canada, and Mexico that contains rules to promote the freer movement of goods, capital, and services between these countries. (7)

Oligarchy A system of government ruled by a few and, according to Aristotle, in their own interests. (2)

Opposition In parliamentary systems, those members of the legislature who do not belong to the party or parties that form the government and cabinet. (9)

Organizational culture Clusters of beliefs about the way groups should be organized. Examples are a belief in hierarchy or a belief in internal democracy. (13)

PAC See *Political Action Committee (PAC)*.

Party discipline The practice that all members in a legislature belonging to the same political party should normally vote the same way, in accordance with their party's stand on the issue at hand. (9, 13)

Party identification An individual's longstanding identification with a particular political party. (11)

Party system The interaction among relevant parties that shapes political competition and the nature of government formation. (12)

Patriotism A sense of pride in one's country. (5)

PCO See *Privy Council Office (PCO)*.

Peacekeeping An undertaking by any group of governments, usually under the sponsorship of the United Nations, to put the forces of a third party between warring parties who have come to a ceasefire, in order to encourage them to keep the peace. (16)

PMO See *Prime Minister's Office (PMO)*.

Policy community A collection of groups and individuals (including both state bureaucrats and interest groups or social movement organizations) who influence each other in an effort to shape policy outcomes in their area of interest. (13)

Political action committee (PAC) A political committee organized for the purpose of raising and spending money to elect and defeat a candidate, especially in the United States. (13)

Political alienation A sense of detachment or resentment that arises in people who have little trust in political leaders and feel unable to influence political decisions that affect their own interests. (5)

Political culture The collection of the understandings, values, attitudes, and principles of a community or society that relate to its political organization, processes, disputes, and public policies. Out of a society's political culture come important beliefs and values that structure the citizens' attitudes and expectations toward such basic political concepts as legitimacy, power, authority, and obedience. (1, 5)

Political development A concept that describes how well a society has developed politically, usually measured by the degree of state capacity to effectively carry out the legislative, executive, and judicial functions of government; the degree of political stability, or ability to resolve political conflicts in a peaceful manner; and the degree of governmental responsiveness to public demands and respect for fundamental rights. (14)

Political dissent Any form of action taken to indicate a rejection of the existing order, such as peaceful protest, domestic violence, or terrorism. (15)

Political economy The study of the relationship between the state, as the leading authoritative actor in affluent societies, and the economy, the site in these societies where wealth is produced and exchanged. (4)

Political efficacy The belief that we as individuals can have some influence upon the political decisions that affect our lives. (5)

Political participation Actions taken by individuals and groups in an attempt to influence political decisions and decision-makers. (11)

Political party An organized group of people with at least roughly similar political aims and opinions that seeks to influence public policy by getting its candidates elected to public office. (1, 12)

Political patronage The awarding of benefits to individuals or companies on the basis of their support for the governing political party. (8, 10)

Political science   The systematic study of government and politics. (1)

Political socialization   The process through which attitudes toward and knowledge about political matters are passed on within a society. (1, 5, 6)

Political trust   The belief that political leaders act in the best interests of society. (5)

Politics   That activity in which conflicting interests struggle for advantage or dominance in the making and execution of public policies. (1)

Polity   A system of government ruled by the many but not—as in a democracy—by all; according to Aristotle, this was the most stable system of government when it was able to balance the interests of the wealthy with those of the poor. (2)

Power   The ability of one actor to impose its will on another, to get its own way, to do or get what it wants. (1, 6, 16)

PR   See *Proportional Representation (PR)*.

Prime minister   The head of government in a parliamentary system who provides political leadership and makes the major decisions, usually in concert with a cabinet. (8)

Prime Minister's Office (PMO)   In Canada, the office that provides political advice to and is staffed by close partisan advisors of the Prime Minister, and whose overriding concern is to safeguard his or her political fortunes. (8)

Prime ministerial government   The notion that the prime minister is now so pre-eminent that the label "Cabinet government" no longer accurately describes how decisions are made in the political executive in Westminster model systems, especially that of Canada. (8)

Private law   A branch of law dealing with relationships between private parties such as individuals, groups of people, and corporations; it includes laws governing contracts, property, and personal injury. (10)

Privatization   Transferring a government program, agency, or Crown corporation to the private sector, for example, by selling shares in the corporation to the public at large or to a private firm. (8)

Privy Council Office (PCO)   In Canada, the office that links the Prime Minister and Cabinet to the world of administration and provides logistical and decision-making support to the government; it is made up of nonpartisan career public servants. (8)

Propaganda   An organized attempt to spread beliefs through a communications campaign. It implies the use of exaggerated facts. (5)

Proportional Representation (PR)   An electoral system that attempts to award seats to parties in proportion to the share of votes earned. Such systems must be combined with multimember constituencies. (11)

Public law   A branch of law involving governments and public authorities; it includes constitutional, administrative, and criminal law. (10)

Public opinion polling   The use of survey interviews, often conducted over the telephone, with a representative, randomly selected sample of people, providing an accurate description of the attitudes, beliefs, and behaviour of the population from which the sample was drawn. (11)

Public policy   A course of action or inaction selected by public officials, usually in response to a specific problem or set of problems. (1, 8, 9, 10, 13)

Question Period   A set period of time in a parliament when members can put questions directly to the prime minister and other cabinet ministers. (9)

Race   Historically, the term *race* was used to speak about differences between people that were supposedly biologically based. Today social scientists completely reject the idea that there are any significant biological differences between people that warrant the use of the term "race." While some suggest that, in the light of this, the term should not be used at all, many contemporary social scientists use the term in quotation marks to refer to differences that, while merely socially constructed, are historically specific and have important consequences in the form of racism. Contemporary discussions of racism highlight the fact that it involves a biological and/or cultural assertion of superiority by one group over another. (3, 6)

Racialization   The historically and culturally specific processes associated with representations or assertions of superiority by one group over another on the basis of purported biological and/or cultural characteristics. (3, 16)

Rational choice An approach to political economy (and political science more generally) which is largely borrowed from economics and in which social processes, including politics, are said to reflect the outcome of interaction among individuals and organizations that each seek to maximize their own self-interest or utility, which may include power and prestige as well as wealth and income. (4)

Rational voting A model that seeks to explain voting decisions by emphasizing the rational evaluation of alternatives (parties and candidates) and the retrospective assessment of the governing party. (11)

Realist theory A foundational theory in international relations, usually identified with Hans J. Morgenthau, that emphasizes the anarchy of the international system and the interaction of states based on their respective power.

Recall A mechanism that allows citizens to petition to remove their political representative before the next election period. (11)

Referendum A mechanism that provides citizens with the ability to vote directly on pieces of legislation or constitutional changes. (11)

Regime The whole decision-making apparatus of the state; the constitutional principles and arrangements according to which government decisions are made; the fundamental rules of the game. (2, 15)

Representation by population The principle suggesting that the allocation of seats in assemblies should occur in a manner that encourages an equal division of the population across electoral districts, so that each vote is of equal weight. (11)

Representative democracy A political system in which citizens hold power indirectly by selecting representatives who render public decisions on their behalf in popular assemblies. (2, 11)

Republic A system of government ruled by a head of state who is not a monarch (generally, in modern times, a president), in which citizens are entitled to participate in decision-making. (2, 7, 8)

Residual powers Powers to pass laws in relation to any matters that the constitution does not expressly assign to any level of government; these powers typi-

cally belong either to the federal government or to the state or provincial governments. (7)

Responsible government A defining principle of Westminster-style parliamentary governments, which states that the cabinet may only hold office as long as it has majority support in the legislature (or lower house in a bicameral parliament) for votes of confidence. (8, 9)

Revolution A sudden, drastic, and usually violent change in the government of a state; the overthrow and replacement of existing political institutions and principles, not merely the forcible removal of the current ruler or government. (2, 5, 6, 7, 15, 16)

Right That part of the ideological spectrum which cherishes individualism and believes in leaving the private sector to operate with minimal government intervention. (6)

Rigid amending formula A constitution whose method of amendment is relatively onerous. (7)

Secular Not connected to or founded on religious beliefs or institutions; in political terms, the separation of church and state is often thought to produce a secular state, which remains neutral on, and does not reflect, issues of religious belief. (2, 6)

Security The peace of mind that comes with a sense of safety from harm of what one values; a sense of well-being that can have economic, environmental, social, linguistic, or cultural dimensions. It can be seen in terms of both individual and community safety. (16)

Self-determination A principle of international law that grants all peoples/nations the right to determine their political status and pursue their economic, social, and cultural development free from external domination or interference. (14)

Separation of powers A principle of constitutional government that is usually taken to mean that legislative, executive, and judicial functions of the state should be carried out by separate branches of government. No one may hold office in more than one branch at the same time. (8)

Sharia law The Muslim or Islamic system of law, both civil and criminal, based on a collection of ancient teachings, the Islamic holy scriptures, the Qur'an, and later scholarly writing, prescribing how people should behave and what punishments are appropriate for particular transgressions. (2, 3, 6, 10)

Single executive   A form of executive in which the posts of head of state and head of government are combined and held by a single officeholder. This arrangement is characteristic of presidential systems, such as those of Argentina, Mexico, and the United States. (8)

Single Transferable Vote (STV)   A proportional electoral system that elects candidates in multimember ridings and provides voters with significant freedom by allowing them to rank-order their choices within and across party lines. (11)

Social movement   An informal network of activists who seek to transform the values of society. (1, 13, 16, 17)

Socialism   The doctrine advocating economic equality of the classes and the use of government to serve the collective good of the whole society. Socialists value the collective good over the private interests of individuals and emphasize cooperation over competition. Socialists support a positive role for government in the economy. They advocate public ownership of key industries, regulation of the market, redistribution of resources, and protection of fundamental social rights and freedoms. (6, 16)

Sovereignty   A legal authority over a population and territory, commonly claimed by the government of a state but ultimately sanctioned by the international system of states. In other contexts, sovereignty can be said to reside in the people or in parliament. (2, 4)

Speech from the throne   The document prepared by the prime minister and cabinet and read by the head of state at the opening of each session of parliament; it outlines the government's legislative proposals for the session to follow. (8)

Staples theory   An interpretation of Canadian economic development, which argues that unlike most other now affluent countries, the production of raw materials for export markets has remained central for the Canadian economy. It is has not been replaced by a focus on manufactured goods and then services. (4)

Stare decisis   The principle of common law systems by which courts are bound to follow prior decisions that involved similar issues of law. A judgment by one member of a court binds other members, and lower courts are bound to follow the decisions of higher courts. (10)

State   A modern form of organizing political life that is characterized by a population, territory, governing institutions, and a government that claims a monopoly of legitimate force; recognition by the international community of states (most often by the United Nations) may also be key. (2, 3, 4, 16, 17)

State failure   A situation in which the structure, authority, law, and political order have fallen apart and must be reconstituted in some form. (2, 14, 15)

STV   See *Single Transferable Vote (STV)*.

Subculture   A cluster of people who share the same basic political values and attributes distinct from those of other groups in society and from the predominant values and attributes of society as a whole. (5)

Supranational   A sphere of politics and political institutions that exists "above" the nation-state but usually "below" the global level. The only supranational polity in the world is the European Union. (16, 17)

Supreme Court of Canada   Canada's highest court and final court of appeal since 1949. (10)

Sustainable development   An approach to development that makes environmental conservation and protection an integral part of development processes, in order to enhance the ability of current and future generations to meet their needs. (14)

Terrorism   The threat or use of violence, usually directed at civilian populations, in order to create some form of political change. (2, 11, 14, 15, 16)

Totalitarian government   A nondemocratic form of government that seeks to wholly control and transform the people through an all-encompassing ideology that speaks to their cultural, economic, political, and social roots and destiny. Totalitarian regimes were responsible for two of the worse genocides of the 20th century, in Europe during the Second World War and in Cambodia in the 1970s. (2)

Transnational corporations   Business firms that are headquartered in one country but have plants or places of operation around the world permitting them to integrate their business activities on a global scale. (1, 4, 16, 17)

Transnational group A group that organizes across the borders of nation-states with the goal of influencing governments, international organizations, or public opinion. (13)

Tyranny of the majority Abuse of the minority by the majority through excessive use of power Many liberals believe that we have as much to fear from the oppression at the hands of unconstrained majorities as we do from the despotic rule of an all-powerful ruler. Today majority tyranny is evident in the social and cultural realms, where the conformity of popular opinion runs counter to individual freedom and the right to be different. As well, ethnic and other minorities feel oppressed by the actions of majorities who can rule through the sheer force of superior numbers. (6, 9)

UN See *United Nations (UN)*.

Unicameral legislature A legislature with only one house, or chamber, to which all members belong. (9)

United Nations (UN) An international organization formed in 1945 as a successor to the League of Nations; it has become the largest and most ambitious international governmental organization in world history, consisting of a vast array of organs and agencies. Its membership now includes almost every country in the world. Less than a world government, it attempts to promote peaceful relations among states and economic and human rights for all people. (2, 14, 16, 17)

Unwritten constitution A constitution whose subject matter is dispersed across a variety of statutes, court rulings, and unwritten political practices known as constitutional conventions. (7)

Varieties of Capitalism (VoC) The foremost contemporary political economy approach to developed countries. These are divided between Coordinated Market Economies (CMEs), where firms rely on coordination with other actors, and Liberal Market Economies (LMEs), where they do not. (4)

Veto The authorized power to block a decision or piece of legislation, especially of a president to reject a law passed by congress or of a province to reject a proposed constitutional amendment. (8, 9)

Weak state The form of state that exists in countries where it did not play an important role in fostering the transition to a market and industrial economy, and in which it continues to play a modest role in guiding overall economic development. (4)

Welfare state A concept that stresses the role of government as a provider and protector of individual security and well-being through the implementation of interventionist economic policies and social programs. The welfare state is regarded as having a positive role in promoting human welfare and in shielding the individual against the economic and social consequences of unemployment, poverty, sickness, old age, disability, and so on. (1, 4, 6, 8)

Welfare state regimes The welfare states of affluent, capitalist countries are said to come in three variants—social democratic, Christian Democratic, and liberal (Anglo-Saxon), which originated in different political party and social coalitions. These result in different levels of poverty and inequality. (4)

World Bank A bank closely linked to the IMF that is one of the world's largest sources of development assistance. Through loans, policy advice, and technical assistance, it aims to improve the living standards in the developing world. (13, 14, 15, 16)

World Trade Organization (WTO) An organization created during the Uruguay Round of GATT negotiations whose goal is to provide liberal trading practices and to reduce protectionism through the development and enforcement of global laws and regulations. (2, 4, 7, 13, 16, 17)

Written constitution A constitution whose fundamental provisions have been reduced to a single document or limited set of documents. (7)

WTO See *World Trade Organization (WTO)*.

Index